Register Now for Online Access to Your Book!

Your print purchase of *Racism in the United States: Implications for the Helping Professions, Third Edition* **includes online access to the contents of your book**—increasing accessibility, portability, and searchability!

Access today at:
http://connect.springerpub.com/content/book/978-0-8261-8557-0
or scan the QR code at the right with your smartphone. Log in or register, then click "Redeem a voucher" and use the code below.

T7WDWXYJ

Scan here for quick access.

SPRINGER PUBLISHING
View all our products at springerpub.com

Racism in the United States

Ann Marie Garran, PhD, MSW, is an associate professor and MSW program director at the University of Connecticut School of Social Work. Her scholarship, teaching, and community work are largely centered on antiracism and other anti-oppression work, as well as inclusive pedagogy in social work education to better understand how power and privilege shape both the instructor and student experience.

Lisa Werkmeister Rozas, PhD, MA, MSW, is an associate professor at the University of Connecticut School of Social Work. Her scholarship, teaching and consulting work focus on various aspects of oppression, coloniality, and antiracism. She teaches courses on Human Oppression, Social Justice and Dialogue, Health Disparities, and a travel study exchange with a University in Germany on Genocide. She has written about intersectional theory, critical consciousness, and dialogue and uses them as pedagogical anchors, which she believes are essential to learning about oppression and advocating for racial and social justice.

Hye-Kyung Kang, PhD, MA, MSW, is an associate professor, MSW program director, and Chair of the Social Work Department at Seattle University. Her scholarship, teaching, and practice focus on cultural citizenship, postcolonial social work practice, Asian American immigrant communities, immigrant mental and social health, and social justice focused social work education.

Joshua L. Miller, PhD, MSW, is a professor at Smith College School for Social Work. He focuses on racial justice in his scholarship, teaching, and community activism. He is the author of *Psychosocial Capacity Building in Response to Disasters* and is working on a new book, *Psychosocial Responses to Socio Political Targeting, Oppression and Violence: Intervention Strategies for Helping Professionals.*

Racism in the United States

Implications for the Helping Professions

Third Edition

Ann Marie Garran, PhD, MSW

Lisa Werkmeister Rozas, PhD, MA, MSW

Hye-Kyung Kang, PhD, MA, MSW

Joshua L. Miller, PhD, MSW

Springer Publishing Company, LLC
11 West 42nd Street, New York, NY 10036
www.springerpub.com
connect.springerpub.com/

Acquisitions Editor: Kate Dimock
Compositor: Transforma

ISBN: 978-0-8261-8556-3
ebook ISBN: 978-0-8261-8557-0
DOI: 10.1891/9780826185570

SUPPLEMENTS:
Instructor Materials:

 A robust set of instructor resources designed to supplement this text is located at http://connect.springerpub.com/978-0-8261-8557-0. Qualifying instructors may request access by emailing **textbook@springerpub.com.**

Instructors' Manual ISBN: 978-0-8261-8558-7
Instructor's PowerPoint Slides ISBN: 978-0-8261-8559-4
Instructor's Podcast Transcript ISBN: 978-0-8261-8561-7

21 22 23 24 / 5 4 3 2 1

Library of Congress Cataloging-in-Publication Data
Names: Garran, Ann Marie, author. | Rozas, Lisa Werkmeister, author. |
  Kang, Hye-Kyung, author. | Miller, Joshua (Joshua L.), author.
Title: Racism in the United States : implications for the helping
  professions / Ann Marie Garran, PhD, MSW, Lisa Werkmeister Rozas, PhD, MA,
  MSW, Hye-Kyung Kang, PhD, MA, MSW, Joshua L. Miller, PhD, MSW.
Identifiers: LCCN 2021045523 | ISBN 9780826185563 (paperback) |
  ISBN 9780826185570 (ebook)
Subjects: LCSH: Racism—United States. | United States—Race relations. |
  Anti-racism—United States. | Human services—Moral and ethical aspects.
  | Social service—Moral and ethical aspects. | Organizational
  change—United States.
Classification: LCC E185.615 .M525 2022 | DDC 305.800973—dc23
LC record available at https://lccn.loc.gov/2021045523

Contact sales@springerpub.com to receive discount rates on bulk purchases.

Publisher's Note: New and used products purchased from third-party sellers are not guaranteed for quality, authenticity, or access to any included digital components.

Printed in the United States of America.

We dedicate this book to those who have been targeted by the myriad oppressive individual, institutional, and structural forces that permeate the very fabric of the United States: Black and brown men and women who have been murdered by the police and are represented in mass incarceration that has plagued the United States.

Asian and Latinx immigrants who have been targets of xenophobia and anti-immigrant violence; Central and South American families who have been separated and whose children have been sequestered on compounds and in cages, Indigenous people who continue to be denied basic rights. This is not an exhaustive list but unfortunately, the tip of a very large iceberg. We also dedicate it to the tireless advocates and activists who work day and night to address systemic inequalities and strive for a more just society.

This book is dedicated, too, to our families, friends, colleagues, students, and all who came before us and will follow us in the struggle against racism.

Contents

Foreword

Forty years of consulting for social justice have taught me a few things. First, racism and other forms of oppression remain prevalent in the United States. Second, we are making some progress. Slow but steady; but progress, nonetheless. Third, too many human services professionals, despite diversity requirements in colleges and universities and cultural competency requirements for licensure, remain inadequately prepared to address the biases, discrimination, and structural racism that they, themselves, and their clients face.

As I consult with human services providers around the country, I hear the following comments and questions. "I don't know how to initiate a conversation with my clients about race." "When should I bring it up?" "How can I avoid being racist?"

A senior manager working with people with disabilities, asks "How do we engage our caregivers so that they believe this is a safe place to talk about the biases they experience?"

A lesbian woman (or a member of the working poor, or a White male) asks, "What about my issues? It can't be all about race."

An executive director (or vice-president or middle manager) asks, "How can I be a leader in these efforts, if I'm not a person of color?"

Do you have a template we can use to guide us through these conversations? Can you chart the end game for us? Help us understand why we are doing this work and where we are going?

Racism in the United States: Implications for the Helping Professions is the book I wish my clients in the human services professions had read. Its comprehensive content covers the fundamental who, what, why, where, and how questions about racism. And it expands beyond that to help us see that there is a spectrum of racism and a web of oppression. It provides readers with both history and tools to enable them to have the critical conversations and to use the reality of intersectionality to hold a "race, and" analysis (racism and classism, racism and sexism), rather than an either/or analysis. The chapters move the reader smoothly and sequentially from individuals, to groups, to social systems. Readers learn about how to work with racism in clinical settings and how to confront it in agencies and organizations. Finally, we are introduced to the web of resistance that encourages continuing antiracism work while exercising self-care.

Though written for students, *Racism in the United States* provides answers to the questions my professional clients are still asking. As this text is adopted more and more widely, I expect those to whom I consult will come with greater understanding. In the meantime, I would love to see human services agencies across the country provide this book to their staff as part of the onboarding process. We are in desperate need of deepening human services workers' understanding of race and racism. The current crises threatening our democracy remind us we have no time to waste.

Patricia Romney, PhD
Amherst, Massachusetts

Preface

Racism has evolved as a persistent part of the human condition. Its obstinacy and intractability are frustrating and at times baffling. We live in a world in which most nations have signed the United Nations' declarations of human rights and claim to be democracies, yet racial and ethnic conflicts abound. Historically, the United States has cherished its Constitution and Declaration of Independence, though in recent years fundamental rights and ideas contained therein have been under fervent attack. Abraham Lincoln is viewed as a great president and the Civil War as an important milestone in the march toward freedom and social justice for all. Yet, it is still unclear as to the motivation for the war; was it a stand against the immorality of slavery or purely about securing the economic interest of a divided nation? Surveys find that today there are vast divisions between USAmericans, particularly in the realm of voting rights, civil rights for all citizens, and whether or not racial prejudice and discrimination are wrong. As this book amply illustrates, racism, White supremacy, and obvious expression of racial hatred are profoundly entrenched in U.S. society, in many ways and forms.

The complexity of racism is part of the problem. Racism is manifested and embedded politically, socially, institutionally, structurally, and culturally in organizations, the economy, social welfare policies, everyday practices, internalized stereotypes, interpersonal and intergroup relations, and public discourse. Despite efforts to eradicate it, racism has demonstrated a remarkable capacity to mutate and evolve, much as bacteria respond to antibiotics. Racism wreaks havoc in many lives—physically, economically, socially, and psychologically. While the continued upsurge in racialized violence has awakened many White people to the privileges they hold, many White people push back against the entire notion of White privilege, while others do not see or acknowledge White privilege at all. Racism divides and alienates people from one another, leaving emotional, psychological, and spiritual wounds. The magnitude and doggedness of racism is demoralizing both to those enduring it and those committed to ending it.

Many people do want to dismantle racism but do not know how. While they recognize the more obvious types of racism, they are not aware of the more insidious, invisible ways that racism exists, nor do they feel they have the skills to intervene. The helping professions—which include social work, psychology, psychiatry, counseling, nursing, medicine, education, and law—usually have codes of ethics that commit practitioners to cultural competence, nondiscrimination, and, in some instances, social justice. Helping professionals interact with millions of people, work in thousands of agencies and offices, and contribute to policy formation and enactment at many levels of society. They can make a real difference in the struggle against racism. They receive training about how to do their jobs, and anti-oppression and antiracism material should be part of the curriculum.

We have been antiracism activists and educators for many years, working with individuals, families, organizations, and communities to dismantle racism. We have pursued our antiracism work as a team, working alone, and in collaboration with many others throughout the United States. In co-teaching antiracism courses for professional social workers for more than a decade, we have been unable to find a text that has attempted to cover the entire spectrum of racism affecting helping professionals and their clients—which motivated us to produce this book. We have now written this third edition, as the face of racism and strategies to confront it are constantly changing. This new edition maintains the essential structure of the first two editions, while presenting updated concepts, graphics, and facts, adding new theories, a chapter on immigration, and increased resources for educators and students alike.

A major change to this edition is the addition of two colleagues, Dr. Lisa Werkmeister Rozas, also a former co-instructor of the racism course, and Dr. Hye-Kyung Kang. Drs. Miller and Garran authored the first two editions based on their having co-taught a course on racism for more than a dozen years. In preparation of this edition, they felt strongly that adding new voices would expand the book's perspective and offer readers new insights. We believe this edition is stronger for their having joined in the writing of this book.

Writing this book has posed a number of challenges. One is that racism is ongoing; while we were writing this book, many examples of extreme racism were occurring on a nearly daily basis—killings of unarmed Black men and women by the police with minimal accountability; a president who, along with his Cabinet, worked to push draconian policies and a racist agenda; and the forced caging of immigrant children along with the deportation of their parents. Another challenge is that there are many levels of racism. We could not concentrate only on racist stereotypes, or institutional racism, or interpersonal and intergroup racism. Knowledge of all forms of racism is relevant to helping professionals, as is knowing how to address them. Therefore, we had to place racism in a historical context and link it to other related forms of oppression, such as classism, sexism, and heterosexism. Thus, this book approaches racism comprehensively, with an emphasis on how helping professionals can respond.

Another challenge is that racism affects people in many different ways, ranging from those who endure it daily to those who are not cognizant of its impact on them and others, and have little awareness of its pervasive and destructive reach. We want to be clear. Racism affects everyone, which is why everyone needs to be a part of eliminating it. Workers and students in the helping professions have had very different experiences with racism and represent a range of racial and social identities, with very different levels of understanding and awareness about racism. We have attempted to write a book from which all helping professionals can benefit. We hope this book will engage those who are new to an exploration of racism while appealing to those who are engaged in antiracism work already.

Race and racism are complex and disputed notions, with varying meanings that are historically situated. In Chapter 2, we explore different ways of understanding and conceptualizing these concepts and conclude that race is a social construction. All social constructions involve the use of language in ways that reflect intersectional social positioning, power, conflict, and contested meanings. These terms shift over time and are interrogated, challenged, and reworked. Thus, in this book we use many words to describe race and ethnicity—White, African American, Black, people of color, Anglo, Latino/a/x, Hispanic, American Indian,

Native American, and BIPOC (Black, Indigenous, and People of Color)—which in many cases are not literally correct or even logically consistent, but they do reflect categories and labels commonly used in public conversations about race and racism. We have chosen to use the terms people of color and BIPOC interchangeably throughout the book, though we understand that there are strong reactions associated with either and, for some, denote an important differentiation. We have also chosen to use the term USAmerican rather than American as we want to bring attention to how U.S. exceptionalism has appropriated the word American, thus rendering South American, Central American, and other parts of North America invisible. Another challenge has been to strike the proper balance between understanding racism and sustaining hope. We cannot confront racism effectively without thoroughly appreciating its complexity. Yet we could easily be demoralized if we were to read only about the history and consequences of racism without addressing how to tackle it. The early chapters explore and map out the contours of racism, and the later chapters place greater emphasis on how to dismantle it.

At the end of each chapter are exercises to help readers explore racism and how it is manifested in their social world, as well as how they have internalized it. Learning about racism and how to challenge it must be experiential and affective, in addition to being cognitive. The exercises are geared toward both introspection and action, as working against racism is in itself empowering.

We believe in many ways of knowing and understanding, and we value multiple and different perspectives. Still, we have a clear and constant bias: We are against racism in all of its manifestations and conceive of this book as an act of resistance to racism. Although we have tried to understand empathically how people are inducted into a social and psychological racial calculus, we stand firmly against racism and White supremacy, and the ultimate purpose of this text is to help readers further their own antiracism work. We have also included an Instructor's Manual, Podcasts, and PowerPoint presentations for each class as a baseline. We welcome the many creative ways that instructors and students will use this material; qualified instructors can request these supplementary materials by email (textbook@springerpub.com).

During our years of antiracism activism, we have had many mentors, teachers, colleagues, compadres/comadres, and students. We have attempted to give credit to anyone who contributed specific ideas used in this book, but much of our own thinking has been forged in collaboration with those with whom we teach, as well as our students; they have evolved collectively. So, although we are listed as the authors of this book, there are many, many people who have participated in constructing its concepts and devising the exercises, and whose voices are woven into the book's narrative fabric. In this spirit, we encourage readers to take the ideas that are presented and to revise, rework, and integrate them into their own antiracism work.

Acknowledgments

We wish to express our gratitude to a number of people.

The four authors of this edition have all taught courses, conducted multiple trainings, and facilitated a range of workshops which promote antiracism. We have been fortunate, too, to work alongside many other talented antiracism teachers and trainers over the course of our careers. We thank the hundreds of colleagues we have collaborated with in antiracism work on campuses and in agencies and communities throughout the United States. Their commitment, ideas, and endless work are inspirational and we are honored to work in solidarity with them.

Any reasonable manuscript requires a good editor, and we were so very fortunate to work with Kate Dimock and assistant editor Mehak Massand for this edition. They offered guidance and flexibility at a time when the country was thrust into a new, challenging way of operating. We would also like to thank our first editor at Brooks/Cole, the late Lisa Gebo, for working with us to realize the first edition of this book. Finally, we thank our family and friends for their support and forbearance while we worked on this project.

Podcasts

The book includes four informative podcasts with the following brief summaries describing the content of the podcasts. Access to the podcast files can be found via the following url: http://connect.springerpub.com/content/book/978-0-8261-8557-0

Podcast 1: Teaching Techniques

Lisa Werkmeister Rozas and Ann Marie Garran

   This podcast shares some thoughts and things to consider when teaching content and topics about race and racism but really are helpful when teaching a range of topics. Some specific techniques we cover address how to create an environment in which students can share in dialogue and learn about their own identities and their place in the larger systems of racism and oppression. We discuss some important concepts like the cycle of socialization, privilege, and agency. We also talk about how to manage and address the differential experiences that people of color and white students may have while taking these courses and the importance of addressing what might be taking place in the larger society and relating it to the course.

Podcast 2: Web of Racism

Lisa Werkmeister Rozas and Joshua L. Miller

   In this podcast we introduce the web of racism and how it functions in U.S. society. We highlight how privilege can act as a barrier to recognizing the powerful structural forces that continue to advantage one group and oppress another. We discuss the importance of the cycle of socialization and critical realism in the rejection of stereotypes and how understanding both can lead to enhanced critical consciousness. The concept of coloniality is also described and proposed as an important framework to recognize how larger structural forces such as White supremacy, capitalism, patriarchy, and Christianity work together to form an intertwined matrix of power.

Podcast 3: Immigration

Lisa Werkmeister Rozas and Hye-Kyung Kang

   This podcast discusses particular elements of the book that have to do with immigration. The concept and practice of immigration is framed around the concept of coloniality. Within this framework we explain our understanding of the powers that are still, to this day, effective in creating groups that are overvalued and undervalued as a result of the power and privilege they have in society. Specifically, we discuss some key historical points in U.S. immigration and how racism continues to manifest itself here in the United States in immigration policy and practice. We also briefly discuss how U.S. imperialist policies continue to push people out of their homeland due to instability and economic strain and pull them as immigrants into the United States.

Podcast 4: Racism and Clinical Practice

Anne Marie Garran and Hye-Kyung Kang

In this podcast we discuss the ways in which race and racism impact clinical practice. We emphasize the importance of making space for exploring and discussing impact of race and racism in all aspects of our clinical practice. In our work with clients, we must ask about and understand racism-based stress and trauma in their lives. We need to be constantly aware of our social identities and how our interpretations and reactions are influenced by racism. We must make space for exploring and understanding impact of racism in our supervision. We also need to address how our agency or organization's policies, procedures, leadership, and environment replicate or address racism. We also emphasize that it is essential for practitioners to make connections between individual troubles and societal problems and structural injustice. Finally, we encourage practitioners to critically analyze power differentials and advocate for change.

Introduction

In a social service agency that offers clinical services to children, adolescents, and adults, a "diversity, equity, and inclusion task force" has been formed to ensure that the agency's clients, more than half of whom are people of color, receive "culturally responsive, intersectional, and socially just" services. The task force generally consists of any individual of color in the agency regardless of position and some clinicians, administrators, and top-level managers. The people of color rarely have much of a choice in whether or not to serve on such task forces and are told that their perspective is essential to the process.

Many people of color on the task force remain frustrated because they see that the agency is riddled with racism, which negatively affects the working environment and the quality of services offered to clients, yet they are told their perspective matters. Knowing that racism is often unconscious within the White staff and that many of those staff members' assumptions and biases result in the agency continuing to be a predominantly White, Eurocentric workplace, serving clients of color, some staff of color use nonparticipation as resistance. They wonder whether the agency is truly interested in meaningful change because the institutional response is generally lukewarm and symbolic, and almost always lacks follow up. Adding to the people of color's concerns is the agency's lack of outward commitment or even statement on the spate of killings of Black and brown men and women and the increased racial tensions locally and nationally.

Many of the White task force participants are frustrated, too. A few share the concerns of their colleagues of color, and others worry that too much emphasis has been placed on racism, which they feel divides and categorizes people. Most of the staff members at the agency have liberal political views and are against discrimination of any kind, so even though they understand the importance of cultural sensitivity toward ethnic and racial "minorities," they are apprehensive about the task force's focus on racism. Some White members also question why more emphasis is not placed on other forms of discrimination and oppression, such as sexism, heterosexism, and ableism.

The conversations in the task force are quite strained at times, with heated confrontations, even expressions of rage and anger. Participants have accused each other of being racist. Feelings have been bruised, characters insulted, working relationships have been negatively affected, and a number of people have become mistrustful and wary of those in the group. They are wondering how much more to invest and risk in this project. Some are concerned that their views may not be considered "politically correct," and they fear being misjudged and attacked, deciding to stay silent to avoid a misstep; unfortunately, the silence only adds to the tension. Others are wary of participants who have all the right vocabulary but still fail to move past a superficial awareness of the reach racism has. One participant says, "I'm a White male with privilege, so no matter what I say, I can't win." Another member thinks, "Will he ever do something meaningful with the privilege he has every day, which I can never take for granted?" A third member wishes that the task force would include discussions about the ways that White supremacy influences policies and administrative decisions in the agency's day-to-day work.

For many helping professionals, this is an all-too-familiar scenario, albeit for the most part well-intentioned. In our example here, an agency has at least tried to consider and discuss issues of racism and inclusion in an attempt to better serve its clients and to foster stronger relationships between colleagues. Yet the domain of what should be under consideration is contested, the assumptions about what is real and important are under dispute, often based on lived experience. The very words used to discuss the topic (such as *racism*) carry different meanings for the participants, who have experienced racial oppression, power, and privilege in different ways. Although they may share certain professional values and ethics, they do not necessarily agree in their worldviews. And no one stands above the fray. All participants are intersectionally situated by virtue of their race, ethnicity, social identities, group memberships, and personal experiences.

This example offers a taste of the complexity of racism in human service organizations today, to illustrate how challenging, if not daunting, is the task of understanding, discussing, and working to overcome it. This is not unique to human service organizations. It is true of racism in the United States in general. Tilly (1998) has described that racism is an example of a "durable inequality"—emulated and adapted by social institutions and organizations, each a synecdoche for society at large.

Tackling racism is compounded by a lack of agreement about what exactly racism is. Racism has been equated with prejudice and bias. By this definition, anyone can be racist or nonracist. Other definitions limit racism to egregious acts of discrimination and oppression, such as the separate facilities and water fountains of the pre-Civil Rights era in the southern United States, or acts perpetrated by overt racists, such as the racially motivated savage murder of Ahmaud Arbery in Georgia in 2020, or the killings of Black men and women at the hands of law enforcement. Others view racism as a comprehensive system of privilege and oppression-an outward manifestation of White supremacy—with rights and privileges for members of some groups but not others.

Even when there is not *de jure* racism, differential access to resources and privileges by virtue of one's skin color, identity, or group membership reflects a racialized calculus. Social psychologists (Dovidio et al., 2002) have described "aversive racism" or the enacting of "racial micro-aggressions" (Pierce et al., 1978; Solorzano et al., 2000), both of which are beyond the consciousness of perpetrators, while wounding the targets of such interactions. We cover these varied definitions of racism in Chapter 2, and we offer our own working definition, but we first wanted to illustrate how confounding it can be to even begin to think about racism.

WHY BOTHER?

Given the complexity and tenacity of racism, and the tremendous resistance (whether this is societal, institutional, group, or individual) to undoing it, why should we even attempt to dismantle it? We can offer many answers—first and foremost, that it is morally wrong and injures everyone, depriving all—perpetrators and beneficiaries alike—of their full humanity.

Racism wounds, traumatizes, and dehumanizes those who are targeted by it and morally compromises those who benefit from it. It also is illegal in the United States, although as we have witnessed, this certainly does not prevent it from occurring. Among other things, racism is political and divides and alienates people, extracting an emotional cost and a social and economic one as well.

In our increasingly multiracial and multiethnic society, corporations lose hours of productivity and cooperative endeavor because of racism and racial tensions. Many lives are truncated and constrained and prematurely ended by racism, reducing the contributions that individuals can make to society while incurring the costs of services or imprisonment. Cities become more dangerous and communities less cohesive as racism exacts its social toll. People voluntarily or involuntarily live in highly segregated neighborhoods, which increases social isolation, reduces social trust, perpetuates vast levels of social inequality, and decreases the capacity of citizens to collaborate and share across racial and ethnic lines. Racism is toxic. Still, most USAmericans would agree that racism is morally wrong and violates modern-day visions of fairness and justice.

We have written this book for another reason as well: Racism violates professional codes of ethics and compromises the capacity of human service professionals to help their clients and to uphold their professional ideals, including social justice. The American Psychological Association's (2017) *Ethical Principles of Psychologists and Code of Conduct* states in Principle D, Justice, that "fairness and justice entitle all persons to access to and benefit from the contributions of psychology and to equal quality in the processes, procedures, and services being conducted by psychologists." Psychologists also are urged to ensure that their biases do not contribute to "unjust practices." The ethical standards further mandate, in paragraph 3.01, that psychologists not engage in discrimination, including by virtue of race.

The American School Counselor Association's (2016) *Ethical Standards for School Counselors* states that each student must have access to a school counseling program that affirms all students, whatever their race or ethnicity. The section on diversity (B.3) includes clauses about how racism affects counselors personally and professionally, including developing an awareness of cultural values and biases. Counselors are expected to achieve "cultural competence."

The most comprehensive professional statement about ethical obligations and social injustices, such as racism, comes from the National Association of Social Workers Code of Ethics (2017). In its Preamble, the code of ethics reminds social workers that the

> … primary mission of the social work profession is to enhance human well-being and help meet the basic human needs of all people, with particular attention to the needs and empowerment of people who are vulnerable, oppressed, and living in poverty.

This code also emphasizes the profession's commitment to social change and social justice. Social workers are expected to achieve "cultural competence" (1.05) and are expected to understand the nature of "social diversity and oppression" (1.05), with prominent mention of race and ethnicity. There is of late, an increasing push for a more intentional commitment to social justice and racial equity.

Paradoxically, while belonging to professions dedicated to upholding ethics and values that are inconsistent with racism, human service professionals are part of a society structured by racism, serving clients who are either beneficiaries or targets of racism, working in agencies that reflect society's institutional racism and that employ practitioners who experience conscious, unconscious, and internalized racism when providing services, and organizing for causes that have divided communities. Practitioners are taught their professional skills in schools that are embedded in a racist society and reflect institutional racism by professors, who are racially positioned in that society and who may or may not have explored the meaning of racism in their work and in their lives.

Professionals such as social workers, too, are agents of social control and, as a result, unintentionally perpetuate racism interpersonally and systemically, despite codes of ethics to the contrary. For example, in working to prevent child abuse and neglect, social workers are participating in child welfare and juvenile justice systems that place children of color disproportionately in substitute care and in juvenile detention centers. When working in health and mental health arenas, social workers are part of a system that allows greater access and more resources to White consumers while disproportionately stigmatizing, misdiagnosing, and underserving clients of color.

OUR OBJECTIVE

Our purpose in writing this book is not to indict helping professionals, accuse individuals, or universally condemn society and its institutions. Nor do we want to instill a sense of hopelessness or a feeling that racism is so overwhelming, ubiquitous, and entrenched that nothing can be done about it. We believe that racism can be undermined, dismantled, and eventually overcome. We have witnessed societal gains (such as passage of the Civil Rights Act of 1964), worked with organizations that have made significant progress toward becoming antiracism institutions, taught students who became more aware of their internalized stereotypes and internalized racism, and worked actively at consciousness raising to become more learned and deeply involved in the struggle against racism. Counselors and clinicians have learned the skills needed to work effectively cross-racially, and human service workers and social service agencies have contributed to coalitions working to address racism in the community.

Yes, we have ample ground for hope. But we also have learned that it is important not to minimize the complexity, obstinacy, persistence, and power of racism in society; its power to shape lives, create wounds, construct areas of unawareness and accompanying rationalizations, and divide and alienate people from themselves and from one another. We cannot challenge racism effectively while wearing rose-colored glasses, but neither can we succeed in confronting it without hope. As Levi (1982) described in his novel, *If Not Now, When?*, even when facing the most overwhelming and dismaying odds, to struggle on behalf of oneself and others is in itself the key to hope and survival; the actual act of resistance is an act of liberation.

Therefore, we intend to examine how racism exists outside of us, as well as inside of us, for we believe that health and human service workers must confront racism in both of these sites. Kendi (2019) posits "that racist and antiracist are not fixed identities. We can be a racist one minute and an antiracist the next. What we say about race, what we do about race, in each moment, determines what—not who—we are" (p. 10). We are ethically obligated to work for a society of fairness and social justice and to provide culturally responsive services to all of our clients, ensuring equal access and quality for all. We also recognize, however, the insufficiency of focusing solely on social structures, services, institutional practices, or on changing other people. We must look within and explore our own wounds, biases, and stereotypes, as these surely will affect how we view ourselves and those whom we are committed to helping. Thus, in this book, we will pursue both themes, analyzing the social and psychological dynamics of racism.

We want to be transparent in our objective of eliminating White supremacy and racism and how our identities position us differently. The first author, Ann Marie Garran, identifies as a straight, cisgender female, Black, Puerto Rican, and a person of color. The second author, Lisa Werkmeister Rozas, identifies as a queer cisgender first generation bilingual/bicultural Peruvian-American Latina with light skin privilege, and a person of color. Hye-Kyung Kang, the third author, identifies as a first-generation Korean American immigrant, a cisgender woman, straight, and a person of color. The fourth author, Josh Miller, identifies as a straight, cisgender male, racially White, and ethnically Jewish.

ORGANIZATION

Chapter 1 introduces the notion of social identity and explains how understanding ourselves—whatever our social identity—is essential in examining racism as we set out to raise our critical consciousness. In Chapter 2, we consider how racism is conceptualized and defined, as this influences perceptions of racism and how it is discussed, and has implications for professional practice, social action, and social welfare policies. This chapter clarifies the terminology, which includes consideration of what "race" and "racism" are. We will draw on two bodies of scholarship: One known as critical race theory, which emphasizes the historical, social, and political constructions of race and racism and how the "racial project" (Omi & Winant, 1994) is constantly shifting and evolving; the other is critical realism (Archer et al., 2013), which seeks to distinguish between the real versus the observable world, and to analyze causal mechanisms. Using critical realism, unobservable structures cause observable events and the social world can be understood only if people understand the structures that generate said events.

Chapter 3 places racism in the United States in a historical context. It considers the foundations of racism in this country from its inception and tracks the legal construction of race (Lopez, 1994, 1996) and how this has shaped the nation economically, politically, and socially. We link the treatment of ethnic and racial "minorities"—such as Native Americans, African Americans, Mexican Americans, Chinese Americans, and Japanese Americans—with domestic policies, as well as with the United States' international role, including the historic and continued impact of colonialism and imperialism. By comparing the experiences of ethnic and racial groups "of color" with those of European-descended immigrants, such as the Irish, Italians, Ashkenazi Jews, and Armenians, we can examine how certain groups "became White" (Guglielmo & Salerno, 2003; Ignatiev, 1995; Sacks, 1996) and how other groups have remained at the margins. Finally, this chapter considers the historical formation of the helping professions and their relationship to the construction of race and racism in the United States.

Chapter 4 introduces a new area of exploration—immigration. The concept of coloniality is used to examine the various ways White supremacy and capitalism have shaped the geopolitical landscape and influenced the push–pull factors that undergird the flow of migration into the United States. It also analyzes the historical racialization of immigrants coming to the United States and how that has furthered xenophobic and racist ideology.

Chapter 5 examines the web of institutional racism in the United States today—its various forms, and how they interact and potentiate one another to create a matrix that allows some people to have access to opportunities and resources while blocking others from these life prospects. The chapter presents data illustrating the scope and incidence of institutional racism in this country and how some policies sustain and reinforce racism while others challenge it, particularly in the past several years where the incidence of disparities between people of color and White people has been realized nationally like never before.

Chapter 6 explores why many White people continue to have difficulty recognizing, acknowledging, and responding to racism, despite both the historical and contemporary ubiquity. We employ concepts such as "the racial contract" (Mills, 1997), "critical consciousness" (Freire, 1996), "white fragility" (DiAngelo, 2018), and "the discourse of denigration and the creation of other" (Miller & Schamess, 2000) to examine how racism is masked, obfuscated, and excused, which can present cognitive challenges for those with race privilege.

Chapter 7 continues in this vein, expanding on the discussion begun in Chapter 1 and presenting and critiquing theories of racial, ethnic, and social identity. We link these concepts with theories about group membership and intergroup relationships and conflict. We feel that this chapter takes on significant import in light of the deep, often violent divisions we have seen in the United States over the past 5 years during the Trump presidency. The chapter explores the impact of racial identity and group membership on clients and practitioners and offers an intersectional model of racial identity formation for human service professionals.

Racism does not exist in a social vacuum. Racial identity is linked to other aspects of social identity, including gender, class, sexual orientation, citizenship status, and immigration experiences. In Chapter 8, we present intersectionality, which highlights the interaction and relationship between race and racism and other facets of social identity and forms of social oppression. Interlocking systems of power and privilege that maintain inequality are discussed. The impact of coloniality both historically and currently is used as a framework to understand White supremacy and privilege.

This leads to a consideration in Chapter 9 of why talking about race and racism is so difficult. We consider the importance of discussions about race and racism, the negative consequences of avoiding these conversations, what impedes them, and how to structure and facilitate racial dialogues. The chapter offers a model for talking about racial reconciliation and reparations (Yamamoto, 1999).

Chapter 10 shifts the focus to the dynamics of racism in communities and how human service professionals can intervene effectively. Chapter 11 continues this theme by examining organizational and agency racial dynamics and how human service workers can strive to create antiracism organizations.

Chapter 12 looks at how race and racism influence clinical work. The chapter includes the connections between social identity (as discussed in Chapter 1) with clinical work, and introduces Anti-Oppressive Practice (AOP), how whiteness continues to be a cultural norm that serves to otherize potential and engaged clients is presented, and the legacies of racism in clinical work are examined. We cover issues such as client rage and "noncompliance," as well as clinician reactivity and defensiveness. We examine racial assumptions and biases in theories, as well as what clinicians must do to raise their critical consciousness en route to becoming more effective with people of color in their practices. We end this chapter with strategies clinicians can use to offer more effective clinical work.

When it comes to understanding race and racism in society and within ourselves, we are all perpetual students and potential teachers. Thus, Chapter 13 offers suggestions for how to teach effectively about race and racism, whether this occurs in classrooms, agencies, or the community. It considers typical teaching problems and challenges and presents helpful pedagogical approaches and teaching techniques.

The final chapter, Chapter 14, is a call to action. We firmly believe that none of us can be neutral in a racialized society and that it is important that citizens—particularly those with race privilege—do not sit on the sidelines (Kendi, 2019). Thus, we articulate a professional imperative for challenging racism and offer various examples of activism and advocacy by which people can work individually and collectively to dismantle racism. These strategies range from broad transformative visions to concrete and specific actions. Racism is an ongoing, dynamic process, with manifestations that never seem to cease. As the result of this reality, we struggled to determine a stopping point as almost each day brought another example that was relevant to this book. We finally had to "put our pencils down" and close our laptops knowing that we would be unable to include most recent incidents of racial violence, discrimination, and racist policies being pushed forward that only serve to further disenfranchise people of color. Writing this book at this particular moment in United States' history challenged all of us to come to terms with the fact that this should be a living manuscript that records the ongoing derision that is placed on people of color in the United States. Originally, our stopping point was January 1, 2021 but that proved problematic, as we heard of murders, illegal assaults during protests, and of course, the insurrection at the Capitol in January 2021. The process of writing the book was demanding because of the psychological and spiritual toll that it exacted on the authors. At times, we found it taxing to be so profoundly immersed in the tragic news cycles, literature focusing on racism, the teaching about racism and antiracism, and the ongoing and heightened need of this book. Yet, we also acknowledge that we have written this book out of solidarity with everyday activists, those people who have been engaged in resisting racism and White supremacy, and those who are very early on the journey toward antiracism.

At the writing of this edition of the book, we are in the midst of highly challenging times: We have borne witness to increased fatal aggression toward Black and brown people, frequently at the hands of the police; the COVID-19 pandemic, which has brought to the foreground profound social inequities, and has exposed deep ruptures in our infrastructure and our systems of care; heartless approaches to immigration, primarily toward Latinos from Central and South America, have served to dehumanize and traumatize a generation of people seeking refuge in the United States; and anti-Asian violence and racism at alarmingly high levels. There are continued deportations, no resolution to DACA, continued attempts at state-sanctioned voter suppression across the country. These and other legislative and executive acts, all rooted in racist policies put in place during the Trump presidency and widely supported by his political party, continue to have long-lasting and deleterious effects.

Racism will not end without recognizing and acknowledging it and taking concerted actions to dismantle it. Helping professionals are ethically obligated to work toward this goal and we all have a great deal to learn, and a great deal to contribute.

REFERENCES

American Psychological Association. (2017). *Ethical principles of psychologists and code of conduct*. Washington, DC: Author.

American School Counselor Association. (2016). *Ethical standards for school counselors*. Author.

Archer, M., Bhaskar, R., Collier, A., Lawson, T., & Norrie, A. (Eds.). (2013). *Critical realism: Essential readings*. Routledge.

DiAngelo, R. (2018). *White fragility: Why it's so hard for white people to talk about racism*. Beacon Press.

Dovidio, J. F., Gaertner, S. L., Kawakami, K., & Hodson, G. (2002). Why can't we all just get along? Interpersonal biases and interracial distrust. *Cultural Diversity and Ethnic Minority Psychology, 8*(2), 88–102.

Freire, P. (1996). *Pedagogy of the oppressed (revised)*. Continuum.

Guglielmo, J., & Salerno, S. (Eds.). (2003). *Are Italians White? How race is made in America*. Routledge.

Ignatiev, N. (1995). *How the Irish became White*. Routledge.

Kendi, I. (2019). *How to be an antiracist*. One World/Random House.

Levi, P. (1982). *If not now, when? (W. Weaver, Trans.)*. Summit Books.

Lopez, I. F. H. (1994). The social construction of race: Some observations on illusion, fabrication, and choice. *Harvard Civil Rights-Civil Liberties Law Review, 29*(1), 1–62.

Lopez, I. F. H. (1996). *White by law: The legal construction of race*. New York University Press.

McIntosh, P. (1989). *White privilege: Unpacking the invisible knapsack*. Peace and Freedom.

Miller, J., & Schamess, G. (2000). The discourse of denigration and the creation of other. *Journal of Sociology and Social Welfare, 27*(3), 39–62.

Mills, C. W. (1997). *The racial contract*. Cornell.

National Association of Social Workers. (2017). *National Association of Social Workers code of ethics*. Washington, DC: Author.

Omi, M., & Winant, H. (1994). *Racial formation in the United States: From the 1960s to the 1990s* (2nd ed.). Routledge.

Pierce, C., Carew, J., Pierce-Gonzalez, D., & Wills, D. (1978). An experiment in racism: T.V. commercials. In C. Pierce (Ed.), *Television and education* (pp. 62–88). Sage.

Sacks, K. B. (1996). How did Jews become White folks? In S. Gregory & R. Sanjek (Eds.), *Race* (pp. 78–102). Rutgers.

Solorzano, D., Ceja, M., & Yosso, T. (2000). Critical race theory, racial micro aggressions, and campus racial climate: The experiences of African American college students. *Journal of Negro Education, 69*(1/2), 60–73.

Tilly, C. (1998). *Durable inequality*. University of California Press.

Yamamoto, E. (1999). *Interracial justice: Conflict and reconciliation in post-civil rights America*. New York University Press.

CHAPTER 1

Background: Social Identity and Situating Ourselves

There are multiple dimensions of the self with which an individual can identify. In the United States, racial and ethnic identity have been important concepts, and, depending on the historical context, have held different and often competing positions of value. Having no biological significance, race is a social construction. Differences in skin color, phenotype, and hair texture, for example, have been used to construct distinct racial categories. Ethnicity is linked with culture as it is an expression of a shared set of cultural symbols, values, behaviors and beliefs.

Due to the legacy of White supremacy, race continues to be the dominant paradigm in the United States. Society has not only determined the number of racial categorizations there are but also their attributions and relevance. The hegemonic structure of race in the United States determines the level of power, privilege, and overall value accessible to different racial groups. Thus, someone's racial identification can result from their affiliation with a socially constructed external classification, or the practice of self-identification due to a sense of belonging or connection. External classifications and self-identifications are not always the same.

At the end of the 20th century and continuing into the 21st century, the United States is experiencing a growth in racial diversity, including those individuals who are identifying as bi- and multiracial (Moadel-Attei et al., 2018). Prominent figures such as President Barack Obama, who declared a biracial identity by situating himself as the son of a Black father and White mother and Tiger Woods, who was frequently seen at golf tournaments with his Black father and Thai mother (both of whom also hold multiracial identities) were both consistently externally categorized as Black by society. However, the trend toward acknowledging multi-racial categorization from external classification forces is growing. For example, the first female Vice President of the United States, Kamala Harris, self-identifies as Black and Indian, and continues to be referred to as such in public forums such as the media and public discourse. Self-identification is not only more accurate but studies have shown that being misclassified has negative psychosocial consequences, including lower self-esteem and social belonging (Barreto & Ellemers, 2003). This remains a challenge because of society's insistence on thinking about race in binary terms.

POWER, PRIVILEGE, WHITE SUPREMACY, AND SOCIAL IDENTITY

Recognizing the role that power and privilege play in the process of racial classification is crucial. As mentioned earlier, because race is a social construct, the overvaluation placed on one end of the racial binary and under or devaluation placed on the other end, is arbitrary. Arbitrary in the sense that the value ascribed to a particular race is determined, not by quantifiable value, but by those who have power and privilege. In the United States, those who are on the White end of the racial binary possess more sociopolitical power. There have been many terms used to illustrate the power differentials that exist on both ends of the social identity binary. We will begin by stating that we feel the terms used do not adequately address the differential and can be problematic. For example, the terms "minority" and "majority" were widely used but eventually found to be misleading because the terms implied a numerical differential and did not account for the differential in power and privilege. The terms "dominant" and "nondominant," while denoting a condition of having power over another, present a relational status that is static, absenting the dynamic aspects of racism that produce inequity and injustice.

One conceptualization that attempts to address the hegemonic structure as well as make evident the ongoing exploits and mechanisms employed by those with power on those with less power is the notion of agent and target (Hardiman et al., 2007). *Agent status* denotes power, privilege, and not only the position to define and determine what is "normal" but the capacity to inflict real harm. *Target status* is used to describe the social identity group that is the intended recipient of intentional or unintentional acts of discrimination, marginalization and oppression. While this conceptualization provides a more robust description of the interplay between social identity group statuses, in naming the identity group that possesses power and privilege, it fails to acknowledge the agency that individuals from the targeted group possess. Figure 1.1 illustrates some aspects of identity that are privileged or oppressed, using an agent/target diagram. Agent identities (privileged) are shown on the left side of center, and the target identities are shown at the right side of center. In the center of the two is a description of the social constructs that create, determine, and maintain the degrees of power and privilege associated with each of the social identities. Figure 1.2 is an example of agent identities that an individual may possess and Figure 1.3 displays some targeted identities of an individual. It is important to remember that most individuals possess a combination of target and agent identities. Figure 1.4 offers an image of a person possessing both target and agent identities.

Although the diagram presents agent and target statuses as taking up separate space, they are not disconnected from each other nor do they imply a lack of interaction. Some people of color have a great deal of target status because of physical characteristics stereotypically associated with a particular racial group (e.g., skin color, hair texture, eye shape, or accent), while other people of color rarely experience racism. A multiracial person may experience the salience of their target and agent statuses at different times based on the larger social context in which they find themselves. A bisexual, nonbinary or transgendered person may not fit into socially constructed essentialist categories. In the end, most people have social identities that comprise a mixture, of some aspects that are targeted and others whose privilege renders them as agents (Hardiman et al., 2007). Some people with a similar mixture of agent/target

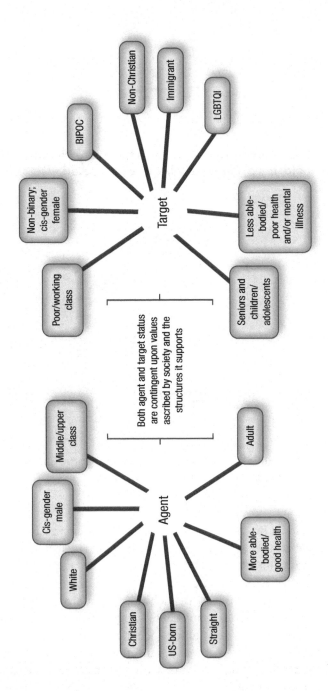

FIGURE 1.1 Agent-target identities. Although presented as static, one-dimensional, and predetermined, people's identities are mostly a mixture of target and agent statuses. Any number of identities that intersect can impact the overall quality and force of target/agent status.

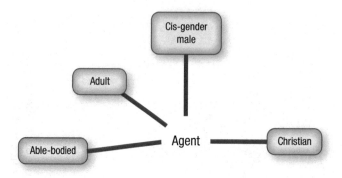

FIGURE 1.2 Agent identities. This diagram represents the agent identities of an individual who is 35 years old, male, Pentecostal, and able-bodied.

FIGURE 1.3 Target identities. This diagram represents the targeted identities of an individual who is Hispanic/Black, bisexual, and a farmworker.

status in their social identities feel privileged, and others in similar circumstances consider themselves to be targeted. We cannot assume that we understand the lived experiences of another person due to their social identity.

It is also important to note that agent and target tells us nothing about a person's internal sense of self and efficacy, or the subjective feelings such as pride or shame that can accompany one's social identity. This concept also approaches identity as something that is possessed by an individual; in many societies and cultures, identity is more collective or familial than in most Western cultures. And the word *target* can imply an idle status, rather than recognizing the strength and resilience that can come with resistance. Our use of *target* and *agent* serve only to illustrate the inequities inherent in U.S. society, and not as assignations of deficit or inferiority.

Despite these caveats, it makes a huge difference to life chances and experiences whether a person's social identity is mostly privileged or is targeted. At the same time, sheer quantity

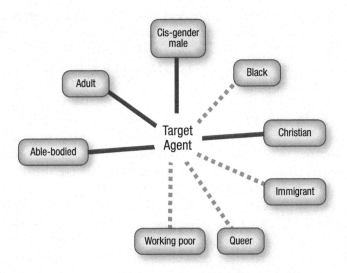

FIGURE 1.4 Intersecting agent/target identities. This diagram represents the identities of an individual who identifies as a male, is Hispanic/Black, Pentecostal, Mexican, bisexual, and a farmworker.

does not always qualify status. In some situations, societal circumstances, or combinations of identity statuses having one particular target status may predict a person's access to equity and inclusion. This explains why racism is further reaching than are consequences of individual biases and prejudices (discussed in Chapter 2). Differences in social identity reflect differential social privilege, power, and access to resources. When talking about social identity and difference, these disparities should always be taken into account. It is not a level playing field of difference but, rather, a tilted landscape of inequality and inequity. Those with the most privilege usually are the least aware of it, as culture and societal norms present agent statuses as central, standard, and most credible. People who have parts of their identity targeted find quite the opposite—their cultural practices, economic standing, sexual orientation, or other aspects of their targeted identity render them as other and often less capable than their privileged counterparts. This is one of the greatest challenges in talking about race and racism. For further work on social identity, see Exercise 1.1. Harro (2018) has drawn a "cycle of socialization" to illustrate how individuals are taught their various social roles in concert with their identity, the ways by which these are reinforced, and how this shapes identity, attitudes, and behaviors (see Appendix 1.1). Reading a book like this takes effort and presents a pathway for developing our critical consciousness. The importance of critical consciousness is that it facilitates our ability to interpret the world and the life experiences of ourselves and others living in the world, within the context of ongoing mechanisms and overall structures of oppression (Freire, 1996). It asks us to examine our society and also to examine ourselves in society. Even though racism in the United States affects us all, we have a variety of individual reactions to this material. Some people of color or people who identify as being multiracial reading this book may think they already know the content or may feel ambivalent about the pain that the content evokes. Some White people will experience resistance, denial, or powerful feelings of guilt and shame. Even the terms *White, BIPOC* or *people of color* (discussed in Chapter 2) are contested and can evoke varied, and at times powerful, reactions. Racism is not a neutral topic. It stirs up strong reactions and feelings in all of us. Yet, if we are to become competent helping professionals, we must take steps to confront racism as it is manifested in society, in our professions, and within ourselves.

None of us is a bystander in a society structured by racism. We may be targeted by racism, benefit from White skin privilege and White supremacy, and, in some instances, experience all of these things, but we are never neutral because racism is never neutral. Ultimately, racism hurts and degrades us all, even those with race privilege. It undermines democracy, scapegoats and dehumanizes people, poisons the wellsprings of interpersonal contact, fosters friction between groups, and causes people to doubt or feel badly about themselves or to unfairly condemn and degrade others. For those in the helping professions, racism undercuts their work with consumers and clients, and creates schisms among colleagues.

Pain, confusion, and other strong emotions will accompany any serious examination of racism—particularly in a context that engages us personally and professionally and is not merely an analytic or academic endeavor. Fear of emotional pain or paralyzing guilt can lead people to engage in profound denial, or to approach the subject of racism with great wariness or detachment. In engaging in this work, we accept the risk of becoming vulnerable to being wounded, and perhaps to wounding others along the way.

Because the spectrum of racism is vast, deep, and far-reaching, some readers may feel overwhelmed or resigned to it. These reactions are understandable, but we should keep in mind that racism has been challenged successfully, in the United States and elsewhere, and maintain the belief that all aspects of racism can be eradicated someday. We cannot allow the complexity of racism to overpower us.

Racism has been part of the DNA of the United States since its inception and is still a major factor today, and all helping professionals have an obligation to work to dismantle racism and overcome its insidious effects. Ultimately, all human beings are entitled to equal rights, and we must visualize a nation in which all people are validated, respected, and included. To that aim, we hope that readers will strive to wrestle with the strong reactions and feelings that this exploration is likely to engender, and not give up. Profound feelings can be a source of motivation and inspiration for changing ourselves and our social world. As we confront racism and struggle to undermine it, we empower ourselves.

Ultimately, it is our enduring belief that dismantling racism will benefit us all individually and will support a better society and nation collectively. In reading this book, learning about and working against racism, it is important to acknowledge that each of us has had different experiences of racism and privilege. For some, this is a new area of exploration; for others, it has been a daily struggle throughout life. This book is for all helping professionals, regardless of race.

Some of the content may appear to be geared more toward one group than another. This is part of the challenge of writing and talking about race and racism. We come to the topic with a range of experiences. Some of us have been targets of racism and others have race privilege. Whether we identify as a person of color, White, or multiracial, or we have a strong or weak ethnic identity, as individuals, we resist being categorized or being subjected to assumptions that do not respect us as unique and intricate beings. At times, though, generalizations are needed when discussing race and racism. We also offer examples to illustrate specific points and concepts, and these should not be construed as conveying the dynamic, multidimensional complexity of people's lives and experiences. Our examples are here as a way for you to more tangibly connect with the ideas, concepts, and dynamics that we discuss. When studying or discussing racism—including while reading this book—you may feel frustrated that your personal experience is seemingly overlooked. We hope that you will channel this frustration into continued learning and communicating and use the frustration as motivation to fuel antiracism activism, including offering feedback and contributing to teaching and leadership roles.

Ultimately, no one reading this book is single-handedly responsible for the systemic racism that has hobbled our nation from its inception. There are, though, ways that many of you reading this book have benefited generationally and currently from systemic racism. As professionals and citizens (of the United States and/or the world), however, we are accountable for how we respond to racism today—in our own lives and in the lives of our clients. Thus, when learning about the nature of racism and counteracting the impact that racism has had on us, we should strike a balance between pushing ourselves to do more while also being gentle with ourselves and others. In any case, in order for things to change, we must press ourselves past our comfort zone to our learning edge and be open to absorbing new content, skills, and insights about ourselves and society.

Racism has a long history and far-reaching tentacles, and overcoming it will take time, humility, and persistence. In the process, we may learn and explore things about ourselves that we do not like, some of which will be unpleasant or even abhorrent. And we will encounter bias and prejudice in others. Although critical self-awareness and self-monitoring are important components of this process, excessive self-criticism can be detrimental. It can lead us to shut down or, if we are unduly impatient with others, cause them to shut down. This does not further the cause of antiracism.

Beyond confronting ourselves and others and taking responsibility for what we say and do, we should work to develop patience and compassion for the struggle that antiracism work involves. We are imperfect beings trying to be decent people doing good work. We will make mistakes. We may hurt people inadvertently or be hurt ourselves. At times, we may think we have regressed or feel more angry or confused than enlightened. All of these reactions are normal and predictable when undertaking a project as complex, challenging, and important as this one. Thus, a balance between pushing ourselves to do more and accepting our limitations is helpful in this work.

Most of us prefer to be viewed as individuals and not placed in social categories or be typecast by others. We do not appreciate people making assumptions about who we are, particularly based on our appearance. This is part of what is so pernicious about racism: It stems from a social construction of race, a system of categorizing and generalizing about people based on physical characteristics and society's ascribed value and meaning. We consider this concept in greater detail in Chapter 2, but for now, it is important to note the tension between the understandable wish to author our own identities and the social reality of how our identities can be constructed or even imposed by others.

When talking about race and racism, we do not want to be viewed solely as racial beings. We are far more complex than that. Our social identity has many facets—gender, social class, age, race, ethnicity, sexual orientation, religion, and ability/disability—which together constitute who we are as social beings—which affects the way we see and experience the world, and the way the world sees us. Social identity is a useful construct as we approach the topic of race and racism. It helps us situate ourselves and be mindful of who we are in relation to students, colleagues, consumers, and others. By examining our social identity we begin the process of developing our critical consciousness which lays the groundwork for us to understand our own biases, privilege, and history in relation to others, which in turn gives us the necessary awareness of the larger systems of which we are a part. It is a crucial concept to grasp in the journey to understanding racism more fully.

What is meant by social identity? This is a central topic in Chapters 7 and 8, but it is helpful to introduce the concept now so we can "situate" ourselves. Tajfel (1981) described social identity as that part of our self-concept that comes from our membership in social groups, the value we and society place on this membership, and what it means to us emotionally.

Society has categorized various aspects of individuals that differ due to appearance, function, development, and circumstance. Each of us has a range of feelings associated with these social categories. The statements about who we are also contain an assumption about another social category—gender—as one author is male the other three are female. Although observers might be able to tell that one of us is White and male and the others are people of color and female, they might not be able to discern that one of us is Jewish, another of us Peruvian, and another of us an immigrant. They also would not know how we feel about our gender, ethnicity, and race, unless we tell them. But, like it or not, people will make assumptions about us when they see us, as this is a normal human response.

Tajfel's definition of social identity has been criticized for being too individualistic (Eriksen, 2001; Kelman, 2001). People do not always choose their social identities. Social identities emerge at certain times under specific conditions; they are shaped by social and cultural contexts, public discourses, national myths, and intergroup relations. For example, the meaning of being Jewish in Europe shifted before, during, and after World War II. A Jewish person who was no longer observant and whose ethnic or religious affiliation as a Jew had little or no personal meaning would have been defined as Jewish during the Nazi era, whether it was salient to their sense of self or not. In Rwanda, which experienced genocidal conflict, the meaning of being a Tutsi or a Hutu was woven inextricably into the relationships, perceptions, and history between the two ethnic groups. A Latinx person who is an immigrant to the United States could find themselves the target of public aggression and humiliation when speaking Spanish in public, particularly in states where polarizing opinions around immigration are high. As we consider in Chapter 3, throughout U.S. history, people have been granted privileges or have encountered barriers or overt oppression based on social constructions of their race. Social identity is how we see ourselves in relation to others. It reflects two powerful social motives: our desire to be included and belong to a group, and at the same time our need for individuation and separateness (Brewer, 2001). This is how we internalize being part of our social world. It influences how we position, align, and categorize ourselves and how we join with and individuate ourselves from others. It is the sense of self that we bring with us to work, to school, in public, at home—every environment and system that we are part of—although what we bring and share about ourselves varies considerably among cultures and depends upon social contexts. Some aspects of our social identity are self-selected, customized, and individualized. Others are collectively constructed, shared with others, and at times imposed.

It is also important to note that social identity is a fluid and changing concept. How we see ourselves or how others view us may be different today than 2 years ago. And social context is another determinant of which parts of our social identities are salient at a given moment; for example, what neighborhood we are walking through, who else is in a classroom with us, and how much we feel others are similar or dissimilar to us, and which people or groups we align ourselves with. Finally, social identity is complex, and it is often difficult to feel comfortable fitting into binary categories assigned by society and others. We consider these issues in greater detail in Chapter 7.

SITUATING OURSELVES

Rather than talk abstractly about social identity, let us explore our social identities together. Figure 1.5 presents a diagram encompassing some aspects of social identity: age, sexual identity, chosen interests, nationality, social class, economic status, gender, health status, religion, ethnicity, race, and political affiliation. Already we can see how some of our social identity is chosen, some is inherited, other parts are imposed, and all aspects have meanings that are socially constructed. On the outer edge of the circle, we have listed some environmental factors that shape social identity: family, culture, institutions, political climate, economy, history, community, religion, and geography. These external contexts are also fluid and are experienced subjectively: Culture may be conscious and huge for one person and either invisible or less relevant for another. And what is on the outside of the circle

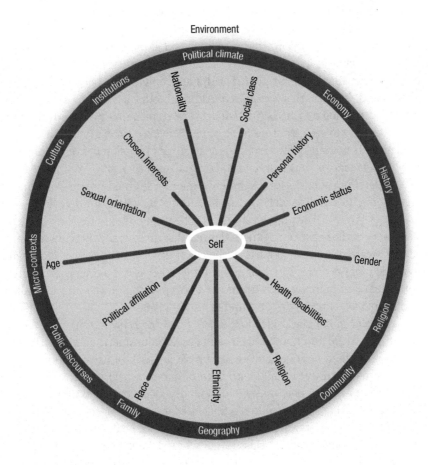

FIGURE 1.5 Social identity pie.

(e.g., religion or geography) can also be internalized as part of a person's social identity; for example, a person may identify as a Southern Baptist. Understandably, there are several of our identities that we find instrumental in defining who we are to ourselves and to others around us. For one person, being a student, father, or spouse may be the primary way they experience themselves moving through the world. While this may be true and very important on an individual level, the identity categories that are outlined in Figure 1.2 are those that carry varying levels of social power and privilege that determine the kind of involvement each has within the overall mechanisms of oppression. Because of the way society is structured, these social identities carry the most weight, or rather, are more likely to determine how much equity, inclusivity and power you have afforded to you.

This might be a good time to draw your own social identity pie (see Exercise 1.2). If you do this exercise in class or in a group, it can be productive to discuss the questions listed in Exercise 1.2 in pairs. After thinking or talking about the questions, some of the following points might emerge:

- ▶ *Identity changes over time.* If we had drawn our pies 5 or 10 years ago, would they have looked the same as they do today? Probably not. Some aspects are mutable, and others have changed or shifted in importance. As we encounter new experiences and the world around us changes, our social identity evolves. It is dynamic, not a static part of ourselves. (We consider phases of social identity development in Chapter 7.)

- ▶ *Some of our identity is chosen, some is imposed, and at times identity is a combination of the two.* We have choices over some parts of our social identity, but we receive other pieces from others and society. Also, there is a dynamic interaction between the parts that are imposed and the parts that are chosen. Although our race may be socially constructed resulting in it being ascribed a particular value or meaning by society, individually we have the agency to create our own meaning. However, the ways which others perceive our identity is not our choice and can be a source of tension or confusion.

- ▶ *Some of our identity is conscious, and other parts are unconscious.* We are always aware of some parts of our identity, and others we take for granted or think about only when we are doing an exercise such as this. It is useful to reflect on *why* we are so aware of some parts of our identity and unaware of others. In our experience, people tend to be more aware of those aspects of their identity that are socially targeted or marginalized and less aware of privileged parts of their identity. This concept of marginalized and privileged parts of our identity is important to note, as it is a theme that runs throughout this text and in many ways forms the underpinning of why it is so challenging for some people to acknowledge and understand racism.

- ▶ *What is salient in our social identities differs from one person to the next.* For example, although my friend and I both may be female, African American, and Puerto Rican, the meaning that these facets of our identity have for each of us may differ considerably. One of us may identify strongly with both of her ethnic heritages, and the other of us may identify only with one heritage and identify most strongly with being a lesbian.

- ▶ *What is salient in our social identities is influenced by social context.* If a White man is in a classroom with a lot of other White men, he may not be conscious of his race or gender. If he is the only man in a class full of women, he is likely to be highly aware that he is male, or in a class where he is the only White person, very aware of his race. Eriksen (2001) offered the construct that social identity is relational, situational, and flexible. We examine this concept more in Chapter 7 as we consider "in group" and "out group" characteristics and behaviors.

▶ *Conflict and oppression can heighten our awareness of our social identity.* Social identities forged in conflict or in opposition to culture and society usually are salient, whereas those that are part of the mainstream or carry a lot of privilege are often less visible. (We consider this dynamic in greater detail in Chapters 6, 7, and 8.)

▶ *Social identity is co-created in microrelations.* Moffat and Miehls (1999) made the point that how we construct our social identity varies from relationship to relationship and from one interaction to another. The parts of self that emerge with an old friend may be very different from the parts that are prominent when meeting with a supervisor.

These points about social identity can be helpful to keep in mind when taking a course on racism, talking about racism in groups, or even reading a book like this. It is helpful to position ourselves, to think about our social identity, and to consider the social identities of people whom we are interacting with or reading about. We all have social identities, which vary considerably from person to person and have different significance and meaning for each individual. We must respect our diversity and appreciate our different experiences through our actions and our deeds, not solely with our words.

PREPARING TO LEARN

Creating a "Safe" Environment?

Often, people embarking on an exploration of race and racism will say they need to feel safe when processing difficult material (Garran & Rasmussen, 2014). The suggestions presented here lend themselves to creating "safer" learning contexts that are conducive to learning and growth. As should be clear by now, learning about racism is not merely an academic enterprise. It combines substantive knowledge with self-awareness and reflection. This involves taking risks, moving out of our comfort zones, and being open to new experiences and to feedback. Psychological and emotional safety are not things that can ever be fully guaranteed, though the expressed desire for safety should be explored with students—with the understanding that definitions may vary widely, often depending on one's social location.

Although the risk of hurt feelings or bruised self-esteem is always a possibility, these reactions can spur growth and self-awareness, particularly as they coax people to their learning edge. Ultimately, we cannot learn about racism without taking some emotional risks, keeping in mind that the risks of exploring racism in a book or class are minor in comparison to the risks that racism poses to people of color day in and day out. Ultimately, exploring racism in a class can be beneficial to everyone, especially when it leads to action to dismantle racism.

CREATING A CONTEXT FOR LEARNING

Certain concepts can assist us when we are trying to learn about racism and other forms of oppression, including the notions of comfort zones, learning edges, and triggers (Hardiman et al., 2007). *Comfort zones* are the safe places from which we generally operate, where things are familiar and predictable, and where we feel most in control. If we stay inside our comfort zones, we have little impetus for change, we surround ourselves with the well-known, and we do not challenge ourselves with new information or experiences. Moving too far away from our comfort zone can feel threatening and evoke a great deal of anxiety. Sometimes this anxiety comes from within and other times, we are overtly or tacitly coached by our family and friends to stay within the bounds of what is known; straying can come with great consequence, such as being mocked at the very least and ostracized at its worst. This fear of rejection can lead people to withdraw, shut down, or simply maintain the status quo.

Hardiman et al. (2007) suggest that the balance we should strive to achieve is our learning edge—that place where we are on the edge of our comfort zone—not so far out that we panic, but looking out at the world and taking small steps away from our safe place. At the learning edge, we try to remain open to new perspectives, enhancing our awareness of self and others, and ultimately learning new information that we can integrate into new understandings. We have achieved a balance between comfort and discomfort, stability and instability, awareness of self and openness to others, having some semblance of an anchor while allowing and pushing ourselves to sail into new waters.

As we move to our learning edge, we usually encounter some internal mine fields that can be activated by *triggers:* words, ideas, or statements that set off a strong emotional reaction (Hardiman et al., 2007). Triggers often strike an emotional vein, either unconscious or conscious, that holds reservoirs of pain, frustration, fear, confusion, guilt, or shame. We all have triggers and should not be alarmed or immobilized by them. The key thing is to learn about what they are, recognize them when they arise, and learn how to handle them rather than have them manage you. When we are emotionally activated in a negative way, we are less likely to be open to new learning and other people and perspectives, and more likely to feel guarded or defensive. Conversely, when experiencing a sense of well-being, we approach people and topics with greater openness and flexibility and generally are less judgmental of ourselves and others (Isen, 2009). (Exercise 1.3 offers some opportunities to think this through.)

Identifying comfort zones and learning edges, as well as identifying and managing triggers, require both self-reflection and awareness of others. It can be useful to identify what fears and hopes people have in group situations, such as when taking a course on racism or working in an agency exploring racism or a related topic. Identifying hopes and aspirations enables individuals to define and express their goals for the course, workshop, or discussion; indicates areas of convergence and divergence; and allows teachers and facilitators to clarify realistic goals for the group. Similarly, having a set of agreements on what each person can expect from the group as they embark on a learning experience together is essential in providing an environment that has predictability.

Expressing fears and concerns also is helpful, as this allows for venting anxiety, as well as providing an opportunity for members to collectively generate ideas for managing the group process effectively. It also can lead to suggestions and ideas about how to proceed if the group becomes stuck, if there is a lack of consensus or compromise, or if excessive conflict arises.

CONCLUSION

This book, as well as courses and workshops on racism and other issues of diversity have the potential to lead to new insights and commitments, but may also engender strong emotional reactions, influenced and moderated by a sense of one's social identity along with challenging or failed attempts at approaching study of this material in the past. A constructive learning environment should encourage openness to new information and experiences, appreciation of differences, recognition of differential social power and privilege, the influence of White supremacy, and self-awareness and examination.

The following exercises can help in identifying and investigating aspects of social identity and the concepts of comfort zone, learning edge, and triggers.

The next two chapters explore how racism is conceptualized and review the history of racism in the United States. Later, we will also explore the manifestations of institutional racism today, highlighting the growing national awareness of vast, life-altering inequities. Using the concepts and techniques presented in this chapter should provide a structure and foundation for engaging with this challenging material.

EXERCISE 1.1 Racial Identity Formation

This exercise should be done in pairs, with each member of the pair interviewing the other.

1. When did you first become aware of your race and ethnicity?
2. Were there any "critical incidents" that shaped your awareness of your identity?
3. How has your racial or ethnic identity affected your life?
4. How does your racial or ethnic identity intersect with other aspects of your identity?
5. In what ways are you targeted, oppressed, or marginalized? In what ways are you privileged? How do these different aspects of your identity interact?

After conducting the interview, write it up or discuss it in class. Consider how your partner's experience with racial identity formation is similar to or different from yours. What did you learn about your partner and yourself? In what ways are you similar and different?

EXERCISE 1.2 Social Identity

On a blank piece of paper, draw your own social identity pie. Look at the pie presented in this chapter and think about which parts are relevant to you. You might draw certain pieces of your pie as being very big and others very small. Some pieces of the pie in this chapter may not be relevant for you, or some aspects of your social identity may be missing. You may want to draw your pie to reflect these differences. Draw your pie in whatever shape, with whatever contents and in whatever proportions, best describes you.

Either on your own or in pairs, consider the following questions:

1. Which parts of your social identity are most important and meaningful for you and why?
2. Which parts are apparent to others and which are more hidden?
3. Which parts did you consciously choose and which parts do you feel were imposed upon you?
4. Which parts of your identity give you the greatest source of pride and satisfaction?
5. Which parts of your identity are ambiguous, in flux, or generate ambivalence?
6. When you are in classes, in your internship, or at work, which parts of your identity come to life and which parts are in the background?
7. Do you ever have to monitor whether you present or hide certain parts of your identity?

EXERCISE 1.3 Exploring Triggers

This exercise can be done in pairs, in small groups, or individually.

1. When discussing race and racism, what are you most apprehensive about?
2. What types of statements or situations do you find triggering?
3. What responses are most typical for you when you are triggered?
4. What gets stirred up for you when you are triggered in discussions of racism?
5. What strategies work for you when you are triggered? Are these strategies adaptive, allowing you to stay in the conversation, or avoidant, giving yourself permission to leave before the work is done?
6. What do you need from those around you in these moments?
7. What guidelines for classroom discussion would you find helpful?

APPENDIX 1.1: The Cycle of Socialization

The cycle of socialization is a key concept in helping us understand how people come to espouse certain values, beliefs, biases, and prejudices.

a. In the beginning (stage 1), we are all born into this world without any biases, ideals, values, or beliefs.
b. We are all taught these things by people we know and love (stage 2). They were also taught *their* set of beliefs by people they love and trusted. As we grow-up we are generally surrounded by people with the same values and beliefs as our families, which is why we often don't realize there are other ways to view the world. The things to which we are exposed (and/or not exposed) become familiar and many outside of our experience become frightening or anxiety provoking.
c. Since the institutions we belong to generally also reinforce what we have already been taught, these beliefs and values are largely held in the unconscious (stage 3).
d. We continue to get rewarded when we do not question these beliefs, and punished when we do (stage 4). Many quickly learn not to question what they have been socialized with.
e. As we become older and venture outside of our familiar environment, we may recognize that not all of what we were taught was complete or truthful. It is at this point where we begin to become aware that differences exist and may feel some confusion and dissonance trying to make sense of the discord (stage 5).
f. Finally, we have the opportunity to assess and reflect on our beliefs and determine whether or not those are what we hold as values at this point in our development or not (stage 6).
g. At this point we can either continue believing what we were taught and think it was "an exception" or we can reflect on how we might have different experiences and ideas than those with which we are raised. This would interrupt the cycle of socialization and begin the cycle of liberation.

Core processes in all parts of the cycle: Fear, ignorance, confusion, insecurity.

Stage 1: The Beginning

▶ Born into a world with the institutional and cultural structures of oppression.
▶ Distorted and limited information about the world.
▶ Incubator of biases, stereotypes, prejudice, habits, traditions.

Stage 2: First Socialization

▶ Socialized into dynamics of oppression by people who are loved and trusted—parents, family, teachers.
▶ Shaping of expectations, norms, values, roles, rules, internalized models.

Stage 3: Institutional and Cultural Socialization—Conscious and Unconscious

▶ Messages come from institutions—churches, schools, media, legal system, mental health system, medicine, and businesses.
▶ Cultural messages—Language, images, practices, norms, music, discourses.

Stage 4: Enforcements

▶ Overt sanctions
▶ Rewards and punishments
▶ Stigma
▶ Privileges (often taken as "normal")
▶ Persecution
▶ Discrimination
▶ Empowerment/disempowerment

Stage 5: Results

▶ Cognitive and emotional dissonance
▶ Silence
▶ Anger
▶ Dehumanization
▶ Guilt, self-hatred
▶ Poor reality testing
▶ Internalized patterns of power
▶ Collusion, bystander behavior
▶ Stress, violence, crime
▶ The normalization of segregation and patterns of power and privilege

Stage 6: A Fork in the Road

▶ Collusion—Do nothing, accept status quo, justify status quo, acquiescing.
▶ Resistance—Raising consciousness, changing behavior, interrupting discourses and patterns of oppression, education, taking stands on issues, raising questions, forming coalitions, liberation through struggle. Adapted from Harro (2013).

REFERENCES

Barreto, M., & Ellemers, N. (2003). The effects of being categorised: The interplay between internal and external social identities. *European Review of Social Psychology, 14*(1), 139–170.

Brewer, M. B. (2001). In-group identification and intergroup conflict: When does in group love become out-group hate? In R. D. Ashmore, L. Jussim, & D. Wilder (Eds.), *Social identity, intergroup conflict, and conflict resolution* (pp. 17–41). Oxford University Press.

Eriksen, T. H. (2001). Ethnic identity, national identity and intergroup conflict: The significance of personal experience. In R. D. Ashmore, L. Jussim, & D. Wilder (Eds.), *Social identity, intergroup conflict, and conflict resolution* (pp. 42–68). Oxford University Press.

Freire, P. (1996). *Pedagogy of the oppressed (revised)*. New York: Continuum.

Garran, A. M., & Rasmussen, B. (2014). Safety in the classroom: Reconsidered. *Journal of Teaching in Social Work, 34*(4), 401–412.

Hardiman, R., Jackson, B. W. & Griffin, P. (2007). Conceptual foundations for social justice education. In M. Adams, L. A. Bell, & P. Griffin (Eds.), *Teaching for diversity and social justice* (2nd ed., pp. 35–66). Routledge.

Harro, B. (2018). The cycle of socialisation. In A. Adams, W. J. Blumenfeld, C. Casteneda, H. W. Hackman, M. L. Peters, & X. Zuniga (Eds.), *Readings for diversity and social justice* (pp. 45–52). Routledge.

Isen, A. (2009). *A role for neuropsychiatry in understanding the facilitating influence of positive affect on social behavior and cognitive processes*. In C. S. Lopez (Ed.), *Oxford handbook of positive psychology* (2nd ed., pp. 503–518). Oxford University Press.

Kelman, H. C. (2001). The role of national identity in conflict resolution: Experiences from Israeli–Palestinian problem solving workshops. In R. D. Ashmore, L. Jussim, & D. Wilder (Eds.), *Social identity, intergroup conflict, and conflict resolution* (pp. 187–212). Oxford University Press.

Moadel-Attie, R., Levy, S. R., London, B., & Al-Rfou, R. (2018). Evolution of social identity terms in lay and academic sources: Implications for research and public policy. *Analyses of Social Issues and Public Policy, 18*(1), 323–352.

Moffat, K., & Miehls, D. (1999). Development of student identity: Evolution from neutrality to subjectivity. *Journal of Teaching in Social Work, 19*(1/2), 65–76.

Tajfel, H. (1981). *Social identity and intergroup relations*. Cambridge University Press.

CHAPTER 2

What Is Racism?

INTRODUCTION

In a class on racism in a graduate school for social workers, students are asked to define themselves racially and ethnically. A White male student from a predominantly White suburb in the midwestern United States responds: "I think of myself as an American. I treat everyone the same, and don't like to see race. I don't care if you're Black, Brown, red, orange, or purple. People are people!"

An African American woman from Los Angeles responds: "I'm Black, African American, part Cherokee Indian. All of my life I've been defined by my race. I'm proud of who I am. When you say you don't see race, you don't see me. It's as if you're telling me to be White, which is racist."

The first student responds, somewhat defensively: "This is what I hate about all of this focus on race and racism. People misjudge me and distort what I say, and before I know it, I'm called a 'racist.'"

A White Jewish woman from Boston adds: "I'm not White, I'm Jewish. I have never felt 'White.'"

A Chicana woman from South Texas responds passionately: "You're a racist! All White people are racists, because you don't even know that you have a race and that your race gives you thousands of privileges I never get!"

The class attendees shift in their seats, and an uneasy silence descends on the class.

This vignette is similar to discussions that have taken place in many, if not most classes about racism that we have taught. It illustrates the difficulty in talking about race and racism, and also reveals the lack of clarity about race and racism and the different perspectives about the salience of these concepts for people today. The conversation also raises questions about the similarities and differences between race and ethnicity and the experiences of people of color and White people, including those who view themselves as neither White nor people of color. Lastly, it illustrates the particular difficulties for White people to engage in a meaningful conversation about race and racism because of fears of being called a racist or being seen as a morally compromised or flawed person (DiAngelo, 2018).

Sources of the tension and confusion are complex and very real for the participants. We also could have added that some people in the class consider themselves to be biracial, multiracial, or multiethnic. They might think that the discussion was encouraging them to define themselves narrowly and in binary terms, and that they were being pressured to make choices that privileged one aspect of their identity while denying, even sacrificing, another. Others might say that neither race nor ethnicity is important to them; they are more concerned with their gender or sexual orientation. Some might think the discussion about race is misguided, as inequality and oppression are really about social and economic class.

What is racism? Is it feeling and thinking with prejudice and bias, or is it something much bigger? If a person treats everyone the same, are they not a racist? Or are all people from a social category racist? Can only White people be racists, or can anyone be a racist? Is racism active, or can it also be passive? We respond to these questions in this chapter.

HOW RACE AND RACISM HAVE BEEN CONCEPTUALIZED

In 1999, the American Anthropological Association (AAA, 1998) published a statement about race that its executive board had adopted previously. The board explained that the statement did not have a consensus but that it was representative of current scholarly thinking by anthropologists about race. The conclusion was that race is not a legitimate biological or genetic construct; rather, it is an ideology used to justify the domination of one identifiable group of people by another—a rationale that has supported many forms of oppression, including genocide, slavery, ethnic cleansing, colonialism, and other forms of domination, mistreatment, and resource and opportunity hoarding.

Throughout history, groups of people have been marginalized, targeted, attacked, enslaved when they are socially constructed as being different and "inferior," based on religion, ethnicity, culture, skin color, phenotype as well as "race" (Painter, 2010). In the United States, however, racism has usually been based on assumptions of biological differences, which could supposedly be identified by skin color, which is a factor of a single gene mutation 8,000 years ago and tells us nothing else about a person (Kolbert, 2018). "Scientific racism" offered a veneer of science confirming the innate superiority or inferiority of "racial" groups, assuming distinct races: Caucasian, Negroid, and Mongoloid. Even though these terms are rarely used today, the assumptions about discrete racial groups lingers. For example, the census continues to classify people by race. Yet the AAA stated:

> Human populations are not unambiguous, clearly demarcated, biologically distinct groups. Evidence from the analysis of genetics (e.g., DNA) indicates that there is greater variation within racial groups than between them … . Throughout history whenever different groups have come into contact, they have interbred. The continued sharing of genetic material has maintained all of humankind as a single species. (AAA, 1998, p. 712)

All human beings evolved from Africa and there is more genetic diversity within groups living in Africa than on all other continents combined (Kolbert, 2018). Thinking of all of humankind as a single species certainly is not how race has been conceptualized, particularly in the Western world. And it certainly does not mesh with how "racial" groups have been treated historically in the United States and many other parts of the world today.

So, how did the notion of distinct races occur, and why did this conceptualization lead to a legacy of racism? This huge question has occupied many historians, anthropologists, sociologists, and psychologists, as well as politicians and a range of citizens. It is such a complex question that it may never be answered completely, and certainly will always be contested. Further, it is not as if anyone who is studying or writing about this subject has a completely "objective" vantage point, because in a racialized society and world, everyone is racially situated. Therefore, all those who write about race and racism must recognize and share their assumptions, values, and biases.

In this chapter, we explain some of the more prevalent theories about race and racism and how these came to be, and then describe the concepts and terms used in this book. Our position, which follows, is that *race* is a social construction-categories such as "White" are fungible, unstable, and in many ways arbitrary but *racism* is a very real, multifaceted, historical, and contemporary sociopolitical force. We also believe strongly that ending racism is a moral, ethical, political, and social imperative for all citizens, but particularly helping professionals. We have been guided in our research, work, and teaching by a body of scholarship by a range of theoretical orientations, particularly critical race theory and critical realism, which we describe as well.

Historical Underpinnings

Throughout history, there has been intergroup conflicts, resulting in enslavement, massacres, and genocide (Kiernan, 2009; Power, 2002). But in order for this dynamic to be a form of racism, there needs to be a concept of race. The historian George Fredrickson, who has spent his career writing about race and racism, traced how racism was linked initially with religious intolerance in Europe (Fredrickson, 2002). Unlike religious bigotry, however, which always held the potential for people to be accepted if they were to change their faith, racism relies on an essentialist, fixed, unchanging view of human beings.

Fredrickson writes that some of the first stirrings of modern racism were in the Iberian Peninsula in the 15th and 16th centuries. During that time, the Spanish, while battling the Moors, conceptualized Jews as having "impure" blood. Along with the Portuguese, the Spanish were beginning to explore Africa and the Americas (Diamond, 1997). This led to Europeans having much more contact with Native American Indians in North America, eventually enslaving and killing them, and with Africans in Africa who were systematically enslaved and shipped to North America. Eventually race became a "scientific" term, and White Europeans would consistently group "races," with Whites at the top of an alleged racial hierarchy (Kolbert, 2018).

In turn, this served as an economic underpinning for European colonization of the Americas, and later Africa and other parts of the world. This condition created a racially oppressive social structure, requiring a legitimizing rationale. The structure of European colonialism endures throughout the world: Former colonial powers are almost always wealthier than their former colonies, often continuing the process of extraction of their natural resources. And the racial hierarchies structured by colonialism continue. For example, domestic servants in Western countries are often people of color from former colonial nations while the reverse is rarely true. Colonialism was the foundation of White supremacy: a system of sociopolitical domination, formal and informal, that led to the subjugation of people from an alleged different race (Yancy & Mills, 2014). While formal European colonialism ended in the mid to late

20th century, White supremacy endures both structurally and as a cognitive and social framework recognized as coloniality, although it is never explicitly named as such; it is so normal for many White people that it is rendered invisible to them.

The Western Concept of Race

The modern Western concept of race had its roots in colonialism's seismic historical disloca-tions and collisions but received a conceptual frame, buttressing the exploitation of distinct groups of people, from the European Enlightenment. The Enlightenment viewed human beings as having descended from animals rather than as being children of God (Fredrickson, 2002). It also was a time of classification, of "scientifically" ordering the world, as well as establishing and privileging Western cultural and aesthetic norms.

All of this led to categorizing people into races, as well as favoring the White (or Caucasian) race as being the most intelligent and having the highest standards of beauty, culture, and conduct. As Fredrickson has pointed out, this coalescing of European thinking about race had the ironic effect of serving as a foundation for the biological determinism and scientific Darwinism of the 19th century while also articulating ideals of equality and justice, which would be used later to question and undermine the rationale for racism.

Certain groups of people do have clear physical differences—such as skin tone, hair color and texture, and facial features. Nevertheless, the genetic evidence cited by the AAA and others is that there is far greater genetic variation *within* "racial" groups than *between* them. Genetic researchers estimate that 88% to 90% of genetic variation occurs within local populations, whereas only 10% to 12% is between populations (Angier, 2000). Much of the perceived variation between races resulted from migration and adaptations to increase survival in a spe-cific region, such as having darker skin in sunnier areas (Angier, 2000; Kolbert, 2018).

Although the conclusions of geneticists and other scientists are not unanimous, the con-sensus is that all human beings descended from the same original ancestors and that we are all, ultimately, of the same race (Angier, 2000; Kolbert, 2018). Lopez (1994) concluded that "the idea that there exist three races, and that these races are 'Caucasoid,' 'Negroid,' and 'Mongoloid' is rooted in the European imagination of the Middle Ages" (p. 13).

Perhaps during some periods of human existence, there was little commingling of distinct human groups, but this has not been the case for thousands of years. In the United States, all "races" have coexisted and interbred for centuries. Or, as Cartmill (1999) stated: "If races are defined as geographically delimited conspecific populations characterized by distinctive regional phenotypes, then human races do not exist now and have not existed for centuries" (p. 651).

Yet, the concept of race, both scientific and cultural, has been used ever since the incep-tion of the United States to justify severe exploitation and terrible economic and social inequalities. Dehumanization and racial denigration served to rationalize the enslavement, murder, and slaughter of American Indians; enslavement and torture of African Americans; dispossession, massacres, ethnic cleansing, and loss of rights of Mexican Americans; exclu-sion of Chinese and Japanese immigrants; and pogroms against many of these groups (Dunbar-Ortiz, 2015; Resendez, 2017; Takaki, 1993). The wedding of racial essentialism, White supremacy, and social Darwinism led to further justifications for social and economic exclusion, as well as to pathologizing the cultures and mental health of groups considered to be "inferior" (Jansson, 2015; Rollock & Gordon, 2000; Steinberg, 2001).

Sadly, social Darwinist tracts, although widely discredited, still survive in our modern era. An example is Hernstein and Murray's (1994) book, *The Bell Curve: Intelligence and Class Structure in American Life*, which explains social inequality by virtue of genetic differences in intelligence (Taylor, 1997). This echoes and articulates a common discourse—it is character, lack of intelligence, or cultural shortcomings that are the source of differential progress between groups socially constructed as being racially different—while ignoring or downplaying the structural systems of racialized barriers and privilege that persist to this day. Thus, the concept of race does not exist or make sense without considering the dynamics of racism. We now consider some principal theories about the nature of racism and its relationship to the construct of race.

THEORIES ABOUT RACISM

A multitude of theories conceptualize racism and race (see Exercise 2.1). For the sake of organizational simplicity, we group them here into the following meta-categories: ethnicity theories, race relations theories, psychological theories (including theories of prejudice and disease theories), and structural theories (including postcolonial, Marxist, and opportunity theories). We then discuss in greater detail critical race theory and critical realism, which are central theoretical frameworks for this book.

One of the conceptual fault lines that runs through most of the literature about racism and race, and which seems to defy theoretical categories, is whether the problem is conceived of in binary or multiracial terms. Scholars advocating the binary concept often examine racism as a Black/White problem, using concepts and data that separate race and racism into these two categories. Multiracialists view race and racism as being part of a larger prism, with many racial and ethnic groups, and a meaning of race that is continually shifting, fluid, contested, and contextual (Omi & Winant, 2014).

Ethnicity Theories

What unites ethnicity theorists is their belief that racism should be seen as a form of ethnocentrism, which can occur in any ethnic group and can lead to conflict or oppression with any other ethnic group. Race is viewed as only one facet of a group's ethnic identity (Omi & Winant, 2014). This theory also emphasizes a group's immigration experience, how rapidly or slowly members of this group assimilate and acculturate into mainstream U.S. society, the cultural capital they carry and have generated, and how well this assists the group in moving forward socially and economically. In keeping with this theory, Chinese Americans, African Americans, Latino Americans, and American Indians are viewed as ethnic groups, as are Jewish Americans, Italian Americans, and Irish Americans, all with their unique histories of oppression, adaptation, survival, and success.

Some of the key scholars within this prototype are Glazer and Moynihan (1963), who coauthored *Beyond the Melting Pot*; Gordon (1964); and Myrdal (1962). One of the achievements of this movement was to shift the predominant racial discourse away from biological determinism to a consideration of cultural pluralism and assimilation (Omi & Winant, 2014). This theory does not place a great deal of emphasis on power and opportunity; rather, the focus is on cultural differences and the degree of fit with Anglo-American culture (Feagin & Feagin, 1994).

Ethnicity theories fit well with a liberal conception of democracy, in which everyone should be afforded equal rights and opportunities. Thus, ethnicity theorists supported the civil rights movements of the 1950s and 1960s, concerned that ethnic groups such as African Americans were being denied full participation in American society, including the capacity to assimilate. They advocated removing legal and institutional barriers and were for equal opportunity (Omi & Winant, 2014).

The ethnicity paradigm has contributed to the discourse on race and racism by elevating the focus from biological determinism to a consideration of culture, values, beliefs, and worldviews. The backing of civil rights and equal opportunity helped to articulate a post-World War II consensus in much of the United States that overt discrimination, racism, enforced segregation, and other forms of racial exclusion and bigotry were wrong and socially destructive. The casting of racial groups in an ethnic framework illuminated the ethnic dimensions of those groups: the importance and structure of family ties, religious meanings, linguistic styles, worldviews, customs, and practices.

The ethnic group paradigm has received a great deal of criticism, which over the past decades has been seen as a limited and conservative way of understanding racism. A major critique is that viewing people of color as similar to White ethnic groups does not explain the level of oppression, exploitation, and exclusion that people of color have experienced in the United States (Feagin & Feagin, 1994; Omi & Winant, 2014; Steinberg, 2001). It also ignores the reasons that ethnic groups emigrated (i.e., White ethnic groups migrated voluntarily while Africans were brought to the United States against their will); the reasons for leaving a host country; and the reception, resources, and social mobility available to a group in the receiving country (Schwartz et al., 2010). Genocide, slavery, loss of legal rights, and legal exclusion are qualitatively different experiences from facing discrimination, stereotypes, de facto quotas, and living in a poor neighborhood for one or two generations. Racism is not the same as ethnic discrimination; the former is more systematic, entrenched, violent, and insidious. To equate it with the negative experiences of some White ethnic groups minimizes its potency.

Another criticism of this model is that it considers Eurocentric, Anglo-American culture as the norm, and that assimilation and acculturation into this culture is a goal. If a group resists assimilation, the implication is that its members are not embracing this country and are erecting barriers to their own success and achievement. In general, this paradigm tends to center on the group's own agency and responsibility for its success or failure, neglecting an analysis of power and structural barriers that oppress and limit the opportunities of people of color. The emphasis is more on culture, and which cultural traits lead to social and economic success and which inhibit a group's advancement. More recent acculturation theorists have attempted to complicate the notion of acculturation and get away from a "one size fits all" conceptual framework (Schwartz et al., 2010). Schwartz and colleagues note that cultural similarity and dissimilarity between the immigrant group and host country, historical patterns of racism and other forms of social stratification that already exist in the host country, and factors such as whether the immigrants are refugees, asylum seekers, and documented or undocumented influence the social construction of the meaning of the group's immigration.

The new wave of acculturation theory encourages examination of the advantages that some ethnic groups have in capital, skills, connections, and power that was missing in earlier iterations of ethnic theory. What becomes problematic is when the success of one immigrant group is compared with that of another: Does culture breed success, or does success shape culture? An associated risk is that the alleged cultural superiority of one group becomes reified in a similar way to biological justifications of racial oppression.

A racial grouping (e.g., Black) may subsume many ethnic groups (e.g., African Americans, Haitian Americans, Jamaican Americans), which is quite different from a White ethnic category (such as Irish Americans; Omi & Winant, 2014). Ethnic theories on their own are unable to explain the advantages or disadvantages associated with skin color, or the phenomenon of White supremacy and privilege

Race Relations Theories

The 1950s through the 1970s saw a burgeoning sociological literature about ethnic and race relations (Berry, 1958; Blaylock, 1967; Epps, 1973; Kinloch, 1974, 1979; McDonagh & Richards, 1953; Segal, 1966; Simpson & Yinger, 1953; Vander Zanden, 1963). Race relations theories form a broad category that encompasses many different perspectives. Some are aligned with ethnicity theorists, others focus on prejudice, and still others consider structural factors that shape race relations. What they have in common is that they recast racism as race relations. The conceptualization and concentration of study is how different ethnic and racial groups interact with one another.

Questions considered by race relations theorists include the initial contact situation between groups; how groups interact and the role of prejudice and discrimination; and the dynamics of conflict, cooperation, and competition between groups. One of the conceptual advantages of this approach is that it goes beyond viewing racism as an individual problem of prejudice or discrimination and recognizes that people have group identities, memberships, and statuses that transcend their personal situations.

These theories usually conceptualize racism in terms of majority–minority group relations; however, the definitions of majority and minority are contested. Are Jews of European descent a minority group because of their religious and cultural status, or are they a majority group by virtue of White privilege, or both? If a group is numerically superior in a community, yet its members are neither White nor of European descent, do they still constitute a minority group? Does the term *minority* imply less than, and, if so, does this mean that this group will always be viewed as existing peripherally to some assumed center or normative mainstream? This seems to be the case when cities with more people of color than Whites are described as "majority minority." Are members of minority groups "minorities" and what does it mean to be a minority? Who gets to define minority–majority? This formulation may burden individuals with a negative identity and can foster a sense of marginalization and alienation. It also implies a center of gravity, the perspective of the "majority" group, which in the United States is socially constructed as White.

In addition to these questions are concerns that the term *race relations* does not adequately describe the institutional, political, and legal basis of racism. A race relations paradigm can focus on relationships between two or more ethnic and racial groups, without acknowledging the power arrangements that shape the interactions. Prejudice and discrimination can be seen as cognitive qualities of majority and minority groups. This lends itself to viewing racism as a reflection of group attitudes and behaviors, minimizing social context. Within this framework, any group potentially can subjugate or discriminate against another group, which is theoretically possible but at odds with the arc of history: In the United States and other

Western nations, there has been a pattern of enduring inequalities, which constructs privileged people as "White" and disadvantaged people as "people of color."

Psychological Theories

After World War II, psychologists and social scientists became more interested in understanding the nature of prejudice. Prejudice was defined as "the holding of derogatory social attitudes or cognitive beliefs, the expression of negative affect, or the display of hostile or discriminatory behavior towards members of a group because of their membership in that group" (Brown, 1995, p. 8). If prejudice could be understood, perhaps the roots of virulent racism would be exposed. How could the Jewish Holocaust have happened? How do ordinary people become complicit in such irrational, hostile, and destructive social movements? What underlying psychological dynamics were at play to explain American racism and anti-Semitism? These were some of the questions that sparked prejudice theory, and research was directed to the psychological aspects of racism and the social psychology of intergroup relations. Freudian and neo-Freudian concepts were employed to further this understanding.

Early Research

Some of the most notable scholars in this tradition were Gordon Allport, Theodor Adorno and his research associates, and Ashley Montagu. They concentrated particularly on prejudice; psychological mechanisms that fueled prejudice, identity, and personality; and how all of this influenced group membership and intergroup dynamics. Allport's (1954) book, *The Nature of Prejudice*, still is regarded as a classic and has spawned much research on psychological facets of racism. Allport's (1948, 1954) work considers drives, attitudes, feelings, and defense mechanisms and how these contribute to stereotypes, prejudice, and discrimination.

This led to articulating the concepts of in-group (where a person sees commonality and sameness) and out-group (where a person perceives difference, otherness, and possible threat). In addition to psychodynamic theory, learning theory was applied to explore the mechanisms by which prejudice was learned and transmitted.

Adorno et al. (1950) were also interested in the concept of in- and out-groups. From their research, they concluded that a certain character type, an "authoritarian personality," predisposes people to prejudicial beliefs and behaviors. Utilizing Freudian concepts, they described how family socialization, particularly harsh discipline, leads to displaced aggression toward members of out-groups. Part of this dynamic is a predilection for ethnocentrism (inordinately favoring and elevating one's in-group) and the tendency to generalize about negative attributes of out-groups. This conceptual stance continues today as researchers try to explain the racism of the modern Republican Party in the United States through the authoritarian tendencies of its supporters (Reid, 2015).

Building on these insights, Montagu (1965/2001) described character traits, such as weak identity and sensitivity to social injury, that predispose people to display prejudice and participate in discrimination. These character traits, coupled with repressed anxiety and displaced aggression, lead to submerging one's identity in groups that are hostile to other groups and engage in racist or anti-Semitic beliefs and actions. Kovel (1970/2001) also used psychoanalytic theory to describe the psychological need of Whites to pinpoint a group—people of color—to view as inferior and feel aversion to, including projecting socially unacceptable drives and bodily functions on them.

Recent Scholarship

A more recent manifestation of the search to understand the psychological mechanisms of racism is to think of it as a disease or addiction (Dobbins & Skillings, 2000; Skillings & Dobbins, 1991). This approach explains how White people are infected with racism and become addicted to White privilege. Surrounded by White privilege and Eurocentric biases that seem to be normative and ubiquitous, Whites develop cognitive distortions about the nature of the world and their place in it.

Some have criticized the metaphors of disease and addiction as explanations for racism. Medicalizing racism has its risks: It depoliticizes racism, depicts it as aberrant rather than normative, and implies the need for psychological or medical responses, or both, rather than social action (Wellman, 2000).

However, psychological theory helps us to understand how racism, particularly modern racism, persists. For example, the concept of defense mechanisms, such as denial and rationalization, can help to explain how Whites are able to sustain illusions, such as the belief that society is fair for all, or that racism is a thing of the past, despite every statistical measure that contradicts this (Miller & Schamess, 2000). When confronted with realities that challenge assumptions, some Whites feel overwhelming guilt and shame or experience cognitive dissonance, which contributes to White denial of racism. Perhaps this helps to shed light on why the majority of Whites in the United States believe that *they* are the victims of reverse racism (Gonyea, 2017; Goodman, 2011; Walsh, 2013), a notion that is challenged throughout this book.

Psychological theories of prejudice and racism have offered important insights and opened illuminating windows. It is important to discern the psychological genesis of racism and to map how it is internalized, managed (or mismanaged), and projected onto the world as a template. Extrapolating these insights to examine how people identify with groups and how identity, drives, impulses, cognitive maps, and feelings become part of the fabric of intragroup cooperation and intergroup tensions has offered fertile seams of research and wisdom for social psychologists, anthropologists, political scientists, and other scholars.

Modifying Stereotypes

Stemming from the study of prejudice, excellent research has been undertaken about the nature of stereotypes and how to modify them. This framework sheds light on how prejudice and stereotypes become mechanisms that help White Americans rationalize their position of privilege and disparage people of color, blaming people of color, rather than racism, for their own racial oppression (Feagin & Feagin, 2011; Miller & Schamess, 2000). Any understanding of racism is incomplete without an appreciation for its psychological dimensions, and we shall consider this in depth in subsequent chapters.

Still, this approach is incomplete, and by itself is insufficient to grasp the scope of racism in the world today. Racism is much more than the sum of individual prejudices and attitudes; it is systemic, institutional, and sustained by a collective discourse of privilege and denigration (DiAngelo, 2018; Miller & Schamess, 2000). Is the mistrust that Blacks feel toward Whites, after repeated negative encounters, the same as the prejudice that many Whites feel toward Blacks, some of it conscious, some of it below the surface of cognition? We think not but reducing racism to simply being a form of prejudice can open up such disparate comparisons. Also, theories of prejudice focus on what is inside of people with less attention to how prejudice is shaped by what is going on outside of people, culturally and in our institutions. When there is political uncertainty or if people experience the world as a dangerous, unstable, and threatening place, there is a greater likelihood of the emergence of prejudicial ideologies to explain this and that give people a greater sense of certainty and security (Fiske, 2013).

While theories of prejudice sometimes consider the imbalance of power and whether the differential lack of opportunity and access to rights and resources for people of color—essential components of racism—are included, prejudice is not adequately emphasized or fleshed out conceptually because the locus of examination is the individual and the group. Also, questions have been raised about the role of social conformity (Brown, 1995): Is prejudice solely a function of personality, frustrated drives, and family upbringing, or does it have a strong element of trying to fit with prevailing social norms? Otherwise, how can we account for the rise and fall of public expressions of prejudice and intolerance over time and the differences in these variables both across and within societies?

Structural Theories of Racism

The structural theory meta-category encompasses a diverse range of conceptual traditions in the study of racism:

- ▶ Colonialism, postcolonialism, and coloniality
- ▶ Marxist theories of class and racism
- ▶ Split labor market theories
- ▶ Economic and social opportunity theories
- ▶ Power and group conflict theories

Although they have different points of emphasis and, in some instances, challenge one another, they also overlap and share some common assumptions. We briefly describe these subsets, but first want to highlight what most of them share and how this distinguishes them from the theories mentioned thus far:

- ▶ Racism is more than the sum of individual or group prejudices. Historical, sociological, political, and economic analyses identify racism as being pervasive, thorough, systemic, and institutional.
- ▶ Like all "durable inequalities" (Tilly, 1998), racism involves "exploitation" and "resource hoarding" by privileged groups such as Whites at the expense of people of color.
- ▶ This leads to widely divergent opportunities for White people and for people of color, where people of color have less access to jobs (particularly well-paying jobs), a range of residential neighborhoods, quality schools, political office, and other positions of power and influence in society.
- ▶ The experience of people of color is qualitatively different from that of White ethnic groups in the United States. Racism and racial oppression are more than merely ethnocentrism and discrimination.

Postcolonialism recognizes the structural legacies of colonialism (Badwall, 2016). Colonialism was a system of exploitation and domination that lasted for centuries and created wealth for colonial powers while subjugating those living in "colonies," which included destroying and suppressing local political and economic systems and cultural practices; extracting and hoarding resources; ethnic cleansing; enslavement; and genocide. The structure of colonialism persists to this day in the form of wealthy so-called first-world nations and poor, developing countries. Colonialism was legitimized and enabled by racist ideologies comparing the colonized subjects to children, justifying the "White man's burden" of paternalistic rule. Racism in the United States is a legacy of colonialism, beginning with genocide of indigenous people; enslavement and forced migration of African Americans; and ethnic cleansing, violence, terrorism, exclusion, and suppression of Latinos living in what is now the United States along with people from Asia and Central and South America.

Whether comparing developing with developed countries, or Whites with people of color, people of European heritage are in positions of power and privilege relative to people of color living in former colonies or in the former colonial powers. Postcolonialists argue that Whites maintain an economic advantage by exploiting the labor of people who have limited economic options and, therefore, are coerced into working for low wages (Blauner, 1969; Feagin & Feagin, 1994), often accompanied by social isolation and cultural stigmatization. Those who are oppressed are forced into having contact with their oppressors; indigenous culture is decimated as part of the process of suppression and subjugation, and racism ultimately is employed as an ideology to justify it (Blauner, 1969).

A contemporary theoretical orientation that captures the enduring legacy of colonialism is "coloniality." Although colonialism and its ruling structure no longer exist in the same form, the hegemonic power structure embedded in the contours of society continues to control all social relations and is known as coloniality of power (Quijano, 2007). Coloniality of power utilizes White supremacy to arrange a social hierarchy that overvalues Whiteness and devalues non-Whiteness. The matrix that makes up the coloniality of power comprises White supremacy, patriarchy, capitalism and Christianity (see Figure 2.1). Together, they create a power structure that subjugates nondominant social identity groups while legitimizing the hegemony of the dominant groups.

According to Fanon (1967), White supremacy is a system of valuation utilized to force non-Whites to occupy the "zone of non-being" and Whites the "zone of being." Categorizing non-Whites as non-being not only relegated them to an inferior status but to a status of non-human. Similarly, patriarchy ascribed a higher status to men over women with the exception of non-White men (Grosfoguel, 2011). As a result, White women garnered more value and privilege than those with darker skin, who were forced to assume an identity of slave. This social order dictated how power was distributed determining what kind of work was valued and performed by whom. Along with gender and race, other social categories such as class and religion have within them a dominant and subjugated status established by the coloniality of power. Superior status is assigned to those individuals who conform to the values, norms, and social roles of those in power. Those with inferior status are acknowledged as "other." The coloniality of power is also the substructure that informs our understanding of intersectionality (Grosfoguel, 2011).

Economic and Class Issues

Other structural theorists emphasize economic and class issues (Omi & Winant, 2014). Racism is viewed not as a central, independent social process but, rather, as an outgrowth of capitalism and a complicating factor in the exploitation of all workers. Instead of workers

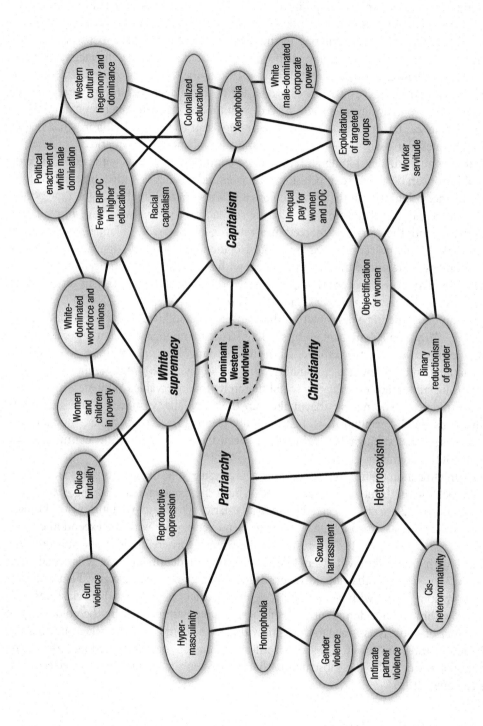

FIGURE 2.1   Web of coloniality of power.

Source: Adapted from Quijano, 2007 and Grosfoguel, 2011.

making common cause with one another across races, together advocating for their rights and benefits, racism offers the lure of White privilege, which splits the working classes.

Relative to people of color, White workers have higher status and advantages in securing occupational niches, from which they expend energy on protecting, rather than fully recognizing and challenging, their own areas of social disadvantage. For example, the history of trade unions in the United States has been one of discrimination by White workers against people of color and women (Schiller, 1998), although there have been recent efforts by trade unions to become more inclusive and less discriminatory. Allen (1994) has described how the practice of dividing indentured servants and laborers from one another during colonial times led to the "invention of the White race," a social identity that divided people sharing common economic interests, in response to the threat of economic and social disorder posed by alliances between poor Whites and present and former slaves.

Some structural theorists emphasize social stratification, status, economic opportunity, mobility, and access to resources (Omi & Winant, 2014). The role of the state in maintaining social divisions is part of this analysis. The mismatch between skills and available jobs—as well as lack of access to the places where jobs are located because of residential segregation, social isolation, the movement of jobs from cities to suburbs, and poor public transportation—create large swaths of severely disadvantaged people of color, particularly African Americans, Puerto Ricans, and other Hispanic groups living in older urban areas (Wilson, 1973, 1987, 2011).

When members of these communities do have jobs, many are in the service sector or in the "secondary" labor market (Schiller, 1998)—under-the-table or illegal work—which is unregulated, is poorly paid, lacks benefits and standards for occupational health and safety, and does not lead to occupational mobility in the primary labor market, where most workers hold jobs. The emphasis on the interaction between class and race is extremely important for a complex understanding of racism. This includes recognition of the economic and social burdens of racism for large segments of people of color, as well as the costs of racism for poor and working-class White people.

Criticisms of Structural Theories

Scholars of racism in the structuralist tradition have contributed greatly to our understanding of the pervasiveness of racism and how embedded it is in institutions, the economy, the political system, and society at large. More than any group, structural scholars have mapped out the contours of institutional racism.

A criticism of those who downplay race and emphasize class is that everything cannot be reduced to class conflict (Omi & Winant, 2014). Racism is a force in its own right and, though perhaps intertwined with class exploitation, operates at all levels of society. Many middle- and upper-middle-class African Americans experience racism regularly in the workplace and in their communities (Cose, 1993); moving up in class does not dissolve racial oppression. Marxists have also been criticized for not sufficiently taking race into account in their structural analysis (Yancy & Mills, 2014). And although coloniality and domestic racial oppression are analogous, they are not exactly the same. Most people of color are U.S. citizens and, at least in formal law, have the same rights as other citizens, although this does not translate into equal treatment under the law.

Seemingly race-neutral laws and policies, such as drug-sentencing laws and transportation policy, disproportionately discriminate against and encumber people of color. Another criticism is that structuralist explanations can be too deterministic and do not acknowledge the agency of oppressed people and their capacity to form cultures of resistance (Omi & Winant, 2014).

Describing the social and economic lines of racism is essential, yet incomplete. In addition to being a structural form of oppression and exclusion, racism is also an ideology shaping public discourses. There are many meanings, signs, and symbols that convey, represent, reproduce, and transmit racism through decades, even centuries, and across regions and communities. Racism in the media, for instance, is not solely about ownership and whose interests are represented (as important as these are) but also concern over what assumptions and stereotypes are embedded in projects, as well as what is ignored and left out. And racism—as scholars of prejudice have articulated—involves attitudes, emotions, and inter-group dynamics.

Though many people would argue that racism today is less blatant and subtler than it was 50 years ago, an increase in open acts of violence throughout the country, including racially motivated attacks on churches and mosques and the murders of Black people by law enforcement officers, during the past decade clearly challenges this idea. Racism remains a damaging force. There continues to be aversive racism (Dovidio et al., 2002, 2001) and racial microaggressions (Solorzano et al., 2000). Racism is a "project" that is constantly shifting and migrating, and "racial formation [is the] socio-historical process by which racial categories are created, inhabited, transformed and destroyed" (Omi & Winant, 2014, p. 55). Racism has subjective as well as objective dimensions, and this is captured in critical race theory and critical realism to which we now shall turn.

Critical Theories

There have been a range of critical theories—critical legal theories, critical feminist studies, queer studies, gender theories, as well as critical theories about racism. We will focus on two critical theories that we find useful for helping professionals: Critical Race Theory (CRT) and Critical Realism (CR).

Critical Race Theory

CRT is founded on the premise that racism has been central to the formation and structuring of the United States, which leads to certain questions. If race is not biological, then what does it mean? How does the way that race is constructed change over time? What are the social, economic, legal, and political implications of how race is constructed? What are the prevailing discourses surrounding race and racism? What is centralized and marginalized in the interrogation of race and racism, visible and invisible? What is outside, concrete, and observable about racism; what is internal and subjective; and how do the public and the personal interact? What can be done to dismantle racism?

These are some of the questions explored by critical race theorists, a loose amalgamation of scholars and social activists. Although the origins of CRT are traced to the late 1970s (Delgado & Stefanic, 1997), there has been an outpouring of books and articles under this umbrella since the 1990s. The impetus for the development of this paradigm was an attempt to reconceptualize and reformulate the understanding of race and racism that had become common wisdom as a consequence of the Civil Rights Movement. Many people committed to ending racism wanted to grasp this phenomenon in a complex, holistic fashion that would contribute to more effective amelioration.

The primary inspirations for this new approach were critical legal studies, critical sociology, and postmodernism (Delgado & Stefanic, 1997). Scholars (McDowell & Jens, 2004; Solorzano et al., 2000) have identified the following five common strands of CRT:

1. The significance of race and racism in U.S. society and how this intersects with other forms of social oppression
2. The importance of deconstructing and challenging dominant racial ideologies, which normalize racism
3. A commitment to racial and social justice
4. The importance and validity of learning from experiential knowledge and recognizing the unique perspectives of people of color
5. The use of an interdisciplinary perspective to understand race and racism

Esposito and Murphy (2000) add that knowledge, understanding, and meaning evolve from intersubjective processes: the interaction of personal meaning systems with historical and social realities and identities, discourses, and connotations drawn from the interactions of racial groups, where race and identity are always relational.

Omi and Winant's germinal work in 1992, *Racial Formation in the United States: From the 1960s to the 1990s, Third Edition* (2014), helped to reconceptualize the meaning of race and its implications for racial formation in what the authors referred to as the American "racial project." They described race not as a fixed, essentialist entity but, rather, as a historically determined, fluid, unstable, contested social construction, continually being deconstructed and reconstructed.

The meanings of race change over time and in different social contexts. For example, Jewish, Irish, and Italian people were considered racial "others" when they first immigrated to the United States, but over time were socially constructed as White (Guglielmo & Salerno, 2003; Ignatiev, 1995; Sacks, 1996).

As Winant (1997) has stated, race is real and illusory; it can both establish and deny one's sense of identity; racial categories can neither be frozen and reified nor completely dissolved. The process of racial construction is not only social and psychological, but legal as well. Some "requisite cases" in U.S. jurisprudence have struggled to define "White" and "Caucasian" by law, allegedly drawing on biological sciences and common sense (Lopez, 1994, 1996; Taylor, 1997). Laws such as these literally have shaped how the population looks, by defining who could enter the country and become a citizen and by prescribing who could and could not intermarry (Lopez, 1996).

Race is a social construction necessary to racism, which has a concrete existence and impact, as well as profound social and psychological consequences. Racism is neither accidental nor an inevitable process. It arises from human ideas, actions, and interactions and is part of a complex human web of interactions imbued with social meanings (Lopez, 1994). Memmi (2000) has described the construction of race and racism as a four-part process:

1. A group of people is perceived as being different (physically, culturally).
2. Value is placed on such differences; the "other" group is thought of as being less advanced, less worthy, less civilized, less trustworthy, and, in some instances, not fully human.

3. The negative differences are generalized to all members of the group.
4. All of this is used to dominate, oppress, and marginalize the targeted group.

Although this is a helpful way to conceptualize the dynamics of racism, we also must recognize the strengths and agency of targeted groups despite these forces and their capacity to resist and undermine dominant racial discourses and racist practices.

This description of racial oppression acknowledges the interaction of psychological and social dimensions, integrating concepts from structural theorists and scholars of the dynamics of prejudice. In a racialized society, we all have racial identities whether we wish to or not. Our sense of ourselves as racial beings and our consciousness about this informs our perceptions of others and social actions (see Exercise 2.2). White people, who have little awareness of White privilege, inhabit a rarefied world by gliding through life without encountering the closed doors or hurdles that people of color navigate daily. This shapes worldviews, values, judgments, behaviors, and beliefs about what is true and fair. One implication, drawn from CRT, is that an interrogation of White privilege and supremacy, and what it means to be White, is necessary when confronting racism. Often, books about race and diversity focus on people of color rather than considering what it is like to live as a White person in a racialized society.

Racial Contract

Critical race theorists also investigate how racism is encoded in institutions, organizations, cultural practices, and the everyday interactions of people. Racism is so ubiquitous and endemic to the fabric of social life that it appears to be ordinary and, for some White people, invisible. The familiarity and imperceptibility of racism for many White people is sustained by a public, cultural discourse that subjugates and marginalizes narratives of racism. Racism is reduced to egregious acts of personal prejudice and bias. Whiteness and European culture are elevated to "normal" stature, placing other cultures and people of color in a status of "minority," located on the borders, as deviations from the center.

One way to understand this dynamic historically is that a "racial contract" has existed from the inception of European colonialism and is encoded in the nation's social contract (Mills, 1997). The racial contract from the beginning determined who was fully human and who was considered to be "savage," "inferior," and not fully human. It determined who had the rights of full citizenship and who was denied those rights. According to Mills (1997), the racial contract is the reality that underlies the lofty ideals and aspirations of the social contract—for example, "all men are created equal"—words written by slaveholders. The contract structured all of society: what is permissible, what is fair, what is normal, what can be debated, and what is rendered invisible or unthinkable.

Mills calls this an agreement to "misinterpret the world," the legacy of which obfuscates and obscures the nature of reality for those who benefit directly from the contract. This leads to White people acting and behaving in ways they believe are ethical and moral without being able to see how they themselves are, consciously or unconsciously, complicit in maintaining a society that benefits them while disadvantaging others—an idea that they would abhor in the abstract. This process sheds some light on how White people, who continue to benefit from the racial contract, believe that *they* are the targets of modern racism (Gonyea, 2017).

Deconstruction and Reconstitution

Critical race theorists are engaged with re-examining and rethinking dominant historical and social narratives. Due to the "racial contract" there are collective cognitive maps and discursive narratives, internalized by many, which centralize and normalize Whiteness and White supremacy. Thus it is important to deconstruct and reconstruct the meaning and understanding of racial categories. Thus CRT seeks to map out subjective states of mind and identity and to link them with the social realities experienced by the targets of racism, which are invisible to so many White people.

CRT leads us to explore and understand the experience of being socially targeted, as well as being socially privileged, and how this shapes and influences social identity. It urges us to examine the hidden "dissensus," veiled by a dominant discourse of accord and consensus (Leonardo & Porter, 2010). Within CRT is a call to action, a recognition that we are not neutral observers but, rather, embedded actors, woven into the social fabric and therefore able to make choices about what we accept or do not tolerate, what we ignore or decide to confront, and whether we are bystanders or social activists.

Critical Realism

CR was developed by Roy Bhaskar as a philosophical approach in the natural sciences, to counter both positivism and postmodernism (Archer et al., 2013). Its principles have since been applied to a number of different disciplines including ethics and social science. Critical realism posits that an objective reality does exist, and it is composed of three levels: "the empirical level consisting of experienced events; the actual level, comprising all events whether experienced or not; and, lastly the causal level embracing the 'mechanisms' which generate events" (Houston, 2001, p. 850). Understanding that the causal level is still real, though not always perceptible, is crucial, as it affects the events occurring on all levels. Without an understanding of the causal level, enactments of social oppression, such as racism, will continue unabated. Archer et al. (2013) offer the concept of magnetism to illustrate the causal level, and its ability to affect the empirical—a mechanism that, though unseen, has real and unyielding influence. CR also describes the world as a set of systems whose influence on one another is variable, significant (or insignificant), and unpredictable. In other words, systems do not operate in a vacuum; they interact with and influence one another, as with intersectional oppressions and identities. Although internal systemic tendencies may exist, multiple systems are operating simultaneously (Houston, 2001) and without a set pattern. Human systems are described as complex due to the countless social and psychological factors that exact influence on individuals and groups at any given time and every given moment.

Using this lens, racism can be seen as a system occurring at the causal as well as the empirical levels; it is a force that has significant influence on all facets of human experience. Hegemonic systems such as White supremacy, patriarchy, Christian-centrism, are unseen mechanisms that construct the empirical and actual levels of experience such as discrimination, racism, sexism, Islamophobia, and anti-Semitism. Often, we presume that unseen oppressive forces influence in one direction only; the oppressor impacting the oppressed. However, as Houston (2001) makes clear, when applied as a social theory CR does not presume individuals to be merely victims of these unseen mechanisms without recourse. Rather, just as these forces impact a group that is targeted, that group can in turn can impact those forces.

Applying critical realist terms, we can understand racism, as comprising three levels: the causal, actual, and empirical. At the causal level power structures serve as unseen forces that shape social life and co-opt differences to create social hierarchy. Such forces include White supremacy, patriarchy, and colonialism (coloniality). In the United States, these interrelated social suprastructures pervade all aspects of social, cultural, political, and economic life. At the actual level these social forces are mechanized through institutions, interactions, self-perceptions, and cultural norms. Privilege, microaggressions, cultural appropriation, residential segregation, and social marginalization are all examples of actual manifestations of White supremacy, colonialism (coloniality), and patriarchy. These physical, socio-political, economic, and cultural structures exist whether or not an individual actor consciously experiences them. We can recognize their existence through our empirical experiences, either personally or in aggregate. Personally, we have empirical experiences informed by racism. Racism is manifested when, for example, one lives in a neighborhood that has been decimated by economic and political divestment. It is present when one strives to attain a standard of beauty that sexually subjugates women and norms beauty to Whiteness. It is also evident when accessing the benefits of privilege by, for example, engaging in self-deception associated with the myth of meritocracy. There are countless empirical examples of racism that impact our everyday lives.

Empirical manifestations of racism can also be visible at the aggregate level. The aggregate empirical level illustrates group patterns as well as individual experiences. For example, racial disparities in health reveal the collective effects of racism on groups of color, as do gender and race-based wealth and wage gaps. Mass incarceration of men of color provides empirical evidence of the aggregate consequences of systemic racism within the policies and practices of law enforcement and the criminal justice system (Alexander, 2010). Tracing one specific form of racism through the various levels explicated in critical realism helps to articulate this framework. In the United States, farm workers from Mexico and Central America often work under exploitative and oppressive conditions. At the empirical level, exploited farmworkers directly experience oppression. They may live in substandard housing conditions (Arcury et al., 2012; Quandt et al., 2013), be exposed to toxic chemicals (Arcury et al., 2001; Robinson et al., 2011), have limited bargaining power (Telega & Maloney, 2010), encounter sexual harassment (Waugh, 2010; Murphy et al., 2015), and lack job security (McLaughlin & Hennebry, 2013). If the farmworkers have access to aggregated information regarding labor abuses in the agriculture sector, they may see that the issues they have encountered do not just impact one or two farms. These issues are present at many farms in many locations (Farmworker Justice, 2017). The actual level consists of the cultural norms, institutions, and practices which solidify power in the hands of agribusiness leaders and away from the worker. This includes laws and policies that perforate the labor rights of farmworkers (Ramos, 2017) and racialized narratives that permit the marginalization of Latinx workers (Nelson, 2008). Capitalism also works at the actual level, creating fundamental structures that commodify labor and demand the extraction of surplus cheap labor of many for the profit of few. Finally, the unseen mechanism at work behind all of this is White supremacy, which denigrates people of color and rationalizes their mistreatment and coloniality (Quijano, 2007), which recasts indigenous land as a natural resource to be manipulated for profit, augmenting the justification for exploitation.

We draw heavily from CR and CRT, although we also utilize elements of all the theoretical approaches summarized in this chapter.

THE CONTOURS OF RACISM

We conceptualize racism as existing along a spectrum, with many different types and forms. Part of the confusion about racism—as the introductory vignette to this chapter illustrates—is that the term is used to describe many different phenomena and is laced with multiple meanings. There are different levels of racism, direct and indirect racism, intentional and unintentional racism, varying sites of racism, and a range of frequencies of racism. We describe these contours briefly before presenting the spectrum of racism.

Levels of Racism

Racism traditionally has been viewed as having at least three levels: (a) individual, (b) group, and (c) institutional. *Individual racism* refers to biases, prejudices, beliefs, or actions that participate in or collude with racism. An example of individual racism is demonstrated by a person who harbors stereotypes of inferiority or difference toward a person who is a member of a group that is different from their own, which leads to exclusionary behaviors or actions, or even telling racist jokes. It can also lead to law enforcement officers using lethal force more quickly when confronting young men of color.

Group racism alludes to actions on the part of one group—often referred to as a dominant, privileged, or agent group—that discriminates against, marginalizes, or in any way oppresses another group that is constructed as being racially different. An example is when White ethnic groups formally and informally control a residential area and will forcefully resist having an ethnic group of color integrate the neighborhood. Another example is the predominantly White composition of many police forces in communities with high numbers of people of color.

Institutional racism indicates systemic, societal, durable racism that is embedded in institutions, organizations, laws, customs, and social practices. Institutional racism forms a web that blocks opportunities for some while offering privilege to others. It leads to a cumulative effect in which groups that are racially targeted are excluded from living in certain neighborhoods and working in numerous jobs and professions, have less access to social assets such as quality schools, and incur greater health risks and other negative consequences and outcomes because of a variety of interacting legal, illegal, direct, and indirect practices. Institutional, group, and individual racism combine when men of color are stopped more frequently than White men by White police officers working in predominantly White police forces and who are more likely to use lethal force.

A final level of racism, *ideological racism*, is pervasive and interwoven into social discourses and narratives. Virulent ideological racism has been enacted throughout history and across the globe through hateful and degrading messages, such as about Muslims in Kosovo by Serbs, Tutsis in Rwanda by Hutus, and Jews in Nazi Germany, and is used to justify horrendous actions against a racial or ethnic group. A modern U.S. example is the vitriol expressed by former President Trump against Muslims and immigrants. By contrast, subtle ideological racism is so familiar that it often passes unnoticed, yet it sustains stereotypes or discriminatory practices. Former President Trump often engaged in this form of racism as well, such as his Tweets about how "no human being" would want to live in Baltimore, implying that those living in Baltimore are not fully human. Ideological racism can be used to reinforce or justify any of the levels of racism mentioned here.

Direct and Indirect Racism

Some racism is overt and direct. Examples of this were the Jim Crow laws and practices in the southeastern United States, which prohibited African Americans from riding in the front of buses, from voting, and even from using the same water fountains as White people. Direct, overt racism can occur at any level. An individual can actively and directly express racial bias or discrimination toward another person and cause bodily, emotional, or psychological harm to the target of racism.

Indirect, or covert, racism seems on the surface to be more passive, but in practice it serves to sustain and maintain racism. An example is seen in the attitudes and biases that inhibit homeowners in a predominantly White suburb from selling their homes to people of color. The cumulative effect can be a segregated neighborhood. Another example is the difference between sentences for possession of cocaine versus crack cocaine, which have no overt indication of racial bias, yet carry the consequence of African Americans being incarcerated disproportionately, more frequently, and for longer periods than their White counterparts.

Intentional and Unintentional Racism

Intentional and unintentional forms of racism are related to active and passive types of racism. The important variable here is motivation. The men who murdered James Byrd, Jr., in 1998, tying him to a vehicle and dragging him along the roads of Jasper, Texas, consciously tortured him because of his race. But many well-intentioned and well-meaning White people engage in racist behaviors of which they are unaware unless confronted. This often comes from unexamined stereotypes or attitudes and consequent microaggressions.

For instance, a White professor, when talking about poverty or single parenthood, may direct her gaze consistently to African American students in the class—a behavior of which she and many White students are unaware but is painfully evident to most African Americans in the class, as well as some White students.

Leong (2012) discusses the concept of racial capitalism; a practice that can include either intentional, unintentional, or both forms of racism. Long offers an examination of a practice where non-Whiteness is valued as a commodity within individual or institutional practices that seek to elevate their own value or value of their institution. Diversity itself has become a valued commodity and most often refers to having Black, indigenous, and people of color (BIPOC) individuals become participants in a predominantly White group or institution. As a result, many institutions intentionally look to hire or accept people of color (POC) in order to be attractive both to White individuals who wish to be in a diverse environment and to POC individuals who do not wish to be the only person of color in an institution. This valuing of non-White racial identity, solely because of the benefits it affords a predominately White institution is *racial captialism*. That is not to say that diversity does not have its merits or that attempts to achieve it are inherently racist. What must be examined is the real objective of an individual or institution.

If the rationale for diversity is only valued to the extent to which it benefits White people, it is commodifying non-Whiteness and has no intention of including POC in the institution's power structure. In this example, the perception is that by merely having POC present, they are, in fact, included. However, the reality is, POC can be present without being included. A desire for diversity that emerges from a belief that remediation is necessary to right the wrongs of past racial discrimination certainly brings with it an intent toward racial justice. Yet, either way, it is the predominantly White institution that possesses the power to place value on non-White identities. What this reveals is that progress for POC in these instances only occurs when it benefits Whites. In order to avoid participating in racial capitalism, when an individual or institution has racial diversity as a goal, they must simultaneously create a plan for how POC individuals will be included in the power structure and supported by the institution.

Sites of Racism

Racism occurs in many different places—on highways when dark-skinned people are stopped "randomly" by the police while light-skinned people drive by; in classrooms, courtrooms, neighborhoods, and streets where White people are more predominant or in positions of power; in television shows and the nightly news, where White people dominate as producers and presenters; in mental health agencies where White people are often in positions of authority and power, even in agencies predominantly serving people of color; in conversations between White people where racial stereotypes and norms or White privilege and supremacy are reinforced backstage; in segregated or racially homogenous neighborhoods; in the privacy of people's homes. Racism operates in all units of society, public and private, institutionally and individually.

Frequency and Magnitude of Racism

Frequency and magnitude refer to the incidence and scale of racism. Is it an everyday occurrence, a legacy that has persisted for decades, or an isolated incident? Does a television show consistently portray Asian Americans in a stereotypical fashion, or did a typecast emerge in a single episode? Is the racist narrative conveyed in a news discussion a part of the network's pervasive culture or a reflection of an individual editor and presenter? When analyzing racism and how to respond to it, an analysis of the frequency and magnitude of racism is useful, and using CRT to identify the hidden patterns and drivers is essential.

THE SPECTRUM OF RACISM

Racism does not fit into neat, exclusive categories. Individual and institutional racism coexist side by side and are interactive; they potentiate one another. The racist attitudes of individuals become reified in institutions, and racist institutions normalize prejudice and oppression, shaping the way in which individuals view the world. Societally, racism is a fluctuating, shifting process, with many examples of societies that have been at the extreme end of the spectrum of oppression during certain eras but not during others. However, when racism and White supremacy are part of a society's history, they will usually re-emerge even if they had seemed to wane. Exercise 2.3 can help with the application of concepts related to the spectrum.

The United States has experienced all of the types of racism described by the spectrum. The spectrum of racism has a core set of practices and a range of levels, as shown in Figure 2.2. The bottom line indicates the level of racism, ranging from the intrapsychic/intrapersonal, to the interpersonal, through the institutional, to the societal/nation state.

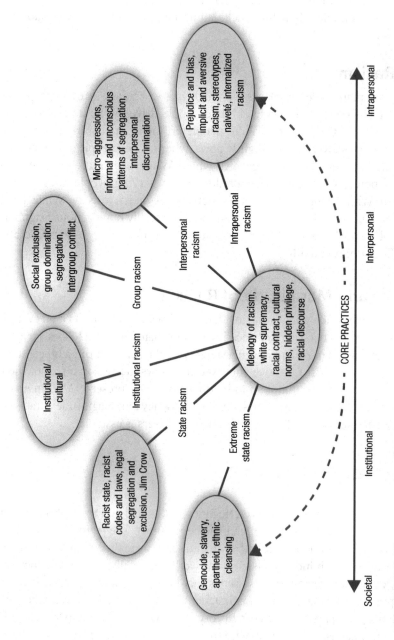

FIGURE 2.2 The spectrum of racism.

In the center of the spectrum is the core, consisting of a racial contract, an ideology of racism, cultural norms, and the oftentimes hidden, invisible privileges of those who benefit from the advantages of the racial contract. The core of racism is part of any facet of the spectrum. The heart of racism is what powers any type or form of racism. Like a human heart, it pumps blood to the various regions of racism, and from them the blood returns.

Intrapersonal

At the intrapersonal end of the spectrum are prejudice and bias, attitudes, beliefs, emotions, ideas, and cognitions. These ideas and responses are what we think of when we see a news story about an armed robbery or what we feel when we pass someone on the street. They are at the core of our internal process and form a reservoir for the stream of messages that we have received from birth, from parents, books, teachers, songs, films, and pictures—messages as ubiquitous as the air we breathe. Our absorption of these messages leads to internalized stereotypes, some of which we are aware but many others of which are unconscious. These stereotypes, in turn, can be a repository of internalized superiority or inferiority—what sometimes is referred to as "internalized racism."

Interpersonal

At this point along the spectrum, we see racism expressed in interactions between people. Racial "microaggressions" occur, unintentional acts of racism often unrecognized by the perpetrator but agonizing and hurtful to the target of the interaction. Or intentional hostile acts take place, resulting in many potential levels of injury. The challenges of having respectful and meaningful interracial conversations and dialogues lead to poor and missed communications. Interpersonal levels of racism create tensions in the workplace and social isolation and even violence in the community.

Intergroup

Intergroup racism refers to the place on the spectrum where people identify with groups defined by socially constructed racial categories. The act of identification shapes the formation of racial identity, and the collective interactions of group members result in domination, exclusion, discrimination, and other forms of group-based oppression.

This level of racism can be manifested in voting patterns and support for voter suppression laws that disproportionately impact members of another racial group, competition for jobs and neighborhoods, and marriage and friendship patterns. This is not a playing field of equals; one group (Whites) has more power, resources, and privilege and exercises this advantage at many levels of interaction and patterns of behavior that appear to be racially neutral and "the way things are."

Institutional

Institutional racism is well documented and is discussed at length in Chapter 5. Institutional racism leads to exclusion from neighborhoods, jobs, schools, politics, healthcare, and mental healthcare; greater exposure to environmental hazards; higher risk of arrest, incarceration, and lethal force; and lower life expectancies. We also include dominant cultural patterns of prejudice and oppression as a form of institutional racism. Institutional racism can occur in any form of society, including democracies.

Official and State

Official and state racism describes situations in which the state is overtly racist. Examples of this, unfortunately, abound. This level of racism includes state-sponsored racism at any level of government. Legal segregation, racist codes and laws, and Jim Crow are all forms of state-sponsored racism that are part of U.S. history. Recently, the U.S. Supreme Court has affirmed the rights of states to racially gerrymander political districts and impose voting restrictions that disproportionately affect voters of color. As long as the policy or law has the veneer of being race neutral, it has been ruled acceptable by the current Supreme Court, despite having documented racialized consequences. Not only has the court allowed practices that disenfranchise people of color from the right to vote, but also those that result in them disproportionately and disastrously being the victims of racial discrimination in the criminal justice system (Alexander, 2010).

Extreme, State Sanctioned

The gloomiest, most appalling end of the spectrum of racism is at the state-sanctioned extreme. Examples include genocide, ethnic cleansing, slavery, and racial apartheid. All of these are part of U.S. history and, sadly, these forms of racism persist in the world to this day. The profound cruelty and terrorism of slavery and the attempts to exterminate indigenous people cannot be glossed over or seen merely as past practices; their legacy persists to this day and is the foundation for the "causal" level of enduring manifestations of White supremacy.

CONCLUSION

In this chapter, we have traced the historical underpinnings of the notion of race and explored the many meanings and interpretations of racism. Various theories of race and racism have evolved, and this chapter highlights several. We have offered a "spectrum of racism" to incorporate the many forms and levels of racism in the United States.

Our understanding of racism, both complex and comprehensive, should not leave us feeling hopeless or overwhelmed. Racism, in its most virulent manifestations, such as during the period of U.S. history when slavery was legal, has been undermined, dismantled, and delegitimized. But racism and White supremacy are always lurking in the shadows, functioning as hidden drivers, and can re-assert themselves in a full-blown way at any moment. The work ahead is hard and challenging, progress is often painfully slow, and we must often take the long view, but the stakes are high and the risks to us all by remaining bystanders and not taking action are even higher.

EXERCISE 2.1 Conceptual Frameworks and You

Consider the different theoretical frameworks presented in this chapter. Which ones best help you to understand the nature of racism? What questions do they raise for you that are still unanswered? Are there any views or assumptions that you hold that were challenged by these theories? Were there any feelings that came up for you while you read about them? What is your theory of racism? If you were explaining to another person the nature of racism, what would you include in a 5-minute presentation?

EXERCISE 2.2 Colonialism and Your Group

Discuss the following question in pairs: Which ethnic and racial group(s) do you identify with? List the ways that coloniality benefited your group and the ways that it harmed or hindered your group. Share this with your partner. Discuss whether and how colonial legacies continue to shape your lives in explicit or subtle ways.

EXERCISE 2.3 Applying the Spectrum of Racism

1. Take each type of racism from the spectrum of racism and apply it to either a current or a historical situation. Consider what types of racism exist in your hometown, college, or university; worksite; website; the United States at large; and other parts of the world. What levels of racism are present in each example (individual, group, institutional)? Can you identify direct and indirect types of racism in your examples? What specific sites of racism are evident in the examples? Note the frequency and magnitude of racism described in your examples.
2. After completing the exercise, reflect on what thoughts and feelings emerged for you as you applied the spectrum of racism. Were any of these reactions surprising or unexpected? Were any parts of this exercise particularly difficult? What questions about racism has this exercise raised for you?

REFERENCES

Adorno, T. W., Frenkel-Brunswik, E., Levinson, D. J., & Sanford, R. N. (1950). *The authoritarian personality.* Harper.

Alexander, M. (2010). *The new Jim Crow: Mass incarceration in the age of colorblindness.* The New Press.

Allen, T. W. (1994). *The invention of the white race.* Verso.

Allport, G. W. (1948). *The ABC's of scapegoating.* B'nai B'rith Press.

Allport, G. W. (1954). *The nature of prejudice.* Addison Wesley.

American Anthropological Association. (1998). AAA statement on race. *American Anthropologist, 100*(3), 712–713.

Angier, N. (2000). Do races differ? Not really, DNA shows. *New York Times.* www.nytimes.com/library/national/science/082200sci-genetics-race.html

Archer, M., Bhaskar, R., Collier, A., Lawson, T., & Norrie, A. (Eds.). (2013). *Critical realism: Essential readings.* Routledge.

Arcury, T. A., Quandt, S. A., Cravey, A. J., & Elmore, R. C. (2001). Farmworker reports of pesticide safety and sanitation in the work environment. *American Journal of Industrial Medicine, 39*(5), 487–498.

Arcury, T. A., Weir, M., Chen, H., Summers, P., Pelletier, L. E., Galvan, L., Bischoff, W. E., Mirabelli, M. C., & Quandt, S. A. (2012). Migrant farmworker housing regulation violations in North Carolina. *American Journal of Industrial Medicine, 55*(3), 191–204.

Badwall, H. (2016). Critical reflexivity and moral regulation. *Journal of Progressive Human Services*, 27(1), 1–20.

Berry, B. (1958). *Race and ethnic relations*. Riverside Press.

Blauner, R. (1969). Internal colonialism and ghetto revolt. *Social Problems*, 16, 393–408.

Blaylock, H. M., Jr. (1967). *Towards a theory of minority-group relations*. Wiley.

Brown, R. (1995). *Prejudice*. Blackwell.

Cartmill, M. (1999). The status of the race concept in physical anthropology. *American Anthropologist*, 100(3), 651–660.

Cose, E. (1993). *The rage of a privileged class*. HarperCollins.

Delgado, R., & Stefanic, J. (1997). Introduction. In R. Delgado & J. Stefanic (Eds.), *Critical white studies: Looking behind the mirror* (pp. xvii–xviii). Temple University Press.

Diamond, J. (1997). *Guns, germs and steel: The fates of human societies*. W.W. Norton Publishing.

DiAngelo, R. (2018). *White fragility: Why it is so difficult for white people to talk about racism*. Beacon Press.

Dobbins, J. E., & Skillings, J. H. (2000). Racism as a clinical syndrome. *American Journal of Orthopsychiatry*, 70(1), 14–27.

Dovidio, J. F., Gaertner, S. L., Kawakami, K., & Hodson, G. (2002). Why can't we all just get along? Interpersonal biases and interracial distrust. *Cultural Diversity and Ethnic Minority Psychology*, 8(2), 88–102.

Dovidio, J. F., Gaertner, S. L., Niemann, Y. F., & Snider, K. (2001). Racial, ethnic and cultural differences in responding to distinctiveness and discrimination on campus: Stigma and common group identity. *Journal of Social Issues*, 57(1), 167–188.

Dunbar-Ortiz, R. (2015). *An Indigenous people's history of the United States*. Beacon Press.

Epps, E. G. (1973). *Race relations: Current perspectives*. Winthrop Publishers.

Esposito, L., & Murphy, J. W. (2000). Another step in the study of race relations. *Sociological Quarterly*, 41(2), 171–187.

Farmworker Justice. (2017). Farmworker justice: Empowering farmworkers to improve their living and working conditions since 1981. Retrieved from www.farmworkerjustice.org.

Feagin, J. R., & Feagin, C. B. (1994). Theoretical perspectives in race and ethnic relations. In F. L. Pincus & H. J. Ehrlich (Eds.), *Contending views on prejudice, discrimination, and ethnoviolence* (pp. 29–47). Westview Press.

Feagin, J. R., & Feagin, C. B. (2011). *Racial and ethnic relations, census update* (9th ed.). Pearson.

Fiske, S. T. (2013). A millennial challenge: Extremism in uncertain times. *Journal of Social Issues*, 69(3), 605–613.

Fredrickson, G. (2002). *Racism: A short history*. Princeton University Press.

Glazer, N., & Moynihan, D. P. (1963). *Beyond the melting pot: The Negroes, Puerto Ricans, Jews, Italians and Irish of New York City*. MIT Press.

Gonyea, D. (2017). Majority of white Americans say they believe whites face discrimination. NPR. www.npr.org/2017/10/24/559604836/majority-of-white-americans-think-theyre-discriminated-against

Goodman, D. (2011). *Promoting diversity and social justice: Educating people from privileged groups* (2nd ed.). Routledge.

Gordon, M. M. (1964). *Assimilation in American life: The role of race, religion, and national origins*. Oxford University Press.

Grosfoguel, R. (2011). Decolonizing post-colonial studies and paradigms of political-economy: Transmodernity, decolonial thinking, and global coloniality. *Transmodernity: Journal of Peripheral Cultural Production of the Luso-Hispanic World*, 1(1).

Guglielmo, J., & Salerno, S. (Eds.). (2003). *Are Italians White? How race is made in America*. Routledge.

Hernstein, R., & Murray, C. (1994). *The bell curve: Intelligence and class structure in American life*. Free Press.

Houston, S. (2001). Beyond social constructionism: Critical realism and social work. *The British Journal of Social Work*, 31(6), 845–861.

Ignatiev, N. (1995). *How the Irish became White*. Routledge.

Jansson, B. (2015). *The reluctant welfare state: Engaging history to advance social work practice in contemporary society* (8th ed.). Cengage.

Kiernan, B. (2009). *Blood and soil: A world history of genocide from Sparta to Darfur*. Yale University Press.

Kinloch, G. C. (1974). *The dynamics of race relations: A sociological analysis*. McGraw Hill.

Kinloch, G. C. (1979). *The sociology of minority group relations*. Prentice-Hall.

Kolbert, E. (2018). There's no scientific basis for race – it's a made up label. *National Geographic*, https://www.nationalgeographic.co.uk/people-and-culture/2018/04/theres-no-scientific-basis-race-its-made-label

Kovel, J. (1970/2001). White racism: A psychohistory. In E. Cashmore & J. Jennings (Eds.), *Racism: Essential readings* (pp. 136–140). Sage.

Leonardo, Z., & Porter, R. (2010). Pedagogy of fear: Toward a Fanonian theory of 'safety' in race dialogue. *Race, Ethnicity and Education, 13*, 139–157.

Leong, N. (2012). Racial capitalism. *Harvard Law Review, 126*, 2151.

Lopez, I. F. H. (1994). The social construction of race: Some observations on illusion, fabrication, and choice. *Harvard Civil Rights-Civil Liberties Law Review, 29*(1), 1–62.

Lopez, I. F. H. (1996). *White by law: The legal construction of race*. New York University Press.

McDonagh, E. C., & Richards, E. S. (1953). *Ethnic relations in the United States*. Appleton-Century-Crofts.

McDowell, T., & Jens, L. (2004). Talking about race using critical race theory: Recent trends. *Journal of Marital and Family Therapy, 30*(1), 81–94.

Mclaughlin, J., & Hennebry, J. (2013). Pathways to precarity: Structural vulnerabilities and lived consequences in the everyday lives of migrant farmworkers in Canada. In L. Goldring & P. Landolt (Eds.), *Producing and negotiating non-citizenship: Precarious legal status in Canada* (pp. 1–15). University of Toronto Press.

Memmi, A. (2000). *Racism*. University of Minnesota Press.

Miller, J., & Schamess, G. (2000). The discourse of denigration and the creation of other. *Journal of Sociology and Social Welfare, 27*(3), 39–62.

Mills, C. W. (1997). *The racial contract*. Cornell.

Montagu, A. (1965/2001). Man's most dangerous myth: The fallacy of race. In E. Cashmore & J. Jennings (Eds.), *Racism: Essential readings* (pp. 98–110). Sage.

Murphy, J., Samples, J., Morales, M., & Shadbeh, N. (2015). "They talk like that, but we keep working": Sexual harassment and sexual assault experience among Mexican Indigenous farmworker woman in Oregon. *Journal of Immigrant and Minority Health, 193*(1), 118–125.

Myrdal, G. (1962). An American dilemma. In M. W. Hughey (Ed.), *New Tribalisms: The resurgence of race and ethnicity* (pp. 61–72). Palgrave Macmillan.

Nelson, L. (2008). Racialized landscapes: Whiteness and the struggle over farmworker housing in Woodburn, Oregon. *Cultural Geographies, 15*(1), 41–62.

Omi, M., & Winant, H. (2014). *Racial formation in the United States: From the 1960s to the 1990s* (3rd ed.). Routledge.

Painter, N. I. (2010). *The history of white people* .

Power, S. (2002). *A problem from hell: America in the age of genocide*. Basic Books.

Quandt, S. A., Wiggins, M. F., Chen, H., Bischoff, W. E., & Arcury, T. A. (2013). Heat index inmigrant farmworker housing: Implications for rest and recovery from work-related heat stress. *American Journal of Public Health, 103*(8), 24–26.

Quijano, A. (2007). Coloniality and modernity/rationality. *Cultural Studies, 21*(2–3), 168–178.

Ramos, A. K. (2017). A human rights-based approach to farmworker health: an overarching framework to address the social determinants of health. *Journal of Agromedicine*. 1059924X.2017.1384419.

Reid, J. (2015). *Fracture: Barack Obama, the Clintons, and the racial divide*. HarperCollins.

Resendez, A. (2017). *The other slavery: The uncovered story of Indian enslavement in America*. Mariner Books.

Robinson, E., Nguyen, H. T., Isom, S., Quandt, S. A., Grzywacz, J. G., Chen, H., & Arcury, T. A. (2011). Wages, wage violations, and pesticide safety experienced by migrant farmworkers in North Carolina. *New Solutions: A Journal of Environmental and Occupational Health Policy, 21*(2), 251–268.

Rollock, D., & Gordon, E. W. (2000). Racism and mental health into the 21st century: Perspectives and parameters. *American Journal of Orthopsychiatry, 70*(1), 5–13.

Sacks, K. B. (1996). How did Jews become White folks? In S. Gregory & R. Sanjek (Eds.), *Race* (pp. 78–102). Rutgers.

Schiller, B. R. (1998). *The economics of poverty and discrimination* (7th ed.). Prentice Hall.

Schwartz, S. J., Unger, J. B., Zamboanga, B. L., & Szapocznik, J. (2010). Rethinking the concept of acculturation. *American Psychologist, 65*(4), 237–251.

Segal, B. S. (Ed.). (1966). *Racial and ethnic relations: Selected readings*. Thomas W. Crowell.

Simpson, G. E., & Yinger, J. M. (1953). *Racial and cultural minorities: An analysis of prejudice and discrimination*. Harper & Brothers.

Skillings, J. H., & Dobbins, J. E. (1991). Racism as a disease: Etiology and treatment implications. *Journal of Counseling and Development, 70*(1), 206–212.

Solorzano, D., Ceja, M., & Yosso, T. (2000). Critical race theory, racial microaggressions, and campus racial climate: The experiences of African American college students. *Journal of Negro Education, 69*(1/2), 60–73.

Steinberg, S. (2001). *The ethnic myth: Race, ethnicity and class in America* (3rd ed.). Beacon Press.

Takaki, R. (1993). *A different mirror: A history of multi-cultural America*. Little, Brown.

Taylor, R. (1997). The changing meaning of race in the social sciences: Implications for social work practice. *Smith College Studies in Social Work, 67*(3), 277–298.

Telega, S. W., & Maloney, T. R. (2010). Legislative Actions on Overtime Pay and Collective Bargaining and their Implications for Farm Employers in New York State, 2009–2010. Charles H. Dyson School of Applied Economics and Management College of Agriculture and Life Sciences Cornell University.

Tilly, C. (1998). *Durable inequality*. University of California Press.

Vander Zanden, J. W. (1963). *American minority relations: The sociology of race and ethnic groups*. Ronald Press.

Walsh, J. (2013). *What's the matter with White people? Finding our way in the next America*. Touchstone.

Waugh, I. M. (2010). Examining the sexual harassment experiences of Mexican immigrant farmworking women. *Violence Against Women, 16*(3), 237–261.

Wellman, D. (2000). From evil to illness: Medicalizing racism. *American Journal of Orthopsychiatry, 70*(1), 28–32.

Wilson, W. J. (1973). *Power, racism and privilege: Race relations in theoretical and sociohistorical perspectives* (pp. 47–67). Free Press.

Wilson, W. J. (1987). *The truly disadvantaged: The inner-city, the underclass and public policy*. University of Chicago.

Wilson, W. J. (2011). *When work disappears: The world of the new urban poor*. Vintage.

Winant, H. (1997). Racial dualism at century's end. In W. Lubiano (Ed.), *The house that race built: Black Americans, U.S. terrain* (pp. 87–115). Pantheon.

Yancy, G., & Mills, C. (2014). Lost in Rawlsland. *The New York Times*. http://opinionator.blogs.nytimes.com/2014/11/16/lost-in-rawlsland/?emc=eta1&_r=0

A Brief History of Racism in the United States and Implications for the Helping Professions

INTRODUCTION

The United States is now well over two centuries old. Considered a nation with an Anglo-Christian tradition, it has been aligned politically and culturally with Europe for much of its history. Waves of immigrants from Europe have melted into the mainstream of "White" American society, even when there was initial hostility, such as that directed at Irish, Italian, and Jewish immigrants when they first arrived. Yet the landmass of the United States has been inhabited for thousands of years by indigenous people (also called Native Americans or American Indians), who settled North America and created tribes, confederations, and nations. For the United States to be established, native peoples had to be subjugated, dispossessed, and in many instances murdered and annihilated.

From early on, the United States was settled with slave labor, which quickly evolved into the institution of chattel slavery, reserved exclusively for people seized from the African continent. Thus, the White race was "invented" in opposition to dark-skinned people who were shackled (Allen, 1994). This, along with the genocide of Native Americans, stands as the most extreme forms of racism associated with the United States.

This was by no means the only state-sanctioned racism in the United States, though. Mexicans, who inhabited what is now Texas, New Mexico, Arizona, Colorado, Nevada, and California, lost their land and rights of citizenship after the Mexican–American War, with the Treaty of Guadalupe Hidalgo in 1848. Chinese workers in the United States, who were instrumental in constructing the transcontinental railway line, were subject to pogroms in cities such as Seattle, where the entire Chinese population was forced to flee at the hands of mobs. Eventually, Chinese people were excluded from immigrating to the United States by the Chinese Exclusion Act of 1882. Japanese immigrants were prevented from entering the United States by what was commonly known as the "Gentleman's Agreement" of 1907 to 1908.

Meanwhile, immigration from Ireland, Germany, Sweden, Poland, Italy, and other European countries was being encouraged, as many cities in the United States industrialized and required cheap labor. From the beginning of this nation state to the present, some groups have been encouraged and recruited—gaining important economic advantages by cornering occupational niches—while other groups have been barred from entering the country, or attacked and shackled once they arrived.

Although this is not a history book, helping professionals will benefit from a brief examination of the past, as its legacy reverberates through our society today. We begin by reviewing the relationship between Native Americans and European settlers, as well as the institution of slavery in the United States. We then consider racial dynamics in the 19th century as the United States industrialized and developed major urban centers, followed by a comparison with European immigrants during this same time span. We also will consider how the development of the helping professions, particularly social work, both reflected and challenged the evolving racial project in the United States. The Progressive Era and the New Deal will receive particular attention, along with the modern Civil Rights Movement, the Great Society of the 1960s, and resurgence of White supremacy at the highest levels of government since 2016.

THE "RACIAL CONTRACT"

The United States was founded on a bedrock of racial exploitation and subjugation. Although most Americans are familiar with the history of "heroic settlers from Europe," braving fierce winters and surviving long journeys to the West across deserts and mountains, Americans are less familiar with the savagery, relentless slaughter, and displacement that accompanied the colonization of North America and the founding of the United States. And while most Americans are able to recall, even recite, the ideals and values of the Declaration of Independence and the U.S. Constitution, the reality of racism during that era remains obfuscated and clouded. We cannot understand racism in the United States today without examining its historical roots and foundations.

The United States was founded on certain principles and values that were ascendant in the European Enlightenment—the rights to freedom, dignity, security, and equality. These aspirations mask the reality of genocide and slavery upon which the republic was founded. By virtue of their race, neither Native Americans nor African Americans were treated with dignity, were afforded security, or were eligible for freedom and equality. They were not considered fully human—an underpinning of severe racism. This dehumanization and social and economic exclusion formed the underbelly of the social contract, the "racial contract" (Mills, 1997), which was used to justify the most extreme forms of state-sanctioned racism while masking its existence for generations to come.

In reviewing some of the most painful chapters in U.S. history, we must not lose sight of the many ways by which subjugated peoples resisted and survived. Whether they were engaged in large-scale conflicts, open rebellions, and massive civil rights movements, or in their day-to-day interpersonal interactions with White people, Native Americans and African Americans have endured the most dreadful conditions imaginable, yet always refused to give in, utilizing whatever means were available to them to care for one another and struggle for dignity and survival.

NATIVE AMERICANS

Indigenous people were living in both North America and South America at least 13,000 years ago, and, by some estimates, tens of thousands of years earlier (Stannard, 1992). Between 75 million and 100 million people were thought to live in both continents, 8 to 10 million of whom were north of what is now Mexico. The number of people living in the Western Hemisphere was comparable to the population of Europe during the same period (Wilson, 1998). The more than 600 autonomous societies in North America had worldviews and a cosmology emphasizing the sacred, interconnectedness, interdependence, and equilibrium. Where farming was practiced, land was not viewed as private property but, rather, as a public resource to be shared.

When the Spanish explorers first encountered the "New World," they were arriving from a country (and continent) that had seen many large-scale wars, as well as the religious and ethnic battles against the Moors, the Crusades, and the expulsion of Jews because of their religious beliefs (Diamond, 1997; Stannard, 1992; Wilson, 1998). They brought sophisticated weapons and a willingness to fight in a brutal, effective fashion—a style of warfare that, unlike that of Native Americans, resulted in huge numbers of casualties.

The Spanish and other European invaders also brought with them devastating germs and illnesses. Diamond (1997) hypothesized that the reason the European diseases were so much more destructive to Native Americans was that the Europeans' exposure to many different peoples from Africa and Asia, as well as Europe, along with the density of the population and the domestication of large farm animals, had "hardened them" to infections. In any case, the mortality rates among Native Americans were overwhelming.

In addition, settlers from all of the major European nations who established colonies and settlements engaged in warfare and, in many instances, genocide. Stannard (1992) estimates a 95% death rate of Native Americans "within no more than a handful of generations following their first encounter with Europeans" (p. x) and declares that this might have been the single worst holocaust in world history. The destruction of Native American villages and communities occurred from the 17th century, when Puritans were slaughtering Pequots and Narragansetts, to massacres by the U.S. cavalry across the nation in the late 19th century.

Early European settlers described Native Americans as "savages" and they often could do nothing to prevent being massacred. Although the Moravian Delaware Indians converted to Christianity in an effort to comply with their White subjugators, their food was destroyed and they were rounded up by American troops and told that they would be taken to safety and offered food. Instead, they were tied up, massacred, and scalped—29 men, 27 women, and 34 children (Stannard, 1992).

In Eastern Colorado in 1863, the *Rocky Mountain News* newspaper urged the extermination of Native Americans a year before what became known as the Sand Creek Massacre of Cheyenne and Arapahoe Indians (Stannard, 1992). When unknown Indians killed a family of settlers, some small skirmishes led to deaths on both sides, although the American Indian losses were much greater. Colonel John Chivington, who likened killing American Indians to "delousing," led 700 heavily armed soldiers to Sand Creek, where there were about 600 American Indians, mostly women and children, as the men were away on a buffalo hunt. The residents of Sand Creek had disarmed themselves voluntarily to show that they were not a threat. Despite repeated efforts by the residents of the village to hoist white flags and other symbols of peace and nonviolence, the soldiers attacked and killed everyone. Stannard (1992) describes how mothers were frantically digging holes to hide their children, but all, from infants to the elderly, were killed and their bodies scalped and further mutilated.

These are but two small examples of widespread and wholesale massacres of Native Americans, ranging from New England to the Southeast, across the Plains to the Pacific Coast. In this way, the land of this nation, which now is occupied mostly by non-Native

Americans, was cleared by mass killings and involuntary relocations. Annihilations were led by high-ranking officers in the colonies, and later the nation. Andrew Jackson, who went on to become president and whose portrait decorates $20 bills, led a particularly brutal massacre of nearly 800 Creek Indians, including women and children, at the battle of Horseshoe Bend in 1814 (Takaki, 1987). After the War of 1812, he pressured "land session" treaties (forced land sales) by the Cherokees, Choctaws, and Chickasaws, which led to the federal government gaining 50 million acres of land by 1820, some of which was sold to White investors at low prices, including Jackson himself (Gonzalez & Torres, 2011).

When Indians were spared death or made peace, they were still subjected to broken treaties and forced relocations when settlers coveted the land they occupied. In the first 90 years of the American republic, White people broke *all* 370 treaties with Native Americans (Wilson, 1998). The Indian Removal Act of 1830 led to five tribes (Cherokee, Choctaw, Chickasaw, Seminole, and Creek) being moved from the Southeastern United States to the Oklahoma Territories, resulting in thousands of deaths during the brutal march (Lum, 2004).

Once the Indians were resettled, the White settlers made further land grabs, especially if the land was found to have natural resources such as oil. The Dawes Act of 1887 allocated land to relocated Indians, attempting to instill a sense of private ownership despite tribal traditions of shared and communal land use, but unscrupulous profiteers cajoled and defrauded Native Americans. Between 1887 and 1932, most of the land grants had passed from Indians to Whites (Lum, 2004; Wilson, 1998).

Once they were "pacified," Native Americans were subjected to additional actions that sought to divest them of their cultural heritage and force them to assimilate into Anglo-American society. From the late 19th century to the present, contested government visions of what would be best for Native Americans have continued. The Bureau of Indian Affairs, led primarily by non-Indians, lurched from one policy to another. Well-intentioned reformers, such as Captain Richard Pratt, sought to "kill the Indian and save the man" through forced assimilation to White ways of living (Wilson, 1998, p. 312). Pratt founded the Carlisle Indian School in Pennsylvania, in 1879, which became the prototype of more than 300 schools, serving nearly 22,000 Indian students, which at the time was about 10% of the Native American population.

The schools attempted to eradicate the students' identity by cutting their traditional hairstyles in favor of the short styles of the Whites; dressing the students in Anglo-American rather than traditional Native American clothing; substituting "American" foods for traditional Indian foods; using unfamiliar forms of physical punishment; and even changing the pupils' names. The psychological and emotional consequences of this forced assimilation were profound, leading to depression, alienation from family and community, severe identity conflict, and high rates of mortality for the children. We know from our first-hand practice that these effects of historical trauma are intergenerational and still haunt indigenous communities in the United States and Canada. In 1924, after losing more than 90% of their people, most of their lands, their capacity to hunt and farm, and much of their traditional cultures, Native Americans were granted full citizenship.

The legacies of genocide and ethnic cleansing toward Native Americans persist to this day. The per capita income for Native Americans living on reservations is one third the national average (Flaherty, 2013). They also have the second shortest life span of any U.S. ethnic or racial group, after African Americans (The Henry J. Kaiser Foundation, 2015). A modern example of this continuing saga of racism is how Native Americans were "relocated," and prohibited from fishing from land near the Columbia River in Oregon, to expedite the building of dams (Harbarger, 2016). Decades later, the relocated tribes still live in squalid, temporary conditions, lacking infrastructure and basic amenities, despite government promises that they would be resettled into equitable, permanent housing. White townships along the river received significantly more federal money and were permanently relocated to new towns with streets, electricity, an adequate water supply, and sewage systems.

AFRICAN AMERICANS

The history of African Americans in the United States is one of survival, resilience, and collective solidarity despite encountering extreme forms of racism. Slavery is a fundamental aspect of the American racial contract. Many of the crafters of the Declaration of Independence and U.S. Constitution, some of whom went on to serve as U.S. presidents, were slaveholders and have become iconic, heroic figures. Twelve U.S. presidents were slaveholders, over a quarter of all U.S. presidents!

Sadly, slavery has existed in one form or another throughout human history (Davis, 1997; Fredrickson, 2002). Slaves were often captured in wars and used by their conquerors as cheap labor. In earlier times, slavery, for the most part, was not racialized. It was deemed bad luck to have been defeated and captured, but the captives were not considered subhuman, inferior beings. The magnitude, duration, and scale of slavery in the Americas were unique in the history of the world. Many scholars believe that slavery began in the United States in 1619, leading to the largest involuntary movement of people ever (Davis, 1997). Although we cannot know exactly how many people were transported from villages in Africa to ships that transported them across the Atlantic Ocean to plantations in New World colonies, an estimated 2,130,000 slaves were imported to the colonies in the New World between 1680 and 1786 (Foner, 1975).

Many European countries participated in the slave trade, including Portugal, Spain, Holland, France, Sweden, Denmark, and England (Foner, 1975). The trade formed a triangle (Foner, 1975; Klinkenborg, 2002), in which manufactured goods first were shipped to Africa from Europe. There, they were traded for people, who in the second leg were transported to the colonies. In the final leg, raw goods such as cotton, sugar, rum, and tobacco were transported back to Europe from the colonies. Because of its ascendancy at sea, England eventually came to dominate the slave trade (Foner, 1975), and more slave ships departed from Liverpool than from any other port (Klinkenborg, 2002). Although slavery came to flourish in the Southeast plantation economy of the United States, it was legalized first in Massachusetts in 1641 (Johnson & Smith, 1998).

Indentured Servitude and Chattel Slavery

In early Virginia, plantation owners sought cheap and stable labor (Allen, 1994; Foner, 1975). Indentured servants from England and Ireland were sold to work on plantations alongside Africans. In the 17th century, 75% of Virginia's settlers came to the state as indentured servants (Takaki, 1993). Indentured servitude was a far cry from chattel slavery, as the former could possibly work off their debts in their lifetime and go on to live freely in society. Chattel slavery treated people as property or livestock, and they and their descendants could be slaves in perpetuity. This had a profound influence on our racial history.

Indentured servants in Virginia during the 17th century were a force to be reckoned with, balking at the yoke of overly harsh working conditions and becoming restive when the prospects of attaining freedom and becoming landholders failed to materialize. Plantation owners and officials feared insurrection, mob violence, and social chaos. This condition culminated in Bacon's Rebellion of 1676, when a multiracial force of indentured servants mutinied over their working conditions and fought with Crown and colonial forces before being subdued (Allen, 1994; Takaki, 1993).

As a result, a full use of the law secured chattel slavery—prohibiting meetings, instituting strict oversight and supervision of slaves, disarming slaves, institutionalizing slavery as a system of intergenerational and perpetual bondage, and barring social and sexual unions between races. This marked the racialization of slavery for African Americans alone. Allen (1994) describes this as the "invention of the White race": In return for the possibility of social mobility—as illusory as this may have been—and backed by the fear of returning to slave status, poor, working Whites exchanged their economic grievances for the privilege of being members of the White race. Plantation owners succeeded in dousing the flames of social unrest while ensuring a steady source of captive labor. While White privilege provided tremendous benefit and power, it came at the cost of diluting their ethnicity and losing their cultural heritage. White skin became the most salient aspect of their identity.

The institution of chattel slavery, reserved solely for African Americans, was fully formed by the time the American Republic was established. George Washington, Thomas Jefferson, James Madison, and James Monroe were all slaveholders, although some expressed ambivalence or misgivings about the institution. Jefferson, who articulated the rights of "man," offers particularly troubling contradictions: He did not free his slaves as did George Washington, only provided for the freedom of five slaves after his death (the descendants of his enslaved mistress Sally Hemmings), and was known for harsh treatment of slaves (Finkelman, 2012). The "three-fifths rule," in which each slave gave the owner an additional three-fifths of a vote in elections, further cemented the disproportionate dominance of the South in American political life, extending the life of formal slavery until the Civil War (Wills, 2003).

It is important to grasp that chattel slavery was a system of unmitigated brutality and terror. Enslaved children were separated from their parents, sometimes at birth and sold (Baptist, 2014; Blight, 2018). Enslaved people were routinely whipped often having to strip and hang from beams with their hands while being brutalized, often left hanging while unconscious and writhing in pain. Slave owners could do whatever they wished with enslaved people, including amputating limbs and killing them. What sometimes prevented them from being lethal was the mercenary desire to preserve their "property." "Slave hunters" patrolled roads and forests to capture and subdue any enslaved people who tried to escape or resist. Enslaved people had no legal rights, no matter how savagely they were treated.

It is also important to note that much of the wealth of this country came from slave labor. Not only did plantation owners become wealthy on the backs of enslaved African American labor, but so did banks, municipalities, shops, and the entire Southern economy (Baptist, 2014). But the industrial North also benefited from having a supply of cheap cotton, as did England and other European countries. Many White immigrant groups immigrated to the United States due to the expanding industrial U.S. economy and were able to find jobs or own land while African Americans were excluded. All White people in the United States were granted advantages due to enslaved African American labor that accrue to this day.

Despite the terrorism of slavery, enslaved people cared for one another, often taking care of children who had been forcibly orphaned (Baptist, 2014; Blight, 2018, Douglass, 1994). They resisted and maintained their dignity, at times directly standing up to slaveholders and often trying to undermine slavery through covert collective action.

Post-Civil War

Although slavery was officially ended at the end of the Civil War, oppression of African Americans in the South was far from over. Immediately following the war, all southern states passed "Black Codes" in 1865 to 1866. These codes were a blatant attempt to continue the indentured, servile status of African Americans (Montgomery, 1993): All Black adults were required to contract for their work in advance each year, and if they quit, they could be arrested and returned to their employers. If they wanted to work commercially or as artisans, they were required to obtain licenses from district courts. Orphans and children under 18 years of age who were deemed to be living with parents unable to support them could be contracted out to White families as laborers and servants.

When these codes were challenged by the federal government under the 14th Amendment to the Constitution, strict vagrancy laws were passed, resulting in high incarceration rates for African Americans (Steinberg, 2001). African Americans were often arrested for minor or spurious charges, and slapped with large fines that they could not pay off, a practice that persisted until the 1940s (Blackmon, 2008). "Convicts," including children, then could be leased out for labor. One convict in four was a child, and children as young as age 6 were leased out (Oshinsky, 1996). Poll taxes and literacy tests also were established to prevent Black people from voting while exempting White voters through "grandfather clauses" (Parrillo, 2012). And anti-miscegenation laws prohibited interracial marriages and sexual liaisons (Fredrickson, 1981). After Reconstruction ended and overt White supremacy once again overtly took control, "Jim Crow" laws instituting strict segregation saturated the states of the Confederacy, and lynching became a gruesome version of southern racial justice. Between 1892 and 1921, about 2,400 African Americans were lynched in the South (Parrillo, 2012).

In the years following the Civil War, African Americans held elected positions during the Reconstruction Era (Gonzalez & Torres, 2011; Higginbotham, 2013). However, within barely more than a decade, the federal government lost the will to continue protecting the rights of African Americans and state laws were quickly passed that made it all but impossible for the majority of African Americans to vote or hold office. These were consistently supported by the U.S. Supreme Court (Higginbotham, 2013). Violence was a central means of reasserting White supremacy in the South. One of many examples was Colfax, Louisiana, in 1873 (Higginbotham, 2013). Elected Black officials and their supporters, who were meeting in the local courthouse, were attacked by White mobs. The courthouse was burned and fleeing people were shot; 65 African Americans died immediately, and 30 who were taken prisoner were shot and thrown in a river. While the leaders of this example of White terrorism were initially convicted of federal crimes, the Supreme Court threw out their conviction upon appeal.

After the end of the Civil War, African Americans could not migrate to the North because racism in employment prevented them from obtaining jobs. While millions of immigrants were arriving from Europe to work in northern factories, African Americans were stranded in the South (Steinberg, 2001). During and after World War I, however, African Americans could move north more successfully, because the flow of European immigrants dried up. Between 1900 and 1930, 2 million African Americans migrated north (Jones, 1985).

The migratory spigot truly opened between the late 1930s, when World War II fueled a strong demand for factory jobs, and the 1960s, with about 5 million people making the journey (Edsall & Edsall, 1991; Leman, 1991). Those who did make it to the North faced de-facto segregation, hostility from White neighbors and White police forces, antagonism from unions, the worst working conditions and the lowest paying jobs on occupational ladders, and were most prone to layoffs when White workers returned from the wars (Jones, 1985; Wilkerson, 2015). Racism against African Americans was so prevalent in the United States during the 20th century that it was necessary to have a guide for safe travel, known as "The Green Book" (McGee, 2010). The guide directed travelers away from unsafe and discriminatory places to those that were more welcoming. There were also 3,000 "Sundown towns" in the mid-20th century, meaning that all Blacks had to leave town by sundown or risk assaults (Higginbotham, 2013). It is important to keep the depth, magnitude, and longevity of discrimination against Black people in mind when the progress of White ethnic immigrant groups is contrasted with the lack of comparable social mobility of African Americans. African Americans had survived slavery, endured Black Codes and Jim Crow, and lacked access to the jobs, resources, and social networks that White immigrant groups were able to leverage.

All of these structural impediments in the South and North constrained the capacity of African Americans to accumulate capital, which further inhibited their social mobility. They also propelled African American women into the workforce in far greater numbers than White women, as African American men had difficulty finding well-paying jobs because of Jim Crow in the South and racial discrimination in the North (Jones, 1985). The ability of African American women to find work as domestic employees led them to an unregulated niche in the low-paying labor market, which echoed the unequal relationships between Blacks and Whites before the Civil War.

In addition to lynching, overt violence continued, in which White mobs attacked Black communities. There were pogroms in East St. Louis, Missouri; Tulsa, Oklahoma; and Rosewood, Florida. Whites massacred more than 100 African Americans in East St. Louis in 1917 (Arnove & Zinn, 2004). In Tulsa, in 1921, Whites rioted, destroying 35 square blocks in an African American neighborhood, murdering about 300 people (Staples, 1999). Days of violence by White mobs in Rosewood, Florida, in 1923 completely destroyed the town. Although the exact number of casualties is unknown, it is thought that dozens perished (Carnes, 1995). African Americans continued to struggle for their rights, despite physical violence, economic exclusion, segregation (official and unofficial), legal disenfranchisement, and overt and covert racism at all levels of the spectrum. After World War II, the modern-day Civil Rights Movement coalesced, gathering momentum in the 1950s and leading to dramatic political responses in the form of the Great Society in the 1960s. Tragically, the killing has not stopped. In the next chapter, we consider a recent wave of violence toward African Americans by law enforcement officials, and the killing of nine African American worshippers in a church in Charlestown, South Carolina, by an avowed White supremacist in 2015. Newt Gingrich referred to President Obama as the "food stamp president," and Donald Trump not only questioned where President Obama was born, but whether he deserved to get into Columbia and Harvard Universities, calling him "the affirmative action president" (Higginbotham, 2013). The degree and amount of racism Obama has been subjected to is enough to fill a book. We have added an exercise (see Exercise 3.1) to help you to consider the depth of this racism and discrimination more fully.

LATINOS/HISPANICS

The terms *Latinos* and *Hispanics* refer to people from Latin America or who have an historical link to Spain. This population is large and extremely diverse, ranging from Mexico to Argentina, and Peru to Venezuela, as well as many islands conquered by the Spanish, including Puerto Rico and Cuba. Although settled by the Portuguese, Brazil often is considered as part of Latin America as well. Hispanics include people from all "racial" groups, encompassing indigenous peoples (Native Americans) from South and Central America, as well as many religions and nationalities. Although Latinx groups have some cultural similarities, and certainly linguistic unity in the predominant use of Spanish, there is a wide spectrum of diversity between cultures and nationalities and ethnic diversity within nations, as well as class variations. While we cannot cover the rich and complex history of all of Latin America, when exploring racism in the United States, it is helpful to understand some critical historical events and how they led to the creation of Hispanic minority groups within the United States, who were constructed as non-White people of color and thus experience continued racism in the United States.

Our discussion here focuses on two major themes: (a) the conquest and control of land occupied by Hispanics and how the people occupying these territories were treated; and (b) the colonization of Hispanic lands, notably Puerto Rico and Cuba. While there have been many instances of U.S. intervention and neocolonialism in other parts of Latin America, for the purposes of this discussion we omit coverage of these events, although immigrants from these countries have been inducted into a racial calculus already in play between Hispanics and White Americans of European descent. It should also be noted that an important concept is that of coloniality—which identified the driving forces of patriarchy, capitalism, White supremacy, and Christianity, which were imposed on indigenous populations throughout the Americas—developed by Quijano (2000) and outlined in more detail in Chapter 2.

Mexican Americans

Spanish colonists, and subsequently Mexicans, were living in much of what is the southwestern part of the United States for many decades before English, Irish, and other pioneers from Europe settled in their territories. Although the antecedents of the Mexican American War are complex, with provocations and human rights abuses on both sides, a racialized discourse was in play even before the outbreak of overt hostilities.

One of the issues was the reluctance of Mexico to allow slavery in the disputed lands; however, American cotton growers had migrated into Mexican territory (what is now East Texas) and were agitating to use slaves to work in cotton fields. Famous Texans used racial imagery to justify the struggle against Mexico: Stephen Austin talked of the "mongrel Spanish-Indian and negro races" versus the civilized "Anglo-American race," and Sam Houston believed that Texas in American hands reflected, "glory on the Anglo Saxon race" (Takaki, 1993, pp. 173–174). The movement to create the state of Texas was fueled in large part by White supremacy.

After defeating Mexico, the Treaty of Guadalupe Hidalgo in 1846 gave the United States what is now California, Texas, New Mexico, and Nevada, as well as parts of Colorado, Utah, Wyoming, Oklahoma, Kansas, and Arizona (Shorris, 1992; Takaki, 1993). The many Mexicans living in these territories were systematically dispossessed from their lands and livelihoods through laws, taxes, and concerted efforts to challenge their property deeds. They were attacked, lynched, and assassinated, including by the revered Texas Rangers, who were an arm of White supremacy (Romero, 2019). Eventually they were forced to work as cheap laborers, hired cowboys, ditch diggers, and miners, at wages significantly below their Anglo counterparts (Feagin & Feagin, 2011; Lum, 2004; Takaki, 1993). Income went down and infant mortality rose (Shorris, 1992). Their language was also suppressed, contributing to social and cultural marginalization (Healey, 1995). Mexicans and Mexican Americans were also attacked by White mobs; between 1848 and 1928, 597 people were lynched (Gonzalez & Torres, 2011)! According to historian Francisco Balderrama, during the Great Depression, up to 2 million Mexicans and Mexican Americans, more than half of them U.S. citizens, were forcibly deported to Mexico in what were known as "repatriation campaigns" (NPR, 2015).

Puerto Ricans

Like the story of Mexican Americans in the United States, the chronicle of Puerto Ricans is one of creating a desperate and dispossessed workforce. In 1898, barely a year after the island had been granted autonomy from Spain, U.S. troops occupied Puerto Rico (Feagin & Feagin, 2011). Puerto Rico became a U.S. territory with patronage-appointed governors, who often knew little of the island's history, culture, and people. At the onset of American occupation, Puerto Rico was an agricultural country, with many Puerto Ricans producing sugar, coffee, and other crops from their own plots of land. However, the United States government's implementation of "Operation Bootstrap," (from 1939–1945) a so-called economic self-help program forced on Puerto Rico, created an inexorable process of corporate takeover through agribusiness and industrialization. This process destroyed the Puerto Rican economy, forcing farmers off the land and into the low-wage, dependent workforce (Feagin & Feagin, 2011; Murillo, 2001).

The collapse of industries such as sugar and needlework in the early to mid-20th century led to high unemployment and migration to the U.S. mainland by individuals in search of work (Glazer & Moynihan, 1963). This migration did not abate. Now, about 3.5 million Puerto Ricans are living in Puerto Rico and about 2.5 million are working and residing on the U.S. mainland (Shorris, 1992). In addition to enduring economic hardship, Puerto Ricans have been subjected to racial and ethnic stereotypes that depict them as docile, overly emotional, and lazy (Feagin & Feagin, 2011; Gonzalez, 2011). This was recently amplified when after Hurricane Maria, much of the island's infrastructure was destroyed and nearly 3,000 people died and President Trump made the following (untrue) statement: "Puerto Rico got far more money than Texas and Florida combined, yet their government can't do anything right, the place is a mess—nothing works" (www.nytimes.com/2019/04/02/us/trump-puerto-rico.html)

Cuban Americans

Although Cuban Americans have not been burdened with the same stereotypes as Puerto Ricans, they, too, have been subjected to typecasting and discrimination in the United States. Many people have considered them a favored minority, and they have achieved a stronger economic position than either Mexican Americans or Puerto Ricans. Still, Cubans have encountered housing and employment discrimination. Many refugees have been unable to retain their occupations and professions from Cuba in the United States, resulting in a lowered economic status (Feagin & Feagin, 2011; Gonzalez, 2011).

Cubans had settled in the United States during the 19th century, often as a result of political upheavals in Cuba and attracted by jobs in Florida (Feagin & Feagin, 2011). Shortly after the Spanish American War, Cuba became a U.S. protectorate in 1902. The United States was strongly involved in influencing Cuban politics and, as in Puerto Rico, controlled the Cuban economy. This resulted in many low-paid, vulnerable workers (Feagin & Feagin, 2011; Gonzalez, 2011).

After the Cuban Revolution in 1959, many of the country's elite fled to Florida. Successive waves of immigration from Cuba swelled the Cuban American community in Florida, and eventually in other states such as New York, New Jersey, Texas, and California (Parrillo, 2012). There was a marked difference in how the 1980 cohort of Cuban refugees was viewed compared to their predecessors, with much attention paid to the numbers of convicts and ex-mental patients in this group (Steinberg, 2001). Most were not criminals or mentally ill but, unlike previous waves of Cuban immigrants, significant numbers of these refugees were of African heritage and darker skinned (Feagin & Feagin, 2011; Gonzalez, 2011; Shorris, 1992).

Sadly, racism has divided the Cuban community in some instances. *The New York Times* ran a story about two friends who immigrated in the early 1990s—Joel, who is dark skinned, and Achmed, who is light skinned (Ojito, 2000). Although they attempted to remain friends in Miami, they both were inducted into the racialized world of the United States. They settled in different neighborhoods that reflected their skin privilege and moved in different cultural directions. Ultimately, Achmed felt uncomfortable visiting Joel in a predominantly Black neighborhood and the friends drifted apart. Of course, one story cannot explain everything, but it does illustrate the complexity and pain accompanying racism in the United States and how it can intersect with other aspects of social identity, such as nationality, ethnicity, and social class.

ASIAN AMERICANS

The history of Asians and Pacific Islanders in America is rich, complex, and diverse. It is a story of many nationalities and their experiences of immigration and settling in the United States from the world's largest and most populated continent. Although many Asian Americans have done well in the United States socially and economically, they still encounter racism. The *New York Times* convened a conversation with about a dozen people with a range of Asian Americans with varied ethnicities about race and many described their frustration with the "model minority" myth, finding that it stereotypes them as always being high achieving and unpolitical, which makes it more difficult when there are struggles and hardships (Gandbhir & Stephenson, 2016). There was also concern voiced about seeing all Asian Americans as being prosperous and how those from ethnic groups with darker skin tones and less social and economic capital experience faced multilayered forms of racism. For the purposes of this brief historical review, we concentrate on two national and ethnic groups, the Chinese and the Japanese, and their experiences of race and racism in America.

The Chinese

The Chinese came in large numbers to the United States in the mid-19th century, because of push factors such as wars and political upheaval, as well as high taxes and poor harvests in China (Takaki, 1993). They were attracted by the lure of jobs with higher wages, as well as the prospect of finding gold. Labor brokers recruited them. They built railroads; mined; constructed agricultural canals, dams, and irrigation systems; and were active in farming (Parrillo, 2012). At one point, 90% of workers building Western railway lines were Chinese, and in 1870, 29% of the population of Idaho was of Chinese descent. Because of federal law in 1790 restricting citizenship to Whites, the Chinese were not able to become citizens.

Although they were welcomed initially, Chinese people encountered nativism, resentment, and eventually outright hostility, discrimination, and violence. In the 1890s, there were anti-Chinese riots in California (Takaki, 1993); during the same period, pogroms in Seattle forced all people of Chinese descent to flee from the city (Morgan, 1962). Racism was further institutionalized by the Chinese Exclusion Act of 1882 (renewed in 1892 and 1902), which prohibited further Chinese immigration and denied citizenship to Chinese individuals already in the country. U.S. leaders set an ominous and derogatory tone, just as they had with Native Americans and African Americans. President Rutherford Hayes referred to the "Chinese invasion" as being "pernicious"; compared the Chinese with other, "weaker" races (African Americans and Native Americans); and committed himself to discouraging further immigration (Takaki, 1993, p. 206). The Chinese Exclusion Act was not repealed until 1943, and large-scale Chinese immigration to the United States did not resume until the 1960s (Feagin & Feagin, 2011).

The Chinese who were already in the United States did band together and form and maintain mutual support networks. Denied access to jobs and farming, they formed their own businesses and settled in what became Chinatowns (Takaki, 1993). Today, Chinese Americans are living in all sectors of society and are a socially and politically diverse group. However, racism remains. When news that the coronavirus (COVID-19) originated in China, a new wave of strong anti-Asian racism came with it. Individuals, such as Donald Trump, wanting to fan anti-immigrant flames, called COVID-19 the "China-virus" and implied that its spread to the United States was intentionally executed by the Chinese, a possible contributor to attacks on elderly Asian Americans in the Bay Area in 2020–2021 (Levinson, Becker & Simon, 2021).

The Japanese

Feagin and Feagin (2011) have observed that Asians immigrated to the United States serially. When immigration for one group was halted or reduced, employers sought Asian immigration from other sources. The Japanese came to the United States later than the Chinese. Many of them initially went to Hawaii to work on the sugar plantations. Then they immigrated to the mainland United States in large numbers from the 1880s until the "Gentleman's Agreement" of 1907 to 1908.

Unlike the early Chinese immigrants, who were largely males planning to return home, the Japanese emigres included significant numbers of women. Japanese settlers were employed mostly in agriculture, railroad construction, mining, and canneries (Feagin & Feagin, 2011; Takaki, 1993). Some worked as farm workers, and others became truck farmers, selling their own produce from truck stands. By 1910, Japanese people were producing 70% of California's strawberries.

Like the Chinese before them, employers who valued their work ethic, skills, and willingness to work in difficult conditions for low wages recruited the Japanese. But the Japanese encountered hostility from White workers and stereotypes and nativism in society at large. A common accusation against the Japanese was that they were "unassimilable" (Feagin & Feagin, 2011; Takaki, 1993). California had statutes prohibiting the Japanese from owning land, intermarrying with Whites, and obtaining citizenship. Similar examples of "blaming the victim" have afflicted many targeted social groups: Legal and structural barriers deny them access to the rights and privileges enjoyed by other groups and cause them to rely on themselves, which confirms the stereotype that they keep to themselves and are unable to assimilate.

Laws and Supreme Court rulings have codified this process. From the inception of this country, a series of Supreme Court decisions, known as the "requisite cases," determined who was eligible for citizenship, predicated on who was considered to be "White" (Lopez, 1996; Taylor, 1997). One such decision was the Ozawa case in 1922, which denied naturalized citizenship to the Japanese plaintiff because he was not Caucasian. An immigration law followed this in 1924 prohibiting the entry of those ineligible for citizenship.

Before this, however, the rising anti-Japanese fervor, fueled by stereotypes in the press, led to what was known as the "Gentleman's Agreement," which essentially was a pact initiated by President Theodore Roosevelt between the United States and Japan that ended new Japanese immigration. It was buttressed by the Immigration Act of 1924, which was not altered significantly until a new immigration act in 1965 prohibited the quotas and restrictions that favored Whites over other ethnic and racial groups (Feagin & Feagin, 2011).

During World War II, one of the most egregious modern acts of racism in this country occurred in 1942. Under Executive Order 9066, Japanese American citizens were barred from "sensitive" places and eventually were interned in concentration camps (Feagin & Feagin, 2011; Takaki, 1993). Although this was a response to the bombing of Pearl Harbor by the Japanese, it is the only time in the 20th century that an ethnic group was singled out for such treatment. German Americans were not interned despite the United States being at war with Germany. This shameful incident led to the confinement of 110,000 Japanese Americans, often in degrading camps, where they were leased out to perform menial work at low wages (Feagin & Feagin, 2011; Takaki, 1993).

The involuntary detention caused great economic, social, and psychological harm. Many Japanese Americans lost their businesses, relinquished their farms, and, after release, found their homes vandalized and damaged. Despite this, 33,000 Japanese Americans served in World War II (Takaki, 1993)! Not until 1987 was a bill passed apologizing to Japanese Americans for this indignation, including the offer of monetary reparations.

Factors Common to Anti-Immigrant Racism

Many other national and ethnic groups from Asia and the Pacific Islands experienced success as well as concerted efforts of prejudice, intolerance, and discrimination after immigrating to the United States. Filipinos, Koreans, and South Asian Indians immigrated in large numbers in the 19th century, followed by modern waves of Vietnamese, Laotians, Hmong, Cambodians, Thai, Malaysians, Indonesians, and individuals from other Asian nations.

The Japanese experience illustrates a cycle of anti-immigrant racism with four factors common to most non-White American groups. This is not a linear process, but all of the elements are usually in place.

1. A public discourse of targeting, scapegoating, and even hatred is amplified by the media.
2. Nativist groups join the conversation with dire warnings about alien cultures and stereotypes about inscrutability, lack of trustworthiness, and coming from a culture at odds with the host country's culture and values. Donald Trump has articulated this while running for president in 2016. Some of these nativist groups are considered quite mainstream, such as the American Legion and major trade unions.
3. Dominant social groups (i.e., Whites) that perceive themselves as victims direct their pent-up anger at the visible racial or ethnic minority. Examples are the White construction and railway workers in the Old West, whose working conditions were abysmal and who blamed Chinese or Japanese workers because of their willingness to endure such conditions without complaint. The White workers' anger was directed at other workers rather than at the employers and owners who created the deplorable conditions.
4. National and local leaders support the targeting and legitimize or even fan the flames of bigotry. American presidents who have engaged in racist demagogy, denigration, and scapegoating include, among others, Thomas Jefferson, Andrew Jackson, Rutherford Hayes, Theodore Roosevelt, and Donald Trump. Trump has reprised discourses about immigrants that were prevalent in the first 150 years of the United States but has not been seen for nearly 100 years.

WHITE ETHNIC GROUPS

After summarizing the historical experiences of prejudice and racism of a number of ethnic and racial groups of color in the United States, we turn to a comparison of these experiences with those of White immigrant groups, such as Jews, Italians, Irish, French Canadians, Armenians, Poles, Greeks, and other groups that have encountered hostility and bias upon arrival in America.

All nonindigenous people, including all White people in the United States, are descendants of immigrants to the United States. Early immigrants included British Puritans, Quakers, and other settlers who left England because of religious persecution. Among the early residents of U.S. colonies were also many Dutch, French, Spanish, and German settlers. Immigrants from Scotland and Ireland, as well as the Scotch–Irish from the area now known as Northern Ireland, were well represented among the early colonists. Class was a critical issue, particularly in the South, as many poor English and Irish emigres entered as indentured servants, as was religion, as most of the earliest settlers were Christian.

Push and Pull Factors

With all voluntary immigrant groups, regardless of race or ethnicity, varying push and pull factors influenced immigration (Steinberg, 2001). Push factors occur in the country of origin and include famine, political persecution, poverty, religious or ethnic intolerance, wars, and other conflicts. Pull factors are the jobs, land, political freedom, recruitment by employers (which can be voluntary or involuntary), and the draw of family or friends who have already immigrated.

In the early United States, major pull factors were land, religious freedom, and economic opportunity. During the 19th century, as the northern part of the country industrialized, many jobs in mills and factories lured immigrants to the United States. While Native Americans, African Americans, and many Hispanics and Asian Americans were being denied access to these jobs as well as facing discrimination in housing, waves of immigrants from Europe and Canada were filling them.

As an example, in Holyoke, Massachusetts, a city that developed as a mill town, first the Irish and Germans were recruited to work in the factories. They were followed by French Canadians and, later, Poles (Miller, 1999). Puerto Ricans did not enter the city in large numbers until after the 1960s. By then, most of the blue-collar jobs had fled to the South or offshore as part of the process of industrialization, leaving boarded up factories and jobless workers. This municipality has never had a significant African American population.

Discrimination Against White Ethnic Groups

Many White ethnic groups migrating to the United States encountered prejudice and hostility, as well as intergroup conflict. Some, such as the Irish, Jews, and Italians, initially were labeled as "non-White" by Whites already in the United States. The Irish, whose Catholicism was also viewed as "alien" by the dominance of Protestantism, were arriving from a region where the English had socially constructed them as racial inferiors. The English had brutally suppressed the Irish for centuries and allowed appalling numbers to starve during a failure of the Irish food staple, potatoes, while the British exported the rest of the Irish food supply for themselves (Takaki, 1987). Although there was a food crisis, it became a famine because of the unwillingness of the British to offer emergency food to starving Irish people. Ireland lost one half of its population through death and immigration, and some recent scholars have asked whether this was actually a genocidal situation (Murphy, 2013). Upon arriving in large numbers to Boston and New York, the Irish were met with signs stating that they should not apply for jobs or rooms in boarding houses.

Jews arrived in this country, particularly from Eastern Europe and Russia, in the late 19th and early 20th centuries, after enduring centuries of religious and ethnic hostility, prejudice, and violence throughout the European continent. Many of the groups who harbored strong anti-Semitic attitudes were well represented in the United States already or were immigrating here at the same time. Jews, too, found certain neighborhoods "unavailable," jobs not open, quotas limiting their attendance at colleges and universities, and inflammatory anti-Jewish rhetoric in newspapers and on the radio (Dinnerstein, 1994). When it became apparent that genocide was occurring against Jews in Germany and other parts of Europe in the 1930s and 1940s, anti-Jewish sentiment in the Roosevelt administration blocked Jewish refugees from fleeing to the United States, which could have saved hundreds of thousands of lives (Wyman, 1984).

Further, Jews in the United States were subjected to hatred and violence from groups such as the Ku Klux Klan. Anti-Semitism has been a theme in intergroup relations ever since Jews arrived in the United States, and many negative ethnic and religious stereotypes have been promulgated and confronted. Jews still are targeted by extreme right-wing organizations such as the Aryan Nations, and incidents of graffiti involving swastikas and anti-Semitic statements still occur and since the election of Donald Trump have risen precipitously, including the single worst massacre of Jews in U.S. history in Pittsburgh in 2018 (Beauchamp, 2019). Italians, Greeks, and other immigrants from Mediterranean countries also have encountered discrimination and nativism. Because many have dark complexions, they initially were not accepted as White (Guglielmo, 2003). This led to difficulty finding well-paying work, residential discrimination, overt hostility from other ethnic groups, and enduring stereotypes and ethnic caricatures.

All ethnic groups need to survive, and they seek upward mobility and prosperity to thrive. When legal and socially acceptable means of success are closed off, groups will move into opportunity structures available to them, including illegal businesses (Cloward & Ohlin, 1960). This surely occurred with Jews and Italians, in particular, upon their arrival in the United States, in which both groups took advantage of criminal opportunities when legitimate economic prospects were sealed off. This is another example of how structural factors in society lead to choices and adaptive strategies that then can be used as evidence of a group's alleged predilection for antisocial behavior.

One of the forms of prejudice that White immigrant groups experienced in the 19th and early 20th centuries was to be viewed as childlike, dependent, and unable on their own to live up to the standards of American civilization. Often forced to live in squalid, overcrowded neighborhoods, with dismal sanitary conditions, they were held responsible for creating those conditions. New immigrants were seen as not being as intelligent as native-born Americans, unable to care for themselves, prone to excessive drinking and violence, having "gross" food habits, and even smelling different—the metaphor of "vile bodies" being one of the most enduring icons of the canon of racism. Social workers and their predecessors were summoned to maintain a semblance of social control through casework and child protective services (Gordon, 1988).

Italians, Jews, and other recent immigrants often lived in neighborhoods in close proximity to African Americans and felt compelled to distance and distinguish themselves by claiming "Whiteness." For an ethnic group that has experienced hostility and oppression, to assume Whiteness means to begin to work toward racial assimilation, assuming that society will permit the group to be socially constructed as White.

Although the group may retain its ethnic identity and practices, racial assimilation means that the group now expects to be treated as White—able to move into affordable neighborhoods, be admitted to colleges and universities, assume that employers will not discriminate against them because of their race or ethnicity, enjoy the privilege of not being stopped by the police because of skin color, and not be subjected to laws or informal barriers that limit intermarriage. Many of the ethnic groups that initially encountered prejudice, stereotyping, and social exclusion now have assumed the status of mainstream Whites, despite retaining aspects of their ethnic identities.

Ethnicity and Race

Several historical factors distinguish White ethnic groups from ethnic groups of color. Although many White ethnic groups encountered and endured serious disapproval and prejudice upon arriving in the United States, there are still some qualitative distinctions between their experiences and those of ethnic groups of color. Exercise 3.2 offers a series of questions to ask members of any ethnic or racial group for comparative purposes. The answers may help to distinguish between the experiences of racism in the United States as encountered by people of color and by Whites. We highlight some of the most important differences here.

Voluntary Versus Involuntary Immigration or Contact

The conditions of the initial contact situation are influential to the dynamics of intergroup relations, the trajectory of a group's success, and a group's identity. All White ethnic groups chose to immigrate to the United States, with the exception of early indentured servants, who were able to discharge their obligations of servitude. This signals group agency and autonomy, some control over one's group narrative, and it offers a much better opportunity to carry resources during immigration, maintain and develop those assets, and acquire new social and economic capital.

Native Americans and Mexican Americans were stripped and divested of the resources they had before their hostile encounters with Whites. African Americans were transported here involuntarily without any belongings, just the resources they carried inside of themselves and the bonds that endured between people. Chinese, Japanese, and other Asian Americans were subject to laws and practices that inhibited their capacity to develop and accumulate resources and secure occupational niches.

Human Versus Not Fully Human

Although some White ethnic immigrant groups were not considered civilized and were viewed as being "uncouth, pagan, greedy, lazy, stupid, and immoral," they were never denied the recognition of their humanity. The same cannot be said for Native Americans and African Americans. Latino Americans and Asian Americans also have been viewed as coming from inferior and less civilized cultures, and their integrity, often with references to genetics, has been questioned during certain historical epochs. They historically have been viewed as being less able to assimilate than White ethnic groups, although there are certainly trends today, such as rates of out-group intermarriage, which indicate that this myth is eroding.

White Versus Non-White

This dichotomy has been one of the most yawning chasms in U.S. immigration history (Kang, 2012). Some groups (such as Northern Europeans) were constructed as White when they arrived, others (such as Irish, Jews, and Southern Europeans) were seen as non-White upon entry but became White within a generation or two, while some have never been considered White (e.g., people of color as described in this book). This dichotomy also influenced whether immigrants were viewed as being desirable/undesirable, deserving/undeserving, and safe/dangerous (Kang, 2012).

The Depth and Breadth of Discrimination

The quality of discrimination is hard to measure, but some differences are important to note. Slavery lasted for centuries, and after it was abolished in this country, Jim Crow and severe discrimination persisted. Native Americans were nearly exterminated by Europeans. This is qualitatively different from the experiences of White ethnic groups, who encountered initial discrimination but within two or three generations were able to move out of poor neighborhoods and gain access to the full opportunities of American society. These groups (e.g., Irish, Jews, Italians) who initially were constructed as not being White, eventually were able to claim membership in the "White race" (Guglielmo & Salerno, 2003; Ignatiev, 1995; Sacks, 1996).

The Perceived Cultural Fit

Although the United States prides itself on being a nation of immigrants, some immigrant groups are viewed as having a better cultural fit with those already living in the country than others, particularly when it comes to values about work, family, and behavior. Is the immigrant group perceived as a threat to American values, physical safety, and economic security (Bikmen, 2015)? Since running for office and becoming president, Donald Trump has described immigrants of color using words such as "alien, predator, criminal, animal, invasion, killer" over 500 times (Fritze, 2019, www.usatoday.com/story/news/politics/elections/2019/08/08/trump-immigrants-rhetoric-criticized-el-paso-dayton-shootings/1936742001/). The quote illustrates the negative statements made about immigrants of color, which are not made about White ethnic immigrants, such as Canadians. In fact, Mukhergee (cited by Bikmen) has found that Americans feel more favorably about undocumented Canadians than they do toward documented Mexican immigrants. The level of mistrust, suspicion, and hostility faced by immigrants of color is much higher than that experienced by White immigrants.

The Degree of Social and Economic Exclusion

Even while living in poor ethnic enclaves, White immigrants were never as segregated as African Americans and never encountered the same depth of social and economic isolation and exclusion (Iglehart & Becerra, 1995; Jansson, 2015; Katz, 1986). While White ethnic immigrants lived in poor, often urban (but for some groups, rural) ethnic enclaves, they did not live in "ghettos," which are characterized by extreme social and economic isolation that is multigenerational. All White ethnic groups had opportunities to achieve social mobility much more rapidly than ethnic groups of color, despite initial hurdles and barriers.

Control or Influence Over the Group Narrative

As White ethnic groups have gained power and resources and have achieved social mobility, they also have gained more control over their group narrative, the story of their ethnic group. The ability to have some efficacy is important for a group's internal sense of self-esteem and worth, as well as in shaping how others view one's group (Thomas, 1994). This does not happen overnight, and success occurs on many fronts. One factor is who owns or produces public narratives, such as television shows, news broadcasts, books, and songs. Another variable is in having watchdog groups, such as the Anti-Defamation League or the Order of the Sons of Italy, to publicly challenge offensive stereotypes or ethnic misrepresentations.

Group leaders and role models can influence public discourse in the way they describe or characterize various social groups. They can extol virtues or exaggerate deficits, include members as part of an in-group of Americans or distinguish them as outsiders and aliens. Control or influence over group narratives is never absolute: White ethnic groups still find that their members are caricatured, just as ethnic and racial groups have experienced extreme racism and yet have struggled boldly to assume some authorship over their own stories.

In summary, although some White ethnic groups experienced prejudice and racism when arriving in the United States, the severity, virulence, and persistence of social oppression pales in comparison to that experienced by people of color. The additional burdens imposed by racism, the toll of regularly experiencing direct and indirect racism, and the personal and social cost of enduring racism have depleted the resources of many people of color and impeded their social progress in ways that are qualitatively different than the experience of White people, even if their ethnic groups initially experienced prejudice.

LIMINALITY

The construction of race and ethnicity is fluid, contested, and contextual. As we have discussed, even the notion of who is White or of color has shifted over time. One of our examples was of two Cubans who immigrated to Miami. Even though Latinos fall within the meta-category of being "of color," one Cuban was considered "White" and the other Cuban was considered "Black." Contradictions, inconsistencies, and irregularities arise whenever we try to group people for the sake of categorization or discussion. People do not appreciate being lumped into a group in a way that is inconsistent with how they define themselves. Yet that is exactly what has happened to many people in the United States. They were offered or denied access, rights, and opportunities based on how they were socially constructed and categorized.

We must acknowledge that some groups more than others occupy a liminal space in a world of socially constructed race, at the boundaries and frontiers of racial typologies. Although there are many examples, we briefly consider three: Arab Americans, Asian Americans, and Jewish Americans.

Arab and Islamic Americans

Since a ruling by an appeals court in 1915 that a Syrian man was White (Gualtieri, 2001), and according to the current categories used by the U.S. census, Arab Americans are considered White by virtue of racial categories that include Caucasian. Although many Arab Americans consider themselves to be Caucasian or White, significant numbers of them find that they are subjected to racism and discrimination. Many Arab Americans are also Muslim and therefore they also experience religious oppression that is akin to racism: Islamophobia. In the years since the 9/11 terrorist attacks, instances of anti-Arab and anti-Islamic sentiment, stereotyping, and hostility have increased. This trend has been exacerbated by an unending "war on terrorism" and direct U.S. military involvement in Afghanistan and Iraq, severe and savage conflict occurring in Syria, and the long-standing, unresolved tensions between Arabs and Jews in the Middle East. Donald Trump has implemented a "travel ban" against people from many predominantly Muslim countries: Libya, Iran, Somalia, Syria, and Lebanon (Gladstone & Sugiyama, 2018). It illustrates how international events as well as internal politics increasingly shape the contours of race and racism in the United States.

Asian Americans

Although we have described the strength of racism experienced by Chinese and Japanese Americans, as well as other Asian nationalities in the United States, there are differences within the diverse Asian American community over their connections and common experiences with people of color or Whites. Many Asian Americans feel the sting of racism, whether it is through racial stereotypes portrayed in the media or outright hostility from Whites in society.

Further, because Asian Americans have a high rate of out-group intermarriage with Whites (nearly 50%), some do not consider themselves to have a lot in common with other ethnic groups of color and may not consider themselves to be people of color, while others have strong identities as people of color. We pass no judgment about how people define themselves; rather, this is a statement about the complexities and vicissitudes of identity, as defined by ourselves and others in a racialized society.

Jewish Americans

Many Jews have experienced forms of racism and oppression. Most, although not all, Jews in the United States are descendants of Ashkenazi Jews in Europe. Many Jews acknowledge that, at this stage in U.S. history, they have access to most if not all of the benefits of other White citizens. Nevertheless, Jews have a lengthy history of oppression and suffered one of the most destructive and egregious acts of racism in modern history, the Jewish Holocaust of World War II.

Jews also have encountered severe anti-Semitism in the United States, and this form of oppression endures, and as stated previously has increased domestically, as well as internationally. Jews are a religious minority in a highly Christian country. And Jews, like Arabs, are impacted by a world context of tremendous tensions and acts of violence stemming from the conflict in the Middle East, which has spread to other parts of the world such as Europe, where Jews have been threatened, targeted, and attacked. These threats contribute to the ambivalence that some Jews have over considering themselves as White Americans, despite the predominant experience of Jews having white skin privilege.

Interracial Families

There has been an increase in interracial families in the United States. In 2010, 15% of all marriages in the United States were interracial, double what it was in 1980 (Afful et al., 2015). Interracial families grapple with having some members with race privilege and others who are targeted due to their race. For example, in some of our own families we have siblings or children with darker or lighter skin than us and have heard from many of our students and colleagues about the different degrees of privilege that light-skinned people than darker-skinned relatives. In short, the historical experiences of groups and the ways by which these experiences shape social identity are laced with tensions, contradictions, and anomalies. In addition, many individuals claim multiple group heritages with their complex racial and ethnic identities. There is also intersectionality (discussed in Chapter 7), where ethnicity and race interact with other aspects of social identity, such as class, gender, and sexual orientation. Thus, the need for caution exists about generalizations and respect for the tremendous diversity within groups.

RACISM AND THE HELPING PROFESSIONS IN HISTORICAL PERSPECTIVE

In the United States, the helping professions were born within a "racial contract" (Mills, 1997) and developed in an evolving, fluctuating, and mutating racial project (Omi & Winant,

1994). All durable inequalities, such as racism, involve adaptation and all institutions society's structural disparities (Tilly, 1998). Thus, it is not surprising to find the nascent helping professions reflecting the racism of society and participating in its maintenance. We consider three seminal eras of social policy enactment: the Progressive Era, the New Deal, and the Great Society, focusing on the influence of race and racism on legislation and social programs, the role of helping professionals (particularly social workers as an exemplar), and the impact of racism on policies and reforms.

PROGRESSIVE ERA

In late 19th-century America, major and profound social trends (e.g., industrialization, urbanization, immigration) interacted, and the helping professions emerged within this milieu. Industrialization was a major economic and social force, attracting large numbers of immigrants, particularly from Europe, and cities became swollen with working and poor people. The fact that most of the immigrants were from Europe in itself reflected the depth of racism in U.S. institutions and the American consciousness as immigrants from other parts of the world were not welcome.

The period from the end of the Civil War to the turn of the 20th century has been called the "Gilded Age" (Jansson, 2015). It was characterized by the development of major cartels and monopolies, the ascendance of an industrialist elite, corruption and greed, extreme economic inequality, and profound labor and social unrest (Axinn & Levin, 1992; Jansson, 2015; Katz, 1986; Trattner, 1999; Zinn, 1980). The extreme economic disparities and the precarious plight of workers and immigrants were justified by "social Darwinism," which saw society as an arena for survival of the fittest. This, in turn, justified the lack of government intervention, because it would buoy and protect the weakest. This social philosophy was fueled by nativist reactions to the masses of immigrants, as well as being overtly racist toward people of color while offering a framework to shape perceptions of the poor, as well as to guide reform efforts.

Cities during this period were squalid, with overcrowding, extreme poverty, poor sanitation, health hazards, and exploitation of children. Urban residents were buffeted by economic depressions and their vulnerability to financial fluctuations. Even reform and social movements had racist and nativist overtones: Trade unions were hostile to people of color; suffragists fought mostly for the right of White women to vote; and the birth control movement was associated with the move for eugenics, which espoused overtly racist ideologies (Jansson, 2015; Trattner, 1999).

The main thrust of the Progressive Movement—which extended from the turn of the century until the end of World War I—was legislation focusing on antitrust activities, instituting economic reforms, introducing a federal income tax, producing health and sanitation standards, enacting women's suffrage and child labor laws, and establishing juvenile courts. Although these universalistic reforms and protections were in theory of benefit to all, they did not challenge institutional or societal racism, which in turn was fueled by prejudice and intergroup hostility. The two major presidential figures of this period, Theodore Roosevelt and Woodrow Wilson, courted White southern racists as part of their political base and overtly expressed racist attitudes in speeches and public statements, as well as in their actions (Iglehart & Becerra, 1995; Jansson, 2015).

The Progressive Era did not respond to Jim Crow in the South or discrimination against the Chinese and Japanese in the West and Mexican Americans in the South, and it was a period of continued land grabs from Native Americans, as well as attempts to destroy their culture. *Plessy v. Ferguson*—the Supreme Court decision in 1896 enshrining the doctrine of separate but equal, which was in reality separate and unequal—stood as the law of the land. African Americans continued to have drastically higher infant mortality rates and shorter life expectancy than Whites, despite the poverty of many White immigrants (Iglehart & Becerra, 1995). Within this context, many helping professions were growing—in particular, social work, public health, juvenile justice, and those associated with public education. We briefly explore two forerunners of social work—the Charity Organization Societies (COS) and the Settlement House movement.

Charity Organization Societies

The COS represented a well-intentioned response by upper middle class, Christian, White reformers, primarily women, to save and elevate the poor, particularly White immigrants. Rather than offering material assistance, the philosophy advocated using social assessment to identify social pathologies and the relationship (a forerunner of the casework relationship in social work) to effect change. The approach, which was riddled with class biases and would be considered patronizing by today's standards, was predicated on and fueled by many ethnic and racial stereotypes. White immigrant groups, and not racial and ethnic groups of color, were the primary targets of the COS.

Settlement Houses

Settlement houses were founded to elevate the poor through contact with their social betters. Upper-middle-class women spearheaded this movement, but there was less social distance between the reformers and their clients than with COS workers, as many settlement house workers actually lived in the settlement houses. The emphasis was on efficacy and empowerment, with a less punitive, morally judgmental attitude. Their use of groups and education and their willingness to fight for needed social reforms reflected an appreciation for the environmental causes of poverty, sickness, and social problems.

Although settlement houses pressed for political and economic protections, they did not work to further social integration or challenge the structure and dynamics of racism (Berman-Rossi & Miller, 1994). And, though some of the settlement house leaders—notably Jane Addams (Jansson, 2015) and Sophonisba Breckinridge (Iglehart & Bercerra, 1995)—acknowledged racism, settlement houses for the most part were established by White reformers, served White clients, and did not respond adequately to the needs of African Americans and other people of color (Berman-Rossi & Miller, 1994). Carson (1990, p. 195) summarized this by saying that "institutionally the settlements failed to make any significant contributions to White Americans' consciousness of racism or the furthering of Black people's rights and opportunities."

Consequently, African Americans worked to establish their own social networks, social service programs, and settlement houses. Unlike White settlement houses, Black settlement houses attempted to foster race pride, promote mutual aid, and tried to integrate micro (personal) issues while responding to macro level social problems (Carlton-LaNey, 1999). There was less social distance between workers and clients, more support for the need of women to work than in White-run settlement houses, and stronger efforts to create the social institutions and programs in the Black community that were more manifest in White communities (Gordon, 1991).

Taking care of one's own people in the face of White indifference and hostility also spurred Japanese and Chinese Americans to form community networks and pool their economic resources. Newly arrived Mexican immigrants in the Southwest often looked back to Mexico for supports and services unavailable in the United States as well as developed local networks in the United States (Jansson, 2015).

Neither the COS nor the White-run settlement houses responded adequately to the needs of people of color. As institutions, they recreated and perpetuated the dynamics of racism found in other sectors of society.

THE NEW DEAL

The New Deal, with its unprecedented number of employment projects and social insurance programs, heralded a new era of government response to need. For the first time in the nation's history, the federal government provided massive grants for people in need, created huge public works projects to provide jobs, and established a system of social insurance and welfare. Yet this, too, was a period in which the racial project was not questioned seriously or undermined and serious acts of racism continued to be perpetrated, including one of the greatest blots in the history of racism in the United States.

The New Deal, more than anything else, was a response to the Great Depression that began with the stock market crash of 1929 and persisted for 12 years. Business and bank failures were staggering, the magnitude of unemployment was unprecedented, the economic challenges to the country were catastrophic, and the social unrest challenged the nation's economic and political systems. When Franklin Roosevelt won the presidential election in 1932, the rate of unemployment in many cities and communities across the country was 20% to a staggering 60% (Jansson, 2015)!

Roosevelt's response in the form of the New Deal was based on three premises (Axinn & Levin, 1992):

1. A belief in the efficacy of the free market system
2. An attempt to maintain a balanced budget
3. An attempt to create an effective demand for employment and consumption through massive government spending

The New Deal also offered three types of relief (Jansson, 2015):

1. Grants to states for direct emergency relief through the Federal Emergency Relief Agency (FERA)
2. Public works programs to stimulate investment, employment, and consumption
3. Eventually, social insurance for the elderly and welfare for children and the blind

Legislation also was passed to reform the economic system, such as the National Labor Relations Act (the "Wagner Act") and the Fair Labor Standards Act, which encouraged unionization, raised the minimum wage, and limited workweeks (Jansson, 2015). The model for all of the programs of the New Deal was for the federal government to funnel resources through states and cities.

Herein lies a fundamental problem for a racially stratified society: Roosevelt sought to retain the political support of many regions of the country, certainly of the South. He also promoted universal programs, because these garnered greater political support. He instituted a few efforts to support fairness for people of color, such as a nondiscrimination statement in the Works Progress Administration (WPA), and African American men eventually did constitute about 10% of the Civilian Conservation Corps (CCC) and 15% of the WPA (Jansson, 2015). However, the CCC camps and housing at other work relief programs remained segregated (Jones, 1985)—which is illustrative of the tensions and contradictions caused by not challenging racism directly.

This pattern rippled throughout the programs of the New Deal. Local agencies administering programs often discriminated against Blacks and Latinos, including delaying the processing of their applications, maintaining racial quotas, and demoting workers to positions that were lower than warranted by their education and training (Abramovitz, 1988). Structurally, the programs excluded many people of color, as the benefits did not extend to those who worked in agriculture, as domestics, or in unregulated, secondary economic sectors (Jansson, 2015; Jones, 1985). By some estimates, three quarters of African Americans were not covered by the social insurance benefits of the New Deal (Brown et al., 2003).

Roosevelt and the New Deal did not challenge poll taxes or lynching in the South (Jansson, 2015). As was mentioned earlier, Mexican Americans, who had been recruited from Mexico to do agricultural and ranching work, were forcibly deported (Jansson, 2015) as were U.S. citizens of Mexican origin (NPR, 2015). Social workers colluded with the forced repatriation, helping to identify people to be exiled.

Native Americans were grappling with the Native American Reorganization Act of 1934. The act sought to establish semitribal governments and encourage economic development but still fostered a client-like, dependent relationship between tribes and the federal government, ceding a great deal of authority to the Secretary of the Interior for Indian affairs. Many Native Americans viewed this act as another step toward losing their culture and heritage, as local chiefs were replaced with tribal councils. As for Asian Americans, most still were unable to immigrate to the United States. As described previously, Japanese American citizens were placed in concentration camps.

So where were the helping professions during this turbulent period? This was a time of growth and expansion for social work and other helping professions. Group work expanded, and the specialty of community organizing was becoming popular. For the most part, social work and other allied professions supported the Roosevelt administration and the New Deal programs (Jansson, 2015). A number of social workers, such as Eveline Burns and Mary Switzer, were active in the Roosevelt administration. A radical group of social workers known as the "Rank and File" criticized the New Deal for propping up capitalism and failing to deal with profound social inequities and injustices, including racism (Abramovitz, 1988). But this small group did not represent the profession as a whole.

In sum, racism was not challenged seriously during the period of the New Deal, and because of a lack of willingness to confront it at the highest levels and the tendency to dispense programs through states and cities, societal racism structured and shaped the contours of the New Deal. Many racial and ethnic minorities continued to suffer from levels of prejudice and discrimination and relief, public works, social insurance, and welfare programs did not reach people of color in the same way that they assisted Whites. And it was during this period that two egregious acts of racism occurred. One was the forced repatriation of

Mexican Americans (described earlier), which is a euphemism for ethnic cleansing. The other was Executive Order 9066, establishing Japanese American internment camps, one of the most blatant acts of American racism in the 20th century and which was not atoned for until an apology was made half a century later. In both of these instances, social workers were collaborators in these gross human rights violations (NPR, 2015; Park, 2019).

THE CIVIL RIGHTS MOVEMENT AND THE GREAT SOCIETY

After World War II, seismic societal changes took place in the United States. People of color served with distinction in segregated military units and were not prepared to resume a subordinate social status when they returned to civilian life; their expectations of fairness and social justice were higher. The painful irony of returning to societal racism after fighting against the racism of Nazi Germany was accentuated by the Cold War between the United States and the Soviet Union, in which the United States was presenting itself as a democracy. At the same time, Japanese Americans, recently released from internment camps, were confronted with challenges to regaining their homes and businesses, which were taken from them by the U.S. government during World War II. They quickly asserted themselves by challenging California's Alien Land Act through legislation in 1948 (Takaki, 1993).

Major demographic changes were at work as well. The dramatic expansion of highways during the Eisenhower years, coupled with the boom in housing fueled by the GI Bill, led to a striking expansion of the suburbs, accompanied by White flight from cities and the growth of de facto segregated neighborhoods. People of color all over the nation and from Puerto Rico migrated to cities seeking jobs, but they encountered poverty, discrimination, and ethnic and racial ghettos (Jansson, 2015). The great migration of African Americans from the South to cities in the Northeast, upper Midwest, and West continued, and between 1940 and 1970, 4.5 million African Americans made this journey (Jansson, 2015).

Major executive orders and Supreme Court decisions furthered the cause of civil rights. President Harry Truman desegregated the armed forces by executive order in 1948 and the *Brown v. Board of Education* ruling in 1954 upended the "separate but equal" decision of *Plessy v. Fergusson* and led to a movement to desegregate schools. One of the consequences of the migration of people of color to northern urban areas was that they had greater access to one another, fostering a sense of solidarity and furthering their ability to communicate and organize to protect themselves and advocate for their own needs (Jansson, 2015).

The Civil Rights Movement that originated in the South often is referred to as the "Second Reconstruction," following the first reconstruction immediately after the Civil War. In 1955, Rosa Parks refused to give up her seat on a bus to a White person, leading to a bus boycott in Montgomery, Alabama, and eventually to court-ordered desegregation of public transportation (Takaki, 1993). Demonstrations at segregated lunch counters and "freedom rides" challenged segregation on buses and at bus terminals. This was met by attacks (including against children trying to integrate schools), bombings (including a church in Birmingham that killed four girls), and assassinations of Black leaders (Juan Williams). In 1963, Dr. Martin Luther King, Jr. led a massive civil rights march in Washington, along with many other acts of resistance to White supremacy (Taylor Branch). Social workers were active in the Civil Rights Movement, and in 1964 a Columbia University social work student, Michael Schwerner, was murdered in Mississippi, along with James Chaney and Andrew Goodman.

Although the Civil Rights Movement initially focused on civil rights rather than economic rights, the two were soon linked. The emergence of Malcolm X as a Black spokesperson and subsequent uprisings by African Americans feeling trapped and frustrated in many cities furthered the impetus for civil and economic rights (Takaki, 1993). In 1967, the National Advisory Committee on Urban Disorders reported eight major uprisings, 33 other serious rebellions, and 123 minor outbreaks; racism was cited as the major cause of this massive social unrest and disorder (Zinn, 1980). Both Malcom X and Martin Luther King, Jr., were assassinated. Black militant groups, such as the Black Panthers, emerged, advocating armed struggle.

The conditions of racism and economic exclusion in cities led to high rates of African American unemployment as migration from the South continued (Miller, 2003). Social workers responded by actively organizing programs to serve people and also precipitated a crisis in the inadequate social welfare system. Richard Cloward, George Brager, Harry Specht, and Sherman Barr, all social workers, were instrumental in converting antigang programs, such as Mobilization for Youth, into antipoverty operations. They devised a strategy of enrolling all those who were eligible for welfare in New York City, most of whom were not receiving benefits, by learning about the city's welfare regulations and educating clients about their rights. The goal was to bankrupt the system and force the federal government to step in with adequate resources, or even establish a guaranteed annual income (Edsall & Edsall, 1991; Katz, 1989; Leman, 1991; Miller, 2003).

All of the strong social currents described thus far, along with the assassinations of President Kennedy, Martin Luther King, Jr., Medgar Evers, and Malcom X, as well as the ascendance of Lyndon Johnson—who won a landslide victory in 1964 and whose party controlled both houses of Congress—created an unprecedented tide of social change and legislation addressing racism, under the awning of the Great Society. The Economic Opportunity Act of 1964 established community action programs, designed to combat poverty and engage citizens with "maximum feasible participation" (Katz, 1989; Miller, 2003; Trattner, 1999).

Programs that emerged from this legislation included VISTA, Job Corps, Neighborhood Youth Corps, Operation Head Start, and Upward Bound. Food stamps were introduced, and Model Cities legislation in 1966 targeted poor urban neighborhoods with federal resources for public schools, nutrition, and health care for women and children. This act, as well as the HUD acts of 1965 and 1968, boosted low-income housing (Axinn & Levin, 1992). Medicaid and Medicare were established in 1965.

All of these programs were aimed at reducing poverty, which indirectly addressed the consequences of institutional racism. Additional legislation directly confronted racial discrimination and supported civil rights. The Civil Rights Act of 1964 prohibited racial, ethnic, or sexual discrimination in employment and established the Equal Opportunity Commission (Axinn & Levin, 1992; Jansson, 2015; Trattner, 1999). Under this act, the Attorney General could file suits against racially segregated court systems and the U.S. government could withhold federal funds for schools and hospitals that practiced racial discrimination (Edsall & Edsall, 1991). The Voting Rights Act of 1965 guaranteed all citizens the right to vote, and Executive Order 11246 required government contractors to "take affirmative action" to redress current and historical patterns of racial discrimination.

The Great Society did not redistribute wealth dramatically; programs were underfunded and there was mismanagement and corruption (Leman, 1991; Trattner, 1999). A guaranteed annual income did not materialize. Although the Great Society did not extinguish the virus of racism, its legacy is profound in the struggle against racism in the United States. The programs aimed at helping the poor and strengthening urban areas benefited people of color as well as poor Whites and those who were city dwellers. Poverty rates were reduced for people of all ages, discrimination was curtailed dramatically, and affirmative action opened doors sufficiently to allow more people of color to enter the middle class (Katz, 1989).

Perhaps one of the Great Society's most notable accomplishments was not in the specific programs that were enacted but, rather, in the attempt by the federal government to challenge and dismantle racism directly. Not since the Civil War and the immediate aftermath of Reconstruction had such a focused and concerted effort to dismantle racism emanated from Washington. As a result of the passion for social justice generated during the 1960s, social workers, lawyers, and other helping professionals often entered their professions with a sense of optimism about their ability to make a difference. Despite flaws and shortcomings, not since Abraham Lincoln was presidential leadership exercised on behalf of people of color as by Kennedy and Johnson.

In today's times, it is difficult to believe that a president, let alone a president from the South, with a prior history of racism, could make speeches endorsing affirmative action with vigor and passion. And herein lies the tragedy of the Great Society—the political and social backlash that has followed it. The Deep South moved inexorably from Democrat waters to become a Republican sea of red, led by White voters associating Democrats with the rights of people of color (Edsall & Edsall, 1991). Across the country, working-class and middle-class White Democrats, angered by what they viewed as preferential treatment for people of color through efforts such as affirmative action, revolted and backed the conservative Republican presidential candidate, Ronald Reagan. Reagan used coded racial imagery while running for president, including initiating his campaign in Philadelphia, Mississippi, (in the county where three civil rights workers had been murdered) in front of a White audience and stressing "state's rights" (Herbert, 2007) and talking about the need to curtail the support of "welfare queens," widely interpreted as referring to Black women. The country became increasingly conservative, cutting taxes and social welfare programs, and dismantling or underfunding many of the Great Society programs.

In 1988, George Bush successfully ran for president using the infamous "Willie Horton" political advertisement. It accused his opponent, Michael Dukakis, of releasing dangerous criminals while governor of Massachusetts, using Willie Horton, a Black man released from prison who subsequently committed murder, to illustrate his point. The advertisement blatantly exploited White Americans' fear of Black men, which was acknowledged by Bush's campaign strategist Lee Atwater, who apologized, as he was dying, for making Willie Horton Dukakis's "running mate" (Associated Press, 1991).

Even after historic achievements, such as the election of Barack Obama, America saw Donald Trump, running after two terms of the first elected Black president, demonizing immigrants and citizens of color as he became the first openly White nationalist president in modern U.S. history (Coates).

Three conservative Republican presidents, serving for a combined 20 years since 1980, were able to appoint conservative Supreme Court justices. In 2015, the Supreme Court gutted the Voting Rights Act, one of the surviving antiracism legacies of the Great Society, by relieving states mandated to produce evidence of fair treatment of people of color of this obligation. Many states with conservative Republican majorities immediately filed and passed restrictive voter laws, which have reduced the number of people of color able to vote in elections, as well as gerrymandering in order to minimize the influence of Black voters. In 2019, the Supreme Court, after Senate Majority Leader blocked even holding hearings for Barack Obama's nominee Merick Garland and subsequently appointing two Trump nominations, voted to not challenge blatant examples of gerrymandering. This rollback illustrates how the nation not only did not finish the work of dismantling racism that was begun during the Great Society, but has actively been turning back the clock.

Today, many White people in the United States view racism as a past legacy rather than a present reality, and themselves as victims of "reverse racism" (Gonyea, 2017)

CONCLUSION

Racism has been part of the history of the United States from the earliest European settlers to the present. Many ethnic groups, including some considered to be White today, encountered prejudice and social exclusion, but the ethnic or racial groups socially constructed as people of color experienced racism that was significantly more extreme and persistent. Painful as it may be, to understand the extent and dynamics of racism today, we must explore and revisit this history if we are to move forward. This is necessary if we are to accomplish true racial healing and reconciliation in this country. Although we have made tremendous progress in confronting racism since the founding of the American Republic, the capacity of racism to adapt, regroup, and endure, and to render itself increasingly invisible to those who are most privileged by it, is a challenge that we consider throughout the rest of this book.

EXERCISE 3.1 Treatment of Presidents

Do a Google search of threats directed at President Obama while he was in office. Compare the results with the threats directed at two other U.S. presidents who held office in the decades after the assassination of President Kennedy. Do the same for public insults and questions about the president's citizenship and religion. If you have found differences, how would you explain the differences?

EXERCISE 3.2 Differential Group Experience

The following questions can be applied to any U.S. ethnic or racial group to understand and compare their historical experiences. This exercise can highlight significant differences between ethnic and racial groups of color and those constructed as White, as well as differences between groups within those categories. Select a White ethnic group and an ethnic group of color and consider the following questions:

1. Was contact or immigration voluntary or involuntary for each of the two groups?
2. Were members of each group ever legally defined as not being fully human?
3. What resources did each group have—linguistic, cultural, or economic? Was there a fit of skills with job opportunities?
4. How destructive was the oppression (e.g., genocide, slavery, exclusion, internment, dispossession, and lack of civil rights)? Have members of each group ever been forcibly

repatriated or barred from immigrating to the United States? Were there laws justifying each group's subordinate status?

5. How far-reaching and severe was the damage caused by racial and ethnic oppression of each group—economic, social, family, psychological, cultural, or legal?
6. How long did each group experience severe oppression in the United States? Was the oppression transitory, in that the group later was enabled to become "White"? Did significant numbers of group members live for generations in socially and economically isolated and deprived neighborhoods? Have poverty rates and other indicators of social well-being been consistently lower for each of these groups than for other groups?
7. Does the oppression of either group endure today?
8. Does either group continue to lack access to resources, as well as to cultural, social, economic, and political capital?
9. Are there enduring denigrating stereotypes and cultural scapegoating for each of these groups?
10. Do members of each group consistently encounter harassment by law-enforcement officials? Are members of each group overrepresented in the criminal justice system and underrepresented at universities and in many occupations and professions?

EXERCISE 3.3 Violence Toward People of Color

Research a specific act of racial violence in U.S. history, such as a White terrorist attack, ethnic cleansing, the use of concentration camps, or a particular lynching.

1. Describe what happened.
2. What led to the event, and what were the conditions that made this possible?
3. What role did law enforcement or the courts play, if any?
4. How was the event covered in the mainstream press or media?
5. Could this happen again? If you think no, what safeguards exist to prevent it from recurring?
6. Is there anything that you can think of that can be done today to honor or make reparations for what happened?

REFERENCES

Abramovitz, M. (1988). Regulating the lives of women. In *Social policy from colonial times to the present*. South End Press.

Afful, S. E., Wholford, C., & Stoelting, S. M. (2015). Beyond "difference": Examining the process and flexibility of racial identity in interracial marriages. *Journal of Social Issues, 71*(4), 659–674.

Allen, T. W. (1994). *The invention of the White race*. Verso.

Arnove, A., & Zinn, H. (2004). *Voices of a people's history of the United States*. Seven Stories Press.

Associated Press. (1991). Gravely ill, Atwater offers apology. www.nytimes.com/1991/01/13/us/gravely-ill-atwater-offers-apology.html

Axinn, J., & Levin, H. (1992). *Social welfare: A history of the American response to social need* (3rd ed.). Longman.

Baptist, E. E. (2014). *The half has never been told: Slavery and the making of American capitalism*. Basic Books

Beauchamp, Z. (2019). Poway and Pittsburgh: The rise of murderous anti-semitism, explained. Vox. www .vox.com/policy-and-politics/2019/5/1/18524103/poway-synagogue-shooting-anti-semitism.

Berman-Rossi, T., & Miller, I. (1994). African-Americans and the settlements during the late 19th and early 20th centuries. *Social Work With Groups, 17*(3), 77–92.

Bikmen, N. (2015). Still a nation of immigrants? Effects of constructions of national history on attitudes towards immigrants. *Analysis of Social Issues and Public Policy, 15,* 282–302.

Blackmon, D. (2008). *Slavery by another name: The re-enslavement of Black Americans from the Civil War until World War II.* Doubleday.

Blight, D.W. (2018). *Frederick Douglass: Prophet of freedom.* Simon and Schuster.

Brown, M. K., Carnoy, M., Curne, E., Duster, T., Oppenheimer, D. B., Shultz, M. M., & Wellman, D. (2003). *Whitewashing race: The myth of a colorblind society.* University of California Press.

Carlton-LaNey, I. (1999). African American social work pioneer's response to need. *Social Work, 44*(4), 311–321.

Carnes, J. (1995). *Us and them: A history of intolerance in America.* Southern Poverty Law Center.

Carson, M. (1990). *Settlement folk: Social thought and the American settlement movement, 1885–1930.* Chicago: University of Chicago Press.

Cloward, R. A., & Ohlin, L. E. (1960). *Delinquency and opportunity.* Free Press.

Coates, T. (2017). The first white president. The Atlantic. www.theatlantic.com/magazine/archive/2017/10 /the-first-white-president-ta-nehisi-coates/537909/

Davis, D. B. (1997). A big business. *New York Review of Books, XLV*(10), 50–52.

Diamond, J. (1997). *Guns, germs and steel: The fates of human societies.* W. W. Norton.

Dinnerstein, L. (1994). *Anti-Semitism in America.* Oxford University Press.

Douglass, F. (1994). *Autobiographies.* Library of America.

Edsall, T. B., & Edsall, M. D. (1991). *Chain reaction: The impact of race, rights and taxes on American politics.* W. W. Norton.

Feagin, J. R., & Feagin, C. B. (2011). *Racial and ethnic relations, census update* (9th ed.). Pearson.

Finkelman, P. (2012). The monster of Monticello. *The New York Times.* www.nytimes.com/2012/12/01 /opinion/the-real-thomas-jefferson.html?emc=eta1

Flaherty, A. (2013). American Indian land rights, rich Indian racism, and newspaper coverage in New York State, 1988–2008. *American Indian Culture and Research Journal, 37*(4), 53–84.

Foner, P. (1975). *History of Black Americans* (Vol. 1). Greenwood Press.

Fredrickson, G. (1981). *White supremacy: A comparative study in American and South African history.* Oxford University Press.

Fredrickson, G. (2002). *Racism: A short history.* Princeton University Press.

Fritze, (2019). Trump used words like 'invasion' and 'killer' to discuss immigrants at rallies 500 times https://www.usatoday.com/story/news/politics/elections/2019/08/08/trump-immigrants-rhetoric -criticized-el-paso-dayton-shootings/1936742001/

Gandbhir, G., & Stephenson, M. (2016). A conversation with Asian Americans about race. *The New York Times.* www.nytimes.com/2016/04/05/opinion/a-conversation-with-asians-on-race.html?emc=eta1

Gladstone, R., & Sugiyama, S. (2018). *Trump's travel ban: How it works and who is affected. The New York Times.* www.nytimes.com/2018/07/01/world/americas/travel-ban-trump-how-it-works.html

Glazer, N., & Moynihan, D. P. (1963). *Beyond the melting pot: The Negroes, Puerto Ricans, Jews, Italians and Irish of New York City.* M.I.T. Press.

Gonyea, D. (2017). Majority of White Americans say that they believe that Whites face discrimination. NPR. www.npr.org/2017/10/24/559604836/majority-of-white-americans-think-theyre-discrimi nated-against

Gonzalez, J. (2011). *Harvest of empire: A history of Latinos in America.* Penguin Books.

Gonzalez, J., & Torres, J. (2011). *News for all the people: The epic story of race and the American media.* Verso.

Gordon, L. (1988). *Heroes in their own lives: The history and politics of family violence, Boston, 1880–1960.* Viking.

Gordon, L. (1991). Black and white visions of welfare: Women's welfare activism, 1890–1945. *Journal of American History, 85*(3), 559–590.

Gualtieri, S. (2001). Becoming "White": Race, religion and the foundations of Syrian/Lebanese ethnicity in the United States. *Journal of American Ethnic History, 20*(4), 29–52.

Guglielmo, J., & Salerno, S. (Eds.). (2003). *Are Italians White? How race is made in America*. Routledge.

Guglielmo, T. A. (2003). "No color barrier": Italians, race and power in the United States. In J. Guglielmo & S. Salerno (Eds.), *Are Italians White? How race is made in America* (pp. 29–43). Routledge.

Harbarger, M. (2016). *Decrepit fish camps built on broken promises*. The Oregonian. www.oregonlive.com /pacific-northwest-news/index.ssf/page/tribal_housing_a_run_of_broken.html

Healey, J. F. C. (1995). *Race, ethnicity, gender and class: The sociology of group conflict and change*. Pine Forge Press.

Herbert, B. (2007, November 13). *Righting Reagan's wrongs? The New York Times*. www.nytimes .com/2007/11/13/opinion/13herbert.html?smid=url-share

Higginbotham, H. M. (2013). *Ghosts of Jim Crow: Ending racism in post-racial America*. New York University Press.

Iglehart, A. P., & Becerra, R. M. (1995). *Social services and the ethnic community*. Allyn & Bacon.

Ignatiev, N. (1995). *How the Irish became White*. Routledge.

Jansson, B. (2015). *The reluctant welfare state: Engaging history to advance social work practice in contemporary society* (8th ed.). Cengage.

Johnson, C., & Smith, P. (1998). *Africans in America: America's journey through slavery*. Harcourt Brace.

Jones, J. (1985). *Labor of love, labor of sorrow: Black women, work and the family, from slavery to the present*. Basic Books.

Kang, H. K. (2012). Re-imagining citizenship, re-imagining social work: U.S. immigration policies and social work practice in the era of AZ SB1070. *Advances in Social Work, 13*(3), 510–526.

Katz, M. B. (1986). *In the shadow of the poor house: A social history of welfare in America*. Basic Books.

Katz, M. B. (1989). *The undeserving poor: From the war on poverty to the war on welfare*. Pantheon.

Klinkenborg, V. (2002, July/August). Liverpool's heart of darkness. *Mother Jones*, pp. 64–67.

Leman, N. (1991). *The promised land*. Knopf.

Levinson, E., Becker, S., & Simon, D. (2021). *Rise in attacks on elderly Asian Americans in Bay area prompts new special response unit*. CNN. www.cnn.com/2021/02/08/us/asian-american-attacks-bay-area /index.html

Lopez, I. F. H. (1996). *White by law: The legal construction of race*. New York University Press.

Lum, D. (2004). *Social work practice and people of color: A process-stage approach* (5th ed.). Brooks/Cole.

McGee, C. (2010). *The open road wasn't quite open to all*. The New York Times. www.nytimes.com/2010/08/23 /books/23green.html?emc=eta1

Miller, J. (1999). Holyoke at the crossroads: Family, ethnicity and community in a de-industrialized small city. Proceedings of the 13th Conference on the Small City and Regional Community (pp. 277–286). Center for the Small City.

Miller, J. (2003). Create a crisis and pray: A narrative interview with Richard Cloward. *Journal of Community Practice, 11*(1), 11–37.

Mills, C. W. (1997). *The racial contract*. Cornell.

Montgomery, D. (1993). *Citizen worker: The experience of workers with democracy and the free market during the nineteenth century*. Cambridge University Press.

Morgan, M. C. (1962). *Skid road: An informal portrait of Seattle*. Viking.

Murillo, M. (2001). *Islands of resistance: Puerto Rico, Vieques, and U.S. policy*. Seven Stories Press.

Murphy, B. (2013). *Was the famine genocide*. The Independent. www.independent.ie/entertainment/books /was-the-famine-genocide-by-the-british-28954929.html

National Public Radio. (2015). Mass deportation may sound unlikely but it's happened before. www.npr .org/sections/codeswitch/2015/09/08/437579834/mass-deportation-may-sound-unlikely-but-its -happened-before

Ojito, M. (2000). *Best of friends, worlds apart*. The New York Times, p. A1.

Omi, M., & Winant, H. (1994). *Racial formation in the United States: From the 1960s to the 1990s* (2nd ed.). Routledge.

Oshinsky, D. M. (1996). *"Worse than slavery": Parchman Farm and the ordeal of Jim Crow justice*. Free Press.

Parrillo, V. N. (2012). *Diversity in America* (4th ed). Routledge.

Park, Y. (2019). *Facilitating injustice: The complicity of social workers in the forced removal and incarceration of Japanese Americans: 1941–1946.* Oxford University Press.

Quijano, A. (2000). Coloniality of power and Eurocentrism in Latin America. *International Sociology, 15*(2), 215–232.

Romero, S. (2019). *Lynch mobs killed Latinos across the West. The fight to remember these atrocities is just starting. The New York Times.* www.nytimes.com/2019/03/02/us/porvenir-massacre-texas-mexicans .html

Sacks, K. B. (1996). How did Jews become White folks? In S. Gregory & R. Sanjek (Eds.), *Race* (pp. 78–102). Rutgers.

Shorris, E. (1992). *Latinos: A biography of the people.* W. W. Norton

Stannard, D. E. (1992). *American holocaust: The conquest of the New World.* Oxford University Press.

Staples, B. (1999). *Unearthing a riot. The New York Times Magazine,* pp. 64–69.

Steinberg, S. (2001). *The ethnic myth: Race, ethnicity and class in America* (3rd ed.). Beacon Press.

Takaki, R. (1987). The metaphysics of civilization: Indians and the age of Jackson. In R. Takaki (Ed.), *From different shores: Perspectives on race and ethnicity in America* (pp. 54–68). Oxford University Press.

Takaki, R. (1993). *A different mirror: A history of multi-cultural America.* Little, Brown.

Taylor, R. (1997). The changing meaning of race in the social sciences: Implications for social work practice. *Smith College Studies in Social Work, 67*(3), 277–298.

The Henry J. Kaiser Foundation. (2015). Life expectancy at birth (in years) by ethnicity. http://kff.org/other /state-indicator/life-expectancy-by-re/

Thomas, L. (1994). Group autonomy and narrative identity: Blacks and Jews. In P. Berman (Ed.), *Blacks and Jews: Alliances and arguments.* Delacorte Press.

Tilly, C. (1998). *Durable inequality.* University of California Press.

Trattner, W. I. (1999). *From poor law to welfare state: A history of social welfare in America* (6th ed.). Free Press.

Wilkerson, I. (2015). *When will the North face its racism?* The New York Times. www.nytimes.com/2015/01/11 /opinion/sunday/when-will-the-north-face-its-racism.html?emc=eta1

Wills, G. (2003). The Negro president. *New York Review of Books, 50*(17), 48–51.

Wilson, J. (1998). *The Earth shall weep: A history of Native America.* Grove.

Wyman, D. (1984). *The abandonment of the Jews.* Pantheon Publishing.

Zinn, H. (1980). *A people's history of the United States.* Harper & Row.

CHAPTER 4

Racism and Immigration

INTRODUCTION

Many of us are familiar with the following lines from *The New Colossus*, a poem by Emma Lazarus, first published in 1883 and in 1903 was cast onto a bronze plaque and mounted inside the pedestal on which Statue of Liberty stands:

> Not like the brazen giant of Greek fame,
> With conquering limbs astride from land to land;
> Here at our sea-washed, sunset gates shall stand
> A mighty woman with a torch, whose flame
> Is the imprisoned lightning, and her name
> Mother of Exiles. From her beacon-hand
> Glows world-wide welcome; her mild eyes command
> The air-bridged harbor that twin cities frame.
> "Keep, ancient lands, your storied pomp!" cries she
> With silent lips. "Give me your tired, your poor,
> Your huddled masses yearning to breathe free,
> The wretched refuse of your teeming shore.
> Send these, the homeless, tempest-tost to me,
> I lift my lamp beside the golden door!"

The sentiment and spirit expressed in this poem is clear: America as an asylum for the "tired" and "poor" "wretched refuse," and the Statue of Liberty as the symbolic mother of the "homeless" "huddled masses." However, during the same period as the poem was published and commemorated, the U.S. policies on immigration and naturalization painted a different picture of America. In particular, history illuminates that the policies differed according to which "ancient lands" those "huddled masses" came from, and the "golden door" narrowed, or sometimes shut completely, depending on which "teeming shores" the immigrant came from. And, the "world-wide welcome" depended largely on the economic and labor needs of the young nation. Moreover, U.S. immigration and naturalization policies excluded Native Americans from citizenship, rendering them foreigners in their own homeland. As we illustrate in this chapter, U.S. immigration and naturalization policies were crucial in implementing racialization (Omi & Winant, 2014) into everyday practices. Immigration and naturalization policies do not just reflect the anti-immigrant racism of the era; they also *legitimize and sanction* them.

COLONIALITY AND CRITICAL RACE THEORY

The theoretical lens of coloniality and critical race theory, which were discussed in Chapter 2, are useful to understand the relationship between racism and immigration. Coloniality (Quijano, 2000) is understood here as a complex system of European (or the "Western") hegemony, established and maintained through European conquest and occupation (colonialism and settler colonialism). It operates through the re-identification and categorization of colonized geocultural regions from the colonizing nations' perspectives and through the production of global capitalism that exploits labor, resources, and products of the colonized. The framework of coloniality also dominates what constitutes legitimate knowledge and epistemologies and what is defined as modern and civilized. Deeply interrelated with and operated through capitalism, Christianity, and gender and economic oppression, coloniality can be seen as an organizing principle for immigration policy in the United States (see Chapter 2 for detailed discussion of coloniality).

The theory of coloniality helps us understand U.S. immigration in the global historical context. Western colonization of Africa, Asia, the Middle East, and the Americas devastated resources and economies of the colonized nations and resulted in geopolitical conflicts and forced migrations in these regions. Western nations continue to influence political and economic states of (formerly) colonized nations through their economic and political power; however, they are rarely accountable to the results of their influence such as global migration. For example, U.S. military and political involvement in Asia, Southeast Asia, Central America, and the Middle East caused sociopolitical destabilization, which resulted in internal displacement and migration. However, the United States has not taken accountability for such global migration, effectively stranding vulnerable populations.

Critical race theorists such as Omi and Winant (2014) contend that race is not a "natural" or biological categorization but rather a historically determined, fluid, unstable and contested social construction. Omi and Winant (1994) termed the process through which a society comes to "signify the extension of racial meaning to a previously racially unclassified relationship, social practice or group" (p. 64) as *racialization*. Racialization is an ideological process that is unique to the society's history. In the United States, the idea of race was constructed and maintained through ascribing racial "identities" that often relied on "scientific" racism that used the faulty narrative of "biologically distinct" races. Historically, the United States has used racialization to exclude and "other" people of color while normalizing and privileging those who were identified as White.

IMMIGRATION AND NATIVE AMERICANS

The story of U.S. immigration must start with acknowledging the deleterious effects of European migration on the indigenous people of this land. This history is beyond the scope of this chapter and as such cannot be adequately addressed. This section only briefly captures nota-ble U.S. policies regarding immigration and naturalization that shaped Native Americans' citizenship rights (https://immigrationhistory.org/).

The push and pull factor theory of immigration (Lee, 1966) explains how different factors prompt transnational migration; the theory posits that immigration is influenced by various push factors of the sending nations and pull factors of the receiving nations, and that immi-gration usually benefits both the receiving country's population and the immigrant popula-tion. The migration of Europeans to what is now known as the United States is unique in that neither the push nor the pull factors had anything to do with the indigenous people. In fact, the European migration to America resulted in near decimation of the indigenous population (Stannard, 1992; Takaki, 1993). As Europeans started migrating in larger numbers and formed a settler colonialist government, they launched a campaign to drive out the indige-nous population by force and through its policies. For example, the Indian Removal Act of 1830, during the presidency of Andrew Jackson, authorized the confiscation of land from Native Americans. The brutal implementation of this law resulted in approximately 4,000 deaths of Cherokees during the forced march in 1838 and 1839, which is known as the Trail of Tears. The settler colonialists' sustained campaign against the indigenous population, which Stannard (1992) termed *American Holocaust*, involved dehumanizing narratives about Native Americans. As stated in Chapter 2, unequal power and domination was created and supported through concepts such as "scientific racism" used to categorize who was not fully human or worthy of full personhood. Similarly, Christianity was employed to define Native Americans as "heathens," denigrating the spiritual practices of non-Christians and justifying genocide and ethnic cleansing (Quijano, 2000).

The Naturalization Act of 1790, the nation's first law regarding citizenship, withheld natu-ralization rights from Native Americans, thus rendering indigenous people of the continent virtual foreigners of their historical homeland. The Naturalization Act of 1870, which granted citizenship to persons of African descent, did not grant naturalization rights to Native Americans because they were neither White nor of African descent. In *Elk vs. Wilkins* in 1884, the U.S. Supreme Court ruled that Native Americans were not citizens by birth and thus the Fourteenth Amendment did not apply to them.

The Dawes Allotment Act (1887) essentially demanded that Native Americans accept the U.S. government-imposed individual landholding system and U.S. citizenship or remain in the traditional tribal system of land tenure and forego U.S. citizenship. Designed to regulate land rights on tribal territories within the United States, this act was aimed to "condition... Native individuals, as well as particular cultural traits or practices... [to fit] into an American 'safety zone' of obedient citizenry" (Lomawaima & McCarty, 2006, pp. 43–44). The act also allowed the U.S. government to sell any remaining lands to non-Native Americans. This not only caused a serious undermining of tribal governments and traditional cultural practices but also caused Native Americans to lose millions of acres of land.

It was not until in 1924 (134 years after the 1790 Naturalization Act) that Native Ameri-cans gained citizenship. The Indian Citizenship Act of 1924 stipulated that all Native Ameri-cans born in the United States were citizens by birth. With this act, Native Americans finally gained the voting rights that were set forth in the Fourteenth Amendment, which was enacted 56 years prior. Also notable is that this act proclaimed that the U.S. citizenship "shall not in any manner impair or otherwise affect the right of any Indian to tribal or other property," essentially allowing Native Americans to hold dual citizenship rights.

HISTORY: IMMIGRATION POLICIES AND RACIALIZATION

In immigration policies, immigrants are referred to as *aliens*. Merriam-Webster dictionary (n.d.) defines *alien* as an adjective as:

a. belonging or relating to another person, place, or thing: strange;
b. relating, belonging, or owing allegiance to another country or government: foreign; and
c. coming from another world: extraterrestrial.

As such, immigrants as "aliens" are imagined as intrinsically different and strange, not belonging to "us" and "here," and not loyal to this country. They may or may not be humans; by definition they have more in common with extraterrestrials than "us." This statement may sound far-fetched, but such racist and xenophobic constructions of immigrants have been conjured up to enact policies and practices that limited rights of racialized immigrants. In turn, those policies and practices solidified racist and xenophobic constructions of racialized immigrants, further marginalizing them.

Kang (2012) argues that the U.S. immigration and naturalization policies operate on a set of binary notions such as desirable/undesirable, safe/dangerous, and deserving/undeserving. Kang contends that these binaries reinforced racialization, had a lasting impact on the racial landscape of the nation, and continue to maintain a racial hierarchy of White as desirable and non-White as undesirable citizens of this country. In this section we illustrate the intertwined relationship between race, racism, and immigration. Due to the limited scope of this chapter, we are not exploring complex similarities and differences between the U.S. immigration and refugee/asylum policies and rely mostly on immigration policies as examples here.

Racialization Through Immigration Policies

The first U.S. policy on immigration and naturalization was the 1790 Naturalization Act, which defined eligibility for citizenship by naturalization to "free, white persons." Until this law was enacted it was assumed that immigrants would be granted citizenship as there were no specific laws that governed it. It is important to note that most immigrants until that era came from Europe, and that Africans who were forcibly trafficked and enslaved were not considered immigrants, or even a full individual. The Article I, Section 2 of the U.S. Constitution of 1787 declared that enslaved Africans were three fifths of a person. In fact, in the *Dred Scott v. Sanford* case in 1857, the Supreme Court dismissed the case brought by Dred Scott, an African American man who attempted to sue in court for freedom from slavery, on this very basis. In this case, the Supreme Court held that "a negro, whose ancestors were imported into [the U.S.] and sold as slaves" could not be a U.S. citizen and therefore could not sue in federal court (Harris, 2001). It was not until the 14th Amendment (in 1868) that formerly enslaved African Americans would be recognized as a citizen of the United States.

The Naturalization Act of 1790 was the first national law to define naturalization eligibility on the basis of race (White) and status (free). Given that the idea of race as a "scientific" categorization was being constructed and socialized during this era, this naturalization policy became crucial to the inculcation of racial categorization as well as establishing the hierarchy of race as a practice. (Please see Chapter 2 for the discussion on scientific racism.) Thus, this first immigration and naturalization law, which linked the idea of race and the idea of citizenship, continues to reverberate throughout U.S. immigration policy.

The ban on "importation" of "any Negro, Mulatto, or other persons of color, not being a native, a citizen, or a registered seaman, of the United States, or seamen, natives of countries beyond the Cape of Good Hope" (Fitzgerald & Cook-Martin, 2014, p. 89) in 1803 was one of the first laws limiting immigration based on race and region. This law specifically targeted free Black people from Haiti, where enslaved Black people revolted against slavery and formed a Black republic, due to the fear of mostly Southern enslavers (but also some White Northerners) that similar revolt would spread to the United States with migration. This law thus linked the idea of race, immigration, and the notion of safety (of the dominant majority, i.e., White people), which is echoed in later and contemporary policies.

The idea of race, specifically what constituted White, did not go uncontested since the designation of White meant many rights, including citizenship. Those who did not easily fit into the Black/White binary, such as Asians and Mexicans, raised a question into such construction of race. One example is the Treaty of Guadalupe of 1848. In settlement of the Mexican-American War, this treaty set Rio Grande as the border between the United States and Mexico (which still remains the case for the most part), and formalized the U.S. annexation of northern Mexico (approximately the present-day California, Nevada, Utah, Colorado, New Mexico, and Arizona). Under this treaty, Mexican residents were allowed U.S. citizenship if they decided to remain within the newly designated U.S. territory. Because Mexicans were not commonly considered White in that era, this policy raised a question regarding the "White" criterion of the 1790 act.

The *People v. Hall* case is noteworthy in this regard. In 1854, the California Supreme Court ruled that the testimony of a Chinese man who witnessed a murder by a White man was not admissible in court. This ruling was based on the California Criminal Procedure's exclusion (1850) that declared, "No black or mulatto person, or Indian, shall be allowed to give evidence in favor of, or against a white man" (Lopez, 1996, p. 51). In this case, the California Supreme Court ruled that while the Constitution and laws did not specify Chinese, "the words 'Black person,' in the 14th section must be taken as contradistinguished from White, and necessarily excludes all races other than Caucasian." It also said that:

> [Chinese are] a race of people whom nature has marked as inferior, and who are
> incapable of progress or intellectual development beyond a certain point, as their
> history has shown; differing in language, opinions, color, and physical conformation;
> between whom and ourselves nature has placed an impassable difference.

Thus, not only did this case codify Chinese (and later interpreted to include all Asians) as non-White but also as distinct and inferior "by nature," echoing "scientific" racism that was being developed and propagated. This focus on the difference ("in language, opinions, color, and physical conformation") between the Chinese and "us" (presumably White, by "contradistinguished") not only reflects the racist and xenophobic sentiment of the era but also makes a lasting impact that produces Asians as perpetual foreigners, which gets repeatedly used to exclude and denigrate Asians and Asian Americans throughout the nation's history.

After the Civil War, and following the passage of the 14th Amendment (1868), the Naturalization Act of 1870 extended naturalization rights to "aliens of African nativity and to persons of African descent." However, this act did not dismantle the race-based naturalization policy. Rather, it upheld the race-based qualification of citizenship by just adding African Americans to those who were already eligible for naturalization (White immigrants). With the Emancipation Proclamation in effect, the only remaining criterion of the 1790 Naturalization Act was race (White), and thus race became the site of determining immigrants' right to naturalization and citizenship.

According to Lopez (1996), there were 52 court cases from 1878 to 1944 that debated whether an immigrant should be considered White or not (and thus should have the right to naturalization or not); these cases are referred to as racial prerequisite cases. The first prerequisite case was an 1878 Circuit Court case regarding Ah Yup, a Chinese immigrant who sought naturalization to become a U.S. citizen. In this landmark case, the Ninth Circuit Court of California denied Ah Yup's right to naturalize citing that the Naturalization Act of 1870 specifically sought to exclude Asians (the "Mongolian" race) on the basis that they were distinct from the "Caucasian" race. Circuit Court Judge Sawyer argued (italics added):

> At that time of the amendment, in 1870, extending the naturalization laws to the African race, Mr. Sumner made repeated and strenuous efforts to strike the word "white" from the naturalization laws, or to accomplish the same object by other language. *It was opposed on the sole ground that the effect would be to authorize the admission of Chinese to citizenship.* (U.S. Circuit Court for the District of Columbia, 1878)

In this case, Judge Sawyer cited Blumenbach's racial classification to argue that the "Mongolian, or yellow race, occupying Tartary, China, Japan, and so forth" was distinct from the "Caucasian or the white race" and argued that "[n]either in popular language, in literature, nor in scientific nomenclature do we ordinarily, if ever, find the words 'white person' used in a sense so comprehensive as to include an individual of the Mongolian race" (U.S. Circuit Court for the District of California, 1878). Thus, this landmark case set the precedent of using "scientific" argument and appealing to "popular" knowledge. Given this decision, it is not surprising that of the 52 prerequisite cases 30 involved immigrants from what is now known as Asia and South Asia and six involved mixed-raced Asians. The rationale in determining prerequisite cases ranged from scientific evidence (which were based on "scientific" racism) to congressional intent (as in the argument in Ah Yup's case) to legal precedent to "common" knowledge (i.e., ideas held by White people since they were the norm), to "ocular inspection of skin." In one case regarding Mallari in 1916, no explanation was offered in terms of why Filipinos were deemed not White. In the cases involving South Asians ("Asian Indians") and Syrians, the prerequisite cases illustrate the instability of racial categorization and how race was socially constructed (Omi & Winant, 2014). Thus, these prerequisite cases reveal the complex interconnection between the idea of race, citizenship, and racism in the society.

The exclusion of immigrants of color from naturalization based on racism also interacted with patriarchy, which placed women of color in double jeopardy. The Expatriation Act of 1907 annulled citizenship of U.S.-born women when they married noncitizen immigrant men under the principle that women assumed citizenship of their husbands. After the Nineteenth Amendment of 1920 that gave the voting right to White women, the Expatriation Act was replaced with the Cable Act of 1922, which restored citizenship of White women who married noncitizen men. However, this restoration did not extend to U.S.-born women whose racial status was determined neither White nor Black and married "aliens ineligible for citizenship." This law disproportionally impacted Asian women; it meant that U.S.-born Asian women still lost their citizenship when they married Asian immigrant men because their husbands were not eligible for naturalization. Once they lost their citizenship through marriage, Asian women also became ineligible for naturalization because of the racial exclusion of the Naturalization Act. Losing citizenship left U.S.-born Asian women, who previously held citizenship, vulnerable to detention and deportation and barred from certain jobs that required licensure since noncitizens frequently were barred from licensure. Given that the *United States v. Wong Kim Ark* decision in 1898 ruled that any person born in the United States is a citizen by birth regardless of race or parents' status, the Cable Act demonstrates the doubly marginalizing effect of the race and gender interaction.

Reflecting and legitimizing such anti-Chinese sentiments, the immigration policies in this era sought to curtail Chinese immigration and limit the rights of those who were already in the country. For example, the Page Act of 1875, which prohibited the immigration of unfree laborers and women brought for "immoral purposes," was primarily enforced against Chinese immigrants. Also, this law specifically targeted Asians by naming them: "...any subject of China, Japan, or any Oriental country...." *No* other countries or races were named. As such, this law implied Asian labor was forced (male) or immoral (female).

The anti-immigrant sentiments toward Chinese (and more broadly Asian) culminated in the Chinese Exclusion Act of 1882, which prohibited immigration by all Chinese laborers for 10 years and explicitly barred the Chinese from naturalization. This act was the first U.S. immigration policy that excluded immigrants based on their ethnicity. Following the Chinese Exclusion Act, the Geary Act of 1892 required Chinese people to carry a Certificate of Residence to prove that they were in the United States legally or be liable for detention or deportation. This certificate was the precursor of the legal alien card (the "green card") and prefigured the more contemporary Real ID Act, which is discussed in a later section.

The Chinese Exclusion Act was extended in 1904 with perpetuity. And finally, the Immigration Act of 1917 (the Barred Zone Act), declared "the Continent of Asia" and most of the Polynesian islands a "barred zone" from immigration (Sohi, 2013). This was the first national act to exclude whole populations based on their geographic locations, and presumably, race. While Pacific Islanders and Asians may not have much in common in terms of shared history or culture, they both represented non-White, inassimilable, exotic "other" in the eyes of the White society's norm. The fact that this policy ties Asians and Pacific Islanders together is notable in that it portended and solidified subsequent constructions of racial categorization in the present-day United States where Asians and Pacific Islanders are usually branded as one group in many official forms and statistics.

The Emergency Immigration Act of 1921 (or the "Quota Law") introduced a quota system, limiting immigration from each European country to 3% of each foreign-born nationality in the 1910 census. The intent of this act was to preserve the particular racial makeup of the United States that was illustrated in the census; the act also upheld the Barred Zone Act that prohibited most Asians and Polynesians from immigrating. Given that the predominant source of immigration was Western and Northern Europe at that time, the quota for Southern and Eastern Europeans were only about 13% of all immigrants allowed per year (Hing, 2004). Reflecting the geo-political tensions that drew the United States into World War I and fanning the anti-immigrant sentiment against Southern and Eastern Europeans, this act made clear that not all Europeans were equally desirable even if they were considered White.

In 1924, the Johnson-Reed Act (the Immigration Act of May 26, 1924) established an official national origins quota system, which based the immigration quotas on the ethnic makeup of the U.S. population as a whole in 1920. The quota system did not apply to Asian immigration since this act denied entry to virtually all Asians. Influenced by eugenics that was popularized by leading White intellectuals (Diamond, 2020), this quota system was lauded as a major accomplishment that halted "the tendency toward a change in the *fundamental* composition of the *American stock*" (Hing, 2004, p. 69, italics added). The Johnson-Reed Act has a significant legacy. It not only contributed to an effort to use immigration policies to determine the ethnic and racial patterns of the country but also resulted in normalizing the narrative of "the fundamental American stock" as predominantly Western and Northern European. Another legacy is that the quota system that privileged certain ethic groups over others prevented many refugees, fleeing the Nazi regime's genocidal campaign based on White supremacy, from entering the United States.

The race and ethnicity-based immigration policies started shifting to reflect the conflicting needs of the nation's political exigencies, economy, and the changing sociopolitical climate. For example, the need for alliance with China during World War II resulted in the Act of December 17, 1943 (the Magnuson Act), which repealed the Chinese Exclusion Act. However, the existence of the Quota Law rendered it practically meaningless. The Luce-Cellar Act of 1946 allowed Filipinos and Asian Indians to become naturalized, but with a quota of just 100 persons per year. The Immigration and Naturalization Act of June 27, 1952, further illustrates this ambivalence. While it ended the race-based ban on naturalization, it also affirmed the national-quota system of 1924, limiting total annual immigration to one-sixth of 1% of the population of the continental United States in the 1920s. In the end, these laws did little to change the racial and ethnic landscape of the U.S. citizenship; in practice, they were merely gestures made to appease the wartime allies.

The Immigration and Nationality Act of 1965 finally repealed the national origins quota system. Influenced by the Civil Rights Movement and civil rights legislations, this post-Vietnam War law prioritized family reunification instead of the national origins that gave primacy to Western and Northern European immigrants. This act had a significant impact on immigration since it finally allowed immigration from the countries that had been excluded or restrained since the Chinese Exclusion Act of 1882. The majority of immigrants who entered the United States since the 1965 act have been people of color (Kang, 2012). Thus, the act had a lasting influence on changing the racial and ethnic landscape of the United States over time. However, the tension among race, racism, and immigration persists, as is discussed in the Contemporary Policies section.

Race, Immigration, and Labor

Coloniality theories highlight the complex relationship among colonialism, racism, and capitalism. A historical look at U.S. immigration policies illustrate this complex relationship. The negative racial sentiment against Chinese immigrants that culminated in the Chinese Exclusion Act of 1882 was partially due to a perceived economic threat to White laborers. After the Emancipation Proclamation, in an attempt to replace enslaved Black labor with another cheaper labor force, the United States and China signed the Burlingame Treaty of 1868 that secured U.S. access to Chinese labor. Under the auspices of this treaty, U.S. labor contractors recruited Chinese laborers from China to work on the transcontinental railroad, in gold mines, agriculture, and other industries to meet the growing labor needs of the American West (Takaki, 1993). As the number of Chinese laborers grew and more White people migrated to the West, White workers saw Chinese immigrant laborers as competitors, which resulted in intense anti-Chinese racism, including lynching, race riots, and even massacres (Takaki, 1993).

It is noteworthy that this anti-immigrant labor sentiment had a specific racial element. In that era, an overwhelming majority of immigrants were still coming from Europe. However, European immigrants, Western European immigrants in particular, were *not* considered a threat to "American" labor because they were White. Since European immigrants were allowed to get naturalized, they were eventually absorbed into the "American" labor force while non-White immigrants such as Asians were prevented from doing so. Thus, the assumption was that White people (especially White men) were entitled to jobs and that non-White immigrants were impinging upon their rights to jobs *even though* Chinese workers were specifically recruited by White labor contractors to work in the United States. As Lowe (1996) argues, there often is a conflict of interest between the project of nation-state and the project of economy. Where a capitalistic economy is not concerned with the source of labor (e.g., race or ethnicity of the labor) as long as it meets its needs, the nation can exploit the narrative of a unified race or ethnicity to construct a fallacious common goal. Therefore, how the immigrant laborer of color in the United States is treated profoundly depends upon the economic exigencies of the nation. Such labor is recruited and tolerated when labor needs are high and cast out when the labor needs shrink. The Labor Appropriation Act of 1924 highlights the coalescence between enforcement of nationalism and "American" labor and economic interests. When the U.S. Border Patrol was established by the Labor Appropriation Act, it specifically mentioned enforcement of the Chinese Exclusion Act. The combination of the demand for labor, racism, and a nation's economic interests reverberates to the present day in the criminalization of racialized immigrant labor ("immigrants are taking *our* jobs").

The complicated relationship between racism, labor needs, and political exigencies are highlighted in the immigration policies pertaining to immigrants from colonized or historically occupied nations such as the Philippines or Mexico. With the Chinese Exclusion Act and the Barred Zone Act cutting off the supply of Asian immigrant labor, the United States again needed another source of cheaper (than White) labor. During the 1910s and 1920s, Mexican immigration increased due to the turmoil in Mexico, fulfilling the U.S. demand for labor. The Johnson-Reed Act (the National Origins Act) did not limit the immigration within the Americas, leaving Mexican immigration unrestricted. However, during the Great Depression, the labor needs sharply declined, and President Hoover's administration implemented a Mexican Repatriation campaign (1929–1936) where the Border Patrol launched raids to detain and expel Mexicans and Mexican Americans across the border. These raid campaigns resulted in the deportation of approximately 2 million people, including 1.2 million U.S.-born Mexican Americans.

Another immigrant act targeting Mexicans was the Undesirable Alien Acts of 1929, which made crossing borders outside an official port of entry a misdemeanor and returning after deportation, a felony. While this law does not specify the U.S.-Mexico border (vs. the U.S.-Canada border), the act, led by a White supremacist and anti-immigrant Senator Blease (D-SC), targeted to curtail Mexican immigration in its enforcement (Hernandez, 2017). The vast majority (sometimes up to 99%) of those imprisoned due to this act were Mexicans

(Hernandez). Similarly, national concerns regarding employment for returning soldiers and anti-Mexican sentiment (which was often based on and further inculcated negative stereo-types of Mexicans) created Operation Wetback in 1954. This program resulted in a stagger-ing mass deportation of Mexicans, including many U.S.-born Mexican Americans (Blakemore, 2019).

The labor shortage, especially in the agricultural sector, during World War II, drove the creation of the Bracero Program in 1942. The Bracero program, which was supposed to pro-tect both Mexican and domestic workers from exploitation by providing the prevailing wages and other reasonable labor conditions, frequently failed in practice. Employers used the pro-gram to bring down wages of both Mexican and domestic laborers (e.g., by using Bracero workers as strike breakers), and the program's implementation problems helped create an undocumented Mexican labor force (Bracero History Archive, n.d.). The Bracero program ended in 1964, but its complicated legacy persists to the contemporary era (e.g., the guest worker programs).

Similarly, after the Barred Zone Act cut off Asian immigrant labor, Filipino immigrants filled the seasonal labor needs in the West Coast and in Alaska (Chin, 2001). Because the Philippines was considered the U.S. territory in that era, Filipinos were exempt from the Barred Zone Act. This again brought on a perceived labor competition in White U.S. workers as well as accusations of Filipino men's romantic interest in White women (which was pros-ecutable under the anti-miscegenation law until 1967). These anti-Filipino sentiments resulted in intense and sometimes violent anti-Filipino campaigns, including lynching and riots (DeWitt, 1979). Finally, in 1934, the Tydings–McDuffie Act made the Philippines a com-monwealth and laid out procedures for Philippine independence. By doing so, this act declared that Filipinos were non-citizens of the United States and limited the immigration to 50 per year, severely curtailing Filipino immigration.

During World War II, however, the need for soldiers caused the United States to reverse this position. The United States re-classified Filipinos as citizens so that they could register for the U.S. military and fight in the war. More than 250,000 Filipinos joined and fought in the U.S. military under this provision, which promised full veterans' benefits (Levs, 2009). However, in 1946, President Truman signed the Rescission Act, which took away the veteran status from those Filipino veterans of World War II and made them ineligible for benefits that were due to them (Levs, 2009). Thus, the case of Filipino immigration illuminates the com-plex relationship among immigration, race, and the nation's political and economic exigences that ultimately marginalized immigrants of color.

Racialized Immigrants as Scapegoats for Social Problems

As illustrated, racialized immigrants have been viewed as both the solution to labor supply needs and the cause of labor surplus (and thus competition for jobs), depending on the nation's economic and political climate. While economy and labor are one of the most visible sites of this phenomenon, the intermingling of racism and social and political climates often results in blaming racialized immigrants for various social problems, and politicians in search for solutions have been quick to turn to immigrants as scapegoats. Immigrants are vulnerable to such exploitation because of their lack of voting rights (until they become natu-ralized), which means less political power. Immigrants of color are particularly vulnerable because racism further marginalizes them in multiple contexts, which we discuss through-out this book.

In the Contemporary section, we discuss how immigration policies targeting racialized immigrants are re-enacted in the contemporary era.

Racialized Immigrants as Economic Scapegoats

We have discussed how racialized immigrants were located in the tension between the nation's need for labor and desire for racial homogeneity and often become marginalized to reconcile them (Lowe, 1996). The flip side of the labor narrative ("immigrants taking our jobs") is the narrative of racialized immigrants as an economic drain and undeserving recipients of welfare. We highlight three historical examples that illustrate how the discourse of "public charge" renders immigrants, especially racialized immigrants, undeserving.

The Immigration Act of August 3, 1882 established a system of central control of immigration through State Boards under the Secretary of the Treasury, thus casting immigration as an economic concern. The same act also expanded the definition of "inadmissible aliens" by adding "persons likely to become a public charge." This provision targeted ethnicized European immigrants (Southern and Eastern Europeans) as well as Chinese and other Asian immigrants (Takaki, 1993), effectively nullifying the spirit expressed in Emma Lazarus' poem ("Give me your tired, your poor...the wretched refuse... the homeless").

A century later, this "public charge" discourse of immigrants as a potential drain in the national economy reverberated in California's Proposition 187 (also known as the Save Our States initiative or Prop 187), a referendum that California voters passed on November 8, 1994. Proposition 187 stipulated that public agencies must deny services to undocumented immigrants ("illegal immigrants") and report them to the Immigration and Naturalization Services (INS). Furthermore, Proposition 187 proposed banning undocumented immigrants from receiving government benefits, including health and social service provisions. The most stunning element of this initiative was barring children (as young as kindergarteners) from public schools until they can prove their citizenship or legal alien status and requiring public schools to verify the immigration status of childrens' parents (Bock, 1994). This controversial law was immediately challenged in a legal suit and ultimately found unconstitutional by a federal district court. Legal challenges continued until 1999 when the new Governor Gary Davis withdrew the appeal, which effectively ended the law (McDonnell, 1999). The Proposition 187 initiative was driven by an unsubstantiated concern that undocumented Latinx and Asian immigrants were draining the state's welfare system (Suarez-Orozco, 1996). The public's anxiety over the economic recession of the early 1990s, coupled with demographic anxiety fueled by a growth in the Latinx and Asian populations in California, scapegoated racialized immigrants as a means to quell the anxiety. Although Proposition 187 ended, its influence was significant, especially on the public discourse on immigrants as undeserving, as was seen in the 1996 Welfare Reform.

In 1996, the Personal Responsibility and Work Opportunity Reconciliation Act (PRWORA) established severe restrictions on the eligibility of legal immigrants for means-tested public assistance. PRWORA was a far-reaching overhaul of public assistance programs fueled by a partisan political competition and influenced by racist messaging (Carten, 2016). PRWORA had many controversial provisions, which are too numerous for this chapter to cover. One significant element of this act was ending or severely restricting public assistance programs for all non-citizens, including legal immigrants. These public assistance programs were largely paid for by taxes, including taxes paid by immigrants. Given the fact that the majority of immigrants in that era were people of color, this law meant that the public benefits were inaccessible to racialized immigrants even though they and their families were paying for the same benefits that citizens, a majority of whom were White, received. This law illustrates the ways in which racism, immigration, and political and economic power dynamics succeeded in scapegoating racialized immigrants, producing harsh inequality for them.

Racialized Immigrants as a Public Health Threat

Immigration policies and processes reveal how racism and xenophobia operate to construct racialized immigrants as public health threats. There is a troubling sense of irony here given that European immigrants, who established a settler colonial government and controlled subsequent populations of immigrants, brought serious and lethal public health consequences to the indigenous population. For example, European settlers brought infectious diseases nonindigenous to the Americas, such as smallpox, measles, and flu, killing an estimated 90% of Native Americans (Diamond, 2005). Historians argued that killing Native Americans by giving them smallpox-infected blankets was an early example of biological warfare (Mayor, 1995). However, European settlers (most of whom were Western European descent) were not constructed as a public health threat to the native population because they regarded themselves as legitimate citizens and rulers of the "new" world.

However, as immigrants from more marginalized parts of Europe and non-European countries came into the country, they were painted with a xenophobic brush as public health problems. The first immigration policy to address this sentiment was the Immigration Act of 1891. Section II, Chapter 551 declared the "classes of aliens" to be excluded from admission to the United States:

> That the following classes of aliens shall be excluded from admission into the United States, in accordance with the existing acts regulating immigration, other than those concerning Chinese laborers: All idiots, insane persons, paupers or persons likely to become a public charge, persons suffering from a loathsome or a dangerous contagious disease, persons who have been convicted of a felony or other infamous crime or misdemeanor involving moral turpitude, polygamists, and also any person whose ticket or passage is paid for with the money of another or who is assisted by others to come ... (Fifty-First Congress, 1891)

This act directly undermined the asylum principle expressed in Lazarus's (1883) poem and spelled out who were not welcomed to come through the "golden door." This policy, which centralized immigration enforcement authority in the federal government, also created the Office of Superintendent of Immigration to supervise immigration inspectors at points of entry within the Treasury Department. As a result, before the entryway to the "golden door" lay intrusive, lengthy, and sometimes painful health screenings, and detention or expulsion for those who were not cleared. Eastern and Southern Europeans, and especially Jewish immigrants, were certainly considered suspect and undesirable as were other Europeans who were poor. However, the number of immigrants who were excluded due to the medical inspection was still fairly small; only 3% of all immigrants at Ellis Island were rejected due to infectious or "loathsome" diseases or mental or physical disability between 1891 and 1928 (Markel & Stern, 1999).

In contrast, on the West coast at Angel Island where immigrants were mostly from China and other Asian Pacific regions, 17% of all Chinese immigrants were deported in

1910–1940. Furthermore, Chinese women were suspected of being prostitutes and were scrutinized for "moral turpitude" and sexually transmitted diseases. This reflects a gendered version of fervent anti-Chinese xenophobia (the "yellow peril") that portrayed Chinese women as immoral prostitutes spreading the "unique, Chinese strain" of syphilis that infused "a poison in the Anglo-Saxon blood" (Chang, 2003). On the Mexico-U.S. border, in late 1910s through 1920s, Mexicans crossing the border were subjected to a humiliating practice of being stripped of clothes to be inspected for lice and nits, disinfected with kerosene, and sometimes submitted to vaccinations even though there was little evidence of contagious diseases (Markel & Stern, 1999).

This characterization of racialized immigrants as a source of communicable diseases (and blaming them for public health problems) is an enduring phenomenon. In the 1980s, the HIV/AIDS panic coincided with the resurgence of xenophobia and anti-immigrant racism, fed by White anxiety about the "Browning of America," and revived the notion of immigrants as public health hazards. In 1986, the United States Public Health Service suggested adding AIDS to the infectious disease list and use it as rationale to turn away immigrants entering the United States (Markel & Stern, 2002). Even though immigrants who were excluded due to HIV/AIDS were few (Markel & Stern, 2002), the linking of racialized immigrants, particularly Africans and Haitians, to a public health crisis reinforced the notion of racialized immigrants as a threat to the nation's health.

During the severe acute respiratory syndrome (SARS) epidemic in the early 2000s, the U.S. discourse erroneously focused on Chinatowns as the epicenters of the disease (Person et al., 2004), reinforcing the notion that Asian ethnic enclaves are dirty and dangerous and that Asians are perilous and perpetually foreign bodies within the nation, threatening "Americans." In other words, Asian Americans became the personification of the virus in the popular imagination. Asians and Asian Americans were racially profiled, stigmatized, and discriminated against even though there was no basis for believing that Asian Americans were more likely to carry the disease than anyone else (Person et al., 2004).

Similarly, during the Ebola outbreak in mid-2010s, in popular discourse, Ebola served as a "rhetorical stand-in for any combination of 'African-ness,' 'blackness,' 'foreign-ness' and infestation'—a nebulous but powerful threat, poised to ruin the perceived purity of Western borders and bodies" (Giorgis, quoted in Zurcher, 2014). African immigrants and U.S. citizens of African origins experienced racial profiling and discrimination even though there was no link between race and vulnerability to the Ebola virus.

Most recently, the COVID-19 pandemic brought back fervent anti-Asian racism and xenophobia. The anti-Asian racism and xenophobia seen and experienced during this pandemic are both a re-escalation of historical mistrust and othering of Asian Americans and an exemplar of powerful political discourses that scapegoated Asians to take the blame away from ineffective management of the pandemic. As the COVID-19 outbreaks started being reported in the United States and the world, the Trump administration downplayed its significance and did little to prepare the nation to manage the potential impact (Shear et al., 2020). Even when scientists and medical experts sounded the alarm and made public health strategy recommendations (such as mask-wearing, quarantining, and social distancing), then-president Donald Trump publicly disregarded or disputed them (Shear et al., 2020). As the nation started seeing a startling number of infections and deaths, Trump evaded responsibility and instead directed blame onto China, calling it the "Wuhan virus" and the "China flu" (Fallows, 2020). Some political leaders such as Senator John Cornyn (R-TX) echoed the president and blamed China and "Chinese culture" for the spread of COVID-19, using a derogatory and stereotypical rhetoric ("where people eat dogs, bats, and snakes"; Wu, 2020).

These political narratives accentuated and perpetuated a centuries-long history of anti-Asian racism and xenophobia built on the stereotype of Asians as "yellow peril" (Lee, 2020), and Asian Americans suffered the consequences yet again. According to the Stop AAPI Hate (n.d.) website, there have been nearly 3,800 reports of anti-Asian hate incidents between March 19, 2020 and March 19, 2021 in the continental United States. These incidents ranged from physical assault (including at least one fatal assault), verbal harassment and threat, civil rights violation, humiliation (e.g., being spat on), to shunning. The victims were predominantly vulnerable populations such as elderly and children, and women were targeted almost 2.5 times higher than men. Many reported being blamed for the pandemic (reflecting the "Wuhan virus" and the "Chinese flu" rhetoric) as well as being called derogatory racial names and told to "go back to China." Race was cited as the primary reason for discrimination, making up 90.3% of incidents (while 60% of the victims were of Chinese descent, others were Asian Americans of non-Chinese background).

These examples illustrate the pernicious persistence of the linkage between racism, immigration, and public health. They also demonstrate how social construction of race and foreignness/otherness become embodied in the literal bodies of racialized immigrants as the United States directs focus on them during public health crises or in an attempt to control the racial and ethnic makeup of the nation.

Racialized Immigrants as a National Security Threat

Constructed as aliens whose allegiance is to foreign nations, immigrants have been placed under scrutiny as a possible threat to national security in times of political upheaval and were often manufactured as a target of fear and suspicion based on xenophobia. The examples in this section highlight how immigrants' rights were curbed in the name of national security.

The Alien and Sedition Act of 1798 is an historic policy that links immigration and national security. Passed amid tension between Democratic-Republicans and Federalists, this law authorized the president to deport any foreigner deemed to be dangerous and made it a crime to speak, write, or publish anything "of a false, scandalous and malicious nature" about the President or Congress (archives.gov, n.d.). The law was directed against Democratic-Republicans, who had the support of many immigrants from non-English speaking parts of Europe, particularly France (archives.gov). Federalists cast Democratic-Republicans' critique of the government as disloyalty to the country in favor of France. With this law, ethnicized (French and other non-English–speaking) immigrants' rights to free speech (which had been created by the Bill of Rights just 9 years before) were annulled as a result of the competition between two political parties.

The Immigration Act of March 3, 1903 reiterated this construction. Following the assassination of President McKinley by a Polish immigrant, it became the first measure to exclude aliens on the grounds of proscribed opinions (e.g., "anarchists"), linking immigrants with anarchists and national security threats. The Alien Registration Act of June 28, 1940 required the registration of all aliens and fingerprinting of those over age 14, further establishing the construction of immigrants as a potential danger to national security.

The link between immigration, racism, and national security reached its peak in 1942 when Executive Order No. 9066 was enacted during World War II, resulting in the incarceration of 120,000 Japanese immigrants and Japanese Americans (Takaki, 1993). Executive

Order 9066 constructed Japanese immigrants and Japanese Americans as disloyal to the United States and as a national security risk. Having been forcibly displaced and put in internment camps, they were forced to sign a document pledging their loyalty to the country that incarcerated them; many were pressured to join the military to fight in World War II against Japan to prove their loyalty while their families were incarcerated (Takaki, 1993). The fact that the internment targeted Americans of Japanese ancestry but not those of Italian or German ancestry, even though the United States was also at war with those countries, reveals the underlying discrimination based on race.

Some 40 years later, the Immigration Reform and Control Act of 1986 reiterated the link between racism, immigration, and national security discourse. While this act was to increase enforcement at U.S. borders and deter illegal immigration, most of the increase was geared toward the Mexican (assumed non-White) border, rather than the Canadian (assumed White) border (Ngai, 2005). By singling out the Mexican border as a risk to national security, this act demonstrates how racism, immigration, and national security intermingled to construct racialized immigrants as a threat.

In the 2000s, an increase in non-White immigration from Asia, Mexico, and South America was accompanied by a uptick in nativism and local and state-driven anti-immigration policies, particularly those aimed at Latinx immigrants. One of the most notorious and controversial was Arizona's Senate Bill 1070 (AZ SB1070), which became the Support Our Law Enforcement and Safe Neighborhoods Act when Arizona's Republican Governor Jan Brewer signed it into law on April 23, 2010. This law had many broad and controversial implications, but two of the most divisive sections were the following:

> Sec. 2. B. For any lawful contact made by a law enforcement official or agency of this state or a county, city, town or other political subdivision of this state where reasonable suspicion exists that the person is an alien who is unlawfully present in the United States, a reasonable attempt shall be made, when practicable, to determine the immigration status of the person.

> Sec. 3. A. In addition to any violation of federal law, a person is guilty of trespassing if the person is both: 1. Present on any public or private land in this state. 2. In violation of 8 United States code section 1304(e) or 1306(a).

Section 2B diminishes the federal control of immigration policy implementation by giving local law enforcement officers and agencies the authority to enforce federal immigration laws. Also, the use of "reasonable suspicion" raised concerns about racial/ethnic profiling. Section 3A in application means that it would be a misdemeanor for immigrants in the State of Arizona to not carry their alien registration documents at all times. Nicknamed "Show me your papers law," AZ SB 1070 was challenged in various courts due to potential civil rights violation; although some of the law's provisions, including Section 3, have been struck down by the courts, Section 2B still stands, resulting in concerns about racial and ethnic profiling by local law enforcement (Peard, 2018). One of the narratives behind AZ SB 1070 was the fear that the drug trafficking and violence in Mexico would spill into the United States, reinforcing the discourse of immigrants as dangerous without evidence linking an increase in immigrants producing an increase in the crime rate (Archibold & Steinhaur, 2010).

The narrative of immigrants as a national security threat became intensified in the 2000s. After the 9/11 attacks, the Homeland Security Act (2002) placed the Immigration and

Naturalization Services under the Homeland Security Department, formally signaling that immigration is a national security issue rather than a humanitarian, population, or economic issue. The Patriot Act (2001) eased regulations around detaining and expelling foreign-born individuals. While it was not written in a race/religion-specific language, this act nevertheless became infamous for its racial-profiling of Muslim Americans (as well as anyone perceived to be Muslim or Middle Eastern). Islamophobia, fear, and hostility directed toward people who are religiously Islamic or who are nationally and ethically associated with the Middle East, was tremendously heightened in political and popular discourses following 9/11 and the "war on terrorism" that focused on "Islamic terrorists." These discourses merged diverse religious affiliations (including religions that are not Islamic but non-Christian, such as Sikh), non-White ethnicities and national backgrounds with terrorism. Numerous people of color were harassed and many immigrants were detained without cause because they were or were presumed to be Middle Eastern or Muslim (ACLU, 2005).

Racism and Immigration in the Contemporary ERA (2016–2020)

In 2016, then-presidential candidate of the Republican Party, Donald Trump, ran for the office with a campaign slogan, *Make America Great Again,* and promising *America First* policies. One of Trump's most prominent campaign promises was to build a wall across the southern border to severely restrict immigration from Mexico and South America; "Build that wall!" became a popular chant at his campaign rallies (Johnson, 2016). Elected on this platform, Trump proposed or enacted numerous anti-immigration and anti-immigrant policies during his administration (2017–2020). Opponents of the president seeking to call out Trump's racist and xenophobic policies re-branded his slogan to *"Make American White Again."* Discussing all of Trump policies on immigration is out of scope of this chapter; we focus on four major policies with far-reaching impact.

The election of Trump was feared and understood as a referendum on racism, sexism, and xenophobia as he capitalized on those sentiments with emboldened actions during and after the campaign (Allen & Goetz, 2000; Craggs, 2016; McElwee & McDaniel, 2017). In this section, we illustrate how Trump reflected and deployed racist and xenophobic discourses on racism and reinforced racism and xenophobia through his immigration policies.

"Build the Wall": Executive Order 13767

On January 25, 2017, five days after the presidential inauguration, Trump issued Executive Order (EO) 13767, Border Security and Immigration Enforcement Improvement. The executive order had the following important components (American Immigration Council, 2017):

▶ Constructing a costly (estimated $15–$25 billion) physical wall across the southern border and allocating more resources to U.S. Customs and Border Protection, including hiring of 5,000 additional agents.

▶ Increasing detention facility construction and expanding the use of detention. Individuals in removal proceedings can be detained to the maximum extent of the law regardless of their court hearing status.

▶ Expansion of the expedited removal, which permits immigration officers to expedite deportation of certain noncitizens without a court hearing with an immigration judge.

▶ Allowing local law enforcement to act as immigration officials. Echoing AZ SB1070, under this executive order, the Department of Homeland Security may deputize state and local law enforcement to perform the functions of federal immigration agents, targeting immigrants inside the border.

▶ Limiting humanitarian protection and access to asylum. Section 11 of the order significantly tightens humanitarian parole authority and heightens the "credible fear" standard for asylum seekers.

▶ Prioritizing criminal prosecution of unlawful entry. The order prioritizes the prosecution of any offenses, including nonviolent offenses such as unlawful entry, connected to the southern border.

The overall impact of EO 13767 is to construct and treat migrants at the southern border as criminals. Also, while the order does not specify race or ethnicity, the fact that it is directed at the southern border (e.g., the wall would be constructed at the U.S.-Mexico border but not at the U.S.-Canada border) reveals its racialized target. In fact, Trump made these points abundantly clear during his election campaign speech: "[W]hen Mexico sends its people, they're not sending their best. ... They're sending people that have lots of problems, and they're bringing those problems. ... They're bringing drugs. They're bringing crime. They're rapists." This narrative drew from a deep-seated yet unfounded xenophobic fear to construct people of Mexican descent (and Central/South Americans who enter the country through the Mexico-U.S. border) as criminals to benefit Trump's election bid. This narrative then became systematized through EO 13767, in turn echoing and reinforcing the perception of racialized immigrants as a threat to national security and safety. By construing immigrants coming from south of the border as undesirable, the United States continues to abdicate its responsibility for creating such mass migration as a result of its role in the destabilization of various Central American governments. The destruction caused by deadly hurricanes and drought as the result of climate change also adds to the push factor of migration but perhaps could have been mollified if the government and economic infrastructures had not been eviscerated by outside forces.

The Muslim Ban: Executive Orders 13769 and 13780

On January 27, 2017, Trump signed EO 13769, Protecting the Nation from Foreign Terrorist Entry into the United States. This order banned people from seven predominantly Muslim countries (Iran, Iraq, Libya, Somalia, Sudan, Syria, and Yemen) from traveling to the United States for 90 days. The order, often referred to as the Muslim ban, also reduced the number of refugees to 50,000, suspended the resettlement of Syrian refugees, and suspended the U.S. Refugee Admissions Program for 120 days. This order was superseded by EO 13780. After a series of court battles and fierce protests across the country, the Supreme Court allowed a third version of EO 13780 to go into force in 2018.

With EO 13769/13780 Trump had argued that terrorists took advantage of the U.S. refugee programs and campaigned for a "total and complete shutdown of Muslims entering the United States" (Greenwood, 2017). By doing so, he equated people from predominantly Muslim countries to terrorists. Trump benefited politically from creating this Islamophobic and xenophobic narrative to consolidate support from White, Christian-identified majority voters.

Even though two non-Muslim majority countries (North Korea and Venezuela) were added to the later version of the order, the effect of the order demonstrated that it indeed had a significant impact on people from predominantly Muslim countries (Niayesh, 2019); for example, long-term U.S. residents who had traveled to their native countries were stranded, and only 2% of travelers, including those who had been fleeing persecution, were able to get a waiver. The Muslim ban policy exemplifies how Islamophobia, racism, and xenophobia interacted to enact a deeply inequitable immigration and refugee policy. It also indicates an enduring effect of historical construction of racialized immigrants as a threat to the nation's safety.

Canceling Deferred Action for Childhood Arrivals (DACA) Program

In September 2017, consistent with his campaign promises, Trump announced that he would "unwind" the DACA program, which provides protection from removal and work authorization to undocumented young people who were brought to the country as children (Pierce & Bolter, 2020). This announcement put the status and future of nearly 700,000 young people in disarray. This decision was contested in courts, and almost a year later, the Supreme Court ruled that Trump could not end the program. A majority of young people who were protected by DACA are people of color, and Trump's decision to cancel the DACA program was part of the sweeping anti-immigrant campaign that targeted racialized immigrants, particularly those coming through the Mexican border. The precarious status of racialized young immigrants on DACA, for many of whom the United States is the only home they know, hearkens back to earlier years where immigrants of color (then targeting predominantly Asian immigrants) were denied a path to naturalization and perpetually barred from gaining their citizenship rights. Thus the Trump administration's attempt at abolishing DACA calls to mind and replays the racialized and ethnicized discourse of a legitimate and desirable citizenry.

Zero Tolerance Policy: Migrant Family Separation

Perhaps the most devastating and unprecedented harsh anti-immigration policy under the Trump administration was the Zero Tolerance Policy. By February 2018, the Trump administration started separating minor children from their parents or accompanying adults when they entered the United States. On May 7, 2018, Attorney General Jeff Sessions announced a "zero tolerance policy" where the Department of Homeland Security and the Justice Department coordinated efforts to stop unauthorized crossings at the U.S.-Mexico border (Horwitz & Sacchetti, 2018). Under this policy, federal authorities separated minor children from their parents or other accompanying adults; adults were then sent to federal jails while children were held in detention shelters. Attorney General Sessions was clear on the purpose and scope of this policy in his remark:

> If you cross the border unlawfully … then we will prosecute you. […] If you smuggle an illegal alien across the border, then we'll prosecute you. […] If you're smuggling a child, then we're going to prosecute you, and that child will be separated from you, probably, as required by law. If you don't want your child separated, then don't bring them across the border illegally. It's not our fault that somebody does that. (Sessions, J., quoted in Horwitz & Sacchetti, 2018)

This policy has created not only tremendous trauma and suffering but also massive complications at the border in terms of lack of necessary personnel and infrastructure. The testimony of Claire Long, associate director of Human Rights Watch, before the U.S. House

Committee on Oversight and Reform, Subcommittee on Civil Rights and Civil Liberties, on July 11, 2019 revealed numerous human rights violations and mistreatment of migrant children who were separated from their adults and detained at the border; children as young as 2 or 3 years old were kept in detention shelters without adult care, and were not provided with necessary basic provisions or medical attention. Facing legal challenges, international criticism, public uproar, and protests over "kids in cages," Trump signed an executive order in June 2018 to end the family separation at the border but replaced it with family detention (Gonzales, 2018). While the Trump administration ended family separation, it did not have a clear plan or correct record keeping to reunite the children with the parents or adult companions of children who were already separated. It has been reported that while the Department of Health and Human Services (DHHS) previously stated that the total number of children separated at the border was 2,737, the actual number may be several thousands higher (Spagat, 2019). Furthermore, DHHS was not able to find the parents of more than 500 separated children, including an estimated 322 parents who were deported (Ainsley & Soboroff, 2021). We may not truly know the real impact of the zero tolerance policy until years to come.

It is important to point out that, like many of Trump's anti-immigration policies, the zero tolerance policy singled out the U.S.-Mexican border, and racialized migrants who tried to cross the southern border. Enacting such policies targeting Mexican and Central/South American migrants would not have been possible without historical narratives constructing Mexicans and other racialized migrants as criminals, problematic, and less qualified, exemplified in policies in previous sections. In fact, Trump-era policies are echoes and reinforcements of previous policies targeting and discriminating against racialized immigrants. Furthermore, Trump-era policies did not simply arise out of thin air; they were informed and buttressed by longstanding and heightened expressions of racism and xenophobia that led to Trump's election. The Trump administration's anti-immigration policies demonstrate that 230 years after the first immigration and naturalization policy in 1790, political and social narratives around race and immigration matter.

Resistance and Activism

While U.S. immigration policies were influenced by racist and xenophobic narratives about deserving and undeserving immigrants and legitimate and illegitimate citizenry, racialized immigrants were neither wholly passive recipients of immigration policies nor simply shaped by them. In each era, racialized immigrants resisted the very discourses that shaped their humanity and limited their rights. The racial prerequisite cases in the history section earlier in this chapter are good examples of racialized immigrants contesting the binary construction of race as Black/White and creating claims for themselves to gain citizenship rights.

Immigrant labor movements (e.g., the Latinx Farmworkers Movement in the 1960s; the Filipino Cannery Workers Movement in the 1970s; the Asian garment industry workers' labor organizing in the 1990s; and the domestic workers' organizing by immigrant women of color in the 2000s) demonstrate racialized immigrants' efforts to resist the dominant discourses that commodified their labor and to negotiate space and rights for themselves in the nation's economic landscape (Kang, 2012). The Dreamers' movement that started in the 2000s and is still active in the present era is an inspirational example of how undocumented young people enacted social and civic citizenship through their engagement in political advocacy and organizing (Hing, 2010).

Even in the Trump era, immigrants and allies resisted and contested Trump's anti-immigration agenda. Numerous immigration rights organizations, social service agencies, student groups, legal groups, religious groups, and other local, state, and national advocacy groups vehemently condemned anti-immigration and anti-migrant policies, advocated for rights of immigrants and refugees, called for policy changes, and raised funds. They used both in-person and online methods to hold rallies, protests and community education events. While these groups may have ideological differences and may deploy different strategies and tactics, they often were able to build alliances and recognize intersectionality in their advocacy (e.g., "no wall, no ban," which recognized both anti-Latinx and anti-Muslim policies; Gleeson & Sampat, 2018).

Helping professionals are well positioned to take part in the immigration activism in their communities and in the national movement. For example, the National Association of Social Workers (NASW) organized to pressure lawmakers to end the Trump administration's "zero tolerance policy" and educated social workers to advocate to protect child migrants at the local, state, and national levels. The American Psychological Association called on lawmakers to end the child separation policy in their statement citing psychological trauma caused by such policies. Numerous social work education programs and educators also utilized their expertise in policy, research, and practice to advocate for more just immigration and refugee policies in partnership with immigrant and refugee rights and service organizations.

CONCLUSION

In this chapter we illustrated how race, racism, and immigration interact to produce and reinforce narratives about who belongs in the United States, who is more desirable and deserving to become citizens, and who should have full rights as a citizen. The history of U.S. immigration cannot be separated from the racial history of the country. This chapter presented the relationship between racism and immigration in the United States through a review of pertinent historical immigration and naturalization policies and their impact on not only the lives of immigrants but also on the nation's demographic and socio-political landscape. We concluded this chapter by demonstrating that narratives about race, immigration, and citizenship are mutable and that activism and advocacy by immigrants and allies can resist racialized anti-immigration narratives and policies and promote social change.

EXERCISE 4.1 Immigration and Colonial History

This exercise is designed for readers who live in the United States. However, it can also apply to readers who live in countries in North, Central, or South America.

1. Who were the Indigenous people of the land where you currently live? What is the original (Indigenous) name of the area where you currently live?
2. Who were the first non-Indigenous migrants that settled in your area (city, county, or state)? Where did they come from? When did the migration start?
3. What impact did the migration have on the Indigenous people and their physical, sociocultural, and spiritual world?

4. Which populations are most dominant (numerically, politically, economically) in your area currently? How did this come about?
5. Where are the descendants of the original people of the land now? If they relocated to other areas, what was the process (e.g., was it voluntary or involuntary)?

EXERCISE 4.2 Mapping the Global Migration

Find out where most recent immigrants or refugees in your area (your city, county, or state) are from. This can be accomplished by researching city, county, or state data or by contacting immigrant-serving agencies in your area.

1. Which countries are they from? What were some possible "push factors" (i.e., the forces that prompted them to leave, such as political destabilization, economic problems, environmental disasters, etc.)? Was the United States involved in any of the push factors, historically or recently?
2. Look at the map of the world to find the countries where the migrants come from. Study the national borders. When and how were the current borders drawn? By whom? What precipitated these borders to come in place (e.g., the border between South Korea and North Korea was initially determined at the Potsdam Conference by the U.S. President Harry Truman, British Prime Minister Winston Churchill, and Soviet Premier Joseph Stalin after World War II, with no Korean representatives)?
3. Had the nations of the migrants been colonized in the past? By which countries? What were the impact of the colonization on the colonized people?
4. What were some possible "pull factors: (i.e., the factors that contribute to the United States/your area to attract international migrants, such as need for labor, need for population growth, etc.)?

EXERCISE 4.3 Policies and Resources

1. What are the current immigration policies that affect the most vulnerable migrant populations?
2. What immigration policy changes are being made or called for?
3. What resources are available to immigrants or refugees of color in your area? How accessible are they?
4. How can helping professionals contribute to changing immigration policies?
5. What can helping professionals do to advocate for resources for immigrants or refugees in your area?

REFERENCES

ACLU (2005 April 20). Homeland Security violates civil rights of Muslim American citizens. ACLU.org. https://www.aclu.org/press-releases/homeland-security-violates-civil-rights-muslim-american -citizens

Ainsley, J., & Soboroff, J. (2021 February 24). *Lawyers have found parents of 105 separated kids in past month.* NBC News. www.nbcnews.com/politics/immigration/lawyers-have-found-parents-105-separated-migrant-children-past-month-n1258791

American Immigration Council. (2017 February 27). *Summary of executive order: Border security and Immigration Enforcement Improvements.* American Immigration Council. www.americanimmigrationcouncil.org/research/border-security-and-immigration-enforcement-improvements-executive-order

Allen, R., & Goetz, E. G. (2000). A home for xenophobia: U.S. public housing policy under Trump. *International Journal of Housing Policy, 21*(1), 127–127. https://doi.org/10.1080/19491247.2020.1803533

Archibold, R. C., & Steinhauer, J. (2010, April 29). *Welcome to Arizona, outpost of contradictions. The New York Times:* A14. www.nytimes.com/2010/04/29/us/29arizona.html

Archives.gov (n.d.). *The formation of political parties: The Alien and Sedition Acts.* https://www.archives.gov/exhibits/treasures_of_congress/text/page5_text.html?_ga=2.145649012.1722372889.1632201915-1463818460.1632201915

Blakemore, E. (2019 June 18). *The largest mass deportation in American history. History.com.* https://www.history.com/news/operation-wetback-eisenhower-1954-deportation

Bock, A. W. (1994 October 2). *Sorting through facts and fiction of immigration. Orange County Register.* p. J.01.

Bracero History Archive. (n.d.). Bracero History Archive. www.braceroarchive.org/about#:~:text=The%20Bracero%20Program%20grew%20out,term%2C%20primarily%20agricultural%20labor%20contracts.&text=The%20Bracero%20Program%20was%20controversial%20in%20its%20time

Carten, A. (2016). *How racism has shaped welfare policy in America since 1935.* The Conversation. www.theconversation.com/how-racism-has-shaped-welfare-policy-in-america-since-1935-63574

Chang, I. (2003 May 21). *Fear of SARS, fear of strangers. The New York Times.* www.nytimes.com/2003/05/21/opinion/21CHAN.html?

Chin, D. (2001). *Seattle's International District: The making of a Pan-Asian American community.* International Examiner Press.

Craggs, T. (2016 November 6). *This election was about the issues: Not the familiar stuff of Washington gridlock, but the most important issues of our time: Misogyny, racism, and xenophobia.* Slate.com. www.slate.com/articles/news_and_politics/cover_story/2016/11/the_2016_election_was_about_the_issues.html

DeWitt, H. A. (1979). The Watsonville anti-Filipino riot of 1930: A case study of the great depression and ethnic conflict in California. *Southern California Quarterly, 61*(3), 291–302. https://doi.org/10.2307/41170831 .JSTOR 41170831.

Diamond, A. (2020 May 19). *The 1924 law that slammed the door on immigrants and the politicians who pushed it back open.* Smithsonian Magazine. www.smithsonianmag.com/history/1924-law-slammed-door-immigrants-and-politicians-who-pushed-it-back-open-180974910/

Diamond, J. M. (2005). *Guns, germs, and steel: The fates of human societies.* Norton.

Fallows, J. (2020, March 18). *A reporter's notebook: A 2020 time capsule.* The Atlantic. www.theatlantic.com/notes/2020/03/2020-time-capsule-5-the-chinese-virus/608260

Fifty First Congress. (1891). An act in amendment to the various acts relative to immigration and the importance of aliens. Fifty-First Congress, Session II, Ch. 551. www.loc.gov/law/help/statutes-at-large/51st-congress/session-2/c51s2ch551.pdf

Fitzgerald, D. S., & Cook-Martin, D. (2014). *Culling the masses: The democratic origins of racist immigration policy in the Americas.* Harvard University Press.

Gleeson, S., & Sampat, P. (2018). Immigrant resistance in the age of Trump. *New Labor Forum, 27*(1), 86–95. https://doi.org/10.1177/1095796017744778

Gonzales, R. (2018 June 20). *Trump's executive order on family separation: What it does and doesn't.* NPR. www.npr.org/2018/06/20/622095441/trump-executive-order-on-family-separation-what-it-does-and-doesnt-do

Greenwood, M. (2017 January 28). *ACLU sues White House over immigration ban.* The Hill. www.thehill.com/policy/national-security/316676-legal-groups-file-lawsuit-against-trump-administration-amid-refugee

Harris, C. I. (2001). Equal treatment and the reproduction of inequality. *Fordham Law Review, 69*(5).

Hernandez, K. L. (2017 April 30). *How crossing the U.S.-Mexico border became a crime.* The Conversation. www.theconversation.com/how-crossing-the-us-mexico-border-became-a-crime-74604

Hing, B. O. (2004). *Defining America through immigration policy*. Temple University Press.

Hing, J. (2010 December 20). *How undocumented youth nearly made their DREAMs real in 2010*. Colorlines. www.colorlines.com/archives/2010/12/dream_movement_profile.html

Horwitz, S., & Sacchetti, M. (2018 May 7). *Sessions vows to prosecute all illegal border crossers and separate children from their parents*. The Washington Post. www.washingtonpost.com/world/national-security/sessions-says-justice-dept-will-prosecute-every-person-who-crosses-border-unlawfully/2018/05/07/e1312b7e-5216-11e8-9c91-7dab596e8252_story.html

Johnson, J. (2016 February 12). *"Build that wall'"has taken on a life of its own at Donald Trump's rallies—but he's still serious*. The Washington Post. www.washingtonpost.com/news/post-politics/wp/2016/02/12/build-that-wall-has-taken-on-a-life-of-its-own-at-donald-trumps-rallies-but-hes-still-serious/

Kang, H.-K. (2012). Re-imagining citizenship, re-imagining social work: U.S. immigration policies and social work practice in the age of AZ SB 1070. *Advances in Social Work*, 13(3), 510–526.

Lazarus, E. (1883). The new colossus. http://en.wikipedia.org/wiki/The_New_Colossus

Lee, E. (1966). A theory of migration. *Demography*, 3(1), 47–57. www.jstor.org/stable/2060063

Lee, M. (2020, March 9). *Corona virus fears show how model minority Asian Americans become yellow peril*. NBC News. www.nbcnews.com/think/opinion/coronavirus-fears-show-how-model-minority-asian-americans-become-yellow-ncna1151671?fbclid=IwAR1zx5x-xyCEwNrauDokqIijklvEeMRt6A0kXP5twb76d6KcWzDJmAz713E

Levs, J. 2009. *U.S. to pay "forgotten" Filipino World War II veterans*. CNN. http://articles.cnn.com/2009-02-23/us/forgotten.veterans_1_philippine-veteran-filipino-world-war-ii-filipino-veterans-equity?_s=PM:US

Lomawaima, K. T., & McCarty, T. L. (2006). *To remain an Indian: Lessons in democracy from a century of Native American education*. Teachers College Press.

Lopez, I. H. (1996). *White by law: The legal construction of race*. New York University Press.

Lowe, L. (1996). *Immigrant acts*. Duke University Press.

Markel, H., & Stern, A. M. (1999). Which face? Whose nation? Immigration, public health, and the construction of disease at America's ports and borders, 1891–1928. *American Behavioral Scientist*, 42(9), 1314–1331.

Markel, H., & Stern, A. M. (2002). The foreignness of germs: The persistent association of immigrants and disease in American society. *The Milbank quarterly*, 80(4), 757–788. https://doi.org/10.1111/1468-0009.00030

Mayor, A. (1995). The Nessus shirt in the new world: Smallpox blankets in history and legend. *Journal of American Folklore*, 54–77.

McDonnell, P. J. (1999 July 29). *Davis won't appeal Prop. 187 ruling, ending court battles*. Los Angeles Times.

McElwee, S., & McDaniel, J. (2017 May 8). *Economic anxiety didn't make people vote Trump, racism did: New data provide a compelling answer to this vexing question*. The Nation. www.thenation.com/article/archive/economic-anxiety-didnt-make-people-vote-trump-racism-did/

Merriam-Webster Dictionary (n.d.). Alien. www.merriam-webster.com/dictionary/alien

Ngai, M. M. (2005). *Impossible subjects: Illegal aliens and the making of modern America*. Princeton University Press.

Niayesh, V. (2019 September 26). *Trump's travel ban really was a Muslim ban, data suggest*. The Washington Post. www.washingtonpost.com/politics/2019/09/26/trumps-muslim-ban-really-was-muslim-ban-thats-what-data-suggest/

Omi, M. & Winant, H. (1994). *Racial formation in the United States: From the 1960s to the 1990s* (2nd ed.). Routledge.

Omi, M., & Winant, H. (2014). *Racial formation in the United States: From the 1960s to the 1990s* (3rd ed.). Routledge.

Peard, B. (2018). *SB 1070 in 2018: what are our rights? ACLU Arizona*. www.acluaz.org/en/news/sb-1070-2018-what-are-our-rights

Person, B., Sy, F., Holton, K., Govert, B., Liang, A., & National Center for Infectious Diseases/SARS Community Outreach Team. (2004). Fear and stigma: The epidemic within the SARS outbreak. *Emerging Infectious Diseases*, 10(2), 358–363. https://doi.org/10.3201/eid1002.030750

Pierce, S., & Bolter, J. (2020 July). *Dismantling and reconstructing the U.S. immigration system: A catalog of changes under the Trump presidency.* Washington, DC: Migration Policy Institute. www.migration policy.org/research/us-immigration-system-changes-trump-presidency

Quijano, A. (2000). Coloniality of power and Eurocentrism in Latin America. *International Sociology, 15*(2), 215–232.

Shear, M. D., Weiland, N, Lipton, E., Haberman, M., & Sanger, D. E. (2020 September 15). *Inside Trump's failure: The rush to abandon leadership role on the virus. The New York Times.* www.nytimes .com/2020/07/18/us/politics/trump-coronavirus-response-failure-leadership.html

Sohi, S. (2013). Immigration Act of 1917 and the "Barred Zone." In X. Zhao, & E. J. W. Park (eds.), *Asian Americans: An Encyclopedia of Social, Cultural, Economic, and Political History [3 volumes]: An Encyclopedia of Social, Cultural, Economic, and Political History* (pp. 534–535). ABC-CLIO.

Spagat, E. (2019 February 3). *U.S. sees limitations on reuniting migrant families.* AP NEWS. www.apnews.com /article/48210bbf243e423ea151ff04e4878ce6

Stannard, D. (1992). *American holocaust: The conquest of the new world.* Oxford University Press, Inc.

Stop AAPI Hate (n.d.). *New Data on Anti-Asian Hate Incidents Against Elderly and Total National Incidents in 2020.* Stop AAPI Hate. www.stopaapihate.org/reportsreleases/

Suarez-Orozco, M.M. (1996). California dreaming: Proposition 187 and the cultural psychology of racial and ethnic exclusion. *Anthropology & Education, 27*(2), 151–161.

Takaki, R. (1993). *A different mirror: A history of multicultural America.* Back Bay Books.

United States Circuit Court for the District of Columbia (1878). *In re Ah Yup, 1F. cas.223, 5 Sawy. 155; 6 Cent. Law J. 387; 17 Alb. Law J. 385; 24 Int. Reve. Rec. 164 (1878).* United States Circuit Court for the District of California. https://cite.case.law/f-cas/1/223/

Wu, N. (2020, March 18). *GOP senator says China 'to blame' for coronavirus spread because of 'culture where people eat bats and snakes and dogs'.* USA Today. www.usatoday.com/story/news/politics/2020/03/18 /coronavirus-sen-john-cornyn-says-chinese-eating-bats-spread-virus/2869342001/

Zurcher, A. (2014 October 14). *Ebola, race, and fear.* Echo chambers. BBC News. www.bbc.com/news/blogs -echochambers-29714657

CHAPTER 5

The Web of Institutional Racism

INTRODUCTION

In the video "True Colors," Diane Sawyer leads a team of journalists/researchers for the ABC television show *Primetime Live* to "test" whether racism is still alive in a "typical" U.S. city (Lukasiewicz & Harvey, 1991). Two testers, one Black and the other White, are filmed secretly while trying to find jobs or apartments, purchasing used cars, and hailing taxis. It becomes clear that the two are consistently treated differently. An advertised job is open to the White man, with great encouragement from the employer, and the same employer denies that the job is available when the Black man with the same credentials applies for the job. The same happens with an apartment that is allegedly for rent.

In a music store, the White man browses without notice while the Black man is followed by an employee wherever he goes. A used car dealer jacks up the price of the same car for the Black man. As the two men leave the television studio after debriefing, a taxi ignores the Black man and screeches to a halt to take the White man.

Many White people who watch this video have expressed shock, while many people of color nod their head because these experiences are all too familiar. Sadly, subsequent research involving "testers" of different racial identities has confirmed that this pattern persists (Freiberg, 2019; Pager & Western, 2012; *The New York Times*, 2018, April 14).

For a significant number of White people, racism *is* a relic of the past and not a salient social issue today. Many Whites believe that the United States has moved to a color-blind society. True racism, in this view, is associated with the overt variety of hostility, aggression, and discrimination that was challenged by the Civil Rights Movement after World War II. Certainly, there has been a great deal of movement toward diminishing some overt forms of racism, although Whites view this progress much more optimistically than people of color.

As visible signs of progress, more people of color have gained access to universities, many police departments now are desegregated, and significantly more people of color are serving in public life as business leaders, actors, athletes, Supreme Court justices, and cabinet officers. However, even given these inroads, people of color still face far less access and opportunity in all sectors of society than White people, but it is important to acknowledge improvements, even when incomplete.

At the same time, some Whites have resented civil rights accomplishments. School busing, often in northern cities, in the wake of the *Brown v. Board of Education* decision in the 1950s, spurred White anger and flight from cities to suburbs, as well as from public schools to private and parochial schools—in many instances reinstituting de facto segregation. And some Whites now feel victimized, believing that their chances of being admitted to elite colleges or of securing jobs are diminished by too much emphasis on race, which they think favors people of color. In fact, today more Whites believe that they are the victims of "reverse racism" than believe in the persistence of racism against people of color (Goynea, 2017; Norton & Sommers, 2011). This is despite the fact that the enduring legacy of segregation continues to benefit Whites, while disadvantaging people of color (Ellen et al., 2016).

To be sure, many White people are well aware of the persistence of racism in the United States. Still, Whites and people of color show marked differences in their beliefs about the extent of racism today, and these disparities indicate a significant perceptual racial divide in this country (Shipler, 1997). For example, while 46% of Whites say that Donald Trump is racist, 80% of African Americans say that he is (Edsall, 2020). African Americans and Hispanics overwhelmingly believe that there is occupational discrimination in favor of Whites, while less than a fourth of Whites agree; and people of color view racism as a deeply entrenched, institutional phenomenon, while many Whites see it as a question of attitudes and behaviors (Bobo, 2001). Whites are victimized by crime far less than African Americans and Latinos but voice far greater support for a criminal justice system and punitive sentencing policies that disproportionately victimize African Americans and Latinos (Ghandnoosh, 2014).

These different observations perhaps belie fundamentally dissimilar experiences with racism, but the perceptual chasm itself becomes a factor in sustaining racism. A danger in having such divergent views about the nature of social phenomena in a highly segregated society is that many people exist in homogenous environments in which it is easy to mistake mirrors for windows.

Revisionist historians and critical social scientists, such as Takaki (1993), Ignatiev (1995), Allen (1994), and Steinberg (2001), have illustrated how members of certain ethnic groups (e.g., Irish, Jews, Italians) initially encountered discrimination but eventually gained access to resources, were granted full citizenship, and assumed the privileges of Whiteness, yet members of other ethnic groups who were socially and legally constructed as "of color" and "other" experienced barriers, exclusion, and at times extreme and brutal repression that has endured. As is still the case today, those who encountered social oppression were, in turn, held responsible for their own misfortunes.

A political backlash erupted in response to the "Great Society" of the 1960s, when there were active government efforts to mitigate racism. One form of this backlash has been the growth of predominantly White exurbs and gated communities, as well as concerted assaults on affirmative action, questioning its use to ensure diverse student representation on college campuses and in graduate human service programs. This backlash also has resulted in a stalling or even backsliding of the gains and momentum created by the Civil Rights Movements of the 1950s and 1960s. For example, we will consider the Supreme Court decision in 2013 that undermined the Voting Rights Act of 1965. The backlash has carried over to views on immigration, with the majority of Whites now feeling negative or ambivalent about immigration, particularly when the media focuses on Latinos or undocumented immigrants (Abrajano & Hajnal, 2015).

In this chapter, we map out the contours of the web of institutional racism in the United States today in the wake of this backlash, illuminating its stubborn and tenacious tendrils. We focus on nine types of institutional racism: residential, educational, employment, accumulation of wealth and upward mobility, environmental and health, mental health, criminal justice, political, and media (immigration racism is considered in Chapter 4). The emphasis here is on how racism remains institutionally embedded in U.S. society and what remains to be done, as opposed to what has been accomplished. We are well aware of other severe forms of social oppression in the United States—for example, income and social class inequities, gender oppression, sexism, heterosexism, transphobia—and that these (and other types of social oppression) are intricately entwined with racism. To completely separate out, for example, the effects of class inequities or those due to racism is difficult. We consider these intersections of oppression in Chapter 7. We also note that in using the category "people of color," we are referring to a very ethnically diverse group and that some aspects of the web have a negative impact on some ethnic groups more than others. For example, criminal justice racism particularly affects African Americans, Latinos, and Native Americans. However, in our view, White people do not encounter the web of racism, even if they are oppressed by economic or gender oppression, and, conversely, all ethnic groups of color have and do experience at least some of the negative consequences of the web of racism.

THE NATURE OF THE WEB OF RACISM

We have diagrammed the web of institutional racism in Figure 5.1. This figure does not cover every type of institutional racism; instead, each circle encapsulates a critical area in which institutional racism is manifested through laws, policies, and formal and informal practices. Each nodule is connected to all others, although some are attached by large, thick cables and others by thin but strong threads. Some strands of the web restrain certain ethnic or racial groups of color more than others, and some individuals and subgroups succeed and prosper despite the web. The web is metaphorical but, as we will illustrate, also very real.

Durable inequalities, such as racism, are replicated in all institutions and practices of a society, although their form adapts and changes (Omi & Winant, 1994; Tilly, 1998). The United States was founded on a "racial contract," which was the shadow side of the social contract (Mills, 1997). The social contract stressed the Enlightenment values of equality, citizenship, and human rights, and the racial contract defined who was human and who was not, who was free and who was enslaved, who could be dispossessed of their lands and often slaughtered, and who would take their place. Thus, we should not be surprised that in a nation founded on a racial contract, racism is reflected in institutions and policies. It is as if the public DNA contains this mutation, which is regenerated and reproduced. Because the racial contract is ubiquitous, it becomes central (i.e., the norm, a given), which makes it all the more difficult to see by those unimpeded by it (Mills, 1997).

In the film *The Matrix*, the hero (who is White) lives in an illusory world that appears pleasing and benign until he has a transformative experience (guided by an African American man) that enables him to view the deceptions and corruption that have always surrounded him. In presenting the web, we hope to make visible the semi-hidden matrix of racism (for most White people) and examine its scope, its depth, and its many connections. Any one chamber of this maze is problematic and of concern, but taken together the sites and

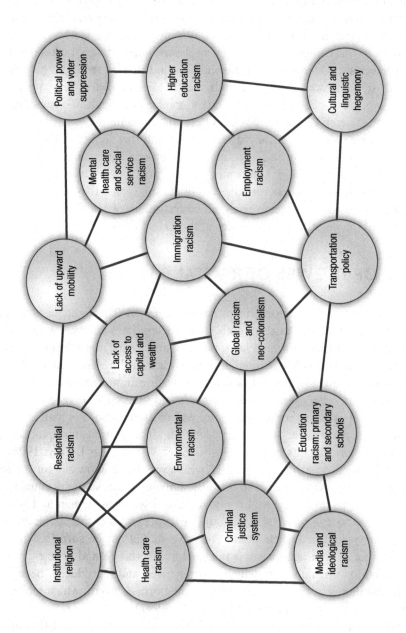

FIGURE 5.1 Web of institutional racism.

Note: Connecting lines are arbitrary and for illustration; in reality, each form of institutional racism connects with each other form in multiple ways.

locations of the web of racism potentiate one another, increasing their ability to exclude and deny. Although some parts of the web, such as racial profiling (in which motorists are stopped because of their race), are overtly racist, what is particularly insidious is that much of the web includes institutions and policies that are viewed as race-neutral, such as transportation and environmental policy.

We emphasize five aspects of the web here:

1. It is systematic and comprehensive, not a case of isolated pockets of "leftover racism."
2. It exists on many levels. For example, educational racism at the macro level shows a racialized pattern of unequal funding for schools, at the mezzo level the insufficient number of teachers and administrators of color working in many school districts, and at the micro level racial microaggressions being perpetrated against students by other students and teachers. Another way to think about this is to use critical realism and see racism operating on three levels: (a) The empirical level of racism—how it is experienced. (b) The actual level—what is actually happening, whether experienced or not. (c) The causal—what conditions and mechanisms lead to certain forms of racism (Houston, 2001).
3. It combines formal and informal practices, some overt and others covert. For example, residential segregation is maintained by formal lending policies and many people of color, particularly African Americans, have more difficulty than Whites qualifying for mortgages. More informally, some real estate agents guide prospective homeowners to some properties and neighborhoods and not to others, or landlords and property sellers are willing or unwilling to do business with people by virtue of their race. Predominantly White communities, in which many White people grew up or live, were not formed by accident or coincidence; they resulted from many strands of the web of racism.
4. It is cumulative, not just contemporaneous. Today's web is built on webs going back hundreds of years, resulting in disinvestment and disempowerment; it is the legacy of generations of outright oppression, systematic exclusion, and loss of opportunity. It has resulted in an inability to generate and maximize social, political, and economic capital and assets (Brown et al., 2003; Shapiro, 2004). Thus, the web is historical, as well as reflecting current social phenomena.
5. It exercises influence and projects power—the power to make laws and policies, to enforce them, to fund them, to define and present them, and to create a public narrative and discourse that normalizes them.

The web of institutional racism encompasses neighborhoods and housing, education, employment, upward mobility, environment and health, mental health, racism within the criminal justice system, political racism, media racism, and immigration racism. We explore each of these parts of the web in turn. Additionally, Exercise 5.1 encourages an expanded understanding of the web.

RESIDENTIAL RACISM: NEIGHBORHOODS AND HOUSING

We discuss residential racism first because it is a bedrock of racism, "normal" yet insidious, influencing other strands of the web and casting a long shadow over those excluded from some neighborhoods and trapped in others. Massey (2016) has called racial segregation the "linchpin" of racial stratification and growing up in poor, hypersegregated communities affects all aspects of life chances, health, and well-being: how long people live, diseases and their consequences, educational opportunities, psychosocial well-being, chances of being incarcerated, drug use, opportunities for upward mobility, and more (Badger & Bui, 2018; Edsall, 2019; Ellen, et al, 2016; Manduca & Sampson, 2019; Massey, 2016; Polikoff, 2015).

There have been some trends toward desegregation in the United States. In 1980, one quarter of census tracts were predominantly White, in 2018 it was only 5%, occurring primarily in rural areas (Badger et al., 2019). African Americans, Latinx people, and Asian Americans have increasingly moved into what were predominantly White areas, although it is less common for Whites to move to areas of high concentrations of people of color and when they do, gentrification is often in their wake, displacing residents from their communities (Badger et al., 2019). The number of hypersegregated communities with predominantly African American populations has dropped (Massey, 2016).

But despite these trends, residential segregation still is a fixture of American life and the effects of racial segregation on life outcomes and opportunity have, if anything, become worse (Ellen et al., 2016). This has been exacerbated by increasing income inequality, which interacts with racial inequality (Massey, 2016). Many poor African Americans continue to live in hypersegregated, deprived, and isolated neighborhoods, and continue to be the most residentially segregated racial group in the country, although the number of Latinx residents living in such communities has grown (Brown et al., 2003; Edsall, 2019; Manduca & Sampson, 2019; Massey, 2016). Whites live in predominantly White neighborhoods, whether in cities, suburbs, or rural areas, and yet are the least convinced of major racial/ethnic groups that segregation still exists (Logan & Stults, 2011). White flight from communities that have increasing numbers of people of color, a demographic trend since the end of World War II, has contributed to racial segregation. This has created "Whitetopias" (Benjamin, 2009), almost exclusively White neighborhoods where residents have fled the burden of poverty and crime that they perceive as being caused by people of color. Residents in these White worlds rarely have contact with poor, urban neighborhoods of color and imagine life in those neighborhoods through the filters of media-amplified, White, middle-class stereotypes. How does this happen?

A combination of public policy, informal real-estate industry and financial lending practices, as well as internalized fears and racist attitudes by White people have led to decades, if not centuries, of racial segregation (Polikoff, 2015). Although the home-ownership rate for African Americans has grown to 49%, it still lags well behind the rate for Whites, which is closer to 76% (Pelletiere, 2005). An example of racialized public policy are zoning laws promulgated by municipalities that prohibit apartments and other congregate housing that would socioeconomically diversify communities (Kahlenberg, 2017). Another that has effectively perpetuated segregation is the federal lending policy from the late 1950s, which has continued to favor loans to predominantly White suburbs (Brown et al., 2003) and transportation policy that has privileged the building of highways that serve suburbs over public transportation in metropolitan areas. Modern segregation is shaped by racial discrimination enacted by real estate brokers and mortgage lenders, along with White racial attitudes that restrict people of color from trying to move into neighborhoods (Edsall, 2019; Freiberg, 2019; Massey, 2016; Shapiro, 2004). The police—or self-appointed vigilantes such as George Zimmerman, who killed a Black teenager, Trayvon Martin, in his predominantly White suburb—monitor their neighborhoods for signs of African Americans who "don't belong here."

This segregation is reinforced by zoning regulations that exclude rental and public housing from some neighborhoods and result in high concentrations of such housing in others.

The use of paired testers (one White, one Black, seeking to rent or buy the same property) continues to document residential racial discrimination (Freiberg, 2019; Oh & Yinger, 2015; *The New York Times*, 2018, April 4). In addition to what has been described earlier, it operates through "racial and ethnic steering" toward or away from certain properties by real estate agents, showing more or fewer units to buyers/renters, willingness or unwillingness to rent or sell by landlords and owners, and in variations in the asking prices for rents and sales. Mortgage lenders are less likely to grant mortgages to people of color, particularly African Americans (Brown et al., 2003; Massey & Denton, 1993; Shapiro, 2004). According to the Urban League (2004), African Americans are denied mortgages at twice the rate of Whites. Credit is harder to establish and the terms of loans are more severe for African Americans (Manning, 1999). Middle-class African Americans also face higher hurdles with home financing than their White counterparts. African American homeowners often have less equity than Whites to begin with and are more likely to borrow "subprime" loans, which allow them to make a lesser down payment but saddle them with significantly higher interest rates and debt (Brown et al., 2003; Pelletiere, 2005; Shapiro, 2004). When African Americans and Latinx people do own homes in poor, segregated areas, the value of their homes often drop rather than grow (Shapiro, 2004).

Social and psychological factors have fueled segregated housing as well. In the 1950s, overt manifestations—including mob violence, intimidation, and acts such as burning crosses on the lawns of African Americans—frightened people of color from moving into predominantly White areas (Brown et al., 2003). Although this is less common, people of color moving to predominantly White neighborhoods often find themselves followed by the police or asked for photo identification when shopping, unlike most White customers. As the numbers of people of color increase in a community, so does White discomfort and the urge of Whites to move to another neighborhood (Edsall, 2019; Massey, 2016). And it is not only at the neighborhood level where suspicion, separation, and segregation occur; people with African American sounding names are 16% more likely to be rejected when seeking rentals through Airbnb (McPhate, 2015).

As mentioned earlier, the consequences of segregation are profound, affecting education, access to jobs, health, economic well-being, and upward mobility. For people of color trapped in hypersegregated neighborhoods, a vicious cycle ensues that further ensnares them and diminishes their life opportunities. Concentrated segregation and poverty interact to create an unhealthy and unsafe environment (Manduca & Sampson, 2019; Samuels, 2014). Because neighborhood stores are sparse, shopping is difficult and prices at those few stores often are higher and there is less healthy food, such as fresh produce. Also, there is a dearth of banks, so residents tend to resort to check-cashing establishments and loan sharks for financial transactions, incurring high fees and rates of interest (Calhoun & Bailey, 2005). Hypersegregated neighborhoods of poor people of color have worse schools, higher crime rates, and falling property values (Logan & Stults, 2011). African American homeowners living in predominantly Black neighborhoods risk having the worth of their property diminish over time, while for White homeowners, the value of their investment usually increases (Shapiro, 2004).

Because fewer jobs are available in these areas, some residents turn to secondary and illegal job markets for employment (outside of the mainstream and the law), and crime rises, making the neighborhood more dangerous (Samuels, 2014). As property values fall, residents lose even more of their equity—if they had any to begin with (Shapiro, 2004). Loans from banks and mortgage companies for repair and renovation become less available, and disinvestment stalks the community, creating an isolated, toxic environment for all who live there (Massey, 2016; Massey & Denton, 1993; Samuels, 2014).

As communities become less safe, people avoid being out in public and keep their children off the streets, which makes the neighborhood even more dangerous (Massey & Denton, 1993; Miller, 2001). Further, the police patrolling the neighborhood often feel threatened, alienated, and prone to overreaction, which contribute to an escalating cycle of tensions between residents and authorities. As residents become more socially isolated, fueled by the absence of adequate transportation and well-paying mainstream jobs, there are fewer role models for prosocial behaviors. Self-destructive subcultures can evolve, including the rise of gang activity (Wilson, 1987, 2011). The focus in public discourse is usually on the values, morals, and behaviors of people responding to residential segregation rather than questioning the pattern of institutional racism that fuels such responses. In sum, the integrity of the community is fractured and the implicit social contract between families and their neighborhood becomes frayed and tattered (Miller, 2001).

This is one side of the tragedy of residential segregation. Another side is the cocoon of Whiteness surrounding many children who grow up in predominantly White lower-, middle- and upper-class neighborhoods, suburbs, and exurbs. Socialized into a world of Whiteness where people of color are often portrayed as a threatening "other," Whites are apt to fear and avoid them (Miller & Schamess, 2000). Even in families that espouse the values of equality, nonprejudice, and goodwill toward all, the actual social arrangements of their lives belie these values. Their behaviors and lifestyles conflict with their social ideals.

Residential isolation ensures that significant numbers of White people will have little or no awareness of their race privilege. Without their necessarily being aware, their success comes at the cost of disadvantage for many people of color (Ellen et al, 2016). As a result, Whites internalize a sense of entitlement to live in a predominantly White world. They will hold stereotypes unchallenged by reality, undisturbed by those who are different from them, and unperturbed by those who suffer the consequences of racism.

EDUCATIONAL RACISM: PUBLIC, PRIVATE, AND HIGHER EDUCATION

Segregated neighborhoods are accompanied by segregation in public education, which exacerbates white flight. It is bad enough when public schools literally reflect residential segregation, but parents have choices about where they send their children to school. Not to mention that even in the same school or school district there is separation and tracking, leading to a pattern of educational segregation that is worse than residential segregation. This is the situation despite numerous attempts following the Supreme Court's 1954 *Brown v. Board of Education* decision to desegregate schools. Efforts to achieve integrated schools, such as school busing, which was designed to offset residential segregation, often provoked a large White backlash. Many White parents withdrew their children from public schools in favor of private schools or moved to Whiter school districts. A more recent development facilitating White flight from multiracial public schools has been the growth of charter school programs (Mickelson, 2014).

These trends emerged in the wake of the court-ordered desegregation; for example, after court-mandated busing in Boston schools in 1974, by 2000 only 25.4% of children under the age of 18 living in Boston were White, and half of those children attended private schools (Logan et al., 2003). The Harvard University Civil Rights Project found that schools are becoming *more* segregated and, on average, Whites are attending schools in which more than 80% of students are White. White racial homogeneity is even more pronounced in private schools (Frankenberg et al., 2003). The same project described a significant number of apartheid schools, character-ized by few White students, substantial rates of poverty, and limited educational resources—a return to "separate and unequal." While some researchers have concluded that there was mild progress toward less school segregation in public schools, recent developments have mitigated that progress (Stroub & Richards, 2013). These include the charter school movement, Supreme Court decisions prohibiting school districts from desegregating their schools within their dis-tricts by using race as a factor for school assignment, and the release of many school districts from supervision orders monitoring segregation. By 2010 only 200 out of 16,000 school districts subject to desegregation supervision orders remained (Stroub & Richards, 2013).

Another correlation between school quality and neighborhood is funding. The amount of spending on students does make a difference—smaller class sizes, ability to attract and retain better trained teachers, as well as the number of support staff such as school counselors and nurses (Sosina & Weathers, 2019). Schools are funded primarily by property taxes, with additional aid from state and federal governments. Thus, the wealthiest communities, which usually are predominantly White, are able to pay more for their school systems and typically spend more per capita per pupil. Researchers have confirmed that schools with predomi-nantly Black or Latinx populations have less money spent on them than schools with pre-dominantly White populations (Sosina & Weathers, 2019). Teachers are also more likely to want to teach in better resourced schools that resemble the kind of school that they attended and that are closer to where they live (Sosina & Weathers, 2019). This means that the pool of teachers willing to work in districts with many poor students of color is smaller to draw upon. Also, due to institutional racism, there are often few teachers of color in a given school so that students of color do not have sufficient role models and White students do not have the opportunity to see people of color in leadership roles (James, 2020) Within schools there is a great deal of racialized segmentation, where White students make up the vast majority of students in honors and advanced placement (AP) classes, even when they are in a minority within the greater school population (Diamond & Lewis, 2015). Native American students are half as likely to be in AP classes as White students in racially mixed schools, have the lowest graduation rate of any racial group, not only facing discrimination and unequal treat-ment but also having their cultures minimized and marginalized (Green & Waldman, 2018).

When students of color find themselves in predominantly White honor's classrooms, usu-ally with a White teacher, they often feel as if they do not belong there (James, 2020). There are also critical differences with which students are severely disciplined. According to the General Accounting Office, Black students are disciplined and suspended at much higher rates than White students (Green, 2018). Data from the U.S. Office of Civil Rights indicate that Black female students in public schools are seven times more likely to receive out-of-school suspen-sions, four times more likely to receive in-school suspensions, over three times as likely to receive corporal punishment, and three times more likely to be referred to law enforcement than White female students (Inness-Thompson, 2018). Both students of color and White stu-dents have reported how they notice the different ways students are dealt with when they break school policies, such as using cell phones when they are restricted; White students may be given a warning while students of color have their phones taken away (James, 2020).

There is increasing "tripartite" segregation by virtue of language, income, and race (Mickelson, 2014). Not surprisingly, segregated schools do not reduce prejudice, do not increase social trust between racial and ethnic groups, and are less likely to produce people committed to living and working in a multiracial society (Mickelson, 2014).

All of these factors contribute to lower quality education for many children of color, particularly those who are poor. Dropout rates and school suspension rates for Hispanics and African Americans are higher than for Whites. College attendance rates are considerably lower. In 1998 nearly 95% of Whites aged 25 to 29 had a high school diploma, and for Hispanics it was just over 60% (Council of Economic Advisors, 1998). Guidance counselors in predominantly White, middle-class school districts, more so than their counterparts in poor school districts of color, expect and encourage their students to attend college. Further, the former have more experience in navigating the application process and far more contacts in college admissions offices to boost the chances of admission for the students that they recommend. Predominantly White schools also are more likely than predominantly non-White schools to have advanced, college preparatory classes (Renner & Moore, 2004).

As if White students did not already have enough advantages over students of color in the college admissions process, state anti-affirmative action efforts have cut minority admissions in colleges. In California's two flagship state schools (UC Berkeley and UCLA), non-Asian minority freshmen dropped from 21.93% to 10.54% in one year after the universities were banned from taking race into account in their admissions decisions (Bronner, 1998). Cutbacks in federal support of financial aid for college also have hurt students of color disproportionately (Brown et al., 2003). In 1995, although African Americans and Latinos comprised 28% of all 18-year-olds, they constituted only 12% of the freshman class in "selective" institutions (Carnevale & Rose, 2003). In 2019, two indigenous high school students, who are brothers, were on a college tour at Colorado State University while wearing traditional tribal clothing; they were challenged by police after being called by a nervous White mother, also on the tour (Chokshi, 2018). They were removed from the tour and returned to their homes in New Mexico without being given a new tour.

Once on campus, students of color frequently face stereotyping, cultural exclusion, and "racial microaggressions" from White students and White faculty (Solorzano et al., 2000). As one consequence, students of color strive to avoid confirming the stereotypes, which creates tension and performance anxiety among them (Leary, 1999). Thus, they face a greater stereotype threat, which undermines their academic performance (Steele, 2011). This dynamic is exacerbated when students of color find themselves few in number in the classroom, at times the only non-White student in a class (Thompson & Sekaquaptewa, 2002). Stereotypes, lower social status, and isolation contribute to their feeling alienated and disengaged and not trusting the fairness and validity of the educational enterprise (Schmader et al., 2001).

Poor students of color are less likely to have had access to computers and the internet before entering college and are less likely to have computers once they attend college (Harmon, 1998; Komar, 2003). In the end, far more Whites than Blacks, Hispanics, and Native Americans graduate from college. Between 2006 and 2010, 29.3% of Whites held bachelor's degrees while the numbers are 17.7% for Blacks, and 13% for Latinos and Native Americans (Ogunwole et al., 2012). Immigrants of color not only face similar disadvantages due to racism and poverty, but also are negatively affected by linguistic and cultural differences (Bottia, 2019).

Although economic and social classes are major variables that lead to educational advantage and disadvantage, race is a significant factor. The majority of poor White students have White teachers as role models, which is not true for many students of color. Although poor White students are often subject to social class stereotypes, they do not encounter racial stereotypes, nor do they encounter racial microaggressions.

All of these factors influencing educational experience and attainment have major implications for employment prospects and for the accumulation of wealth. We consider these two areas of institutional racism next.

EMPLOYMENT RACISM

People of color face residential segregation and educational segregation, leading to unequal opportunities for developing skills and employment networks, but then face another layer of racism when seeking jobs and workplace discrimination when they find jobs. This has been a historical pattern that continues well into the 21st century. For African Americans it is a legacy from the period of enslavement, through the failure of Reconstruction and the Jim Crow era, that persists to this day (Lee, 2019). In the past, legislation and informal practices prevented African Americans, Native Americans, Mexican Americans, Chinese Americans, and Japanese Americans, among other non-White ethnic groups, from competing with White people in an allegedly free-market economy and accumulating property and other resources. These barriers included Jim Crow and Black Codes, outright discrimination, hostility in the workplace, exclusionary immigration and labor laws, hostility from trade unions, and a range of roadblocks limiting access to jobs. Residential and educational segregation blocked access to job networks. As important as qualifications, merit, and access are, many jobs are acquired through the connections of family and friends. This is how, over time, various ethnic groups have cornered occupational niches and have accessed specific businesses, trades, and professions (Steinberg, 2001; Sullivan, 1989). This also created a vicious cycle because with a lower presence in the formal job sector, there were fewer social networks to facilitate employment for job seekers of color. It was harder for people of color to learn about jobs, successfully apply for jobs, have the same job conditions as White workers when they were employed, get paid the same as White workers, and to benefit from promotion and upward mobility. All of these factors conspired to limit economic opportunity and reduced opportunities to generate capital and intergenerational wealth.

As we mentioned earlier, in modern times, many well-paying jobs have moved to the suburbs and exurbs, where many African Americans, Latinos, and Native Americans didn't live. In the absence of adequate public transportation linking employment to urban centers, many residents were stranded without the means to earn a living (Wilson, 1987, 2011). This dynamic was driven by deindustrialization. For example, Holyoke, a small industrial city in western Massachusetts, saw an influx of Latino, primarily Puerto Rican, residents in the 1960s to the present, drawn by the low cost of housing (rental apartments built for mill workers) and family networks (Miller, 1999, 2001). But Puerto Ricans arrived in Holyoke when jobs were disappearing. While the Irish, French Canadian, and Polish immigrants who preceded them also arrived poor and without resources, they were able to gain a foothold on an economic ladder through factory work. For Puerto Ricans, the mills were moribund, with no entry-level jobs. Also, public transportation was insufficient to take people to jobs in surrounding cities and communities. Further, the Puerto Rican population was young and poorly educated. They often did not have the qualifications to be hired for some of the high-tech and white-collar jobs in the area. Finally, the quality of the public school system was and still is far below that of more affluent nearby communities, and the rate of college attendance is low. This pattern stalks many older, metropolitan areas in the United States.

Another barrier is not having the requisite cultural capital to thrive in the workplace. Many people of color living in poor, isolated urban neighborhoods have few role models in how to talk, dress, and act in ways that fit with many predominantly White mainstream business establishments (Wilson, 2011). Discouraged, some may feel more comfortable operating in the informal, secondary labor market, which is less humiliating but carries more risks and little security (Bourgois, 1995). Cultural norms, too, erect a barrier to middle-class people of color, who may feel pressured to conform to White, middle-class norms at work, giving up some of their identity and sense of personhood (Cose, 1993).

But, employment racism goes beyond culture. Promotional opportunities are fewer and salaries lower for people of color engaged in the same professions as Whites. College faculty members of color earn, on average, about 75% of what their White colleagues make with similar qualifications (Renzulli et al., 2006). Kivel (2011) explains this by referring to a number of factors: the legacy of past discrimination that keeps people of color out of the academy; inadequate public schools and needing more time to complete postsecondary studies; having fewer colleagues of their race, ethnicity, and culture to form support networks within universities; and prejudice and discrimination by White faculty and administrators. There are assumptions about what is academically valued that reflects "White logics," which in turn shape rules and practices combined with "White racial framing": stereotypes, beliefs, and emotions that reinforce a White racial hierarchy in academia (Moore et al., 2018). All of these factors form an academic web of discrimination. Other considerations include the way that the web is internalized when a person is isolated in academia and the pressure caused by "stereotype threat" (Steele, 2011).

People of color are underrepresented in many professions and occupations. The U.S. Bureau of Labor Statistics (BLS, 2016) provides many examples of this pattern. (Keep in mind that African Americans make up about 12% of the U.S. population and Hispanics about 16%.)

▶ Among chief executives, 90.6% are White, 3.6% are Black, and 5.5% Latino.

▶ Among architects, 85% are White, 5.8% Black, and 5.7% Hispanic.

▶ In health care, 6.4% of doctors and 2.9% of dentists are Black, and the figures are 6.4% and 8.6% for Hispanics.

▶ In elementary, middle, and high school classrooms, about 9% of teachers are Black and 8% Hispanic.

▶ Social work is an exception: African Americans comprise 22% of social workers, and the number of Latinos, 12.6%, is improving.

▶ In the legal profession, 89.6% of lawyers are White, 4.1% are Black, and 5% are Hispanic.

The New York Times has researched how White people dominate key positions of power in U.S. society and found that eight of 102 CEOs of the biggest American firms are people of color (Park et al., 2016). A similar pattern holds true for high-tech Silicon Valley companies. Only 1% of Google's and Yahoo's tech workers are Black, and Hispanics make up 3% of Yahoo's tech force (Brown, 2014, 2015). According to the U.S. BLS (2016), 39% of Whites and

49% of Asians and Asian Americans are employed in managerial and professional positions, while only 21% of Hispanics and 30% of Blacks are working at these levels. The unemployment rate for Native Americans and Alaska Natives is 9.9%; for African Americans, 9.6%; and for Latinos, 6.6%, compared to 4.6% for Whites. These indicators are stark and powerful reminders of the barriers that still exist for people of all ethnicities and races to participate fully in the entire range of occupational opportunities.

Once people of color have made it into law firms and corporations, they often do not progress as quickly as their White peers (Cose, 1993). For example, General Electric, representative of many other major U.S. corporations, has little racial, ethnic, or gender diversity in the top echelons of management. In 2000, only 6.4% of its corporate officers were women, and of the 20 businesses that contributed 90% of the company's earnings, only one was headed by a person of color (Walsh, 2000). This pattern persists today.

Employment racism is not a historical vestige; rather, it is an active dynamic in American society. When "testers" of different racial backgrounds, using names that tend to connote White or Black identities, apply for jobs, they are less likely to be given an interview; even when they are interviewed, they are less likely to be hired (Bell et al., 2018; Pager & Western, 2012). Ultimately, employment racism has led to a situation where the unemployment rate for African Americans is steadily twice that of Whites (Higginbotham, 2013). African Americans not only have more challenges in getting interviews and being hired, receive lower salaries, find it harder to be promoted, and have higher rates of unemployment but also are unemployed for longer periods of time, becoming "discouraged workers" at twice the rate of unemployed White workers (Bell et al., 2018).

Discrimination is notoriously difficult to prove, particularly in the eyes of the current U.S. Supreme Court, which demands actual specific evidence of intent to discriminate and will not accept the validity of proving racist patterns (Alexander, 2010); therefore, there is little recourse for those who face systemic discrimination. In modern-day USAmerica, White people do not acknowledge that they discriminate by race, which means it is nearly impossible to prove discrimination under the current standards set by the Supreme Court. While White managers who are responsible for hiring deny ever discriminating by race, asserting that they hire the most qualified person for the job, when interviewed about their attitudes toward different racial and ethnic groups they evince a great deal of prejudice toward African Americans and Latinos, indicating that "aversive" and "implicit" (both terms are discussed in later chapters) racism are at work (Pager & Western, 2012).

All of the nodes of institutional racism mentioned thus far—residential, educational, and occupational—interact with one another and contribute to the next nexus of institutional racism. We turn to disparities in accumulation of wealth and upward mobility.

RACISM AND WEALTH ACCUMULATION AND UPWARD MOBILITY

We acknowledge that there has been significant progress over many decades in lowering the income differential between people of color and Whites (Roberts, 1995). From 1960 to the mid-1970s, the gap between the median income for African Americans and Whites narrowed because of the Civil Rights Movement, Great Society legislation (including affirmative action), and a tight labor market (Stoll, 2004). And in the 1990s, African Americans also made some less dramatic gains toward reducing the wage gap (Stoll, 2004). However, there are still significant disparities in earnings by virtue of race. In the fourth quarter of 2019, the median usual weekly earnings for Hispanics was $712, for Blacks $756, for Whites $976, and for Asian/Asian Americans $1166 (BLS, 2020). Yet these divergences pale when compared to racial discrepancies by virtue of net worth, or cumulative assets held by families.

Assets are accumulated over time, and are passed down from one generation to another in the form of college tuition payments and loans, gifts, and, of course, inheritances. The capacity to accumulate wealth is so racially disparate that it is one of the most profound examples of the opportunity hoarding that characterizes durable inequalities (Brown et al., 2003). For African Americans, asset accumulation was stripped by enslavement, the post-Civil War period of racial codes, Jim Crow and White supremacist terror, exclusions from asset generating programs during the New Deal, discrimination in the implementation of the GI Bill after World War II (Lee, 2019), and ongoing racism and discrimination as described in the previous three sections.

Two of the most important assets in accumulating wealth are home ownership and higher levels of education. As we have learned, homeownership is more difficult to achieve for African Americans and Latinx Americans, and the web of racism prevents many African Americans, Latinx Americans, and Indigenous Americans from educational achievement comparable to that of Whites. Even when people from these groups are able to own their homes, interest rates for mortgages are higher and property values lower, contributing to a hemorrhaging rather than an increase in assets (Brown et al., 2003). "The way homes are bought and sold, where they are located, how the market values them, provides a contemporary foundation for racial inequality" (Shapiro, 2004, p. 53).

The same holds true for small businesses. African Americans are less able to secure loans and capital, denying them another way by which families and communities grow their assets (Urban League, 2004). All told, residential and occupational segregation continue to further the existing racial wealth divide because of historical barriers and disadvantages.

No matter what measures are used, African Americans and Hispanics earn less than Whites and have significantly fewer financial assets (Oliver & Shapiro, 2013). The income wealth gap is twice as great for Whites as Hispanics and Blacks, but the wealth gap is six times as high when comparing Whites to Hispanics and Blacks (McKernan et al., 2013). While inequalities in wealth have grown for all racial groups, the ratio for White wealth compared to Black and Hispanic wealth has increased. White wealth in 2016 ($171,0000 was 10 times higher as Black wealth ($17,150; McIntosh et al., 2020)! The disparities are similar for Hispanic families (McIntosh et al., 2020). In addition to the factors already discussed, inheritances continue and amplify the pattern of disproportionate White wealth when compared with most families of color (McIntosh et al., 2020). As described in the previous section, even having a college degree does not close the gap: The median net worth of African Americans who held college degrees dropped by 56% between 1992 and 2013 while for Whites it rose 86% (Cohen, 2015)!

Financial assets can be "transformative" over the life cycle, helping family members purchase houses and attend college without incurring massive debt, which can boost a family beyond where their jobs and earnings alone would land them socially (Shapiro, 2004). The flip side is that poverty rates are higher for most groups of color, particularly Native Americans, Blacks, and Latinos, than they are for White families (Blank, 2001). The racial wealth gap is a profound consequence of racism. Shapiro (2004) concludes that "it is virtually impossible for people of color to earn their way to equal wealth through wages" (p. 2).

ENVIRONMENTAL AND HEALTH RACISM

All aspects of the web of racism discussed thus far are linked with environmental and health racism. Whether it is through exposure to toxic conditions or brown fields facing the ongoing stress of racism and segregation, having employment without healthcare benefits and overall access to healthcare resources, or being treated differently by medical providers by virtue of race, racism interacts with health and longevity. Although all forms of institutional racism are abhorrent, environmental racism and health racism are particularly lethal. Together, they expose people of color to greater health risks: injuring, hurting, and maiming bodies and spirits; depleting and devastating communities; and abrogating life chances—a graphic reminder that racism literally kills people. It can be argued that environmental racism began when Europeans began to settle North America, replacing a Native American cosmology where people are not separate from their environment with a pre-capitalist and eventually capitalist orientation where the environment could be exploited and pillaged for settlement and profit (Robyn, 2002). Examples of this range from White settlers indiscriminately shooting buffalo from the windows of trains, nearly exterminating a species and important food source and cultural wellspring for Native Americans, to cheating Native Americans out of land rights in places where oil was discovered.

Environmental racism today intersects with residential racism as White families continually moved farther from communities of color, leading to ribbon development (where homes are built along a main roadway), longer commutes, and further environmental degradation and pollution (Powell, 1999). Environmental racism correlates with race and class. Poor people of color are more likely to live in neighborhoods sandwiched by highways, where they are subjected to increasing levels of noise and air pollution. And they are more likely to live near toxic chemical dump sites, in neighborhoods with elevated rates of cancer and other major diseases. African Americans are 75% more likely than White Americans to live near hazardous waste (Villarosa, 2020). One example is the elevated rates of cancer in the Hyde Park neighborhood in Augusta, Georgia, thought to be a consequence of the carcinogen polychlorinated biphenyl (PCB) from a wood treatment plant dumped in a community that was 90% African American by a company called Chemical Waste Management in the late 1970s (Loomis, 2015).

One of the largest uranium contamination zones in the United States is around a village on a Navajo reservation in New Mexico (Frosh, 2014). This comes from debris from over 500 abandoned uranium mines from the Cold War era. The land has social, cultural, and historical meaning to its residents whose health is endangered and yet they are loath to abandon their home.

A more recent example of environmental racism is the toxic water supply for Flint, Michigan, a deindustrialized, predominantly African American city near Detroit. In January 2016, the state of Michigan changed the source of the city's water from Lake Huron to the Flint River. The Flint River is highly corrosive and soon the levels of lead in the drinking water were high enough to cause lead poisoning (Ganim & Tran, 2016). This threat was identified by outside researchers and a local pediatrician because the state kept reassuring residents that the water was safe. State officials not only tried to cover up the catastrophe but initially condemned those who blew the whistle (*The New York Times*, 2016). It is difficult to imagine that this would have happened in a community of White, middle-class residents. Communities that are wealthier and Whiter have greater lobbying ability and more social connections with politicians and decision-makers, allowing concerns about illness and exposure in their situations to be taken seriously and receive a helpful response (Lerner, 2019).

Hazardous exposure is a consequence of the interaction of race and class. In Massachusetts, communities with a median household income of less than $30,000 had triple the cumulative exposure to hazardous locations and facilities than communities with higher income levels (Faber & Krieg, 2001). Race exacerbates the problem: If people of color make up more than 25% of a community's population, the hazardous exposure rate is nine times the rate of communities with less than 5% people of color (Faber & Krieg, 2001).

Poor people of color are more likely to live in areas prone to natural disasters, such as low-lying floodplains, as was sadly illustrated by the "social ecology" of Hurricane Katrina (Park & Miller, 2006). Poor people of color are more apt to live in apartments with lead paint, more likely to live in roach-infested apartments, and have much higher rates of asthma than do White, middle-class children (Acevedo-Garcia & Osypuk, 2004; Yinger, 2000).

A report by the Natural Resources Defense Council (Quintero-Somaini & Quirindongo, 2004) documented environmental health risks for Hispanics. Many Latinos live in cities with high levels of air pollution, which increases the risks for cancer and asthma, and older housing stock results in Hispanic children having twice the rate of dangerous lead levels as White children. A significant number of Latinos live in "colonias," unincorporated communities near the U.S.–Mexico border, where inadequate drinking water and sewage disposal increase the risks of waterborne diseases such as giardiasis, hepatitis, and cholera. In Western states, many Latinos drink water contaminated by arsenic, chemicals, and fertilizers. Those working as farm workers face high exposure to pesticides, which increases the risks for cancer.

Taken together, these environmental hazards create major health risks for Hispanics, who as a group are the least likely to have health insurance, although this also is a problem for African Americans and some Asian American groups such as Koreans (Brown et al., 2000). Racial disparities in health begin before birth (as mothers are exposed to more hazards), continue through childhood and persist through adulthood and old age, driven by differential exposure to environmental risk and less access to needed health care resources (Assari, 2018). An extreme example of this is the contamination of Vieques, Puerto Rico, where in 1941, the U.S. military took over most of the island, displacing many families living close to the beaches in order to run military training exercises. As a result of running these training operations, complete with live munitions and unexploded bombs, the island was left contaminated with heavy metals and toxic waste. Today, Puerto Ricans living on Vieques have experienced higher levels of birth defects and cancer rates due to these toxins. The U.S. government has yet to assume responsibility for this superfund waste site (Roman, 2003).

People of color, particularly African Americans, Latinos, and American Indians, receive lower quality healthcare than Whites (Assari, 2018). In addition to having less insurance, people of color have less access to health services due to not having sufficient doctors nearby and the cost. Health facilities that are used are often more crowded, with longer waiting periods and in older and less well-kept facilities. People of color are less likely than Whites to find doctors who mirror them ethnically and have a good understanding of their culture, which can affect interpersonal trust. People of color also are more likely to be misdiagnosed and less likely to have necessary tests, while being more vulnerable to undergoing invasive surgery such as amputations and castration. For example, African American women have a 40% higher death rate than White women from breast cancer due to significant delays in diagnosis and treatment when compared to Whites (Freeman, 2014).

Doctors and other healthcare providers, as with the population at large, may be unaware of their own stereotypes, biases, and prejudices. For example, one stereotype is that Black men do not feel pain as severely as White men and thus receive less pain medications (Villarosa, 2019). Tervalon and Murray-Garcia (1998) report that emergency department doctors give Latinos anesthesia for long-bone fractures half as often as White patients; yet a follow-up study with the same physicians indicated that they did not think that Latinos were in any less pain. Healthcare providers are themselves often the target of racism (Garran & Rasmussen, 2016), with very little institutional support, in the form of training or other interventions.

Despite progress in public health initiatives over the years, people of color endure more illness and injury from birth until death. African American babies are more than twice as likely as White babies to have a low birth weight (Acevedo-Garcia & Osypuk, 2004; McLoyd & Lozoff, 2001). This, in turn, contributes to higher rates of infant mortality and lifelong developmental challenges and learning difficulties. This trend is exacerbated as poor children of color face higher risks of injury in hazardous living situations, along with more exposure to lead paint (Acevedo-Garcia & Osypuk, 2004). Poor, isolated neighborhoods also are more dangerous, placing residents at higher risk for being victims of violence. All of these factors have negative consequences for developmental, medical, behavioral, educational, and social outcomes. African Americans, as well as Latinx people and Native Americans experience many health challenges in higher numbers than Whites across the life span; for example, heart disease, hypertension, and obesity (Assari, 2018). Continual exposure to the stress and trauma of racism also results in higher cortisol levels, hypertension, inflammation, and premature aging (Assari, 2018). Blacks are more likely to die from heart disease (Williams, 2001), have a significantly lower survival rate from cancer (Joiner, 2004), and, along with Native Americans and Latinos, have higher death rates than Whites from diabetes (Williams, 2001). African Americans also have much higher rates of hypertension, which may be related in part to the ongoing stress of racism (Kingston & Nickens, 2001).

In research by Woody and Green (2001), African Americans of all social classes reported that they confront constant stereotypes and discrimination in all spheres of their lives and are concerned about losing jobs. Thus, they work longer hours and take less time for vacations, which affect health as well as family life. African American men in particular report strong feelings of vulnerability as well as an acute awareness of their lower life expectancies and higher risk factors in all aspects of life, leading to a diminished sense of well-being compared to Whites.

African American men also are more likely than Whites not to have a doctor, a consequence of the conditions mentioned earlier and also borne of mistrust about the aims of the medical profession, generated in part by revelations about medical abuse. During the Civil War, Black people were allowed to die of smallpox (Interlandi, 2019). Another example is the infamous Tuskegee experiment, in which Black men were left with untreated syphilis for research purposes (Joiner, 2004). Given this accumulation of risk factors, it is not surprising that 40% of Black men die prematurely, compared to 21% of White men, and that Blacks have a significantly shorter life expectancy than Whites (Joiner, 2004; Muhammad et al., 2004).

All of these factors, and more, have contributed to the much higher mortality rates for people of color during the COVID-19 crisis of 2020 and 2021. Early statistics during the pandemic indicate that in places like Chicago and Louisiana, African American fatalities account for over 70% of COVID-19 deaths while only making up about one third of the population (Oppel Jr. et al., 2020). For the reasons previously discussed, African Americans (and Latinos and Native Americans) are more likely to be working in jobs where sheltering in place or using virtual technology is not possible and also more likely to have pre-existing conditions that create greater risk for the virus (Oppel Jr. et al., 2020). They also suffer from accelerated aging from the unending stresses of racism (Eligon et al., 2020). Across the United States, Native Americans are at greater risk from the pandemic due to lack of running water on some reservations, pre-existing health conditions, and less access to medical facilities, many of which were closed in recent years, than other populations (Ebbs & Hazlett, 2020).

The structural conditions for this pattern also include the faltering of the U.S. welfare state, because so many White people oppose programs that benefit brown and Black people (Porter, 2020). In many southern states with large Black populations, there has not been Medicaid expansion, often due to White racism, which lowers access to medical services for many Black people. Nine of the 14 states who have denied Medicaid expansion since the passage of the Affordable Care Act are in the South, corresponding with Jim Crow states (Newkirk II, 2020). The COVID-19 virus also threatens migrants of color on both sides of the U.S. border as they are crowded together in unsafe and unsanitary conditions, lacking access to protective gear and medical care (*The New York Times*, 2020, March 3). The same is true for prisons, with huge numbers of inmates of color, which will be discussed. The racial profiling of Black men is relevant for a discussion about racism and COVID-19. Black men are wary about wearing masks, which are part of the Centers for Disease Control and Prevention protective guidelines against COVID-19, for fear of racial profiling, inviting police attention and harassment (Taylor, 2020). If fewer masks are worn for this reason, Black men are then at greater risk of infection and transmission. Asian Americans have also suffered additional stress, since President Trump intentionally named COVID-19 the "Chinese virus"; attacks against Asian Americans have increased while, like everyone else, they are trying to survive the pandemic (Tavernise & Oppel Jr., 2020). The racialized politics of stoking fear and targeting racial/ethnic groups is discussed in the following.

MENTAL HEALTH RACISM

The same structural barriers to healthcare that affect people of color disproportionately also apply to mental health services. Mental health services, however, sometimes are offered on a sliding-fee basis, a policy that expands the pool of people who are covered. At the same time, managed care has reduced the number of counseling sessions available to consumers, except those with the means to pay out of pocket. Provider biases and prejudices operate with mental health workers as they do for medical personnel, but the essence of therapy and counseling involves intersubjective meaning-making, so the corrosive impact of such biases erodes the relational foundation of clinical services. Internalized, unconscious stereotypes loom large when White practitioners engage in cross-racial or cultural counseling because of its intimate, interpersonal nature (Goggin et al., 2015).

Wade (1993) has argued that institutional racism is present in mental health policy and has a significant impact on diagnostic and treatment issues. Institutional racism is at hand in the following areas: (a) access, (b) services offered, (c) who provides services, (d) the structure of services, (e) theoretical biases, (f) racism between people in the clinical encounter, (g) culturally insensitive counseling facilities, (h) lack of representation on policy-making boards, (i) lack of access to private practitioners, and (j) the misuse of diagnosis.

Access

The same issues of access apply to mental health services as to other health services (Davis, 1997). The uninsured have fewer mental health options and, due to the intersection of race and health coverage, the rates of insurance coverage are lower for many groups of color. Other considerations include the location of clinics and whether they are easily accessible by public transportation.

Middle-class consumers have a choice when selecting providers, whereas poor communities of color often have access to only one mental health agency. A recent emphasis on faith-based initiatives may lead to more religious agencies offering counseling services, although people from different denominations or who are not religious may feel uncomfortable about accessing them. Another inequity is that waiting lists for clinics serving poor clients of color are often longer.

Services Offered

Managed care has medicalized counseling. To receive reimbursement, a client requires a diagnosis acceptable to Medicaid or to a managed care company. Less counseling is available for the stresses of daily living, to help people cope with the consequences of illness and disability, to improve interpersonal communication, and to address developmental delays and learning disabilities—all of which are needs exacerbated by institutional racism. And there is not yet a diagnostic category that includes race-based trauma despite clinical evidence of its existence (Carter, 2007).

Who Provides Services

The issues facing community mental health centers are similar to those in public education who are concerned about the quality of services offered and who provides them. Counseling in clinics located in poor communities of color is stressful, with low pay, long hours, and stringent productivity requirements. Although some dedicated clinicians remain in these agencies, more often we see an exodus of qualified counselors seeking better working conditions and salaries by going into private practice or working in agencies in more affluent communities. This leads to high staff turnover. Overall, clinicians with less experience and training work in poor communities of color.

Seeking therapy involves trust and making oneself vulnerable in the presence of another. It is helpful for clients to feel mirrored by those who are providing services; to feel like there is "someone like me who can understand me and my experiences." For those who are targeted by racism, it is often more challenging to develop a trusting relationship with a White clinician or a clinician of color from another ethnic group. Will the clinician understand the dynamics of racism? Will there be racial enactments in the clinical encounter? Is it safe to be vulnerable with this person? These are salient questions raised by the specter of racism in the clinical encounter.

Also, when clients speak languages other than English, there is a need for translation and interpretation, which is difficult to arrange and frequently unavailable. In some agencies, when indigenous workers are hired, cultural competency increases but clinical services may be offered by people with less professional training. Also, agencies have racial hierarchies. Although a significant number of line workers may be people of color, the staffing pattern Whitens in the supervisory, managerial, and leadership ranks. The exceptions are agencies run by people of color, for people of color, with representative boards of directors.

The Structure of Services

Individual counseling and 50-minute sessions make certain assumptions about cultural styles, worldviews, and values. Many Asian American, Hispanic, and African American communities have more of a collective orientation, which de-emphasizes the individual and stresses the importance of family and community. Yet, most U.S. counseling centers offer individual counseling in a 50-minute hour. This is reinforced by a financing and billing structure in which most clients are seen individually rather than in families (nuclear and extended), friendship clusters, or groups.

The emphasis on regular appointments, though important to staff, assumes a certain level of organization, adequate transportation, and does not allow for irregular working patterns or sudden and debilitating stressful events. The length of sessions, with an emphasis on starting and ending on time, also reflects middle-class Eurocentric norms of communication and social behavior.

Theoretical Biases

The counseling enterprise in the United States is founded on values, expectations, and beliefs derived from European psychologists and White practitioners in this country. As mentioned earlier, the focus on the individual and the value placed on separation-individuation is a clear example of this cultural and social bias. As Summerfield (2004) has argued, help-seeking is culturally informed—what do we seek help for, who do we seek help from, what do we expect when we seek help, what are the risks of seeking help from outsiders? These are questions often left unexplored and unanswered by theories of Western psychology.

These assumptions are exacerbated by expectations about disclosure and communication, as well as by Western notions of egalitarianism, which sometimes run counter to expectations about deference and hierarchy in other cultures. Even the notion of confidentiality, as important as it is, reflects cultural norms about privacy and the rights of the individual transcending those of the family. The same is true of the concept of professional boundaries, which evolved in Western European countries; not eating with or socializing with clients may be normative in Western counseling but is alienating and even perceived as being rude or disrespectful in other cultural contexts.

Finally, Western theories of counseling and therapy have often focused on deficits and problems, rather than strengths, cultural sources of wisdom, and resilience (Miller, 2012). Resisting racism takes courage and strength, which need to be validated in clinical encounters. Otherwise, the act of making oneself vulnerable, particularly with a person who may not "get it," carries the risk that this will undermine one's resistance in the face of racism.

Racism in Clinical Encounters

Therapists already hold a great deal of power in their relationships with clients, and this is magnified when clinicians are not mindful of the power and privileges that their race or ethnicity convey. A danger when White clinicians are working with people of color is that non-Western cultural patterns and behaviors might be pathologized or viewed as dysfunctional. This contributes to the potential for nonempathic, unhelpful services, ranging from culturally insensitive services to actual racist encounters during sessions (Carter, 1995, 2007; Pinderhughes, 1989; Ridley, 1995). Clinicians, like everyone else, have internalized stereotypes, thus, the transactional patterns of racism can involve implicit or aversive racism by White clinicians, which contribute to microaggressions (see Chapter 6) in the clinical encounter. Racial transference and countertransference is operating in all cross-racial and cultural work, whatever the race or ethnicity of the client or therapist. Sometimes clients of color, understandably, are slow to trust White clinicians: Will the White therapist be able to not only tolerate this dynamic but have the skills and foresight to take active steps to name and work with the cross racial nature of the relationship?

Clinical work also involves a third party, the clinician's supervisor. Even when there are clinicians of color, they often have White supervisors. It is important for supervisors to be able to open up space for explorations about power, privilege, cultural patterns, and other aspects of ethnic/racial diversity and to be able to model a stance of cultural humility (Lipscomb & Ashley, 2017). Having a supervisor of color is important for understanding sociocultural factors but in the case of Spanish-English bilingual (SEB) clinicians having a supervisor who speaks Spanish is essential.

Culturally Insensitive Facilities

Waiting rooms and offices, like the clinicians themselves, typically reflect cultural biases and assumptions, as well as power relationships. They often reflect the centrality of White, heterosexual, cis-gender, able-bodied people (Al-Hassan et al, 2018). Where a receptionist sits, how they treat clients, and how they are treated in return by professional staff send many messages. The reception area also communicates respect or disrespect for clients. What pictures or genres of art, if any, are on the wall, and what do they convey? Is there a television in the waiting room and, if so, what channel is it tuned to? What toys and magazines are in the waiting room? Is the telephone message in English only? Even the softness or harshness of lighting can affect the comfort level of consumers (Al-Hassan et al, 2018). While there have been improvements over the past decade in mental health facilities having a more culturally welcoming atmosphere, many of our clients of color have expressed unease and discomfort about waiting for and receiving services in facilities that for them encode White, middle-class ideas about how offices should be structured.

Lack of Representation on Policy-Making Boards

Most mainstream clinical agencies that are not established specifically to serve a specific ethnic or racial group do not have adequate representation of people of color on their boards, even when their clients are predominantly people of color. Boards of directors often do not offer enough board positions for consumers. Managed-care panels and Medicaid decision-making committees also are prone to exclude people of color or to have only token representation. This interacts with the Whiteness of the staff hierarchy at the higher levels of the organizational chart. All of this contributes to policymaking and administration that lacks an understanding of racism or a commitment to racial justice.

Lack of Access to Private Practitioners

Very few private practitioners, particularly White practitioners, work with poor people of color, and if they do, they often limit the hours of availability. This leads to a tremendous gap in potential clinical services for clients. It also limits the options of poor clients of color. If a consumer has had a bad experience with the only mental health agency serving their neighborhood and does not want to return to that organization, or if in turn the agency has dismissed the consumer as a client, the option of seeing a clinician in private practice is often not available. And there are even fewer practitioners of color than in public mental health facilities, making it even more likely that a person of color can find a private practitioner who they anticipate will mirror and understand them.

The Misuse of Diagnosis

One of the biggest obstacles to having a racially just mental health system is that clinicians often practice as if there can be pure, psychological conditions that are somehow divorced from the daily reality of experiencing racism. Mental health is always part of a larger psychosocial context. Diagnosis is an essential part of offering mental health services, particularly given the need to justify services to insurance companies and Medicaid in order to be reimbursed for services. As we illustrate in Chapter 12, racism itself is a cause of stress, emotional tension, and can even cause trauma (Carter, 2007). And yet, there is no diagnostic category used by insurance companies to capture this. Thus, people of color seeking services for problems that accrue from experiencing ongoing racism are often given other psychological diagnoses that are decontextualized from their lived experiences and have the capacity to be pathologizing; the consequences of social targeting and oppression are construed as psychological or reflecting characterological vulnerabilities and weaknesses. Even the efforts to resist and confront racism can be negatively interpreted as evidence of an "oppositional defiant disorder," or anger management problems, or even paranoia.

In short, institutional racism, particularly when combined with class inequities, is pervasive at all levels of the mental health system, from policy making to what happens in the consulting room. The result is that people of color, who suffer the additional life stresses of racism, often have the fewest options for mental health services. And when they do receive counseling, it often reflects cultural biases and leads to further racist encounters and experiences.

RACISM IN THE CRIMINAL JUSTICE SYSTEM

All forms of institutional racism are wrong and dangerous. Criminal justice racism is a stain on American society akin to apartheid. African Americans and Latinos constitute only 30% of the general population, yet comprise 58% of the prison population (Ghandnoosh, 2014). African Americans comprise 42% of the death row population (Higginbotham, 2013). If the victim is White, African American men are 22% more likely to receive the death penalty

(Stevenson, 2019). When people of color are imprisoned so disproportionately, something is terribly amiss. When there are such gross racial disparities among death row inmates, an appalling caricature of justice is enacted in the name of all U.S. citizens.

These discrepancies cannot be explained by blaming the victims of institutional racism. What is taken as a normative pattern today was not yesterday's prototype. In 1950, at the height of Jim Crow and virulent Southern racism, African Americans constituted 30% of the prison population; by the early 1990s, they made up about half (Hawkins, 2001). Ultimately, this is a crushing indictment of the web of institutional racism, in which all of the strands contribute to more vulnerability for involvement in the criminal justice system and experiencing the pervasive racism within it.

On a macro level, segregated, isolated, economically depleted neighborhoods lack opportunities for quality education, well-paying jobs, and pathways to economic self-sufficiency (Massey, 2001). Absent sufficient legitimate opportunities, some residents turn to illegal activities, such as drug dealing. (In predominantly White suburbs, there are also many drug dealers, but they are far less likely to be under surveillance and arrested.) As these activities become more prevalent, the neighborhood becomes more dangerous. This, in turn, leads to fewer citizens venturing out to public places, which makes streets even more dangerous (Geis & Ross, 1998; Miller, 2001).

Police officers, many of whom are White, patrol these neighborhoods and develop or reinforce negative stereotypes toward people of color, who report far more negative interactions with police than do White people (Ghandnoosh, 2014; Weitzer & Tuch, 2004). Stereotypes and implicit bias lead to dehumanization of people of color, particularly Black people, who are viewed by law enforcement as being in need of control, discipline, and punishment (Bustamante et al., 2019). Ironically, Whites live in neighborhoods where they are far less likely to be victimized by crime than are people of color and yet they fear crime more than people of color and have more punitive attitudes toward the punishment of criminals (Ghandnoosh, 2014). The police guard urban neighborhoods with high concentrations of poor people of color in much the way the military guards occupied territory. They may overreact and sometimes commit brutal and sadistic acts, such as the well-publicized beating of Rodney King, the slaying of Amadou Diallo, and the rape and torture of Abner Louima. Experimental studies have documented how White people, whether police officers or civilians, hold implicit biases toward African American men and are more likely to shoot an unarmed Black person in an ambiguous situation than an armed White person (Sadler et al., 2012).

In the past few years there have been well-publicized murders of unarmed young Black men by police officers: Tamir Rice, John Crawford III, Freddie Gray, Michael Brown, Rumain Brisbon Alton Sterling, Philando Castile, Ahmaud Arbery and many more. In 2015, out of 965 people killed by the police, 60% were unarmed Blacks or Latinos (Reinka & Leach, 2017). Black people are about 15% of the population but 40% of suspects killed by the police (Scott et al., 2017). An unarmed Black man is seven times more likely to be killed by the police than an unarmed White man (Reinka & Leach, 2017). Neighborhood residents, then, not only fear drug dealers and gangs but also the law enforcement officers who are supposed to "protect" their community. This is all a prelude, occurring before many wheels of institutional racism in the criminal justice system begin to turn.

Not only are unarmed Black and Latino men more likely to be killed by the police but the victims are often blamed for what happened. Research indicates that it is police bias, not victim behavior, that leads to fatal shooting (Scott, et al, 2017). Media portrayals focus on the victim's background, size, lifestyle, and the neighborhood where the murder occurred, as if this explains or justifies the outcome (Dukes & Gaither, 2017). This is a process of dehumanization and demonizing and criminalizing men of color (Dukes & Gaither, 2017), which in turn creates fertile conditions for justifying further police violence against unarmed Black and Latino men.

Within the population of African Americans differentially treated by the criminal justice system, there are also differences. Men with darker skin color and more afrocentric facial features are more likely to trigger a quicker shooting response in implicit bias tests and are also more likely to receive longer sentences and death penalty verdicts (Bennett & Plaut, 2017).

Prior involvement with the child welfare and juvenile justice systems are risk factors for adult association with the criminal justice system. African American children are more likely to be the subjects of protective investigations, more likely to be placed out of their homes, less likely to have permanent placement or reunification plans, and on average spend a longer time in foster care (Lu et al., 2004; Roberts, 2002). In Chicago, 95% of foster children are Black (Roberts, 2002).

Black children, too, are more likely to be moved from one foster home to another. Children without family or stability in substitute care, living in more dangerous neighborhoods, and attending underresourced schools, are more prone to educational difficulties. This leads to a greater likelihood of becoming involved with the juvenile justice system, gangs, and, thus, greater risk of police harassment.

African American children are disproportionately represented in the juvenile justice system. Youth of color are treated more severely at every stage of the juvenile justice system (Building Blocks for Youth [BBFY], 2001; Poe-Yamagata & Jones, 2000). African American youth are more likely than White youth to be charged for the same offense, and more likely to be placed out of home. They are given longer sentences, are more likely to be referred to adult court, and are less likely to receive probation (Poe-Yamagata & Jones, 2000). In Cook County, Illinois, 99% of juvenile offenders referred to adult courts are African American or Latino (BBFY, 2001).

One of the single most important factors in determining whether a youth offender does not reoffend as an adult is to be able to change either the peer group or the community (Laub, 2000). But with disproportionate sentencing and incarceration of youth of color, combined with less social mobility, the peer group becomes entrenched and increasingly deviant. These factors, along with systemic racism in policing, increase the risks for engagement with the criminal justice system as adults (Laub, 2000).

Although African American men do have slightly higher rates of engagement in violent crimes than White men, this difference is not large enough to explain the discrepancies in the demographics of the prison population (Ghandnoosh, 2014). The majority of prisoners are not incarcerated for brutal crimes (Alexander, 2010), and while the prison population has grown dramatically over the past 20 years, the murder rate has been dropping (Massey, 2001).

Many people are in prison for violating drug laws, which have built-in racial biases. Crack cocaine carries mandatory minimum sentences, whereas powdered cocaine does not (Kennedy, 2001). The 2010 Fair Sentencing Act reduced the ratio between crack and powder cocaine in order to levy the same sentence for possession of either substance. Although this has resulted in less disparity, federal law still imposes a harsher sentence on possession of crack cocaine.

Because Whites use powdered cocaine proportionately more than Blacks do, the sentencing patterns are racially divergent. In 2000, African Americans constituted 80% to 90% of those imprisoned for drug offenses (Alexander, 2010). Although the majority of drug users and dealers are White, three quarters of those imprisoned for drug offenses are Black and Latino.

Recently, there has been a lot of public discussion about the opioid crisis and how drug addicts, now increasingly White, have an illness and should receive treatment rather than incarceration. There are public discourses asking for addicts to be treated with compassion and sympathy, but where were these voices when the crack epidemic was sweeping predominantly African American communities? African American addicts were characterized as pathological thugs and criminals and the response of the criminal justice system was to arrest and incarcerate them (Yankah, 2016). Alexander (2010) asks how the United States would have responded if the "war on drugs" had been conducted in White suburbs, where equally high rates of drug use were occurring, resulting in the incarceration of young, White, middle-class men.

In addition to "drug sweeps," Alexander (2010) has described the process that results in such high rates of Black and Latino imprisonment. People of color are more likely to be stopped by the police if walking and pulled over if driving. For example, in Florida in 2014 Black people were twice as likely as White people to be stopped and given a ticket for not wearing a seatbelt (Alvarez, 2016). The rate of being stopped by the police while driving is up to five times as high for Black drivers in some parts of the country and is a problem throughout the nation (LaFraniere & Lehren, 2015). If there is a legal problem, such as unpaid traffic tickets, this is more likely to be uncovered. African American and Latino men are more likely to be searched and if carrying a drug, such as marijuana, have it discovered. They are more likely to be charged and face higher charges. They are less likely to have the resources or adequate legal representation to enable them to settle charges without punitive consequences. They are more likely to be viewed as a threat by the police officers who stop them and through the interaction of implicit bias (see Chapter 6) and external violence suffer the consequences. They are more likely to face trial (often with White judges and predominantly White juries that harbor implicit bias) than White defendants and more likely to be convicted and given stiffer punishments. They are more likely to be placed on probation or parole when not in prison. At every step of the criminal justice system—being stopped, being searched, being charged, being arrested, facing trial, sentencing, incarceration, and parole—African Americans and Latinos are disproportionately represented and face stiffer penalties (Ghandnoosh, 2014; Johnson et al., 2010). Accordingly, Black men are five times more likely than White men to be under the supervision of the criminal justice system (Council of Economic Advisors, 1998; Human Rights Watch, 2000). In 2006, one in every 14 Black men was in prison compared with one in every 106 White men (Alexander, 2010).

Other contributing factors to the high Black prison population are states' "three strikes" laws, which disproportionately affect African Americans because they are more likely to have been arrested and charged in the past for reasons already stated. This is part of a trend that favors punishment over treatment. Once in prison, there has been a move to deny prisoners' educational services, disadvantaging their job and career prospects when released (Boyd, 2001; Western, 2001).

Here is how the vicious cycle occurs (Ghandnoosh, 2014). Whites, many of whom have very little contact with African Americans and Latinos, harbor negative stereotypes about

African Americans and Latinos and view them as dangerous and predatory. Much of this comes from media stereotypes and many studies have confirmed that there is internalized implicit bias within the general White population. This has accelerated with the symbiotic relationship between President Trump and Fox News (discussed later), which promulgate stereotypes and fan the flames of fear about people of color and immigrants, also often of color. Politicians often respond to these fears by promising and promulgating more punitive legislation. Consequently, more African Americans and Latinos are stopped, charged, sentenced, and imprisoned, reinforcing White stereotypes of criminality. Because of unfair treatment, many people of color mistrust the criminal justice system and are less likely to cooperate with it, while Whites have fewer and more positive interactions with law enforcement. The media selectively reports on crime by people of color, continuing to fuel White fears, overplaying the threats of men of color toward White victims, underplaying the racist criminal justice system, and the cycle continues.

Consequences of racism in the criminal justice system amplify racism in the political process, as more and more states are depriving felons of the right to vote—in some instances for the rest of their lives. Even when there are referenda to return the right to vote, such as in Florida in 2018, politicians devise ways to stall or derail reinstatement of this basic right (Michaelson, 2020). Although the referendum passed by a 2:1 margin, the Republican controlled legislature is proposing that all former felons pay outstanding fines and fees before being reinstated. This was not in the original referendum and by some estimates would deny the right to vote for up to 80% of those who were to have had their right to vote restored.

By 2000, more than 4.2 million Americans had been disenfranchised from voting because of past or present incarceration; and in Alabama and Florida, 31% of African American men have lost their right to vote (Sengupta, 2000). This right is often forfeited for very minor crimes (Alexander, 2010). The United States is the only democracy in the world that disenfranchises convicted felons, which has disturbing echoes of the Jim Crow era (Boyd, 2001; Simson, 2002). In fact, voter disenfranchisement for felons has more effectively suppressed Black votes than at the height of the Jim Crow era (Alexander, 2010).

The costs of all of this to individuals and communities are immense. The consequences of constant surveillance and brutal treatment by law enforcement, which is often repetitive, is humiliating and can lead to feelings of shame, sadness, and anger (Bustamante, et al, 2019). There is a sense of cumulative dehumanization, which can also be accompanied by the well-grounded fear of being killed.

Many men who are socially integrated in their communities and who are fathers are taken out of their communities (Sabol & Lynch, 1997). This means that potential breadwinners are no longer available, which contributes to the family's inability to accumulate social capital, as discussed. It also leads to a loss of eligible marriage partners for heterosexual couples. It is also more difficult for former felons to find jobs and receive social welfare benefits (Alexander, 2010). Children lose father figures. Reintegration programs are few and inadequate, so those who try to return to their communities after incarceration often lack skills, counseling, training, and other necessary supports, all of which contribute to high rates of recidivism. And because of hypersegregation, most of the men in prison come from a small number of urban communities of color (Sabol & Lynch, 1997). Ironically, according to former Attorney General Eric Holder (2015), states that saw their prison population decrease had lower crime rates.

It has not always been this way— in the early 1970s there were fewer than 300,000 people in prison but now there are 2.2 million (Stevenson, 2019). The United States has 4% of the world's population and 22% of the world's prison population (Stevenson, 2019). This is only the tip of the iceberg, as there are over 7-million people under some form of correctional supervision (Alexander, 2010). The United States incarcerates 25% of the world's prisoners, and if all prisoners were brought together in one place, they would constitute the 35th most populous American state (Boyd, 2001). Black men in the United States are incarcerated at four times the rate that Black men were imprisoned during the apartheid era in South Africa, and that number is now more than that of Black men enslaved during the height of the U.S. slave era (Alexander, 2010). In the past quarter century, the United States has created a racial gulag through its criminal justice system (Boyd, 2001) and has reinstituted racial apartheid.

POLITICAL RACISM

Power in society resides in many sites—industry, the military, the media, among the wealthy-and, when there are social movements, among the people. One of the most visible and significant locations of power lies in government and politics. Over the course of its history, this nation has repeatedly denied political representation and power to people of color, such as denial of citizenship and the right to vote by legal and illegal means. Accordingly, racism not surprisingly extends throughout the political system. It is manifested in who is elected (and who is absent), who is appointed, who can and cannot vote in elections, and who wields power behind the scenes.

Since writing the first edition of this book, the United States elected its first non-White president, Barack Obama, who is a multiracial African American, won two terms as president, achieving a milestone that deserves recognition and celebration as a significant marker in the struggle against racism. However, this accomplishment was marred by overt racism and hostility toward President Obama by his political opponents (Boule & Kruse, 2019; Mcllwain & Caliendo, 2014), the formation of the Tea Party in direct response to having an African American president (Zeskind, 2012), White flight to the Republican Party (Abrajano & Hajnal, 2015), and the election of Donald Trump, who challenged the legitimacy of President Obama by questioning his citizenship and whose many instances of racism will be discussed. We first consider some historical trends and then examine current efforts to suppress the votes of people of color.

Racism was built into the U.S. electoral system from the beginning of the republic. The development of the Electoral College involved invoking the "3/5 rule," which counted enslaved people as 3/5 of a person for the allotment of political representation even though they were unable to vote, giving the slave-holding South disproportionate political power (Keyssar, 2020). This continued throughout the Jim Crow Era, as Southern states blocked Black people from voting while having their representation based on the entire population of their state, enabling White supremacists to erase Black political power and enhance their national political influence (Keyssar, 2020). The U.S. Electoral College continues to be inherently undemocratic, allocating disproportionate electoral advantages to sparsely populated, predominantly White states like Wyoming and Vermont, because they have a minimum of three electoral votes, compared to racially diverse states such as California and New York. It also means that Wyoming and Vermont have as many senators as California and New York, despite having far fewer people than the more populous states. The Electoral College ensures that White people continue to wield more political influence than people of color.

After the Civil War, the first African American senators and representatives were elected, but the backlash to Reconstruction and successful efforts by White Southerners to restrict voting meant that shortly afterward, no African Americans served in Congress until the election of an African American representative from Illinois in 1928 (Patrick et al., 2001). In the entire history of the U.S. Senate, there have been only 26 senators who were people of color (Park et al., 2016). In the 2016 U.S. Senate, the number was six out of 100 senators (Park et al., 2016). In the history of the Supreme Court, there have been two Black justices. In recent decades, there have been a number of firsts: Colin Powell became the first African American to serve as the head of the Joint Chiefs of Staff and the first Black Secretary of State under the second President Bush, followed by Condoleezza Rice. The numbers of people of color in cabinet-level positions increased under both Presidents Bill Clinton and George W. Bush, and even further under President Obama, including his appointment of Eric Holder as the first non-White U.S. Attorney General. President Obama also appointed the first Latina to the Supreme Court, Sonia Sotomayor.

The first Latinx cabinet members were appointed in the 1970s. However, the few Hispanic congressmen and senators holding national office in the United States today do not mirror the percentages of Hispanics in the general population, which is about 16%. Hispanics only constitute 5% of federal judges (Patrick et al., 2001). There have been three Native American congressmen, two of whom went on to serve in the Senate, although at this writing there are no Native American senators. There have been no Native American nor Asian American Supreme Court justices. Asian Americans were not elected to Congress or the Senate until the 1950s, when their numbers were boosted by the admission of Hawaii as a state in 1959. Few staffers of color work for elected officials. For example, in a survey taken in 2000, in Massachusetts, of 151 congressional staffers, only 15 were "minorities" and no congressional office from any state was headed by a person of color (Associated Press, 2000). In 2015, the combined numbers of people of color in the U.S. House of Representatives and Senate were the highest ever (17%) but did not reflect the growing diversity of the U.S. population (38% people of color; Krogstad, 2015). Only four out of 50 U.S. governors are people of color (Park et al., 2016).

The dearth of adequate representation of people of color does not stop with the federal government. Many cities and states lack a fair proportion of elected and appointed people of color. One mechanism that supports this inequity at the local level is the practice of electing at-large candidates to city councils and school committees. In a city where perhaps one third of the residents are people of color, this practice can mean that people of color will be in the minority for every contested seat and, therefore, unable to elect people representing their interests.

In suburbs around Hartford, Connecticut, for example, people of color have moved to Bloomfield, East Hartford, West Hartford, Newington, Wethersfield, and Windsor in significant numbers; yet a number of these communities have only—or mostly—White city councilors and school board members (Altimari et al., 2001). This underrepresentation goes beyond elected officials, extending to the warrens of commissions and city departments, often staffed by people who are patrons of the elected people who appoint them.

This lack of access to political offices at the local level means that people of color do not gain the experience and develop resumes propelling them to state and national office. The high costs of campaigning coupled with the unrestricted growth of Political Action Committee (PAC) donations also hampers the capability of people of color to forge political careers.

There have been recent negative trends that have weakened the power of people of color in the political process: unbridled spending, the evisceration of the Voting Rights Act, voter suppression laws passed at the state level, and taking away the vote from people convicted of criminal behavior. The Supreme Court decision known as Citizens United allows PACs to spend unlimited amounts of money to influence elections; in many cases, PACs do not need to identify their donors (Vandewalker, 2015). Given that people of color have much less wealth than White people in the United States, their ability to participate in this free-for-all buying political advertisements is much more limited. PACs have allowed for more heated rhetoric, including negatively coded messages directed toward White voters about people of color. PACs are also less accountable for being factually accurate. Political advertisements can be racialized in many ways (McIlwain & Caliendo, 2015):

- ▶ Associating people of color with racist stereotypes—such as presidential candidate Romney's advertisement that "Obama is not working"—not directly accusing Obama of being lazy but activating a racial stereotype about Black people not working with White voters.
- ▶ By deploying props—such as showing candidates talking with White voters or voters of color to prime feelings about whom their allegiances are to.
- ▶ By spreading racialized rumors, such as the advertisement during the 2012 Presidential Election run by a PAC associated with the Tea Party showing an African American woman crowing about Obama giving out free phones to supporters, which not only distorted facts but activated a number of racial stereotypes.

The Voting Rights Act, passed in 1965, ensured that in states and localities that historically denied African Americans the right to vote, there was federal supervision of the voting plan that ensured full participation of all racial and ethnic groups. It dramatically increased the political participation of African Americans and other groups of color that had been systematically excluded from the political process for many decades. Shortly after its passage, 800,000 African American voters were registered and the number of Black office holders jumped to 10,000 from 300 (Higginbotham, 2013). Although there were attempts to dismantle the act from its inception, there was overall support for the Voting Rights Act from all three branches of government and both major political parties (Berman, 2015). However, this changed in 2014 when the U.S. Supreme Court voted to overturn the need for these places to have federal approval of their voting plans unless there were overt attempts to subdue votes based on race or ethnicity. In the United States today, no policy explicitly states that it is racist, but many policies that purport to achieve other goals are intentionally racialized (McIlwein & Caliendo, 2015). The Supreme Court decision effectively permitted the passage of a slew of laws that not only made it more difficult for registered voters to exercise their constitutional right to vote, but carried restrictions particularly suppressing the votes of people of color (Waldman, 2015). In our view, this was intentional, as were efforts to suppress the votes of people of color before the Voting Rights Act was passed. Since 2010, 24 states have passed voter suppression laws and there is a very strong correlation between Republican control of the state political process and the passage of restrictive voting legislation (Weiser & Opsal, 2015).

Many of the laws were passed in response to alleged, largely uncorroborated "concerns" about voter fraud. Former President Donald Trump, who has voted by mail himself, has claimed that voting by mail, which would make it easier for voters of color to vote, leads to potential fraud, despite no evidence that this is the case (Michaels, 2020). Voter ID laws disproportionately suppress the votes of people of color, the youngest and oldest of voters, and voters with disabilities (Weiser & Opsal, 2015). The laws make it more difficult for people who move more frequently and are less likely to have driver's licenses or other "acceptable" documentation, where the cost of obtaining the ID may be prohibitive (Waldman, 2015). Many of the laws also did away with early voting, which was more utilized by the groups listed earlier (Weiser & Opsal, 2015). In addition to this, precincts with large populations of poor voters of color have longer lines to wait before voting due to fewer available voting sites and machines or less modern voting equipment (Famighetti et al., 2015), which is why voting by mail would enable more people of color to vote.

A congressional investigation found that voters in "low-income, high-minority" districts were sometimes 20 times more likely than voters in other districts to have their votes discarded in the 2000 national election (Minority Staff, Special Investigations Division, Committee on Government Reform, U.S. House of Representatives, 2001). In South Dakota, American Indians complained that certain maneuvers, including complicated registration procedures and dubious identification requirements, were attempts to suppress their vote (Cohen, 2004). Tactics such as these are eerily reminiscent of voting restrictions that characterized the Jim Crow era.

It is not surprising that the Republican Party is committed to voter suppression of people of color. As the party has increasingly tacked to the right and appealed to those who are White, while opposing legislation that provides social, educational, and health services supported by many people of color, there has been an exodus of people of color to the Democratic Party and Whites to the Republican Party (Abrajano & Hajnal, 2015). Thus, there is a vicious cycle where the Republican Party increasingly relies on White voters and their political hegemony is threatened by people of color voting in large numbers. And as the party supports restrictions in voting, it pushes voters of color further into the Democratic camp. Sadly, voter suppression has worked and probably influenced the outcome of the 2014 senatorial race in North Carolina in the Republican's favor, along with the gubernatorial elections in Kansas and Florida (Weiser, 2015). Having one party that has become so blatantly associated with White privilege and power in this modern era has been a stunning setback in the struggle for racial equity and justice (Wines & Fernandez, 2016).

This trend is not new and began in the 1960s when Richard Nixon pursued his "Southern strategy," which shifted White voters from the Democratic camp to the Republican Party through explicit and implicit racially coded messages to White voters (Edsall & Edsall, 1991; Polikoff, 2004). President Ronald Reagan used coded racialized imagery when he talked about "welfare queens," and the first President Bush appealed to similar sentiments in his now infamous Willie Horton advertisements while running for president against Michael Dukakis. This raised the specter of unbridled sexual and physical assault by Black felons, a stereotype promulgated throughout the history of the racial project of the United States. Although his son, George W. Bush, had a better track record of appointing a more diverse cabinet, both of his election campaigns were marred by numerous efforts to suppress the Black vote, and many of his policies increased the tax burden on poor people of color while cutting health and human services.

The lack of adequate representation has consequences for people of color. The nation's leaders do not fully grasp the experiences and implications of racism. Consequently, at best, these issues are neglected, and actually exacerbated by support for anti–affirmative action initiatives, restrictive immigration laws, miserly social benefits, and stiff, unequal drug penalties. There has not been a serious attempt to implement an urban policy since the Great Society.

Leaders set a tone and offer role models. When leaders legitimize coded racist imagery, they encourage and permit others to do so as well. Leaders can divide and exacerbate social schisms (Miller & Schamess, 2000). They are highly visible opinion shapers in what becomes a public discourse that no longer is concerned about racism and inequities but, instead, focuses on how people of color are freeloaders and "cheating the system," gaining unfair advantage through government programs and affirmative action policies, while the rights of "good, hardworking" White people allegedly are under siege. In the primary election of 2016, most Republican candidates talked about "taking back our country" to largely White audiences. Who were they trying to take the country back from?

Such populist discourse has been taken to unprecedented levels, not seen since before the Civil War, by Donald Trump. Journalist German Lopez (2019) has catalogued Trump's racism before he was president, while he ran for president and since becoming president. In the 1970s, his real estate company was sued by President Richard Nixon's Justice Department for refusing to rent to Black tenants and violating the Fair Housing Act. In the 1980s he called for the death penalty for five teenagers of color who were falsely accused of raping a white jogger in New York City's Central Park; they served 13 years in prison and as recently as 2016 he continued to say that they are guilty despite DNA evidence to the contrary. In 2011 Trump falsely claimed that President Barack Obama was not born in the United States and contributed heavily to the "birther" movement. While running for president, Donald Trump called Mexican immigrants rapists and drug dealers, called for a ban on all Muslims immigrating to the United States, and argued that a judge of Mexican descent was prejudiced against him because of his ethnic heritage. Since becoming president this is a partial list of his racially charged statements:

▶ Claimed that White supremacist demonstrators in Virginia, who killed a counter-demonstrator, had some "very fine people."
▶ Said that immigrants coming from Haiti and Nigeria were from "shithole countries."
▶ Mocked Senator Elizabeth Warren, who claims some Native American heritage, by calling her Pocahontas.
▶ Called for four Congresswomen of color to "return to their countries," three of whom were born in the United States.
▶ Retweeted a video of a supporter yelling "White power."

When the president of the United States regularly employs racist tropes and is beloved by White supremacists, then racism has a cheerleader at the highest level. This came to a violent and dramatic climax when Donald Trump lost the 2020 election and continued to try to overturn election results from predominantly Black districts in key states. His "big lie" culminated in a violent insurrection on January 6, 2021, where Trump exhorted his followers to overturn the election. The U.S. Capitol was breached by an angry, predominantly White mob, carrying symbols of White supremacy such as Confederate flags and a make-shift gallows. A number of people were killed including a police officer. Many of the insurrectionists were allowed to leave the Capitol, in stark contrast with peaceful Black Lives Matter protestors who were tear-gassed and beaten by police and military in combat gear in order to clear room for President Trump to pose in front of a predominantly Black church with a bible.

Despite Trump's attempts to subvert the election and his incitement of a mob populated by members of many White supremacist organizations, Republican Senators, all of whom are White save one, overwhelmingly voted to dismiss Trump's second impeachment. Sadly, the Republican party in its current iteration has embraced White supremacist organizations, sanctioned extremism and attempts to suppress votes and steal elections, and no longer holds people accountable for racist attempts to subvert democracy.

MEDIA RACISM

What inner models do people internalize to understand race and racism, and where do those images and concepts come from? People are exposed to a racial discourse from birth. The discourse is not hegemonic, but the dominant narrative is one that privileges White people and presents doing so as fair and normal. This narrative is transmitted by parents to children, and they are not alone: Children's books help to tell the story with racialized choices of characters, settings, and plots (van Dijk, 1995).

The narrative is furthered in preschool and school, where teachers, books, videos, and other media presentations continue the saga of White supremacy, often without reference to race and racism. In some U.S. states, such as Texas, history textbooks used in public schools, in a form of historical "erasure," do not mention Jim Crow or the Ku Klux Klan, and treat slavery as a peripheral issue during the Civil War (Sehgal, 2016). Children are exposed to an idealized history, such as *The Story of Thanksgiving* and the relationships between Pilgrims and Indians, which neglect to describe the Native American holocaust. This discourse shapes attitudes and encodes stereotypes that people often carry with them for life. The distorted narratives lead in turn to cognitive distortions that often remain unchallenged given the degree of residential and educational segregation that persists in the United States, as described earlier. The narratives subtly diminish people of color and establish White people as society's dominant group (van Dijk, 1995).

Adults are exposed to the racial discourse through television shows, news broadcasts, films, books, magazines, advertisements, music, and the internet. Most people have internalized stereotypes from childhood, and they continue to be bombarded with complementary stereotypes: Whites presented as heroes, leaders, decision-makers, central characters, experts, and talking heads; while people of color frequently are constructed as "other," different, deviant, quaint, exotic, and stereotyped (van Dijk, 1995). Or people of color are just missing. Whether it is the lack of people of color nominated for Hollywood Oscars or the paucity of people of color as "talking heads," White dominance is the norm, even in liberal news outlets. Specialized news shows on public radio—for example, "Only a Game," "On Being," "Wait-Wait, Don't Tell Me," "On the Media"—offer a preponderance of White presenters and White people being interviewed.

The technology used by all forms of media have racist assumptions baked into them; given how pervasive racism is within society, this is unsurprising. For example, even the lighting settings for photographs, centers whiteness (Lewis, 2019). When film was being used for analog pictures, there was a lighting template to guide film developers called "The Shirley Card," which used a White woman with brown hair as the norm: If "Shirley's" face looked good, then the lighting was correct. This marginalized lighting settings for Black or brown people. And with the switch to digital photography, the same biases have found their way into algorithms. A good example is facial recognition programs, where African American and Asian Americans were misidentified 100 times more often than White people, with an even higher error rate for Native Americans (Harwell, 2019). This has serious implications for misidentification in both civil and criminal proceedings.

In 2020, actor Christopher Rivas wrote an op-ed piece for *The New York Times* (2020) describing how he constantly needs to have his hair cut short so that he does not have curls and look less Latino and more White, in order to fit in with what casting directors seek. This is not unique and is part of an ongoing pattern. A recent study by the Media, Diversity, & Social Change Initiative and the University of California's Annenberg School for Communication and Journalism is particularly damning about Hollywood (Coyle, 2016). After analyzing hundreds of films and television shows from 2014 to 2015, the researchers found that only 28.3% of actors in speaking roles were "minority," although people of color makeup about 37% of the population. Directors were 87% White and broadcast television directors are 90.4% White. There was also severe underrepresentation of women and lesbian, bisexual, transgender, queer, and intersex (LBTQI) identified actors, directors, and characters. Over 50% of the content that was examined did not feature one Asian/Asian American character. This may be due to only two people of color out of 19 people being involved in deciding which television shows will be made (Park et al., 2016). When it comes to deciding which films are made, only one of 20 major studio executives in those positions is a person of color (Park et al., 2016). And in the music industry, of Billboard's 20 most influential music executives, only one is a person of color (Park et al., 2016).

The print media is another area that erases the presence of people of color, including books as well as popular media. Most major poetry anthologies in the 1960s and 1970s ignored major poets of color (Michael Thurston, personal communication). When *The New York Times* selected the most powerful people in the publishing industry who decide which books are published, two out of the 20 were people of color (Park et al., 2016).

When people of color are visible for media discussions, it is often because the focus of the story is about "minority" issues. And in the rare moments when racism is directly addressed, it is often portrayed as a question of individual attitudes and behaviors determined by whether White people and people of color can talk to one another and be friends (DeMott, 1995). The realities of the web of institutional racism and the legacy of the "racial contract" are rendered invisible. There is little or no historical context. A fantasyland of individual relationships without reference to historical and sociological legacies and constraints dominates many storylines.

Dynamics at ESPN, the major sports network now owned by the Disney Corporation, illustrate some of these racialized patterns. Although compared to other networks, there are many Black, Indigenous, and people of color (BIPOC) faces on shows, Black employees have been complaining for years about systemic racism within the network that has led to lower rates of promotion, microaggressions from White workers, and a cultural and political worldview that is White (Draper, 2020). This has affected how movements—such as Colin Kapernick's "taking a knee" are covered or not covered. When Black presenters tried to bring a Black consciousness into discussions about such issues, this was viewed as being "too political" by the mostly White executives at the network, bolstered by fears of alienating the parent company, Disney (Draper, 2020).

When it comes to the news, people of color consistently are portrayed in a negative, stereotypical fashion. Sometimes this is done through codes that do not refer to race and yet have racial meanings for readers and viewers, as was described earlier in Mitt Romney's campaign slogan "America is not working." Or it can come from having threatening visuals of men of color when there are stories about crime in a local community (Ghandnoosh, 2014). The terms *broken families, teenage mothers, welfare mothers, inner-city crime,* and *crack* all conjure up racial stereotypes (van Dijk, 1995), as did the Willie Horton advertisements used in the election campaign of the first President Bush (described earlier).

Most staff working for mainstream magazines and journals are White. According to *The New York Times*, of the 12 most powerful executives in both print and network media, only two are people of color (Park et al., 2016). Even liberal and left-leaning publications have only about 10% of people of color working for them (Arana, 2014). When most editors and television producers are White, they may not recognize that they are colluding with racial stereotypes (Gillens, 1999). Some media executives, however, do know what they are promoting, and they strive to maintain high ratings through news that titillates and stirs people up (Westin, 2001). White editors, executives, and reporters also shape what issues are covered ("agenda setting") and how issues are framed—such as focusing on "illegal immigration" while flashing images of immigrants of color, even though this is a small percentage of all immigrants (Abrajano & Hajnal, 2015). Even in liberal news outlets—such as *The New York Times*—negative stories on immigration outnumber positive stories 3:1 (Abrajano & Hajnal, 2015). What gets lost is how we are a nation of immigrants and how many contributions immigrants make to U.S. culture and society.

Given the negative media portrayals of people of color, particularly Black and brown people, it is not surprising that people of color are wary about telling their stories because there is so much potential for distortion, mischaracterization, erasure, and a lack of empathy and understanding by White journalists and their editors. In order for BIPOC to feel safe and secure enough to engage with media representatives, trust must be fostered. For this to happen, reporters may need to undergo anti-bias training and examine their worldviews, assumptions, and biases (Chaney, 2017).

Another problem that continues to promulgate racist stereotypes and that fails to deconstruct and address that society is structured by the "racial contract" and White supremacy is the myth of neutrality and objectivity that organizes main-stream media reporting. While reporters need to be responsible, thorough, and do their research, there are no objective reporters. All decide what their starting point is, what the narrative frames will be, whose stories are told and how they are narrated. Given the normality of White dominance in society, neutrality will reinforce this structural reality. Thus, media reporters, whose work is always guided by working assumptions, which in turn are shaped by the reporter's experiences, can actively take an antiracism stance to inform their work (Chaney, 2017). This will take an active effort by the mainstream media to unlearn the parts of their heritage that maintain White supremacy and to see their work as situated and therefore calling for an antiracism stance.

Some stories do seriously engage with racism. There are some actors of color who are recognized and many artists of color in the music industry. There are some models who are not White and news anchors who are people of color. But these are *exceptions*; rarely does the media reflect the actual demographics of U.S. society. And exceptions can give cover to media industries that consistently and systematically exclude and demean people of color, creating the illusion of equal opportunity and equity, while serving to maintain a racialized institution and society which it reflects.

Whatever the motivation, the choice of images and words, how stories are presented, and who presents them create a racialized tapestry of meaning. When people of color are used as presenters or "talking heads," they often are enlisted to talk about issues seen as pertinent to racial issues, while mainstream, allegedly nonracialized issues more often are the domain of White experts. When people attempt to present programs that feature people of color in a positive light, they encounter barriers, including concerns from producers that the programs will not appeal to Whites and, thus, will not fare well in the ratings derby (Westin, 2001). Advertisements, too, are prone to portraying White men in leadership roles and African American men as aggressors (Coltrane & Messineo, 2000).

While much of this section has focused on mainstream news, entertainment, and media outlets, the growth of social media—Facebook, Twitter, Youtube and so forth—have, not surprisingly, amplified and magnified society's racial biases and inequities. There is less accountability than in more traditional media outlets, which can lead to greater liberatory narratives and journalism but also serve as a forum for overt and covert racism and racists. The internet has allowed organizations and individuals of color to tell their own stories, directly, without White filters, and to reach a diverse range of audiences. Websites and apps can be used to mobilize people, raise money and challenge White media hegemony. In many ways, the insurrections of the spring and summer of 2020 in response to the death of George Floyd and others at the hands of the police, depended on the power of social media to inform and mobilize.

On the other hand, the internet is also a gathering place for White supremacists. Overt racists have always found media channels and outlets to spew their messages of hate, using websites, chat rooms, networking sites, and discussion boards to spread misinformation, groom and recruit new members, and reassure their fellow travelers (Faulkner & Bliuc, 2018). There are usually narratives about Whites being victims, promulgation of racist stereotypes, a misguided vision of patriotism, an emphasis on White purity, and the recycling of racist myths and tropes (Faulkner & Bliuc, 2018). Sadly, they have found an ally in Donald Trump who not only does not condemn them but who actually retweets and amplifies some of their hateful messages.

In summary, the overall saturated ubiquity of Whiteness in the media promulgates an ongoing narrative reinforcing racism while rarely drawing attention to racism as a central social problem. It is nearly impossible to withdraw or escape from this unending drumbeat that normalizes White culture, style, morality, and meaning. It is the cloak that shrouds and obscures the web of racism by making it seem as if this is just the way things are. Recognizing, decoding, and resisting the web takes a great deal of time and effort. Fortunately, the internet has created openings to engage in this work.

Islamophobia

A particular form of immigration racism that is prevalent in the United States today is fear and hostility directed toward people who are spiritually Islamic or who are nationally and ethnically from the Middle East. Islamophobia is directed not only toward immigrants but also toward people who share this religious or ethnic identity and who have lived for generations as U.S. citizens. This is a good example of how racism toward immigrants is also directed toward citizens with similar ethnic identities and vice versa. Islamophobia affects who is allowed to immigrate to the United States, how they are treated when they arrive, and how native Muslims are treated. Like other forms of racism, Islamophobia is fueled by myths and distortions about the nature of Islam and generalizations about Middle Eastern and

Muslim people. This response has grown since 9/11 and the seemingly endless "war on terrorism." It became a flash point issue during the 2016 race for the U.S. presidency as Republican candidates clamored for restrictions against Muslim or Middle Eastern immigrants, despite the humanitarian crisis afflicting millions of refugees.

Studies of Muslim Americans document the extent of racism, hatred, and fear that they encounter. In one study, nearly 60% of Muslim participants stated that they have encountered discriminatory acts, 4% have been physically assaulted, 86% were subjected to anti-Muslim comments, and 68% experienced excessive security checks while flying (Abu-Raiya et al., 2011). Anti-Muslim behaviors can range from microaggressions (see Chapter 6) to attacks, including murder. People who White Americans think look like Muslims or Arabs, such as Sikhs, have also experienced such assaults (Ahluwalia, 2011). As with all forms of racism, the media plays a complicit role, often portraying Muslims and Arabs as violent, heartless, different, and untrustworthy (Halse, 2012). What is particularly insidious is the portrayal of Muslims as terrorists. The vast majority of Muslims reject terrorism, as do the majority of Christians, Jews, Buddhists, and Hindus, although terrorist acts have been perpetrated in the name of all of these groups. In the United States, according to Federal Bureau of Investigation (FBI) statistics for 1980 through 2005, 96% of domestic terrorist attacks were carried out by non-Muslims (Global Research, 2013).

Concerns about Muslims by White Americans echo discourses about other immigrants who are viewed as being different from mainstream White America. Such nativist discourses have been activated when Jews, Italians, the Irish, and other ethnic groups now socially constructed as White immigrated to the United States. They are consistent with the anti-immigrant discourses that are affixed to immigrants from Latin America, Africa, and Asia. They reflect a pattern of "othering" and intergroup conflict that is discussed in Chapter 7.

IMPLICATIONS OF THE WEB OF RACISM FOR THE HELPING PROFESSIONS

The web of institutional racism is painfully obvious for the people of color caught in its strands, yet nearly invisible to many White people who pass through it unimpeded. White people hold the illusion that many societal institutions, policies, living and working arrangements, programs, and organizations are race neutral. As we have argued, this is not possible in a racialized society. Thus, identifying and mapping the web of institutional racism, pinning it on the wall of individual and collective consciousness, is a step toward confronting racism. It no longer can be denied or relegated to museums and history.

Recognizing and understanding institutional racism is particularly essential for the helping professions. Exercise 5.2 builds on this point. Clinicians must appreciate that racism affects everyone. No one is immune. Some are targeted by it, others benefit from it, and still others have experiences of both privilege and oppression; all internalize structural racism as part of cognitive maps, emotions, and what seems normal and predictable Even though some can ignore racism, it is always present and certainly is a dynamic involving those in the helping professions. Essential questions include: Who is offering the services, and to whom? How are the services being provided? What assumptions are being made about the nature of the problem, what will be helpful, and where should that help come from? And where do these assumptions come from?

A second implication is that every organization is affected by the web, and all are part of it. The web influences which agencies or programs are funded and under what conditions. Racism is part of the mission statement of every organization, whether by commission or omission: Is there an explicit commitment to antiracism, multiculturalism, and social justice, or are these factors absent in the organizational mission? The web shapes who works in organizations, what qualifications they have, how they enter the organization, what capital they bring with them, and how quickly or slowly they progress after they arrive. It influences where organizational power resides.

A third implication is that the web shapes interactions between providers and consumers and also between colleagues. The web operates in everyone's lives, albeit differentially. It influences worldviews, values, and assumptions. A person's experience with the web will shape their beliefs about how fair and equitable the world is, which in turn will influence how open or guarded, trusting or skeptical a person is. One way that social service organizations can deal with this dynamic is to have ongoing dialogue groups among staff members, as well as workshops that help them identify their cultural and social assumptions and values.

The web also influences training and qualifications. Racism increases the challenge for some people of color to gain an education or acquire the resources necessary to become professionally qualified. The web enables many White people to receive a college education, increase their professional training, and find jobs where they gain important experience. In turn, these inequities influence what jobs people are qualified to take within organizations; what they are paid, even with similar credentials and work history; and, of course, who is positioned to move into supervisory and management positions.

The web of racism also determines what is taught when people receive their training, how they are trained, and what is viewed as normative professional behavior, including what emotions are permissible. In the helping professions, racism is always present and may be tackled, partially confronted, or ignored. As Kivel (2011) has written, institutionalized racism in organizations determines what gets addressed, how it is addressed, who participates in addressing it, and what options are considered viable or untenable. See Exercise 5.3 to consider how the web can change over time.

CONCLUSION

Higginbotham (2013) posits that racism and White supremacy have been upheld by three interlocking dynamics throughout U.S. history: (a) a belief in White superiority and Black inferiority; (b) separation and segregation of the races; and (c) assaults on people of color, particularly African Americans. The web of racism is the structure by which racism endures and persists. It is historical and contemporary; some parts shift the surface in ways in which they are manifested, but one thing has endured throughout U.S. history— it benefits White people while hurting and holding back people of color. It limits opportunity for many people of color, while increasing risks for individual bodies, minds, and spirits, disrupting systems of collective unity and support. Many White people are unaware of it. It is a direct descendent of the implicit racial contract undergirding the foundation of the United States. Although public and political discourses place the locus of responsibility for racial differences in wealth, power, incarceration rates, and success with individual effort and cultural and ethnic work ethics, the web of racism demonstrates that society is structured unequally, and how racism continues to privilege White people and oppress people of color. That the web is so ubiquitous and yet so invisible to the majority of White people in the United States is perplexing. The reasons for this and how this ignorance helps to ensure that racism in the United States remains so entrenched is the subject of the next chapter.

EXERCISE 5.1 The Web of Racism and Passports of Privilege

Consider the web of racism. Have you had experiences where you have been caught in the web, or have you had a passport of privilege that has permitted you to pass through it? For those who have experienced the web, which parts have been most problematic? For those with privilege, which parts were you least aware of?

Discuss your experiences with the web in small groups. Are parts of the web evident in your school or agency? What steps could be taken to unravel the web of racism on a local level?

EXERCISE 5.2 The Trajectory of Institutional Racism

The dynamics and manifestations of institutional racism are always shifting. Some aspects of institutional racism have been ameliorated or diminished while others have barely changed at all. Rarely does change or progress happen in a straight line; there are cycles of repression and liberation. For example, when post–Civil War Reconstruction ended, all states from the former Confederacy passed voter suppression laws that were presented as race neutral but virtually eliminated the votes of African Americans. The Supreme Court at the time upheld the legitimacy of the state's claims to race neutrality. From 1965, when the Voting Rights Act was passed, until 2013, a consensus among the president, Congress, and Supreme Court upheld the act, which led to dramatic increases in the participation and election of people of color. The trajectory during this period was one of progress against political racism. But in 2013, the Supreme Court gutted the Voting Rights Act and numerous states passed "race-neutral" laws that are effectively suppressing the votes of people of color and have influenced elections—what was accomplished is now being undone.

Take any aspect of institutional racism covered in this chapter and research its effects during certain historical periods and continuing to the present.

1. What has been its trajectory? Has it remained the same, gotten better or worse, or have there been cycles? Has it changed form and has the language justifying it shifted?
2. If there has been progress, contrast the most racist periods with the most progressive periods. What social and political conditions contributed to repression or progress?
3. What conclusions or lessons do you draw from your research about what is needed to ameliorate institutional racism? What can undermine successes in the struggle against racism? What can be done to prevent backsliding?

EXERCISE 5.3 Update the Web!

The data for the web of racism are often contested and always changing. Once we have written this book, it is frozen in time and always needs to be updated. Research a particular aspect of the web of racism and consider how data can be used to support or undermine arguments used in this chapter. How would you organize the data and frame the issues? What changes have already occurred in data and patterns that you would use to update a particular section of this chapter?

REFERENCES

Abrajano, M., & Hajnal, Z. L. (2015). *White backlash: Immigration, race and American Politics.* Princeton University Press.

Abu-Raiya, H., Pargament, K. I., & Mahoney, A. (2011). Examining coping methods with stressful interpersonal events experienced by Muslims living in the United States following the 9/11 attacks. *Psychology of Religion and Spirituality, 3*(1), 1–14.

Acevedo-Garcia, D., & Osypuk, T. L. (2004, July/August). Racial disparities in housing and health. *Poverty & Race, 13*(4), 1–2, 11–13.

Ahluwalia, M. K. (2011). Holding my breath: The experience of being Sikh after 9/11. *Traumatology, 17*(3), 41–46.

Alexander, M. (2010). *The new Jim Crow: Mass incarceration in the age of colorblindness.* The New Press.

Al-Hassan, K., Hornell, K., Moon, A., Pasternak, M., Scott, D., & Simon, J. (2018). Physical environment as an indicator of cultural validation in counseling and psychological services and the Center for Human Growth at Indiana University. *Journal of the Student Personnel Association at Indiana University.* www.scholarworks.iu.edu/journals/index.php/jiuspa/article/view/25695

Allen, T. W. (1994). *The invention of the White race.* Verso.

Altimari, D., Budoff, C., & Davis, T. (2001, July 15). *Suburbs more diverse, but not town halls.* Hartford Courant, A1, A6.

Alvarez, L. (2016, January 27). *Black drivers in Florida face far stricter seat-belt enforcement, report says.* The New York Times. www.nytimes.com/2016/01/28/ us/florida-police-black-drivers-aclu.html?emc=eta1

Arana, G. (2014, May 12). *The unbearable Whiteness of liberal media.* The American Prospect. http://prospect.org/article/unbearable-whiteness-liberal-media#.U3Ntt-d-_m4.email

Assari, S. (2018). Health disparities due to diminished return among Black Americans: Public policy solutions. *Social Issues and Policy Review, 12*(1), 112–145.

Associated Press. (2000, June 26). Mass. congressmen lag in number of minority hires. *Daily Hampshire Gazette,* B1.

Badger, E., & Bui, Q. (2018, October 1). Detailed maps show how neighborhoods shape children for life. *The New York Times.* www.nytimes.com/2018/10/01/upshot/maps-neighborhoods-shape-child-poverty.html?action=click&module=Top%20Stories&pgtype=Homepage

Badger, E., Bui, Q., & Gebeloff, R. (2019, May 1). All-white neighborhoods are dwindling as America grows more diverse. *The New York Times.* www.nytimes.com/2019/05/01/upshot/all-white-neighborhoods-are-dwindling-as-america-grows-more-diverse.html

Bell, M. P., Leopold, J., Berry, D., & Hall, A. V. (2018). Diversity, discrimination and persistent inequality: Hope for the future through the solidarity economy movement. *Journal of Social Issues, 74*(2), 224–243.

Benjamin, R. (2009). *Searching for Whiteopia: An improbable journey to the heart of White America.* Hyperion Books.

Bennett, M. W., & Plaut, V. (2017). Looking criminal and the presumption of dangerousness: Afrocentric facial features, skin tone, and criminal justice. *U.C. Davis Law Review, 51.* Available at SSRN: https://ssrn.com/abstract=3078065

Berman, A. (2015). *Give us the ballot: The modern struggle for voting rights in America*. Farrar, Straus & Giroux.

Bikmen, N. (2015). Still a nation of immigrants? Effects of constructions of national history on attitudes towards immigrants. *Analysis of Social Issues and Public Policy, 15*(1), 282–302.

Blank, R. M. (2001). An overview of trends in social and economic well-being, by race. In N. J. Smelser, W. J. Wilson, & F. Mitchell (Eds.), *America becoming: Racial trends and their consequences* (Vol. I, pp. 21–39). Washington, DC: National Academies Press.

Bobo, L. D. (2001). Racial attitudes and relations at the close of the twentieth century. In N. J. Smelser, W. J. Wilson, & F. Mitchell (Eds.), *America becoming: Racial trends and their consequences* (Vol. I, pp. 265–301). Washington, DC: National Academies Press.

Bottia, M.C. (2019). Educational and residential segregation of immigrants in the United States. *Poverty & Race, 28*(10) 1–2, 6, 8.

Boule, J., & Kruse, K. M. (2019, August 18). Undemocratic democracy. *The New York Times Magazine*, 51–55.

Bourgois, P. (1995). *In search of respect*. Cambridge.

Boyd, G. (2001, July 31). *The drug war is the new Jim Crow*. American Civil Liberties Union.

Bronner, E. (1998, April 1). Black and Hispanic admissions off sharply at University of California. *The New York Times*, Al.

Brown, D. A. (2014). Diversity and the high-tech industry. *Alabama Civil Rights and Civil Liberties Law Review, 6*, 95.

Brown, E. R., Ojeda, V. D., Wyn, R., & Levan, R. (2000). *Racial and ethnic disparities in access to health insurance and health care*. UCLA Center for Health Policy Research.

Brown, M. K., Carnoy, M., Curne, E., Duster, T., Oppenheimer, D. B., Shultz, M. M., & Wellman, D. (2003). *Whitewashing race: The myth of a colorblind society*. University of California Press.

Brown, P. L. (2015, September 3). Silicon Valley, seeking diversity, focuses on Blacks. *The New York Times*. www.nytimes.com/2015/09/04/technology/silicon-valley-seeking-diversity-focuses-on-blacks.html?emc=eta1

Building Blocks for Youth. (2001). *Drugs and disparity: The racial impact of Illinois' practice of transferring young drug offenders to adult court*. Washington, DC: Author.

Bureau of Labor Statistics. (2020, January 17). *Usual weekly earnings of wage and salary workers Fourth Quarter 2019*. U.S. Department of Labor. www.bls.gov/news.release/pdf/wkyeng.pdf

Bustamante, P., Jashnani, G., & Stoudt, B. G. (2019). Cumulative dehumanization in everyday policing: The psychological, affective and material consequences of discretionary arrests. *Analysis of Social Issues and Public Policy, 19*(1). http://doi.org/10.1111/asap.12187

Calhoun, M., & Bailey, N. (2005). Predatory lending: Undermining economic progress in communities of color. *Poverty & Race, 14*(1), 17–19.

Carnevale, A. P., & Rose, S. J. (2003). *Socioeconomic status, race/ethnicity, and selective college admissions*. Century Foundation.

Carter, R. T. (1995). Race and psychotherapy: Clinical applications in a sociocultural context. In The influence of race and racial identity in psychotherapy: Toward a racially inclusive model (Chap. 13, pp. 225–241). Wiley.

Carter, R. T. (2007). Racism and psychological and emotional injury: Recognizing and assessing race-based traumatic stress. *Counseling Psychologist, 35*, 13–105.

Chaney, C. (2017). How crisis journalists can magnify the voices of poor, marginalized communities of color. *International Journal of Crisis Communication, 1*, 2–8.

Charles, C. Z. (2000). Processes of racial residential segregation. In A. O'Connor, C. Tilly, & L. D. Bobo (Eds.), *Urban inequality: Evidence from four cities* (pp. 217–271). Russell Sage Foundation.

Chokshi, N. (2018, May 5). *Native American brothers pulled from campus tour after nervous parents call police*. The New York Times. www.nytimes.com/2018/05/05/us/native-american-brothers-colorado.html?module=WatchingPortal&region=c-column-middle-span-region&pgType=Homepage&action=click&mediaId=wide&state=standard&contentPlacement=19&version=internal&contentCollection=www.nytimes.com&contentId=https%3A%2F%2Fwww.nytimes.com%2F2018%2F05%2F05%2Fus%2Fnative-american-brothers-colorado.html&eventName=Watching-article-click

Cohen, A. (2004, June 21). *Indians face obstacles between the reservation and the ballot box*. The New York Times, A18.

Cohen, P. (2015, August 16). *Racial wealth gap persists despite college degree, study says*. The New York Times. www.nytimes.com/2015/08/17/business/racial-wealth-gap-persists-despite-degree-study-says.html

Coltrane, S., & Messineo, M. (2000). The perpetuation of subtle prejudice: Race and gender imagery in 1990s television advertising. *Sex Roles, 42*(5/6), 363–389.

Cose, E. (1993). *The rage of a privileged class*. HarperCollins.

Council of Economic Advisors. (1998). *Changing America: Indicators of social and economic well-being by race and Hispanic origin*. Washington, DC: Author.

Coyle, J. (2016, February 22). *Damning study finds a "whitewashed" Hollywood*. The Associated Press. http://bigstory.ap.org/article/3fa20ecbb5884649acfe22c0324fff99/report-finds-epidemic-invisibility-throughout-hollywood

Davis, D. B. (1997). A big business. *New York Review of Books, XLV*(10), 50–52.

DeMott, B. (1995). *The trouble with friendship: Why Americans can't think straight about race*. Atlantic Monthly Press.

Diamond, J.B., Lewis, A.E. (2015). Despite the best intentions: Making school integration work in integrated schools. *Poverty & Race, 24*(6), 1–2, 14–17

Draper, K. (2020, July 13). ESPN employees say racism endures behind the camera. *The New York Times*. www.nytimes.com/2020/07/13/sports/espn-racism-black-employees.html?action=click&module=Top%20Stories&pgtype=Homepage

Dukes, K.N., & Gaither, S.E. (2017). Black racial stereotypes and victim blaming: Implications for media coverage and criminal proceedings in cases of police violence against racial and ethnic minorities. *Journal of Social Issues, 73*(4), https://doi.org/10.1111/josi.12248.

Ebbs, S., & Hazlett, S. (2020, April 3). *Indian country faces higher risks, lack of resources in COVID-19 fight*. ABC News. https://abcnews.go.com/Politics/indian-country-faces-higher-risks-lack-resources-covid/story?id=69957760

Edsall, T. B. (2020). *How racist is Trump's Republican party?* The New York Times. www.nytimes.com/2020/03/18/opinion/trump-republicans-racism.html

Edsall, T.B. (2019, July 17). Integration vs. white intransigence. *The New York Times*. www.nytimes.com/2019/07/17/opinion/integration-politics.html

Edsall, T. B., & Edsall, M. D. (1991). *Chain reaction: The impact of race, rights and taxes on American politics*. W. W. Norton.

Eligon, J., Burch, A.D.S., Searcy, D., & Oppel Jr., R.A. (2020, April 8). Black Americans face alarming rates of Coronavirus infection in some states. *The New York Times*. https://www.nytimes.com/2020/04/07/us/coronavirus-race.html?action=click&module=Top%20Stories&pgtype=Homepage

Ellen, I. G., Steil, J., & De La Roca, J. (2016). The significance of segregation in the 21st century. *City and Community*. https://doi.org/10.1111/cico.12146

Faber, D. R., & Krieg, E. J. (2001). *Unequal exposure to ecological hazards: Environmental injustices in the Commonwealth of Massachusetts*. Northeastern University, Philanthropy and Environmental Justice Research Project.

Famighetti, C., Melillo A., & Perez, M. (2015). Why long lines on Election Day? In D. R. Reiner, J. Lyons, E. Opsal, M. Terrell, & L. Glaser (Eds.), *Democracy and justice: Collected writings* (Vol. VIII, pp. 74–76). Brennan Center for Social Justice.

Faulkner, N., & Bliuc, A. (2018). Breaking down the language of online racism: An analysis of communication in racist, anti-racist and non-activist groups. *Analysis of Social Issues and Public Policy*. https://doi.org/10.1111/asap.12159

Frankenberg, E., Lee, C., & Orfield, G. (2003). *A multiracial society with segregated schools: Are we losing the dream?* Harvard University Civil Rights Project.

Freeman, H. P. (2014, March 13). Why Black women die of cancer. *The New York Times*. www.nytimes.com/2014/03/14/opinion/why-black-women-die-of-cancer.html?emc=eta1

Freiberg, F. (2019). Prove it! *Poverty and Race, 28*(4), 1–2, 7–8.

Fritz, N. (2001, March). Electoral debacle: Our response. *Civil Liberties*, 2–6.

Frosh, D. (2014, February 19). Amid toxic waste, a Navajo village could lose its land. *The New York Times*. www.nytimes.com/2014/02/20/us/nestled-amid-toxic-waste-a--navajo-village-faces-losing-its-land -forever.html?emc=eta1

Ganim, S., & Tran, L. (2016, January 13). *How tap water became toxic in Flint, Michigan.* CNN. www.cnn .com/2016/01/11/health/toxic-tap-water-flint-michigan

Garran, A. M., & Rasmussen, B. M. (2016). In the line of duty: Racism in health care. Commentary. *Social Work*, 61(2), 175–177.

Geis, K. J., & Ross, C. E. (1998). A new look at urban alienation: The effect of neighborhood disorder on perceived powerlessness. *Social Psychology Quarterly*, 61(3), 232–245.

Ghandnoosh, N. (2014). *Race and punishment: Racial perceptions of crime and punishment.* Washington, DC: The Sentencing Project.

Gillens, M. (1999). *Why Americans hate welfare.* University of Chicago Press.

Gjelten, T. (2015, October 2). *The immigration act that inadvertently changed America.* The Atlantic. www .theatlantic.com/politics/archive/2015/10/immigration-act-1965/408409

Global Research. (2013, May 1). *Non-Muslims carried out more than 90% of terrorist attacks in America.* Centre for Research on Globalization. www.globalresearch.ca/non-muslims-carried-out-more-than-90-of -all-terrorist-attacks-in-america/5333619

Goggin, E., Werkmeister Rozas, L., & Garran, A. M. (2015). A case of mistaken identity: What happens when race is a factor. *Journal of Social Work Practice.* http://doi.org/10.1080/02650533.2015.11005961-15

Gonyea, D. (2017). *Majority of white Americans say they believe whites face discrimination.* NPR. www.npr .org/2017/10/24/559604836/majority-of-white-americans-think-theyre-discriminated-against

Green, E.L. (2018, April 4). Government watchdog finds racial bias in school discipline. *The New York Times*. www.nytimes.com/2018/04/04/us/politics/racial-bias-school-discipline-policies.html?emc=edit_th _180405&nl=todaysheadlines&nlid=207144620405

Green, E.L., & Waldman, A. (2018, December 28). I feel invisible': Native students languish in public schools. *The New York Times*. www.nytimes.com/2018/12/28/us/native-american-education.html

Halse, R. (2012). The Muslim-American neighbor as terrorist: The representation of a Muslim family in *24. Journal of Arab & Muslim Media Research*, 5(1), 3–18.

Harmon, A. (1998, April 17). Racial divide found on Internet highway. *The New York Times*, A1.

Harwell, D. (2019, Dec. 19). Federal study confirms racial bias of many facial-recognition systems, casts doubt on their expanding use. *The Washington Post*. www.washingtonpost.com/technology/2019/12/19/fed eral-study-confirms-racial-bias-many-facial-recognition-systems-casts-doubt-their-expanding-use/

Hawkins, D. F. (2001). Commentary on Randall Kennedy's overview of the justice system. In N. J. Smelser, W. J. Wilson., & F. Mitchell (Eds.), *America becoming: Racial trends and their consequences* (Vol. II). Washington, DC: National Academies Press.

Higginbotham, H. M. (2013). *Ghosts of Jim Crow: Ending racism in post-racial America.* New York University Press.

Holder, E. H. (2015). Shifting law enforcement goals to reduce mass incarceration. In D. R. Reiner, J. Lyons, E. Opsal, M. Terrell, & L. Glaser (Eds.), *Democracy and justice: Collected writings* (Vol. VIII, pp. 36–41). Brennan Center for Justice.

Houston, S. (2001). Beyond social constructionism: Critical realism and social work. *The British Journal of Social Work*, 31(6), 845–861.

Human Rights Watch. (2000). *United States—Punishment and prejudice: Racial disparities in the war on drugs.* Author.

Ignatiev, N. (1995). *How the Irish became White.* Routledge.

Inness-Thompson, M.N. (2018). *Summary of discipline data for girls in U.S. public schools: An analysis from the 2015–2016.* U.S. Department of Education Office for Civil Rights Data Collection. National Black Women's Justice Institute. WWW.NBWJI.ORG

Interlandi, J. (2019, Aug. 18). A broken health care system. *The New York Times Magazine*, 45. https://www .nytimes.com/interactive/2019/08/14/magazine/universal-health-care-racism.html

James, B. (2020). *Shortage of teachers of color in Western Massachusetts has its costs.* New England Public Radio. www.nepr.net/post/shortage-teachers-color-western-mass-has-major-costs

Johnson, J. E., Austin-Hillery, N., Clark, M., & Lu, L. (2010). *Racial disparities in federal prosecutions.* Brennan Center for Justice.

Joiner, L. L. (2004, November/December). The state of Black health. *The Crisis, 111*(6), 17–27.

Kahlenberg, R. D. (2017, August 3). The walls we won't tear down. *The New York Times*, www.nytimes .com/2017/08/03/opinion/sunday/zoning-laws-segregation-income.html

Kennedy, R. (2001). Racial trends in the administration of criminal justice. In N. J. Smelser, W. J. Wilson., & F. Mitchell (Eds.), *American becoming: Racial trends and their consequences* (Vol. 2, pp. 1–20). Washington, DC: National Academies Press.

Keyssor, A. (2020, August 3). How has the Electoral College survived for this long? *The New York Times.* www.nytimes.com/2020/08/03/opinion/electoral-college-racism-white-supremacy.html

Kingston, R. S., & Nickens, H. W. (2001). Racial and ethnic differences in health: Recent trends, current patterns, future directions. In N. J. Smelser, W. J. Wilson, & F. Mitchell (Eds.), *America becoming: Racial trends and their consequences* (Vol. 2, pp. 253–310). Washington, DC: National Academies Press.

Kivel, P. (2011). *Uprooting racism: How White people can work for racial justice* (3rd ed.). New Society Publishers.

Kochar, R., & Fry, R. (2014, December 12). *Wealth inequality has widened along racial, ethnic lines since end of Great Recession.* Pew Center for Social Research. www.pewresearch.org/fact-tank/2014/12/12/racial -wealth-gaps-great-recession/

Komar, B. (2003, January/February). Race, poverty and the digital divide. *Poverty & Race, 22*(1), 1–2, 5.

Krogstad, J. M. (2015). *114th Congress is most diverse ever.* Pew Research Center. www.pewresearch.org/fact -tank/2015/01/12/114th-congress-is-most-diverse-ever

LaFraniere, S., & Lehren, A. W. (2015, October 24). The disproportionate risks of driving while Black. The New York Times. www.nytimes.com/2015/10/25/us/racial-disparity-traffic-stops-driving-black .html?emc=eta1

Laub, J. (2000). Crime over the life course. *Poverty Research News, 4*(3), 4–7.

Leary, K. (1999). Passing, posing and "keeping it real." *Constellations, 6*(1), 85–96.

Lee, J., & Bean, F. D. (2007). Reinventing the color line: Immigration and America's new racial divide. *Social Forces, 86*(2), 561–586.

Lee, T. (2019, August 18). The wealth gap. *The New York Times Magazine, 83.* https://www.nytimes.com/ interactive/2019/08/14/magazine/racial-wealth-gap.html

Lerner, S. (2019). *A tale of two toxic cities: The EPA's bungled response to an air pollution crisis exposes a toxic racial divide.* The Intercept. https://theintercept.com/2019/02/24/epa-response-air-pollution-crisis -toxic-racial-divide/

Lewis, S. (2019, April 25). The racial bias built into photography. *The New York Times.* www.nytimes .com/2019/04/25/lens/sarah-lewis-racial-bias-photography.html?fallback=0&recId=1KdOGglpZn2t yDafeE74sJkikOi&locked=0&geoContinent=NA&geoRegion=MA&recAlloc=story&geoCountry=U S&blockId=home-featured&imp_id=278343739&action=click&module=editorContent&pgtype=A rticle&region=CompanionColumn&contentCollection=Trending

Lipscomb, A. E., & Ashley, W. (2017). Colorful disclosures: Identifying identity-based differences and enhancing critical consciousness in supervision. *Smith College Studies in Social Work, 87*(2/3), 220–237.

Logan, J. R., Oakley, D., & Stowell, J. (2003, September 1). *Segregation in neighborhoods and schools: Impacts on minority children in the Boston region.* Unpublished paper presented at Harvard Color Lines Conference, Boston, MA.

Logan, J. R., & Stults, B. J. (2011). *The persistence of segregation in the metropolis: New findings from the 2010 census (Census Brief prepared for Project US2010).* Brown University. https://s4.ad.brown.edu/Projects /Diversity/Data/Report/report2.pdf

Loomis, E. (2015). *Out of sight: The long and disturbing story of corporations outsourcing catastrophe.* The New Press.

Lopez, G. (2019, July 15). *Donald of Trump's long history racism from the 1970's to 2019.* Vox. www.vox .com/2016/7/25/12270880/donald-trump-racist-racism-history

Lu, Y. E., Landsverk, J., Ellis-Macleod, E., Newton, R., Ganger, W., & Johnson, I. (2004). Race, ethnicity and case outcomes in child protective services. *Children and Youth Services Review, 26,* 447–461.

Lukasiewicz, M. (Producer), & Harvey, E. (Director). (1991). *True colors [Video recording].* MTI Film and Video.

Manduca, R., & Sampson, R. J. (2019, April 16). Punishing and toxic neighborhood environments independently predict the intergenerational social mobility of black and white children. Proceedings of the National Academy of Scientists. https://doi.org/10.1073/pnas.1820464116

Manning, R. D. (1999). Poverty, race, and the two-tiered financial services system. *Poverty & Race, 8*(4), 1–2, 11.

Massey, D. S. (2001). Segregation and violent crime in urban America. In E. Anderson & D. Massey (Eds.), *Problem of the century: Racial stratification in the United States* (pp. 317–344). Russell Sage Foundation.

Massey, D. (2016). Residential segregation is the linchpin of racial stratification. *City Community*, https://doi.org/10.1111/cico.12145

McIlwain, C. D., & Caliendo, S. M. (2014). Mitt Romney's racist appeals: How race was played in the 2013 presidential election. *American Behavioral Scientist, 58*(9), 1157–1168.

McIntosh, K., Moss, E., Nunn, R., & Shambaugh, J. (2020, February 27). *Examining the Black-White wealth gap*. The Brookings Institute. www.brookings.edu/blog/up-front/2020/02/27/examining-the-black-white-wealth-gap/

McKernan, S. M., Ratcliffe, C., Steuerle, E., & Zhang, S. (2013, April). *Less than equal: Racial disparities in wealth accumulation*. The Urban Institute.

McLoyd, V. C., & Lozoff, B. (2001). Racial and ethnic trends in children's and adolescents' behavior and development. In N. J. Smelser, W. J. Wilson, & F. Mitchell (Eds.), *America becoming: Racial trends and their consequences* (Vol. 2, pp. 311–350). National Academies Press.

McPhate, M. (2015, December 11). Discrimination by Airbnb hosts is widespread, report says. *The New York Times*. www.nytimes.com/2015/12/12/business/discrimination-by-airbnb-hosts-is-widespread-report-says.html?emc=eta1

Michaelson, J. (2020, March 20). *What referendum? Florida GOP set to exclude up to 80% of felons from voting*. Daily Beast. www.thedailybeast.com/what-referendum-florida-gop-set-to-exclude-up-to-80-of-felons-from-voting

Mikelson, R.A. (2014). The problem of the color lines in twenty-first-century sociology of education: Researching and theorizing demographic change, segregation and school outcomes. *Social Currents, 1*(2), 157–165.

Miller, J. (1999). *Holyoke at the crossroads: Family, ethnicity and community in a de-industrialized small city* (pp. 277–286). Proceedings of the 13th Conference on the Small City and Regional Community, Stevens Point, WI: Center for the Small City.

Miller, J. (2001). Family and community integrity. *Journal of Sociology and Social Welfare, 28*(4), 23–44.

Miller, J. (2012). *Psychosocial capacity building in response to disasters*. Columbia University Press.

Miller, J., & Schamess, G. (2000). The discourse of denigration and the creation of other. *Journal of Sociology and Social Welfare, 27*(3), 39–62.

Mills, C. W. (1997). *The racial contract*. Cornell.

Minority Staff, Special Investigations Division, Committee on Government Reform, U.S House of Representatives. (2001, July 9). *Income and racial disparities in the undercount in the 2000 presidential election*. Washington, DC: U.S. House of Representatives.

Moore, K. K., Cid-Martinez, I., Toney, J., Smith, J. A., Kalb, A. C., Shin, J. H., & Spalter-Roth, R. M. (2018). Who climbs the academic ladder? Race and gender stratification in a world of whiteness. *The Review of Black Political Economy, 45*(3), 216–244.

Moreno, C. (2015, August 31). *9 outrageous things Donald Trump has said about Latinos*. The Huffington Post. www.huffingtonpost.com/entry/9-outrageous-things-donald-trump-has-said-about-latinos_us_55e483a1e4b0c818f618904b

Muhammad, D., Davis, A., Lui, M., & Leondar-Wright, B. (2004). *The state of the dream 2004: Enduring disparities in black and white*. United for a Fair Economy.

Newkirk II, V. R. (2020, April 2). *The Coronavirus' unique threat to the South*. The Atlantic. www.theatlantic.com/politics/archive/2020/04/coronavirus-unique-threat-south-young-people/609241/?fbclid=IwAR0wELjk2ifExUaGQEuVSCD6WOYu36gZPOQ-hm-ZDqqSezzIW3bJNueokJQ

Norton, M. I., & Sommers, S. R. (2011). Whites see racism as a zero-sum game that they are now losing. *Perspectives on Psychological Science, 6*, 215–218.

Ogunwole, S. U., Drewery Jr., M. P., & Rios-Vargas, M. (2012, May). The population with a bachelor's degree or higher by race and Hispanic origin, 2006–2010. In American Community Survey Briefs (ACSBR 10–19). Washington, DC: U.S. Census Bureau.

Oh, S. J., & Yinger, J. (2015). What have we learned from paired testing in housing markets? *Cityscape, 17*(3), 15–59.

Oliver, M. L., & Shapiro, T. M. (2013). Race, wealth, and equality. In M. Adams, W. J. Blumenfeld, R. Casteñeda, H. W. Hackman, M. L. Peters, & X. Zúñiga (Eds.), *Readings for diversity and social justice* (3rd ed., pp. 164–170). Routledge.

Omi, M., & Winant, H. (1994). *Racial formation in the United States: From the 1960s to the 1990s* (2nd ed.). Routledge.

Oppel Jr., R. A., Searcey, D., & Eligon, J. (2020). Black Americans face alarming rates of Coronavirus infection in some states. *The New York Times.* www.nytimes.com/2020/04/07/us/coronavirus-race .html?action=click&module=Top%20Stories&pgtype=Homepage

Pager, D., & Western, B. (2012). Identifying discrimination at work: The use of field experiments. *Journal of Social Issues, 68*(2), 221–237.

Park, H., Keller, J., & Williams, J. (2016, February 28). The faces of American power: Nearly as white as the Oscar nominees. *The New York Times.* www.nytimes.com/interactive/2016/02/26/us/race -of-american-power.html

Park, Y., & Miller, J. (2006). The social ecology of Hurricane Katrina: Rewriting the discourse of natural disasters. *Smith College Studies in Social Work, 76*(3), 9–24.

Patrick, J. J., Pious, R. M., & Ritchie, D. A. (2001). *The Oxford guide to the United States government.* Oxford University Press.

Pelletiere, D. (2005, May/June). House of cards: The state of Black housing. *The Crisis, 112*(3), 16–19.

Pinderhughes, E. (1989). *Understanding race, ethnicity, and power: The key to efficacy in clinical practice.* Free Press.

Poe-Yamagata, E., & Jones, M. A. (2000). *And justice for some.* Washington, DC: Building Blocks for Youth.

Polikoff, A. (2015). Housing mobility: Why is it so controversial? *Poverty and Race, 24*(4), 33–8.

Polikoff, A. (2004). Racial inequality and the black ghetto. *Poverty and Race, 13*(6), 1–2, 8–12.

Porter, E. (2020, April 13). Race/Related. *The New York Times.* https://messaging-custom-newsletters.nytimes. com/template/oakv2?campaign_id=37&emc=edit_rr_20200328&instance_id=17147&nl=race%2Frela ted&productCode=RR&regi_id=261671&segment_id=23179&te=1&uri=nyt%3A%2F%2Fnewsletter %2F564403ec-d7f4-4bc5-a962-745397b86820&user_id=c40644cf79330c01b71cc3ebdbcb62f9

Powell, J. A. (1999). Achieving racial justice: What's sprawl got to do with it? *Poverty & Race, 8*(5), 3–5.

Quintero-Somaini, A., & Quirindongo, M. (2004). *Hidden danger: Environmental health threats and the Latino community.* National Resources Defense Council.

Reinka, M. A., & Leach, C. W. (2017). Race and reaction: Divergent views of police violence and protest against. *Journal of Social Issues, 73*(4), 768–788. https://doi.org/10.1111/josi.12247

Renner, K. E., & Moore, T. (2004). The more things change, the more they stay the same: The elusive search for racial equity in higher education. *Analyses of Social Issues and Public Policy, 4*(1), 227–241.

Renzulli, L. A., Grant, L., & Kathuria, S. (2006). Race, gender, and the wage gap: Comparing faculty salaries in predominately White and historically Black colleges and universities. *Gender and Society, 20*(4), 491–510.

Ridley, C. R. (1995). *Overcoming unintentional racism in counseling and therapy.* Sage.

Rivas, C. (2020, July 13). I'm an actor of color. My curls are not wanted. *The New York Times.* www.nytimes .com/2020/07/13/opinion/hollywood-latinos-diversity.html?action=click&module=Opinion&pgtyp e=Homepage

Roberts, D. (2002). Racial harm: Dorothy Roberts explains how racism works in the child welfare system. *Color Lines, 5,* 19–20.

Roberts, S. (1995, June 18). The greening of America's Black middle class. *The New York Times, Sec. 4,* pp. 1, 4.

Robyn, L. (2002). Indigenous knowledge and technology: Creating environmental justice in the twenty-first century. *The American Indian Quarterly, 26*(2), 198–220.

Roman, I. (2003, June 10). *Study: Vieques cancer rates higher than Puerto Rico.* Orlando Sentinel. www.orlan dosentinel.com/news/os-xpm-2003-05-10-0305100194-story.html

Sabol, W. J., & Lynch, J. P. (1997). *Crime policy report: Did getting tough on crime pay?* Urban Institute.

Sadler, M. S., Correll, J., Park, B., & Judd, C. M. (2012). The world is not black and white: The decision to shoot in a multiethnic context. *Journal of Social Issues, 68*(2), 286–313.

Samuels, B. (2020, April 7). *Trump defends his mail-in ballot after calling vote-by-mail 'corrupt'.* The Hill. https://thehill.com/homenews/administration/491674-trump-defends-his-mail-in-ballot-after-calling-vote-by-mail-corrupt

Samuels, B. (2014). "Nowhere to live safe": Moving to peace and safety. *Poverty and Race, 23*(6), 1–2, 11.

Scott, K., Ma, D.S., Sadler, M.S., & Correll, J. (2017). A social scientific approach toward understanding racial disparities in police shooting: Data from the department of justice (1980–2000). *Journal of Social Issues, 73*(4), 701–722. https://doi.org/10.1111/josi.12243

Schmader, T., Major, B., & Gramzow, R. H. (2001). Coping with ethnic stereotypes in the academic domain: Perceived injustice and psychological disengagement. *Journal of Social Issues, 57*(1), 93–111.

Sehgal, P. (2016, February 2). Fighting erasure. *The New York Times.* www.nytimes.com/2016/02/07/magazine/the-painful-consequences-of-erasure.html?emc=eta1

Sengupta, S. (2000, November 3). Felony costs voting rights for a lifetime in 9 states. *The New York Times,* A18.

Sentencing Project. (2004, May). *New prison figures demonstrate need for comprehensive reform.* Washington, DC: Author.

Shapiro, T. M. (2004). *The hidden cost of being African American: How wealth perpetuates inequality.* Oxford University Press.

Shipler, D. (1997). *A country of strangers: Blacks and Whites in America.* Knopf.

Simson, E. (2002). *Justice denied: How felony disenfranchisement laws undermine American democracy.* Washington, DC: Americans for Democratic Action Education Fund.

Solorzano, D., Ceja, M., & Yosso, T. (2000). Critical race theory, racial microaggressions, and campus racial climate: The experiences of African American college students. *Journal of Negro Education, 69*(1/2), 60–73.

Sosina, V. E., & Weathers, E. S. (2019). Pathways to inequality: Between-district segregation and racial disparities in school expenditures. *AERA Open, 5*(3), 1–15. https://doi.org/10.1177/2332858419872445

Steele, C. (2011). *Whistling Vivaldi: How stereotypes affect us and what we can do.* W. W. Norton.

Steinberg, S. (2001). *The ethnic myth: Race, ethnicity and class in America* (3rd ed.). Beacon Press.

Steinhorn, L., & Diggs-Brown, B. (1999, November/December). By the color of our skin: The illusion of integration and the reality of race. *Poverty & Race, 8*(6), 1–5.

Stevenson, B. (2019, August 18). *Mass incarceration. The New York Times* Magazine, 81.

Stoll, M. A. (2004). *African Americans and the color line.* Russell Sage Foundation.

Stroub, K. J., & Richards, M. P. (2013). From resegregation to reintegration trends in the racial/ethnic segregation of metropolitan public schools, 1993–2009. *American Educational Research Journal, 50*(3), 497–531.

Sullivan, M. (1989). *Getting paid: Youth, crime and work in the inner city.* Cornell University Press.

Summerfield, D. (2004). Cross-cultural perspectives on the medicalization of human suffering. In G. Rosen (Ed.), *Posttraumatic stress disorder: Issues and controversies* (pp. 233–247). Wiley.

Takaki, R. (1993). *A different mirror: A history of multi-cultural America.* Little, Brown.

Tavernise, S., & Oppel Jr., R.A. (2020, April 10). Spit on, yelled at: Chinese citizens fear for their safety. *The New York Times.* www.nytimes.com/2020/03/23/us/chinese-coronavirus-racist-attacks.html?campaign_id=37&emc=edit_rr_20200411&instance_id=17561&nl=race%2Frelated&regi_id=261671&segment_id=24776&te=1&user_id=c40644cf79330c01b71cc3ebdbcb62f9

Taylor, D. B. (2020, April 14). For Black men, fear that masks will invite racial profiling. *The New York Times,* https://www.nytimes.com/2020/04/14/us/coronavirus-masks-racism-african-americans.html?action=click&module=News&pgtype=Homepage

Tervalon, M., & Murray-Garcia, J. (1998). Cultural humility versus cultural competence: A critical distinction in defining physician training outcomes in multicultural education. *Journal of Health Care for the Poor and Underserved, 9*(2), 117–125.

The New York Times. (2016, March 25). The racism at the heart of Flint's crisis. www.nytimes.com/2016/03/25 /opinion/the-racism-at-the-heart-of-flints-crisis.html?emc=eta1

The New York Times. (2018, April 14). Blacks still face a red line on housing. Author. www.nytimes .com/2018/04/14/opinion/blacks-still-face-a-red-line-on-housing.htm

The New York Times. (2020, March 31). The Coronavirus does not care where you come from: Trump still does. Author. www.nytimes.com/2020/03/31/opinion/immigration-coronavirus-border.html

Thompson, M., & Sekaquaptewa, D. (2002). When being different is detrimental: Solo status and the performance of women and racial minorities. *Analysis of Social Issues and Public Policy*, 2(1), 183–203.

Tilly, C. (1998). *Durable inequality*. University of California Press.

U.S. Bureau of Labor Statistics. (2016, September). Labor force characteristics by race and ethnicity, 2015. (BLS Report 1062). Washington, DC: Author.

Urban League. (2004). *The state of Black America*. Author.

Vandewalker, I. (2015). Outside spending, dark money dominate toss-up Senate races. In D. R. Reiner, J. Lyons, E. Opsal, M. Terrell, & L. Glaser (Eds.), *Democracy and justice: Collected writings* (Vol. *VIII*, pp. 15–17). Brennan Center for Social Justice.

van Dijik, T. A. (1995). Elite discourse and the reproduction of racism. In R.K. Whillock & D. Slayden (Eds.), *Hate speech* (pp. 1–27). Sage.

Villarosa, L. (2019, August 18). *Medical inequality. The New York Times* Magazine, 57.

Villarosa, L. (2020, July 28). Pollution is killing Black Americans: This community fought back. *The New York Times Magazine*. www.nytimes.com/2020/07/28/magazine/pollution-philadelphia-black -americans.html

Wade, J. C. (1993). Institutional racism: An analysis of the mental health system. *American Journal of Orthopsychiatry*, 63(4), 536–544.

Waldman, M. (2015). How the Supreme Court made a mess of our voting system. In D. R. Reiner, J. Lyons, E. Opsal, M. Terrell, & L. Glaser (Eds.), *Democracy and justice: Collected writings* (Vol. *VIII*, pp. 10–14). Brennan Center for Social Justice.

Walsh, M. W. (2000, September 3). Where G.E. falls short: Diversity at the top *The New York Times*, Sec. 3, p. 1.

Weiser, W. (2015). What difference did voting restrictions make in 2014's close races? In D. R. Reiner, J. Lyons, E. Opsal, M. Terrell, & L. Glaser (Eds.), *Democracy and justice: Collected writings 2014* (Vol. *VIII*, pp. 18–19), Brennan Center for Social Justice.

Weiser, W., & Opsal, E. (2015). The state of voting in 2014. In D. R. Reiner, J. Lyons, E. Opsal, M. Terrell, & L. Glaser (Eds.), *Democracy and justice: Collected writings* (Vol. *VIII*, pp. 6–9). Brennan Center for Social Justice.

Weitzer, R., & Tuch, S. A. (2004). Race and perceptions of police misconduct. *Social Problems*, 51(3), 305–325.

Western, B. (2001). Incarceration, unemployment and inequality. *Focus*, 22(3), 32–36.

Westin, A. (2001). The color of ratings. *Brill's Content*, 4(3), 82–85, 129–131.

Whillock, R. K. (1995). The use of hate as a stratagem for achieving political and social goals. In R. K. Whillock & D. Slayden (Eds.), *Hate speech* (pp. 28–54). Sage.

Williams, D. R. (2001). Racial variations in adult health status: Patterns, paradoxes, and prospects. In N. J. Smelser, W. J. Wilson, & F. Mitchell (Eds.), *America becoming: Racial trends and their consequences* (Vol. 2, pp. 371–410). National Academies Press.

Wilson, W. J. (1987). *The truly disadvantaged: The inner-city, the underclass and public policy*. University of Chicago.

Wilson, W. J. (2011). *When work disappears: The world of the new urban poor*. Vintage.

Wines, M., & Fernandez, M. (2016, May 1). Stricter rules for voter IDs reshape races. *The New York Times*. www.nytimes.com/2016/05/02/us/stricter-rules-for-voter-ids-reshape-races.html?emc=eta1

Woody, D. J., & Green, R. (2001). The influence of race/ethnicity and gender on psychological well-being. *Journal of Ethnic and Cultural Diversity in Social Work*, 9(3/4), 151–166.

Yankah, E. N. (2016, February 9). When addiction has a White face. *The New York Times*. www.nytimes .com/2016/02/09/opinion/when-addiction-has-a-white-face.html?emc=eta1

Yinger, J. (2000). Housing discrimination and residential segregation as causes of poverty. *Focus*, 21(2), 51–55.

Zeskind, L. (2012). A nation dispossessed: The Tea Party movement and race. *Critical Sociology*, 38(4), 495–509.

CHAPTER 6

Why Is It So Difficult for People With Privilege to See Racism?

INTRODUCTION

Thus far, we have considered what racism is, its lengthy and central place in the history of this nation, and the pervasive web of institutional racism today. People of color often face racism daily. It is important to describe pervasive, enduring, and measurable racism, which has been statistically documented and consistently confirmed by research. Even so, most White people (and some people of color who have sufficient privilege to buffer them from the onslaught of racism) believe that racism is essentially a thing of the past. Bobo (2001) cites the Los Angeles Survey of Urban Inequality, conducted in 1994, which found that slightly more than 20% of Whites believe that discrimination prevents Blacks and Hispanics from getting good-paying jobs, whereas 65% to 70% of Blacks and Hispanics believe they face such discrimination. Further, as was mentioned in the previous chapter, most Whites think that so-called "reverse racism" is a bigger problem than racism (Norton & Sommers, 2011). How is this possible?

In this chapter, we discuss how one of the most verdant elements of the coloniality of power, White supremacy, allows for the existence of White privilege. White hegemony and racism have become so "normal" and central in our society that, for those with race privilege or partial race privilege, it is accepted as the way things are—as familiar as the air one breathes. It shapes the streets people walk down, the neighborhoods they live in, the offices where they work, the food sold in supermarkets and who sells it, the news people watch, and the characters and stories in television shows, books, and films. White supremacy is the "invisible knapsack" that contains, fodders, and harbors the various aspects of race privilege that White people carry (Leonardo, 2004).

Focusing on White privilege without the examination of White dominance advances a narrative that colludes with the oppressor's version of history, conceals the agents of domination and masks the transparency of whose actions are harmful to whom. In other words, centering the understanding of privilege on the advantages White people receive instead of the appropriation suffered by people of color allows for the actions of such agents to be overlooked (Leonardo, 2004). The lacunae which exist in the face of this privilege are reinforced by a constant public "discourse of denigration" toward people of color and treating them as an "other," while producing narratives that manage to both deny and justify racism. Also, if White privilege were truly to be recognized, intrinsic to its process and persistence is the existence and function of White domination and White supremacy. This connection is often difficult for White people to concede. Such admission and conscious declaration challenges the discourse around White privilege from an emphasis on the unearned advantages that White people are afforded, without their asking for them, to the ongoing domination they have as a result of the coloniality of power. It is critical that people's awareness includes how the current day power relations were created not only through individual acts of bias, prejudice, or hate, but primarily through a historical process that strategically and intentionally created sub-human categories for racial groups of color. White dominance created these sub-human categories which constructed and allowed for the socially unjust treatment of people of color while deeming White people's humanity to be universal. The source of racial privilege is White supremacy and domination. This symbiotic relationship cannot be postscript when discussing White privilege as it undergirds an abstruse system of racism that permeates our world.

This denial and obfuscation of racism is encoded in the mental and cognitive maps that people use to navigate their social worlds—maps that shade and distort reality so that racism is barely a shadow or a whisper, maps that make it difficult for many well-meaning and well-intentioned White human service workers to accept the extent of racism that some of their clients experience or to recognize how they themselves have benefited from race privilege. Acknowledging that they have unearned racial advantages they did not ask for is easier than to consciously accept their role—even if unintentional—in a process that continues to maintain White domination and its product, White privilege.

CONSCIOUSNESS

Understanding the nature of consciousness is an ongoing human quest that perhaps never will be completed successfully. But recent progress in neurobiological imaging and advances in our knowledge about how the human brain works have generated new hypotheses and understandings about consciousness. Damasio (2000) persuasively speculated that consciousness has two essential components: (a) an awareness of self as an actor who is both the author and reader of any narratives that constitute consciousness and self-awareness, and (b) an awareness of "objects" outside of ourselves that impinge on us and modify and alter how we think and feel. Thus, we have a sense of ourselves as actors and of objects (and people) outside of us; and consciousness involves a secondary, meta-awareness of the interaction of self and other and the resulting transformations.

If we apply this model to consciousness about race and racism, it helps to explain why people of color are more aware of racism than White people. People of color have three advantages with race consciousness:

1. They are more likely to have an ongoing racial self-awareness.
2. They are highly aware of the social world outside of them and how it can encroach upon them.
3. They are more likely to have greater empathy for all people because they are less likely to suffer from implicit bias toward others (Ojiaku, 2016).

Consequently, people of color are more likely to be aware of racism and themselves as racial actors.[1] White people can move through the world believing that they are deracinated, that they are just people, or USAmericans, but with little core awareness of being White and what that means in this society. This means that White people can view themselves as individuals rather than as members of groups whose identities are imposed on them by society (Groot & Marcus, 1998). White writers can think of themselves as USAmerican writers and not have to respond to assumptions that they are writing White books for White people because of their race, but writers of color often are seen as being Black writers, or Latinx writers, or Chinese American writers. At the same time, there is often a differential response to works of literature by authors of color. A recent publication of a book called *American Dirt* (2020) by author Jeannine Cummins sparked a maelstrom among literary critics and authors. The book is about a middle-class Mexican woman and her young son who flee Mexico to escape the threat of violence caused by drug cartels. Although Jeannine Cummins acknowledges having a Puerto Rican grandmother, she identifies as White. Some questioned the legitimacy of her characters and their experiences, but the largest outcry was about the value that was placed on her work because of her White identity. Several Latinx authors have written about the harrowing events of border crossings and undocumented immigration but none had received so much attention and such high accolades. Such acts of appropriation are not new. When Harriet Beecher Stowe wrote *Uncle Tom's Cabin*, the works of Frederick Douglass were largely ignored and criticized by White readers. It was when a White, socially well-established woman wrote about the immorality of slavery that other Whites felt compelled to take a stand. Among Whites, there is an assumed confidence and ownership not only of having a dominant identity in society (Wenger, 2013) but also of the nondominant identities of others.

Let us explore this a bit further. If a White person grows up in a predominantly White suburb, attends a predominantly White school, encounters mostly White teachers and administrators, sees mostly White actors on television and in films—who for the most part are not portrayed as negative stereotypes or deviant—there is little dissonance between their positive sense of self and the world they experience. Whether people of color grow up in a racially or ethnically homogenous neighborhood or in a predominantly White neighborhood, they are likely to come up against racism that is at odds with their positive sense of self. Children of color who grow up in a predominantly White neighborhood most likely encounter racial stereotypes and slurs from other children, interact with mostly White teachers and administrators, and observe that students of color have higher detention, suspension, and expulsion rates and are saddled with lower expectations. White people are in the majority and experience no disconnect between who they are and what they are surrounded by. The ideology of White supremacy, the cultural frameworks, and assumptions that mediate between people and institutions can be taken for granted (Ferber, 2012).

If children of color grow up in a racially homogenous neighborhood, it is more likely to be poor, and the schools probably will have significantly fewer resources than those in White neighborhoods. These children are more likely to have had negative encounters with the police, many of whom are White. People of color, when watching television news, will find people of their color largely absent from some stories and featured stereotypically in others. This will be true of other media as well.

In Damasio's (2000) theory of consciousness, he also asserts that people strive toward a homeostatic state when they encounter outside influences that stir them up. It follows that people of color will be more aware of the salience of their race and how this can threaten their well-being in a racist society. Race is more likely to be on the radar screen of their consciousness. Meanwhile, White people will encounter less dissonance between their race and their social world and experience less disequilibrium, so they likely will not have to be conscious of their race constantly. If they do experience discomfort, it is often due to being confronted with their White privilege and often experience feelings of confusion, guilt, or shame, which can lead to attempts to reset their equilibrium through strategies such as withdrawing from discourses about race, becoming angry at those who draw attention to issues of race, dismissing accounts of racism, or blaming and deprecating the victims of racism. White people may become angry when confronted with racism and White privilege, as this conflicts with the notion of "color blindness," that racism is a thing of the past, that people earn jobs and other resources through their effort, skill, and talent, not because of the persistence of racism and White privilege (Ferber, 2012). In truth, in a racialized society, no one can escape a racial discourse, but people of color are more likely to recognize this.

   Much of our consciousness has been formed by our interactions with individuals, families, groups, and the larger societal structure. The messages we carry on a subconscious level are derived from these interactions. Since these messages are, for the most part, not overtly relayed, many people are unaware that they hold subliminal attitudes, ideas, values for or against different social groups. An individual may recognize that people are treated differently but not be curious about why. What is needed is an understanding of the larger social forces that create, maintain, and perpetuate White supremacy and racism. Freire (1996) describes this ability to perceive and analyze the influence of oppressive social structures on an individual's lived experience. Critical consciousness is also understood as the development of critical awareness of personal dynamics in social and political situations (Freire, 1996).

INVISIBLE KNAPSACKS OF PRIVILEGE

One of the best metaphors for illuminating the cognitive challenges that White people face in regard to racism was coined by McIntosh (1989, 1992). She described how Whites carry an "invisible knapsack" of White privilege. As a White woman, she drew an analogy from her frustrations with males who are taught not to recognize their gender privilege, and realized that she had learned to ignore her race privilege. White people carry race privilege as "an invisible weightless knapsack of special provisions, maps, passports, codebooks, visas, clothes, tools, and blank checks" (1989, p. 10).

This invisible knapsack has been available to White people since the inception of this country, the implicit racial contract upon which the nation was founded (Mills, 1997). The "special provisions" have been encoded into laws from the outset, when White people were granted citizenship and this right was denied to people of color (Lopez, 1996). The social construction of Whiteness was reaffirmed consistently and reinterpreted by U.S. courts, which had a profound influence on who could enter this country and what rights they were afforded if they did get in (Lopez, 1996).

McIntosh (1992) listed up to 46 examples of the knapsack's provisions. Here is a sample:

▶ To be able to consistently arrange to be in the company of people of your own race; this would not be true of a person of color working in a mostly White office.

- ▶ To be able to move to live in whatever neighborhood you could afford.
- ▶ To not be followed when shopping.
- ▶ To see yourself widely (and for the most part positively) represented in the media.
- ▶ To be taught that people of your race had created a civilized democracy.
- ▶ To not consistently have to prove your creditworthiness (such as when shopping) because of your race.
- ▶ To not have to protect your children from racism.
- ▶ To not be considered a "credit to your race" when you excel.
- ▶ To not be viewed as representing or speaking for your racial group.
- ▶ To not have to worry if stopped by the police or if audited by the IRS because of your race.
- ▶ To find greeting cards, dolls, and toys depicting people who look like you.
- ▶ To see that "flesh-colored" adhesive bandages more or less correspond to the color of your skin.
- ▶ To be able to be late for a meeting without it reflecting on your race.

McIntosh could have added: to have your way of speaking assumed to be the correct way and not to have your speech monitored (Hill, 1999). Or if reading literary histories of postwar American poets, finding that most if not all feature White poets, thereby "erasing" many Black poets (Michael Thurston, personal communication). Ultimately, these privileges allow White people to feel "more at home in the world," better about themselves, and to "escape penalties or dangers that others suffer" (McIntosh, 1992, p. 76).

Why does this knapsack remain so invisible? There are many possible reasons, and understanding them might help human service professionals to work more effectively against racism. Many pressures and social and psychological forces combine to minimize the visibility of White privilege. Deconstructing White privilege threatens the ideals and myths about this nation that many take for granted; it challenges the notion of meritocracy and equal opportunity, which are cornerstones of democracy (McIntosh, 1992; Miller & Schamess, 2000). Acknowledging White privilege is at odds with the world that many White people think that they inhabit. Examining White privilege can threaten a person's sense of self—the belief that they are a good person who does not condone nor collude with racism.

McIntosh (1992, p. 76) believes that the knapsack remains invisible because of the erroneous assumption that its contents are "neutral, normal and universally available to everybody." This view echoes the myth that racism results from individual acts, perpetrated by bad people, and not from a web of systemic privilege. This is part of a liberal ideology infused with abstract concepts, such as equality or color blindness, or "realistic" justifications about how this is the way that the world is, or a belief in cultural and social differences between racial groups (rather than institutional advantages and disadvantages) that explains inequality (Bonilla-Silva, 2009).

Another factor that we and others (Goodman, 2011; Kaufman, 2001; Wenger, 2013) have noticed is that many, if not most, White people do not feel powerful. Actually, many feel disempowered because of their gender, social class, sexual orientation, religion, and personal misfortunes and tragedies, so there is resistance to assuming the mantle of race privilege. Our adaptation of Damasio's (2000) theory of consciousness illustrates that it is often easier to be aware of how advantages are structured when we feel disempowered because we do not have passports of privilege.

SOCIALIZATION INTO WHITE PRIVILEGE

To further our understanding of why the knapsack remains so invisible, we should examine ways by which we are all socialized into a racialized society, founded on the racial contract and structured by the web and discourse of racism. To paraphrase antiracism activist Andrea Ayvazian (personal communication, July 27, 1993), it is in the air we breathe, and we all need to breathe. And as with air, it seems normal and taken for granted that many Americans live in virtually segregated communities or attend segregated schools; it is the known world.

Thus, by as early as age 4, White children have begun to internalize a sense of White racial superiority (Group for the Advancement of Psychiatry [GAP], 1987). By adolescence, teenagers are forging their identities, which are closely related to their sense of who is inside and outside of their group. Thus, one's group identity is associated with a sense of privilege and superiority.

In her book *Why Are All the Black Kids Sitting Together in the Cafeteria?* Tatum (2017) considered this process and what it is like for students of color who are minorities in predominantly White environments. Sitting together can reflect a need for students of color to bond, support a positive sense of identity, and buffer themselves from the stresses and wounds of racism, as well as be a response to being considered devalued out-group members for many White students. Here we consider the role of the family in socializing White people into taking their race privilege for granted.

THE ROLE OF THE FAMILY

Families are nested in the racialized society that we have been describing. The relationship between family and community is reciprocal, and to completely filter out societal racism from the family is difficult if not impossible. Society and community provide parameters for what families can and cannot access, such as safe streets and superior schools, and they influence how families think by offering discursive narratives about the meaning of living in this society. Families and communities have a profound influence over our development and daily lives, instilling us with values, sorting out what is normal and abnormal, and defining what is possible and impossible (Miller, 2001). Many of the inner maps that we carry to orient ourselves to the world are minted by our families.

Families have explanatory systems, internal to the family system although strongly influenced by systems external to the family (e.g., families of origin, workplaces, ethnic groups, churches, the media), which become a shared meaning-making process to interpret (or misinterpret) the world (Reiss, 1981). This is important to keep in mind when we consider the nature of stereotypes in the following. According to Reiss (1981), these explanatory systems form "naive psychologies," in that they are subjective and often untested and uncontested, but they are experienced as being truthful and objective maps of the world. When naive psychologies are carried outside of the family, they are liable to clash with different or contradictory explanatory systems or may be inadequate to explain phenomena outside of the family. This can lead to confusion and a state of disequilibrium, a form of cognitive dissonance.

People strive toward explanatory systems that reduce internal tension and maintain equilibrium (Ferber, 2012). Allport (1948, 1954) considered ways by which White people deal with the tension caused by discord due to being confronted by racism. One of the strategies that he identifies is to "re-fence," to explain the difference as an exception without changing the explanatory system. A classic example is the White person whose explanatory system orients them to believe that African Americans do not work as hard as White people, yet one African American work colleagues is a hard worker. This person might "re-fence" by concluding that the colleague is an exception and is not like "those people," while the prejudiced belief system remains in place. Another way of dealing with the tension caused by racial cognitive dissonance is to blame victims for their own misfortune, which is consistent with and contributes to derogatory public discourses.

For people of color, the process also is one of dissonance between family explanatory systems and the outside world, although for different reasons. From their parents and extended families, children of color learn explanatory systems about their self-worth and value. Some families attempt to prepare their children for the racism they are likely to encounter and also provide strategies for responding to it. Even if forewarned, however, most people of color are unprepared for the magnitude, depth, and persistence of racism. This leads to an even greater consciousness about how society devalues people and does not treat them fairly or equally by virtue of race and ethnicity. It also can cause strong emotional reactions, such as anger, rage, despair, sorrow, estrangement, isolation, and confusion. To be the "other" in a discourse of denigration is a particularly uncomfortable and alienating feeling.

THE DISCOURSE OF DENIGRATION AND THE CREATION OF OTHER

The matrix of coloniality was not only central in instituting the racial contract, the web of racism, and White privilege, it also established the categories of "Being" and "non-Being" (Grosfoguel, 2013). Such categorizations coalesce in a public discourse of denigration and creation of "other" (Miller & Schamess, 2000). Most societies project an image of fairness, particularly if the society views itself as a beacon of democracy for the world. And members of society want to feel good about their country because this also makes them feel better about themselves (Brewer, 2001). Thus, a discourse that emphasizes a nation's greatness, magnanimity, generosity of spirit, and commitment to equal justice serves to enhance both social stability and collective self-esteem. Citizens feel proud about being members of a compassionate, just, and great nation. Often, such a discourse emphasizes the unique nature or character of a nation, such as "manifest destiny."

So, if there is dissonance between the narrative and reality, how is this resolved? How do citizens who are proud of their country reconcile slavery, annihilation, exclusion, subjugation, and a pervasive system of race privilege? If feelings of confusion, guilt, or even shame are present, how are these expressed or resolved?

Renounced Targets

One psychological strategy, be it individual or collective, is to have "common renounced targets" (GAP, 1987; Kaufman, 2001; Volkan, 1988). These become receptacles for projections of what is too painful or conflictual for an individual, or society, to tolerate. These unacceptable aspects of self or society are passed on to individuals or groups who are denigrated and fulfill the role of "other." It is a psychological mechanism that leads to blaming the victim and exonerating the beneficiaries of racism. Thus, politicians will extol the virtues and greatness of a nation while directly or implicitly targeting subgroups within a society for commendation. Donald Trump has been a master of this process. They craft a discourse that elevates the country in the face of discrimination and unearned race privilege, connecting some people to its success and greatness and enhancing collective self-esteem while marginalizing and denigrating others. As Coates (2015) has argued, it is not an accident or unintended consequence that so many African American men are in prison; it is the result of deliberate public policy. Providing similar disparities is the disproportionate number of African American deaths from COVID-19 pandemic. Laughland and Zanolli (2020) draw the despairing conclusion that, "[i]n 2020, COVID-19 has begun to divide the country between those ready to explore the structural racism ingrained in America's public health outcomes, and those who are not." Public policies that affect contextual conditions such as education, child care, employment, housing, and transportation (known as social determinants of health) are largely responsible for racial health inequities (Adler & Rehkopf, 2008). These policies, with their supporting public narratives, enact and encode White superiority and the deviance and marginality of many people of color (Higginbotham, 2013).

As individuals, we also construct discourses about our lives, authoring stories of ourselves, which are revised and rescripted (Bruner, 1990). Because we want to feel good about ourselves, we will go to great lengths to avoid censure and blame (Douglas, 1995), including self-criticism. Then, when confronted with unearned privilege or complicity in the oppression of others, particularly when we view ourselves as good, nonprejudiced, well-meaning people, we tend to split off those parts of ourselves that are incompatible with our self-narrative and project them onto denigrated targets (GAP, 1987; Miller & Schamess, 2000; Volkan, 1988). The targets and victims of racism become the problem: They are "lazy," "demanding," "overly sensitive when it comes to race," or "playing the race card." (In the past, the terms were *inferior, savage, and subhuman.*) This process occurs on all levels—intrapersonally, interpersonally, between groups, and on community and national levels. It serves to strengthen social cohesion and makes those who are not targeted feel better about themselves.

Triangulation

Bowen's (1976) concept of "triangulation" furthers our understanding of this process. In triangulation, two parties (individual or groups) join together against a third party, which brings the two groups together at the expense of the scapegoat. It is a way to reduce or oversimplify complex reality and can lead to an "emotional cutoff" from the pain and suffering of the scapegoated party, who is held responsible for their social oppression. When it comes to race, it is a process that allows people and groups with race privilege to come together to feel good about themselves, denying any gains or benefits from their race while lacking empathy for those facing racial discrimination.

Conversely, when people of color are confronted with an unfair society, such as a biased school or organization, they can, in turn, psychologically disengage, resulting in less investment in systems where they are experiencing the hypocrisy of racism, or from society at large (Schmader et al., 2001). Ironically, this self-affirming and protecting response then becomes the target of criticism from White people—"Why do they always hang out together?"—and further reinforces the sense that people of color are too sensitive about race and racism.

For people of color, such disengagement can be part of a process of shedding and disowning an imposed, falsely negative identity and developing a positive identity—an act of rebellion and self-empowerment. But it also can lead to disengagement, alienation, and even self-destructive and oppositional behavior—such as what Dr. Richard Majors termed the "cool pose" of young African American men, creating the illusion of control in the face of severe environmental threats (Goleman, 1992). The aforementioned manifests itself in internalized stereotypes which must be recognized and responded to.

STEREOTYPES AND WHAT CAN BE DONE ABOUT THEM

We all harbor stereotypes. Stereotypes are a set of beliefs and cognitions about the characteristics of members of a social group (Bobo, 2001). Some are positive, but many are derogatory. They stem from our need to generalize and form categories as we navigate the world. Stereotypes about other people do not evolve in a vacuum. They reflect social structures, cultural norms, and public discourses about ethnic and racial groups, informing attitudes and guiding behaviors, while also staking out social boundaries. So, in our racialized society, stereotypes have been used to discredit the victims of racism and to justify their mistreatment and social exclusion, masking privilege and unequal and unfair access to resources.

As with "naive psychologies," those who hold stereotypes often assume them to be objective truths rather than subjective prejudices. They appear as fixed reference points and involve group generalizations. They go beyond merely being cognitive constructions, drawing on deep emotions while operating as programs filtering what we see and how we make meaning of what we perceive. They often are unconscious and can be at odds with our conscious values and beliefs. In fact, people who view themselves as valuing equity and justice are often more vulnerable to unconscious stereotypes *because* they do not align with their conscious values (Banaji & Greenwald, 2013). Although all people harbor stereotypes, they are particularly damaging when supported by power and group dominance, as they then go beyond personal attitudes and justify and reinforce societal oppression.

One form of stereotyping, known as "group attribution theory" (Brewer, 2001), involves giving people in your own group the benefit of the doubt when they encounter misfortune while blaming members outside of your group for their travails. An example of this would be if a White person knows of another White person receiving public assistance (welfare) and assumes that the recipient encountered some bad luck or was treated unfairly by the economy while believing that when a person of color collects the same benefit, that recipient is lazy or manipulating the system. Racialized attitudes such as these are shaped by segregation and family explanatory systems, and inflamed by media depictions and discourses.

Gillens (1999) found that newspaper editors and television producers, who were mostly White, helped to manufacture deprecating stereotypes about African Americans and welfare, thereby influencing the White public to become unsupportive and antagonistic to the social value of offering such assistance to families in need. This undoubtedly contributed to survey results in the mid-1990s, which found that between 65% and 70% of Whites believed that Blacks and Hispanics preferred welfare to working (Bobo, 2001). Similarly it was difficult for President Obama's administration to convince states that voted for Mitt Romney in the 2012 presidential election to establish healthcare exchanges as part of the Affordable Care Act (ACA; Jones et al., 2014). Research on White racial attitudes and resistance to the ACA indicate that there is a strong correlation between White racial resentment to African Americans receiving government-supported health benefits and lack of support for the ACA (Maxwell & Shields, 2014).

Sources of Resistance

We discussed earlier the cognitive dissonance or emotional conflict that can result from confronting evidence about one's unearned privilege or the pervasiveness of racism in society. Stereotypes can allay the tension caused by cognitive contradictions and emotional discomfort because they relieve the holder of responsibility, projecting culpability for misfortune onto those who are oppressed. It follows that White people need not feel guilty about social inequality or the benefits of race privilege if they rationalize that they worked hard for what they have achieved and that people of color have not tried hard enough (an example of group attribution theory). This is one reason that people resist challenges to their stereotypes.

If stereotypes are at odds with people's conscious view of themselves, or with their values and principles, they may feel shame or discomfort about actually holding a stereotype and, therefore, attempt to deny or suppress it. If White people view themselves as enlightened, liberal, fair, and lacking prejudice, a recurring negative stereotype about people of color can be disturbing if it is recognized. It can cause an identity crisis, leading a person to try to stifle the stereotype as it challenges their positive self-identity.

This can be problematic, as the stereotype is still operating but now below the radar screen of self-awareness. For people of color, holding stereotypes—particularly if they are about their own group or other groups of color—can be unsettling when they also have been on the receiving end of such distortions.

Resistance to examining and challenging stereotypes is stiffened further by the source of many stereotypes—trusted, respected, even beloved relatives, friends, teachers, and colleagues. Confronting stereotypes can cause us to lose faith in people we have believed and relied on and can lead to our feeling alienated from important relationships. Even acknowledging stereotypes, then, can cause an identity crisis, casting a flawed light on essential people in our lives as well as on ourselves.

DiAngelo (2018), in her book *White Fragility*, presents ways to understand the defensive and emotional processes race-privileged individuals go through when confronted with their stereotypes and distortions. Since Whites have been socialized to believe in their superiority, any challenge made to their world views can be experienced as a threat to the perception they have of themselves as a morally good person. Such stress, particularly related to their White racial identity is uncommon and as a result can trigger unfamiliar feelings of anxiety and disease. DiAngelo (2018) writes that this fragility to discomfort "is born out of superiority and entitlement…it is not a weakness per se [but] a powerful means of white racial control and the protection of white advantage." She explains how emotions such as anger, guilt, and fear often result from the lack of critical consciousness Whites have around race and also from unwillingness of Whites to unsettle the status quo our society has around race. Wanting to avoid conversations as a result of both or either of these reasons people with race privilege often defer to silence as a way to manage their uncertainty, fear, and discomfort. Remaining silent on the subject of race, in turn, blocks racial dialogue and prohibits them from developing their own critical consciousness.

While White defensiveness and avoidance can be understood as behaviors in which Whites engage in order to manage their anxiety, guilt and/or fear, it is imperative that we acknowledge how this colludes with oppressive systems and continues to put people of color at risk. A clear example of this is the behavior of Amy Cooper, a White woman on May 26, 2020 as she was asked by Christian Cooper, a Black man to put her dog on a leash, as she was in an area of Central Park where this was required. Upon his request, Ms. Cooper becomes agitated, walks toward Mr. Cooper and asks him to stop recording her. When he asks her not to come close to him, Ms. Cooper states, "Then I am taking a picture and calling the cops" to which Mr. Cooper replies "Please call the cops." Amy Cooper takes out her phone and says, "I am going to tell them there is African American man threatening my life." Ms. Cooper does just that. She contacts the police, gives her location and states that "There is an African American man who is recording me and threatening myself and my dog." As she continues her voice becomes more frantic, as she uses her emotions as a weapon. While Amy Cooper may have felt fear and anger, her actions demonstrated how White privilege can intentionally be used to put a Black man in danger of being killed. Acknowledging her overt racism would have required Ms. Cooper to reckon with her White privilege and fragility. Albeit often unconscious, there is a certain awareness that individuals like Amy Cooper have been socialized to possess: that they are "good," their lives are worth saving, they will be believed.

Consequences of Unexamined Stereotypes

One of the greatest risks of unacknowledged stereotypes is that rather than being reflected upon, they will be acted out, often in ways that are unconscious but having the potential to wound and harm others. They are the source of implicit racism, aversive racism, and racial microaggressions. They contribute to racial anxiety and stereotype threat (Godsil, 2015). Figure 6.1 illustrates this process.

Implicit and Aversive Racism

Implicit racism is when there are unconscious negative racial beliefs that shape attitudes and behaviors held by people who consciously espouse egalitarian racial values (Banaji & Greenwald, 2013). Implicit racism is measured by implicit association tests (IATs), which examine associations among pictures, names, actions, and emotions. This test has demonstrated that White respondents are more likely to "shoot" a picture of an unarmed African American man than an armed White man when rapidly shown pictures in simulated experiments (Sadler et al., 2012). After taking an IAT, research participants are then evaluated by observers in test situations with people of different races for comfort and discomfort, warmth or coolness, confidence versus hesitation, and other observable measures. People who showed racial bias on the IAT demonstrated through their behavior in the test situations and in their everyday lives that they would also be less likely to hire African Americans and less likely to vote for President Obama, but consciously would not think that race was a factor in their decision-making process.

Implicit racism influences political party affiliation, and predominantly Republican districts have more people with higher levels of implicit racial bias (Vedantum, 2010). While education and training influence conscious attitudes and values, they do not seem to reduce implicit bias. Ojiaku (2016), in her review of implicit bias research, notes that when White participants viewed pain being experienced by Black people, the parts of the brain associated with empathy

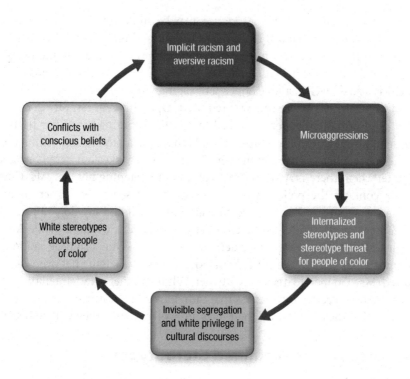

Implicit racism and aversive racism

Microaggressions

Internalized stereotypes and stereotype threat for people of color

Invisible segregation and white privilege in cultural discourses

White stereotypes about people of color

Conflicts with conscious beliefs

FIGURE 6.1 **From stereotypes to stereotype threat.**

were less active than when they viewed pictures of White people experiencing pain. Banaji and Greenwald (2013) have found in their research what we mentioned earlier: A disconnect between conscious values and implicit bias leads to cognitive dissonance. This causes tension and discomfort, which people try to resolve, often by reinforcing their stereotypes.

One type of implicit bias is aversive racism. It occurs when White people hold implicit attitudes about people of color—often at odds with a White person's conscious beliefs or intentions—that lead to negative interactions with people of color (Dovidio et al., 2002, 2016). Aversive racism is when Whites act on their implicit biases and prejudice. It can be subtle—such as standing further away from people of color when talking with them—but it is often felt or experienced by the person of color while the White person is unaware of it. Aversive racism involves harboring negative stereotypes and attitudes toward people of color that are not only unconscious but reflect a lack of awareness about the lived realities of racism of people of color. It also involves evaluating people of your own racial group more positively and feeling a greater sense of comfort and trust (Dovidio et al., 2016). When aversive racism occurs, it often is enacted by White people who hold egalitarian views and who would, by the process of White fragility, be defensive, upset, even shocked to be confronted with racism, which is why it is difficult to address. It influences a range of practices and institutions such as hiring and admission decisions, and support or lack of support for public policies. In interactions with people of color, however, the anxiety, discomfort, or prejudice can be manifested sufficiently to be picked up by the person of color, much to the surprise and dismay of the White person, leading to interpersonal strains and difficult interactions. In turn, people of color can become increasingly watchful about their interactions with Whites, and wary of the impact of subtle biases.

When one of the authors (Miller, 2001) was conducting research in a liberal Northeast city, he interviewed a Hispanic police officer, who worked in another community and who had run unsuccessfully for political office in his hometown. The respondent described how, when he entered White, suburban neighborhoods to campaign, he would have to wear a T-shirt emblazoned with his campaign logo, so as not to cause undue alarm to residents or to the police patrolling the neighborhood. Yet, the majority of White respondents living in that neighborhood viewed themselves as being without prejudice.

Kaufman (2001) describes the subtlety of interactions with an underlying current of aversive racism:

> The actions that create the racist atmosphere in society can be so small that each action in itself is almost imperceptible. For many people of color, whenever they walk into a mostly White space, they are looked at. The looks are not necessarily hostile. But they are looks nevertheless. The person of color's presence has a charge and, if the tension is to be eased, it falls on the person of color to initiate this. Each individual White person doesn't do much. A meeting of the eyes that is broken off a split second too quickly; a slight pulling in of the arms; a smile that is just a millimeter too forced at the edges. Each action is almost imperceptible. Together they are enough to create a force field of discomfort. (p. 33)

Racial Microaggressions

Racial microaggressions are related to implicit and aversive racism. They are "subtle, stunning, often automatic" verbal and nonverbal put-downs and social assaults that wound people of color unbeknownst to the perpetrator (Pierce et al., 1978). As with aversive racism, microaggressions stem from unconscious acts, but they have painful consequences. They occur repetitively, and their impact can be cumulative, like a thousand paper cuts as opposed to one deep wound. Microaggressions can occur whenever a person with social power (e.g., Whites, men, or heterosexual people) interact with people who have minority or targeted identities (e.g., people of color; women; people with lesbian, gay, bisexual, transgender, questioning, and indeterminate [LGBTQI] identities; Sue, 2010). In all of these dynamics, the person with greater social power holds implicit biases and enacts them, usually without being aware of it. Examples of racial microaggressions are: ignoring people of color in a group or classroom, having lower expectations, being mistrustful, expecting people of color to speak on behalf of their own race, expecting a person of color to "act and talk White," and repeatedly denying the relevance of race and racism (Solorzano et al., 2000).

Consider the following examples: A Korean American student is taking a sociology class that includes no other Asian Americans. Whenever Asian Americans are mentioned in the class, the other students and the professor turn their attention to this student. A Native American student describes how racism contributes to the high poverty rates in her community and is told by other students that she is making too big a deal about racism and using it as an excuse to justify the plight of her people.

Being on the receiving end of racial microaggressions can leave people of color feeling hurt, mistrustful, angry, beleaguered, and exhausted (Solorzano et al., 2000). One way of dealing with such regular and commonplace assaults is to seek refuge in groups that are composed predominantly of people of color to lessen the chances of encountering microaggressions and to offer buffering, mutual support, and positive validation and confirmation (Solorzano et al., 2000; Tatum, 1997).

This, in turn, can lead to White people thinking that people of color are preoccupied excessively with race, are excluding themselves and fostering racial divisions, are manufacturing problems that do not exist, or are exacerbating conflicts because they are seen as being unwilling to discuss issues with Whites.

There are some challenges with using a microaggression metaphor. One is that it frames an interaction as having an aggressor and a victim. While this characterization is somewhat accurate, it can dichotomize what are often complex interactions (Kang & Garran, 2018). By doing this, it can minimize the agency of the "victim" of the microaggression. Also, many microaggressions take place in groups so there are many other actors in the interaction, some of whom can be seen as "bystanders" (Staub, 2001). What is their role in the events leading up to the microaggression and in its aftermath? How can "bystanders" play a helpful part in the interaction and not exacerbate the negative consequences? Lastly, some verbal and social assaults go beyond being a microaggression—they are really macroaggressions.

Despite these challenges, we have found in our practice that microaggressions do occur with regularity and that the concept can offer a conceptual frame for unpacking and ameliorating the effects of interpersonal racism.

Confronting Stereotypes

Completely eradicating stereotypes is often unrealistic, particularly because they are continually reinforced by institutions, as well as social and cultural discourses (Banaji & Greenwald, 2013; Hu et al., 2015). Thankfully, research by social psychologists has confirmed a number of effective strategies for confronting stereotypes and minimizing their impact. We discuss each of these tactics, as they are essential for workers in the helping professions to use with themselves and others (see also Box 6.1).

1. *Dissonance with beliefs.* We must have conscious beliefs that counteract stereotypes. People who are comfortable with their stereotypes will either not recognize them as such or have no motivation to modify them. This is why it is so important to expose people to experiences that confront their prejudiced, but often unconscious, explanatory systems. To create the dissonance necessary to motivate people to work to dispel their stereotypes and to enable self-monitoring, people have to acknowledge, examine, and explore a stereotype rather than try to suppress it and act as if it does not exist (Monteith et al., 1998; Moskowitz et al., 1999). One of our students put it this way: A stereotype is like a pop-up screen on your computer desktop—you have an urge to click the X and close it. The more the stereotype conflicts with one's conscious beliefs and positive self-image, the greater is the impulse to erase it. But we are suggesting that it is better to leave it open and examine it, comparing it with what you consciously value and believe.

2. *Self-monitoring.* Related to allowing the stereotype to surface and to experience the discord with conscious ethics and viewpoints is the value of self-monitoring (Monteith, 1993). This self-awareness has two aspects: (a) the cognitive component, and (b) the feelings that accompany the stereotype. Self-awareness about the "thought" part of a

BOX 6.1 Strategies for Confronting Stereotypes

1. Monitor dissonance with conscious beliefs.
   ▶ Do not suppress the stereotype. Examine it.
   ▶ Experience the discomfort and discord with values and beliefs to create motivation to confront the stereotype.
2. Monitor thoughts and feelings that accompany the stereotype.
   ▶ How did you learn the stereotype?
   ▶ How did you come to disagree with it?
   ▶ What feelings accompany the stereotype?
   ▶ What feelings accompany your desire to counter the stereotype?
3. Perspective taking.
   ▶ Think of individuals who defy the stereotype.
   ▶ Imagine how *you* would feel if you were them.
   ▶ Imagine how *the other person* feels.
   ▶ Practice empathy in groups as well as alone.
4. Use replacement thoughts.
   ▶ Think of something or someone that contradicts the stereotype.
   ▶ Give the counter-stereotype a positive image or sound.
   ▶ Whenever the stereotype emerges, try to counter it with the positive association.
5. Practice.
   ▶ Recognize that unlearning stereotypes takes time.
   ▶ Keep in mind that any of these techniques must be practiced.
6. Develop egalitarian goals.
   ▶ Cultivate goals that contradict racial stereotypes.
   ▶ Use professional codes of ethics and standards, as well as organizational mission statements and commitments, to support egalitarian goals.
7. Surround yourself with allies.
   ▶ Find allies to support you in unlearning racism.
   ▶ Suppressing stereotypes usually is not helpful, because it can interfere with self-awareness (Moskowitz et al., 1999), and there also is a danger of a "rebound effect" (Galinsky & Moskowitz, 2000). By trying so hard to smother a stereotype, the stereotype gains more potency and resonance than if it is aired and explored.

stereotype can involve tracking back the source of the stereotype—where it was learned, who also holds this stereotype, what experiences you have had that reinforced the stereotype, and how you came to disagree with it.

The emotional component of self-awareness can take the form of exploring what feelings accompany both the stereotype and your awareness that you hold the stereotype. Do feelings of fear and anxiety spark the stereotype? Do feelings of guilt or shame immobilize you when you are trying to work on the stereotype? Are there other people who hold this stereotype with whom you have strong emotional attachments? Do you have feelings that cause you to resist letting go of this stereotype?

3. *Perspective taking.* Empathy is an excellent antidote to stereotypes (Stephan & Finlay, 1999). Empathy puts us in the shoes of others, infusing their humanity with our personhood, so constructing them as a denigrated "other" becomes much more difficult. When stereotypes are operating, empathy often is lacking and will not flow easily. Thus, a conscious effort is necessary to try and empathize to offset a racial stereotype.

You can leaven the process of empathy by: (a) treating people as individuals and trying to empathize with the individual, rather than attempting to make a general connection with a group; and (b) imagining how *you* would feel and experience the world if you were the other person, rather than empathizing only with how that person experiences the world (Galinsky & Moskowitz, 2000). Todd and Galinsky (2014) have also recommended that White people not only think about how *they* would feel in similar circumstances to a person of color but try and mentalize the situation of the person of color—how *the other person* feels. They have found in their research that the second type of empathy leads to a greater engagement and willingness to participate in antiracism activities. People with lower social status always need to take the perspective of people with more social power but those with racial privilege need to be encouraged to engage in empathic perspective taking. As we have described earlier, there is often resistance to doing this due to cognitive dissonance, guilt and shame, and feeling badly about oneself.Empathy can be achieved in different ways, such as: (a) participating in diverse groups and forming relationships with people who are racially or ethnically different, and structuring conversations to evoke mutual and reciprocal empathy; (b) using techniques such as focused, single-point meditation to concentrate on putting oneself in another's place and to experience, as nonjudgmentally as possible, what this feels like; and (c) reading vignettes, watching videos, hearing stories, and then responding to structured questions that guide people toward using their empathy to understand the other person's experience (Todd & Galinsky, 2014).

4. *Replacement thoughts.* One way to confront a stereotype is to substitute another thought in its place, which negates or contradicts the stereotype (Kawakami et al., 2000). This is a way of "imagining a stereotype away" (Blair et al., 2001). Some researchers (Hu et al., 2015) have found that if there is a positive association with the counterfactual to the stereotype, such as a sound, then hearing this sound while sleeping helps to solidify the counterfactual and reduce the potency of the original stereotype. The first step is to consciously think of something that contradicts the stereotype, bringing into conscious awareness a person who is a counterfactual to the stereotype (e.g., a friend, colleague, public figure) who is inconsistent with the negative stereotype toward their ethnic group. Given Hu et al.'s research, it might also be helpful to give the counterstereotype a positive association, such as music or a visual image.

Next, practice tagging the positive association to the stereotype every time the stereotype arises, so eventually when the stereotype bubbles up, so does its antidote. If you do this repeatedly and self-consciously, it eventually may become a process of automatic self-monitoring in which the replacement thought becomes ascendant (Kawakami et al., 2000).

Ultimately, the replacement thought may cancel out the stereotype even before the stereotype reaches the level of consciousness (Moskowitz et al., 1999).

5. *Practice.* With all of the aforementioned techniques and strategies, practice is of paramount importance (Blair et al., 2001; Monteith et al., 1998). Stereotypes have accrued over many years and are reinforced constantly by the webs and discourses of racism. Thus, it is not as if a person can just decide to expunge a stereotype and—poof—it's gone! It is also frustrating to work on challenging a stereotype only to have it pop up again. So persistence is essential.

   Thus, it is important to engage in a variety or combination of the previously described strategies and continue to identify dissonance, develop self-monitoring, actively engage empathically, and substitute replacement thoughts over time. This may take years and may never be complete; however, the research cited thus far indicates that these strategies do work and are worth the investment.

6. *Cultivating egalitarian goals.* All of the stereotype-reduction approaches discussed here are dependent on cultivating egalitarian goals that clash with the stereotypes. This is not always as easy as it sounds, because the stereotypes themselves can inhibit a person from developing empathy or egalitarian goals (Monteith et al., 1998; Moskowitz et al., 1999). This is where professional codes of ethics, training, and standards of practice can be helpful. They provide a mandate for ethical practice as well as templates for how to achieve that standard in practice. All human service and helping professionals are expected to practice according to the principles of their professions, and this can be the incentive for learning about content that challenges assumptions and stereotypes and can facilitate the development of nonprejudicial goals.

   Another helpful tool is for organizations and institutions to make a formal commitment to social justice and/or antiracism. This serves as a constant reminder to all staff about the vision and aspirations of the organization, with expectations of staff commitment.

7. *Surrounding oneself with allies.* Because motivation, time, and persistence are required to unlearn stereotypes, surrounding oneself with allies, people who have already done similar work, or are also engaged in an unlearning process, is beneficial. This creates a space where people can take risks and collectively explore internalized stereotypes about themselves and others. Allies can set an example for one another and together create an impetus and momentum for unlearning racism. Confronting stereotypes is an emotional endeavor and requires courage and persistence.

CONCLUSION

Because of the cognitive and emotional tensions between explanatory systems and the reality of the historical and social worlds that people inhabit, all people, regardless of race, are conscripted as actors in a racialized social discourse, which grants in-group status to some while casting others into socially targeted and maligned roles. All of these processes lead to stereotypes about oneself and others, internalizations of external social inequities and ideologies of supremacy. Implicit racism and unexamined stereotypes can lead to aversive racism, White fragility, and racial microaggressions. A variety of strategies can be used to counteract stereotypes.

Two exercises further the experience of self-awareness and detoxification of stereotypes. Exercise 6.1 is a cultural audit that permits you to explore how you learned about yourself as a social actor and your encounters with people from different cultural and racial backgrounds.

Exercise 6.2 can be done alone or in groups, with discussion enabling participants to examine their stereotypes and begin the process of empathy, perspective taking, and replacement thoughts.

NOTE

Some people of color have experienced sufficient partial race privilege, which can derive from a variety of factors (class privilege, having grown up in another country, being able to pass for White, etc.), so they do not have a highly developed racial consciousness.

EXERCISE 6.1 Personal Audit

This is a tool to explore your socialization with people from different racial and ethnic groups—often a source of positive and negative stereotypes.

1. Describe your first contacts with members of other racial and ethnic groups. When did these occur?
2. What values and attitudes did you learn from your family about people from other racial and ethnic groups? Were there discrepancies between what was said and what was done?
3. How diverse was your neighborhood? School? College?
4. What other experiences have you had with people of different races and cultures?
5. What were some positive encounters with people from other ethnic or racial groups?
6. What were some negative encounters with people from other ethnic or racial groups? What did you think or feel? If you could replay the tape of what happened, what do you wish you would have done differently?
7. Which clients from different racial and ethnic groups have you found to be most challenging? Why?

EXERCISE 6.2 Confronting Stereotypes

1. Think of a racial/ethnic stereotype you hold that makes you feel uncomfortable. If you have difficulty identifying one, try to think of something about a person from a different racial or ethnic group that you would *not* want to discuss with them but would be willing to confide to somebody who shares your racial or ethnic identity.
2. What is the stereotype? If you were trying to teach this stereotype to someone else, how would you explain it?
3. What uncomfortable feelings surface when describing this stereotype? It can help to list them.
4. Where might you have learned this, and from whom? (Include multiple sources if you like.)
5. What might have been the historical and social contexts from which this stereotype evolved?

6. What in society or your daily life perpetuates and reinforces the stereotype?
7. What do you *know* or *believe* that contradicts this stereotype?
8. Who do you know that counters the stereotype?
9. What positive image or sound can you associate with the counterstereotype?
10. Where can you continue to work on this with other allies?

REFERENCES

Adler, N. E., & Rehkopf, D. H. (2008). US disparities in health: Descriptions, causes, and mechanisms. *Annual Review of Public Health, 29*, 235–252.

Allport, G. W. (1948). *The ABC's of scapegoating.* B'nai B'rith Press.

Allport, G. W. (1954). *The nature of prejudice.* Addison-Wesley.

Banaji, M. R., & Greenwald, A. G. (2013). *Blindspot: Hidden biases of good people.* Delacorte Press.

Blair, I. V., Ma, J. E., & Lenton, A. P. (2001). Imagining stereotypes away: The moderation of implicit stereotypes through mental imagery. *Journal of Personality and Social Psychology, 81*(5), 838–841.

Bobo, L. D. (2001). Racial attitudes and relations at the close of the twentieth century. In N. J. Smelser, W. J. Wilson, & F. Mitchell (Eds.), *America becoming: Racial trends and their consequences* (Vol. 1, pp. 265–301). Washington, DC: National Academies Press.

Bonilla-Silva, E. (2009). *Racism without racists: Color-blind racism and the persistence of inequality in America.* Rowman & Littlefield.

Bowen, M. (1976). Theory and practice in psychotherapy. In P. J. Guerin (Ed.), *Family therapy: Theory and practice* (pp. 42–90). Gardner Press.

Brewer, M. B. (2001). Ingroup identification and intergroup conflict: When does ingroup love become outgroup hate? In R. D. Ashmore, L. Jussim, & D. Wilder (Eds.), *Social identity, intergroup conflict, and conflict resolution* (pp. 17–41). Oxford University Press.

Bruner, J. (1990). *Acts of meaning.* Harvard University Press.

Coates, T. (2015). *Between the world and me.* Spiegel & Grau.

Damasio, A. (2000). *The feeling of what happens: Body, emotions and the making of consciousness.* Vintage.

Douglas, T. (1995). *Scapegoats: Transferring blame.* Routledge.

DiAngelo, R. (2018). *White fragility: Why it's so hard for white people to talk about racism.* Beacon Press.

Dovidio, J. F., Gaertner, S. L., Kawakami, K., & Hodson, G. (2002). Why can't we all just get along? Interpersonal biases and interracial distrust. *Cultural Diversity and Ethnic Minority Psychology, 8*(2), 88–102.

Dovidio, J. F., Gaertner, S. L., Ufkes, E. G., Saguy, T., & Pearson, A. R. (2016). Included but invisible? The darker side of "we." *Social Issues and Policy Review, 10*(1), 6–46.

Ferber, A. (2012). The culture of privilege: Color-blindness, Postfeminism, and Christonormativity. *Journal of Social Issues, 68*(1), 63–77.

Freire, P. (1996). *Pedagogy of the oppressed (revised).* Continuum.

Galinsky, A., & Moskowitz, G. B. (2000). Perspective–taking: Decreasing stereotype expression, stereotype accessibility, and in group favoritism. *Journal of Personality and Social Psychology, 78*(4), 708–724.

Gillens, M. (1999). *Why Americans hate welfare.* University of Chicago Press.

Godsil, R. D. (2015, January/February). Breaking the cycle: Implicit bias, racial anxiety and stereotype threat. *Poverty & Race, 24*(1), 1–2, 8–10.

Goleman, D. (1992, April 21). Black scientists study the "pose" of the inner city. *The New York Times,* p. CI.

Goodman, D. (2011). *Promoting diversity and social justice: Educating people from privileged groups* (2nd ed.). Routledge.

Groot, M., & Marcus, P. (1998). Digging out of the White trap. *Poverty & Race, 7*(2), 1–2, 5.

Grosfoguel, R. (2013). *Decolonizing post-colonial studies and paradigms of political economy: Transmodernity, decolonial thinking and global coloniality.* Transmodernity. www.escholarship.org/uc/item/21k6t3fq

Group for the Advancement of Psychiatry [GAP]. (1987). *Us and them: The psychology of ethnonationalism.* Brunner/Mazel.

Higginbotham, H. M. (2013). *Ghosts of Jim Crow: Ending racism in post-racial America.* New York University Press.

Hill, J. (1999). Language, race and White public space. *American Anthropologist, 100*(3), 680–689.

Hu, X., Antony, J. W., Creery, J. D., Vargas, I. M., Bodenhausen, G. V., & Paller, K. A. (2015). Unlearning implicit social biases through sleep. *Science, 348*, 1013–1015.

Jones, D. K., Bradley, K. W. V., & Oberlander, J. (2014). Pascal's wager: Health insurance exchanges, Obamacare, and the Republican dilemma. *Journal of Health Politics, Policy, and Law, 39*(1), 97–137.

Kang, H. K. & Garran, A. M. (2018). Microaggressions in social work classrooms: Strategies for pedagogical intervention. *Journal of Ethnic & Cultural Diversity in Social Work, 27*(1), 4–16.

Kaufman, C. (2001). A user's guide to White privilege. *Radical Philosophy Review, 4*(1/2), 30–38.

Kawakami, K., Moll, J., Hermsen, S., Dovidio, J. F., & Russin, A. (2000). Just say no (to stereotyping): Effects of training in the negation of stereotypic associations on stereotype activation. *Journal of Personality and Social Psychology, 78*(5), 871–888.

Laughland, O., Zanolli, L., (2020). *Why is coronavirus taking such a deadly toll on black Americans?* www.theguardian.com/world/2020/apr/25/coronavirus-racial-disparities-african-americans The Guardian.

Leonardo, Z. (2004). The color of supremacy: Beyond the discourse of "white privilege." *Educational Philosophy and Theory, 36*(2), 137–152.

Lopez, I. F. H. (1996). *White by law: The legal construction of race.* New York University Press.

Maxwell, A., & Shields, T. (2014). The fate of Obamacare: Racial resentment, ethnocentrism and attitudes about health care reform. *Race and Social Problems, 6*, 293–304.

McIntosh, P. (1989, July/August). White privilege: Unpacking the invisible knapsack. *Peace and Freedom,* pp. 10–12.

McIntosh, P. (1992). White privilege and male privilege: A personal account of coming to see correspondences through work in women's studies. In M. Anderson & P. H. Collins (Eds.), *Race, class and gender: An anthology* (pp. 70–81). Wadsworth.

Miller, J. (2001). Family and community integrity. *Journal of Sociology and Social Welfare, 28*(4), 23–44.

Miller, J., & Schamess, G. (2000). The discourse of denigration and the creation of other. *Journal of Sociology and Social Welfare, 27*(3), 39–62.

Mills, C. W. (1997). *The racial contract.* Cornell.

Monteith, M. (1993). Self-regulation of prejudiced responses: Implications for progress in prejudice-reduction efforts. *Journal of Personality and Social Psychology, 65*(3), 469–485.

Monteith, M. J., Sherman, J. W., & Devine, P. G. (1998). Suppression as a stereotype control strategy. *Personality and Social Psychology Review, 2*(1), 63–82.

Moskowitz, G. B., Gollwitzer, P. M., Wasel, W., & Schaal, B. (1999). Preconscious control of stereotype activation through chronic egalitarian goals. *Journal of Personality and Social Psychology, 77*(1), 167–184.

Norton, M. I., & Sommers, S. R. (2011). Whites see racism as a zero-sum game that they are now losing. *Perspectives on Psychological Science, 6*, 215–218.

Ojiaku, P. (2016, March 21). *Is everybody a racist? Aeon.* www.aeon.co/essays/unconscious-racism-is-pervasive-starts-early-and-can-be-deadly

Pierce, C., Carew, J., Pierce-Gonzalez, D., & Wills, D. (1978). An experiment in racism: T.V. commercials. In C. Pierce (Ed.), *Television and education* (pp. 62–88). Sage.

Reiss, D. (1981). *The family's construction of reality.* Harvard University Press.

Sadler, M. S., Correll, J., Park, B., & Judd, C. M. (2012). The world is not black and white: The decision to shoot in a multiethnic context. *Journal of Social Issues, 68*(2), 286–313.

Schmader, T., Major, B., & Gramzow, R. H. (2001). Coping with ethnic stereotypes in the academic domain: Perceived injustice and psychological disengagement. *Journal of Social Issues, 57*(1), 93–111.

Solorzano, D., Ceja, M., & Yosso, T. (2000). Critical race theory, racial microaggressions, and campus racial climate: The experiences of African American college students. *Journal of Negro Education, 69*(1/2), 60–73.

Staub, E. (2001). Individual and group identities in genocide and mass killing. In R. D. Ashmore, L. Jussim, & D. Wilder (Eds.), *Social identity, intergroup conflict, and conflict resolution* (pp. 159–184). Oxford University Press.

Stephan, W. G., & Finlay, K. (1999). The role of empathy in improving intergroup relations. *Journal of Social Issues, 55*(4), 729–743.

Sue, D. W. (2010). *Microaggressions in everyday life: Race, gender and sexual orientation.* Wiley.

Tatum, B. (1997). *"Why are all the Black kids sitting together in the cafeteria?" And other conversations about race.* Basic Books.

Tatum, B. D. (2017). *Why are all the Black kids sitting together in the cafeteria?: And other conversations about race.* Hachette UK.

Todd, A. R., & Galinsky, A. D. (2014). Perspective taking as a strategy for improving intergroup relationships: Evidence, mechanisms, qualifications. *Social and Personality Psychology Compass, 8*(7), 374–387.

Vedantum, S. (2010). *The hidden brain: How our unconscious minds elect presidents, control markets, wage wars, and save our lives.* Spiegel & Grau.

Volkan, V. D. (1988). *The need to have enemies and allies: From clinical practice to international relationships.* Jason Aronson.

Wenger, M. R. (2013, July/August). White privilege. *Poverty & Race, 22*(4), 1–2, 6–7.

CHAPTER 7

Social Identity Formation and Group Membership

INTRODUCTION

When did you first think of yourself as having a race and ethnicity, or multiple races and ethnicities? Were you aware of this as a child? When you went to school? College? How well do you think your racial and/or ethnic identity is respected and validated in society? Are you able to be your complex self, or does society try to label you, reduce and constrict who you are or restrict you to only one part of your identity? Are there other people "like" you in your immediate social world? Do you have regular interactions with people of different racial backgrounds? If so, do you experience them as mostly comfortable or uncomfortable? If not, what are some reasons in your experience that lead to cross-racial interactions occurring less often than those of the same race?

These questions begin to address our racial and ethnic identities. They invite us to reflect about who we are, who we identify and interact with, how we perceive our group's place in society, and all of the feelings that accompany these contemplations, as well as how we are defined by others. Such questions may feel awkward or uncomfortable or, upon introspection, yield valuable insights. They can help us to explore and validate our sense of self while also highlighting our differences and social divisions. We believe that these are essential lines of inquiry for all who work in the helping professions.

Chapter 1 introduced the concept of social identity and asked readers to situate themselves and reflect on how various aspects of our identity carry differential power and privilege. In Chapter 5, we described the paradox of White privilege, ubiquitous yet often invisible to those who benefit from it. In this chapter, we continue to explore the internalization of ethnicity, race, and racism and examine how this influences group allegiances and intergroup dynamics. We present a comprehensive model of social identity that is holistic, flexible, adaptable, and useful in the work of the helping professions.

Because all of the helping professions involve interpersonal contact and the use of self, exploring our social identity and how we came to be who we are is essential as we try to work across race and culture. We also have to try to understand the identities of the people with whom we work and how they are similar to and different from us.

After considering classical notions of identity and some major principles of racial identity theory, this chapter presents a model of social identity development. Identity is related intricately to the groups we feel attached to and those we feel different or excluded from, so we also look at the dynamics of group membership and how this affects intergroup relations. Last, we consider the implications for work in the helping professions.

IDENTITY

We all have an identity, a sense of who we are in relation to other people. Identity is an integral part of self. It is a consistent way by which we organize the various aspects of ourselves as we negotiate relationships and the social world. Identity can be adaptive or maladaptive. It can be a vehicle for successfully negotiating relationships, social roles, and social tasks or a train on the wrong track that never seems to be cruising at the right speed or in the right direction. Some aspects of identity are quite stable and enduring, while others are more fluid or situationally activated. Identity engages us as both actors and observers; we reflect on ourselves and are able to name and classify who we are and what we do in relation to other people and how we fit with social categories (Stets & Burke, 2000). Identity is the narrative we construct about who we are, which we present to ourselves as well as to others.

Identity shapes what we see, think (about the world, ourselves, and others), feel, believe, and value. It also directs our social roles, skills, occupations, and our group affiliations and allegiances (Erikson, 1963; Stets & Burke, 2000).

Erikson (1963, 1968) is one of the most recognized identity theorists. He offered a developmental, epigenetic, psychosocial model of development from birth until death. He believed that identity is the resolution of adolescence, the bridge between childhood and adulthood. Adolescence is a time of physical, endocrinological, and social turbulence, which involves dismantling our child-self and laying down tracks for our adult-self, but we are neither beyond our childhood nor have we reached adulthood. It is a period of transition.

This transition involves a heightened sense of self-awareness. We are concerned with how we look and present ourselves, sensitive to how others perceive us. During this period, we clarify what is good and bad, whom we feel attached to and to which groups we belong, and whom we distance ourselves from and scorn and disparage.

The process of individuation and differentiation, along with the desire to belong, are powerful sources for creating in-groups and out-groups and fueling social divisions. According to Erikson (1963), identity is formed by the interaction of a developmental process and the cultural and social context in which this occurs. In the United States, identity is fashioned in a relatively heterogeneous society. Even if many neighborhoods are segregated and socially homogeneous, society at large is quite diverse ethnically and racially. This contrasts with identity formation in many other societies, which are more ethnically and racially homogeneous (Hoare, 2003).

Identity formation incorporates a sense of power, privilege, and marginalization. Erikson (1968) believed that those with privilege project their unconscious, negative identities onto those who are oppressed, which has the effect of buttressing their sense of superiority at the expense of those who are "other" and, further, socially constructed as "less than." Identity formation involves internalizing a subjective sense of social order, a hierarchy with a "we" and "they" (Smith, 1991). Thus, in a society riddled with racism, people have difficulty achieving a positive sense of self without disparaging others or being recipients of unowned and unacceptable projections from others (Myers et al., 1991; Volkan, 1988).

Erikson's sense of identity reflected a localized, Western notion of self that is not representative of many of the world's cultures. Although he was aware of this, his own thinking and the preponderance of his clinical experience was in a Western, Eurocentric context. Thus, his strong emphasis on an autonomous, individuated self, with its roots in Western history, philosophy, and culture, is at odds with most of the world's cultures, which emphasize a more collective and interdependent sense of self and identity (Roland, 2003; Yeh & Hwang, 2000). It has been critiqued as a very male vision of identity (Gilligan, 1977, 1982). Erikson's model also did not focus sufficiently on individual agency in forging an identity or on how individuals with multiple ethnic and racial strands of identity integrate those parts of themselves (Santos, 2015).

Erikson also did not address the impact of social targeting—racism, sexism, homophobia, transphobia, and so forth—on identity formation. His vision of identity is often written from the perspective of society's privileged, rather than from the vantage point of those who are socially targeted. Partially in reaction to these concerns, racial identity theory emerged.

RACIAL AND ETHNIC IDENTITY THEORY

Racial and ethnic theories of development go beyond generic conceptualizations of identity and attempt to consider the impact of cultural differences and societal oppression. Ethnic and racial identity theories originally had different premises, with ethnic identity theories focusing on cultural differences in worldview, values, and relationship of self to family. Power, privilege, and oppression were taken into account by considering how identity formation was influenced by reacting to a racist environment (Sellers et al., 1998). Racial identity theory took as its starting point the experience of African Americans (Cross, 1978, 1991; Helms, 1990; Helms & Cook, 1999) and, later, other people of color, seeking to understand how a positive and adaptive sense of identity could emerge for Black people living in a racist society. This perspective was attempting to understand the internal experience of people of color (Sellers et al., 1998).

Racial identity theorists disagreed over whether a theory could be applied to only one specific racial or ethnic group or if universal theories could be developed for people with race privilege and those who are racially targeted. But theories of ethnic and racial identity development also had much in common. The distinctions between ethnicity and race are far from clear-cut. For example, African Americans are an ethnic group, with traditions, customs, and other cultural distinctions, but also are the targets of racism and have been socially constructed racially as Black (Taylor, 1997). Latinx people in the United States are an amalgamation of ethnic groups racialized by the calculus of U.S. racism, who also experience nativism and also colorism (Alcoff, 2012).

On a personal level, some people distinguish between their race and ethnicity and others do not. For example, a Mexican American born in the United States could view herself as Mexican American, U.S. American, Chicana, Latina, Latinx, a person of color, or have a fluid and flexible identity depending on the social context. She also may identify with Indigenous, European, Asian, or African heritage. As both race and ethnicity are social constructions and a person's identity includes personal, subjective meanings, the distinction between race and ethnicity is not always clear. Thus, we find it more useful to consider ethnic and racial theories of identity formation together rather than as separate entities. Santos (2015) has proposed a meta-concept of "ethnic–racial identity," which we continue to use in this book.

Classical theories of ethnic and racial identity map out phases or stages that a person moves through. Stage theories tend to be more linear and epigenetic, with a clear progression of stages in which each stage subsumes previous stages in a hierarchy of stages. In most stage theories, a person is in one stage at a time.

Phase theories are more fluid and can view a person as having certain statuses or constellations of attitudes and behaviors. These theories allow more leeway for a person to have qualities of more than one phase and for development to proceed in a nonlinear fashion.

Most theories of ethnic and racial identity development, whether stage or phase, have different trajectories for White people and for people of color. In the early days of theorizing, little was written about multiracial and multi-ethnic identity development although this has changed in the past 15 to 20 years (e.g., Albuja et al., 2019; Binning et al., 2009; Cheng & Lee, 2009; Jackson, 2009; Miville et al., 2005; Rockquemore et al., 2009; Santos, 2015). In this context, we consider both stage and phase theorists together and use insights from multiracial identity theorists to explore ethnic–racial identity.

In our review of stage theories and building on an earlier review by Phinney and Kohatsu (1999), we have found a number of commonalities in the theories for people of color (Atkinson et al., 1993; Cross, 1991; Helms, 1990; Malott et al., 2015; Marcia et al., 1994; Phinney, 1989, 1993; Sue & Sue, 2015; Yi, 2014):

- ▶ *Initial, pre-aware phase.* Different theorists have described this as "pre-encounter" (Cross, 1991; Helms, 1990), "unexamined" (Phinney, 1989), and "conformity" (Atkinson et al., 1993; Sue & Sue, 2015). All refer to an unexamined ethnic or racial identity where the person is unaware of themselves as an ethnic–racial person in a racialized society.
- ▶ *Transition/dissonance phase.* This phase has been termed "encounter" (Cross, 1991; Helms, 1990), "exposure" (Phinney, 1989), "dissonance" (Atkinson et al., 1993; Sue & Sue, 2015), and "identity crisis" (Marcia et al., 1994). It implies a critical re-evaluation, a period of transition, often precipitated by a crisis or intense encounters that challenge previously held assumptions. This often is accompanied by cognitive confusion and emotional distress.
- ▶ *Intermediate/resistance phases.* These phases are often characterized by "exploration" (Phinney, 1989) of a new identity and its implications, as well as "immersion/emersion" (Cross, 1991; Helms, 1990), which means wanting to be with people, groups, and cultures that reflect one's new identity and avoiding painful encounters with those who are different or antagonistic. This involves self-protective, self-validating, and buffering maneuvers.
- ▶ *Introspection stages* (Yi, 2014)—At this point, a person is weighing who they are in relation to others in a more nuanced and complex fashion. There is greater self-validation coupled with wider tolerance for people with different racial identities.
- ▶ *Final phase.* The final phase involves internalizing and establishing a positive and adaptive identity and a means of functioning within the dominant culture and being able to manage racism and other threats to self.

Hardiman (1994) performed a similar service for models of White racial identity development, comparing her own model (Hardiman, 1982) with those of Marcia (1980), Helms (1990), Ponterotto (1988), and Sabnani et al. (1991). All illustrate movement from being racially unaware, to encounters that create crisis and confusion, to eventually achieving a nonracist, positive racial identity—an awareness of what Whiteness and White privilege mean in society, without subscribing to the tenets of racism. Malott et al. (2015) summarized some of the characteristics of Whites in the more "advanced," "autonomous stages": a sophisticated awareness of oneself as a White person and White privilege; complex, flexible, and meaningful cross-racial friendships; abandonment of personal racism and racial privilege; understanding the impact of racism on people of color; taking an antiracism stance; and engaging in antiracism activities. When interviewing White antiracism activists they found that some questioned whether Whiteness as a social category can ever be separated from oppression. However, Sullivan (2014) argues that it is important to humanize White people without condoning racist actions; in other words, forgiving the person but not their deeds.

Hardiman employs the metaphor of wearing new eyeglasses at each stage, enabling people to see themselves and the world with greater clarity. Of course, there is never a straight progression between realizing that racism in the United States continues to exist to becoming a White ally and antiracism activist. In fact, racial identity theorists believe that the majority of White people do not make it to these "higher stages." Helms (1990) and Helms and Cook (1999) include a stage called "reintegration," which is a time of great resistance to acknowledging racism, understanding one's place in a racist society, and accepting a nonracist identity. In our experience, many White people land here. This is consistent with what we described in Chapter 5 about the difficulty many White people have in seeing and acknowledging the extent of racism and their White privilege.

Theories of racial identity development share many characteristics: They are developmental, have discrete stages or phases, and ideally lead to a positive and adaptive sense of self. Phinney (1992) identified four common elements found in most theories of racial/ethnic identity:

1. How a person self-identifies
2. The ethnic behaviors and practices that accompany identity
3. How strong or weak a person's sense of belonging to a group is, and an affirmation of one's own ethnic or racial identity
4. The actual process that one goes through to achieve an ethnic or racial identity

Adolescence clearly is a fertile time for developing a racial and ethnic identity, but the process actually begins in childhood and is lifelong (Smith, 1991). As we described in Chapter 5, the family plays a crucial role by shaping attitudes, conveying ethnic practices and values, and employing explanatory systems and narratives to explain how family members fit with their social world. But research has indicated that the biggest factor shaping children's attitudes about race and ethnicity is their sociocultural environment (Hirschfield, 2012). As children attend school, socialize with friends, play sports, are exposed to the media, and eventually move on to college, they are ingesting the values, narratives, and structural privileges and barriers associated with racial identities. Although all theories of racial and ethnic identity development have some elements in common, they also have fundamental differences in the tasks assigned for White people and for people of color. People of color and multiracial people work to develop an identity that encompasses self-esteem and positive self-regard despite societal ambivalence or hostility toward their identity; White people face different challenges involving recognizing White privilege and supremacy and owning their own racism. People of color face the dual challenge of understanding how Whiteness operates in society and how they can survive in this world, while also having to learn about their own racial and ethnic group, resolving their relationship to both; White people need to make a commitment and effort to understand and confront racism.

With so many negative stereotypes in society at large, it is difficult for people of color and multiracial people not to internalize some of them. They also face identity denial and stereotypical reductions of their identities (Moadel-Attie et al., 2018). These factors can lead to higher stress and cortisol levels and consequent health risks (Yang et al., 2018). Therefore, part of the task for developing a positive racial identity is to dislodge internalized stereotypes and to externalize them. Ultimately, the hope is that people of color will achieve an identity that will enable them to survive and prosper in a social world where they encounter oppression and to feel good about who they are.

White people face the challenging task of unlearning racism. This involves forging a nonracist White identity. As we described in Chapter 5, White people do not see racism or the scope of White privilege for many reasons. Racial identity formation relies on being able to perceive this eventually and to place oneself in this racialized matrix. One of the biggest challenges for White people is that unlearning racism and coming to terms with White privilege cuts across the grain. Racism, not antiracism, is reinforced in society, with many pressures, both overt and subtle, to continue to assume White privilege and to discourage White people from challenging entrenched racial systems of advantage. This is one reason that support groups for unlearning racism can be so helpful, in the same way that groups and associations for people of color can offer mutual support and buffering from racism.

Multiracial/Biracial Identity Development

A problem with classic theories of racial and ethnic identity development is that many people today identify as biracial, multiracial, and multiethnic. In 2010, 15% of all marriages were multiracial, which is double what the percentage was in 1980 (Afful et al., 2015). Classical theories of ethnic and racial identity development do not capture the fluidity, importance of context, and unique ways of integrating different aspects of identity that are central to the identities of multiracial people. And all ethnic–racial identity development occurs in the context of multiple social identities (e.g., gender, social class) and how they uniquely interact and fit together within individuals (Santos, 2015).

There are many factors that shape the ethnic–racial identities of multiracial people. These include skin color and phenotype, family dynamics, social relationships, educational and community contexts, and the availability (or lack of) sociohistorical–cultural roles, as well as one's inner process of consciousness and decision-making (Santos, 2015). One's appearance influences how one is perceived by others in the world and can even influence intra-family dynamics. Students who are light-skinned Latinos or African Americans have described to us how they have been able to "pass" as White while their siblings or parents with darker skin are treated as people of color. Family dynamics are shaped by relations and alliances among parents, siblings, and extended family. These in turn are influenced by family history (including migration and where people settled), the nature of the neighborhood, and which social and community groups family members identify with and have relationships with (Aldarondo,

2001). Some multiracial and multicultural people grow up in an environment that predominantly stresses one side of their heritage, because of family dynamics, or perhaps the nature of the community in which they grow up (Poston, 1990). For other people, all aspects of their racial and ethnic identity are acknowledged and validated. There are times and places where there is a great range of possible social roles, which are fluid and flexible, or conversely where there are limited, rigidly proscribed options for the complex expression of identity.

Family dynamics do not develop in a vacuum, they reflect the sociocultural contexts in which families live. For example colorism, where lighter skin is more highly valued in a family than darker skin, reflects the values of coloniality and capitalism, where lighter-skinned people of color have more access to predominantly White institutions, corporations, and professions (Alcoff, 2012).

Rockquemore et al. (2009) have reviewed multiracial identity theory and found that there are four distinct conceptual approaches. One is focused on how multiracial individuals face more problems than other people. A second approach is to treat multiracial people as being the same as mono ethnic–racial people. A third way of approaching this topic has been to see the identities of multiracial people as always being different than those of mono ethnic–racial people—the "variant" approach. The fourth way, which Rockquemore et al. (2009) prefer, is an ecological approach. With this model, identity is fluid and situation and context dependent. There is no privileging of one aspect or identity state over another. Multiethnic–racial people may identify with one aspect of racial/ethnic identity, all aspects, no aspects, or, in some instances, continually shift from one identity to another, depending on a given situation or context (Rockquemore & Brunsma, 2004). Rockquemore et al. (2009) describe how multiracial people can occupy the border zone between their identities, live in one part of their identity, claim all aspects of their identity, or even reject all aspects of their identity.

Miville et al. (2005) conducted research with multiracial people to see what themes were prominent in their identity development. Many of their respondents described their regular encounters with racism and the unsettling experience of always being seen as different or asked "What are you?" Many also identified with one group (e.g., African American) as well as being multiracial. President Obama often describes himself as a multiracial African American man. Such identifications are influenced by reference groups as well as social categories and norms. Respondents also described how they were like "chameleons" and had learned how to adapt to a range of situations where they code-switched and accented or de-emphasized different parts of their identity. For many multiethnic–racial people, parts of their identities may be privileged or targeted (Binning et al., 2009; Cheng & Lee, 2009). Thus, identity resolution not only involves integrating disparate ethnic and racial identities but also reconciling higher or lower social statuses.

Albuja et al. (2019) have found that multiracial people often feel that they are denied membership in any of their identity groups. This has a negative impact on stress levels, health, and psychological well-being. There are also higher rates of substance abuse. Resistance to the erasure of identities through self-assertion helps to ameliorate some of this. Yang et al. (2018) have also found mindfulness- attending to the present moment, and attention and emotion regulation—to be helpful in such situations.

The ecological approach (Rockquemore et al., 2009) is one that we favor not only for multiracial people but for all people. Identity always involves intersectionality (see Chapter 8) and all people are adapting to situations and contexts as they construct and reconstruct their social identities. Helping professionals should be careful not to privilege any specific resolution of racial identity development for any people, as this creates additional pressure to conform to the others' expectations. With all aspects of social identity development, a transcendent goal is for people to feel positive and secure about themselves and to feel competent in negotiating their social world.

SOCIAL IDENTITY FACTORS

Using an ecological approach, we consider ethnic–racial identity formation in a nonlinear, nonjudgmental fashion. We strongly support people having agency over how they construct their social identities and shy away from hierarchies. However, we also believe that in order to dismantle racism, White people need to strongly consider, reflect on, and take steps to respond to their inherent White privilege. Failure to do so means collusion with White supremacy, which most White people consciously reject. Thus, we embrace an approach to ethnic–racial identity development, for both clients and helpers, which focuses on tasks rather than stages or phases. Before describing our model of multidimensional social identity development we would like to focus on factors that are important to consider.

- ▶ *Identity is internal and external* (Kwan & Sodowsky, 1997). Internal concepts of identity include people's views of themselves and their ethnic group, as well as their awareness of the history and values of their ethnic group. External identity refers to observable customs, behaviors, cultural practices, traditions, and rituals. Social identity combines internal and external aspects of identity, what is inside and what we show and express, and how we see ourselves and are seen by others.
- ▶ *Some aspects of identity are more enduring while others are fluid, situational, and contextual* (Arredondo, 1999; Rockquemore et al., 2009; Sellers et al., 1998). Some parts of our identity, such as a religious orientation, may feel fairly constant and enduring from situation to situation. However, other parts of identity, perhaps gender or sexual orientation, change over time or are activated by certain contexts and are suppressed and erased by others.
- ▶ *Identity connects us with our past and future* (Myers et al., 1991). Having a sense of racial and ethnic identity can tie people to ancestors, as well as descendents, with whom they can identify. Landau (2007) has referred to these connections among past, present, and future as "transitional pathways." If children or grandchildren modify, complicate, or abandon their ethnic and racial identities, this can be viewed by others in the family as threatening this connection—which often is why there can be emotional struggles over retaining historical and traditional identities.
- ▶ *Some aspects of identity are in the forefront* (Reynolds & Pope, 1991; Sellers et al., 1998). Many people have a hierarchy of aspects of their identity, in which some parts are more conscious and important for the individual. We often hear White students describe their social class, gender, or sexual orientation as being more significant for them than their racial identity. This is less common for students of color. When parts of identity are socially targeted and not mirrored by mainstream society, they tend to be salient and are more likely to enter conscious awareness.
- ▶ *Helping professionals should accept the validity of an individual's definition of their own identity* (Rockquemore et al., 2009; Sellers et al., 1998). Identity is subjective and

socially constructed, and when using relationships to help people, we must honor a consumer's self-constructions of identity. Unfortunately, society defines and generalizes about people, placing them in categories whether they choose to be in these groupings or not. The dignity and worth of each individual is affirmed when we begin by asking them how *they* socially define themselves. Validation in interpersonal relationships is vital to achieving a positive sense of identity (Rockquemore & Brunsma, 2004).

▶ *Identity development is not linear* (Henriksen & Trusty, 2004; Myers et al., 1991; Rockquemore et al., 2009; Sellers et al., 1998). Identity does not progress neatly through a series of linear steps. It is most helpful to track each person's own journey through identity development, which may proceed elliptically, in a spiral or zigzag formation, as well as step by step. Some people remain in the same place, skipping phases or stages altogether, while at other times people revisit earlier identity phases.

▶ *A person's identity has many dimensions* (Arredondo, 1999; Myers et al., 1991). Examples of identity dimensions are self-regard, salience and meaning, affect, worldview, opinions, and values and beliefs about one's identity.

MULTIDIMENSIONAL SOCIAL IDENTITY DEVELOPMENT

We have fashioned a model of social identity development that draws on many of the concepts just presented as well as our own clinical and teaching experience. We have focused on social identity rather than a narrower view of racial and ethnic identity development, as we have found that race and ethnicity are inseparable from other aspects of identity. Our model considers dimensions and clusters of identity, but we have consciously abandoned the notion of phases or stages because of the tendency to rank them hierarchically, which we believe is judgmental and proscriptive (see Figure 7.1). Instead, we discuss tasks associated with identity.

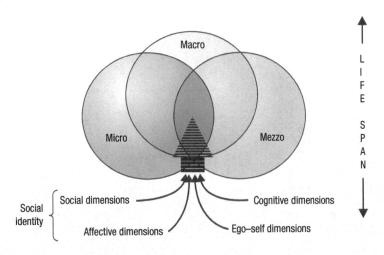

FIGURE 7.1 Multidimensional social identity development.

The model is holistic and values the complexity of social identity, the conflicts and contra-dictions among different aspects of a person's social identity, an individual's phenomenologi-cal experience and meaning, available and unavailable social roles, and the significance of the historical and material context in which identity emerges. We share the assumptions that underpin our model and then present its various components: axes of social identity, dimen-sions, contexts (both life span and environmental), and potential resolutions and stances for each axis (see Box 7.1). We then consider different tasks for both targeted and privileged parts of identity. (See Exercise 7.1 for a framework to explore this model.)

BOX 7.1 Social Identity Variables

Dimensions

1. Social: Who you affiliate with
2. Emotional: How you feel about who you are
3. Cognitive: How your social identity influences how you see the world (and vice versa)
4. Ego-self: How you view and describe yourself

Life-Span Context

Social identity is influenced by and shaped by life-span development: phase of life, health status, social situation, and living situation.

Environmental Context

1. *Macro:* Social identity is shaped by history, politics, nationality, cohort, and economics.
2. *Mezzo:* Social identity is shaped by where we work, live, our professions, schools, and social groups.
3. *Micro:* Social identity is contingent and interactional and is activated (or deacti-vated) by relationships, interactions, places, billboards, songs, books, and films.

Resolutions/Stances

1. Integrated to unintegrated
2. Complex to simple
3. Stable to fluid
4. Flexible/adaptable to fixed
5. Activist to passive
6. Collaboration to conflict

Axes of Social Identity

Race, ethnicity, gender, sexual orientation, class (both social and economic), religion, nationality, regional identity, immigration status, language capacity, physical ability/health

Adapted from Donner and Miller (2007).

ASSUMPTIONS

Most theories of identity development are predicated on assumptions about what is healthy and normal. Following are some of the assumptions underpinning the multidimensional social identity development model.

▶ *There are targeted and privileged identity statuses.* There is a spectrum ranging from being privileged to being targeted for every aspect of social identity. For example, White people are not stopped by the police while driving because of their race.

Many people have a mix of targeted and privileged statuses. For example, someone feels targeted by virtue of being a woman but is privileged by being middle class and White. Having a targeted or privileged status is a matter of degree and falls on a continuum rather than being limited to absolute categories.

The extent of racial oppression that people of color experience varies considerably, as does the amount of privilege for White people. For example, a dark-complexioned African American man may experience many forms of racism that a Japanese American woman does not, although each of them identifies as a person of color and has encountered some degree of racial prejudice. Similarly, a White man working as a custodian in a factory may have White skin privilege but lack economic security and class privilege.

How people view themselves in relation to others is highly subjective, as is their personal sense of having privilege or being socially oppressed. Much depends on their unique experience, which parts of their identity are most salient over time, and their exposure to specific social situations—such as repeatedly being stopped and searched by the police.

Croteau et al. (2002) found that having some aspects of identity that are socially targeted helps people connect with people from other oppressed groups, as well as having a more realistic understanding of the dynamics of oppression. Many variables, including how various axes of identity interact, personal experience, available resources, and the meaning one ascribes to one's identity, render a person's identity more complex than a binary classification of oppressed or privileged.

Those with privileged aspects of social identity may have the capacity to understand the experience of those with oppressed identity statuses by virtue of intimate and personal relationships. A White partner of a person of color can empathize deeply with the experience of racism. A White mother of biracial children can better understand her own racial identity and privileges through her children's experiences with oppression (O'Donoghue, 2004). However, this is not always the case and we know multiracial people who do not feel understood by their White parent.

There are also aspects of identity in which a person experiences both privilege and being targeted within the same axis. Examples are multiethnic–racial people or those who identify as bisexual who might experience privileged and targeted aspects of their identity simultaneously. Also, some people consciously change an aspect of their social identity—such as those who are transgender or transsexual—and in the process shift their social status. A transgender woman experienced herself as being male during one phase of her life before becoming female. Even within the category of "women," she may experience minority status. A working-class White male who becomes a college professor has shifted his social class and, although his inner sense of self still may be working class, his economic and social status have risen in society.

We have given these examples to illustrate how targeted and privileged identity statuses are relative, fluid, and contextual and not always clear-cut. Therefore, although societal privileges are attached to different social identity statuses, virtually any axis of social identity can change over time and can be personally reconstructed or redefined in different contexts.

▶ *Identity is holistic and personal.* People may be highly aware of race or gender, and this may be central to their self-concept and lived experiences. But most people do not appreciate being characterized by one aspect of their identity, because they view themselves as more complex and holistic beings. All aspects of identity intersect, including those parts that are unconscious. In addition, people do not appreciate when other people make assumptions or judgments about who they are.

▶ *Understanding the complexity of social identity of oneself and one's clients is vital for helping professionals.* Although we have tried to honor the phenomenology and subjectivity of social identity development, we are writing to an audience of helping professionals. To enhance their capacity to help others without conscious or unconscious prejudice, helping professionals must strive to reach a point of personal comfort and self-esteem, as well as respect and empathy for those who are different. Helping professionals should continually strive to understand their own complex social identities, as well as those of clients and consumers.

AXES OF SOCIAL IDENTITY

Our model of social identity posits that we all have social identities that can be separated into distinct axes. Among the more common coordinates that form a person's social identity are race, ethnicity, gender, social class, economic class, sexual orientation (and performance), nationality, religion, age, and health or disability status. This is not an inclusive list. For example, we have worked with clients and students whose regional identity, such as coming from the southeastern United States, was salient for them. One of us also consulted with a social service agency staffed by Asian and Asian American clinicians, for whom immigration status and linguistic preferences and competency were significant social identity factors.

And even within our list of social identity coordinates, the valence and relevance of various aspects of social identity vary considerably among individuals and groups. Helping professionals should understand the *meaning* that each aspect of social identity has for themselves as well as their clients, and appreciate the social advantages and baggage carried by each axis.

Dimensions

The following four dimensions—social, affective, cognitive, and ego-self—are part of each axis of social identity:

▶ *Social.* The social dimension refers to groups and people with whom a person identifies or dis-identifies and which groups of people they spend time with. This includes what people often refer to as their "community," which is more a socially constructed sense of community and less a geographic rendering of area or district.

▶ *Affective.* The affective, or emotional dimension of identity development refers to the feelings people have about an aspect of their identity, such as pride, joy, ambivalence, shame, rage, sorrow, acceptance, indifference, attraction, and denial. Feelings about our identity are influenced as well by the affective reactions that *others* have in response to our identity.

▶ *Cognitive.* Feelings influence thoughts (and vice versa), and people have cognitive reactions at different phases of social identity development. This literally means the way one thinks about and understands the world at large. Social identity influences perception and analysis—how one sees, what one hears, and the sense and meaning one makes of experience.

▶ *Ego-self.* The final dimension refers to how we perceive, think about, and describe ourselves. We observe ourselves as actors engaged with the social world and this, in turn, leads to metanarratives, the story of our identity in action that we tell ourselves and others. The ego-self dimension responds to the question, "Who am I in relation to others?"

Social identity dimensions interact and cluster together. Sometimes, they are synchronized and in accord and contribute to a sense of clarity and consistency but may also clash and lead to internal conflict. There is no right or wrong assemblage for these dimensions, but how they coalesce has implications for social identity at a specific point in time as well as the salience of a given axis of social identity.

Life-Span Context

Social identity development occurs throughout the life span. As a person grows and matures, the meanings of different aspects of one's social identity are revised, reviewed, and reworked. For example, the meaning and sense of one's gender probably will be quite different at ages 2, 5, 16, 25, 40, and 65. Yet everyone does not have the same experience at a certain age. Some women become aware of their targeted gender status as children or adolescents, others in middle age, and still others may not pay much attention to status differences at any age. At whatever age people grapple with some aspect of their social identity, their life span development influences how they process and come to terms with their social identity. Age is itself an axis of social identity.

Life-span development can also influence a person's social status. For example, older couples who are still in the workforce tend to be wealthier than younger, single people who have been employed just recently. Or some retirees find themselves sliding downward economically. Psychological tasks vary considerably throughout the life course and have a bearing on social identity development. Thus, the meanings of race and ethnicity are likely to be very different for an adolescent who is struggling to establish an identity and joining peer groups than for a retired person who is grappling with retirement and impending issues of mortality.

Environmental Context

Who we are and how we see ourselves are influenced profoundly by environmental contexts, past and present. Even future contexts shape the contours of social identity, as we imagine where we want to go or who we hope to be. Environments affect who we encounter and what we see or do not see, and create a gestalt in which some aspects of identity become figure and others become ground. For example, a White teenager from a predominantly White suburb may not have thought much about her racial identity until she finds herself taking a subway through a predominantly African American section of a city, with few other White riders, and has a sudden surge of awareness of herself as a White person. Or a working-class male may not have thought about the ways in which he is privileged until he attends a social work program that is predominantly female. Middle-class participants in the same program may not have paid much attention to their class status until they were engaged in discussions with the aforementioned working-class male.

Different social roles are available during different historical epochs and these limit or expand which social identities can be claimed as well as the existence or absence of social communities that support aspects of social identity (Rockquemore et al., 2009; Santos, 2015). For example, the social role of being a transgender person is available today in a way that was not a social concept or category for people a century ago. The social identity of multiracial was expanded by adding it as a census category, which offers a range of social identity possibilities unavailable when the "one drop rule" was shaping how people were racially constructed and counted. Social stereotypes tend to constrict and inhibit the range of possibilities for social identity.

Environmental contexts fall into the following three categories:

▶ *Macro contexts.* Macro contexts encompass large historical and societal contexts. For example, if a country is at war, its people may be much more aware of their citizenship, gender, and age than during peacetime. Political environments affect social identity, as witnessed by the influence of the Civil Rights Movement and the Great Society on raising awareness about racial oppression and racial identity. Another macro context is geographical—one's community, region, or country.

▶ *Mezzo contexts.* Examples of mezzo contexts are professions, schools, agencies, and other organizations in which we find ourselves throughout much of our lives. Children attending highly diverse and integrated schools are likely to have a very different consciousness about their racial identity than are students who attend homogeneous schools. A social service agency in San Francisco is likely to have an entirely different discourse about sexual orientation than one in a rural town in Mississippi—which will influence how workers think about themselves and interact with one another.

▶ *Micro contexts.* Micro contexts include families, as well as the small, quotidian, and ubiquitous fabric of everyone's lives. They are the streets we walk down, the stores we pass or shop in, the songs we hear on the radio, and the food available (or unavailable) in the supermarket. Micro contexts contain social and cultural markers that privilege certain social identities while marginalizing others.

Although identity has autonomous and enduring aspects, it also is co-constructed and reconstructed in the micro context of relationships with others (Moffat & Miehls, 1999). Each interaction has symbolic meanings in which we are aware not only of how we want to present ourselves but also how the other person expects us to present ourselves (Cooley, 1922; Goffman, 1959; Pfuetze, 1954). All of us have found that some aspects of ourselves come to life in one friendship but not in other friendships or in a work environment. Thus, the aspects of our social identity that are present, conscious, understood, and validated vary between relationships and even in different encounters with the same person or groups.

Resolutions/Stances

We have identified six resolutions/stances for a person's social identity that transcend any one axis of social identity. Exploring these identity standpoints can be useful when considering interpersonal and intergroup relationships. We do not place a value on these stances, and they are not binary, either/or dichotomies; rather, they offer a spectrum of overlapping possibilities.

- ▶ *Integrated to unintegrated.* There are times when people find that they integrate most aspects of their social identity, and others when there are less integrated parts, which may include zones outside of conscious awareness or areas of great ambivalence. For example, one person may feel passionately about their class background and work to challenge class oppression while having done little thinking about racial identity, gender, and sexual orientation. Another person may have made many connections between the various parts of their social identity and been able to integrate targeted and agent axes, gaining a sense of how their identity reflects privileges and areas in which they also are oppressed.

- ▶ *Complex to more simple.* The complexity or simplicity of a person's social identity relates to the previous discussion. A person with a clear sense of one aspect of their identity but not others may have a straightforward sense of who they are in the world, while someone else might see themselves as having many identity strands that cohere in intricate, multifaceted ways. Environmental contexts influence this stance. Heterogeneous societies are more likely to foster complex identities than are more homogeneous or fundamentalist societies, where there are more limited social roles.

- ▶ *Stable to fluid.* In addition to some social identities being integrated or unintegrated, or complex or simple, they may be stable or fluid. This resolution is influenced by lifespan development, environmental contexts, and the availability of social roles. Some people have identities that endure over time, while others experience a great deal of flux and transition, which may raise more questions than provide answers.

- ▶ *Flexible/adaptable to fixed.* Although this stance relates to stability, it is not exactly the same. Some social identities, even when stable, are able to continually take in new information about oneself and others and have the capacity for plasticity and adaptation. For example, someone's ethnic identity may remain stable in its central importance to the person but has been modified in terms of what it means and how it is integrated into a person's lifestyle. By contrast, another person's social identity may have cohered at a certain life-span phase (e.g., adolescence) and be constructed in such a way that new information or critical experiences will do little to change or alter it.

- ▶ *Active to passive.* The stability, adaptability, and complexity of a social identity can have implications for how empowered people feel and whether or not they believe they have the capacity to exert agency about their social identity. This also involves a cognitive appraisal of the social conditions in which identity is grounded and whether or not a person believes that there is value in asserting who they are, particularly if this runs counter to cultural and social expectations.

- ▶ *Collaboration to confrontation.* The final stance that has implications for interpersonal and intergroup dynamics is whether social identity inclines people to approach change through collaboration with others, including people with diverse social identities, or wariness about working with those who have divergent social identities, which is more likely to lead to confrontation or isolation. This can be manifested in interpersonal relationships, small groups, and large groups, all the way up to how nations conduct their affairs with other nations.

SOCIAL IDENTITY: LEVELS OF AWARENESS, PERFORMANCE, AND TASKS

Thus far, we have described the various dimensions, contexts (life span and environmental), and resolutions/stances of each axis of social identity development. We now consider different ways that identity is experienced by people as well as how people choose to perform their social identities. This involves how people see themselves and others, the feelings that accompany this, behaviors, and the actions that people choose to take.

Each aspect of social identity has corresponding degrees of social status, and these statuses carry different levels of privilege and degrees of oppression. Although we do not subscribe to a binary, either/or way of conceptualizing the differences in these social statuses, for the purposes of illustrating this model, we have presented potential social identity tasks using the concepts of *target* and *agent* identities as we did in Chapter 1 (Hardiman & Jackson, 1997). Target identities are those aspects of identity that correspond to social statuses that are more on the marginalized and scapegoated end of the spectrum, in which groups of people suffer exclusion and oppression. Agent identities correspond to social statuses that are more privileged by society and reflect dominant norms and assumptions and are afforded unearned and unequal rights by virtue of this status.

Even though we present only one aspect of a person's social identity development to illustrate our model, we should keep in mind that each axis of social identity is interacting with other axes; most people are grappling with a process that may involve a highlighted aspect of their social identity but in concert with other axes of identity.

Identities That Are at the Socially Targeted End of the Spectrum

TASKS: The most important task for those wrestling with a targeted aspect of their identity is to ultimately embrace who they are while externalizing and rejecting the webs of social oppression they may have internalized in the form of stereotypes, low self-esteem, self-doubts, and self-alienation. Internalized social oppression is destructive to individual and collective well-being, and a primary task of social identity development for those who are targeted is to have pride in, respect for, and comfort with their social self. This in turn frees people to make decisions about how to perform their identity and to make choices regarding personal resistance and the means and levels of social activism.

Identities That Are at the Socially Privileged End of the Spectrum

TASKS: While a task for people with a targeted identity is to shed internalized stereotypes and negative self-images, for people with agent identity, the charge is to recognize their agent status, which often is initially invisible to them, and to discard internalized feelings of superiority. Although people with targeted identity status usually have to confront that status in the face of oppression, those with agent status can ignore their privileged identity and social group membership more easily. Thus, it also is easier *not* to move through many of the later phases, as society is structured to mirror the agent identity status; to disown agent status poses risks and challenges.

As we mentioned earlier, grappling with privilege often involves cognitive dissonance between a person's conscious values and their realization of unearned privileges or unearthed stereotypes, which raises feelings of guilt, shame, and anger that need to be processed in order to become a colleague, ally, and responsible world citizen. People with high levels of social identity privilege can easily retreat into their privileges and displace these feelings onto people with less privilege; in other words, socially withdrawing while blaming the victim. At times, while grasping the levels of social oppression of others and one's unearned privilege that were heretofore not conscious, a person may feel very alienated from friends, family, and society. While having such reactions, it is important to not direct one's pain or rage at others while not examining oneself; to call out rather than call in. Ultimately, people with high degrees of social privilege need to make conscious decisions about how they live their lives and how this intersects with the lives of people who are socially targeted or with less social privilege.

As we have mentioned in earlier chapters, White supremacy is now expressed more openly since Donald Trump became president of the United States. Far-right White supremacist groups have been winked at and even embraced at the highest levels of government and are now represented within the Republican party at all levels of government. This makes it even more challenging for some White people to shed their internalized White supremacy as it has now been legitimized and many White people, aggrieved by the perception of "reverse racism," have political, social, and psychological space to not only avoid examining White privilege but to take pride and celebrate it. Identities bathed in White privilege and supremacy rely on "artificial origin stories and strategic forgetting" (Alcoff, 2012). This has implications for intergroup relations, which we will now consider.

IDENTITY AND INTERGROUP RELATIONS

So far, we have been considering the process of social identity development from the perspective of the individual. Social affiliations—how people feel part of or separate from groups—are intricately related to social identity. We also have described the process of racism as one of group inequality. Thus, it is useful to consider how social identity leads to group affiliation (and vice versa) and how this contributes to durable inequalities such as racism. Stephan (2008b) has identified five factors that shape "prejudice" in intergroup relations: historical contexts, sociocultural structures and reality, situational factors (such as competing for limited resources), personality factors (research has consistently confirmed that people with more authoritarian personalities are more prone to prejudice), and phenomenological factors (e.g., meaning, discourses that shape how people interpret and understand events). We have covered all of these factors in earlier chapters but would like to delve more deeply into intergroup dynamics.

"Optimal distinctiveness theory" postulates that humans have a need to both individuate and affiliate (Brewer, 2001). Groups potentially offer members many benefits: a sense of identity and belonging, validation, support, resources, security, buffering, and a source of meaning. At times of social change, turbulence, and uncertainty, it feels reassuring to have the security of a group social identity (Abrams, 2015). Political, religious and community leaders can articulate categories of identity and what it means to be part of a particular group. Inclusion in a group can meet the need for belonging; in turn, the group can meet the need for differentiation by stressing the differences between in-group and out-group members. Feeling a sense of in-group pride and solidarity can be healthy and validating, but when it is predicated on demeaning members of the out-group, it can lead to intergroup strife and conflict.

This can be accompanied by disowning negative and undesirable traits from the in-group and displacing them and projecting them onto the out-group members, describing them as being lazy, untrustworthy, morally deficient, and even less than human (Erikson, 1968; Fisher, 1990; Group for the Advancement of Psychiatry [GAP], 1987; Miller & Schamess, 2000; Volkan, 1988). Viewing members of another group in such negative terms enhances the positive identities of members of the in-group (Crocker & Luhtanen, 1990; Triandafyllidou, 1998). This in turn accentuates differences between in-group and out-group members, further fueling intergroup mistrust and tensions (Brewer, 2001). Leaders such as Donald Trump, who are prone to splitting people into good and evil, are adept at exploiting in-group/out-group tendencies. In-group tendencies can be so strong that group members can inhabit an alternative universe of reality and accept lies as facts, such as the falsehood that Trump won the 2020 election.

When identifying with a group, members usually ascribe positive "group prototypes" to those within the group and negative stereotypes about members in other socially constructed groups (Dovidio et al., 2016). Accentuating positive attributes to in-group members and negative connotations to out-group members can lead to "misattribution" of the motives of out-group members (Brewer, 2001). An example is imputing malevolent intent to another group—surmising that its members mean to do harm to "us"—which can justify engaging in destructive, pre-emptive actions toward "them," legitimized by fear of those categorized as "other." This dynamic has been in play domestically since the founding of the United States; for example, legitimizing the near genocide of Native Americans because of their perceived threat to European settlers. It is very salient today in public discourses about building walls to keep out "undesirable" Mexican immigrants and in discussions about banning Muslims and people from the Middle East from entering the United States. And it is part of the dynamic where many Donald Trump supporters believe that the people who stormed the U.S. capitol were not really his supporters, but were Democrats and members of left-wing groups, such as ANTIFA. This also exemplifies the moral rectitude of in-group members: There is a naive realism—for example, a belief that Trump must have won the election, and bad behavior, like a violent insurrection directed at the government, must be the work of members of the out-group (Hughes, 2017). When there are such polarized in-group/out-group dynamics, compromise, or even seeing members of the outgroup as decent human beings, is nearly impossible.

This is part of a process that ascribes positive motivations to in-group members and bad morals and behaviors to out-group members. There are positive stereotypes about in-group members and negative stereotypes to explain similar situations (Dovidio et al., 2016; Todd & Galinsky, 2014). For example, let's look at a person who is unemployed and requires public assistance. If the unemployed person is a member of the same racial–ethnic in-group as the observer, the narrative may stress circumstances outside of one's control—the person was unfairly fired, or the economy was tight—making that person a worthy victim of external forces. For out-group members, however, the storyline might stress the lack of a work ethic and a tendency to seek government handouts. Misattributions such as this further fuel a sense of group differences and distinctions and increase the difficulty for members of one group to respond empathically to members of another group. During the presidential campaign of 2016, a frequent theme voiced by Republican candidate Trump was "taking back our country" in the wake of the first African American president. Who is taking back the country and from whom?

Leaders can exploit group conflict by further demonizing and demeaning out-group members. The group that is being oppressed is viewed by the oppressors as a threat, justifying pre-emptory aggression (Bar-Tal, 2007). This dynamic has many historical examples, one of the most egregious of which was the Nazis' targeting of Jews as being subhuman. Nazi propaganda focused on the threat posed by Jews to non-Jewish Germans, which then was used to justify unspeakably brutal treatment toward Jews.

In the United States, leaders fanned similar flames to justify slaughtering Native Americans, enslaving African Americans, and placing Japanese Americans in concentration camps during World War II. To this day, invidious group distinctions have been used to justify wars and civil rights violations. In 2016, presidential candidate Donald Trump talked about Mexican immigrants to White audiences: "They're not sending their best. They're not sending you … . They're sending people with lots of problems, and they are bringing those problems with us. They're bringing drugs. They're bringing crime. They're rapists. And some, I assume, are good people" (Moreno, 2015). Many of Trump's supporters were working-class White voters who felt that they were losing "their" country (Porter, 2016). A more recent example of Trump's rhetoric leading to violence against members of a racial/ethnic group was his repeated insistence of calling COVID-19 "the Chinese virus." Since then, Asian Americans have been cursed at, spit at, and attacked, with some even leading to death (Tavernise & Oppel, Jr., 2020).

Group conflict reinforces in-group and out-group distinctions and fosters in-group solidarity, making dissent and disagreement more difficult, with less tolerance for difference. As President George W. Bush famously said after the attacks of 9/11, "either you are for us or against us." The rights of the individual are sacrificed in the name of group security. Many factors can either promote or reduce group conflict. For example, competition for scarce resources or territory (such as jobs or apartments) can heighten group conflict. This has been referred to as "realistic" group conflict, as contrasted with "unrealistic" group conflict, which occurs by virtue of the symbolic demonizing of another group (Bayor, 1988). An example of "unrealistic" group conflict would be the fears and prejudices of White people living in exclusively White communities, where they have no contact with people of color, and yet do not want them moving into their community. Ironically, the greatest levels of prejudice toward people of color are found among White people where there is little intergroup contact (Oliver & Wong, 2003).

Unequal power and privilege between groups can deepen group conflict, as can exploitation and monopolization of resources. Group dominance theory speculates that members of the dominant group learn to normalize and tolerate their superior position, while group norm theory complements this by illustrating how the dominance by one group then becomes what is considered "normal" by in-group members (Pratto & Stewart, 2012). It can also lead to a sense of existential threat by those used to power when there is the perception that previously subordinated "others" are exerting power and influence. Many Trump supporters have expressed the concern that they are losing their country (Hochschild, 2016). The January 6, 2021 attempt to overthrow the Democratic process occurred on the same day that the first African American ever elected as a Senator from Georgia, was declared the winner, tipping the balance of the Senate to Democrats. With the losses of Trump and control of the Senate, states controlled by the predominantly White Republican party are moving to pass restrictive voting requirements to make it more difficult for people of color to vote (Wines, 2021). The rationale is allegedly to cut down on "voter fraud," which consistently has been investigated and is not a major problem in U.S. elections: There are loud echoes here from the Jim Crow era, when racialized restrictive voting restrictions were legislated under the guise of protecting democratic elections.

However, intergroup conflict does not occur only between majority and minority groups, or between those with power and those facing oppression. The 1930s in New York City saw a fierce ethnic conflict between the Jews and the Irish, both recent immigrants, as they competed for jobs, apartments, occupational niches, and political power (Bayor, 1988). A similar process is occurring today in major U.S. cities between African Americans, Latinos, and Asian/Asian Americans because of "demographic restructuring, social dislocations, and spatial isolation" (Johnson & Oliver, 1994, p. 197).

The perception of having efficacy can buffer the stress of perceived hostility from members of other groups (Dion, 2002), so another factor in intergroup relations is the control, or lack of control, over a group's narrative (Thomas, 1994). It is often remarked that history is written by the victors, and this dynamic certainly is true of racial and ethnic relations. Although there are revisionist history books, such as Takaki's (1993) A Different Mirror or Lepore's (2018) *These Truths,* most U.S. citizens have been schooled on historical narratives emphasizing the positive virtues of early White European settlers and have erased the depth and extent of racism throughout U.S. history. The stories of the exploitation and suffering of people of color are accorded insufficient space in mainstream history courses and public discourse, and as mentioned earlier are intentionally erased from school history books in the state of Texas. The ability to tell the story of one's group and to present it to others, and for it to be received empathically, is an important step toward resolving intergroup conflict, as we shall consider in Chapter 8.

What Can Prevent or Alleviate Intergroup Conflict?

Conflict between groups and exploitation of one group by another is not inevitable, nor is it a hopeless historical inheritance. Just as processes of identity and group behavior foster mistrust and tension, steps can be taken to reduce this conflict (see Box 7.2). Ultimately, stressing our commonalities and similarities can bridge differences and offer a framework to heal wounds, as long as we do not erase inequalities that continue to persist (Dovidio et al., 2016). We mention briefly some steps that work in this direction.

▶ *Overarching, common goals.* It is helpful to establish superordinate objectives and purposes that unite, rather than divide (Brewer, 2001). For example, a course that uses this book should establish that the purpose of conducting an in-depth examination of racism, which is such a divisive social force, is to prepare all readers entering the helping professions to be better professionals. We are united in our desire and commitment to become better social workers, psychologists, psychiatrists, counselors, therapists, nurses, and social service workers. We all share this goal, and even if we have had experiences that divide us or face challenges when trying to talk about this topic, we are unified in our professional identity and codes of ethics.

▶ *Recategorization to achieve a "superordinate" identity* (Dovidio et al., 2016). A superordinate identity means that there is a higher level of identity uniting people rather than accentuating group differences. Examples are being a psychologist or social worker, or a U.S. citizen. However, there is also a risk that such an identity resonates with Whites more than people of color if the structural conditions that privilege Whites and

---

BOX 7.2 What Can Prevent or Alleviate Intergroup Conflict?

1. Having overarching, common goals that emphasize what members from different groups have in common.
2. Separating positive group identities from negation of members of other groups.
3. Facilitating contact and fostering relationships between members of different groups.
4. Fostering healing and reconciliation rather than demonizing and accentuating differences.
5. Fostering empathy for the pain of members of other groups and recognizing the historical narrative of their suffering.
6. Resolving both the practical and symbolic issues that foster conflict.
7. Establishing a process for intergroup dialogue, taking group responsibility, reconciliation, and reparations.
8. Focusing on shared concrete and long-term goals.

---

oppress people of color persist. Dovidio et al. (2016) have found that one way of mitigating this dilemma is to have both the superordinate identity as well as retaining a subgroup identity. Yes, all psychiatrists share a superordinate identity, but psychiatrists who are people of color also may want to maintain ethnic and racial identities that mark unique positioning within the profession.

▶ *Positive identity not predicated on negation of the "other."* It is normal for people to want to feel good about the groups of which they are members, as this increases their own sense of self-esteem (Brewer, 2001; Crocker & Luhtanen, 1990; Kelman, 2001). But this need not lead them to denigrate other groups. Thus, we must distinguish between having pride in oneself and one's group and needing to disparage other groups. Actually, vilification of others is frequently a warning sign that collective self-esteem is low and requires an external target to boost it.

▶ Focus on concrete examples as well as abstract principles (Verkuyten et al., 2019)— This helps when there is in-group moralizing about out-group members. It helps to look at shared goals, which can lessen the demonization of adversaries (Hughes, 2017).

An example on a national level is Staub's (2001) distinction between "constructive" patriotism, which is thoughtful pride in one's nation, and "blind" patriotism, which views the outside world as inherently dangerous or evil and does not question the policies or actions of one's own nation.

▶ *Contact and relationships.* Regular, respectful, and real contact between people mitigates against stereotypes by offering real relationships as the basis for understanding other people (Stephan, 2008a). People from different ethnic and racial groups have more commonalities than differences, so actual relationships, whether they are between individuals or within groups, create more opportunities for exploring what people have in common. Relationship allows people to interact verbally and cognitively, emotionally and behaviorally (Stephan, 2008a). Working on overarching goals places people in the position of working together, and intergroup dialogue creates structured opportunities to listen and share.

Friendships have the effect of making it more difficult to misattribute motives and intentions (Shelton & Richeson, 2005). Being in relationship with people is not without its challenges, particularly when there is a history of mistrust and out-group denigration, but actual connection is preferable to the dehumanization that is more possible when there is no affiliation. However, positive relationships are not a substitute for engaging in meaningful social action to challenge racial inequalities (DeMott, 1995) and only improving interracial relations without accompanying structural changes can help Whites to feel better about themselves without addressing racism (Dovidio et al., 2016).

It is also possible to have structured opportunities for virtual intergroup contact by the use of online forums, chat rooms, exercises, and other cyber means of engaging people together (White et al., 2015).

▶ *Leadership that fosters healing and reconciliation.* Leadership can sow seeds of divisiveness and hatred or can be a voice for compassion, empathy, and healing (Staub, 2001; Whillock, 1995). We have witnessed this phenomenon repeatedly in the United States and throughout the world. We have offered many examples of the racist, anti-immigrant, anti-Muslim, anti-Asian rhetoric of Donald Trump. It has given voice to latent racial hatred and legitimized it. One of many examples is when high school students in Indiana held up a picture of Trump while yelling "build a wall" at students from a largely Hispanic high school during a basketball game (Egan, 2016). Leaders shape public narratives and give voice to fears and hopes.

Leadership can humanize those who are different or can demonize them, justifying oppression and aggression.

▶ *Empathy for the suffering of the other group and recognition of its historical narrative.* The absence of empathy is most apparent during times of group exploitation and intergroup conflict. When people are described as "lazy," "violent," "criminal," "inscrutable," "subhuman," "savages," or coming from "shithole countries," it is difficult to engender understanding and compassion. "Brother," "sister," and "fellow human being," conversely, prompt compassion. Groups must develop processes to listen to one another empathically and to hear and validate wounds and suffering (Staub, 2001). Each group also should control the narrative it presents and have autonomy and authorship of the story being told (Thomas, 1994). "Perspective taking" is one way to increase intergroup empathy (Todd & Galinsky, 2014). This involves listening to stories from members of the other group (these can also be in the form of vignettes, recordings, or pictures) and imagining how the other person feels or how one would feel if you were that person (Todd & Galinsky, 2014).

▶ *Resolving practical and symbolic issues alike that foster conflict.* Intergroup conflict often involves "realistic" areas of competition and disagreement, as well as powerful symbols, historical and contemporary, that hold great meaning for group members. Failure to respond to both of these areas of divergence can lead to partial or unresolved conflict (Kelman, 2001). The enduring negative stereotypes that burden people of color in the United States need to be named, deconstructed, and discarded.

▶ *Establishing a process to take group responsibility.* Most intergroup conflict has arisen between groups with unequal power and resources, resulting in the subjugation and domination of one group by another. Reconciliation requires acknowledging past wrongs and taking responsibility for prior exploitation and current reparations.

Yamamoto (1999) conceptualized a four-step process involving:

1. Recognizing the humanity of the other group
2. Taking responsibility for past wrongs
3. Reconstructing fractured relationships
4. Establishing a process for reparations and healing

Each of these steps is challenging and requires enlightened leadership and collective commitment, but the rewards can be to heal wounds that have festered for centuries.

IMPLICATIONS FOR THE HELPING PROFESSIONS

The process of racial identity formation and of intergroup relations is a central, ongoing dynamic for workers in the helping professions. All human service and health care occupations rely on interpersonal contact and the centrality of the worker–consumer relationship. In a multiracial, multiethnic society, professionals must be committed to fairness, equity, and social justice, to take race and culture into account when providing services.

Racial identity and social identity theory are helpful in understanding ourselves, as well as our clients and colleagues. Ultimately, using relationships to help people thrive when we have a good understanding of who we are, who our consumers are, and how this influences our relationships with one another. If we can situate and position ourselves by reflecting on our social identity, we are more likely to have a sense of self-awareness and less likely to act out our prejudices unconsciously or to think and behave in a way that meets our own identity needs rather than responding to those of our clients.

If we can develop a greater sense of comfort with ourselves, as well as an awareness of and respect for cultural differences, we can own our assumptions and worldviews without imposing them on others. If we are mindful of our own experiences of power, privilege, oppression, and marginalization, we can respond more empathically to our clients, who have had their own mix of these experiences and are engaged in their own quests for identity and self-esteem.

Some theorists have attempted to map out the potential dynamics between clients and workers, depending on the racial identities of both parties (Carter, 1995; Helms, 1990; Helms & Cook, 1999). We are reluctant to present such equations, as they can lead to prejudgments and overgeneralizations. Nevertheless, we do share our belief that practitioners—on their own, as well as through supervision and consultation—should explore and assess their social identities and, when working with clients, be mindful of how social identities interact in the helping relationship.

We all can benefit from the perspectives of trusted others, whether they are similar or different from us in their social identities, as we reflect on ourselves and in our work with clients. People with similar social identities can be empathic and understanding of challenges and struggles, hidden biases, and areas of resistance, as they may have traveled over similar terrain. Consulting with colleagues of different social identities offers diverse perspectives, encouraging us to view things in different ways and to leave familiar comfort zones. It is also helpful to consult with colleagues who are familiar with the social identities of consumers.

Working with social identity is not just about working with clients. It involves our relationships with colleagues, too. At work, we interact as individuals, and midsize and larger organizations have subgroups and cliques of workers. Interpersonal tensions and misunderstandings at work often are related to differences in social identity and the consequent intergroup dynamics.

Workplaces often fail to recognize these dynamics, or they do not have the capacity to explore and respond to intergroup discord when it arises. We have explored this topic and offered recommendations in Chapter 11. Often these tensions escalate beyond individual miscues and become part of an organizational culture characterized by mistrust and group splintering, which ultimately harm professional cohesiveness and productivity. It also can lead to low morale, suspicion, wariness, and alienation from the agency. Understanding the dynamics of intergroup conflict can shed light on tensions between subgroups of colleagues working together within an organization, as well as interactions between staff and consumers.

CONCLUSION

It is important for helping professionals to have a good sense of their own identity as well as those of their clients. As social identity is closely aligned with groups, it also is useful for helping professionals to appreciate the dynamics of conflict and cooperation between groups with differing social identities. Social identity is a foundational concept for helping professionals trying to work effectively cross-racially and concerned with undoing racism. Therefore, we develop this concept in subsequent chapters.

In Chapter 8, we continue our consideration of social identity by exploring intersectionality—the relationship between racism with social class, gender, sexual orientation, and immigration status. We build on this foundation in Chapter 9, further examining the impact of social identity on relationships with colleagues and how to talk about racism and other issues surrounding social identity.

The discussion of social identity and intergroup conflict will be helpful in understanding Chapters 10 and 11, as we consider antiracism work by human service professionals in the community and in agencies. Social identity also is a central concept in Chapter 12, where we discuss cross-racial/cultural clinical work, and Chapter 13, which describes teaching about race and racism. All antiracism work is enhanced by an appreciation of the complexity of social identity.

EXERCISE 7.1 Multidimensional Social Identity Exercise

This exercise helps you map out your own social identity.

General Questions/Life-Span Context

1. Which axes of your social identity have the most meaning for you today?
2. Which axes had the most meaning for you during the following periods of your life: preschool, elementary school, high school, or college?

3. What experiences or social and historical factors have been most influential in the evolution of your social identity?
4. What family influences have had a strong effect on your social identity?
5. When you are with your best friend, which parts of your social identity most come to life?
6. When you are in a public situation (e.g., work, school), which parts of your social identity are you most aware of? Least aware of? Which parts are other people aware of?
7. Do you feel that there are other people like you? Do you have connections with them?

Dimensions

Taking one axis of your social identity that is relatively *privileged* and one that is relatively *targeted*, respond to the following questions:

1. When you have a choice, which people do you seek to be with?
2. What groups do you feel a part of that connect with this aspect of your social identity?
3. What feelings do you have about this aspect of your social identity? Do some situations evoke certain feelings about this aspect of your social identity?
4. How does this aspect of your social identity influence how you see the world?
5. What does this aspect of your social identity say about who you are in relation to others?

Contexts

1. Think of a macro context (historical events, social movements, wars, community, etc.) that had a big influence on some aspect of your social identity. How did it influence the evolution of your social identity? Can you imagine living in a different place or at a different time and how your social identity development might have been different as a result?
2. Think of a mezzo context (school, workplace, organizational setting) that influenced your social identity development. What occurred in this context that had an impact on your identity?
3. Think of a relationship (a form of micro context) in which you find certain aspects of your social identity coming to life, then think of another relationship in which these aspects of your identity are not expressed. Which factors in the two relationships have an influence on your identity expression?

Resolutions/Stances

Think about how the following statements apply to you. What are some reasons they do or do not apply?

1. All parts of my identity are integrated and fit well together.
2. My social identity is straightforward and easily explained to other people.
3. My social identity has not changed much in the past 20 years.
4. I am happy with the way my social identity fits me and am not seeking to adapt or change any aspects of it.

5. I believe that I have the capacity to change and improve the social conditions that shape my social identity.
6. I feel completely comfortable and like working with people on issues of social identity and social oppression, however similar or dissimilar they are to me.

REFERENCES

Abrams, D. (2015). Social identity and intergroup relations. In M. Mikulincer & P. R. Shaver (Eds.), *APA Handbook of personality and social psychology: Group processes* (Vol. 2, pp. 203–228). American Psychological Association.

Afful, S. E., Wholford, C., & Stoelting, S. M. (2015). Beyond "difference": Examining the process and flexibility of racial identity in interracial marriages. *Journal of Social Issues, 71*(4), 659–674.

Albuja, A. F., Gaither, S. E., Sanchez, D. T., Straka, B., & Cipollina, R. (2019). Psychophysiological stress responses to bicultural and biracial identity denial. *Journal of Social Issues, 75*(4), 1165–1191. https://doi.org/10.1111/josi.12347

Alcoff, L. M. (2012). Anti-Latino racism. In A. D. Isasi-Diaz & E. Mendieta (Eds.). *Decolonizing epistemologies: Latina/o theology and philosophy.* Fordham University Press.

Aldarondo, F. (2001). Racial and ethnic identity models and their application: Counseling biracial individuals. *Journal of Mental Health Counseling, 23*(3), 233–255.

Arredondo, P. (1999). Multicultural counseling competencies as tools to address oppression and racism. *Journal of Counseling and Development, 77*, 102–108.

Atkinson, D., Morten, G., & Sue, D. (1993). *Counseling American minorities* (4th ed.). W. C. Brown.

Bar-Tal, D. (2007). Sociopsychological foundations of intractable conflicts. *American Behavioral Scientist, 50*(11), 1430–1453.

Bayor, R. H. (1988). *Neighbors in conflict: The Irish, Germans, Jews and Italians of New York City, 1929–1941.* University of Illinois Press.

Binning, K. R., Unzueta, M. M., Huo, Y. J., & Molina, L. E. (2009). The interpretation of multiracial status and its relation so social engagement and psychological well-being. *Journal of Social Issues, 65*(1), 35–49.

Brewer, M. B. (2001). Ingroup identification and intergroup conflict: When does ingroup love become outgroup hate? In R. D. Ashmore, L. Jussim, & D. Wilder (Eds.), *Social identity, intergroup conflict, and conflict resolution* (pp. 17–41). Oxford University Press.

Carter, R. T. (1995). Race and psychotherapy: Clinical applications in a sociocultural context. In The influence of race and racial identity in psychotherapy: Toward a racially inclusive model (Chap. 13, pp. 225–241). Wiley.

Cheng, C., & Lee, F. (2009). Multiracial identity integration: Perceptions of conflict and distance among multiracial individuals. *Journal of Social Issues, 65*(1), 51–68.

Cooley, C. H. (1922). *Human nature and the social order.* Scribner.

Crocker, J., & Luhtanen, R. (1990). Collective self-esteem and ingroup bias. *Journal of Personality and Social Psychology, 58*(1), 60–67.

Cross, W. (1978). The Thomas and Cross models of psychological nigrescence. *Journal of Black Psychology, 4*, 13–31.

Cross, W. (1991). *Shades of Black: Diversity in African-American identity.* Temple University Press.

Croteau, J. M., Talbot, D. M., Lance, T. S., & Evans, N. J. (2002). A qualitative study of the interplay between privilege and oppression. *Journal of Multicultural Counseling and Development, 30*, 239–258.

DeMott, B. (1995). *The trouble with friendship: Why Americans can't think straight about race.* Atlantic Monthly Press.

Dion, K. L. (2002). The social psychology of perceived prejudice and discrimination. *Canadian Psychology, 43*(1), 1–10.

Donner, S., & Miller, J. (2007). The complexity of multidimensional social identity development. In S. Borrmann, M. Klassen, & C. Spatscheck (Eds.), *International social work: Social problems, cultural issues and social work education* (pp. 75–94). Barbara Budnch Publishers.

Dovidio, J. F., Gaertner, S. L., Ufkes, E. G., Saguy, T., & Pearson, A. R. (2016). Included but invisible? The darker side of "we." *Social Issues and Policy Review, 10*(1), 6–46.

Egan, T. (2016, March 4). The beast is us. *The New York Times*. www.nytimes.com/2016/03/04/opinion/campaign-stops/the-beast-is-us.html

Erikson, E. H. (1963). *Childhood and society* (2nd ed.). W. W. Norton.

Erikson, E. H. (1968). *Identity, youth and crisis*. W. W. Norton.

Fisher, R. J. (1990). *The social psychology of intergroup and international conflict resolution*. Springer-Verlag.

Gilligan, C. (1977). In a different voice: Women's conceptions of self and morality. *Harvard Educational Review, 47*, 481–517.

Gilligan, C. (1982). *In a different voice: Psychological theory and women's development*. Harvard University Press.

Goffman, E. (1959). *The presentation of self in everyday life*. Anchor.

Group for the Advancement of Psychiatry (GAP). (1987). *Us and them: The psychology of ethnonationalism*. Brunner/Mazel.

Hardiman, R. (1982). *White identity development: A process-oriented model for describing the racial consciousness of White Americans*. Unpublished doctoral dissertation, University of Massachusetts, Amherst, MA.

Hardiman, R. (1994). White racial identity development in the United States. In E. P. Sallett & D. R. Koslow (Eds.), *Identity in multicultural perspective* (pp. 117–140). Washington, DC: National Multicultural Institute.

Hardiman, R., & Jackson, B. W. (1997). Conceptual foundations for social justice courses. In M. Adams, L. A. Bell, & P. Griffin (Eds.), *Teaching for diversity and social justice: A sourcebook* (pp. 16–29). Routledge.

Helms, J. (1990). *Black and White racial identity: Theory, research and practice*. Greenwood Press.

Helms, J. E., & Cook, D. A. (1999). *Using race and culture in counseling and psychotherapy*. Allyn & Bacon.

Henriksen, R. C., Jr., & Trusty, J. (2004). Understanding and assisting Black/White biracial women in their identity development. *Women & Therapy, 27*(1/2), 65–83.

Hirschfield, L. (2012). Seven myths of race and the young child. *De Bois Review, 9*(1), 17–39.

Hochschild, A. R. (2016). *Strangers in their own land: Anger and mourning on the American right*. The New Press.

Hoare, C. H. (2003). Psychosocial identity development in United States society: Its role in fostering exclusion of cultural others. In E. P. Salett & D. R. Koslow (Eds.), *Race, ethnicity and self: Identity in multicultural perspective* (2nd ed., pp. 17–35). Washington, DC: National Multicultural Institute.

Hughes, J. (2017). When cooperation and compromise fail: Distrusting and denigrating the moral character of those who disagree. *Analysis of Social Issues and Public Policy*. https://doi.org/10.1111/asap.12131

Jackson, K. (2009). Beyond race: Examining the facets of multiracial identity through a life-span developmental lens. *Journal of Ethnic and Cultural Diversity in Social Work, 18*(4), 293–310.

Johnson, J. H., & Oliver, M. L. (1994). Interethnic minority conflict in urban America: The effects of economic and social dislocations. In F. L. Pincus & H. J. Ehrlich (Eds.), *Race and ethnic conflict: Contending views on prejudice, discrimination, and ethnoviolence* (pp. 194–205). Westview Press.

Kelman, H. C. (2001). The role of national identity in conflict resolution: Experiences from Israeli-Palestinian problem solving workshops. In R. D. Ashmore, L. Jussim, & D. Wilder (Eds.), *Social identity, intergroup conflict, and conflict resolution* (pp. 187–212). Oxford University Press.

Kwan, K. K., & Sodowsky, G. R. (1997). Internal and external ethnic identity and their correlates: A study of Chinese ethnic immigrants. *Journal of Multicultural Counseling and Development, 25*(1), 51–68.

Landau, J. (2007). Enhancing resilience: Communities and families as agents of change. *Family Process, 41*(1), 351–365.

Lepore, J. (2028). *These truths: A history of the United States*. Basic Books.

Malott, K. M., Paone, T. R., Schaefle, S., Cates, J., & Haizlip, B. (2015). Exploring White racial identity theory: A qualitative investigation of Whites engaged in antiracist action. *Journal of Counseling and Development, 93*, 333–343.

Marcia, J. E. (1980). Identity in adolescence. In J. Adelson (Ed.), *Wiley series on personality processes: Handbook of adolescent psychology* (pp. 159–187). Wiley.

Marcia, J., Waterman, A., Matteson, D., Archer, S., & Orlofsky, J. (1994). *Ego identity: Handbook of psychosocial research*. Springer-Verlag.

Miller, J., & Schamess, G. (2000). The discourse of denigration and the creation of other. *Journal of Sociology and Social Welfare, 27*(3), 39–62.

Miville, M. L., Constantine, M. G., Baysden, M. F., & Go-Lloyd, G. (2005). Chameleon changes: An exploration of racial identity themes of multiracial people. *Journal of Counseling Psychology, 52*(4), 507–516.

Moadel-Attie, R., Levy, S. R., London, B., & Al-Rfou, M. (2018). Evolution of social identity in lay and academic sources: Implications for research and public policy. *Analysis of Social Issues and Public Policy, 18*(1), 323–352.

Moffat, K., & Miehls, D. (1999). Development of student identity: Evolution from neutrality to subjectivity. *Journal of Teaching in Social Work, 19*(1/2), 65–76.

Moreno, C. (2015, August 31). *9 outrageous things Donald Trump has said about Latinos.* The Huffington Post. http://www.huffingtonpost.com/entry/9-outrageous-things-donald-trump-has-said-about-latinos_us_55e483a1e4b0c818f618904b

Myers, L. J., Speight, S. L., Highlen, P. A., Cox, C. I., Reynolds, A. L., Adams, E. M., & Hanley, P. (1991). Identity development and worldview: Toward an optimal conceptualization. *Journal of Counseling and Development, 70,* 54–63.

O'Donoghue, M. (2004). Racial and ethnic identity development in White mothers of biracial, Black–White children. *AFFILIA: Journal of Women and Social Work, 19*(1), 68–84.

Oliver, J. E., & Wong, J. (2003). Intergroup prejudice in multiethnic settings. *American Journal of Political Science, 47*(4), 567–582.

Pfuetze, P. E. (1954). *Self, society and existence.* Harper Torch Books.

Phinney, J. (1989). Stages of ethnic identity development in minority group adolescents. *Journal of Early Adolescence, 9,* 34–49.

Phinney, J. (1992). The multigroup ethnic identity measure: A new scale for use with diverse groups. *Journal of Adolescent Research, 7*(2), 156–176.

Phinney, J. (1993). A three-stage model of ethnic identity development. In M. E. Bernal & G. P. Knight (Eds.), *Ethnic identity: Formation and transmission among Hispanics and other minorities* (pp. 61–79). State University of New York Press.

Phinney, J., & Kohatsu, E. L. (1999). Ethnic and racial identity development and mental health. In J. Schulenberg, J. L. Maggs, & K. Hurelmann (Eds.), *Health risks and developmental transitions during adolescence* (pp. 420–443). Cambridge University Press.

Ponterotto, J. G. (1988). Racial consciousness development among White counselor trainees: A stage model. *Journal of Multicultural Counseling and Development, 16,* 146–156.

Porter, E. (2016, January 5). Racial identities, and its hostilities, are on the rise in American politics. *The New York Times.* www.nytimes.com/2016/01/06/business/economy/racial-identity-and-its-hostilities-return-to-american-politics.html?emc=eta1

Poston, W. S. C. (1990). The bi-racial identity development model: A needed addition. *Journal of Counseling and Development, 69,* 152–155.

Pratto, F., & Stewart, A. L. (2012). Group dominance and the half-blindness of privilege. *Journal of Social Issues, 68*(1), 28–45.

Reynolds, A. L., & Pope, R. L. (1991). The complexities of diversity: Exploring multiple oppressions. *Journal of Counseling and Development, 70,* 174–180.

Rockquemore, K. A., & Brunsma, D. L. (2004). Negotiating racial identity: Biracial women and interactional validation. *Women & Therapy, 27*(1/2), 85–102.

Rockquemore, K. A., Brunsma, D. L., & Delgado, D. J. (2009). Racing to theory or retheorizing race? Understanding the struggle to build a multiracial identity theory. *Journal of Social Issues, 65*(1), 13–34.

Roland, A. (2003). Identity, self, and individualism in multicultural perspective. In E. P. Salett & D. R. Koslow (Eds.), *Race, ethnicity and self: Identity in multicultural perspective* (2nd ed., pp. 3–15). National Multicultural Institute.

Sabnani, H. B., Ponterotto, J. G., & Borodovsky, L. G. (1991). White racial identity development and cross-cultural counselor training: A stage model. *Counseling Psychologist, 19,* 76–102.

Santos, C. E. (2015). Current and future directions in ethnic-racial identity theory and research. In C. E. Santos & A. J. Umana-Taylor (Eds.), *Studying ethnic identity: Methodological and conceptual approaches across disciplines.* American Psychological Association.

Sellers, R. M., Smith, M. A., Shelton, N., Rowley, S. A. J., & Chavous, T. M. (1998). Multidimensional model of racial identity: A reconceptualization of African American racial identity. *Personality and Social Psychology Review*, 2(1), 18–39.

Shelton, J. N., & Richeson, J. A. (2005). Intergroup contact and pluralistic ignorance. *Journal of Personality and Social Psychology*, 88(1), 91–107.

Smith, E. J. (1991). Ethnic identity development: Toward the development of a theory within the context of majority/minority status. *Journal of Counseling and Development*, 70, 181–188.

Staub, E. (2001). Individual and group identities in genocide and mass killing. In R. D. Ashmore, L. Jussim, & D. Wilder (Eds.), *Social identity, intergroup conflict, and conflict resolution* (pp. 159–184). Oxford University Press.

Stephan, W. G. (2008a). The road to reconciliation. In A. Nadler, T. Molloy, & J. D. Fisher (Eds.), *The social psychology of intergroup reconciliation: From violent conflict to peaceful co-existence*. Oxford University Press.

Stephan, W. G. (2008b). Viewing intergroup relations in Europe through Allport's lens of prejudice. *Journal of Social Issues*, 64(2), 417–429.

Stets, J. E., & Burke, P. J. (2000). Identity theory and social identity theory. *Social Psychology Quarterly*, 63(3), 224–237.

Sue, D. W., & Sue, D. (2015). *Counseling the culturally diverse: Theory and practice* (7th ed.). Wiley.

Sullivan, S. (2014). *Good White people: The problem with middle-class White antiracism*. University of Albany Press.

Takaki, R. (1993). *A different mirror: A history of multi-cultural America*. Little, Brown.

Tavernise, S., & Oppel, Jr. (2020, March 23). Spit on, yelled at, attacked: Chinese-Americans fear for their safety. *The New York Times*. www.nytimes.com/2020/03/23/us/chinese-coronavirus-racist-attacks.html

Taylor, R. (1997). The changing meaning of race in the social sciences: Implications for social work practice. *Smith College Studies in Social Work*, 67(3), 277–298.

Thomas, L. (1994). Group autonomy and narrative identity: Blacks and Jews. In P. Berman (Ed.), *Blacks and Jews: Alliances and arguments*. Delacorte Press.

Todd, A. R., & Galinsky, A. D. (2014). Perspective taking as a strategy for improving intergroup relationships: Evidence, mechanisms, qualifications. *Social and Personality Psychology Compass*, 8(7), 374–387.

Triandafyllidou, A. (1998). National identity and the "other." *Ethnic and Racial Studies*, 21(4), 593–612.

Verkuyten, M., Yogeeswaran, K., & Adelman, L. (2019). Intergroup toleration and its implications for diverse societies. *Social Issues and Policy Review*, 13(1), 5–35. https://doi.org/10.1111/sipr.12051

Volkan, V. D. (1988). *The need to have enemies and allies: From clinical practice to international relationships*. Jason Aronson.

Whillock, R. K. (1995). The use of hate as a stratagem for achieving political and social goals. In R. K. Whillock & D. Slayden (Eds.), *Hate speech* (pp. 28–54). Sage.

White, F. A., Harvey, L. J., & Abu-Rayya, H. M. (2015). Improving intergroup relations in the Internet age: A critical review. *Review of General Psychology*, 19(2), 129–139.

Wines, M. (2021, February 7). In statehouses, stolen-election myth fuels a GOP drive to rewrite rules. *The New York Times*. wwsw.nytimes.com/2021/02/27/us/republican-voter-suppression.html

Yamamoto, E. (1999). *Interracial justice: Conflict and reconciliation in post-civil rights America*. New York University Press.

Yang, A. V., Ludvik, M. B., Sax., C. L., Garcia-Navarrete, S., Bracken, W., Wood, J. L., & Iyoho, C. (2018). Exploring whether mindfulness can enhance ethnic identity among undergraduate and graduate students. *Journal of Research in Innovative Teaching and Learning*, 11(1), 67–93. https://doi.org/10.1108/JRIT-08-2017-0016

Yeh, C. J., & Hwang, M. Y. (2000). Interdependence in ethnic identity and self: Implications for theory and practice. *Journal of Counseling and Development*, 78, 420–429.

Yi, K. (2014). Toward formulation of ethnic identity beyond the binary of White oppressor and racial other. *Psychoanalytic Psychology*, 31(3), 426–434.

CHAPTER

Intersectionality: Racism and Other Forms of Social Oppression

INTRODUCTION

Racism is very real, and although based on a fiction—the social construction of race—it has profoundly damaging consequences for individuals, groups, and society. Race is the dominant paradigm in the United States, and as a result so much of how things are perceived and experienced by individuals socialized here is through the lens of race. Race became a categorical identity in the United States in order to "reconcil[e] chattel slavery—as well as the extermination of indigenous peoples—with the ideals of freedom preached by Whites in the new colonies" (Alexander, 2010, p. 23). It was then "scientifically" reified to further distinguish Anglo-Aryan residents from the influx of Eastern and Southern Europeans, to prevent Asians and Latinx people from emigrating to the United States, and as a justification for "Jim Crow" (Painter, 2010). As such, race is a significant dimension of social identity, and racism, although an independent social and psychological force, does not stand alone. As far as social recognition is concerned nobody is defined solely by race. The dimensions of social identity comprise gender, social class, sexual orientation, and other social group memberships, each of which holds a particular level of power and privilege. While each identity is situated on its own axis of stratification and inclusion, all are simultaneously entangled in systems of inequality. The same holds true for racism in society. It is strongly interconnected with other forces of dominance such as sexism, colonialism, homo/transphobia, and social status. In this chapter, we discuss three social forces that interact significantly with racism: socioeconomic class, gender, and sexual orientation. An intersectional analysis is incomplete if it only examines identities that exist on the margins of society. Only when all social identities are included can intersectionality facilitate an understanding of how social stratification results from the intertwined systems of oppression that exist. However, not all possible intersections will be examined here but we will offer a road map and examples of how this concept can be applied. Although we consider each identity separately in its relation to racism, in truth all interact simultaneously, although to different degrees. Therefore, considering even two forms of social oppression and how they interact leaves out their interaction with other sorts of social oppression.

So, even though we consider each of these factors and their conjunction with racism separately, we describe briefly how all forms of social oppression have certain similar qualities.

It is important to note that intersectionality can be defined and applied in more than one way. McCall (2005) describes three different approaches to intersectionality: anti-categorical, intercategorical, and intracategorical. The anti-categorical approach is based on an understanding that all social identities are socially constructed and have limited utility in dealing with the complexity of our sociopolitical reality. It posits that by continuing to use categories it reifies the stereotypes inherent in them and simplifies complex aspects of the human in environment experience. By deconstructing these categories and rendering them obsolete it requires that the multiplicity within each person is acknowledged as a whole. The intercategorical approach maintains the usefulness of social identity categories because they are rooted in current-day social structures that maintain relationships of inequality among different groups. This approach is less interested in teasing out the mutability and complexity within each social group but rather focuses on analyzing the relationship between categories in order to reveal the source of the inequality. It accepts that no categories are static but can be used strategically as a placeholder to analyze the relationships that exist among them. Finally, the intracategorical approach is most in keeping with the concept outlined by Crenshaw (1989; 2005) who critiqued gender-based and race-based affirmative action policies that failed to allow for the overlap of subordinate identities. It rejects the singularity of individuals' lived experiences as reflected only by a single category and sheds light on how an individual's multiple subordinate identities put them "at the neglected point of intersection" between them (McCall, 2005, p. 1780). This approach also highlights that individuals who belong to more than one oppressed group often have the added form of discrimination, which is invisibility (Remedios & Snyder, 2018). Although emphasizing different aspects, each approach has something to offer—an understanding of how social forces of oppression create and shape the lived experiences of individuals with varying social identities.

We use the term *intersectionality* to describe the relationship between these factors because it captures the connections and junctures that occur both inside a person (manifested in their identity) and in society (as evidenced by inequities and disparities in power and privilege). Recognizing that each social identity has its own level of power and privilege, intersectionality refers to the ways that these varying levels of power and privilege interact with one another and create a context for an individual's lived experience. In intersectional terms, this context is considered to be a person's unique social location in society (Garran & Werkmeister Rozas, 2013). One's social location not only exists on the microlevel of individual interactions but also on the macrolevel as social identities are always interacting with structural forces and cultural meanings (Stevens-Watkins et al., 2014). The element of power is always at the center of discussions on intersectionality (Yuval-Davis, 2006) and when exploring race, it is important to recognize White supremacy as one of the pre-eminent mechanisms of social control, undergirding all systems of oppression (Alexander, 2010). Similarly, the interrelatedness of hegemonic hierarchies rooted in colonial patriarchy allows race, class, and gender to shape and be shaped by one another (Wade, 2009).

Each approach to intersectionality has something to offer when examining the effects of power and privilege. What is essential to all is the placement of race within the context of "an imperial/capitalist/colonial world-system [whose] transversal dividing line … cuts across multiple power relations such as class, sexual and gender at a global scale" (Grosfoguel, 2016, p. 11). As a result of the coloniality of power (which will be described), race holds a prominent and differential position in the lived experience of all. Coloniality constructed a racial hierarchy where non-Whites were not only inferior but subhuman, and according to Fanon occupied a "zone of non-being" and Whites as superior, human, occupying a "zone of being"

(Fanon, 1967 as cited in Grosfoguel, 2016 p. 11). Which zone you occupy dictates whether the lived experience of your other social identities are mitigated by race, in the case of White privilege, or aggravated by race, in the case of racial oppression (Grosfoguel, 2016).

Exercise 8.1 builds on the concept of social identity that was explored in Chapter 1.

COMMON ASPECTS OF SOCIAL OPPRESSION

First, we examine Tilly's model of categorical inequalities. This model highlights particular characteristics inherent in structural forces that lay the framework for oppression to function. This leads into discussion of Quijano's (2000) coloniality of power which offers an overarching framework describing a set of assumptions that form a political, social relational, economic, and epistemological structure of subjugation, exploitation, and domination that determine social roles and status.

Tilly's Model of Categorical Inequalities

It is important to identify the operant forces that are most significant in how and to whom power and privilege are awarded and maintained. Tilly (1998) sought to extract the essential dynamics and structures that create and maintain "durable inequalities" and came up with four enduring traits:

1. Exploitation
2. Opportunity hoarding
3. Emulation
4. Adaptation

He argued that these "categorical inequalities" are manifest in many organizational and institutional settings, and evidenced by categorical disparities (e.g., by race, gender, and class) in wages, healthcare, political power, and all of the institutions central to the "web of racism."

Although each class of categories has its own historical legacy, the categories have a common pattern:

> Over and over again, exploitation by powerful people and resource hoarding by less powerful people combine to favor the establishment of unequally rewarded categories, whereas emulation and adaptation secure such categories in place. The creation of interior categories and the matching of interior with exterior categories build durable inequality into organizations and attach them to networks—internal and external—in ways that favor their reproduction, even their transmission to new members of the categories. (p. 169)

Readers are familiar with the notion of *exploitation*, which involves centralization and use of power, controlling and deploying resources, granting rights and privileges, and creating categories that include and exclude groups of people (Tilly, 1998). Implicit in *opportunity hoarding* is ideological control, as well as domination of social institutions and resources (Hardiman et al., 2007). Tilly describes how "networks" of less powerful people who have been granted privileged status by decision makers and power holders reinforce their control over hoarded resources by means of their power to include or exclude other members with respect to language, kinship, courtship, marriage, housing, sociability, religion, ceremonial life, credit, and political patronage ... Race, gender, schooling, professional training, political affiliation, and sexual preference all, at times, constitute the networks and categorical distinctions on which opportunity hoarding builds (pp. 154–155).

Emulation, in Tilly's model, refers to the structures of categorical inequalities operating in society at large that are replicated in various social sectors, institutions, and organizations. The pattern of inequality is found in most social units. As people are socialized into these familiar disparities, they become normative and commonplace. *Adaptation* refers to the interactive rituals, social scripts and narratives, and interpersonal practices that facilitate social interaction while maintaining categorical boundaries and their accompanying inequities. An example that Tilly (1998) offers is the use of humor in offices as males sexually harass females.

Adaptive strategies lead to compliance and complicity with the social structure of durable inequalities. Tilly's framework offers us the possibility that durable inequality is not only a macrostructural phenomenon but is also one residing in smaller scale institutional forms, which then are extended to other settings. We have durable inequalities not because of the sum of economic and social transactions but, rather, because of the stability of structures. Exercise 8.2 further helps to elucidate Tilly's model.

Durable inequalities help to create in-group and out-group allegiances and identities (Tilly, 1998). The psychological and social psychological process of creating a denigrated "other" further justifies and rationalizes social inequality, reinforcing categorical group distinctions (Miller & Schamess, 2000). Social categories and social identity though distinct, are mutually reliant. Some individuals complain that discontinuing the use of social categories would inevitably cause social divisions to die away: If there is no category of race there can be no racism. However, it is not the existence of social categories that creates social divisions but society's over- and/or under-valuation of certain social identities that exist within each category. Such socially constructed and sanctioned appraisal confers social roles and statuses on people, such as being targeted or having privilege (Hardiman et al., 2007). Sometimes individuals who possess a social status that has less power due to society's undervaluation, internalize their oppressed status, mirroring and reinforcing external social divisions. At the same time, social identities often serve as a strong source of collective identity and pride for individuals whose social identity holds less power and privilege. Both have been considered to be important factors when confronting the deleterious effects of oppression on a person's health and well-being by offering some protection and resilience.

Coloniality of Power

Quijano (2000) presents an understanding of coloniality of power through the codification of race and subsequent racial social classification as demonstrated through the distribution and valuation of work based on racial identities. Quijano contends that "the concentration of the control of productive resources and capital, as social relations, including salary, as a privilege of 'Whiteness' ... affected the entire distribution of power among the world population" (p. 218). Basically, race and racism become the organizing principles of how hierarchies are structured in the modern world (Grosfoguel, 2011). According to Grosfoguel, patriarchal valuation of gender is also affected by this as some women who would be classified as "White," in some circumstances are granted superiority over men who would be classified as "non-White." Race becomes the lens through which all people are ascribed value. Grosfoguel adds to Quijano's matrix by contending that "race, gender, sexuality, spirituality, and epistemology are not additive elements to the economic and political structures of the capitalist world-system, but an integral, entangled and constitutive part of the broad webbed 'package' called the European modern/colonial capitalist/patriarchal world-system" (Grosfoguel, 2011, p. 11). By situating individuals within the context of these power structures we are able to more fully analyze how they experience society and how society experiences them. All individuals are classed, sexed, gendered, and racialized; each identity carries with it its own varying levels of power and privilege, which makes up our social location (Garran & Werkmeister Rozas, 2013). Grosfoguel makes the point that individuals whose social location may comprise social categories that primarily carry less power and privilege may possess a subjugated view of their own identities. Bell and Griffin (1997) identify the espousal of the oppressor's world views and beliefs by the oppressed as internalized oppression.

It is impossible to explore every intersection of identity that exists. When looking at any social category or intersection of social categories it is essential to avoid a one-dimensional analysis. Each category has characteristics that are multi-dimensional and must be analyzed as such. There is a temporal dimension, which establishes the *when*, and a geographic component, referring to the *where*, and the process dimension of *how* (Haschemi Yekani et al., 2008). Each dimension plays a role in establishing an individual's experience that is created by the intersection of various levels of power, privilege (or lack thereof), and dimensions of time, place, and process. There is a difference between being poor in Burundi or India than being poor in the United States; being racialized in Brazil versus racialized in the United States; being a non-citizen in Germany or a non-citizen in the United States. The next section offers examples of the intersection of race and class, gender, and sexuality while acknowledging there are always more key dimensions that can be added, including other social identities. Most important to keep in mind is, as Grosfoguel states, "The intersectional entanglement between class, sexual, gender or national/colonial oppressions that exist in the zone of non-being are … qualitatively distinct from the ways these oppressions are lived and articulated in the zone of being" (2016, p. 12). Therefore, fundamental to an intersectional analysis of social categories within the United States is an a priori acknowledgment of the existence and distinct difference that these two zones create for their inhabitants. Individuals who experience oppression because of their class, gender, or sexuality but have White privilege inhabit the zone of being and are mutually recognized for their humanity within the coloniality of power. However, their targeted or marginalized social identity places them in opposition to the dominant gendered, classed, and/or sexual hegemonic groups and for this they become the "Other Being." When a racially oppressed individual inhabits one of these targeted or marginalized identities that conflict with the hegemony they become the "Non-Being Other" with no mutual recognition of humanity and no race privilege to mitigate their position (Grosfoguel, 2016, p. 14).

RACE AND CLASS OPPRESSION

The framework of the coloniality of power illustrates the overdetermined role race has on class, by highlighting how the two have been intertwined from the inception of this country and continue to be tightly woven together today. Theorists of class conflict and oppression, particularly Marxists, tend to emphasize the primacy of class, whereas scholars of racism often call attention to the significance of race. However, the matrix of coloniality makes visible the symbiosis that created the two social categories and their ongoing interdependence today. Although the actual classification of race may find its roots in the age of the Enlightenment, Indians, Negroes, and Mestizos had been robbed of their various historic identities long before by the Spanish. A diverse group of people with their own unique language and history whose identities stemmed from tribal or land association, were put into one of two general race categories: Indian and Negro (Quijano, 2000). Stripped of their way of life and survival through enslavement these two groups became the crucial target for exploitation needed for a capitalist structure to take hold. Once dominant Whites controlled the economic structure they determined the monetary value of the workers within the hegemonic structure. Almost immediately, the economic structure ascribed value and worth to Whites, rewarding them with generous pay, and insignificance to the Blacks and Indigenous deeming them only fit to be slaves, relegating them to the zone of being.

Although people of color are not the only group exploited within the United States capitalist system because of the cycle of socialization (see Harro, 2018; Chapter 1), characteristics ascribed to slaves continue to be attributed to people of color today, particularly African Americans, which allows for the cross-cutting nature of racism and class. People of color in the middle class experience racism, whether it determines where they live, work, or in how they are treated when they are shopping or driving (Cose, 1993), and many poor people are White. In fact, the largest ethnic–racial group of poor people are White (Sakamoto & Wang, 2015). But class-based factors, when combined with race, make it even harder for people of color to achieve upward social mobility. And from the country's inception, being considered White has granted certain social privileges, even to those who were economically considered poor or working class (Allen, 1994; Fredrickson, 1988; Takaki, 1993). Economic success for people of color in the United States has not always afforded the same access to social privileges as it has for Whites.

We use the term *class* to mean socioeconomic status and positioning. This has not only an economic dimension as determined by employment, income, and assets, but also a social and spatial dimension, such as where people live, how they dress, if they have a car, what vehicle they drive, the level and quality of their education, how they speak, with whom they socialize, and the types of recreations they favor. There is an "objective" economic class position but "class identification" is the subjective sense that a person has of their social class (Speer, 2015). As discussed in the preceding chapter, class also involves an axis of identity. Like race, class is a social construction, influenced by history and context, and its meanings are disputed, as are the ways by which people see and define themselves. Even the way that classes are conceptualized and discussed varies and is contested.

For example, how is class divided and measured? Is it by income or by lifestyle or some other factor? Access to important resources such as education or employment? Why do so many people describe themselves as "middle class"—ranging from blue collar workers to highly paid professionals and managers? Socioeconomic class is a relative concept, and its meaning often is in the eye of the beholder.

Race and Class Visibility

Within limits, class can be less visible than race. We can dress similarly and even learn to talk in the same way. As a result, people can carry "hidden injuries of class" and feel as if they are "passing" (Sennett & Cobb, 1972). For example, in the elite college where one author teaches, students from lower-middle-class or working-class backgrounds have expressed ambivalence over whether they "truly" belong there as much as students from higher-class backgrounds.

Certain values, norms, and expectations are shaped through the influence of class by way of the cycle of socialization. Class also influences developmental processes; as such, we carry within us the memories and sense of self based on our constructions of class from earlier phases of our life into the present. Class, too, has a future orientation, as people set their sights on upward mobility. The belief in class mobility is what may diminish class resentment for some USAmericans, as they hold to the idea that they can alter their class standing. But we should not minimize the limits of opportunity that many people face by virtue of their social and economic class, regardless of race.

From the beginning of this country, race and ethnicity shaped which class positions were availed to whom. Quijano (2000) describes the intersection of race and class in this way:

> That specific basic element of the new pattern of world power that was based on the idea of "race" and in the "racial" social classification of world population—expressed in the "racial" distribution of work, in the imposition of new "racia" geocultural identities, in the concentration of the control of productive resources and capital, as social relations, including salary, as a privilege of "Whiteness"—is what is basically referred to in the category of coloniality of power. (p. 218)

The coloniality of power meant that Native Americans, Chinese Americans, Japanese Americans, and Mexican Americans had less access to the full range of economic opportunities afforded to ethnic groups constructed as White, and faced restrictive laws as well as informal discriminatory practices. African Americans were restricted from any semblance of economic mobility through the institution of slavery and, after the Civil War, through Black Codes, Jim Crow, and segregation, both formal and informal.

Ransford (2000) has proposed a racial/ethnic hierarchy that has characterized U.S. society, with Anglo Saxons at the top; next, White ethnic groups; then Asian Americans; and finally, African Americans, Native Americans, and Mexican Americans. The factors influencing those at the bottom of the socioeconomic scale include groups with a history of having been enslaved, colonized, or conquered; people having fewer resources, less power, and less efficacy in their communities; and those having to confront pervasive discourses that legitimize denigration.

Slavery was instituted as a commodity and served the capitalist system that required a workforce to be paid less than their value in order for a profit to be made by those that own the capital (Quijano, 2000). By using enslaved labor to grow cotton, White Southern plantation owners enriched themselves while White Northern capitalists had a source of cheap cotton, fueling their industrial economies which were only open to White workers (Baptist, 2014). Assigning no economic value to the work produced by slaves but rather to the slaves themselves as property, a form of capital only those not enslaved could possess, created an entire underclass of people that were considered subhuman. As slaves, they were deemed unintelligent and ineducable, immoral and aggressive. Without a legal right to education very few slaves could read or write, reinforcing the belief that slaves did not possess the same degree of intellect as Whites. Slavery with all of its less-than-human associations became synonymous with Blackness. As a result even after the formal end of the institution of slavery, discrimination by labor unions was utilized as a mechanism for White ethnic groups to maintain their rungs on the socioeconomic ladder, much to the disadvantage of people of color (Fenton, 1999; Lacy, 2015; Omatsu, 2000). This was in the context of not being able to climb society's highest steps. Coupled with discriminatory hiring and employment practices, this practice severely limited the class mobility of people of color, particularly African Americans, Native Americans, and many Hispanic Americans.

Class mobility was blocked further by residential segregation, lack of access to good schools, being unable to attract as much credit to obtain homes and businesses, paying higher interest rates for loans, and having homes and businesses situated in areas where their value was lower and appreciated more slowly (Oliver & Shapiro, 2013). There has been a great deal of debate among scholars about whether residential segregation is primarily caused by economic inequality or racial discrimination. Certainly, middle-class African Americans live in more integrated neighborhoods than poor Black Americans but still encounter more residential isolation than Whites, leading some to conclude that class stratification and racism interact to contribute to a lack of full residential integration (Lacy, 2015; Sakamoto & Wang, 2015; Spivak & Monnat, 2013). Last, social policies such as the New Deal had built-in inequities, disadvantaging low-income people of color by not covering many of the occupations in which they were employed (Jansson, 2015; Jones, 1985; Lieberman, 1998; Quadagno, 1994).

Cox (1948) and Quijano (2000) believed that racism is the inevitable by-product of capitalism, and as such it can be argued that race determines class relations and status (Omi & Winant, 1994). We cannot say whether racism or classism is the more pre-eminent social force; they are both powerful social dynamics in their own right. Ultimately, ethnicity and race have strongly influenced a group's socioeconomic position in society (Eriksen, 1996). Conversely, an ethnic group's socioeconomic standing has profoundly influenced a group's ethnic character and interactions with other groups (Fenton, 1999).

Because race and ethnicity are more visible than socioeconomic class, class exploitation often has been obfuscated by racial and ethnic scapegoating. In order for coloniality to function, the varied White ethnic/racial identities were surrendered in exchange for the power and privilege possessed by the larger White group. There were very clear distinctions made between different types of work with Whites occupying the "capital-salary" work (Quijano, 2008, p. 219) and other races the less socially desirable work. By controlling which groups belonged in which racial/ethnic category as well as which were eligible to assume what type of work, Whites maintained their domination over people who were not classified as White. As economic power was reserved to Whites the wish to belong to this racial group intensified. During colonial times, as well as in the early days of the Republic, poor White workers felt a greater allegiance to the White elite of owners than to Black slaves, who also were being economically exploited (Allen, 1994; Fredrickson, 1988; Takaki, 1987). Thus, the focus on race and the alleged inferiority of Black slaves served to divide potential class allies and perhaps forestall and pre-empt a genuine class-based struggle that might have resulted in better conditions for all workers.

Racial and ethnic scapegoating as a subtext of public discourse continues to this day. Although there are class-based stereotypes that are similar to racial stereotypes, such as "White trash" (Sullivan, 2014), class-based inequities are not covered in a complex fashion by the mainstream media. Social ills are often blamed on immigrants or depicted as being perpetrated by "violent" people of color. These subtexts all occur as the government promulgates policies that redistribute wealth upward. All of this has been done by refuting the intersectional nature of race and class created by the coloniality of power.

Race, Class, and Politics

Rather than acknowledge that the connection between race and class had been created by a White dominant class in order to maintain their superiority, politicians have been able to link race and class in ways that detract from class issues and that ultimately diminish the discourse on social class in the United States. There are political rewards for "playing the race card" and punishments for those who support civil rights. President Lyndon Johnson, more than any other modern president, actively sought legislation to respond to racism and ensure greater equality for African Americans and other people of color. He worried that his policies would turn the South into a Republican stronghold.

Thus far, President Johnson's concerns have been validated. Since 1968, when he declined to run for reelection, Republicans have won the presidency in 8 of 13 elections. By 2020, they have held the presidency for 32 of 50 years, with a substantial swing of southern and midwestern states to support their success. Twice they have lost the popular vote but won the election due to the electoral college, a system intentionally set up to benefit slave holding states. President Nixon openly played the race card, fomenting White working-class resentment toward people of color who benefited from the policies of the Great Society (Edsall & Edsall, 1991; Quadagno, 1994), only to be surpassed by the unadultured racism of Donald Trump.

Speaking of the Great Society, Quadagno stated:

> The positive liberties it extended to African Americans were viewed by the working class as infringements on their negative liberties, the liberty for trade unions to discriminate in the selection of apprentices and to control job training programs; the liberty to exclude minorities from representation in local politics; the liberty to maintain segregated neighborhoods. (p. 195)

President Reagan used racially coded discourse when he described "welfare queens" and received working-class White support from so-called "Reagan Democrats" (Edsall & Edsall, 1991; Quadagno, 1994). During his successful presidential campaign, George H. W. Bush exploited the "Willie Horton" issue, blaming the release of a "dangerous" Black felon on the liberal policies of his opponent. Even President Clinton, who had tremendous Black support, had to prove himself to White people by publicly denouncing Sister Souljah when running for president and by taking the lead in dismantling the country's welfare system. When critics complained that the tax policies of President George W. Bush grossly redistributed wealth upward, they were immediately denounced as fomenting "class warfare." Despite the trend of greater inequality in the country in favor of the very rich over the past 35 years, the term *class warfare* is only used to refer to efforts to protect middle- and working-class Americans.

As has been mentioned in Chapter 5, President Obama, the only person of color to hold the office of President of the United States, faced unprecedented obstruction and hostility, including an entire "birther" movement questioning where he was born. A leading purveyor of the birther movement, Donald Trump, used race regularly as a divisive trope during his successful—though openly hostile at times—run for president in 2016, denouncing Mexican immigrants and threatening to ban Muslim immigrants. For instance, he did not immediately denounce an endorsement of his candidacy by David Duke, a former Grand Wizard of the Ku Klux Klan. As president, he told four congresswomen of color, three of whom were born in the United States, to return to the country from where they came. Throughout the campaign, some of his core supporters were working-class White Americans. Ironically, Trump is a wealthy White male who has often been cited for unfair labor practices and yet received substantial support from working class Whites, a potent example of how racism can mask class exploitation.

Interaction of Race and Class Today

On the level of political discourse, then, race is used to cloak and veil class exploitation. How does the interaction of race and class affect people who live in the United States today? We have identified seven major areas to explore in more detail.

1. *Residential apartheid.* Neighborhoods always are segmented by class, as determined by income, wealth, and the cost of homes. Neighborhoods are also still segregated racially, especially leaving poor people of color, particularly poor African Americans and Latinos, living in hypersegregated, poor neighborhoods (Feagin, 1999; Massey & Denton, 1993; Spivak & Monnat, 2013; Wilson, 1996).

2. *Access to jobs and segmented labor markets.* Working-class people of color, particularly those living in highly segregated neighborhoods, have less entrée to decent jobs than other people, even poor or working-class Whites. Deindustrialization, expanding suburbanization, and poor public transportation give them less access to jobs, and racism and discrimination add another layer of impermeability for poor people of color seeking employment.

   Poor urban Blacks reside in neighborhoods where they lack access to social and professional networks conducive to employment, more so than other ethnic and racial groups in the inner city (Wilson, 1996). Both residential segregation and lack of access to employment contribute to segmented labor markets, with poor neighborhoods of color offering more illegal and marginal work, carrying fewer benefits, if any; greater risks; and little opportunity for advancement and employment security (Bourgois, 1995; Sakamoto & Wang, 2015; Schiller, 1998; Wilson, 1996).

3. *Racialized financial services.* Credit and loans are essential for class mobility, yet both are less available and more expensive for people of color (Manning, 1999). Poor neighborhoods of color have fewer banks and more check-cashing companies and informal loan sharks, which charge much higher rates of interest. People of color have more difficulty securing the credit to buy a home—which is one of the most basic assets that people acquire as they move up in class—and, as we have mentioned, when people of color acquire homes in these areas, the value of these homes is less likely to go up and more likely to fall (Shapiro, 2004). The PBS series *Race: The Power of an Illusion* (2003) documents the lasting effects of racist government and business practices in the post-World War II financial and residential limitations imposed on people of color who should have been eligible for funds through the GI Bill.

4. *Lack of assets.* All of the aforementioned conspire to hamper poor people of color in accumulating assets (Oliver & Shapiro, 2013; Shapiro, 2004; Wolff, 2001). More than income, assets create the great wealth divide in the United States between Whites and African Americans, Hispanics, and Native Americans (Oliver & Shapiro, 2013; Shapiro, 2004). The status of middle-class African Americans reflects their income rather than their comparative net worth (Oliver & Shapiro, 2013).

5. *Increasing inequality within and between racial groups.* The overall class divide is greatest in the United States since 1928 (Lacy, 2015). And since the 1970s the chasm between

the poorest and wealthiest African Americans has widened (Lacy, 2015). However, there is still a major wealth gap between racial and ethnic groups with Whites and Asian Americans doing much better than African Americans, Latinos, and Native Americans. Some of the reasons for this are greater wealth transfers for White and Asian American families (Shapiro, 2004; Speer, 2015), lower and often falling property values for people of color at the low end of the economic spectrum (Shapiro, 2004), and racial discrimination (Speer, 2015). The class divide has increased in the United States, partly due to the income tax rates for the wealthiest Americans falling from 72% in 1928 to 39% in 2015 (Lacy, 2015). Many African Americans, Latinos, and Native Americans rely on their salaries for their income, not dividends from their wealth; in addition, the rates for capital gains tax have fallen from 67% to 20%, exacerbating wealth disparities between ethnic–racial groups (Lacy, 2015).

6. *Racism and classism in state policy.* Federal policies can take class or race into account in a remedial fashion, such as having a progressive income tax or laws supporting affirmative action. But state policies can do the opposite, widening class and race divisions.

   The policies under President Reagan of reducing progressive income taxes while increasing flat payroll taxes did exactly this, as wealth was redistributed upward (Phillips, 1990), and predominantly to White people. Under President George W. Bush, policies were promoted that dramatically reduced the income tax burden on the wealthiest, as well as reducing wealth and estate taxes while cutting services for the poor, which further widened the class and race divide with respect to assets. The cutting of income taxes for the wealthiest and exacerbating class inequality was accelerated by President Trump and his Republican allies.

7. *A vicious cycle.* All of these factors leave concentrated neighborhoods of poor people of color with higher poverty rates and more social disorganization. This becomes "evidence" to outsiders of the cultural dissoluteness of people living in these neighborhoods, reinforcing stereotypes and making them suitable targets for scapegoating (Wilson, 1996). A "discourse of denigration," blaming the victims of these policies for laziness and lack of moral fiber, is then used to mask the policies that contribute heavily to this situation (Miller & Schamess, 2000). It also fuels suburban sprawl, as White people of all socioeconomic strata and middle-class people of color seek to move away from the perceived sources of social disorder. This has the effect of despoiling the environment and also reinforcing residential segregation with all of its economic, social, and psychological consequences.

RACE AND GENDER

Using the coloniality of power to analyze the intersection of race and gender in the United States today highlights the important role patriarchy and White supremacy play in society's marginalization or centering of an individual's lived experience. White supremacy and patriarchy are foremost systems that are essential to the social construction of race and gender and have significant consequences as independent social forces. Racism and sexism are two of the most basic forms of durable inequalities and, in combination, have profound consequences for how a person experiences the world. Together, they straddle all aspects of social life—public and private, at the workplace, and in the home. Although everyone has a socially constructed race, as we have discussed, many White people are unaware of this.

In this section, we will be considering gender, and in the next sexual orientation and performance. Although gender and sexual orientation are often closely related, they are also separate constructs. The concept of gender throughout history has shifted from being associated with biology to a social construction (Butler, 1997; Feinberg, 1993; Langer & Martin, 2004) with emphasis on self-identity after World War II (Herdt, 1994). Gender identity is a sense of one's masculinity, femininity and anything in between or neither (Richards et al., 2016; Singer, 1997; Zandvliet, 2000). Butler (1997) defines gender as "the mechanism by which notions of masculine and feminine are produced and naturalized, but gender might very well be the apparatus by which such terms are deconstructed and denaturalized" (p. 43). Related to this is gender expression—how one dresses, behaves, talks, and, in general, presents oneself. This is related to but distinct from sexual orientation, which is who a person is attracted to and involved with emotionally, socially, and sexually.

Gender, like race, has historically been portrayed in binary, essentialist terms, but this has been contested and problematized in the 21st century. Themes, such as gender neutral, non-binary, gender nonconforming, transgender, gender expansive, acknowledging different combinations of masculinity and femininity have created a gender order that promotes gender as diversity rather than a difference (Annandale & Hunt, 2000). Distinctions are also made between those who are cisgender, meaning that their biological sex assigned to them at birth matches their self-identified gender and others who have either transitioned from one gender to another (transgender) or those who identify outside, between, or/and both the categories of man and woman referred to as gender nonbinary (Lorber, 2018).

So there are multiple discourses occurring about gender, which enrich our understanding of the intricacies of gender identity and oppression while also making it more complicated to analyze the social dynamics of gender. The majority of people still identify as either male or female, and there is a great deal of evidence about gender inequality using these constructs. But there are also a growing number of people who are transgender and transsexual or who view themselves as gender nonbinary/gender expansive who face even greater discrimination. We will attempt to be mindful of these different discourses as we consider the intersection of race and gender. Gender is not only manifested and contested in the public domain but in private spaces as well. While there are homogenous racial communities, such as all or predominantly White communities or schools, many domestic relationships (partners, relatives, and friends) involve the interaction of people with differing gender identities.

For most people, biological sex is the earliest axis of social identity to which a person becomes categorized, often before they are even born. For many, while still in utero or after the birth of a baby, the first question is often "is it a boy or a girl" (Lorber, 2018). Biological sex and gender have immediate social consequences involving dress and playmates, as well as social roles and expectations. This is not to imply that everyone is comfortable with their assigned sex; there are some people who feel at odds with and constricted by their sex and the gender assignment and socialized roles that accompany them. However, every culture and society throughout history has had gender norms and expectations throughout the life course ascribed to biological sex, primarily through the lens of a masculine-feminine binary. Although some cultures prescribed less rigid rules about gender conformity, to the point where some indigenous cultures acknowledged some possessing "two-spirits" or both genders, most reverted to a traditional binary patriarchal structure where men are superior to women.

In considering the intersection of gender and race, we highlight the organizing role race and White supremacy has on the larger, well known global hegemonic hierarchies (Grosfoguel, 2011). According to McClintock (1995), "race, gender and class are not distinct realms of experience, existing in splendid isolation from each other; nor can they be simply yoked together retrospectively like armatures of Lego. Rather, they come into existence *in and through* relation to each other" (1995, p. 5, emphasis in the original).

Similar to how race was used to demarcate which racial/ethnic groups were eligible for what kind and status of work, it proffered a social order that made all Whites superior to all people of color regardless of gender. Whereas women were considered categorically inferior to men, the privilege of being superior to men of color elevated the status of White women to a higher social order (Grosfoguel, 2011). Women of color remained at the bottom of the social-political hierarchy. By elevating White women to a status above Black men they were obligated to support and uphold the "colonial power matrix" where "race organizes the world's population into a hierarchical order of superior and inferior people that becomes an organizing principle of the international division of labor and of the global patriarchal system" (Grosfoguel 2011, p. 11).

The previous chapter considered some contradictions and paradoxes: White women subjected to sexism can be racists, whereas men of color who are subjected to racism every day can have sexist attitudes and behave in sexist ways toward women. These paradoxes can cause tensions and divisions between individuals and groups, splinter social movements, and fracture potential political alliances. Such contradictions can be better understood when put up against the context of the coloniality of power. As McClintock (1995) explains, "imperialism cannot be fully understood without the theory of gender power. Gender power was not the superficial pationa or empire, and ephemeral gloss over the more decisive mechanics of class or race. Rather, gender dynamics were, from the outset, fundamental to the securing and maintenance of the imperial enterprise" (pp. 6–7). Although the hierarchy of gender was essential to the social hegemonic structure, its salience differs when coupled with race (Harnois, 2010).

The surge of the Women's Movement in the 1960s has been criticized as primarily a White, middle-class movement, with little awareness by its leaders of their race privilege or of the multiple struggles endured by women of color, which exemplifies this fissure (Remedios et al., 2011; Wilkinson, 1995, 1997). Many women of color worked hard for women's rights, yet found that White women often did not understand the intersection of racism and sexism. Harnois (2010) argues that because Black women's experience has been shaped much more by racial segregation than the gender segregation White women experienced, the gendered world of White feminists was not theirs. Having a more gender-integrated experience afforded Black men and women the ability to recognize the need to join economic and personal resources in an effort to survive the coloniality of power. Aware that historically, the structures of patriarchy and White supremacy required the emasculation of Black men, Black women distanced themselves from White feminist rhetoric (Benard, 2016). Many White women were not aware of how the coloniality of power determined their social superiority causing them to be unmindful of the unique needs and social relations of women of color. The hierarchy of race once again controlled the social relations among women even though they are all subjugated by patriarchy. Though many White women were unaware of their own racial identity and privilege it allowed them to be less invested in affiliating with women of color in the struggle for women's rights.

Social Consequences of Racism and Sexism

European masculinity was created by White men "othering" colonized men of color and placing themselves in opposition to them. In order to assert their power over indigenous men they colonized, they had to render them weak, irrational, effeminate (Schiwy, 2007). The sexist structure was not added on top of the racist one, but came with it or through it.

The socioeconomic consequences of the coloniality of power include lower pay scales for women than men, underrepresentation in many professions and overrepresentation in lower-paying occupations, sexual harassment and sexual objectification, and domestic violence. Although more than half the country's population is female, the U.S. Senate in 2018 includes only 25 female senators out of a total of 100, and this is the largest number of women in the history of the Senate. It is a newsworthy exception when a woman heads a Fortune 500 company. Needless to say, there have never been openly transgender senators or presidents.

Thus, women earn less than men and a greater percentage of the poor are women. Women also are more likely to have major child-rearing and other domestic responsibilities than men, often in addition to their work in paid employment. For people who are transgender or nonbinary there are more barriers to inhabiting social roles historically designated for the female or male gender, less social and cultural mirroring and support, and face more employment discrimination and social targeting.

The consequences of the coloniality of power are apparent through the intersection of sexism and racism: limited economic opportunities, stereotypes connected to alleged biological differences, and restricted access to positions of power and influence. Women of all races and men and women of color have had to struggle for rights, opportunities, and the status of full citizenship. Repressive institutions, such as slavery, relied on an interaction of racism and sexism to create socially stratified roles and positions. As a result of discrimination and oppression, people of color, women, and people who are transgender, nonbinary, or gender fluid have endured diminished economic, political, and social status (Reid & Comas-Diaz, 1990).

Some research seems to indicate that both sexism and racism operate as independent forces and are additive (Stevens-Watkins et al., 2014); however, when observed within the colonial matrix of power it can be seen that although they were historically constituted they are concomitantly contemporarily operative as linked forms of oppression. A woman of color is affected by White supremacy and patriarchy. There are certain opportunities and resources that are afforded to men of color because they are men and certain opportunities and resources that are accessible to White women because they are White. Crenshaw (1989) gives an example of intersectionality that demonstrates this dynamic. Using the example of Black women being barred from the industrial workforce because they were being discriminated against for being women who were Black and for being Black but not a man. The narratives created by African American men and White women about employment discrimination were heard and although there was affirmative action laws that were meant to correct the effect of discrimination on women and African Americans the laws failed to address the narratives of Black women. In 1976 Emma Degraffenreid attempted to gain employment in a car manufacturer. Bound by the Affirmative Action legislation the company had been hiring Black men to work on the factory floor and White women to do clerical work when Ms. Degraffenreid applied for a clerical position. Although Black, she was not a man and therefore not "equipped" to work on the factory floor. Although a woman, she was not White and therefore deemed ineligible for office work. Following the coloniality of power matrix, White supremacy had controlled which type of work was eligible for Blacks and patriarchy had controlled which types of work were accessible to women. Emma fit the criteria for office work as a woman, but not as a Black and she fit the criteria for being a factory worker as a Black but not as a woman. She sought help from the court and sued, claiming she was discriminated against because she was a Black woman. The court did not side with her, claiming the company did employ Blacks and did employ women. The court failed to take into consideration that someone like Emma could fall outside both of these two categories. As a result of the two simultaneous mechanisms of patriarchy and White supremacy Emma was marginalized, falling between the cracks of the legislation meant to rescue her from discrimination.

Cho et al. (2013) succinctly state that what an intersectional analysis offers is a way of "thinking about the problem of sameness and difference and its relation to power" (p. 795). They go on to explain how when an intersectional framework is utilized, "This framing—conceiving of categories not as distinct but as always permeated by other categories, fluid and changing, always in the process of creating and being created by the dynamics of power—emphasizes what intersectionality does rather than what intersectionality is" (p. 795). Other perspectives that referred to a person inhabiting more than one targeted identity as having additive or cumulative disadvantage lacked the factor of the dynamic interplay that exists within each identity category and between their relationships to power. To help understand this ever-evolving process we will use an example of unarmed men of color and unarmed women of color shot by police. By examining the relations each has to power we can see how their sameness and difference places them in different social locations.

Historically, in the United States, women have endured oppression and unequal treatment but were not targeted for extermination or slavery as a result of their gender. At the same time, the various plights of women of color have not been given the same amount of attention as those that have plagued men of color. An example of this is the police shooting of unarmed Black USAmericans. Since the fatal shooting of an unarmed Michael Brown by a police officer in 2015, much attention has been given to fatal interactions with police (FIP). However, what gets primarily reported are the deaths of the Black men and little is said about the myriad deaths of Black women who died at the hands of police. Johnson et al. (2018; available at: www.futurity.org/police-killings-unarmed-black-women-1675912-2/) point out that there are very few studies that examine the number of unarmed Black women who have died as a result of excessive force used by police. While it is true that more Black men are involved in FIP than Black women, what is disturbing is that Black women seem to have been left out of the prevailing narrative. One reason may be that Black women do not fit the violent and threatening stereotype as do Black men, making it more troubling for some that unarmed women are being killed. Not fitting the frame of what kind of person, according to the matrix of coloniality, seems reasonable to be perceived as a threat renders Black women victims of FIP invisible. Intersectionality enables us to recognize the marginalization of Black women because although they are women living in a patriarchal society and therefore vulnerable to violence committed by men, they are Black and do not hold the same power and privilege as White women due to White supremacy. Also, although they are Black and as a result of White supremacy, more vulnerable to FIP they are women, and do not hold the same status as men in a patriarchal society. With victimization rates continuing to rise even more vulnerable to gender violence are transwomen of color (Fitzgerald, 2017).

Social Roles and Social Identity

Gender roles are shaped by culture and historical and social contexts. The meanings of being one's gender are far from fixed and have transmuted over time and across societies. Racial roles and gender roles both are contested by groups and social movements, as well as by individuals in their daily interactions. They also are intricately interconnected. As the use of nonbinary and gender expansive terminology increases, the entrenched associations between a social role with a gender identity may diminish.

If we consider race and gender for African Americans, through lens of the coloniality of power, White patriarchy initially placed severe constraints on the range of available social roles, and gender influenced what forms of labor slaves were expected to perform (Jones, 1985). This also meant that African American women worked outside of their families in jobs that White women did not—a pattern that continued for many decades following the Civil War, a clear example of how White patriarchy continued to maintain control over who is eligible for what type of work.

Racism also contributed to public visions of stereotypical social roles for Black men and women. Although African Americans challenged and contested these distortions, the structures of White supremacy and patriarchy continued to limit access to more variety. This necessitated a great deal of struggle, requiring African Americans to create and value their own self-definitions over those that were foisted upon them and to generate collective self-respect and self-reliance (Collins, 1990).

Lack of respect is an important notion, as racism can be thought of as a collective lack of respect for the dignity and worth of human beings based on their race and ethnicity (Miller & Ferroggiaro, 1996). Lack of respect makes it all the more difficult to achieve a positive sense of identity, including gender identity. Bourgois (1995) has described young male Puerto Rican drug dealers seeking the respect that was absent from office jobs by becoming involved in their illegal but self-validating entrepreneurship. Cose (1995) has speculated that because men of color, particularly African American men, receive so little respect in society at large, they may, at times, feel as though they need to seek respect in ways that can be construed as very intense or damaging to themselves, or that others seek in an intense way with their domestic partners, as they are the closest people at hand. This dynamic further weakens cross-gender relationships and provides an example of how racism and gender interact.

For people of color, particularly African Americans, Latinx, Asians, and Native Americans, gender becomes another source of oppression and is aggravated by the racial oppression they experience. Although all women are subject to sexist stereotypes, women of color find that these negative images are distorted further through the lens of racism, leading to exoticism, denigration, and visions of hypersexuality or hyposexuality. Idealized female images of body, weight, and dress are laden with Eurocentric distortions, compounding the challenges of developing a positive, integrated body image and gender identity.

Men of color also face racialized gender distortions with reference to their sexuality, fidelity, and potential for violence. People may internalize images such as these, with the result that many White women acknowledge fear if they pass an African American man on the street at night.

Thus, gender stereotypes have psychological consequences for women and men of color, affecting their sense of psychological well-being (Carter, 2007; Stevens-Watkins et al., 2014).

To internalize a positive sense of both race/ethnicity and gender becomes more of a challenge, as the world is lined with distorted mirrors and narrated by demeaning discourses.

Woody & Green (2001) has found that the most salient factor in psychological well-being is race, followed by its interaction with gender, with African American men being the most adversely affected. They face a greater likelihood of police harassment and aggression while simply walking down a street, and they experience projections at work and elsewhere. They face lethal consequences by simply reaching for their wallet. Many know friends and relatives who have been incarcerated. This lack of control over their life is further exacerbated if domestic relations are tense, conflictual, and unstable. This is not to say that Black women do not live with the same consequences of racism. What differs is the way race is mitigated by gender.

RACE AND SEXUALITY

Shortly before the presidential campaign of 2004 had begun in earnest, the Massachusetts Supreme Judicial Court reached a decision that ignited a firestorm around the nation. The court delivered an opinion that to deny gay and lesbian couples the right to marry was a violation of state law. Soon thereafter, lines of couples registered for marriage at town halls from Cambridge to Northampton, accompanied by public celebrations of marriage.

In other parts of the country, the scene was less cheerful. The court's decision sent a shockwave through many communities and homes where many people believed that marriage was a right reserved exclusively for heterosexual couples. Although a few religious denominations supported the decision, some believed that it violated fundamental teachings of their faith. Many politicians exploited the issue, seeking a ban on same-sex marriages through a constitutional amendment and placing antigay marriage propositions on state ballots. It was a factor in how some people voted in the presidential election. And then in 2015, the Supreme Court of the United States ruled that there is a constitutional right to gay marriage, legalizing it in all 50 states. This is now under threat with the rightward drift of the Supreme Court after Donald Trump appointed three justices. Although the right to marry someone of the same sex ostensibly carries with it the same rights and social status as a heterosexual couple, queer individuals do not have federal protection against employment or housing discrimination awarded to women and people of color.

Even though there have been tremendous strides in the movement for the rights of gay, lesbian, bisexual, and transgender people, including the right not to be seen as deviant from a heterosexual norm, there remain strong rivers of heterosexism and homophobia flowing in our society. Heterosexism is a formidable form of social oppression, a durable inequality that intersects with sexism and racism, as well as other types of social oppression. Sexual orientation cannot be considered without also taking gender into account, along with gender roles and expectations. Also important to consider are the contexts of culture, ethnicity, and race.

The gay, lesbian, bisexual, transgender, queer, questioning, and indeterminate communities comprise a highly diverse grouping of people—not a homogenous or monolithic cluster of the populace (Catalano & Griffin, 2016). This heterogeneity is akin to trying to describe ethnic and racial communities: There is not an African American or Black community—rather, many communities (Hooks, 2000). What is shared by these groups is that they are not heterosexual, or "straight." Even within any one of these categories are many differences, as sexual orientation can refer to identity, sexual attractions, and behaviors that, although they overlap, are not exactly the same (Morales, 1990).

Diamond (2003, p. 491) describes *sexual orientation* as a stable and enduring pattern of sexual attraction and distinguishes this from *sexual identity*, a "culturally organized conception of the self." Sexual orientation describes attraction but does not necessarily tell us about a person's behaviors and lifestyle (Morales, 1996). For example, a man who is attracted to other men may marry and live his life as a straight, heterosexual person because of societal pressures, or live with a male partner, or work out a lifestyle that accommodates his sexual orientation while protecting him from homophobic harassment. Diamond also distinguishes sexual orientation and sexual identity from *same-sex sexuality*, in which a person may have a same-sex sexual liaison in certain situational conditions, such as living in a college dormitory or serving time in prison, but not have a gay sexual identity or sexual orientation.

For purposes of this discussion, we will consider anyone and any groups that do not see themselves fitting within the dominant paradigm of heterosexuality, and we refer to them as lesbian/gay/bisexual/transgender/queer/questioning/indeterminate (LGBTQI), recognizing that this term involves lumping together a highly diverse, disparate group of people. We also will use the terms *straight* (to describe heterosexuals) and *queer* (in reference to those who are gay), as these are common terms within LGBTQI communities. The term that researchers use for all those who are not straight or heterosexual is *sexual minorities* (Diamond, 2003), so we employ that term as well.

Sexual Oppression-Heterosexism

Sexual oppression occurs when an individual's sexuality (sexual relations, identity, behavior) does not conform to the dominant model of a male-female relationship. As a result, individuals are deemed morally inferior, depraved, and marginalized within dominant society. They are targets of verbal and physical violence and are often not afforded the same privileges as those who conform to what is considered heteronormative; for example, having a spouse invited to a business dinner or being eligible for a family discount. Heterosexism is the presupposition that heterosexual relationships are normative and that all other sexual attractions and gender identities are divergent. Heterosexism is an ideology, a dominant discourse that is manifest on many levels. It is a set of attitudes and belief systems that organizes interpersonal relationships, particularly dating and family formation, while also evident in institutions and the social ordering of society. Many subcultures within society also have their own meaning-making systems about gender and sexual relationships, which are transmitted intergenerationally through families, influencing how people feel about their own sexual identity and how they react to those of others (Morales, 1996). For instance, in Latino and Hispanic culture, even language is gendered, ordering an entire matrix of social relations between masculine and feminine.

As with every form of durable inequality, a web of oppression covers those who are considered sexual minorities. Heterosexism has many social consequences for those who are queer: being the target of stigma and violence, encountering discriminatory laws, lacking access to partner benefits, facing employment discrimination, having to fight for parental rights, and being denied the capacity to serve as foster or adoptive parents in many states—to mention a few. Perhaps the recent Supreme Court decision legalizing LGBTQI marriage will change this over time. LGBTQI people encounter hostility, discrimination, and exclusion from a significant number of religious denominations. Many openly LGBTQI people also have difficulty succeeding in politics in many parts of the country.

Homophobia is often viewed as an aspect of heterosexism but is more closely connected to sexism. Expressed through fear or aversion to LGBTQI people, it can take the form of prejudice, discrimination, or harassment and can operate intrapersonally, interpersonally, institutionally, and culturally (Blumenfeld, 2000). An individual does not have to identify as queer or have a relationship with someone of the same sex to be a target of homophobia. Straight men have been victims of hate crimes because they were perceived to be gay. In the United States men who are viewed as "effeminate" or unmasculine are often determined to be gay. Masculinity is associated with maleness, and maleness is associated with heterosexuality. Consider the coloniality of power and the importance the patriarchy placed on masculinity and virility, particularly as it pertained to White men. Similarly, when women do not conform to the gender norms associated with femininity, they are suspected to be lesbians. The codification of masculinity and femininity often expressed through attire, mannerisms, vocal patterns, gender role conformity, limits the range of identity expression for all individuals regardless of gender or sexual orientation. Heterosexism and homophobia place pressures on LGBTQI people that people who are straight do not face. This causes those who are LGBTQI to have to make decisions about disclosure and lifestyle, weighing the risks and balancing them with their desire to live openly. Herek (2000) talks of "internalized homophobia," which accrues from a constant discourse of heteronormativity, creating conflict and internal tensions. People can feel guilt or shame about their identity if they are "out," or experience the same emotions if they remain in the closet. Unlike social class, race, and gender, which are considered primarily inherited attributes, sexual orientation sometimes is constructed as a choice that people make about their lifestyle (Lim-Hing, 2000).

Although people do make decisions about the details of their lifestyle, most LGBTQI people strongly believe that their sexual orientation is part of their core self and being, that they are being themselves. Again, straight people do not have to justify their sexual and partnership lifestyles as "choices." It is *assumed* that they are being true to their genes and character.

The struggle against heterosexual norms and sanctions and to achieve one's authentic social and sexual self has its psychological costs. Many studies have documented higher rates of depression, drug use, and suicide in the LGBTQI population, particularly youth struggling to achieve their identities in hostile environments, such as high schools, and often without the support of their families (Consolacion et al., 2004; Gipson, 2002; Harper et al., 2004).

The Interaction of Racism and Sexual Oppression

When sexual oppression is faced by someone who inhabits the non-being zone it is aggravated by the racial oppression to which they are also subjected. A queer individual of color does not occupy the same being zone as someone who is White and queer, differentiating their lived experiences. As a result, racism exists within LGBTQI communities and homophobia is present in communities of color. Although experiencing social oppression can help to sensitize a person to the impact of being targeted, this does not necessarily negate internalized prejudice or discriminatory behaviors along another axis of social identity (Morales, 1990). And though all forms of durable inequalities have similar structures (Tilly, 1998), they also are distinct.

For example, the social construction of race and gender is often visible to others, while sexual orientation is often hidden and unseen. People of color can feel resentment toward

White women or lesbians who believe they grasp the experience of racism because of their own social disenfranchisement (Hooks, 2000). For reasons expressed in the preceding, the lived experience of someone who is racially oppressed is qualitatively different than those who experience White privilege (Grosfoguel, 2016). The status of being at the bottom of the sociopolitical hierarchy afforded to people of color through coloniality power continues to this day. Any form of social exclusion or oppression reduces its target to an inferior status that is detected and known; each is experienced in the lives of each person in concert with various systemic and structural forms of oppression.

People of color who are LGBTQI usually have to operate in at least three communities— their ethnic and racial communities, LGBTQI communities, and society at large—which privileges Whiteness and heterosexuality (Morales, 1990). LGBTQI people are both a visible and an invisible minority and often find that neither of these worlds has the space for them to be their complete and complex self. LGBTQI people of color often encounter tensions that White people and straight people of color do not. These may be loyalty conflicts or pressure to choose one community over the other, as their LGBTQI and ethnic communities often do not overlap and may even be wary of one another (Harper et al., 2004).

Because of invisible White privilege and the internalization of racist stereotypes and prejudices, people of color may feel alienated from LGBTQI friends and even partners. At the same time, a LGBTQI person of color may feel estranged from their own family and community. People of color often find support from their families for their race and ethnicity, but this regularly is not the case for their sexual orientation (Consolacion et al., 2004). There are many reasons for this, in addition to general societal heterosexism.

Some ethnic and racial groups, such as Native Americans and African Americans, have survived systematic attempts to destroy their families and cultures, including enslavement and genocide. Homosexuality can be perceived as a threat to the survival of the race (Greene & Boyd-Franklin, 1996). Some racial and ethnic groups have traditional values about gender roles, some of which may have been adopted from the coloniality of power (Schiwy, 2007) and may see gayness as a threat to their culture (Morales, 1990), which can place a great deal of pressure on a person not to let down their family.

In a study of adolescent boys and their views on the word "fag," Pascoe (2005), observes how White racial privilege has succeeded in colonizing how sexuality is represented. As a result of the coloniality of power, this critique on masculinity carries different consequences based on a person's racial classification as Pascoe (2005) states, "gendered power works through racialized selves" (p. 331). Being treated as a non-Being, Black men have been socialized to rely on masculinity as a source of power because of the high value a White supremacist and patriarchal culture places on it (Pascoe, 2005). As a result queer Black men will choose to align themselves with their race over their gender or sexuality. Being a Black man without masculinity means not being Black. Many men of color who are gay, transgender, or gender fluid, are viewed by many in their families and communities as embracing White culture. As a result of racing gender men of color often find themselves on the outside of their racial group (Pascoe, 2005).

Such internal conflicts, accompanied by negative or even hostile reactions from loved ones can make the coming-out process painful and tendentious and can alienate a person from their family, culture, and ethnic community. This can result in LGBTQI people of color seeking support from other LGBTQI people who are not ethnically or culturally similar and who may or may not grasp the unique tensions and strains experienced by queer people of color. For example, a young Latino man may not act in a way that is visibly gay because, in his family and community, this is linked with being alien, feminine, and inferior (Morales, 1996). His behavior, in turn, can precipitate a negative reaction from White gay friends who are disappointed that he is acting straight (Merighi & Grimes, 2000).

The emotional and psychological costs of various loyalties can cause LGBTQI people of color to act as if they are being segmented and parceled out into fragmented identities (Gipson, 2002; Harper et al., 2004). Yet there are anomalies and crosscurrents. Balsam et al. (2004) found that American Indians who were "two spirits" (having male and female spirits in one body) had more psychological symptoms and more mental health needs, but they also were highly identified with their traditional ethnic culture.

We should be mindful, too, that many LGBTQI people, whether of color or White, receive support and validation from their families. There are White allies for people of color and LGBTQI allies from straight communities of color. Groups can serve as a buffer from micro aggressions and as a locus of mutual aid and support. People gain many survival skills and sources of strength and resiliency from their experience of oppression, which can be of use when they encounter other types of discrimination. Even though they certainly experience high stress levels, people who encounter multiple oppressions do not necessarily have more emotional and psychological problems than people who have more social privilege (Consolacion et al., 2004; Mitchell et al., 2014).

Although it is important to explore the complex interactions of different axes of social identity and diverse forms of oppression, it is also prudent not to overly generalize. When working with individuals, groups, and families, it is most fruitful to seek to understand the unique constellations of identities and oppressions and how they are manifested with specific people in a given situation.

CONCLUSION

Racial identity does not exist in isolation from other aspects of identity. It is intersects with other aspects of social identity in different ways depending on the varying levels of power and privilege afforded to them. The systems and mechanisms that make up and fuel the coloniality of power affect every social identity and form durable inequalities and social oppression. We have structured our intersectional analysis to include intersections of race with social class, gender, and sexual identity. We have done this not only because the focus of this book is on racism but because the lived experience of people who face racial oppression in the United States is distinct from those who experience White privilege, due to their early classification of Non-Being through the coloniality of power. When people of color possess other targeted identities that demarcate them as "other" in the eyes of the hegemony, their lived experience of these targeted identities, as a Non-Being Other, is aggravated because each social oppression is concurrently being perpetuated. All forms of social oppression and axes of social identity are worthy of many volumes of analysis and discussion on their own. What we have done in this chapter is to explore some of the most significant ways by which race and racism intersect with these social phenomena and how racism in the United States, whether inside or outside of us, touches and transforms everything else.

EXERCISE 8.1 Intersectionality

Intersectionality involves the interactions between different axes of identity and of different types of social privilege or oppression.

Returning to the Social Identity Pie that you drew for Chapter 1, consider how your racial identity interacts with different aspects of your identity (e.g., gender, social class, sexual orientation, immigration status). You can do this on your own, in pairs, or in small groups.

1. How significant is your racial identity for you in relation to other aspects of your identity?
2. With which parts of your identity does your racial identity feel most integrated? With which parts do you feel tension? How would you explain the places of fit and disjuncture?
3. What social forces have supported or undermined the different aspects of your social identity? What social policies would you like to see changed to support yourself, your family, and your friends?
4. As a helping professional, what about your social identity will you want to be particularly mindful of when working with consumers?

EXERCISE 8.2 Dynamics of Durable Inequality

Examine an aspect of social identity and/or a form of social oppression that is not covered in this chapter. Describe how this durable inequality operates in U.S. society today. Who is privileged and targeted within society and in what ways? What are the kinds of dynamics—tasks, challenges, internal struggles—that occur with this aspect of identity? How is this similar and different to the dynamics of race and racism? How does it intersect with race and racism?

REFERENCES

Alexander, M. (2010). *The new Jim Crow: Mass incarceration in the age of colorblindness.* The New Press.

Allen, T. W. (1994). *The invention of the White race.* Verso.

Annandale, E., & Hunt, K. (Eds.). (2000). *Gender inequalities in health* (Vol. 214). Open University Press.

Balsam, K. F., Huang, B., Fieldand, K. C., Simom, J. M., & Walters, K. L. (2004). Culture, trauma, and wellness: A comparison of heterosexual and lesbian, gay, bisexual and Two-Spirit Native Americans. *Cultural Diversity and Mental Health, 10*(3), 287–301.

Baptist, E. E. (2014). *The half has never been told: Slavery and the making of American Capitalism.* Basic Books.

Bell, L. A., & Griffin, P. (1997). Pedagogical frameworks for social justice education. In M. Adams, L. A. Bell, & P. Griffin (Eds.), *Teaching for diversity and social justice: A sourcebook* (pp. 44–58). Routledge.

Benard, A. (2016). Colonizing Black female bodies within patriarchal capitalism: Feminist and human rights perspective. *Sexualization, Media, & Society, 2*(4), 1–11.

Blumenfeld, W. J. (2000). How homophobia hurts everyone. In M. Adams, W. J. Blumenfeld, R. Castañeda, H. W. Hackman, M. L. Peters, & X. Zúñiga (Eds.), *Readings for diversity and social justice* (pp. 267–275). Routledge.

Bourgois, P. (1995). *In search of respect.* Cambridge University Press.

Butler, J. (1997). *The psychic life of power: Theories in subjection.* Stanford University Press.

Carter, R. T. (2007). Racism and psychological and emotional injury: Recognizing and assessing race-based traumatic stress. *The Counseling Psychologist, 35,* 13–105.

Catalano, D. C. J., & Griffin, P. (2016). Sexism, heterosexism, and trans* oppression. In M. Adams, & L. A. Bell (Eds.), *Teaching for diversity and social justice* (3rd ed., pp. 183–211). Routledge.

Cho, S., Crenshaw, K. W., & McCall, L. (2013). Toward a field of intersectionality studies: Theory, applications, and praxis. *Signs: Journal of Women in Culture and Society, 38*(4), 785–810.

Collins, P. H. (1990). *Black feminist thought: Knowledge, consciousness and the politics of empowerment.* Routledge.

Consolacion, T. B., Russell, S. T., & Sue, S. (2004). Sex, race/ethnicity, and romantic attractions: Multiple minority status adolescents and mental health. *Cultural Diversity and Ethnic Minority Psychology, 10*(3), 200–214.

Cose, E. (1993). *The rage of a privileged class.* HarperCollins.

Cose, E. (1995, June 5). Black men, Black women. *Newsweek,* pp. 66–69.

Cox, O. C. (1948). *Caste, class and race: A study in social dynamics.* Doubleday.

Crenshaw, K. (1989). Demarginalizing the intersection of race and sex: A black feminist critique of antidiscrimination doctrine, feminist theory and antiracist politics. *University of Chicago Legal Forum, 1989,* 139.

Crenshaw, K. (2005). Mapping the margins: Intersectionality, identity politics, and violence against women of color (1994). In R. K. Bergen, J. L. Edleson, & C. M. Renzetti (Eds.), *Violence against women: Classic papers* (pp. 282–313). Pearson Education New Zealand.

Diamond, L. M. (2003). Special section: Integrating research on sexual-minority and heterosexual development: Theoretical and clinical implications. *Journal of Clinical Child and Adolescent Psychology, 32*(4), 490–498.

Edsall, T. B., & Edsall, M. D. (1991). *Chain reaction: The impact of race, rights and taxes on American politics.* W. W. Norton.

Eriksen, T. H. (1996). Ethnicity, race, class and nation. In J. Hutchinson & A. D. Smith (Eds.), *Ethnicity* (pp. 28–31). Oxford University Press.

Fanon, F. (1967). Black skin, white masks, trans. *Charles Lam Markmann (New York: Grove, 1967),* 109, 98.

Feagin, J. R. (1999). Excluding Blacks and others from housing. *Cityscape: A Journal of Policy Development and Research, 4*(3), 79–91.

Feinberg, L. (1993). The life and times of a gender outlaw: An interview with Leslie Feinberg. *TransSisters: The Journal of Transsexual Feminism, 1*(1), 4–8.

Fenton, S. (1999). *Ethnicity, racism, class and culture.* Rowman & Littlefield.

Fitzgerald, K. J. (2017). Understanding racialized homophobic and transphobic violence. In S. E. Weissinger, D. A. Mack, & E. Watson (Eds.), *Violence against black bodies* (pp. 53–70). Routledge.

Fredrickson, G. (1988). *The arrogance of race: Historical perspectives on slavery, racism, and social inequality.* Wesleyan University Press.

Garran, A. M., & Werkmeister Rozas, L. (2013). Cultural competence revisited. *Journal of Ethnic and Cultural Diversity in Social Work, 22*(2), 97–111.

Gipson, L. M. (2002). Poverty, race and LGBT youth. *Poverty & Race, 11*(2), 1–6, 11.

Greene, B., & Boyd-Franklin, N. (1996). African American lesbians: Issues in couples therapy. In J. Laird & R. J. Green (Eds.), *Lesbians and gays in couples and families: A handbook for therapists* (pp. 251–271). Jossey-Bass.

Grosfoguel, R. (2016). What is racism? *Journal of World-Systems Research, 22*(1), 9–15. https://doi.org/10.5195/jwsr.2016.609

Grosfoguel, R. (2011). Decolonizing post-colonial studies and paradigms of political-economy: Transmodernity, decolonial thinking, and global coloniality. *Transmodernity: Journal of Peripheral Cultural Production of the Luso-hispanic World, 1*(1). https://doi.org/10.5070/T411000004

Hardiman, R., Jackson, B. W., & Griffin, P. (2007). Conceptual foundations for social justice education. In M. Adams, L. A. Bell, & P. Griffin (Eds.), *Teaching for diversity and social justice* (2nd ed., pp. 35–66). Routledge.

Harnois, C. E. (2010, March). Race, gender, and the Black women's standpoint. *Sociological Forum, 25*(1), 68–85.

Harper, G. W., Jernewall, N., & Zea, M. C. (2004). Giving voice to emerging science and theory for lesbian, gay and bisexual people of color. *Cultural Diversity and Mental Health*, 10(3), 187–199.

Harro, B. (2018). The cycle of socialization. In A. Adams, W. J. Blumenfeld, C. Casteneda, H. W. Hackman, M. L. Peters, & X. Zuniga, (Eds.), *Readings for diversity and social justice* (pp. 45–52). Routledge.

Haschemi Yekani, E., Hrzán, D., Husmann-Kastein, J., Junker, C., Krasuska, K., & Michaelis, B. (2008). Where, when, and how? Contextualizing intersectionality. *New Subjectivities: Negotiating Citizenship in the Context of Migration and Diversity*, 19–47.

Herdt, G. (1994). *Third Sex and Third Gender: Beyond Sexual Dimorphism in Culture and History.*

Herek, G. M. (2000). Internalized homophobia among gay men, lesbians, and bisexuals. In M. Adams, W. J. Blumenfeld, R. Castañeda, H. W. Hackman, M. L. Peters, & X. Zúñiga (Eds.), *Readings for diversity and social justice* (pp. 281–283). Routledge.

Hooks, B. (2000). Homophobia in Black communities. In M. Adams, W. J. Blumenfeld, R. Castañeda, H. W. Hackman, M. L. Peters, & X. Zúñiga (Eds.), *Readings for diversity and social justice* (pp. 283–287). Routledge.

Jansson, B. (2015). *The reluctant welfare state: American social welfare policies: Past, present and future* (8th ed.). Cengage.

Johnson. (2018, February 9). http://www.futurity.org/police-killings-unarmed-black-women-1675912-2/

Jones, J. (1985). *Labor of love, labor of sorrow: Black women, work and the family, from slavery to the present.* Basic Books.

Lacy, K. (2015). Race, privilege and the growing class divide. *Ethnic and Racial Studies*, 38(8), 1246–1249.

Langer, S. J., & Martin, J. I. (2004). How dresses can make you mentally ill: Examining gender identity disorder in children. *Child and Adolescent Social Work Journal*, 21(1), 5–23.

Lieberman, R. C. (1998). *Shifting the color line: Race and the American welfare state.* Harvard University Press.

Lim-Hing, S. (2000). Dragon ladies, snow queens, and Asian-American dykes: Reflections on race and sexuality. In M. Adams, W. J. Blumenfeld, R. Castañeda, H. W. Hackman, M. L. Peters, & X. Zúñiga (Eds.), *Readings for diversity and social justice* (pp. 296–299). Routledge.

Lorber, J. (2018). Paradoxes of Gender Redux. *Gender Reckonings: New Social Theory and Research*, p. 297.

Manning, R. D. (1999). Poverty, race, and the two-tiered financial services system. *Poverty & Race*, 8(4), 1–2, 11.

Massey, D. S., & Denton, N. A. (1993). *American apartheid: Segregation and the making of the underclass.* Harvard University Press.

McCall, L. (2005). The complexity of intersectionality. *Signs: Journal of Women in Culture and Society*, 30(3), 1771–1800.

McClintock, A. (1995). *Imperial leather. Race, gender, and sexuality in the colonial conquest.* Routledge.

Merighi, J. R., & Grimes, M. D. (2000). Coming out to families in a multicultural context. *Families in Society*, 81(1), 3, 2-Al.

Miller, J., & Schamess, G. (2000). The discourse of denigration and the creation of other. *Journal of Sociology and Social Welfare*, 27(3), 39–62.

Miller, S. M., & Ferroggiaro, K. M. (1996). Respect. *Poverty & Race*, 5(1), 14.

Mitchell, J. D., Simmons, C. Y., & Greyerbiehl, L. A. (Eds.). (2014). *Intersectionality & higher education.* Peter Lang.

Morales, E. S. (1990). Ethnic minority families and minority gays and lesbians. *Marriage and Family Review*, 14(3/4), 212–239.

Morales, E. S. (1996). Gender roles among Latino gay and bisexual men. In J. Laird & R. J. Green (Eds.), *Lesbians and gays in couples and families: A handbook for therapists* (pp. 272–297). Jossey-Bass.

Oliver, M. L., & Shapiro, T. M. (2013). *Race, wealth, and equality.* In M. Adams, W. J. Blumenfeld, R. Casteñeda, H. W. Hackman, M. L. Peters, & X. Zúñiga (Eds.), *Readings for diversity and social justice* (3rd ed., pp. 164–170). Routledge.

Omatsu, G. (2000). Racism or solidarity? Unions and Asian immigrant workers. In M. Adams, W. J. Blumenfeld, R. Casteñeda, H. W. Hackman, M. L. Peters, & X. Zúñiga (Eds.), *Readings for diversity and social justice* (pp. 407–412). Routledge.

Omi, M., & Winant, H. (1994). *Racial formation in the United States: From the 1960s to the 1990s* (2nd ed.). Routledge.

Painter, N. I. (2010). *The history of white people.* WW Norton & Company.

Pascoe, C. J. (2005). "Dude, you're a fag": Adolescent masculinity and the fag discourse. *Sexualities, 8*(3), 329–346. https://doi.org/10.1177/1363460705053337

Phillips, K. (1990). *The politics of rich and poor: Wealth and the American electorate in the Reagan aftermath.* Random House.

Quadagno, J. (1994). *The color of welfare: How racism undermined the war on poverty.* Oxford University Press.

Quijano, A. (2000). Coloniality of power and Eurocentrism in Latin America. *International Sociology, 15*(2), 215–232.

Quijano, A. (2008). Coloniality and modernity/rationality. *Cultural Studies, 21*(2–3), 168–178.

Ransford, E. (2000). Two hierarchies. In M. Adams, W. J. Blumenfeld, R. Casteñeda, H. W. Hackman, M. L. Peters, & X. Zúñiga (Eds.), *Readings for diversity and social justice* (pp. 412–418). Routledge.

Reid, P. T., & Comas-Diaz, L. (1990). Gender and ethnicity: Perspectives on dual status. *Sex Roles, 22*(7/8), 397–408.

Remedios, J. D., & Snyder, S. H. (2018). Intersectional oppression: Multiple stigmatized identities and perceptions of invisibility, discrimination, and stereotyping. *Journal of Social Issues, 74*(2), 265–281.

Remedios, J. D., Chasteen, A. L., Rule, N. O., & Plaks, J. E. (2011). Impressions at the intersection of ambiguous and obvious social categories: Does gay+Black=likable? *Journal of Experimental Social Psychology, 47*(6), 1312–1315. https://doi.org/10.1016/j.jesp.2011.05.015

Richards, C., Bouman, W. P., Seal, L., Barker, M. J., Nieder, T. O., & T'Sjoen, G. (2016). Non-binary or genderqueer genders. *International Review of Psychiatry, 28*(1), 95–102.

Sakamoto, A., & Wang, S. X. (2015). The declining significance of race in the twenty-first century: A retrospective assessment in the context of rising class inequality. *Ethnic and Racial Studies, 38*(8), 1264–1270.

Schiller, B. R. (1998). *The economics of poverty and discrimination* (7th ed.). Prentice Hall.

Schiwy, F. (2007). Decolonization and the question of subjectivity. *Cultural Studies, 21*(2–3), 271–294.

Sennett, R., & Cobb, J. (1972). *The hidden injuries of class.* Knopf.

Shapiro, T. M. (2004). *The hidden cost of being African American: How wealth perpetuates inequality.* Oxford University Press.

Singer, B. (1997, November 11). Trans identities: Language has the power to erase or self-define. Au Courant, pp. 3–17.

Speer, I. (2015). Race, wealth and class identification in 21st-century American society. *The Sociological Quarterly, 57*(2), 356–379.

Spivak, A. L., & Monnat, S. M. (2013). The influence of race, class and Metropolitan area characteristics on African American segregation. *Social Science Quarterly, 94*(5), 1414–1437.

Stevens-Watkins, D., Perry, B., Pullen, E., Jewell, J., & Oser, C. B. (2014). Examining the associations between racism, sexism, and stressful life events on psychological stress among African American women. *Cultural Diversity and Ethnic Minority Psychology, 20*(4), 561–569.

Sullivan, S. (2014). *Good White people: The problem with middle-class White antiracism.* University of Albany Press.

Takaki, R. (1987). The metaphysics of civilization: Indians and the Age of Jackson. In R. Takaki (Ed.), *From different shores: Perspectives on race and ethnicity in America* (pp. 54–68). Oxford University Press.

Takaki, R. (1993). *A different mirror: A history of multi-cultural America.* Little, Brown.

Tilly, C. (1998). *Durable inequality.* University of California Press.

Wade, P. (2009). *Race and sex in Latin America.* Pluto Press.

Wilkinson, D. Y. (1995). Gender and social inequality: The prevailing significance of race. *Daedalus, 124*(1), 167–178.

Wilkinson, D. Y. (1997). Reappraising the race, class and gender equation: A critical theoretical perspective. *Smith College Studies in Social Work, 67*(3), 261–276.

Wilson, W. J. (1996). When work disappears. *Political Science Quarterly, 111*(4), 567–595.

Wolff, E. N. (2001). *Public policy brief 66: Racial wealth disparities; Is the gap closing? Annandale-on-Hudson,* Levy Economics Institute of Bard College.

Woody, D. J., & Green, R. (2001). The influence of race/ethnicity and gender on psychological well-being. *Journal of Ethnic and Cultural Diversity in Social Work, 9*(3/4), 151–166.

Yuval-Davis, N. (2006). Intersectionality and feminist politics. *European Journal of Women's Studies, 13*(3), 193–209.

Zandvliet, T. (2000). Transgender issues in therapy. In C. Neal, & D. Davies (Eds.), *Issues in therapy with lesbian, gay, bisexual, and transgender clients* (pp. 176–189). Open University Press.

CHAPTER 9

Racial Dialogue: Talking About Race and Racism

INTRODUCTION

I say hi to everybody, touch everybody, but that's normal. I don't even see what color you are when I do that. But when a White student comes up to me in the cafeteria where I'm sitting, minding my own business, and wants to talk about her burning issues of race, that's another level for me, and I can't do that if I'm not in a good space. It's hard when I get angry and voice it. I'm getting angry with the people I love and kiss. That's a horrible feeling for me.
                    —**Latina participant in a racial dialogue (Miller & Donner, 2000)**

I need to check my own internalized oppression and voice it. I need the opportunity to talk about how I feel and how offended I am by constant references to [White] people's privilege and safety that I don't ever have the safety to experience. I need to allow myself to be angry.
—**African American woman participant in a racial dialogue (Miller & Donner, 2000)**

It's the longest process you are going to go through probably in your life, if you are really committed to it. It means unlearning something so codified in the culture. It's both interrupting a racist joke and making a racist joke and being interrupted and hearing that; somebody having the courage to say to me "you're screwing up."
                    —**White woman participant in a racial dialogue (Miller & Donner, 2000)**

The aforementioned quotes are from a facilitated racial dialogue held at a graduate school of social work in 1998 (Miller & Donner, 2000). They convey many things: strong emotions such as anger and fear, the desire to be left alone, ambivalence about caring for someone who is intruding in an oppressive fashion, and the importance of confronting other people. The statements also suggest inner resiliency, the courage to face oneself and others, the importance of being authentic, and the value of listening and self-reflection. The quotes illustrate both the benefits and the challenges of having dialogues about race and racism.

Talking directly about race and racism in racially mixed groups does not occur often in society (Miller & Donner, 2000; Shipler, 1997). Residential segregation limits interracial contact in public. The web of racism opens doors for White people while creating filters for people of color, further limiting opportunities for interracial dialogue. Even when people are working or studying together, however, these dialogues usually do not take place, and if they emerge spontaneously, they can be so painful or difficult that people disengage and withdraw. An African American resident life leader at a prestigious women's college once told one of our research assistants: "The problem is that the conversations often end up with White people talking about their own oppression." Why is talking about race and racism so difficult?

This chapter explores the possible answers to that question, but begins by considering why racial dialogues are even worth the time, effort, and investment. We first look at the ways that people avoid talking about race and racism and the consequences of such evasion. We then suggest ways to have fertile interracial conversations. Last, we consider how these conversations can be part of a larger process of repair and reconciliation.

When we talk of racial dialogue, we refer to structured, group conversations and discussions that focus on race, racism, ethnicity, and culture. Some dialogues take place in large groups, others with small clusters of people. These dialogues can comprise participants of the same race or ethnicity, two different races or ethnicities, or more. A racial dialogue can be a one-time event or a series of meetings, structured or unstructured. We examine some of these variables and their potential impact. What all racial dialogues have in common is a commitment by all participants to listen respectfully, accompanied by a desire to learn about oneself and others in the milieu of a racialized society. For the purposes of this chapter, we focus on in-person racial dialogues. With the limitations placed on the formation of in-person groups due to COVID-19 and the urgent need for dialogue opportunities, online racial dialogue has become crucial. Many of the principles and guidelines described in this chapter can be used with online or web-based racial dialogues.

WHY UNDERTAKE RACIAL DIALOGUES?

What is to be gained by talking about race and racism? In many ways, racism itself is the antithesis of this question: Racism is predicated on not having respectful interracial dialogue. Racism is a condition of dehumanization and alienation; by contrast, genuine dialogue relies on recognizing the fundamental humanity and equality of the person or groups of people engaged in dialogue. It has been tied to the pursuit of social justice and democracy as it subverts the bifurcation of "us" and "them" (Cooks, 2020).

Racism isolates and silences people, even alienating them from themselves. Dialogues connect people, some by highlighting commonality and others by posing the question of what each of our accountability is to others (Cook, 2020). Racism relies on obfuscation and masking privilege. Dialogue can lead to exploration and revelation. Racism justifies inequities by alleged genetic or cultural flaws. Dialogue unmasks these fictions while exposing people to personal stories and experiences. Racism is a system of power, privilege, and exploitation that benefits one or a number of groups at the expense of others. Dialogue, even if only temporarily, can establish a level playing field. Racism marginalizes the voices of people of color while promoting a hegemonic, White discourse. Dialogue allows all to tell their stories and to hear the narratives of other people. Racism depends on uninvolved bystanders. Dialogue encourages everyone to participate. Racism relies on ignorance. Dialogue contributes to knowledge. Without dialogue, racism seems to be the normal state of affairs. With dialogue, the madness of racism is laid bare. Racism leads to feeling overwhelmed and resigned to failure. Dialogue sparks optimism. Racism divides people and pits them against one another. Dialogue offers opportunities for cooperation and trust building that may lead to collaborative social action.

Dialogue will not dismantle racism on its own. In fact, dialogue on its own leaves intact structural and institutional racism (Leonardo & Porter, 2010). The most significant civil rights victories have resulted from organized social movements and heroic struggle, in which lives were risked and lost. It took a Civil War to officially end slavery in the United States. What dialogue can do is challenge racism that has been internalized and that poisons interpersonal relationships, and can help groups of people, whether in the workplace, school, or community, learn to understand, respect, and collaborate with people who are different.

Dialogue can also disrupt the static definitions of and boundary between self and other because the process involves the constant creation and deconstruction of one's identity. Bakhtin's (1981) concept of the dialogic profers a particularly important aspect of how dialogue operates. He states, "Understanding and response are dialectically merged and mutually condition each other; one is impossible without the other" (1981, p. 282). In Bakhtin's (1981) world, not only is it impossible for individuals to exist without each other, they exist because they are the result of all of the interactions, relationships, and experiences they have with others. Recognizing that in dialogue the very act of sharing a thought, a feeling, or "utterance" includes connections with the past, present, and anticipated future. Listening to and exchanging testimonies of people's life experiences is exactly what dialogue participants identify as salient and transformative to their understanding of self and other within a larger sociopolitical context (Rozas, 2004).

Interracial and intercultural dialogue encourages individuals and groups to reflect on who they are in relation to other people within the context of a racialized society (Aldana et al., 2012; Ford & Malaney, 2012; Gurin et al., 2014; Gurin-Sands et al., 2012; Miller & Donner, 2000; Werkmeister Rozas, 2007). These encounters immerse our social identities in a social situation with people who have similar and dissimilar social identities. Dialogues take people out of their own ethnocentrism.

Dialogue has been used to enhance understanding and resolve conflict between groups experiencing severe tensions, misunderstandings, and conflict. Examples include discussions between Koreans/Korean Americans and African Americans in Los Angeles (Norman, 1994), Jews and Arabs in the Middle East (Bargal & Bar, 1994), Jews and Germans (Nadan et al., 2015), Protestants and Catholics in Northern Ireland (Templegrove Action Research Limited, 1996), Whites and people of color in many U.S. communities (Ford & Malaney, 2012; McCoy & Sherman, 1994; Study Circles Resource Center, 1997, 1998), and in many other parts of the world marked by enduring patterns of ethnic, religious, or racial conflict (Fisher, 1990).

Researchers have found that intergroup dialogue helps participants to collaboratively analyze varied social-historical-political contexts and unequal power relations (Aldana et al., 2012; Ford & Malaney, 2012; Gurin-Sands et al., 2012; Nadan et al., 2015). This happens through letting go of essentialist viewpoints and moving to a more constructivist framework, learning to reflect on oneself rather than focusing on others, acknowledging the complexity of intersectionality for all participants, and building concepts and theories from what is offered in exchanges rather than understanding the dialogic process through the lens of preexisting theories (Nadan et al., 2015).

Dialogue groups also offer a forum to discuss charged and controversial issues, such as abortion and the death penalty (Becker et al., 1995; Chasm et al., 1996). They have been held on a national level as well as on the local level (Lawson et al., 1998).

Zúñiga et al. (2002) identified three beneficial consequences of dialogues:

1. Sustained communication
2. Consciousness raising
3. Bridging differences

Ford and Malaney (2012), who conducted qualitative research with college students who identified as being multiracial and/or people of color, in a historically White college (HWC) describe how interracial and intraracial dialogue groups rely on forming relationships, exploring differences and commonalities in social identities, tackle difficult topics, and can contribute to forming alliances. People of color and multiracial people participating in such conversations evinced a better sense of their social identities, a recognition of the fluidity and intersectionality of social identity, greater pride in their identity, increased awareness of their biases toward others, and greater confidence about taking action to confront racism. Similarly research conducted by Dessel & Rodenborg (2017) found that one of the most helpful aspects of dialogue is when it is designed to examine and interrogate one's own social identity (Dessel & Rodenborg, 2017; Garran & Werkmeister Rozas, 2013). Recognizing your own and others' social identities promotes involvement on a cognitive level, a sense of having a common fate, and develops a collective self-esteem. All of this enables a broader sense of community and increased desire to interact with a racially diverse group.

Sustained communication usually brings together people from diverse backgrounds and with varying social privilege, status, and power, and encourages them to keep talking with one another about their differences. This involves listening, taking risks, raising questions, and moving beyond static positions. It also requires developing a language and skills for participating in these conversations. Consciousness raising implies learning about history, sociology, and cultural differences, and further suggests the importance of self-awareness and learning about the experiences of members of different groups.

Consciousness raising also has a value orientation, as it is meant to lead to social-justice commitments and changes in how people think, act, and interact. A central goal of racial dialogues is to bridge differences. The dialogue offers a space where conflicting perspectives and strong emotions can be expressed, shared, and interrogated. The conflicts that arise in these exchanges can lead to greater understanding, self-awareness, and compassion for others. At the same time, it is important to respect and validate the real differences in experiences, power, and privilege that exist among participants (Dovidio et al., 2016; Leonardo & Porter, 2010).

When examined from a communications perspective, dialogue can be seen as an ethical form of communication because it requires reflection, each person acting as a witness to our own and others' words. It demands continuous deliberation, asking the question of why we uphold our values and how we enact them (Cooks, 2020).

Ultimately, dialogue is an alternative to the use of force as a means of conflict resolution. These conversations can offer hope, no matter how deep the conflict or how long the odds. Most participants in the dialogue referred to at the beginning of this chapter found "that the dialogue provided hope that constructive and substantive conversations could take place across racial lines," which encouraged them to take risks (Miller & Donner, 2000, p. 46). Optimism that people can work together and challenge oppression is an essential ingredient in the struggle against racism.

Critical Conversations

Critical Conversations is a model developed by Kang and O'Neill (2018) that invites participants to explore how power is noticed, named, reflected upon and discussed, leading to action to address power imbalances and inequities. It is a useful model to use when talking about race and racism as it creates a scaffolding for all members of a group to be self-reflexive and for there to be sharing and negotiation. It offers a conceptual analysis and an analytic process that helps people to experience how structural aspects of racism and other forms of oppression are manifested in interactions between people. Engaging in a critical conversation is an intentional process where all participants consent to having a critical conversation about race and racism

Critical Conversations involves four steps:

1. *Tuning in and noticing*—Participants are invited to pay attention to their own experiences during a conversation, including assumptions that they are making about themselves and others. As the model acknowledges the centrality of power, this phase involves noticing the various ways that power is manifested and how this lands with different participants.
2. *Reflect*—Participants are encouraged to reflect on their thoughts, feelings, assumptions, and reactions. How might their social identities and the social identities of others influence the conversation and people's reactions to it?
3. *Sharing*—Participants are encouraged to share their reflections; both what they are experiencing but also what they are witnessing, in specific and behavioral terms. Sharing with others allows participants to express their needs and values without blaming others. And importantly, sharing or naming observations about the power dynamics that are present, being replicated or in some way being played out among people, allows for the social/structural dynamics to be externalized and examined. This creates opportunities for participants to shift their perspectives about assumptions, thoughts, and ways of interacting with each other.
4. *Requests*—What concrete, doable requests can someone make of someone else engaged in a critical conversation? Participants are encouraged to be affirmative—what they would want—rather than critical—what they don't want. They are also encouraged to be aspirational—what are their hopes about how a critical conversation can lead to a better outcome where unacknowledged power and privilege are not shaping the conversation.

The value of critical conversations is that participants practice paying attention to themselves and others and are encouraged to share this with a group, where humility is a virtue, as well as authenticity and respect for different identities, values, experiences and world views. It can help people to both understand and manage their emotions without withdrawing from genuine engagement. It encourages listening, self-reflection, and can reduce unproductive, hostile conflict. It avoids reductionist ways of thinking and doing and embraces complexity and ambiguity. Ultimately, such conversations can lead to greater understanding as well as an enhanced capacity to take action.

The Critical Conversations model is being field-tested at a number of colleges and universities, with professors, graduate students, and undergraduate students from a range of disciplines and more data will be gathered about its effectiveness.

WHY ARE RACIAL DIALOGUES SO CHALLENGING?

Because racial dialogues are not common and are not always successful, we should endeavor to understand why. Without awareness, we are likely to have sterile or fruitless conversations or to avoid the discussions entirely. One impediment to racial dialogue is pessimism on the part of people of color who believe that they will not benefit or gain anything by raising painful feelings, and that White people will remain uninterested and unmotivated. Another barrier is that some White people lack the incentive to participate in a process that could involve conflict or painful realizations.

Part of what makes racism so pernicious is how "normal" it seems and how everyone living in a racist society is socialized into roles and internalizes beliefs, attitudes, and values shaped by racism. Yet many people are willing to risk talking about racism because they are committed to challenging it. In our view, for anyone entering one of the helping professions, engaging in these discussions is imperative, because effective cross-racial and cross-cultural work requires the ability to talk about race and racism.

"The Web of Institutional Racism" helps to describe how U.S. society continues to be segregated. This is one of the fundamental reasons that people do not have cross-racial conversations about race. This is not the only reason, because even when occasions present themselves, many people are wary or skeptical. Or when such conversations do occur, they do not engage people in meaningful, collaborative, and critical conversation and may reinforce existing power relations and recycle predictable, unproductive, and stereotypical discussions about race and racism. Dominant public discourse often denies and masks racism, which can feel more dispiriting than not talking about it at all. Racism becomes a taboo subject, a discursive "third rail."

Some people may have tried to talk about race and racism with people of other races and had bad experiences that left them feeling vulnerable and misunderstood (Stone et al., 1999). When our few experiences are negative, we begin to lack trust and confidence in the process, increasing the potential for misunderstanding. If people enter into such conversations with suspicion and their guards up, they are likely to encounter miscommunication and missed opportunities.

In addition to their fear of being misunderstood, people are dissuaded from engaging in racial dialogues because they think their identity is on the line (Miller et al., 2004a; Stone et al., 1999). Race and racism pivot on the construction of racial identity. Most people seek situations in which their identity is affirmed and valued and avoid situations in which their identity is dismissed, disrespected, and denigrated. People of color often maintain a positive identity despite social stereotyping and cultural devaluation. As we described in Chapters 1 and 6, one strategy for withstanding assaults on selfhood is to form support groups with other people of color, which can serve as a buffer (Dion, 2002; Solorzano et al., 2000; Tatum, 1997). In response to this, intraracial dialogue is an effective strategy (Ford & Malaney, 2012) at least temporarily. Engaging in interracial dialogue carries the risk of experiencing microaggressions and having painful social interactions with White people.

Most White people see themselves as unbiased and tolerant. White people talking about racism are fearful of being viewed as racists. There is a difference between saying something racist and "being" a racist, but many White people believe that their moral integrity as a person is on the line when criticized about saying something racist. Thus, they resist entering social situations in which their view of themselves might be challenged, in which they may be called something that they consciously abhor and that induces feelings of shame. This can threaten a person's identity and self-concept, as well as generate cognitive dissonance from being exposed to information that challenges both the person's identity and their perception of the world (Miller et al., 2004b).

People of color and White people alike risk being emotionally hurt or wounded in conversations about race and racism. As the opening quotes illustrate, they also are concerned about inadvertently hurting other people or having to confront friends or colleagues. Shelton and Richeson (2005) found that Whites held back from participating in intergroup dialogue for fear of appearing prejudiced, undesirable, and selfish; and Blacks were reticent to risk confirming negative stereotypes held by Whites. So it is not surprising that people try to avoid these situations.

Nevertheless, people have a concomitant desire to understand more about themselves and others, and those in the helping professions are concerned about serving their clients, as well as having a commitment to social justice. So people do enter into such conversations or take classes and workshops in which racial dialogues are a part. But as the conversation heats up, if someone feels under attack or misunderstood or becomes angry over another person's insensitivity, what happens?

At this juncture, the risk is that people will withdraw, shut down, or become pessimistic or even despondent. As people experience more negative affect, they become less engaged and willing to invest in intergroup dialogue (Miles et al., 2015). As people become guarded and mistrustful, defense mechanisms such as denial or projection can kick in (Miller et al., 2004a). A climate of blame and shame can overshadow attempts to listen and be self-reflective. Sometimes this leads to frustration and anger directed toward the facilitator or teacher. A conspiracy of silence can settle over the group, as its members no longer feel safe to talk or take risks (Davis, 1992; Miller et al., 2004a).

Another typical roadblock to productive racial dialogues is that the learning curve for White people is much steeper (Miller & Donner, 2000). While people of color are highly aware of racism, many White people are cocooned by their White privilege. This creates a paradox: White people need space to learn and explore about racism in the world and inside of them, a place where they will not be attacked or humiliated. Yet, when people of color observe this unfolding, it can be painful or frustrating, particularly during the early phases of discussion, which might expose significant White naiveté about racism and the ambivalence felt by people of color about not wanting to have to teach White people about racism. One of the biggest challenges for racial dialogues is how they can be productive for all participants, not just a learning situation for White people in which people of color bare their souls to help White people "get it" (Miller & Donner, 2000). We reflect on this dilemma as we consider how to structure successful dialogues.

CONDUCTING SUCCESSFUL RACIAL DIALOGUES

What constitutes a successful racial dialogue? A number of criteria can be employed in responding to this question. One is that participants leave the dialogue thinking they have learned something about racism. Another is that they feel willing and able to engage in social action to confront racism. What is learned will vary considerably among participants, but this may include enhanced self-awareness; greater understanding of others' experiences;

more knowledge about the dynamics of racism; and a sense that one has been heard, respected, and understood. This will not always feel good. A successful racial dialogue can cause discomfort and unease, and these feelings can be overwhelming.

Interracial dialogues that feel too comfortable run the risk of maintaining the hierarchies of privilege that divide participants because they reinforce rather than resist dominant patterns of racial privilege (Leonardo & Porter, 2010). To be able to experience deep learning, one must leave one's "comfort zone," but it is not productive to be so uncomfortable that defense mechanisms take over and shut a person down. Research has indicated that Whites and people of color have different expectations for racial dialogues (Miller & Donner, 2000; Study Circles Resource Center, 1998). White people often think a dialogue has been successful if race and racism were discussed openly and respectfully and they learned something. People of color may value this experience, too, but they also have reported that they think it is important to see how the discussion has led to action, more than just talk. Other criteria for successful dialogue include less suspicion toward and greater respect for others, a reduction in negative stereotypes, greater awareness of structural racism, and lower levels of ethnocentrism (Aldana et al., 2012; Gurin-Sands et al., 2012; Miller & Donner, 2000).

Ford and Malaney (2012) contend that dialogues are successful if they structure interaction, foster engaged listening, and facilitate a learning environment. Yet, a recent study by Tittler and Wade (2019) indicated that it can depend on racial group composition (as discussed in the following). Sometimes that involves sharing information and helping participants to develop and utilize a sharper critical consciousness. The dialogue mentioned at the beginning of this chapter had 53 participants—11 people of color and 42 White people (Miller & Donner, 2000). It was co-facilitated by two women—Beverly Tatum, who is African American, and Andrea Ayvazian, who is White. Both had facilitated many racial dialogues, often together. They structured the dialogue by first mapping out the contours of the conversation and then having an exchange between themselves about race and racism, describing their own feelings, struggles, fears, and missteps, using anecdotes to illustrate their points. They modeled respectful listening and the courage to take risks and make mistakes and acknowledged their different experiences and expectations by virtue of their race.

Then they set up a "fishbowl," a circle within the larger group circle. Six chairs were placed in the fishbowl with the expectation that one chair always would remain empty so people outside of the fishbowl could enter it to participate in the conversation. This meant that if someone were to enter the group, someone else would have to leave, to maintain the empty chair. Then the facilitators asked for volunteers to fill the initial fishbowl and asked the first question: "What do you need to be able to respond to cross-racial dialogue at [this school for social work]?" After 15 minutes, they asked a second question: "How do I use what I have learned here beyond the gates of [this school for social work]?"

After this, the facilitators asked those in the larger group, who had not participated in the fishbowl, to relate their reflections about what they had heard. Next, the facilitators had another conversation between themselves, reflecting on the discussions that had taken place, highlighting issues and themes; then moving to a "brainstorming" activity in which the participants were asked to generate examples of active and passive racism and ways to resist racism. They concluded with a video showing faces of different ethnic and racial groups melting into one another.

The participants filled out questionnaires immediately after the event, utilizing Likert-scale responses (see Table 9.1). All participants found the event to be helpful and gave it high

TABLE 9.1   Results of Questionnaire

Percent of respondents who strongly agree (1) or agree (2)			
	Total	People of Color[a] (n = 11)	White People (n = 42)
I found this event to be helpful.	98.1	90.9	100
My experience in this dialogue increased my desire to participate in further racial dialogues.	98.2	90.9	100
A person's race is a central element in one's experience in this society.	98.1	90.9	100
Racial dialogues are one important way to deal with racism in this country.	100	100	100
This dialogue increased my understanding of how people from a racial background different from my own think and feel about racial issues at [school of social work].	77.4	45.5	85.7
Perspectives were put forward that I had not considered before.	56.6	18.2	66.7
The dialogue increased my hope that people from different racial backgrounds can listen to each other.	92.4	72.8	97.6
The dialogue gave me hope that people from different racial backgrounds can learn from each other.	90.5	54.6	100
My experience with this event will better enable me to talk about racial issues on campus and in the classroom.	80.8	36.4	92.7
The dialogue was just an exchange of monologues.	0	0	0
The dialogue complements other antiracism activities on campus.	86.3	72.8	90
The dialogue helped me clarify some of my own thoughts and feelings about race and racism.	84.6	45.5	95.1
The dialogue challenged some of my feelings and opinions about race.	55.8	27.3	63.4
Participating in this event motivated me to want to become more involved in antiracism efforts.	82.7	45.5	92.7
The facilitators were skilled at assisting the expression of diverse points of view.	100	100	100

Reprinted with permission from Miller & Donner (2000).
[a]African American, Asian, and Latina.

positive ratings. But White participants were more enthusiastic about how helpful the event was and significantly more positive about learning to better talk about race and racism, being exposed to new perspectives, and feeling more motivated to engage in antiracism activities. White participants also indicated that they felt more challenged about their feelings and opinions about race and racism and more hopeful that people from different racial backgrounds can listen to one another. At the same time, more than 90% of the participants of color found the experience to be helpful and wanted to participate in more dialogues, and more than 70% indicated that the dialogue had given them hope that people from different racial backgrounds can learn from one another.

The results of this dialogue, although based on a small sample, offer an example of one way that a discussion can be structured. The responses on the questionnaire indicate that the experience was different for Whites and people of color, but the majority of the participants seemed to get something from it and, at the very least, this would motivate them to participate in further racial conversations. Alimo (2012) has documented how White high school students deepened their critical awareness and were more likely to take social action from participating in dialogues. And Ford and Malaney (2012) found that students of color and multiracial students at a traditional White college found racial dialogues to be validating and empowering. So what can we extract from this and the experience of others to suggest ways to manage effective dialogues?

Important Dimensions of Dialogue

Before turning to how to conduct successful dialogues, some dimensions and parameters to consider in planning such conversations will be helpful.

- ▶ *The participants.* Dialogues can occur in small groups or large groups. People may know each other already or be brought together specifically to participate in the dialogue. This will affect the dynamics of the discussion as well as follow-up to the conversation. Some dialogues feature prominent people and others consist of ordinary folks sitting down and talking with one another.

- ▶ *The sponsor and the location.* The credibility of a dialogue often rests on the sponsoring organization and the perceived motives and intentions for holding a dialogue. If people tend to trust and respect the sponsor, this is more likely to carry over to the actual discussion. The location also is important, so all participants feel comfortable. For example, holding a dialogue in a public school may feel more familiar and comfortable for some participants than others; conversely, holding a dialogue at a public housing project might seem more secure for some and less amenable for others. Successful dialogues can be facilitated in high schools (Alimo, 2012) or colleges (Ford & Malaney, 2012) as credit-bearing classes or stand-alone workshops.

- ▶ *The duration and frequency.* Some racial dialogues, such as the one we have described in this chapter, are single, contained events. Others are structured encounters that meet over time, often following a curriculum (Study Circles Resource Center, 1998). A dialogue can take place as part of an ongoing class or as a part of a 2-day workshop. This dimension influences what is discussed, how it is talked about, and how deep the conversation will become, and also can affect who can participate or wants to participate.

▶ *The context.* What is the context for having the dialogue? Is it in response to tensions or conflict? Is it being offered to improve understanding in an effort to avoid clashes? Is it part of an organization's desire to be more culturally competent or to engage in antiracism activities? Is the discussion the vision of a few people, or is it part of an organizational or community movement to increase interracial understanding? Is the dialogue a required part of professional training, in which all students are expected to participate?

Whatever the reasons for having the dialogue, the context in which it occurs shapes the expectations and the actual discourse. Dialogue has more value and resonance when it takes place in the context of a strong institutional or community commitment to challenge racism.

▶ *The goals.* Clarifying the goals of a racial dialogue is helpful. Is the dialogue being used for educational purposes or to resolve conflict between two clashing groups? Is the goal to encourage people to think in a more complex and nuanced way about complicated issues or to motivate them to become more socially active? Will the dialogue have a follow-up, or is it a single event?

These are examples of goals that can shape how a dialogue is set and determine what questions are asked. Some dialogues combine many of these objectives. If one dialogue is attempting to accomplish too much, however, it can become confusing, so prioritizing goals can provide coherence and focus. Exercise 9.1 serves as a guide to help prepare for dialogue.

Models and Stages of Intergroup Dialogue

Zúñiga and Nagda (2001) have created a typology of four different types of intergroup dialogue.

1. *Collective inquiry model.* This model encourages participants to suspend their usual assumptions and judgments and examine challenging issues, such as race and racism, from new perspectives. In many ways, this model is one attempted in many educational classrooms teaching about diversity across the country. The Public Conversations Project (Becker et al., 1995; Chasm et al., 1996) falls within this category. With this model, all participants are given a chance to listen and respond to questions about challenging social issues. Engaging in this process will help participants loosen rigid thinking and be able to see and understand different perspectives. Ultimately, collectively interrogating and examining an issue will facilitate meaningful relationships.

2. *Critical-dialogical education models.* These models assume a social-justice perspective with multiple goals: increasing knowledge and understanding; raising awareness about social inequities; consciousness raising about privilege and oppression, which includes self-introspection and gaining perspectives about intergroup dynamics; and creating alliances among participants that lead to social action. Although these models are used primarily in classrooms, they also are found in campus-wide orientation programs. They are allied with critical race theory, which is a major theoretical perspective informing this book.

3. *Community building and social action models.* These models seek to engage community members, citizens, and workplace employees in conversation about big issues, such as racism, but primarily to ground the discussion in local concerns and to mobilize

people to take constructive collective action to redress social problems. A good example of this model is Everyday Democracy, summarized in Appendix A.

4. *Conflict resolution and peace-building models.* These models apply when distinct groups are in conflict with one another, usually racial/ethnic, religious, or national groups. The goals are to identify sources of conflict; to understand competing group narratives; to engage in conflict mediation, resolution, and transformation; and to eventually generate action plans that reduce conflict and promote intergroup understanding, healing, and resolution (Bar-Tal, 2007; Miller, 2012a; Stephan, 2008; Zehr, 2002). Examples of this model are attempts to improve Korean American and African American relations in Los Angeles (Norman, 1994), to work with Arabs and Jews in the Middle East (Bargal & Bar, 1994), and to improve relations between Catholics and Protestants in Derry/ Londonderry (Templegrove Action Research Limited, 1996). The model of racial reconciliation summarized at the end of this chapter (Yamamoto, 1999) falls within this category.

Zúñiga et al. (2002) have developed a model for intergroup dialogue along the lines of the critical-dialogic educational model (see Appendix B). It is designed as a class or ongoing workshop for small groups of 12 to 16 students who correspond to both targeted and agent identities within the topic being discussed; if possible, both should be equally represented. The classes are co-facilitated and the facilitators represent each of the social-identity groups within the context of the dialogue topic. So for race and racism, the co-facilitators ideally would include a facilitator of color and a White facilitator.

The first stage creates an environment for dialogue and sets the stage for the type of dialogue that will ensue. The second stage involves developing a common base, which can include defining terms, identifying the issues on which to focus, clarifying the nature of problems, and identifying beliefs and assumptions that participants bring to the table. The critical-dialogic model places more emphasis on exploring the complexity of social identity at this stage.

In the third stage, participants explore questions, issues, or conflicts, which may include consideration of conflict and social justice, the meaning and significance of social identity, and the nuances of intergroup dynamics. The final stage in all of the models is for the group to move from discussion to some form of alliance building and action, whether that means changing the way people lead their everyday lives, planning local community events, or committing to major action plans to resolve conflicts and further social justice. Exercise 9.2 encourages thoughtful collaboration around the importance of rituals as they relate to this work.

Managing Effective Racial Dialogues

The important ingredients for establishing fruitful conversations are summarized as follows (see Box 9.1).

▶ *Skilled facilitation.* This is one of the most important factors in fostering a successful racial dialogue, often determining if a dialogue is a positive learning experience that engages participants or a negative encounter that wounds people, leading to alienation and withdrawal. Preferably, facilitators should be from the outside rather than members of the group. Group members should be free to participate rather than have to take on the dual role of facilitator and participant. The facilitator should not be

BOX 9.1 Key Ingredients for Successful Racial Dialogues

▶ *Skilled facilitation*—Preferably biracial or multiracial teams.
▶ *Egalitarian space*—Ensuring a group composition of parity of people of color and White participants, or at least having a "critical mass" of either group (30%).
▶ *Establishing a dialogic framework*—Generating group norms that facilitate respectful listening and self-reflection.
▶ *Understanding the historical, social, and political context in which the conversation occurs*—Presenting group narratives; distributing advance readings for group discussion.
▶ *Creating conceptual categories*—Such as racial identity development, worldviews, cultural values; predicting strong emotions; seeing the dialogue as part of an ongoing process.
▶ *Emphasizing superordinate identities and overarching goals*—Identifying what people have in common and what goals can be collectively tackled.
▶ *Having mechanisms to deal with stuck conversations.*
▶ *Collectively grieving the losses suffered from racism*—This is an important step in joining together to acknowledge the destructive power of racism while working to overcome it.
▶ *Engendering hope; considering solutions as well as problems*—Considering strategies, action plans, and individual commitments.

Source: Many points are adapted from Miller et al. (2004a) and also reference Dovidio et al. (2016), and reflect our own thinking about racial dialogues.

someone who is in a position to evaluate participants, as this will inhibit honest conversation.

Whenever possible, the dialogues should have co-facilitators and multiracial teams. Co-facilitators can plan together, support one another, and act as live consultants. They also can model respectful cross-racial conversation. Two facilitators can demonstrate sharing and collaboration and offer a variety of role models for various people in the group to connect with (Miller et al., 2004a). Ideally, facilitators should know something about racism and about the nature of the participants in the conversation and have skills in presenting, facilitation, mediation, and creative problem solving. Good interpersonal skills are always an asset.

▶ *Egalitarian space.* A racial dialogue cuts against the grain, in that inequality and talking past one another is more the norm in many social venues. Racial conversations can take place in groups that are racially mixed, all White, or all people of color. The conversations should be adapted to the nature of the group and emphasize the experiences of the participants, not those of people who are not present for the discussion. Thus, for an all-White group, suitable topics for discussion include White privilege, or stereotypes, or the feelings associated with being White. This can be challenging for White participants because many believe that they can only learn about issues of race and racism from people of color. Not only does this place the burden on people of color to teach White people but places the emphasis on the experience of people of color, reinforcing the belief that racial identification is not relevant to Whites. This allows for the mechanisms of Whiteness, race, and power to go undetected, unrecognized, and unchallenged. For a group that is composed of people of color, topics might be internalized racism, racism between people of color, strategies for resisting White racism, and how to survive in predominantly White environments. There are times that even within racially diverse groups, there are advantages to breaking into racially/ethnically homogenous "caucus" or "affinity" groups. For some people, it is easier to speak frankly when it is not in front of people with substantially different social identities: There are perceived risks about being too vulnerable, feeling misunderstood, or being judged and criticized. However, there are also risks when doing this. For example, we have heard from some students of color that they wonder if an all-White caucus group will hold people sufficiently accountable or confront implicitly racist thinking and comments. In our experience, the act of breaking into affinity groups can cause some discomfort, particularly for White participants who have yet to interrogate their own racialized self. Multiracial-ethnic students have also discussed loyalty conflicts about which group they belong in or resentment over having to choose one group over another.

Tittler and Wade (2019) examined the differential effects that racial make-up has on White participants and Black, Indigenous, and people of color (BIPOC) participants and found a difference when the dialogue groups were structured or unstructured. For White participants they reported being able to share more honestly in mixed-race groups where dialogue was more structured. Alternatively, White participants in all-White dialogue groups reported feeling less likely to honestly share their thoughts when the group was structured. What the research suggests is that the way dialogues are comprised and facilitated should not be seen as "one-size-fits-all." Dialogue group structure, facilitation, and composition should be carefully considered when devising a plan for the group (Tittler & Wade, 2019).

Notwithstanding the benefits of homogenous caucus groups, we ultimately must move to interracial dialogues—and this is where egalitarian space becomes important. A racial dialogue composed of mostly White people and only a few people of color is not advisable, as this recreates the demography of many social situations in which people of color find themselves. In such circumstances, the danger is that people of color will become marginalized as the needs of White participants dominate, or find themselves in the roles of teachers or as exemplars for the experience of the racial "other."

Proportion matters. Davis and Proctor (1989) found that African Americans prefer dialogue groups with equal numbers of Whites and Blacks, whereas White people feel more comfortable in groups that reflect the demographics of larger society. Miller et al. (2004b) recommend striving for parity between people of color and White participants, but otherwise that at least one third of the group is composed of people of color. Parity presents a greater likelihood of a balanced and complex conversation, as participants will be more likely to speak up, take risks, and present a greater variety of viewpoints.

▶ *Emphasizing superordinate identities and overarching goals.* Research about what helps people to respect and engage with one another when there is intergroup conflict has found that establishing a superordinate, or "common group," identity is helpful

(Dovidio et al., 2001, 2016). For example, in a multiracial class of social work students, the common group identity is that of social workers. It is also helpful to have group members identify and work toward goals that all group members can agree on and commit to (Miller, 2012a).

▶ *Establishing a dialogic framework.* Many people are not used to talking about race and racism and can feel anxious when engaging in such conversations. And the expression of strong emotions can make people uncomfortable listening to other people and different perspectives. Sometimes participants deliver prepackaged speeches and are reluctant to embrace new ideas, grandstanding on soapboxes. To create a climate that fosters dialogue and deep listening, norms and guidelines should be established for discussion, and participants asked to abide by them (Miller et al., 2004a; Muldoon, 2011).

Miller et al. (2004a) have suggested guidelines for establishing a dialogic framework (see Box 9.2). Facilitators may want to work with the group to generate the norms for discussion, as this leads to greater ownership. The facilitator also might suggest important guidelines if the group fails to identify them on their own, and to remind them that the purpose of the conversation is to listen and explore, promoting what Stone et al. (1999) have referred to as a "learning conversation" in which people do not already know all the answers. This promotes a stance of genuine curiosity, encourages empathy for people and positions that are different, and establishes a commitment to self-reflection and respect for others (Miller et al., 2004a).

BOX 9.2 Norms for Establishing a Dialogic Framework

▶ *Maintaining confidentiality.* Outside of the group it is acceptable, even useful, to share the themes that emerged within the group, but it is important to strive to maintain the confidentiality of who said what about whom, particularly when participants have expressed strong emotions.

▶ *Sharing time and not taking up too much air space.* A few individuals dominating the discussion will choke and stifle a dialogue. Although facilitators should monitor the group process, group members should agree on this norm and observe it to ensure contributions by all members.

▶ *Speaking for oneself and not representing one's group.* In a dialogue, people should speak from their own experiences and not try to represent the views of others or think they must speak for all people of their racial or ethnic group. "I" statements are helpful here.

▶ *Listening carefully to others.* Dialogue depends on listening. Particularly listening to understand another person's point or perspective rather than using listening to filter out information that can be used to negate or support one's own perspective. Frequently, in other types of conversation, people are thinking about their responses while another person is talking. Allowing a moment of reflective silence after each speaker is a good idea. If listening is problematic, the facilitator might ask each speaker to paraphrase the remarks of the previous speaker to foster careful listening.

▶ *Striving for open-mindedness.* Group members should be asked to reflect on their usual positions and stances and to acknowledge areas of ambivalence and ambiguity. The facilitator might remind participants that if everyone already knows the answers, there is no need for dialogue.

▶ *Challenging behavior and ideas without attacking people.* Meaningful dialogue requires an exchange of ideas, including disagreements. If group members start attacking one another, however, participants will be less likely to take the risk of participating and the conversation may shut down. The distinction between challenging behavior and ideas without putting down the speaker is subtle but important. The facilitator should remind participants that everyone is imperfect and that they are permitted to take risks and make mistakes because this is how we learn and grow.

Adapted from Miller et al. (2004a).

▶ *Understanding the historical, social, and political context in which the conversation occurs.* Conversations about race and racism inevitably draw upon the racial axis of social identity (Miller et al., 2004b). As these identities are grounded in subjective interpretations and group narratives about history and the nature of sociopolitical reality, sufficient time must be allotted to discuss these topics. One way to do this is to allow different groups represented in the dialogue group to present their social and historical narratives while members of other groups listen (Bargal & Bar, 1994; Miller et al., 2004a; Norman, 1994).

Another way to prepare the ground is to distribute articles beforehand, for participants to read and comment on. Chapters from *critical* history books, such as Takaki's (1993) *A Different Mirror*, can offer counternarratives to prevailing historical discourses and elicit critical thinking and historically grounded dialogue.

▶ *Creating conceptual categories.* Concepts can help participants to cognitively grasp common challenges and dynamics that appear in racial dialogues. They can be used to predict misunderstandings before they occur, which renders them less disturbing and toxic. The nature of racism is that people have had different experiences and varied understandings about the role of race in American society. Strong feelings are attached to these differences, as well as perceived threats to one's social identity (Stone et al., 1999).

Many concepts presented in this book can be helpful when promoting racial dialogues. The formation of racial identity is one such notion that can assist participants in understanding varying aspects of racial identity development and how these influence self-concept, emotions, meaning making, and interpersonal needs and relationships.

Other examples of useful concepts include differences in worldviews and cultural values (Sue & Sue, 2015) and naming certain defense mechanisms, such as denial and projection (Miller & Schamess, 2000). Predicting strong emotions and perceived threats to identity also may reduce their potency. The conversation should be seen as part of an ongoing process in which participants engage before the actual dialogue and will continue to do afterward, so they will face less pressure to solve and resolve everything in this encounter.

▶ *Having mechanisms to deal with "stuck" conversations.* Facilitators should enter racial dialogues with the expectation that misunderstandings, conflicts, or withdrawal and disengagement may arise. Fortunately, a number of strategies are available to prevent or respond to jammed conversations. Use Exercise 9.3 as a guide to navigate when difficulties, which are inevitable, do arise.

- *Divide into caucus groups.* Temporarily dividing the participants into separate caucus groups of people—color-multiracial people and White people—allows participants to discuss painful and challenging material without fear of hurting others or being attacked when expressing vulnerabilities. Whites can discuss racist stereotypes and ways to respond to them, while people of color can talk about their mistrust of White people or the psychic wounds of racism.

  We have discussed some of the challenges to forming caucus and affinity groups earlier. Another reason that participants sometimes balk at forming affinity groups is that interracial relationships and friendships are temporarily interrupted by dividing the group in this fashion. Being flexible and allowing participants to choose which caucus group they wish to work in can be helpful, while also acknowledging in advance that tensions can arise by dividing the group in this manner.

  A mechanism for summarizing the caucus group discussions and sharing them with the larger group is important. This should include the chance to debrief about what the experience of dividing up was like for different people. The large-group discussions about both the process and the content of caucus groups can uncover important issues and emotions that occur in daily social intercourse.

- *Take a "fishbowl" approach.* We have already shared the use of this method in the racial dialogue described by Miller and Donner (2000). Having a smaller circle with five to eight people talking in front of a larger audience can allow for more focused and intimate conversation. An empty chair allows people outside of the fishbowl to enter the conversation. Allowing the larger group to comment on the conversation observed in the fishbowl is important.

- *Use structured "go-rounds."* Sometimes dialogues become heated or unproductive when a few individuals become locked in conflict. This can freeze a conversation and lead to disengagement and alienation. One way of preventing this is to ensure that all participants are given a chance to speak by sequentially asking each person to respond to a question that has been posed. Depending on the nature and expansiveness of the question, giving all participants 2 minutes to gather and jot down their thoughts and another 2 minutes to share sequentially can provide a good balance of brevity and multiple perspectives. Having a secondary go-round that allows a participant to ask another participant a question or share a comment on what they heard. When using this method, facilitators should institute a "pass rule," so anyone who does not want to speak at a given moment can pass and wait for another round of questions. Going around in a circle also cuts down on reactive, defensive, and attacking responses and usually leads to a more complex and nuanced conversation (Becker et al., 1995; Chasm et al., 1996).

- *Use structured exercises.* Having participants engage in a structured activity, such as brainstorming, can unify them in working toward a common target or goal. Or, when difficult material, such as White privilege, is being covered, a helpful exercise involves having participants stand up and walk a step forward or backward as questions are posed about access to education, housing, jobs, and other resources, as this visually conveys the differential impact of racism and stimulates thoughtful and reflective conversation.

▶ *Collectively grieving the losses suffered from racism.* Racism is insidious and it is also a tragedy. It is important to not gloss over the suffering and personal and collective losses that accrue from racism. It can be helpful for the group to design a collective mourning ritual that acknowledges the sorrows and suffering wrought by racism.

▶ *Engendering hope, and considering solutions as well as problems.* Racism is pernicious but not hopeless, a common state of affairs but not an inevitable one. If people are led to believe that nothing can be done about it, they will feel demoralized and discouraged from taking action. Thorny and sensitive discussions about social identity can leave participants feeling dispirited and overwhelmed if the discussion ends in a thicket of unresolved problems, thereby fostering tendencies to blame rather than take responsibility (Miller et al., 2004a, p. 390).

This can be the consequence of a racial dialogue that discusses only problems and does not offer solutions. At least part of the racial dialogue should be devoted to considering resiliency, empowerment, and ways to dismantle racism. It must consider strategies, action plans, and individual commitments to engage in future antiracism work. Still, while racial dialogues are valuable, they are not an end in themselves. They are just one part of a larger process of decommissioning racism. And it is also important to avoid painting too rosy a picture of how the group can dismantle racism or minimize the losses, challenges, and struggles that lie ahead.

RACIAL RECONCILIATION AND INTERRACIAL JUSTICE

Perhaps the highest aspiration of racial dialogue is that it will lead to racial reconciliation and racial justice. On a substantive level, this necessitates healing wounds, addressing wrongs, meeting needs, honoring obligations, and instituting mechanisms that prevent future racial targeting and human rights violations (Zehr, 2002). And such a process requires an ongoing commitment to a process of reconciliation and reparation involving all major stakeholders (Zehr, 2002). This integrates working toward social justice and engaging in psychosocial healing, which are intricately related: Without genuine social justice psychosocial healing will not occur (Miller, 2012a).

Most dialogues will not achieve this level of reconciliation. Reaching this goal would require commitment at the highest and deepest levels, and the power to implement restorative justice and make reparations. However, we briefly consider some basic steps in this process here so readers can imagine what the process will look like when it does eventually occur.

Yamamoto (1999) has conceptualized interracial justice as a four-step process, which we employ in our discussion. It refers to what has to happen on the institutional, discursive, and intergroup levels, as well as between individuals.

Recognition

One of the most painful facets of racism in the United States is the denial and lack of awareness and acknowledgment by many White people. Racial reconciliation cannot begin until there is a recognition of the historical and collective legacy of racism and acknowledgment and validation of the terrible damage it has inflicted on generations of people of color. This acceptance precedes any formal apologies. White people will have to listen to the narratives of racism and its consequences as told by people of color, without denying, negating, or rejecting these stories. This is the foundation of racial rapprochement.

Responsibility

Taking responsibility for colluding with racism and structural White supremacy follows the recognition of racism. This often is a difficult step, as many White people do not concede their racial privilege, and this is accompanied by common mechanisms of denial, such as slavery being a thing of the past, or distancing through statements such as, "My relatives never owned slaves." Such denials ignore the reality of White racial group privilege, a form of White supremacy, and the systematic denial of full human rights and equity to people of color in the United States.

Responsibility in the process of racial reconciliation goes beyond individual culpability. It refers to group exploitation and domination and the racial privileges that settlers and immigrants alike accepted as they were socially constructed as White. Taking responsibility means acknowledging the racial contract, the failure of Reconstruction, the litany of broken treaties with Native Americans, the exclusion of Chinese immigrants, the placing of innocent Japanese citizens in concentration camps, and the many other instances of racism. It also means taking responsibility for the web of racism today and committing to dismantling it.

Reconstruction

Only after the first two steps have been achieved can interracial groups work on reconstructing the relationships torn asunder by racism. This is where formal apologies can be offered. Yamamoto, however, warns that apologies can be self-serving and a way of avoiding responsibility, and are susceptible to insincerity, misapprehension, poor timing, and inadequacy. Thus, apologies should be grounded in the first two steps, recognition and responsibility.

A sincere apology involves seeking forgiveness. Healing will not occur unless forgiveness is requested and the apology is accepted in turn. This does not mean that there is absolution or a universal pardon. Rather, these are significant gestures by those who have benefited, as well as those who have suffered from racism to restore relationships and institute justice. When leaders publicly take these steps, it sets an example for others to follow.

Reparation

Apologies and forgiveness are important steps in the process of racial reconciliation and can lead to the final stage of reparations. The notion of reparations is complex and controversial (Coates, 2014). *Reparations* refer to the repair of frayed human relationships on the individual and group levels, as well as to material compensations. To respond only to the historical legacy of racism without dismantling the web of institutional racism, racist discourses, and racist attitudes is insufficient. Resources have to be redeployed.

If material reparations were offered, however, who would receive them and where would the line of eligibility be drawn? What would be a fair amount of financial or economic reparations for centuries of exclusion? These are complex questions, with no simple answers, yet they are not insurmountable barriers to having race-based reparations.

Even if the government pledges itself to such actions, this does not ensure that the web of racism will dissolve. Local governments, institutions, organizations, policies, practices, intergroup relations, and individual attitudes and behaviors are slow and resistant to change. Nevertheless, as we learned from the successes of the Great Society in the 1960s, however incomplete and transitory these may be, when the federal government makes a commitment of this nature, it can lead to profound social changes.

CONCLUSION

Talking about race and racism is challenging. Racial dialogue usually does not occur spontaneously and requires planning, resources, commitments, and skilled facilitation. Dialogue is an alternative to alienation and conflict. It is a tool that we, as helping professionals, can use to understand ourselves, the people we help, and the social world we all inhabit. Racial dialogues engage people in a process that renders visible what often is unseen, puts words to what is unsaid, and has the potential to connect people of all races to work together as allies to dismantle racism.

If local dialogues occur in communities, schools, religious organizations, and workplaces, they may generate momentum for larger-scale, society-wide conversations. Ultimately, the hope of having a genuine national process of racial reconciliation may be a dream deferred, but not a dream denied.

EXERCISE 9.1 Preparing for Dialogue

1. Think of a topic pertaining to race and racism that you would like to discuss with others.
2. Who do you think should be part of this conversation? How will you ensure sufficient balance between people targeted and privileged by racism?
3. What dialogue norms or ground rules would you find helpful?
4. What preparatory reading would be useful for the dialogue? What concepts will be useful to introduce before the conversation? Are there historical or social narratives that should be shared early in the discussion?
5. What dialogue model would you like to use?

6. Who might facilitate this dialogue?
7. Are you concerned that the conversation might become "stuck"?
8. What mechanisms or interventions will be helpful if the conversation does stall?
9. What would you like to see come out of the dialogue? How might the conversation be followed up?

EXERCISE 9.2 Designing Rituals

Break into work groups that have different assignments:

▶ Group 1: Design a grieving and mourning ritual that honors losses and suffering due to racism.
▶ Group 2: Design a ritual that has people with racial privilege accept responsibility for their unearned White privilege and a mechanism for people of color to recognize the responsibility that has been taken.
▶ Group 3: Design a ritual that emphasizes shared group identities and goals and the unity needed to accomplish these goals.

Return to the large group, present the rituals, and then enact them with the larger group.

EXERCISE 9.3 Addressing Tensions or Misunderstandings in Discussions of Race and Racism

There will likely be times when having discussions about race and racism cause tension, misunderstandings, and strong or hurt feelings. Racism divides people and there are insufficient opportunities to have meaningful discussions about race and racism. So for many people, such discussions are a new or infrequent experience. Some authors (e.g., Leonardo & Porter, 2010) argue that striving for safety, good feelings, and a consensus reinforces dominant hierarchies and social inequities; Confronting racism involves challenging a false consensus and disrupting the normal ways of conducting business. If it feels too comfortable, it may not be meaningful.

We have designed a process that encourages people to pause, reflect, and process when there are bumps in the road during discussions about race and racism, employing suggestions from others (Miller & Donner, 2000; Miller et al., 2004a; Rosenberg, 2003; Stephan & Finlay, 1999; Stone et al., 1999).

1. For oneself:
   a. Try to be clear on what you observed and why this did not make you feel good, safe, trusting, or respected. Is it possible to share this with the other person to check this out? Are there any questions that you would like to ask the other person?
   b. It helps to reflect on how this made you feel. What emotions were raised by the tension or conflict? Have you been here before? Can you share these feelings with the other person? How can you move forward?
   c. What were the issues of power, privilege, and/or social identity involved in this interaction? Can you and the other person examine these together?

    d. What do you want from the other person (e.g., to be understood, to feel appreciated, for the other person to let you be yourself, to be respected, to be left alone, to be listened to)?

    e. What would you like to ask the other person to do that would be helpful to you? Are there requests that you would like to make of the other person?

    f. Are there any contributions that you made to what happened? Was there any baggage from a relationship with this person or interactions with others that this reminded you of? Are there any stereotypes that you harbor that influence how you see this person? Do you want to share any of your self-reflections with the other person?

2. For the other person:

    a. Can you cognitively empathize with the other person? This means, can you intellectually understand or relate to their intentions, motivations, mistakes, or actions?

    b. Can you emotionally empathize with the other person? Can you relate to the other person's feelings when the interaction began or perhaps after you confronted them? (If you do not want to emotionally empathize with the other person, which can be a valid, self-nurturing stance to take under certain circumstances, then can you still cognitively understand them?)

3. For third parties:

    a. How can you be an ally and a helper, rather than a bystander?

    b. Do you have a relationship with either party where you might be helpful?

    c. Were you able to empathize (cognitively or emotionally) with either or both of the other parties?

    d. Is there anything that you can say or suggest that can be framed in such a way that a person is likely to hear what you are saying?

    e. Is there any experience that you have had that can be used as a story to express empathy and illustrate a point? (Be careful about putting people down.)

    f. Are you able to clarify parts of the interaction that appear to be misunderstood?

    g. Can you help either party articulate their feelings, needs, or requests?

REFERENCES

Aldana, A., Rowley, S. J., Checkoway, B., & Richards-Schuster, K. (2012). Raising ethnic-racial consciousness: The relationship between intergroup dialogues and adolescent's ethnic-racial identity and racism awareness. *Equity and Excellence in Education*, 45(1), 120–137.

Alimo, C. J. (2012). From dialogue to action: The impact of cross-race intergroup dialogue on the development on White college students as racial allies. *Equity and Excellence in Education*, 45(1), 36–59.

Bakhtin, M. M. (1981). Epic and novel. *The Dialogic Imagination, 33*.

Bargal, D., & Bar, H. (1994). The encounter of social selves: Intergroup workshops for Arab and Jewish youth. *Social Work With Groups*, 17(3), 39–59.

Bar-Tal, D. (2007). Sociopsychological foundations of intractable conflicts. *American Behavioral Scientist*, 50(11), 1430–1453.

Becker, C., Chasm, L., Chasm, R., Herzig, M., & Roth, S. (1995). From stuck debate to new conversation on controversial issues: A report from the public conversations project. *Journal of Feminist Family Therapy*, 7(1/2), 143–161.

Chasm, R., Herzig, M., Roth, S., Chasm, L., Becker, C., & Stains, R. R., Jr. (1996). From diatribe to dialogue on divisive public issues: Approaches drawn from family therapy. *Mediation Quarterly*, *13*(4), 323–345.

Coates, T. (2014, May). *The case for reparations*. The Atlantic. www.theatlantic.com/features/archive/2014/05/the-case-for-reparations/361631

Cooks, L. (2020). The communicative ethics of racial identity in dialogue. *Communication Theory*.

Davis, L. E., & Proctor, E. K. (1989). *Race, gender and class for practice with individuals, families, and groups*. Prentice-Hall.

Davis, N. J. (1992). Teaching about inequality: Student resistance, paralysis, and rage. *Teaching Sociology*, *20*, 232–238.

Dessel, A. B., & Rodenborg, N. (2017). An evaluation of intergroup dialogue pedagogy: Addressing segregation and developing cultural competency. *Journal of Social Work Education*, *53*(2), 222–239.

Dion, K. L. (2002). The social psychology of perceived prejudice and discrimination. *Canadian Psychology*, *43*(1), 1–10.

Dovidio, J. F., Gaertner, S. L., Niemann, Y. F., & Snider, K. (2001). Racial, ethnic and cultural differences in responding to distinctiveness and discrimination on campus: Stigma and common group identity. *Journal of Social Issues*, *57*(1), 167–188.

Dovidio, J. F., Gaertner, S. L., Ufkes, E. G., Saguy, T., & Pearson, A. R. (2016). Included but invisible? The darker side of "we." *Social Issues and Policy Review*, *10*(1), 6–46.

Fisher, R. J. (1990). *The social psychology of intergroup and international conflict resolution*. Springer-Verlag.

Ford, K. A., & Malaney, V. K. (2012). "I now harbor more pride in my race": The educational benefits of inter and intra-racial dialogues on the experiences of students of color and multiracial students. *Equity and Excellence in Education*, *45*(1), 14–35. http://doi.org/10.1080/10665684.2012.643180

Garran, A. M., & Werkmeister Rozas, L. (2013). Cultural competence revisited. *Journal of Ethnic and Cultural Diversity in Social Work*, *22*(2), 97–111.

Gurin-Sands, C., Gurin, P., Nagda, B. A., & Osuna, S. (2012). Fostering a commitment to social action: How talking, thinking and feeling make a difference in intergroup dialogue. *Equity and Excellence in Education*, *45*(1), 60–79.

Gurin, P., Sorensen, N., Lopez, G., & Nagda, B. A. (2014). Intergroup dialogue: Race still matters. In R. Bangs & L. Davis (Eds.), *Race and social problems: Restructuring inequality* (pp. 39–59). Springer-Verlag.

Kang, H. K & O'Neill, P. (2018) Teaching note—constructing critical conversations: A model for facilitating classroom dialogue for critical learning. *Journal of Social Work Education*, *54*(1), 187–193. http://doi.org/10.1080/10437797.2017.1341857

Lawson, K., Koman, B., & Rose, A. (1998). *Building one nation*. Washington, DC: Leadership Conference Education Fund.

Leonardo, Z., & Porter, R. K. (2010). Pedagogy of fear: Toward a Fanonian theory of "safety" in race dialogue. *Race, Ethnicity and Education*, *13*(2), 139–157.

McCoy, M. L., & Sherman, R. F. (1994). Bridging the divides of race and ethnicity. *National Civic Review*, *83*(2), 111–119.

Miles, J. R., Muller, J. T., Arnett III, J. E., Bourn, J. R., Johnson, M. C., & Recabarren, D. (2015). Group member affect and session evaluations in intergroup dialogue. *Group Dynamics: Theory, Research and Practice*, *19*(4), 225–242.

Miller, J., & Donner, S. (2000). More than just talk: The use of racial dialogue to combat racism. *Social Work With Groups*, *23*(1), 31–53.

Miller, J. (2012a). *Psychosocial capacity building in response to disasters*. Columbia University Press.

Miller, J., Donner, S., & Fraser, E. (2004a). Talking when talking is tough: Taking on conversations about race, sexual orientation, gender, class, and other aspects of social identity. *Smith College Studies in Social Work*, *74*(2), 377–392.

Miller, J., Hyde, C., & Ruth, B. J. (2004b). Teaching about race and racism in social work: Challenges for White educators. *Smith College Studies in Social Work*, *74*(2), 409–426.

Miller, J., & Schamess, G. (2000). The discourse of denigration and the creation of other. *Journal of Sociology and Social Welfare, 27*(3), 39–62.

Muldoon, B. (2011). *The heart of conflict.* G.P. Putnam's Sons Publishers.

Nadan, Y., Weinberg-Kurnik, G., & Ben-Ari, A. (2015). Bringing context and power relations to the fore: Intergroup dialogue as a tool in social work education. *British Journal of Social Work, 45,* 260–277.

Norman, A. J. (1994). Black-Korean relations: From desperation to dialogue, or from shouting and shooting to sitting and talking. *Journal of Multicultural Social Work, 3*(2), 87–99.

Rosenberg, M. B. (2003). *Nonviolent communication: A language of life* (2nd ed.). Puddledancer Press.

Rozas, L. W. (2004). On translating ourselves: Understanding dialogue and its role in social work education. *Smith College Studies in Social Work, 74*(2), 229–242.

Shelton, J. N., & Richeson, J. A. (2005). Intergroup contact and pluralistic ignorance. *Journal of Personality and Social Psychology, 88*(1), 91–107.

Shipler, D. (1997). *A country of strangers: Blacks and Whites in America.* Knopf.

Solorzano, D., Ceja, M., & Yosso, T. (2000). Critical race theory, racial microaggressions, and campus racial climate: The experiences of African American college students. *Journal of Negro Education, 69*(1/2), 60–73.

Stephan, W. G. (2008). The road to reconciliation. In A. Nadler, T. Molloy, & J. D. Fisher (Eds.), *The social psychology of intergroup reconciliation: From violent conflict to peaceful co-existence.* Oxford University Press.

Stephan, W. G., & Finlay, K. (1999). The role of empathy in improving intergroup relations. *Journal of Social Issues, 55*(4), 729–743.

Stone, D., Patton, B., & Heen, S. (1999). *Difficult conversations: How to discuss what matters most.* Viking.

Study Circles Resource Center. (1997). *Facing the challenge of racism and race relations: Democratic dialogue and action for stronger communities* (3rd ed.). Author.

Study Circles Resource Center. (1998). *Year 1—1997. A report on the focus groups.* Author.

Sue, D. W., & Sue, D. (2015). *Counseling the culturally diverse: Theory and practice* (7th ed.). Wiley.

Tatum, B. (1997). *"Why are all the Black kids sitting together in the cafeteria?" And other conversations about race.* Basic Books.

Takaki, R. (1993). *A different mirror: A history of multi-cultural America.* Little, Brown.

Templegrove Action Research Limited. (1996). *Public discussions on aspects of sectarian division in Derry Londonderry.* Author.

Tittler, M. V., & Wade, N. G. (2019). Engaging White participants in racial dialogues: Group composition and dialogue structure. *Group Dynamics: Theory, Research, and Practice, 23*(2), 75.

Werkmeister Rozas, L. M. (2007). Engaging the dialogue in our diverse social work student body: A multilevel theoretical process model. *Journal of Social Work Education, 43*(1), 5–28.

Yamamoto, E. (1999). *Interracial justice: Conflict and reconciliation in post-civil rights America.* New York University Press.

Zehr, H. (2002). *The little book of restorative justice.* Good Books.

Zúñiga, X., & Nagda, B. A. (2001). Design considerations in intergroup dialogue. In D. Schoem & S. Hurtado (Eds.), *Intergroup dialogue: Deliberative democracy in school, college, community and workplace* (pp. 306–327). University of Michigan Press.

Zúñiga, X., Nagda, B. A., & Sevig, T. D. (2002). Intergroup dialogues: An educational model for cultivating engagement across differences. *Equity and Excellence in Education, 35*(1), 7–17.

CHAPTER 10

Responses to Racism in the Community

INTRODUCTION

This chapter begins with the fictional community of Millville, a composite community based on our research and activism. Throughout this chapter, Millville is used to illustrate how racism is manifested in a community and how human service professionals can respond to it. Millville's fictional residents are based on people we have interviewed and worked with, but every community is unique and the dynamics of race and racism vary considerably in different communities and regions. We encourage you to plug your own community into this chapter and to explore how the dynamics of racism are manifested where you work and live.

This chapter builds on basic skills of macro and community-based practice and an analysis of multidimensional and intersecting ways in which racism manifests and operates. As is true of work with individuals, families, and groups, community-based practice relies on understanding history, conducting an assessment, a carefully planned strategy, and ongoing evaluation. As our description of Millville illustrates, racism and White supremacy in the community is manifested in many ways—in neighborhoods, schools, political processes, intergroup conflict, internalized self-concepts, and consciousness about inequality and privilege. Racism shapes where people are able to live, educational opportunities, occupational options, and economic fortunes. Racism contributes to intergroup tensions and conflicts. Combined with poverty and lack of economic opportunity, racism leads to unsafe streets and feelings of disempowerment, compelling people to stay indoors, which makes the streets even more dangerous.

Racial and ethnic groups are blamed for the very urban decay and economic deterioration that plagues their lives and circumscribes their potential. Racism causes people to feel disrespected, unwanted, and wary of the motives of others. It can cause feelings of powerlessness. It can fuel anger and alienation. Places, events, and public spaces, such as murals, serve as community canvasses inscribed with highly charged symbols and meanings that validate or threaten social identity.

Those in the helping professions—social workers, community nurses, psychologists and psychiatrists, guidance counselors, religious leaders, and community organizers—work with systems, institutions, and programs, as well as with individuals, groups, and families. Workers use clinical and interpersonal skills coupled with their ability to work systemically. Their efforts to effect change must respond to local conditions, but with an eye toward national policies and global trends, which provide the context for inexorable historical patterns such as the deindustrialization that swept the United States and stranded many cities such as Millville with high social needs, lack of adequate jobs, and reductions in social and health services.

MILLVILLE

Millville is a mid-sized city, a deindustrialized mill town in the northeastern United States. Although the mills have closed, their hulking buildings remain. Some have been "repurposed" into music venues, restaurants, industrial museums, artist studios and professional offices. The city used to be mostly White, with people of predominantly Irish, French Canadian, and Polish descent, but now is 52% Latinxs, mostly Puerto Rican. Many Latinx residents live in low-rent tenement housing abutting the abandoned mills and proximate to downtown. Millville has had a small African American community ever since the mills first opened in the late 19th century, currently constituting about 2% of the population. Most African Americans live in a low-rent area known as the Lincoln Square district, about a half-mile from downtown on the other side of an unused canal. A small number of middle-class African Americans and Latinx residents live in a predominantly White, middle-class area. Recent immigrants include Cambodians and Russians, and a local charity has resettled clusters of refugees from Syria and Somalia in the city.

Children of color constitute 79% of the public school population. The poverty rate in this community has been one of the highest in the state for the past 35 years. This is accompanied by high rates of unemployment, illiteracy, school dropout, single-parent families, low-birth-weight infants, teen pregnancy, gang activity, and reports of child abuse and neglect. The Puerto Rican population tends to be younger and less educated than both the Black and White populations, with less capital, fewer resources, and less access to jobs and political power. Although Latinx people make up 52% of the population, they hold only four of 13 city council seats. One reason is that they are concentrated in certain neighborhoods and there are six at-large seats, all held by Whites. The city council president is White, as is the mayor of the city. The mayor is considered a progressive politician who has reached out to the Latinx community and won office with significant Latinx support. He is openly gay and the first openly queer person to hold a major leadership position in the city's government. The majority of appointed city officials are White, including the chief of police, but the superintendent of schools (where 79% of students are Latinx) is Latina, the first non-White person to hold that position.

Millville has gone from being an industrial city to a social service city. The building that formerly housed its largest department store is now headquarters for the Department of Social Services. All residents agree that downtown Millville is not safe at night. The city's biggest cultural event is an annual St. Patrick's Day parade, which marches through many predominantly Latinx neighborhoods.

Snapshots of Millville Residents

Martin

Martin, is a 52-year-old, White, straight, cisgender male, and upper middle class, owns his home and lives with his family in a mostly White neighborhood of stately homes on a hill.

His family has owned a local lumberyard for three generations. He is committed to remaining in Millville, where he grew up, but is concerned about the economic deterioration of the city and issues of safety. His children attend private school.

Miguel

Miguel, a 33-year-old Puerto Rican, straight, cisgender man, owns a home in a lower-middle-class neighborhood, where neighbors are White and Puerto Rican. The neighborhood had been predominantly White but now is increasingly Latinx. Miguel is a police officer in another city. He and his wife grew up in Millville after their parents migrated from Puerto Rico. He ran for city councilor and lost. During the campaign, when he entered White neighborhoods, he had to wear a T-shirt with his campaign logo emblazoned on it so that residents did not continually call the police. He has battled the school department after they tried to place his children in bilingual education classes, even though they were being reared in an English-speaking home. He is frustrated when he is followed in stores while shopping and is insulted that grocery stores label Hispanic food as "ethnic food" and put it next to the pet food.

Sarah

Sarah is 45, a White, straight, cisgender woman who is divorced and a mother of two. She grew up downtown but now lives in a subdivision on the outskirts of the city in a mostly White neighborhood of small, lower-middle-class homes. She works for the water department of Millville. Enraged by the deterioration of her old neighborhood, she blames this on Hispanic residents, whom she believes do not care about their environment. She wanted to continue to reside within the city limits because of her pride in the Millville that she grew up in but is wary of living too close to downtown. One of her sons attends parochial school and the other, who has a learning disability, was transferred to the public school system.

Yaldira

Yaldira is a 23-year-old, cisgender, straight Puerto Rican woman with three children. She was born in Puerto Rico and speaks English with difficulty. Her partner has found work in Puerto Rico and lives there while Yaldira remains in Millville, caring for her children and her parents, who give the appearance of being elderly although they are in their early 50s. Her father used to work as a janitor but now is disabled and legally blind. Yaldira obtained her high school diploma after being in mostly bilingual classes. She does not have a job outside her home, and her lack of proficient English is problematic for many potential employers. She and her family feel connected to their immediate neighbors but not to the larger community. Both she and her parents are wary of leaving their apartments during the day and rarely venture out at night, as they perceive the city as dangerous and unsafe.

Herbert

Herbert, a 62-year-old, cisgender African American man who identifies as gay, grew up in Millville and presently is the director of a large antipoverty/civil rights organization in the city. He was reared in what is now a mixed neighborhood of African Americans and Puerto Ricans but currently lives in the same, predominantly White neighborhood as Martin. He has been working with local business leaders to try to form a consortium that will improve the high school graduation rate and college acceptance rate. He graduated from a regional parochial high school, and his three children attended college.

Patience

Patience is 25 years old, cisgendered, single and straight and is the eldest daughter of a Somali family that settled in Millville 3 years ago. Before moving to Millville the family had lived in a refugee camp in Eastern Congo for 12 years. They are Sunni Muslim. There is no mosque in the city, and they have to travel 12 miles to a neighboring city to worship. Patience and her family run a restaurant that serves East African food in a predominantly Latinx neighborhood. Patience and her family were settled in the same apartment complex as a family from a rival clan when they were in Somalia, and there are tensions between the families.

Racism in Millville

Racism plays out in various ways in Millville, as shown in the following brief example. A group of schoolchildren painted a public mural as a school project, attempting to display the joining of cultures and nationalities in Millville. The mural included both the American flag and the Puerto Rican flag. A White city councilor was offended that the Puerto Rican flag was higher than the U.S. flag in the mural and threatened to paint over the whole thing. On their own, the children repainted the flags, before the councilor could deface their artwork. A number of White councilors were elected because they support "safety, law and order" and emphasized the threat of gangs.

THE DYNAMICS OF RACISM IN COMMUNITIES

In this chapter, we briefly review structural and institutional manifestations of racism and White supremacy in communities, considering the relationship between social identity and group membership, and the phenomenology of racism in the community—how it is experienced and what it means to people. Then we consider the value of the concepts of social cohesion, community efficacy, and community integrity for helping professionals engaged in community-based work that confronts racism.

Structural/Institutional Racism

The Millville vignette describes a small city that is severely segregated residentially. Some neighborhoods, such as the one where Miguel lives, could be described as "transition zones" of racial integration, but even these neighborhoods have a tendency to become more segregated. As more Puerto Ricans move in, more Whites move out. New tract developments are carved out, such as the predominantly White enclave where Sarah resides. Other Whites move to outlying communities, spurring further ribbon development, where homes, malls, and highways are strung out increasingly farther from urban centers.

Many Whites still living in the city remove their children from the public school system and place them in private and parochial schools, which diminishes community support and resources for quality public education. Meanwhile, poor people of color find themselves stranded increasingly in high-poverty, mostly non-White neighborhoods, where the quality of public education is poor. They face obstacles to finding jobs, and many services that make up the infrastructure of a community (banks, stores, health providers, public transportation) and that generate community capital (wealth, knowledge, resources, recreation) are in short supply.

Residential Segregation

It is helpful to highlight some relevant factors of the discussion of residential segregation in Chapter 5. Across the nation, the specific dynamics of residential segregation vary from community to community, although they have some trends in common. After the Great Recession of 2008, not only did more people become poor but more poor people lived in areas of concentrated poverty (over 40% of residents) and high poverty (20%–40% of residents; Kneebone & Holmes, 2016). But while 5.5% of Whites live in concentrated poverty areas since 2008, 25.1% of Black people and 12.9% of Latinx people live in such neighborhoods (Kneebone & Holmes, 2016). This leads to much higher numbers of poor people of color living in communities with fewer jobs and job-seeking networks, poorer performing schools, higher crime rates, greater health risks and more people suffering from financial insecurity (Kneebone & Holmes, 2016). Residents of such communities are increasingly alienated and isolated from mainstream society, with upward mobility like a receding tide and downward mobility pulling like a strong undertow (Massey & Denton, 1993; Wilson, 2011). The value of houses declines (Logan & Stults, 2011) and mortgage defaults since the Great Recession have increased. Racial segregation is underpinned by racial discrimination enacted by real estate brokers and mortgage lenders, along with White racial attitudes that restrict people of color from trying to move into less poor neighborhoods (Edsall, 2019; Freiberg, 2019; Massey, 2016). Rusk (cited by Polikoff, 2004) describes the consequences as if a crowd of people is trying to run up a descending escalator; a few make it to the top, but most are dragged downward.

Subcultures evolve, and informal economies and services develop to fill the economic and social vacuum. Those who are working or trying to buy homes have to rely on loan sharks, predatory mortgage dealers, or subprime mortgages from major institutions who charge exorbitant interest rates and set financial traps for late payments, depleting the fragile resources of families (Association of Community Organizations for Reform Now, 2002; Calhoun & Bailey, 2005). Denials of mortgages occur at much higher rates for Blacks and Latinx people than Whites, even when income levels are held constant (Glantz & Martinez, 2018). Concentrated segregation and poverty interact to create an unhealthy and unsafe environment (Manduca & Sampson, 2019; Samuels, 2014). As supermarkets move out, small grocery stores, with higher prices and sparse selections of healthy foods, take their place. Drug dealing increases and neighborhoods become more dangerous, which inhibits civic and community life. This in turn leads to a perception of community disorder in the three critical areas—changing ethnic demographics, residential instability, and increasing crime (Kleinhans & Bolt, 2013)—which are strong contributors to "White flight" from neighborhoods. While economic disparity plays a central role in residential segregation, it is a much more complicated phenomenon because of the web of intersections between economics, political power, and racism. For example, although 2015 census data indicate a decrease in the poverty rate for all racial groups, including African Americans (Semega et al., 2017), African Americans remain more highly segregated than any other racial groups (Firebaugh & Ferrell, 2016). In fact, research (Ellen, 2008, cited in Greene et al., 2018) suggests that residential segregation along Black-White racial lines would be significantly decreased if income was the only determinant of residential distribution. George Galster of Wayne State University has articulated a vicious cycle that ensues (as cited in Polikoff, 2004). Spatial, economic, and social isolation lead to "behavioral adaptations" for residents, who are trying to survive under increasingly harsh conditions. The media then highlights these "deviant" lifestyles, fostering negative stereotypes and depicting poor people of color as different from mainstream Americans and culturally aberrant. This, in turn, validates pre-existing White prejudice, such as that expressed by Sarah in the vignette, and fuels bigotry and prejudice, which promotes White discrimination and withdrawal from support of neighborhoods and public services, further deepening the plight of those stranded in impoverished, segregated neighborhoods.

Political Power

Residential and economic exclusion intersects with a lack of political power. As mentioned earlier, Millville has only four out of 13 elected Latinx city councilors and few Latinx or African Americans in appointed political positions. Recent arrivals, such as Patience and her family, are even less represented politically. At-large systems of voting often prevent people of color from gaining political power because their votes represent a numerical minority in the general electorate of a local city or county, which poses a significant challenge to electing their members in contested political positions. Ward-style voting also can dilute political power, as people of color are confined to densely populated city wards where they elect one or two local politicians but are unable to have any influence in the many other districts where they are underrepresented. The result is a city hall where people of color have diminished influence. The situation only worsens with state and national elections, in which people of color are even more severely underrepresented.

Lack of political power is a crucial dimension of community racism. In the recent years there has been a resurgence by Republican-controlled state legislators to suppress the votes of people of color through limiting the hours of polling, closing polling stations in poor neighborhoods populated predominantly by people of color, felon disenfranchisement, removal of "inactive" voter rolls, gutting the Voting Rights Act of 1965, and through a raft of new voter identification laws (Astor, 2018; Berman, 2015; Cobb, 2018; Famighetti et al., 2014; Waldman, 2015; Weiser & Opsal, 2015). And the problems with electoral fairness go deeper than intentional voter suppression. People living in economically deprived communities of color are much more likely to have outdated voting technology—with a greater likelihood of lost or miscounted votes. And there also have been outright attempts to intimidate voters of color and suppress their votes both before and during Election Day (Cohen, 2004; Fritz, 2001; Raskin, 2004). This can be done by offering misinformation about where and when elections are being held, deceiving people about their voter eligibility, and intimidating voters with challenges as they attempt to vote, or illegally filming voters as they cast their ballots (Astor, 2018; Overton, 2005; Reimann, 2020). In 2020, President Trump and the Republican Party have openly encouraged voter suppression by challenging without basis mail-in voting, even during a pandemic, limiting the number of polling places in poorer communities of color, placing falsely labeled "ballot" boxes in neighborhoods of people of color, and asking for self-appointed poll watchers, who are often aggressively challenging voters (Hakim & Saul, 2020; Thrush & Medina, 2020).

Attempts to purge voter rolls of convicted felons also have been documented (Raskin, 2004), which presents two problems (Boyd, 2001; Overton, 2005; Raskin, 2004; Sengupta, 2000):

1. People often are falsely accused and yet are still denied the right to vote.
2. With the disproportionate numbers of people of color who are incarcerated, and with the increasing trend in states to deny voting privileges for a convicted felon's lifetime, many people of color are legally being denied their right to vote.

Even when laws are passed to restore voting rights to convicted people, such as Florida in 2004, Republican dominated legislators have reverted to requiring people, many of whom are poor, to pay their outstanding fines before being re-enfranchised, a modern-day form of poll tax (*The Washington Post*, 2020).

Corporate Executives

Along with having less political power at all levels of government, people of color are dramatically underrepresented as high-level corporate executives, particularly as CEOs; and many groups of color—particularly African Americans, Native Americans, and various Latinx groups—are poorly represented among small business owners. Corporate and business leaders work together with elected and appointed politicians to make decisions that strongly shape a community's destiny. Together they decide what programs are funded, where things get built, which social service agencies are worthy of capital campaigns, where hospitals and healthcare will be located, where highways will be constructed, and through which neighborhoods bus routes will pass. Local corporate elites also have influence over the direction of charitable funding, through mechanisms such as the United Way.

To be sure, politicians and the local business elite do not always have the same agenda, and how they exercise their power varies considerably in different communities. Some communities work vigorously to engage all citizens in civic life, while others actively exclude and marginalize people of color. And some business leaders may live in a highly segregated, predominantly White neighborhood or community but at the same time be committed to improving public education, strengthening local job-training programs, and making the streets safe for everyone. This may stem from the need for local businesses to have an educated and trained workforce, as well as a safe community for people to live, work, and shop in, but also can reflect genuine compassion and concern for all community residents.

Other positions of power in communities may offer more access for people of color—including religious leaders, educators, social service agency directors, and local community activists. Herbert's stature and status as a community leader in Millville provides an example. Ethnic and racially minoritized communities also can create their own newsletters and radio stations to contest the hegemony of a local newspaper or television station, in which their voices have been ignored or distorted. This has been a way of resisting racism in the United States since the founding of the Republic: Native Americans, Asian Americans, Latinxs, and African Americans have been publishing counternarratives to White racism and supremacy in the United States for centuries (Gonzalez & Torres, 2011). Communities are entities with many nodes of power and influence, some formal and others informal. Analyzing and understanding the unique mix of players and power in a given community is essential for workers in the helping professions who are hoping to have an impact.

Social Identity and Group Membership

Social identity and group allegiance emerge in relation to other people and groups. Communities are often sites of competition between ethnic and racial groups for housing, jobs, cultural events and rituals, and political power. In Millville, Black, Indigenous, and people of color (BIPOC) people, particularly poor African Americans and recent Puerto Rican immigrants, face many barriers to achieving economic success—such as impoverished schools, lack of capital, inability to secure loans—yet they are blamed for living in poor, underserved neighborhoods. Residential segregation and the dystopic characterization of poor urban neighborhoods and their residents fuel a "discourse of denigration and the creation of other" (Miller & Schamess, 2000). Positive social identities are forged at the expense of those seen as less capable and worthy and whose cultures are misperceived as not fostering a work ethic or civic responsibility. This not only happens to people of color, but blame is often apportioned to poor and working class White people. They are often portrayed as bigoted by the "narrating" class while the systemic racism of political, business, civic, and media elites is insufficiently interrogated (Metzgar, 2016).

Effective community interventions must take into account dynamics between social identity formation and intergroup competition and conflict, as they spawn a great deal of anger, alienation, and scapegoating. In Millville, as in many cities, the decades-long process of deindustrialization and the accompanying loss of jobs, a declining city tax base, and ancient and inadequate infrastructures clearly are not the fault of any ethnic, racial, or class group, let alone those who have arrived recently. Yet, as can be seen from Sarah's comments, the group becomes the symbol of the city's decline and the target of her sadness, rage, and discomfort. Apples are compared to oranges; the vibrant industrial city that Sarah recalls from her youth is contrasted with the decaying urban landscape in which Puerto Ricans are trapped, yet, in Sarah's view, blamed. While the blame is laid on those who are seen as the "other," larger societal and structural causes of the city's decline go unquestioned.

A trend in intergroup relations in the community is that Whites and people of color frame the community narrative differently. People of color, particularly in poor neighborhoods, report consistent encounters with prejudice. They describe feeling stereotyped, excluded, and denied access to resources. They say they are followed in stores, are stereotyped by their children's teachers, and encounter police brutality, among other examples of overt and covert racism and bias. They are aware of the social and economic barriers they face daily. Miguel, the police officer, felt humiliated and stereotyped when the school department kept trying to place his children, born in the United States, in less academically oriented bilingual classes simply because they were identified as Latinx. Not only does this happen but civic elites are often in denial, creating a secondary wound from the denial of the experiences and personhood of people of color. That may explain why an ad campaign posting billboards in Brooklyn, New York, which confirmed the existence of racism, such as redlining, subprime mortgages, and separate and unequal education, validated the experiences of people of color living in the neighborhood and led to a decline in race-related stress (Kwate, 2014).

Whites, by comparison, frequently downplay or ignore the structural impediments to success and their own White privilege and focus more often on values (DiAngelo, 2018; Gurin et al., 2014). African Americans and Hispanics are seen by White critics as having an "alien culture," one that is antithetical to mainstream American values and behaviors (Miller, 1999). The storyline goes, "If only they would work harder, if only they weren't so loud, if only they were good parents, if only they weren't so violent—this would be a better place to live."

This is not a new response to immigrants. Actually, the Irish, who were discriminated against when emigrating to the United States, had the same reaction to French Canadian immigrants in communities, such as Millville in the 19th century, and this pattern has been replicated by ethnic groups across the nation. The view that recent arrivals are culturally deficient and responsible for urban decay has been around for a long time and was a driving force in the founding of professions such as social work (Gordon, 1988; Jansson, 2015). But when ethnic conflict arose in places like Millville and other American cities 50 or 100 years ago, sufficient blue-collar jobs were available so ethnic groups could move up the occupational and economic ladder and achieve social mobility.

This is not the case today. Historically, White ethnic groups were quickly able to assume the mantle of White privilege, an option not available for many people of color, particularly African Americans, Asians, and dark-skinned Latinxs.

The Phenomenology of Community Racism

In addition to structural and intergroup racism, every community has a phenomenology of racism. A phenomenological approach considers the subjective meanings of history and experience (Seidman, 1991). What we mean by this for communities is a *historical* story of race and race relations in the community and the way residents currently *experience* race and racism; the *storying* and the *meaning* of race and racism for residents.

Every community has historical narratives about how it was founded, what it represents and stands for, who lives there and how they arrived, and a story about the character of the community (Miller, 2001). Such collective group myths are part of a community's DNA, encoded in neighborhoods, inscribed on buildings, drawn on murals, written in books, and stamped on the psyches of its residents. For many communities, the narrative is positive, validating, and self-affirming, but for others the narrative is one of deep poverty, unrelenting crime, and social isolation. It becomes a negative story about a community and its residents.

The larger community narrative contains specific group narratives and, within those, family narratives. Thus, stories are constructed *within* groups about how the Irish, African Americans, French Canadians, and Puerto Ricans came to live in a city such as Millville. Often cited are the hardships they left and initially encountered, and pride in the achievements and successes the ethnic group gained over time. Other stories are spun *about* groups by other groups, which often are more critical and less generous.

Within families, myths frequently are invoked about how a grandparent or great-grandparent, despite dismal conditions and severe hardships, was able to overcome adversity and create the conditions, often through self-sacrifice, for descendants to thrive. These myths and stories often are invoked to create invidious comparisons with recent immigrants, and they tend to ignore or minimize significant differences in social and economic opportunity as well as structural limitations such as social, economic, and legal policies. Moreover, these stories all but erase the historical presence of Indigenous peoples, who were massacred or forced out of their traditional lands by European settlers.

The phenomenology of race and ethnicity in the community is articulated by public narratives, both formal and informal, about the citizens and the groups living there. These narratives guide news coverage, are expressed from the pulpits of churches, are printed in pamphlets and brochures, are woven into conversations with family and friends, and become part of the story that people tell themselves about who they are and where they live. The stories are reconstructed in public rituals—parades, holiday celebrations, civic events, community gatherings—as well as in micro interactions, such as when the police stop a car and search the passengers. The public narrative is affirmed and embodied in civic associations and their activities: Daughters of the American Revolution, Rotary Club, Shriners, Elks, discussion groups, salons, United Way campaigns, charity road races, or school spelling bees.

All of these are part and parcel of community life, and vibrant communities have rich lattice works of associations, events, and installations—the capillary systems of the civic body. How these tie in with race and racism becomes clearer when we ask and explore certain questions:

- ▶ Who is represented in a parade and who is ignored?
- ▶ What neighborhoods does the parade move through?
- ▶ What varying meanings does the parade have for different groups in the community?
- ▶ Who is a member of the Chamber of Commerce and who is missing?
- ▶ Which drivers are stopped and searched consistently and which continue unimpeded?
- ▶ Who stops the drivers?
- ▶ Whose history is taught in public schools?
- ▶ Whose holidays are celebrated as public holidays?
- ▶ Who are the reporters on the local newspaper and what worldviews, assumptions, and values underlie their writing?

These and similar questions will guide our suggestions for ways by which people in the helping professions can strengthen community unity and inclusivity.

Social Cohesion and Community Integrity

As we consider how to respond to racism in the community, we must reflect on what contributes to healthy and vibrant communities. When conducting needs assessments and analyzing enduring inequalities and oppressions, we tend to focus on what is wrong and what is missing. Yet all communities have resources, assets, and sources of hope and inspiration (Kretzman & McKnight, 1996). Some communities with high poverty rates and residential and occupational racism are more cohesive than others with similar demographic characteristics (Miller, 2001). Why is this so?

Social cohesion is defined as the process of people feeling connected and bound to one another and forming an entity (Petrosino & Pace, 2015), such as a block, neighborhood, or community. Wilson (2011) in his research concluded that social cohesion results when residents are able to achieve communal objectives while maintaining effective social control. To achieve both of these goals, residents should have some efficacy, an ability to assert their agenda and supervise it, facilitated by richly cross-joined social networks (Sampson et al., 1997). People are more likely to develop a sense of collective efficacy and engage in social action if they feel as if they have shared values with other members of the community (Petrosino & Pace, 2015), trust one another (Driscoll et al., 2015), and are able to perceive the structural forces that contribute to social problems (as opposed to seeing them as a function of individual character or moral failing) and believe that taking collective action can effect meaningful change (Corcoran et al., 2015; Stewart et al., 2010).

An example of such an agenda is to have safe streets with no drug dealing. This must be articulated as a common goal, accompanied by the capacity to change and monitor the situation. It relies also on adults working collectively to supervise the activities of children and other adults (Sampson et al., 1999). For issues such as these, an intergenerational approach is more likely to contribute to a sense of collective efficacy and healthy outcomes (Kang, 2015). Such collective endeavors also require resources—economic, financial, political, and social.

A major barrier to social cohesion is an unequal approach to law enforcement. As the Black Lives Matter (BLM) movement has illustrated, Black and Brown people not only do not view the police as a safe and trusted community institution but are far too often the victims of police brutality and may live in fear of being stopped for minor offences, such as traffic violations, and ending up arrested, shackled, tasered, and even killed. As we indicated in Chapter 5, the entire criminal justice system reflects racial bias against BIPOC people, so the legitimacy of law enforcement as a force for good in a community is questionable and there is often a lack of social trust. And yet many BIPOC residents of communities want to have a sense of safety and suffer when their neighborhoods lack any semblance of consistent and fair law enforcement.

Thus, Whiter and wealthier neighborhoods find it easier to develop collective efficacy because they not only have more social and economic capital but greater social trust of community institutions such as the police.

Sampson et al. (1999) identified five dimensions of social capital:

1. Organizations and services (e.g., mental health services, crime-prevention programs, after-school programs)
2. Kinship/friendship ties
3. Voluntary associations (e.g., local religious organizations, tenant associations, business and civic groups, ethnic/nationality clubs)
4. Neighborhood activism
5. Mutual trust

Social networks are lubricated by mutual trust and fostered by articulating common norms and goals and working together in pursuit of those goals (Putnam, 2000). There is greater social stability when communities have spaces and processes that foster interaction between people from different sectors of the community and with different social identities (Tach, 2014). But when communities are divided by racism and intergroup conflict, and entire populations are targeted and excluded by key community institutions, the trust essential to these networks is difficult to generate. Multiple disadvantages, such as high concentrations of poverty and racism, compromise the ability to form such networks and take collective action (Sampson et al., 1999). With diminished trust, overwhelming social disorganization, and fewer collective resources, residents can readily feel disempowered and be less optimistic about their capacity to work together to improve the quality of their lives. This is not only a local issue—lack of social trust reverberates throughout all levels of nation and society, particularly when there is a political regime that actively targets and scapegoats people based on race, ethnicity, and religion (see Chapter 5 for a discussion about White supremacy in national political leadership and discourses).

Social capital, community efficacy, and the integrity of families all interact with each other (Miller, 2001). *Family integrity* implies "the ability of the family to consistently provide its members with the emotional, psychological, social, and economic foundations to support their engagement with the community" (Miller, 2001, p. 29). Families are unable to achieve this when they have few economic opportunities, when danger is ubiquitous, and when hope is extinguished. Thus, family integrity depends on community integrity, "the capacity of a community to provide for its families a safe, economically viable and meaningful place to live, with equal justice for all" (Miller, 2001, p. 29). Family integrity and community efficacy and integrity are intricately related to one another—it is difficult to have one without the other. They are also deeply impacted by structural forces in the society such as social, political, economic, and legal policies and trends (e.g., an economic recession or boom, welfare reform, civil rights legislation, racially biased policing, immigration policies, a president refusing to condemn White supremacists, etc.). In examining how to confront racism in the community, we will articulate in greater detail what community integrity means and what workers in the helping professions can do to foster it.

RESPONDING TO RACISM IN THE COMMUNITY

We have considered four major dimensions of racism in the community: structural and institutional racism, intergroup conflict and its relation to social identity, the phenomenology of racism (how it is experienced, storied, and its different meanings), and the interaction of racism with social capital and community integrity. Meaningful interventions against racism in the community should address each of these dimensions. Consequently, our recommendations for action fall into four topical areas: (a) public dialogue, (b) re-storying the community, (c) structural interventions, and (d) generating social capital in the quest for community integrity. We have also provided two exercises (Exercises 10.1 and 10.2) to help you understand and map your community.

Public Dialogue

Intergroup misunderstanding and conflict contribute greatly to racism, as they lead to alienation and seeing the "other" as different and less than, and foster stereotypes and scapegoating. Add to this structural White supremacy, which will be discussed, and there are many factors that contribute to residential segregation. These factors contribute to White people moving out of cities to suburbs, exurbs, and gated communities, which leaves poor, segregated communities bereft of resources. Thus, Whites are less likely to support needed reforms and services and may even be moved to obstruct these efforts. Hochschild (2016) in her research continually heard from her White respondents that they were unwilling to pay taxes that help fund services that would benefit them because they did not want to support their stereotyped notion of people of color receiving benefits that "they do not deserve"! Meanwhile, intergroup conflict between groups such as African Americans and Korean Americans drains and depletes groups already targeted by racism and misdirects their anger and frustration toward one another rather than helping them to unite and work together for a more socially just community.

Whites are less likely to support needed reforms and services and may even be moved to obstruct these efforts. Hochschild (2016) in her research continually heard from her White respondents that they were unwilling to pay taxes that help fund services that would benefit them because they did not want to support their stereotyped notion of people of color receiving benefits that "they do not deserve"! Meanwhile, intergroup conflict between groups such as African Americans and Korean Americans drains and depletes groups already targeted by racism and misdirects their anger and frustration toward one another rather than helping them to unite and work together for a more socially just community.

Structured opportunities to discuss race and racism are highly beneficial in communities where race or ethnicity-based intergroup conflict is present as they offer a mechanism for community members to be heard and recognized as well as to engage with one another. Community dialogue about race, ethnicity, and racism creates space for revisiting historical narratives, airing grievances, and going beyond frozen, dichotomized positions. Understanding can replace finger-pointing and blame. Myths and stereotypes can be interrogated.

Local leaders can support such conversations, formal and informal, and model their capacity to engage in them. Public discussions can be augmented by presentations, exhibits, and oral history projects (Miller, 1999).

While no single model of intergroup dialogue is applicable to all communities as every community has its own unique history and current intergroup dynamics, a critical dialogic model achieves a number of goals that have the potential to improve intergroup understanding and relationships (Gurin-Sands et al., 2012). By engaging in dialogue, citizens have an opportunity to tell their own stories while also listening to those of others, acknowledging sameness (e.g., wanting safe neighborhoods) while recognizing differences (e.g., being repeatedly stopped and frisked by the police). This may lead to critical reflection and an exploration and potential re-evaluation of assumptions and values. This in turn can lead to collective action, which engages residents in a shared social identity (Dovidio et al., 2016) as concerned local citizens.

Without critical dialogue, groups may engage in diatribe and conflict. Without a mechanism for being heard and recognized, people who are targeted are left with the options of acquiescing to their subordinate status or challenging it through confrontational tactics. We have witnessed the need for this during the summer of 2020 after repeated calls to protect Black people from police violence were ineffective. Confrontation often is called for, and the Civil Rights Movement is a good example of what that can achieve. Whenever possible, though, constructive dialogue should also be attempted to build bridges, heal wounds, repair broken relationships, and develop interracial coalitions.

It is important that racial dialogues, regardless of which model is used, serve to produce antiracist action and change, on the individual, interpersonal, and community levels. Conversations that illuminate people of color's experiences of racism but produce no change or actions on the part of White people may become counterproductive. Such conversations may further marginalize people of color's experiences and inadvertently elevate the need of White people (to access the lived experiences of people of color) over the need of people of color to see tangible changes, which produces a paradoxical result of upholding White privilege (DiAngelo, 2018).

Re-Storying the Community

One positive outcome of dialogue is that new stories about the community emerge as old narratives are questioned. Community narratives are akin to individual narratives of self in that both rely on stories that explain who we are, and both reflect our experiences. Both also shape our actions and reactions by giving meaning to our reality. If our self-narrative is one of incompetence and failure, we are less likely to have the confidence to succeed when confronted by challenges. This also holds true for communities. If the public storyline accentuates the decline of community, dangers lurking in the streets, and the antisocial behavior of targeted ethnic and racial groups, businesses will consider relocating, city government may neglect schools and parks, children will be kept inside, and the community will confirm the story of being a bad environment with little hope for improvement.

All communities go through demographic and economic changes, yet public narratives about the community often are slow to map these transformations and unable to translate the shifts into an adaptable community identity (Miller, 2001). Thus, the community identity can become a frozen, idealized, unattainable, air-brushed portrait of the past, with which current residents are saddled.

A community identity emerges from history, an economy, cultural traditions, and political leadership, and is formed in relation to surrounding communities. An identity can link a community to similar communities while also differentiating it, celebrating it, or decrying its uniqueness. Thus, terms are employed that resonate for residents as well as people who have never set foot in the community (Miller, 2001):

> "thriving industrial city"
> "decaying neighborhood"
> "inner city"
> "wealthy suburb"
> "safe place"
> "nice place to raise a family"
> "college town"
> "bedroom community"

Collective self-definitions like these give meaning to the lives of people within and outside the community.

When working with individual consumers, helping professionals seek to uncover troubling beliefs such as "I'm unworthy" or "It's my fault that this happened to me." Consumers are helped to articulate a positive, affirming self-narrative—for example, "I'm competent" or "I have the strength to overcome adversity." In certain ways, this is what communities should be working toward as well: to identify and desensitize negative and pessimistic public narratives while facilitating public discourses that foster an identity that is hopeful and inclusive of all residents, one that is able to confront new challenges, so a community can validate its honorable past while also embracing its future (Miller, 2001). Helping professionals can work with a cross-section of residents and leaders intentionally and collectively to craft new visions of the community—a story of what the community would like to become.

Structural Interventions

Structural interventions are the most important initiative for community change, but they are unlikely to succeed without the groundwork being laid by the first two proposals. To put it simply and directly, none of the other dimensions of community intervention will have any meaningful impact without structural interventions that address racism and poverty in the community. The other suggestions may help to achieve a consensus for change and generate the narratives and networks to effect change, but ultimately the community must undergo concrete, material changes that support racial justice.

One of the most essential, unfinished tasks of the Civil Rights Movement at the community level is the need to desegregate communities. This entails many factors, including the following:

▶ The ability of people to move out of racially isolated zones and into other neighborhoods.

▶ An end to residential redlining and restrictive covenants, including informal restrictive agreements among homeowners and residents.

▶ The presence of and equitable access to banks, stores, and services in all neighborhoods.

▶ An end to the practice of predatory lending.

▶ The capacity for all people to generate sufficient capital to eventually own their homes
and businesses, gain equity, and achieve social mobility.

Supporting Economically and Racially Mixed Communities and Upward Mobility

One of the most challenging aspects of residential racism is the way that poor people of color
can find themselves in neighborhoods where there are high rates of poverty, underperform-
ing schools, dangerous streets, lack of shops and services, and a paucity of doors and ladders
leading to upward social mobility. It is important to emphasize that such residential racial
segregation is not based on individual choices but rather due to intentional government policies, from violent removal of Native Americans from their homeland, to forced segregation of
Chinese immigrants, which resulted in forming of Chinatowns, to formal and (often violent)
informal restriction of Black residents from moving into "White neighborhoods" (Salomon,
2019). This does not mean that there have not been people of color neighborhoods that
thrived economically and socially. However, even thriving middle-class, people of color
neighborhoods were not exempt from the forces of racism. One chilling example is the
Greenwood neighborhood in Tulsa, Oklahoma, which was a thriving wealthy Black community (nicknamed the Black Wall Street) in the early 1900s. It was destroyed by angry White
mobs who fire-bombed the neighborhood, killing many residents and burning homes and
businesses to the ground, with law enforcement in collusion (Bruney, 2020). Furthermore,
many people of color neighborhoods were often bisected or demolished to build new highways during the urban renewal period, resulting in diminishment of those neighborhoods'
social and economic capital and stymieing growth (Beyer, 2020; Kang, 2010).

One successful program aimed at breaking up racially and economically isolated urban
areas has been the Gautreaux program in Chicago (Polikoff, 2004). This was the result of
a desegregation lawsuit that began in 1966, claiming that the Chicago Housing Authority
had employed racially discriminatory policies (Rosenbaum et al., 1991). This led to a U.S.
Supreme Court consent decree in 1976 and a demonstration project known as the
Gautreaux program (Keels et al., 2005). The program gave vouchers to low-income African
Americans living in Chicago housing projects to enable them to live in private apartments.
About half moved to predominantly Black city neighborhoods and half to predominantly
White suburbs.

This project has been one of the most studied desegregation efforts in the nation. Between
6 and 22 years after being initially placed, the majority of program participants, most of
whom have since moved, were living in neighborhoods that reflect the socioeconomic conditions of the neighborhood to which they had moved originally, rather than the housing projects from whence they came (Keels et al., 2005). Living in safer areas with better resourced
and higher achieving schools and more jobs produced dramatic improvements in educational
attainment, college attendance, employment status, and upward mobility, particularly for
those who were moved to the suburbs (Gaumer et al., 2014; Keels et al., 2005). Upon their
initial entry into their new neighborhoods, the residents did experience prejudice and harassment from White residents but, despite that, have made substantial socioeconomic progress
after moving.

The program has served as a model for other cities, including Boston, Cincinnati, Dallas, and Hartford (Rosenbaum, 1995). It has led to calls for establishing a national Gautreaux program to break up high-density, inner-city neighborhoods of extreme segregation and poverty while also serving to integrate predominantly White areas (Polikoff, 2004). Such a program is unlikely to make much headway in the current deadlocked political environment, and the original program would not have been possible without the desegregation movement of the 1960s and a Supreme Court committed to furthering that agenda in the 1970s. These factors point to the importance of political activism at the local community level.

Another way of supporting racially and economically mixed communities has been the development of Community Development Financial Institutions Funds (CDFI), which have directly invested billions of dollars in poor communities while also facilitating investments by the private sector (Julian, 2015). Building on this, Julian has proposed that there be a national Inclusive Communities Federal Institution (ICFI) that would have as its mission to support racially and economically integrated communities with a focus on opportunity for all. This would be a counterweight to the entropy of institutional forces that contribute to poor, segregated communities. This would combine revitalizing poor communities while also increasing access to more affluent neighborhoods (as happened with the Gautreaux program) through making available financial assistance. This would be targeted toward increasing the quality of existing housing stock, ensuring diverse residential options when building new housing, making affordable loans available to poor people of color, and providing the kinds of support services needed to help poor people make successful transitions to more affluent neighborhoods. Julian lists a number of possible programs, such as counseling, financial assistance, advocacy, help with developing "micro-enterprises" that address important social gaps (such as affordable day care), fostering greater parental involvement in schools, and offering advice and opportunities for investing so that equity and wealth accumulation are possible. Such a program has the advantage of supporting people who continue to live in low-income communities while also helping people to move to more affluent communities, increasing opportunity through a range of programs while decreasing all levels of segregation (Henneberger, 2015).

Political Activism

As long as people of color are denied political power, programs such as Gautreaux that reduce segregation will be difficult to enact. Political activism involves registering voters, an activity in which many health and human service agencies can actively engage as long as they remain nonpartisan. This is particularly important in light of massive voter suppression efforts by the Republican party. The overt attempts to intimidate voters of color in the 2000 and 2004 presidential elections and subsequent voter suppression laws passed in states under Republican political control underscore the importance of creating nonpartisan election commissions, which are found in most Western democracies (Overton, 2005). In 2013, the Supreme Court decision in Shelby County vs. Holder significantly weakened the Voting Rights Act of 1965. Since that landmark case decision, Republican-led efforts to suppress the minority vote have proliferated. According to the Brennan Center for Justice (2017), 99 bills that aimed at restricting access to registration and voting have been introduced in 2017 alone. Voter ID laws, closure of polling places in neighborhoods of people of color, and purging of "inactive" voters from the voter rolls all result in restriction of access to registration and voting for people of color (Astor, 2018). Efforts by the current Republican party—not allowing convicted felons to vote, limiting polling places in poor neighborhoods and communities with many people of color, aggressive purging of voter rolls, limiting early voting and mail-in voting—to name a few of their strategies, have been accelerating since (Fessler, 2020; McIlwain & Caliendo, 2014; Weiser & Opsal, 2015).

With the current system, the party in control of a state's executive branch appoints a commissioner, often a political partisan actively working for a campaign, who may have a vested interest in curbing the votes of people of color. And challenges must be mounted to the odious practice of lifelong voter disenfranchisement because of a felony conviction. Coupled with the disproportionate numbers of African American men who are convicted of felonies, this has become a backdoor way to reintroduce a Jim Crow-like system of denying people of color the right to vote, which has had major local and national repercussions (Alexander, 2010).

Working with voters' rights organizations, trade unions, and other groups concerned with a political voice for the disenfranchised is also necessary, as many registered voters do not vote. It is important that registered voters of color are educated about voter suppression efforts and about the steps that can be taken to ensure that their democratic right is not abrogated. Also, human services professionals can help educate voters about candidates' positions and the relevance of various issues and initiatives.

People of color also must be represented on local city councils and school committees. As described, residents of color in far too many communities are not elected or meaningfully represented in appointed positions. Interethnic struggles over political power have been occurring ever since the first major waves of European immigrants arrived in the United States, and groups do not easily share or yield power once they have attained it. Among the many ways to work to achieve local representation are registering voters; forming coalitions; and organizing, demonstrating, and mounting legal challenges to at-large systems of voting that end up stifling minority representation.

Creating Jobs

Another structural area calling for ongoing activism is to create jobs, ensure adequate public transportation to take people to work, and strengthen public education. A community without sufficient jobs is simply not a viable community. Business leaders and politicians know this as well, and recognize the importance of public education in preparing a competent workforce. A related need is to advocate for more vocational, health, and human services. Without these, many families and individuals will be unable to take advantage of educational and occupational opportunities.

Safety

Safety is an essential ingredient for community integrity for all residents. What constitutes a safe community is defined differently by different groups and is influenced by relative experiences of privilege and oppression. However, those who endure the least safe environments are poor people of color. They live farther from protection from crime and violence, coupled with the added risk of abuse by law enforcement authorities. One of the reasons the Gautreaux initiative has been so successful is that people moved to safe enough environments to be able to leave their houses, attend schools, and commute to work (Keels et al., 2005), which also allows social networks to evolve and public life to flourish. Adequate representation on police review boards, as well as citizen-driven efforts to maintain safe streets and neighborhoods, contribute to safer communities, and the process of participation in itself is empowering and offers hope.

Generating Social Capital in the Quest for Community Integrity

It is important that there is cross-racial interactions through the routine activities of daily living (Tuch, 2014) although there is also a need for more intentional initiatives. Engaging in interracial dialogue, producing new narratives, and implementing structural interventions help to generate social capital by encouraging social networks among people. The *process* of working and contributing together is in its own right an important achievement; the efficacy fostered by working together against racism and offering opportunities for all residents is a major accomplishment in itself. It results in what McKnight (1997) refers to as an "associational community," in which people with diverse backgrounds and identities work together to share capacities, skills, and resources to solve problems and spawn solutions as connected citizens rather than being isolated in the role of clients. This encourages collective efficacy as trust evolves between individuals and groups and as residents work collaboratively to solve pressing social needs (Sampson et al., 1997).

Kretzman and McKnight (1996) have developed a "community assets" map with three levels of resources:

1. Local institutions (businesses, schools, parks, libraries, hospitals, community colleges)
2. Citizen associations (churches, block clubs, cultural groups)
3. Gifts from individuals (people, income, art)

Every community has assets, or potential assets, but fears for safety, alienation, and inability to sustain oneself and family cause disruptions and ruptures in the social fabric; therefore, assets are never mined and polished. Racism fosters community fissures, which is why dialogue and healing are so essential for creating the conditions for structural changes and development of assets.

Community integrity is boosted further by having civic associations and public institutions that "braid" families to the community and to one another (Miller, 2001). Community institutions such as schools and libraries can foster meaningful and inclusive public participation through parent associations, after-school programs, and public lectures, dialogues, exhibitions, and concerts. Developing and securing public spaces, such as parks, playgrounds, community centers, and swimming pools, provide safe public places where children, families, and other residents can gather. Public places offer sites where people are able to congregate and develop relationships and networks, which are essential for antiracism activities.

Civic associations can contribute to dismantling racism when they include people from all ethnic and racial groups in the community. Organizations such as the Elks, Knights of Columbus, Rotary Club, and Junior League often have gender, class, and ethnic biases that deter people of color from even considering joining or participating in them. People need to feel welcomed, respected, and comfortable to join civic associations, and believe their participation is a meaningful way to contribute to the community.

Professionals in the helping professions can work with civic associations by offering anti-racism and equity and inclusion training, and by facilitating dialogue and public conversations to explore institutional White privilege and supremacy. These efforts may meet with resistance, but without practicing cultural diversity, equity and inclusion and opening doors to previously excluded groups, traditional civic organizations are unlikely to survive as vibrant organizations. If they do not become interracial, multicultural institutions and intentionally move toward racial justice, new civic associations that are inclusive will emerge to take their place.

Other important community resources that can promote exclusion or inclusion include public events and rituals—parades, celebrations, murals, and holiday decorations. These are part of a community's public narrative and can convey respect and appreciation for all cultures rather than privileging or marginalizing certain ethnic and racial groups. Traditions evolve over time but do not always keep up with demographic changes in the community. Thus, community leaders have to work actively to reconfigure public events and rituals to acknowledge the contributions of all of the community's ethnic and racial groups, prompting greater inclusivity (Etzioni, 1997).

Having presented a vision of a community with integrity, we now consider concrete actions that people in the helping professions can take to make this a reality.

ANTIRACISM WORK IN THE COMMUNITY

To challenge racism in the community, people in the helping professions are well positioned to work in any or all of the four areas just outlined and to make significant contributions. Social workers, nurses, psychologists, psychiatrists, counselors, and other helping professionals are part of a community's social capital. They can sponsor and facilitate community dialogues about race and racism and contribute to the construction of inclusive, antiracist community narratives. People in the helping professions working for agencies, associations, schools, and businesses can ensure that their organizations work to decolonize, to become antiracism institutions and act as partners in community-wide efforts to dismantle racism. We briefly describe some general principles of community-based antiracism work, all of which are appropriate for individuals and organizations pursuing an antiracism agenda. We have provided an assessment tool to act as a guide (see Box 10.1).

BOX 10.1 Antiracism Community Assessment Tool

Demographic information: Track population changes, racial and ethnic makeup of the community, public school students, and teachers.
Sources: Census data, state agencies, planning organizations, United Way, Chamber of Commerce.
Political information: Research the race and the ethnicity of elected and appointed officials, voting patterns by party, and race and number of registered voters.

Sources: City or county government, League of Women Voters, community journals or newspapers (oversample periodicals published by minoritized groups).

Transportation systems: Trace public transportation routes, highways, and local streets.

Sources: Local department of transportation, maps.

Residential patterns: Analyze neighborhoods and towns by race and ethnicity.

Sources: Planning departments of local government, census data geomapping.

Religious patterns: Determine existing religious organizations and who attends them by race and ethnicity.

Sources: Interfaith councils, Chamber of Commerce.

Surrounding community: Compile similar information for county and nearby communities.

Key informants: Seek information from residents, consumers, commuters, politicians, health and human service workers, business leaders, shopkeepers, teachers and school administrators, college professors, clergy community leaders, youth, community volunteers and "natural helpers," and local media. Key informants should be racially and ethnically diverse.

Questions to Ask:

1. What is it like to live (or work) in this community?
2. How would you describe relations between different ethnic and racial groups? Please be specific. What do you surmise about race and racism in the community?
3. How would you describe the community? How would you describe your community if you had less than 5 minutes with someone who had never visited your community?
4. Who or what groups hold power in the community? In what ways is their power visible? How is power expressed?
5. What are the community's problems?
6. What are its strengths and assets?
7. What social networks exist?
8. What organizations are important in civic life?
9. How do you and other people get your local news?
10. How safe is the community? Has it remained the same or is it changing? What makes you feel safe or unsafe in your community?
11. What do various groups say about law enforcement in the community? How do you feel about law enforcement in your community? What would you like to see happen to improve law enforcement in your community?
12. What is your vision of what you would like to see your community become?

Assessment and Prioritization

Assessment should be the starting point with any activism or change project. No community is the same. We described Millville to you to illustrate some issues of which you should be aware when examining racism in your community. Collecting demographic information is useful and often available from census reports, planning organizations, state and local agencies, the United Way, and the Chamber of Commerce.

▶ What racial and ethnic groups live in the community?

▶ Are patterns changing, or is the current population stable and enduring?

▶ How does the demographic makeup of the community match the race and ethnicity of the children attending public schools?

▶ How does the race and ethnicity of teachers and administrators correspond to those of the children attending the school?

▶ Do those who are in elected and appointed positions mirror the ethnic and racial demographics of the community?

▶ When planning and decision-making groups are formed, who is missing from sitting at the table? Who controls who gets invited or ensures certain groups are invited?

Answering these questions provides simple statistical data for tracking local racial and ethnic patterns. Some of this information will be difficult to find, but a lot of data should be readily available without having to spend too much time searching for it. Areas of focus should include the racial dynamics of politics (both elected and appointed), jobs and employment, residential patterns, transportation systems (particularly public), and social and health indicators. We should identify those community institutions that have power, as well as the source of their power. For example, in one community the power brokers may be the Democratic Party, the corporate elite, and the Catholic Church, and in another community a farmer's cooperative, county government, and a local extended family may wield considerable influence.

Drawing a religious map of the community is another valuable tool in ascertaining whether ethnic and racial patterns coincide with religious affiliation and church participation. Also, we can place the community in a larger context, its social ecology (Miller, 2012): How does it compare with neighboring communities? What are the county, region, and state demographics? This should include an assessment of national and international developments, as well as historical trends. Piven and Cloward (1993) have argued that at some times in history there are seams when certain changes are possible, such as the era of civil rights and Great Society programs (Miller, 2002) and the recent movements like the Me-Too movement and the Black Lives Matter movement. These windows of opportunity do not last long, and when they close, so do the opportunities for large-scale changes. Therefore, we have to attempt the right strategy at the right time.

A statistical assessment is only part of the overall process. We can learn much from hearing from a variety of people about their experience of living in the community and what meaning it has for them. We can do this formally or informally, by talking with consumers, residents, local leaders, health and social service workers, religious leaders, politicians, youth, community volunteers, and people from the media. At this stage, the goal is to gather a range of perceptions and opinions about race and the community, not to try to change anything or influence anyone. Mapping an array of experiences can help us to see which groups might work well together in coalitions and which issues are likely to be controversial or thorny.

As part of the assessment, priorities have to be established. Racism is ubiquitous, enduring, and complex, so it will not be possible to do everything at once. Based on the initial assessment, what are the most pressing community needs concerning racism? Which issues are likely to engage people, and which are likely to cause severe conflict and tension? Where are you and your organization positioned in all of this?

Helping professionals should evaluate the resources that they and their agencies can bring to the table, and should recognize their limits and liabilities. Working on racism in the community always will involve using assets and resources while also navigating and negotiating inevitable roadblocks and setbacks. We must be strategic, expect resistance, persist, and take a long-term view. We should work on issues that have a greater chance for success, at least initially, to generate the momentum that will allow for relationships and networks to develop and to achieve at least partial success that will motivate people to continue their efforts. The accompanying antiracism assessment tool can help human service workers begin this process.

As Kang (2015) has argued, all community work, including assessment and research, should be done collaboratively with community members. Professionals or outsiders should be cautious about taking an "expert" stance and assessing community needs from a distant vantage point. Community members should design and implement their own needs assessments in collaboration with professionals who bring assets, such as expertise, agency resources, and possible funding, to the process.

Working With Existing Groups and Organizations

When engaging in antiracism work, helping professionals understandably want to design their own change project. Usually, existing groups and organizations already are working on meaningful projects that they can join or affiliate with. Although antiracism depends on individuals making their own contributions and engaging in self-reflection, community change efforts are more successful if they are driven by coalitions of organizations and people.

Sometimes meaningful change has not begun, and helping professionals can initiate change. Before taking this step, however, they should carefully review what is in place already. Starting a project when other change efforts are in motion already can become competitive and even elicit bad feelings from those who are engaged in antiracism work already. This can dilute the effort and weaken the antiracism actions.

A major exception is when existing change efforts are stalled and not gaining traction. Perhaps a coalition has been co-opted and is being promoted for the sake of good public relations rather than confronting racism in the community in a meaningful way. Maybe the coalition reflects White power and the leadership and voices of BIPOC people are not seen or heard. When this is the case, creating a new structure or vehicle makes sense to move the process forward. One should assess possible actions carefully, because establishing alternative change projects can generate problems, such as competition or dilution of effort. Even so, meaningful social actions capable of making progress and achieving results are equally important.

Whether working with an existing group or establishing a new one, helping professionals can expect to encounter resistance, differences, tensions, and conflicts. These dynamics are found in any organization or coalition, and when the topic is racism, feelings run high, and these tendencies may become exacerbated. Just because people working together share a larger vision does not necessarily mean that their work together will be harmonious. Well-intentioned people bring their biases and interactional patterns to antiracism work. Well-meaning coalitions can still re-enact patterns of coloniality and White supremacy.

Whatever the situation, we must remain in the fray and work through disagreements, possibly using some of the racial dialogue mechanisms.

Working in Coalitions

Coalitions offer advantages in antiracism work. They bring together many individuals and organizations, multiplying the impact of any actions or initiatives. Coalitions provide legitimacy for a change project if they include a wide representation of stakeholders. An example is a coalition to improve the academic performance of children of color in the public school system, which could be reframed as improving the academic performance of schools serving children of color. Obvious core participants in this project are teachers, parents, and high school students. Civil rights and antiracism organizations are other likely members.

If business leaders, the Chamber of Commerce, religious organizations, the United Way, colleges, community colleges, and universities become involved as well, the coalition gains more magnitude and political stature. Politicians also can be members of coalitions, but this carries the risk of alienating their political rivals, who may be helpful to the change efforts at some time. We should approach with caution the notion of including politicians directly in coalition efforts, as they might seek to hijack the coalition's work to support their own political agendas.

Coalitions increase the amount of resources available and are able to develop effective communication and action networks. Coalitions can lessen the load on any one person or organization by pooling resources and sharing organizational burdens. By working together, coalition members learn from one another and develop relationships that help to sustain change efforts. There is also a critical mass of effort, a center of gravity of momentum that coalitions can muster, keeping things moving even when some groups or people are feeling burned out and de-energized. Coalitions, too, can model interracial, cross-cultural collaboration for the community. The multi-racial and ethnic coalition of communities of color against racist policies and practices in Seattle in the 1970s (Santos, 2002) is a successful example of such efforts.

Working in coalitions can present both challenges and advantages. Having more people and players can entail more work to develop a consensus. They must devote more time to the process and work to achieve a consistent level of knowledge and commitment to the coalition's goals. Differences of opinion about outcomes and tactics may lead to conflicts.

If participants reach a consensus that is acceptable to all, it may dilute the capacity of the coalition to subvert the existing social order. This risk increases as more mainstream and conservative organizations join the coalition. Although their participation can enhance the credibility of the coalition's work, it carries the risk of slowing or even co-opting the coalition's mission.

Multiracial coalitions are most effective when engaging in antiracism work. This ensures a range of perspectives and validates the importance of racism being tackled by White people along with people of color. Talking and working together cross-racially and cross-culturally is rare, which may necessitate structured dialogues and confidence and relationship-building exercises among group members. The coalition must strive not to re-create the racist imbalances of society at large but to ensure that people of color hold meaningful and influential leadership positions. If a coalition starts off predominantly White, chances are that it will remain that way.

Disruptive Strategies

A collaborative approach such as a coalition usually is the strategy of choice. In many situations, however, this method simply will not be effective. A blatant example existed in the southern United States between the end of the Civil War and the legislation of the Great Society. In this entrenched, openly racist, essentially caste system, collaboration was not possible. The existing local and state political and civic power systems were not open to meaningful partnership and compromise. Confrontation was the only means available to further the cause of civil rights.

In some communities today, the efforts of progressive people to redress racial imbalances through collaborative efforts have not met with success. Instead, they have encountered blatant segregation, along with racially targeted police harassment and school systems failing the needs of children of color. Thus, at times the tactics of disruption are necessary. Piven and Cloward (1993) have argued that throughout history, the most significant social changes have resulted from disruption and social unrest, not from compromise and collaboration. Disruption is one of the most effective means available to those without power and privilege.

If a class action lawsuit had not been initiated in the 1960s in Chicago, the Gautreaux program described in this chapter would not have been initiated. Lawsuits and other legal actions often have paved the way for significant and large-scale efforts to dismantle racism. Another disruptive tactic initiates boycotts against employers with intransigent records of racist practices.

Protests and sit-ins are effective approaches for gaining public attention and putting pressure on leaders to respond to concerns and demands. While effective, these methods also carry risks. Even peaceful demonstrators can get hurt and face the threat of arrest. Disruptive actions, too, can alienate potential supporters who are not comfortable with confrontational styles. And, though disruptive tactics can attract attention and garner publicity, the media might spin a negative narrative about the change project, which could alienate potential supporters and place those working for racial justice on the defensive. Prevalent and unmonitored social media may mean that goals and purposes of the protest may be co-opted and altered by those who are not organizers of the protest. In short, disruptive strategies are important devices in the toolkit of antiracism activists, but should be used judiciously and purposefully.

The Black Lives Matter (#BLM) movement, and the #BLM-organized public protests and rallies to confront systematic violence against African Americans, is a good example of purposeful and intentional use of disruptive strategies. #BLM essentially changed the practice of protest from a concrete-agenda model to a radical method of organizing to demand racial justice and to strive for liberation of all African Americans (Black Lives Matter, n.d.; Copeland, 2015).

Participatory Efforts

Antiracism activists can be involved directly in the community in many ways. Given the significance of political power, becoming involved politically is a vital facet of antiracism activity in the community. A person can do this in many ways: run for office, join a political party and become an active participant, contribute to political organizations that support antiracism, and hold meetings to brief and inform politicians about important issues. Running for office may seem daunting and takes time and resources, so it may not be appropriate for everyone. Still, running for city council or the school committee is feasible for many people and can have a significant impact on local policy decisions. And running for higher office, such as mayor or congressperson, usually follows service in a local elected capacity.

People and organizations can identify viable candidates—those committed to an antiracism platform—and work to get them elected. Antiracism activists can volunteer for appointed political positions, such as serving on human rights commissions or local planning boards. Nonpartisan political organizations need volunteers to ensure fair and free elections and political parties need help to help get out the vote at election time.

Other ways of furthering an antiracism agenda in the community include being a poll-watcher and driving people to the polls. Also, people can serve on agency boards, commissions, and coalitions. It is imperative that consumers be represented on the boards of health and human service agencies. Professionals and other citizens can volunteer to work with people targeted by racism through mentoring, recreational skill-building, and relationship-building programs.

At times, people in the helping professions can take a direct leadership role in community efforts, and at other times they can more effectively identify someone else to take this role. For example, helping professionals may have formed a relationship with a volunteer on their agency's advisory board who is vice president of a local bank and has indicated a strong commitment to antiracism ideals and principles. Encouraging this board member to take a high-profile role in community-wide antiracism efforts can be productive. Health and human service workers may be expected to advocate for progressive policies, but having a bank official take a leadership role in antiracism projects offers a different type of legitimacy and credibility.

Antiracism policies are not the only goal of direct community change efforts. As already discussed in this chapter, changing the way people think about racism and about the community represents a significant intervention. Art projects, such as murals or exhibits, can draw attention to issues of antiracism. Writing workshops and poetry presentations serve this function as well. Even a well-placed letter to the editor of a local newspaper or an op-ed piece can create a ripple of reflection. Planning inclusive community-wide events and celebrations are other venues for antiracism activists. Conferences and workshops can bring attention to issues of racism while serving as forums to generate creative ideas for addressing social inequities.

CONCLUSION

Millville is one example of how racism is manifested in a community. As with racism in other domains, this fictional town represents the concrete, institutional, and structural manifestation of racism in the community. All levels of race and racism intersect with personal and social identities.

Given the complexity of how racism is manifested in communities, we recommend four domains of intervention: engaging in public dialogue; reconstructing inclusive community narratives; intervening directly to ameliorate the structural manifestations of racism; and working to generate and utilize community resources, assets, and capital. Helping professionals can engage in antiracism work in the community in a number of ways, beginning with assessment and prioritization. This can be expanded to working with coalitions, political activities, and making direct social, interpersonal, and artistic contributions.

Antiracism work at the community level involves understanding all facets of racism, past and present, and the ability to intervene with multiple systems at many levels. As daunting as this may seem, helping professionals can contribute in many ways to create inclusive and equitable communities. Ultimately, when it comes to dismantling racism, we must have a national and international perspective even though most of our meaningful actions and activities will take place at the community level.

EXERCISE 10.1 Mapping Your Community

Consider these questions about the community where you are currently living or where you grew up.

1. Which indigenous nations or tribes historically resided in this geographic community? How is their heritage recognized (or not recognized)?
2. When did different ethnic and racial groups arrive in the community, and what were their reasons for moving there?
3. What jobs were available in the community when specific ethnic and racial groups moved in?
4. Did ethnic and racial group members remain in the neighborhoods where they originally settled, or have they moved to new neighborhoods?
   - How would you characterize relationships among the different ethnic and racial groups in your community?
   - What ethnic and racial groups are represented in local city government, and which are not represented (e.g., mayor, selectmen, city councilors, school committee members, appointed officials)?
   - What major businesses are in your community, and what are their ethnic and racial staffing patterns? Are there differences between higher and lower status positions?
   - Who are considered the "civic elite" in your community, and what ethnic and racial groups do they represent?
   - What challenges in your community hinder antiracism work and progress toward social justice?
   - What assets does your community have that further racial equity, justice, and reconciliation?

EXERCISE 10.2 Community Walk Through

Walk (or if this is not feasible, ride a bicycle or drive) with a notebook through the community where you work or live. Imagine that you are viewing it as a news reporter. Jot down your impressions every few minutes. In addition, you may take photos to capture your impression of the community and later jot down reflection notes for this exercise.

What do you notice about the streets? Are they pedestrian and wheelchair friendly? What kinds of buildings do you see and what kind of condition are they in? What stores and services are visible? Are there people on the street? What are some things that you notice about them—age, what they are doing, gender, ethnicity/race, how they are dressed.

Are there public spaces where people can congregate? Are there parks and other recreational areas? What can you see that connects you with natural beauty? What makes you feel healthy or unhealthy when in the community?

How do you feel in different parts of the community? Are there places where you feel safe or less safe? What do you make of this? Do you notice a police presence? What do you notice about the interactions between residents and police? What makes you feel good about walking through your community? What would make you feel better?

Compare your journal entries with the results of the community mapping exercise.

REFERENCES

Alexander, M. (2010). *The new Jim Crow: Mass incarceration in the age of colorblindness.* The New Press.

Association of Community Organizations for Reform Now. (2002). *Separate and unequal: Predatory lending in America.* Author

Astor, M. (2018). Seven ways Alabama made it harder to vote. *The New York Times.* www.nytimes.com/2018/06/23/us/politics/voting-rights-alabama.html

Berman, A. (2015). *Give us the ballot: The modern struggle for voting rights in America.* Farrar, Straus & Giroux.

Beyer, S. (2020, April 2). How the U.S. government destroyed Black neighborhoods: Post-World War II urban renewal replaced thriving Black hubs with highways and public housing. *Catalyst.* https://catalyst.independent.org/2020/04/02/how-the-u-s-\

Black Lives Matter (n.d.). *About Black Lives Matter.* https://blacklivesmatter.com/about/

Boyd, G. (2001, July 31). *The drug war is the new Jim Crow.* American Civil Liberties Union.

Brennan Center for Justice. (2017). *Voting laws roundup 2017.* www.brennancenter.org/our-work/research-reports/voting-laws-roundup-2017

Bruney, D. (2020). *A very abbreviated history of the destruction of Black neighborhoods.* Esquire. www.esquire.com/news-politics/a32719786/george-floyd-protests-riots-black-comminity-destruction-history/?utm_campaign=esq-2020-tradetracker&utm_medium=affiliate&utm_source=tradetracker&utm_term=137180

Calhoun, M., & Bailey, N. (2005). Predatory lending: Undermining economic progress in communities of color. *Poverty & Race, 14*(1), 17–19.

Cohen, A. (2004, June 21). Indians face obstacles between the reservation and the ballot box. *The New York Times,* p. A18.

Cobb, J. (2018). *Voter suppression tactics in the age of Trump.* The New Yorker. www.newyorker.com/magazine/2018/10/29/voter-suppression-tactics-in-the-age-of-trump

Copeland, P. (2015). Let's get free: Social work and the movement for Black Lives. *Journal of Forensic Social Work, 5*(1–3), 3–19. http://doi.org/10.1080/1936928X.2015.1109397

Corcoran, K. E., Pettinicchio, D., & Young, J. T. N. (2015). Perceptions of structural injustice and efficacy: Participation in low/moderate/high-cost forms of collective action. *Sociological Inquiry, 85*(3), 429–461.

DiAngelo, R. (2018). *White fragility: Why it is so hard for white people to talk about racism.* Beacon Press.

Dovidido, J. F., Gaertner, S. L., Ufkes, E. G., Saguy, T., & Pearson, A. R. (2016). Included but invisible? The darker side of "we." *Social Issues and Policy Review, 10*(1), 6–46.

Driscoll, M. W., Reynolds, J. R., & Todman, L. C. (2015). Race related stress and African American life satisfaction: A test of the protective role of collective efficacy. *Journal of Black Psychology, 41*(5), 462–486.

Edsall, T. B. (2019, July 17). Integration vs. white intransigence. *The New York Times.* www.nytimes.com/2019/07/17/opinion/integration-politics.html

Ellen, I. G. (2008). Continuing isolation: Segregation in America today. In J. H. Carr & N. K. Kutty (Eds.), *Segregation: The Rising Costs for America,* (pp. 261–277). Routledge.

Etzioni, A. (1997). A new fourth: A national unity day? *Responsive Community, 7,* 6–8.

Famighetti, C., Melillo, A., & Perez, M. (2014). Election day long lines: Resource allocation. *Brennan Center for Justice at New York University School of Law.* https://www.brennancenter.org/publication/election-day-long-lines-resource-allocation

Fessler, P. (2020). Trump's calls for poll watchers raise fears about voter intimidation. NPR. www.npr.org/2020/09/30/918766323/trumps-calls-for-poll-watchers-raises-fears-about-voter-intimidation

Freiberg, F. (2019). Prove it! *Poverty and Race, 28*(4), 1–2, 7–8.

Firebaugh, G., & Farrell, C. R. (2016). Still large, but narrowing: The sizable decline in racial neighborhood inequality in Metropolitan America, 1980–2010. *Demography, 53*(1): 139–164.

Fritz, N. (2001, March). Electoral debacle: Our response. *Civil Liberties,* 2–6.

Gaumer, E., Jacobowitz, A., & Brooks-Gunn, J. (2014). Building ties: The social networks of affordable-housing residents. *Cityscape, 16*(3), 47–68.

Glantz, A., & Martinez, E. (2018, February 17). *Modern day redlining: How banks block people of color from home ownership.* The Chicago Tribune. www.chicagotribune.com/business/ct-biz-modern-day-redlining-20180215-story.html

Gonzalez, J., & Torres, J. (2011). *News for all the people: The epic story of race and the American media.* Verso.

Gordon, L. (1988). *Heroes in their own lives: The history and politics of family violence* (pp. 1880–1960). Viking.

Greene, S., Turner, M.A., & Gourevitch, R. (2018). *Racial residential segregation and neighborhood disparities.* U.S. Partnership on Mobility from Poverty.

Gurin, P., Sorensen, N., Lopez, G., & Nagda, B. A. (2014). Intergroup dialogue: Race still matters. In R. Bangs & L. Davis (Eds.), *Race and social problems: Restructuring inequality* (pp. 39–59). Springer-Verlag.

Gurin-Sands, C., Gurin, P., Nagda, B. A., & Osuna, S. (2012). Fostering a commitment to social action: How talking, thinking and feeling make a difference in intergroup dialogue. *Equity and Excellence in Education, 45*(1), 60–79.

Hakim, D., & Saul, S. (2020, October 9). *Trump told voters to 'watch' voting: His staff is more than watching.* The New York Times. www.nytimes.com/2020/10/09/us/politics/trump-campaign-poll-watch.html

Henneberger, J. (2015). False choices in housing policy. *Poverty & Race, 24*(5), 3–4.

Hochschild, A. (2016). *Strangers in their own land: Anger and mourning on the American right.* The New Press.

Jansson, B. (2015). *The reluctant welfare state: American social welfare policies: Past, present and future* (8th ed.). Cengage.

Julian, E. K. (2015). Inclusive communities financial institutions: Investing in a more ambitious vision for the future. *Poverty & Race, 24*(5), 1–2, 6, 11–12.

Kang, H.-K. (2010). *Cultural citizenship and immigrant community identity: constructing a multi-ethnic Asian American community.* LFB Scholarly Publishing, LLC.

Kang, H.-K. (2015). We're who we have been waiting for: Intergenerational community organizing for a healthy community. *Journal of Community Practice, 23*(1), 126–140.

Keels, M., Duncan, G. J., Deluca, S., Mendenhall, R., & Rosenbaum, J. (2005). Fifteen years later: Can residential mobility programs provide a long-term escape from neighborhood segregation, crime, and poverty? *Demography, 42*(1), 51–73.

Kleinmans, R., & Bolt, G. (2013). More than just fear: On the intricate interplay between perceived neighborhood disorder, collective efficacy and action. *Journal of Urban Affairs, 36*(3), 420–446.

Kneebone, E., & Holmes, N. (2016). *U.S. concentrated poverty in the wake of the Great Recession.* The Brookings Institute. www.brookings.edu/research/u-s-concentrated-poverty-in-the-wake-of-the-great-recession

Kretzman, J., & McKnight, J. P. (1996). Assets-based community development. *National Civic Review, 85*(4), 23–29.

Kwate, N. O. A. (2014). "Racism still exists": A public health intervention using racism "Countermarketing" outdoor advertising in a Black neighborhood. *Journal of Urban Health, 91*(5), 851–872.

Logan, J. R., & Stults, B. J. (2011). *The persistence of segregation in the metropolis: New findings from the 2010 census (Census Brief for Project US 2010).* Brown University. https://s4.ad.brown.edu/Projects/Diversity/Data/Report/report2.pdf

Manduca, R., & Sampson, R. J. (2019, April 16). Punishing and toxic neighborhood environments independently predict the intergenerational social mobility of black and white children. Proceedings of the National Academy of Scientists. https://doi.org/10.1073/pnas.1820464116

Massey. (2016). Residential segregation is the linchpin of racial stratification. *City & Community, 15*(1), 4–7.

Massey, D. S., & Denton, N. A. (1993). *American apartheid: Segregation and the making of the underclass.* Harvard University Press.

McIlwain, C. D., & Caliendo, S. M. (2014). Mitt Romney's racist appeals: How race was played in the 2013 presidential election. *American Behavioral Scientist, 58*(9), 1157–1168.

McKnight, J. L. (1997). A 21st-century map for healthy communities and families. *Families in Society, 78*(2), 117–127.

Metzgar, J. (2016, March 14). *Misrepresenting the White working class: What the narrating class gets wrong.* Working Class Perspectives. https://workingclassstudies.wordpress.com/2016/03/14/misrepresenting -the-white-working-class-what-the-narrating-class-gets-wrong

Miller, J. (1999). *Holyoke at the crossroads: Family, ethnicity and community in a de-industrialized small city.* Proceedings of the 13th Conference on the Small City and Regional Community (pp. 277–286). Center for the Small City.

Miller, J. (2001). Family and community integrity. *Journal of Sociology and Social Welfare, 28*(4), 23–44.

Miller, J. (2002). I do what I write about and I write about what I do: A narrative interview with Richard A. Cloward. *Reflections, 8*(1), 44–64.

Miller, J. (2012). *Psychosocial capacity building in response to disasters.* Columbia University Press.

Miller, J., & Schamess, G. (2000). The discourse of denigration and the creation of other. *Journal of Sociology and Social Welfare, 27*(3), 39–62.

Overton, S. A. (2005). Stealing liberty. *The Crisis, 112*(1), 15–18.

Petrosino, C., & Pace, J. (2015). Social cohesion, collective efficacy, and the response of the Cape Verdean community to hate crime: Learning a new reality. *American Behavioral Scientist, 59*(13), 1681–1697.

Piven, F. F., & Cloward, R. A. (1993). *Regulating the poor: The functions of public welfare (updated edition).* Vintage.

Polikoff, A. (2004). Racial equality and the Black ghetto. *Poverty & Race, 13*(6), 1–2, 8–12.

Putnam, R. D. (2000). *Bowling alone: The collapse and revival of American community.* Simon & Schuster.

Raskin, J. (2004). From slave republic to constitutional democracy: The continuing struggle for the right to vote. *Poverty & Race, 13*(6), 3–4, 13–18.

Reimann, N. (2020). *Report: Trump campaign has videotaped Philadelphia voters in potentially illegal voter intimidation.* Forbes. www.forbes.com/sites/nicholasreimann/2020/10/22/report-trump-campaign-has -videotaped-philadelphia-voters-in-potentially-illegal-voter-intimidation/?sh=18b3c959a1d6

Rosenbaum, J. E. (1995). Changing the geography of opportunity by expanding residential choice: Lessons from the Gautreaux program. *Housing Policy Debate, 6*(1), 231–269.

Rosenbaum, J. E., Popkin, S. J., Kaufman, J. E., & Rusin, J. (1991). Social integration of low-income Black adults in middle-class White suburbs. *Social Problems, 38*(4), 448–461.

Salomon, D. (2019). *Systemic inequality: Displacement, exclusion, and segregation.* Center for American Progress. www.americanprogress.org/issues/race/reports/2019/08/07/472617/systemic-inequality-displacement -exclusion-segregation/

Sampson, R. J., Morenoff, J. D., & Earls, F. (1999). Beyond social capital: Spatial dynamics of collective efficacy for children. *American Sociological Review, 64*, 633–660.

Sampson, R. J., Raudenbush, S., & Earls, F. (1997). Neighborhoods and violent crime: A multilevel study of collective efficacy. *Science, 277*, 918–924.

Samuels, B. (2014). "Nowhere to live safe": Moving to peace and safety. *Poverty and Race, 23*(6), 1–2, 11.

Santos, B. (2002). *Ham bows, not hot dogs! Memoirs of a savvy Asian American Activist.* Chin Music Press.

Seidman, I. E. (1991). *Interviewing for qualitative research: A guide for researchers in education and the social sciences.* Teachers College Press.

Semega, J. L., Fontenot, K. R., & Kollar, M. A. (2017). Income and poverty in the United States: 2016. Current Population Reports. United States Census Bureau. https://census.gov/content/dam/Census/ library/publications/2017/demo/P60-259.pdf

Sengupta, S. (2000, November 3). Felony costs voting rights for a lifetime in 9 states. *The New York Times,* p. A18. http://nyti.ms/2ihvHSP

Stewart, T. L., Latu, I. M., Branscombe, N. R., & Denney, H. T. (2010). Yes we can! Prejudice reduction through seeing (inequality) and believing (in social change). *Psychological Science, 21*(11), 1557–1562.

Tach, L. (2014). Diversity, inequality, and microsegregation: Dynamics of inclusion and exclusion in a racially and economically diverse community. *Cityscape, 16*(3), 13–46.

The Washington Post (2020). The racist anti-vote effort by Florida Republicans hits a new low. Author. www .washingtonpost.com/opinions/the-racist-anti-vote-effort-by-florida-republicans-hits-a-new -low/2020/09/27/5d5a7450-fe9d-11ea-8d05-9beaaa91c71f_story.html

Thrush, G., & Medina, J. (2020, October 12). California republican party admits it placed misleading ballot boxes around state. *The New York Times*. https://www.nytimes.com/2020/10/12/us/politics/california -gop-drop-boxes.html

Waldman, M. (2015). How the Supreme Court made a mess of our voting system. In D. R. Reiner, J. Lyons, E. Opsal, M. Terrell, & L. Glaser (Eds.), *Democracy and justice: Collected writings,* (Vol. *VIII,* pp. 10–14). Brennan Center for Social Justice.

Weiser, W., & Opsal, E. (2015). The state of voting in 2014. In D. R. Reiner, J. Lyons, E. Opsal, M. Terrell, & L. Glaser (Eds.), *Democracy and justice: Collected writings,* (Vol. *VIII,* pp. 6–9). Brennan Center for Social Justice.

Wilson, W. J. (2011). *When work disappears: The world of the new urban poor.* Vintage.

CHAPTER 11

Racially Just Agencies and Organizations

INTRODUCTION

Most helping professionals work for agencies and organizations. They represent the organizations for which they work, and their workplaces give meaning and direction to their professional efforts. Agencies, through their missions, charters, policies, and practices, define the parameters of what workers can and cannot do, and by paying salaries and offering resources, they make possible the work of helping professionals.

Health and mental health clinics, family service agencies, counseling centers, and hospitals are the junctions where clients, workers, and services intersect. None of these sites are immune to the many forms of racism described in this book. In fact, health, human service, and educational facilities emulate the dynamics of racism in society at large. They encode the power of coloniality and historical legacies of White supremacy in many ways: Who has power and who feels as if they belong; what is considered good professional practice; what services are offered and how they are offered; what models of treatment are sanctioned or not taken seriously. As Ahmed (2009) says, when people of color are part of the staff of agencies that have not excavated and examined their core practices of Whiteness, they are treated like "guests" or a commodity in a system of racial capitalism. In either case, people of color are expected to be grateful for being a part of the organization. Thus, as important as it is for every human service professional to work individually to dismantle racism, equally important is to act collectively to decolonize our organizations. Having a strategy for pursuing social justice will ultimately lead to greater organizational effectiveness and better services to consumers (Barak, 2000; Donner & Miller, 2005). Workplaces tend to be more ethnically and racially mixed than racially segregated neighborhoods (Donner & Miller, 2005). While this situation offers both opportunities for interracial cooperation and understanding and perhaps racial justice, it also poses challenges, particularly for Black, Indigenous, and people of color (BIPOC) staff who are more likely to be aware of assumptions, structures and patterns of White supremacy than their White colleagues. There is also a heavy emotional toll for BIPOC staff working or teaching at traditionally White institutions, which not only harms workers but also weakens organizational respect and cohesion (Anthym & Tuitt, 2019; Jaurique et al., 2018). In this chapter, we examine how people in the helping professions can work to make racial justice central to their organizations. We consider what becoming a racially just institution means and reflect on the areas an organization should think about to make significant progress toward this target. The chapter also briefly considers different types of organizations in relation to racism and delves into the necessary tasks upon which organizations seeking to become antiracism entities can embark, and offers tools for tracking progress.

HOW TO FRAME COMMITMENTS TO CHANGE ORGANIZATIONS?

There are many different types of human service organizations. Some were established to serve communities of color and not only have a mission statement that directs services to certain communities but also have significant leadership and representation from members of those communities on their board, administration, and in their staffing patterns. These organizations may have a non-Eurocentric philosophy, such as an Afrocentric orientation, or a non-Western–centered approach while emphasizing sensitivity and cultural competence.

Antiracism is often a part of the agency's mission. Exemplifying such an organization is the Martin Luther King, Jr. Community Center in Springfield, Massachusetts, which serves families in a catchment area that is predominantly African American and Latino. Another is the Asian Counseling and Referral Service in Seattle. Both agencies were established to offer social, educational, vocational, health, and recreational services with specific populations in mind, using models of service provision that stress cultural responsiveness and a commitment to confronting oppression.

In a sense, these are social service organizations created in opposition to White European hegemony. However, even these organizations grapple with matters of diversity, including issues of class and immigration status, as well as prejudices and biases between ethnic groups. In addition, funding sources stipulate the nature of service provision, which can put pressure on ethnically focused agencies to compromise their principles and values and lead to unwillingly or inadvertently emulating discriminatory practices found in mainstream agencies.

But most human service agencies, social service organizations, college counseling centers and hospitals are "mainstream" organizations that are supposed to serve everyone but as we discussed in Chapter 5, they have histories and current practices of racialized discrimination. Leadership in such organizations is often predominantly White, and power, philosophies of providing services and care, and the overall assumptions and worldviews reflect Whiteness. Chapter 5 considered the differential impact that such organizations have on clients of color; they also are experienced very differently by White staff and staff of color. We will call such organizations traditional White organizations (TWO). In this chapter we will focus on TWOs, which employ the majority of human service workers.

TWOs often respond to concerns about racism by taking a "color-blind" approach; meaning that everyone should be treated the same. A color-blind approach minimizes the embedded racism and racialized power and privilege that continues to exist in the organization (Block, 2016). Another frame is that of a *multicultural organization*. A multicultural organization seeks to value all consumers and employees, attempting to be responsive to the varying cultures that are part of its human mosaic. There is an emphasis on understanding and respecting all cultures. However, by not contesting the structural, institutional, and programmatic means of power and privilege, it not only leaves institutional racism in place but creates the appearance of being an agency committed to social justice (Block, 2016). An *antiracism organization* goes further and acknowledges the destructive power of racism in society, which it attempts to ameliorate, maintaining a critical stance toward its own organizational racism. An antiracism organization includes a commitment to multiculturalism but goes beyond this to examine inequities of power and privilege in addition to building cultural responsiveness and competency. We intentionally use the term *antiracism* rather than *antiracist*. The former implies a commitment to dismantling racism, which has dimensions that are institutional and social as well as attitudinal and behavioral. Using the term *antiracist* carries the risk that change efforts will be directed toward trying to uncover or reform "racists," which can lead to severe conflict while leaving important areas for examination and change unattended (K. Basham, personal communication, March 24, 1994).

There are two limitations of an antiracism framework. One is that it does not articulate the central problem of White supremacy in the organization. Racism derives from White supremacy, it is not simply a set of beliefs or behaviors; as we have argued, White supremacy permeates every part of U.S. society and is replicated in all of its organizations. It is structural but also central to organizational culture (The Centre for Community Organizations [CCO], 2019). White supremacy is a legacy of coloniality and thus calls for an active process of decolonization, rather than simply working toward not being racist. A second critique of an antiracism framework is that it is against something, but what is the positive vision that guides organizational change? We will argue that a truly inclusive organization, equitable for both staff and clients, should be viewed as a Racially Just Organization (RJO) and we describe what that looks like in this chapter.

HOW RACISM IS MANIFESTED IN MAINSTREAM SOCIAL SERVICE ORGANIZATIONS

As with any durable inequality (Tilly, 1998), racism is emulated in all mainstream agencies and can suffuse any part of that organization. Although some organizations overtly discriminate against people because of their race and ethnicity, this is comparatively rare in the United States today. Much more common are organizations that collude with racism by making choices, such as about what funding to pursue, which politicians to work with, which clients to serve, who is hired to serve them, what theories and assumptions shape what is offered. Similarly, racism can be maintained by how services are delivered, having predominantly White executives and boards, and unexamined policies and practices that are considered "normal." We look at some commonplace policies and practices that are problematic.

Policies

Most policies are implicitly rather than overtly racist. Chapter 5 explored how transportation policies and housing policies, for example, may seem to be race neutral yet promulgate programs and practices that serve to deepen racial divisions and inequalities. The same is true for health and human service agencies.

As mentioned, many mainstream agencies strive to be "color blind," viewing this as a commitment to fairness and equity (Block, 2016). But such an approach leaves in place the implicit racism that is internalized by White managers, supervisors, and workers and the structural racism that is externalized (Block, 2016). Thus, fewer people of color applying for jobs are called in for interviews; are hired, promoted, or receive positive performance reviews; and are represented in the higher management positions and on boards of directors (Block, 2016). A color blind approach also ignores the microaggressions that occur between colleagues as well as the macroaggressions that are encoded in policies, such as a directive that all staff are to speak in English only (Rocco et al., 2014).

Recent scholarship has considered "White supremacy culture" (CCO, 2019). Implicit in this culture is the belief that the way that White people do things is the right way and that people of color-clients and staf-need to conform to this. White supremacy culture is characterized by:

- ▶ Focusing on the person rather than the systemic and structural aspects of racism and White supremacy, which therefore problematizes people of color who either do not feel that they fit in or engage in resistance to these systems.
- ▶ Emotional tone policing and setting standards of "civility" and discourse reflecting White, middle-class values. Blackwell (2018) writes about how people of color are often judged by White people in organizations as being too loud or too quiet, too direct or indirect, too passionate or too disengaged.
- ▶ Concentrating power with White people and having hierarchical systems of functioning that minimize the input, agency, and efficacy of BIPOC staff.
- ▶ Creating an environment where White people feel more at home and comfortable than people of color.
- ▶ Fear of openly discussing racism and White supremacy and a wariness of disagreement and conflict.
- ▶ Defensive responses when racism and White supremacy are called out.

A question to be considered is: Do the agency's policies and structure continue racial inequities, whether intentional or not, or does the agency actively attempt to do anything to dismantle racism? We consider two examples: hiring and retention, as well as policies for clients.

Hiring and Retention

As described in the previous chapters, people of color face many more hurdles and barriers in their efforts to become members of the helping professions. If hiring policies of a predominantly White agency consist merely of placing an advertisement in a local newspaper for an opening, will this result in more racial and ethnic diversity within the agency? The chances are that it will not. One issue to consider is who reads the local newspaper or has access to a computer to check its website. If the newspaper readership is weighted toward White readers, the chances of recruiting an applicant pool of people of color are lessened.

A frequent way that people hear about jobs is through friends and colleagues. If the staff is predominantly White, the people who learn about the opening most likely will be White as well. And it always helps to have someone inside of an agency advocating for a job applicant, so the default drift of a predominantly White organization will be to have White employees advocating for White applicants. It also helps to have people on the inside who can give an applicant the "inside scoop" about an agency, which can help the applicant prepare for interviews. And some BIPOC applicants are wary of joining predominantly White organizations where they may feel isolated or tokenized.

As we have considered in previous chapters, implicit racism influences the choices, decisions, and behaviors of White people in many contexts. This includes hiring and there has been much research, often using paired testers of different races, demonstrating that people with White-sounding names are more likely to be called in for an interview than people with African American–sounding names, even when their qualifications are equal (Block, 2016).

And if a person of color is invited for an interview, who will conduct the interview? Who will make the hiring decisions? Unless this is considered carefully, the tendency will be to have a staff that recreates itself racially and ethnically as well as culturally. Social groups are inclined toward feeling more comfortable and inclusive with people whom they perceive as similar.

What qualifications are being sought for the job, and will people of color have attained education and experience comparable to that of White people? This question can make some people feel uneasy, for it brings into the forefront the issue of qualifications and racism. One of the ways that White privilege works in society is to increase the social and educational capital of White people, so they are more likely to present as applicants with "better" qualifications, although as we said earlier, even when qualifications are equal White applicants have implicit advantages. It was not a "race neutral" society that led to this. It is the cumulative result of institutional racism and social privileges favoring White people. To then approach hiring as a race-neutral enterprise favors people who have had race advantages all of their lives.

Now this, of course, raises other issues. For one, consumers must be served by skilled, competent people. We are not suggesting that agencies forego issues of competence in favor of a blanket policy of racial diversity. The choices are seldom either/or, yet the "competency" argument often is cited as a justification for not considering more applicants of color. If many clients are people of color and they are receiving services from predominantly White clinicians, would it not be in their interests to have more clinicians of color on staff who can empathize with their experiences of racism more readily, are more likely to understand them culturally, and also can serve as positive role models? Perhaps a person who can fulfill these expectations has had less actual job experience than a White candidate for the job. On paper, the White applicant might look better, but in practice, reality is more complex.

We have raised these questions and issues to illustrate how a "race-neutral" hiring policy actually can collude with a system of preferences that favors White people and may diminish the capacity of an agency to best serve its clients. This conundrum has no easy solutions, but even just considering the problem can lead to an agency rethinking its overall recruitment strategy, which can make a difference in the long run. The agency can place advertisements in local neighborhood newspapers. Its employees can ask colleagues of color if they know any interested applicants. They can pay attention to the racial/ethnic composition of the search committees. The job qualifications can be expanded beyond the usual academic and work expectations to include intimate familiarity with cultural practices or the experiences of racial targeting and marginalization. Another strategy is to engage in cluster hiring, bringing in cohorts of BIPOC workers which would address the issues of isolation, tokenism, and racial capitalism.

Staffing issues go well beyond hiring, as retention is just as important. Creating systems for mentoring younger and newer workers of color is essential. Because many workers of color are assigned to some of the agency's most challenging cases, the agency should monitor their caseloads to prevent burnout. In-service training can help to increase the bank of social and professional capital that some workers lacked before joining the organization. The comfort level of co-workers and the atmosphere of the workplace make a difference as well. As we have described in previous chapters, bridging differences, embracing diverse cultural styles, and promoting an interracial and ethnic dialogue require a conscious effort, which many people have not experienced. It is also important to be sensitive to the phenomenon of "stereotype threat" (Steele, 2011), which is heightened in organizations espousing a color-blind ideology, which de-emphasizes racism (Block, 2016).

But even more should be done to support retention of staff of color. A common dynamic is that staff of color have more informal demands placed on them; for example, mentoring and supporting other BIPOC staff or being overstretched by assigning large caseloads of clients of color. There is also the additional burden of emotional labor for BIPOC staff (Kawaii-Bogue, 2020). This comes from feeling responsible for clients of color who are not being well treated by the organization and society at large as well as having to deal with their own experiences of racism and repeated microaggressions.

Agencies also must consider where staff members of color are placed within the organization. A common staffing pattern for mainstream agencies, which have made an effort to recruit a diverse staff, is to have many staff members of color clustered in lower-status jobs or working within teams that are more marginalized and less central to the agency's mission. With large agencies, patterns of segregation can emerge, replicating the segregation patterns of society. What is often most challenging for mainstream agencies is to have significant racial and ethnic diversity among the supervisory and management team and in leadership positions on the board of directors.

According to Leong (2012), hiring people of color to increase diversity within the organization often occurs as the result of racial capitalism described in Chapter 2. What is important to determine is what version of diversity is being applied. Leong (2012) describes the "thin version of diversity" (p. 2169) as one where the outcome is an increase in the number of people of color hired. This version can very quickly offer an aesthetic accomplishment which can be highly appealing for leaders and clients of the organization. It has high social and monetary value and overall could enhance the worth of the organization. However, just because there are additional people of color does not ensure their benefit. In other words, it benefits the TWO more than the people of color who were hired. With the thin version of diversity, the actual causes of racial inequity and barriers to racial equity are not addressed and remain buried beneath the superficial progress of employing more people of color. Additionally, this type of diversity relies on people of color presenting themselves in stereotypical versions of their identity in order to warrant their taking up space in the organization. People of color who do not possess stereotypical attributes (e.g., articulation of language that is associated more with White middle-class groups; phenotypes typically associated with Whites such as light skin, straight hair, blonde hair, blue eyes) may not be seen as valuable on a racial capitalist market because they do not enhance the "look" of diversity, even though their lived experience and perspective is that of a person of color (Ford, 2009). Similarly, when organizations employ a numbers-driven goal of diversity, some racial groups, such as Asians and Asian Americans, may possess less value because of their perceived "overrepresentation" in fields that are more lucrative and highly desirable.

There is another option. Agencies can also attempt to apply a "thick version of diversity" (Leong, 2012, p. 2169). Here, there is an understanding that the value is not based just on numbers but on the ability for cross-racial interactions and relationships to occur fostering inclusivity which benefits all races. The thick version also includes an intention to remedy the discriminatory acts of past hiring practices by employing more people of color. Both versions, thick and thin, require hiring more people of color, thus superficially appearing to accomplish the same. However, the "thick" version has as its goal real, empirical progress toward racial equity, justice, and inclusion of people of color in all aspects of the organization.

Client Policies

The client policies that are considered race neutral can cause difficulties in practice for people of color. Most organizations have policies about eligibility, expectations for client conduct, and protocols and methods for helping people. All should be examined for possible racial and cultural biases. Racism and cultural bias can manifest themselves in many ways. Pervasive racial and ethnic stereotypes can influence expectations for clients as well as their actual treatment (we consider these dynamics in clinical settings in Chapter 12). This, in turn, can make clients feel as if they are misunderstood, invalidated, and experiencing racial microaggressions. In response, clients become more guarded and defensive or even terminate their involvement with the agency, which will fulfill stereotypes that they indeed are "less motivated." Missing appointments and showing up late for appointments can be seen as indicators of client reactions to unexamined racism. As with much of racism, individuals are blamed for their "irresponsible" behaviors rather than considering the structural factors, such as those described in Chapter 5, that create barriers for BIPOC clients. For instance, inadequate or unreliable public transportation can affect the ability of clients to make it to appointments on time.

Theoretical biases can lead to misunderstanding clients of color or even pathologizing them. Eurocentric biases about human behavior and conduct can cause clients to feel unwelcome or unfairly judged. Attendance policies can contain biases. Some agencies give primacy to individuals, and confidentiality rules discourage seeing clients accompanied by relatives and friends. This might be consistent with many European cultural orientations but is less compatible with cultural orientations for people of color from Asia, Africa, and Latin America. As explored further in Chapter 12, cultural biases can influence expectations about disclosing intimate information; expressing emotions; internal family roles, relationships, and hierarchy; and typical responses to authority.

Seemingly minor environmental factors can make clients feel welcome or unwelcome. The layout of waiting areas, where the receptionist sits, who the receptionist is, and their demeanor all contribute to client comfort or discomfort. Are chairs clustered together to accommodate family groups, or are they all lined up against the wall? The type of artwork displayed, the magazines in the waiting room, what music is playing, or what TV channel is on—all serve as markers to clients, conveying information about the culture of the agency and who is being welcomed. In addition to these physical factors, the language spoken by the receptionist and clinicians has a big impact on client trust and comfort.

Interpersonal Relationships

Within agencies that have made a commitment to diversity, interpersonal relationships often require attention. In our consultation work with agencies, we have found, not surprisingly, that people do not trust one another automatically and many misunderstandings and miscommunications arise. These disagreements can lead to open conflict or workers walking on eggshells, monitoring what they say, or retreating from social interactions. This atmosphere is not conducive to effective teamwork and high staff morale.

Many people have not had a lot of practice working closely with people from different racial and ethnic backgrounds. Every staff member has their own social identity; as discussed in Chapter 7, social identity is fluid and contextual and is co-constructed by interactions with colleagues. The wider the range of social identities, the more complex the interpersonal relationships become. Some White staff members have not thought a great deal about their White privilege or internalized stereotypes, which can lead to difficult and painful interactions for people of color. Some people of color are wary or mistrustful of White people and approach interactions guardedly. Microaggressions are likely to occur, further fueling tensions and more alienation. As a result, cliques and factions may form, widening divisions and inhibiting collaboration.

Therefore, organizations must actively and proactively initiate discussion and dialogue groups along the lines recommended in Chapter 9. In the workplace, these dialogues should not be open-ended considerations of social identity, group membership, and intergroup relations but, instead, should be grounded in a consideration of the agency's mission, services to clients, working conditions, and ability of employees to effectively work together. Employees may be reluctant to share too much personally and emotionally in a work environment, and this should be respected. Despite this hesitation to disclose, dialogues still can include a myriad of issues connected to racial and ethnic differences and the pervasiveness of racism in society. Thus, we must consider the socioeconomic contexts that have an impact on clients and workers alike.

It is also important to have "affinity groups" where staff members are given opportunities to meet with other people sharing their social identities to talk about race and racism within the organization. In mainstream agencies and predominantly White spaces, it is likely that White cultural patterns and norms will be dominant (Blackwell, 2018). White people can often choose to engage or not engage in conversations about race and racism, a luxury unavailable for people of color (Blackwell, 2018). Affinity groups can offer spaces for BIPOC employees where they have the freedom to be themselves and do not have to conform to or perform for White people (Blackwell, 2018).

Affinity groups are helpful for people of all racial and ethnic identities. For example, there can be different affinity groups for White staff and staff of color, or subdivided even further by gender or other social identity markers. White affinity groups provide spaces for White people to self-reflect about racism and to support one another, without the pressure of performing for people of color while also protecting people of color from exposure to stereotypes and microaggressions. Blitz and Kohl (2012) describe how one agency offered structured opportunities in three affinity groups—White, men of color, and women of color. They found that those in the White group initially had difficulty with the term *White* affinity group and that the group worked more effectively to explore racism within the agency if their work was shared with the affinity groups of color. All three groups explored issues such as overt and covert White privilege within the organization and their independent work eventually led to better cross-racial collaboration. White people often fear that affinity groups will divide people within an organization but by offering homogeneous spaces, agencies may actually increase the comfort and well-being of all staff, which can ultimately lead to both greater social cohesion as well as contributing to greater diversity within the organization (Blackwell, 2018).

Exercises such as those suggested in many of the previous chapters can help staff members get in touch with their own experiences with people from different backgrounds, whether colleagues or clients, and reflect on their internalized attitudes, fears, biases, and stereotypes. This can be connected to systemic organizational racism that is institutionalized. Developing ground rules and norms for talking about these issues is crucial and may carry over from a discussion group to the agency as a whole.

Organizational Power

Organizational power probably is the most challenging issue for mainstream agencies. Although many organizations make well-intentioned efforts to diversify their staff and to offer training in cultural competency, the challenge of examining and shifting organizational power is exceedingly difficult. Power inequities are at the heart of racism. Therefore, it is not surprising to encounter great resistance to redistributing power, along with organizational inertia. Yet without a meaningful effort to consider power and decision-making within an organization, there is little likelihood of organizational transformation.

What does reordering power mean and how can it be achieved? In most mainstream agencies, power is manifested in many ways. Clients have the power to go elsewhere, file complaints, or not follow service plans. Receptionists can bend the rules and make it easier or more difficult for clients to access the program, and administrative assistants can rush or delay critical assignments. Line workers have the power to organize collectively, to work more slowly, and to censor what they share with their supervisors and management. Supervisors have the power to offer inducements or disincentives and to evaluate workers. Middle managers evaluate supervisors and make decisions about policies.

But the higher one looks at the pyramid of formal power in an agency, the Whiter it looks. The highest levels of power involve program directors, executive directors, and boards of directors. They have the most authority for determining the organization's mission, ensuring its fiscal viability, setting the terms and conditions of employment, and hiring and firing staff members. If the upper echelons of management exercise their power in a hierarchical and arbitrary fashion, it results in low morale and high staff turnover. When this happens, line staff may organize and resist formally, but more often informally. But even when there is the veneer of fairness, of color blindness, the basic structure of unequal relationships remains; even if staff acquiesces on the surface, there is underlying disharmony and services suffer.

Thus, an organization committed to racial justice should consider all of the ways by which power is exercised and where it resides, and be prepared to make changes and adjustments. This does not mean that the executive director necessarily has to step down, but it does imply reconsidering how decisions are made and working toward power sharing among more of the agency's stakeholders. For example, in hiring, who makes the ultimate decision? If the executive director or board of directors makes the final decision, how much influence will the search committee or the middle managers have? When considering the office waiting room, who makes decisions about the decor and seating arrangements? Will the receptionist and line workers be part of this decision-making? Will clients?

In our view, a racially just organization implies that those in the agency will take care in all decisions to include people of color in a meaningful way and recognize and avoid institutionalized racist patterns, implicit White privilege, and unexamined racial biases and stereotypes influencing the outcome. There should be an assumption that racism is prevalent and proactive measures taken to lessen its impact. Value should be placed on hearing and validating the voices of those in the minority (Stewart, 2018). It is also important to be wary of pushing for a consensus that does not reflect the diversity of identities and opinions in the room (Stewart, 2018). And given the Whitening of mainstream agencies at the higher ends of the organizational staffing pattern, power and decision-making should be shared and decentralized wherever and whenever possible.

One direct way to achieve this is to empower work groups and committees. Another is to engage in open and honest discussions about power and decision-making as part of an organization's antiracism commitment, including when setting future goals. While this often meets with resistance and, in the short-term, White people may resent their diminished influence within the organization, establishing clarity about who will make decisions, who will be consulted, and what criteria will be used is ultimately helpful to everyone because the agency will be a fairer, more just, and less oppressive place to work and clients will receive superior services.

Another pattern in many mainstream agencies is that there are more clients who are people of color than agency workers. Thus, seeking clients' ideas and forming client advisory groups are ways to ensure that people of color have input into the agency's decisions and policies. Also, having some clients serve on the agency's board of directors is valuable. In this way, boards have more community representation as well as racial and ethnic diversity. Further, recruiting other community members, such as local business owners and professionals, promotes a spectrum of diverse community representation.

Setting numerical goals for boards eventually can result in more diversity. One author (Miller) worked with the board of a United Way organization that was virtually all White, despite serving a community with significant populations of people of color. This caused major community tensions and mistrust of the United Way by many people of color, as well as by progressive White people in the community. After sometimes tense discussions and power struggles, the White board of the organization eventually voted to ensure that at least a third of its members would be people of color. This was followed by hiring a man of color as executive director, the first non-White director of the agency, who was, in turn, followed by a woman of color as chief executive. The organization's standing with citizens and agencies of color in the community improved significantly and many more projects were funded that addressed racism and its consequences.

This example illustrates a power shift over time. Tensions between the organization and the community led to a vote to change the racial and ethnic representation of the board of directors. This resulted in hiring a person of color as the chief executive and reallocating funds. It also created a communitywide culture shift, as every agency receiving United Way funding was put on notice that serving communities of color was a priority. Every step of this process was marked by power struggles, yet the United Way achieved meaningful agency and communitywide change, set in motion by one vote of the board of directors.

Resources Devoted to Antiracism

A meaningful antiracism change initiative by organizations requires resources. A commitment without devoting sufficient resources is a Potemkin village—a shell of a commitment perhaps made more for good public relations than a meaningful pledge for change. Racial justice work requires many different kinds of resources and while all agencies have their limits, a realistic discussion about what resources are necessary and what resources are available is an important step when making a racial justice commitment.

Staff time is one precious resource in this process. The time spent in meetings, planning initiatives, and engaging in dialogues and training sessions requires a major agency commitment. If staff members are not given sufficient time to participate in these activities, they will not be invested in the outcome or will become disillusioned or burned out, or their antiracism work could clash with their other agency responsibilities, including seeing clients. Thus, middle and upper managers, as well as board members, should carve out time to partake in racial justice activities. This sends a strong message to the rest of the staff that the organization makes this issue a high priority. It is also crucial for White staff to actively participate in antiracism efforts. As mentioned, there is an identity tax on staff of color, who often have extra responsibilities such as offering linguistic and culturally tailored services to clients, through having to represent their ethnic–racial group on internal or community committees, and also are the ones who directly experience the stress of unresolved organizational racism. For antiracism efforts to be meaningful, all staff, but particularly White staff, need to be genuinely and authentically engaged in the process.

Agencies can demonstrate their commitment to antiracism by providing training resources, such as books and videos, and hiring facilitators and consultants. Other resources are needed as well: funding for outreach for hiring; money for mentoring, and other mechanisms designed for staff retention; and support for the continuing education of staff members, including pursuing credit-bearing degrees. Scholarship and fellowship money targeted to support training for students and workers of color are other examples of how resources can be assembled to support antiracism efforts.

Reallocating resources to support an antiracism commitment entails complex decision-making. Some programs may lose resources, and the staff members who operate them understandably will become uneasy as their assets are shifted and reprioritized. Board members who supported certain programs or who were comfortable with an existing agency culture may become perturbed. Supporters of the agency in the community (e.g., business leaders, politicians) also may become dismayed at the organization's shift in direction.

Funding bodies, including managed care organizations and insurance companies, may impose restraints that limit the amount of staff time available for antiracism work. Whatever the obstacles, working with staff, board members, and community supporters to explain and negotiate these changes is essential. And antiracism efforts must be linked to larger policy trends, by advocating and lobbying to change oppressive practices.

MODELS OF ORGANIZATIONAL CHANGE

When embarking on the road to becoming a racially just organization, a map can be useful. The map will help to track what has been accomplished and offer a route for forward progress. We suggest an audit tool for both of these purposes, after summarizing some developmental models of organizational movement toward becoming antiracism institutions that will help in assessing what next steps will be realistic.

Unfortunately, most models of how to become a racially just organization follow a linear, developmental sequence, in which attaining subsequent stages depends on having resolved prior stages. As with theories of individual racial development, these paradigms are too rigid, linear, and inflexible. An organization may not be involved entirely in one "stage" or another, and change does not necessarily follow a strict linear progression. Many developmental models describe organizational pathways to becoming multicultural, diverse, or anti-oppression and antiracism institutions (Golembiewski, 1995; Jackson & Hardiman, 1994; Jackson & Holvino, 1988; Minors, 1996; Sue et al., 1998; Valverde, 1998). Some stress diversity and multiculturalism, and others challenge racism and highlight social justice (Chesler, 1994). As we stated earlier, working toward multiculturalism without focusing on structural forms of racism, including unequal power and privileges, within the organization is insufficient and risks creating the illusion of meaningful change without the substance (Block, 2016). Sue et al. (1998) compared models of multicultural organizational development and extracted three metastages of development:

1. Overt (through outright hostility) or covert (through ignorance) dismissal or denial of diversity. These organizations are considered "monocultural": The centrality of Whiteness and Eurocentric norms are so embedded and "normal" that they are invisible and unquestioned. We would add that White privilege and power are not even named, let alone confronted.
2. Overt commitment to diversity, yet with many unexamined, unconscious, White (Eurocentric) male biases and assumptions. Structural forms of racism are often unaddressed.
3. Embracing and valuing diversity. It has become part of the organization's DNA, with a decentering of White race privilege and Eurocentric culture, metabolized by the organization and its staff. As important as this is, if the essential power structures remain unchanged and White supremacist culture unexcavated, then this is insufficient.

Becoming a racially just organization at minimum involves these activities:

▶ Addressing structural factors within the organization and proactively addressing the default of White supremacy.
▶ There should be a process for healing and reconciliation for all of those harmed by racism in the past and present (Kawaii-Bogue, 2020).
▶ Compensating BIPOC staff for the emotional labor and identity taxes that they inevitably experience (Kawaii-Bogue, 2020).
▶ Illuminate how the agency culture reflects White assumptions and values and work to change it.
▶ Work to address anti-Blackness, and other forms of stereotyping and microaggressions directed at BIPOC staff and clients (Kawaii-Bogue, 2020).
▶ Reallocate budget and other resources to be applied to racial justice initiatives (Spry, 2020).
▶ Create affinity group and caucus spaces (Blackwell, 2018).
▶ Decentralize power and ensure that it is shared among stakeholders (CCO, 2019).
▶ Have a process for conflict resolution and interpersonal reparations.
▶ Have reflexive opportunities that foster learning, critical reflection, and growth and development in the service of racial justice for all employees (CCO, 2019).
▶ Prioritize the voices, security and safety of BIPOC staff (Stewart, 2018).
▶ Offer mentoring for all staff about racial justice and how to achieve it (Stewart, 2018).

We will develop these ideas further in the next section.

THE PROCESS OF BECOMING A RACIALLY JUST ORGANIZATION

There is no one way to become a racially just organization and genuine transformation is a long-term, ongoing project, but some steps can be taken early, and certain activities are more likely to spell success. First, an organization should openly and honestly discuss whether it is willing to commit itself to this goal and consider what it will entail (Donner & Miller, 2005). This is not as simple as it sounds: Becoming a racially just organization is not a short-term fix and requires a long-term commitment (Hyde, 2004). Working to become an racially just organization requires buy-in from all major stakeholders. If an agency director is willing to make the commitment but the board and staff are not supportive, it is unlikely to be successful.

Organizational antiracism work takes time and effort, must be multifaceted, requires resources, and involves overcoming hurdles and roadblocks. The effort is easily stalled or marginalized, with inevitable setbacks, disagreements over what constitutes meaningful change, and even conflict. Rocco et al. (2014) have described three broad tasks that will help with this process: (a) Increasing awareness about the differential impact of agency structure and policies on the *experiences* of staff and clients, depending on their social identities. (b) Analyzing how these differences *influence decision-making* in the organization. (c) Being attentive to the differential *impact of any changes* on specific groups of people in the organization by virtue of their social identities and group identifications.

Although the commitment to becoming a racially just organization is worth making, it is not without its risks, the biggest being that the organization will abandon its efforts without making substantive progress. This abandonment can prove to be demoralizing to all who have committed to the change process. Therefore, an organization should carefully consider why it wants to embark on this journey, what its goals are, what will serve as landmarks for success, what resources may be needed, and what potential turbulence it can anticipate and how it will respond (see Appendix D).

If a consensus is not reached about moving to become a racially just organization, the next move is to work to create the conditions for making this commitment. An antiracism change effort can originate with any level or sector of an organization and initially may face opposition from other parts of the agency. In the previous example of the United Way, the agency's leadership and many of its board members fiercely resisted the change at the start. Fortunately, significant numbers of people, some with power and influence, supported the change effort. Any organizational change project requires tactical and realistic thinking about how to move an antiracism agenda forward and to enlist critical players as the project moves along. And any antiracism commitment should be tied to providing superior services for clients (Hyde, 2004).

Ultimately, for the venture to succeed, people with formal power in an organization, such as the executive director and board, must support it (Hyde, 2004). Bringing all sectors of an organization on board is essential, yet complicated, and it will take time to educate people about the issues and discuss the importance of the commitment. Everyone will not be equally committed, but a critical mass of support is needed to maintain sufficient momentum. Exercise 11.1 provides a road map to consider in assessing readiness for organizational change.

Necessary Conditions for a Genuine Commitment

Mission Statement

Codifying in writing the commitment to becoming a racially just institution is extremely helpful. Ideally, it should become part of the mission statement of an organization. This makes it fundamental to the *raison d'etre* of an organization and means that it will be a central focus of activity. Other ways to enshrine the commitment are to include it as part of the agency's written policies and to have an antiracism commitment statement that becomes part of all or most of the organization's literature and marketing materials, including websites.

Putting the commitment in writing serves to notify everyone who is inside the organization or comes in contact with it that this is a fundamental philosophy of the agency. This commitment, in itself, causes people to think about its meaning and their own positioning in the change effort. It also serves as a reminder of the commitment when setbacks are encountered and energy and motivation flags. It is a tool for holding the organization accountable.

Project Group

The next step after making a commitment is to form a group that will be responsible for enacting the project and monitoring its progress. Ideally, this group will have diversity of composition, influence within the organization, access to agency leaders, and sufficient time and resources to operate. By "diverse composition" we mean that it should be racially and ethnically diverse but also organizationally diverse, drawing people from all sectors of the agency. It should include some people who have power and influence within the organization including access to the agency director and board. Placing board members and consumers on the committee can be helpful, too, as they can maintain links with people inside and outside of the system.

Needed resources for the group include a time to meet, a place to meet, and use of administrative services (copying, email, etc.). The project group also requires access to information—such as demographic information about clients and staff members, workloads, and funding—and must be able to interview the various organizational stakeholders. The project should not be tied down through usual organizational bureaucratic procedures. It must have a mandate to cut through organizational barriers. One group member should be responsible for convening meetings, ensuring follow-up, and reporting regularly to the entire organization.

Assessment and Prioritization

One of the initial tasks for the group is to assess the organization (as suggested previously) for racism and antiracism. This assessment may involve pulling together disparate views and opinions and will elicit value judgments that are likely to raise strong feelings, such as guilt, anger, and defensiveness. The project group should try to seek as wide a range of viewpoints as possible without discrediting or negating any perspectives, and try to balance subjective opinions with hard facts. It is critical that the voices of BIPOC staff are prioritized as part of any assessment and action planning, with significant and meaningful BIPOC leadership (Kawaii-Bogue, 2020).

The data can be drawn from many of the documents mentioned in Chapter 10 (census reports, statistics from state agencies, etc.) as well as agency reports and statistics. We suggest using the audit developed by Donner and Miller (2005; Appendix C) to ensure that the assessment touches all of the bases and because using an audit can make the process more objective and less emotionally driven. But we do not want to minimize the likelihood or importance of feelings, as racism should arouse strong passions. Problem-solving and dialogue mechanisms, such as those mentioned in earlier chapters, are helpful to respond to strong emotions, particularly if some issue is splitting the group or causing conflict.

As part of the assessment, prioritization is essential, as everything cannot be done at once. Setting short-term and long-term goals is useful. The group should consider each area separately but also think about how all of the pieces of the organization fit together when it comes to antiracism. This is where a developmental model can be useful to put the organization's progress in perspective.

Recall that few, if any, mainstream agencies have achieved so much progress that they have become completely racially just organizations. More work can always be done. At the same time, measuring progress is essential so the organization can see that, as challenging as antiracism work is, their efforts can produce forward movement. By reporting back to the larger organization regularly, the group can ensure that it does not move too far ahead of other employees. Part of its job is to engage people in the process, as well as to achieve certain goals and objectives. Last, written progress reports, at least annually, should be used to chart progress and to ensure that the antiracism agenda is always on a front burner.

Hiring BIPOC Staff and Ensuring Equity in Leadership

There is much more to racial justice than solely bringing more BIPOC people into an organization. But in far too many mainstream organizations, there are insufficient people of color and their numbers often dwindle in the higher realms of an organizational chart. It is exceedingly difficult for BIPOC people to flourish when they are numerically small in an organization and they end up shouldering too much responsibility, including helping the organization to move toward racial justice. And what opportunities exist for advancement, leadership development, and power sharing? If an organization simply ensures equal opportunity, this will be insufficient. Because of historical legacies and structural patterns, there are far more obstacles for BIPOC staff (discussed throughout this book) to ascend within the organization. There need to be concrete compensatory measures put into place which expand opportunities for BIPOC staff and resources to support them in their careers.

Attention to the Needs and Experiences of BIPOC Staff

In addition to having BIPOC participation in the assessment and planning for racial justice initiatives, it is important to have mechanisms to honor and support BIPOC staff working in organizations. As mentioned earlier, this should include affinity group spaces where BIPOC staff can meet and caucus together (Blackwell, 2018). Any assessment should include consideration of safety for people of color in the organization and undue burdens and identity taxes (which include emotional burdens as well as extra work expectations; Stewart, 2018). It is also important to consider self-care for all staff, but particularly for BIPOC staff (Anthym & Tuitt, 2019).

Forums for Discussion and Sharing Findings

While it is important to have affinity spaces for people of color to support one another it is also essential to have spaces for White staff to reflect on and process internalized stereotypes and White supremacy, which is often invisible. It is also important to bring people back together and to have what Anthym and Tuitt (2019) refer to as "courageous conversations" about race and racism. It can be helpful to bring in outside facilitators for such conversations. There may be a need for a process of truth sharing about the experiences of BIPOC staff in the organization as well as consideration of repair, reconstruction of relationships and reparations, if called for. It is also important to have forums for stakeholders where findings are presented and there is an opportunity for reactions and feedback (Spry, 2020).

Deconstructing White Supremacist Culture

As discussed, White supremacy and Eurocentrism pervades most organizations and isoften assumed to be "normal," "professional," and how things should work. Deconstructing this is an important task (CCO, 2019; Kawaii-Bogue, 2020). Such an excavation should include examining notions of time, boundaries, "civil and professional discourse," clinical theories and assumptions, and also understandings of "personhood" (Summerfield, 2004)—what it means to be a healthy person and what people need in order to heal and recover from trauma, including racial trauma.

An Antiracism Audit

Appendix C shows an antiracism audit, based on Donner and Miller (2005) but expanded for this book, which can be used to ensure that all critical areas mentioned herein are addressed as part of the agency's antiracism effort. The audit can be reordered to fit the priorities of any organization, and specific areas or issues can be added as well. Although this chapter has highlighted the importance of many of the areas mentioned in the audit, all of the topics are worth considering.

The audit has a rating system of *accomplished, in process*, and *unaddressed*, but these are broad and categorical. For each item that will be dealt with, more concrete goals and objectives can be set. For example, with staff hiring, establishing specific targets—such as a percentage goal of the staff as well as time frames—can help to make the work more concrete and focused and less abstract. Or consider raising awareness about barriers to communication about race: What specific barriers are identified, and what strategies are suggested to overcome them? The audit is a starting point for gaining an overview of organizational tasks and progress and can be used as a tool for ongoing monitoring.

CONCLUSION

Agencies are a prime site for racial justice work for human service professionals. If our organizations can move toward becoming racially just institutions, this will have a profound impact on workers, clients, communities, and society at large. The United Way example showed how antiracism work can create a big ripple within a community. We have geared the analysis and recommendations in this chapter specifically toward mainstream health and human service agencies because they employ the majority of human service workers. Seemingly benign and race-neutral policies in organizations often have significant implications for racism and social justice because of the racialized nature of U.S. society. Hiring policies and services toward clients can appear to be universal and equitable while reinforcing pervasive social inequities. It is important to directly confront issues of power when doing antiracism work and securing sufficient resources to ensure success.

Antiracism work in agencies depends on commitment, buy in, and working to improve and deepen interpersonal and intergroup relationships. Disagreement, frustration, roadblocks, and setbacks will require structured processes to manage conflict and to help people to remain in alignment with the antiracism commitment. Although a concerted and sustained effort is necessary to work toward antiracism in agencies, progress is achievable and the contributions to client services and antiracism work in society are significant.

EXERCISE 11.1 Racial Justice Agency Assessment

1. Apply the Racial Justice Audit (Appendix C) to an organization in which you are currently involved (college, agency).
2. If you were to initiate an antiracism change project in this organization, who would you approach to work with you?
3. What would be your first steps?
4. How will you ensure participation and adequate time and resources?

REFERENCES

Ahmed, S. (2009). Embodying diversity: Problems and paradoxes for Black feminists. *Race, Ethnicity and Education*, 12(1), 41–52.

Anthym, M., & Tuitt, F. (2019). When the levees break: The cost of vicarious trauma, microaggressions, and emotional labor for Black administrators and faculty engaging in race work at traditionally White institutions. *International Journal of Qualitative Studies in Education*, 32(9), 1072–1093. https://doi.org/10.1080/09518398.2019.1645907

Barak, M. (2000). Beyond affirmative action: Toward a model of diversity and organizational inclusion. *Administration in Social Work*, 23(3/4), 47–68.

Blackwell, K. (2018, August 9). *Why people of color need spaces without white people*. The Arrow. www.arrow-journal.org/why-people-of-color-need-spaces-without-white-people/

Block, C. (2016). The impact of color-blind ideology on maintaining racial disparities in organizations. In H. A. Neville, M. E. Gallardo, & D. W. Sue (Eds.), *The myth of racial color blindness: Manifestations, dynamics, and impact* (pp. 243–259). Washington, DC: American Psychological Association.

Blitz, L. V., & Kohl Jr., B. G. (2012). Addressing racism in the organization: The role of White racial affinity groups in addressing change. *Administration in Social Work*, 36, 479–498.

Centre for Community Organizations. (2019). *White Supremacy culture in organizations*. Montreal. www.coco-net.org/wp-content/uploads/2019/11/Coco-WhiteSupCulture-ENG4.pdf

Chesler, M. A. (1994). Organizational development is not the same as multicultural organizational development. In E. Y. Cross, J. H. Katz, F. A. Miller, & E. W. Seashore (Eds.), *The promise of diversity* (pp. 240–251). Irwin.

Donner, S., & Miller, J. (2005). The road to becoming an anti-racism organization. In A. Lightburn & P. Sessions (Eds.), *Community based clinical practice*. Oxford University Press.

Ford, R. T. (2009). *Racial culture: A critique*. Princeton University Press.

Golembiewski, R. T. (1995). *Managing diversity in organizations*. University of Alabama Press.

Hyde, C. (2004). Multicultural development in human service agencies: Challenges and solutions. *Social Work*, 49(1), 7–16.

Jackson, B., & Hardiman, R. (1994). Multicultural organizational development. In E. Y. Cross, J. H. Katz, F. A. Miller, & E. W. Seashore (Eds.), *The promise of diversity* (pp. 231–239). Irwin.

Jackson, B., & Holvino, E. (1988). Developing multicultural organizations. *Creative Change: The Journal of Religion and the Applied Behavioral Sciences, 9*(2), 14–19.

Jaurique, A., Ryan, D. A., Smith, H. J., & Paolucci-Calahan, M. (2018). Observing discrimination: Implications for group-based respect and morality. *Social Issues and Policy Review, 13*(1), 125–153. https://doi.org/10.1111/sipr.12050

Kawaii-Bogue, B. (2020). *Combatting anti-Blackness and White supremacy in organizations: Recommendations for anti-racist actions in mental health care.* Community Action Partnership, Sonoma State University. https://caps.sonoma.edu/sites/caps/files/combating_anti-blackness_and_white_supremacy_in_organizations_-_recommendations_for_anti-racist_actions_in_mental_healthcare.pdf

Leong, N. (2012). Racial capitalism. *Harvard Law Review, 126*, 2151.

Minors, A. (1996). From university to poly-versity: Organizations in transition to anti-racism. In C. E. James (Ed.), *Perspectives on racism and the human service sector: A case for change* (pp. 196–208). University of Toronto Press.

Rocco, T. S., Bernier, J. D., & Bowman, L. (2014). Critical race theory and HRD: Moving race front and center. *Advances in Developing Human Resources, 16*(4), 457–470.

Spry, A. (2020, June 15). *Beyond the obligatory statement: Here are 5 things organizations can do to meaningfully combat racism.* WBUR. www.wbur.org/cognoscenti/2020/06/15/business-anti-racist-amber-spry

Steele, C. (2011). *Whistling Vivaldi: How stereotypes affect us and what we can do.* W. W. Norton.

Stewart, D. L. (2018). Minding the gap between diversity and institutional transformation: Eight proposals for enacting institutional change. *Teachers College Record, 120*, 1–16.

Sue, D. W., Carter, R. T., Casas, J. M., Fouad, N. A., Ivey, A. E., Jensen, M., LaFromboise, T., Manese, J. E., Ponterotto, J. G., & Vazquez-Nutall, E. (1998). *Multicultural counseling competencies: Individual and organizational development.* Sage.

Summerfield, D. (2004). Cross cultural perspectives on the medicalisation of human suffering. In G. Rosen (Ed.), *Posttraumatic stress disorder: Issues and Controversies* (pp. 233–247). John Wiley.

Tilly, C. (1998). *Durable inequality.* University of California Press.

Valverde, L. A. (1998). Future strategies and actions. Creating multicultural higher education campuses. In L. A. Valverde & L. A. Castenell (Eds.), *The multicultural campus* (pp. 19–29). Altamira Press.

CHAPTER 12

Racism and Clinical Work

INTRODUCTION

In this chapter, we focus on implications of racism on clinical practice. This chapter assumes that readers have some foundational knowledge in clinical theory and practice. Clinical practice, in this chapter, refers to counseling and therapy with individuals, couples and families, and small groups. The terms therapy, counseling, and clinical practice are used interchangeably, as are therapist, clinician, and (clinical) worker.

Because of the pervasiveness of racism in our society the topics addressed in this chapter should be considered in all clinical situations. We recognize that some clinical situations may involve cross-racial clinical work, in which clinicians engage with clients who have racial and ethnic identities that differ from their own, and that racial dynamics may be more manifest in those situations. Cross-*cultural* counseling involves working with people from different cultural backgrounds (such as socioeconomic class, religion, geography, and the like) who may or may not be of the same race. Working cross-racially often (but not always) involves working cross-culturally but always implies differences in racial privilege, power and status, and social experiences.

Recognizing the saliency of social identities in shaping life experiences and the impact of race and racism on clinical practice, we recommend a relational, intersubjective, critical, and anti-oppressive approach to clinical practice. By *relational,* we mean that a helping professional is using the relationship with a client to help the client; the interpersonal connection serves as a foundation for change and growth.

Intersubjective refers to the intersecting inner worlds of clinician and client (Fort, 2018). Every person brings to the relationship their unique psychologies, social identities, perspectives, and lived experiences. An intersubjective approach acknowledges ways by which our social identity shifts as it is co-constructed in the clinical encounter (Moffat & Miehls, 1999). It invites us to reflect on who we are and our internal processes as well as those of the client. So there are at least two sets of intersecting social identities, and each person is reconstructing their social identity in the presence of the other. This means that the workers as well as clients are potentially changed by the clinical encounter.

By *critical* we employ what Fook (2002, 2016) refers to as critical reflection. Critical reflection involves a constant process of examining our own practice and our assumptions about truth, reality, and power. It requires a reflexive stance that considers our social identities and positionalities and their influence on our thinking and actions (Fook, 2016). Each aspect of social identity is shaped by social contexts with differential power and privilege. Thus, Zúñiga and Nagda (2001) emphasize the importance of understanding history and the social world and how they differentially shape our experiences, leading to the development of a *critical social awareness*. Bringing to bear our critical social awareness to our own social identities and positionalities in relation to those around us is crucial for those engaged in clinical work. Critical social awareness and critical reflection help us gain more contextual understanding of our own and our clients' intersectional positionalities, attend to the power dynamic in the therapeutic relationship, and work toward challenging existing power relations and structures within which both the clinician and the client are located.

An *anti-oppressive practice (AOP)* approach involves a critical examination of the various power imbalances that are found in our society, within organizational structures, and between the clinician and their clients (Morgaine & Capous-Desyllas, 2014). AOP emphasizes the interconnection between individual struggles, structural inequalities, and historical oppression, and how those struggles are connected to social identities and intersectionality. Therefore, AOP compels clinicians to go beyond psychological services to strategize ways to diminish power imbalances through their practice, promoting equity and empowerment for their clients in all contexts.

Clinical relationships are intense and intimate. Intimacy brings into focus many issues of identity, relationship, and dialogue that were discussed in earlier chapters. How do workers negotiate therapeutic relationships in which social identity and race are salient? There are challenges, to be sure, but this chapter offers some suggestions and encourages workers to be open to a relational, intersubjective, critical, and anti-oppressive approach to clinical practice.

In this chapter, we discuss the importance of attending to how our experiences and perspectives are shaped by our social identities and the role of power in the clinical process. We examine legacies of racism seen in clinical work and the ways in which racism can place barriers to effective clinical work. We conclude with strategies for practice and organizational interventions that enhance the effectiveness of clinical work.

FIRST STEPS

When embarking on clinical work, helping professionals should consider social identity and power.

Social Identity

Clinicians must recognize the ways by which social identity manifests itself in the clinical relationship. Because clinical relationships do not occur only in a psychological sphere but also within the context of our society, considering social identity in the framework of intersectionality is essential. Intersectionality is described in Chapter 8 as the relationship between different factors in our social identities, which captures the connections and junctures that occur both inside a person (manifested in their identities) and in society (as evidenced by inequities and disparities in power and privilege). Recognizing that each social identity has its own level of power and privilege, intersectionality refers to the ways that these varying levels of power and privilege interact with one another and create a context for an individual's lived experience.

This understanding begins with the worker having insight and awareness of the salient parts of their own social identity and how they shape their perspective and lived experiences. Consider the following example. An African American mother of a 12-year-old son tells her counselor about a conflict she had with her son. Her son had disobeyed her rule for him not to ride his bike past certain areas in the evening. She chastised him, and he pushed back at her saying that he was not a little kid anymore. The worker, who identifies as White and middle class and has a teenage son, tells the mother that it is developmentally appropriate for a 12-year-old to push for more independence. She offers the mother psychoeducation on developmental stages and tasks, after which she adds with a warm smile, "I know it is hard to let go of our sweet little boys, but they all grow up whether *we* like it or not!" The mother looks down, shakes her head, and says, "well, I want to make sure that my son *gets to* grow up."

In this case, while the worker focused on psychological development needs of the boy she failed to consider the sociopolitical context of the mother's concerns. The long history and recent incidents of racism-based murder of African American youth, such as Trayvon Martin and Tamir Rice, while engaged in age-appropriate activities, provide the context to why the mother was worried about her son riding his bike to an unfamiliar, White-dominant area of the suburbs.

As discussed, the web of racism presents multiple barriers, which the worker probably has not encountered and of which she is unaware. Not being critically aware of how her social identity and positionality shape her perspective and experience led the worker to miss that the same age-appropriate behavior can lead to seriously different consequences for the client's son who is Black than for her son who is White. If she does not grasp this before intervening with her client, it could lead to an unrealistic service plan, and also to empathic failures that threaten the effectiveness of the clinical relationship.

Most workers are sincere in their commitment to respect clients' dignity and worth. Many workers, however, face challenges when conversations turn more directly to race and ethnicity or miss the crucial context of race and racism. Many in the United States, particularly those who identify as White, have been reared and socialized to believe that people are people and that we should not treat one another differently. A common refrain is, "To me, we're all just people. I don't see color. I don't care if you're Black, Brown, White, or purple; people are people, and talking about differences just drives us apart."

This "color-blind" notion tends to be well-intentioned and ironically emerges from a person's desire to not discriminate by virtue of a person's race or ethnicity (Goodman, 2011), but it is hazardous to good clinical practice. As we have discussed throughout this book, we are not all "just people," as the aphorism would indicate. We all have complex, intersecting social identities, including race and ethnicity. We come to each clinical encounter with rich and diverse cultures and heritages and different lived experiences with how society responds to our racial identity. We *do* notice differences, though some of us have been socialized not to talk about them. Statements that seek to "equalize" us all by ignoring our differences, however well-meaning, minimize and devalue the experiences of many people, especially people of color, and erase the legacies of many groups in this country. Rather than denying our differences or either consciously or unconsciously negating them, we should find ways to value and acknowledge clients' varied perspectives, histories, cultures, and experiences while also being critically aware that our own intersectional social identities will have an impact on the clinical encounter.

Thus, all clinicians should be aware of the impact of social identity on the clinical relationship. Part of having race privilege is being less likely to have thought about this aspect of their social identity daily. For many White workers in training or new to the field, this exploration may be new to them and feel uncomfortable. Many White people in the United States do not often consider the influence of race and ethnicity on their own and other White peoples' lives or the impact of racism on people of color. A worker's critical awareness of race and ethnicity, along with other aspects of social identity, both privileged and marginalized, and their willingness to explore these issues in an open and non-defensive fashion can have a positive influence on levels of trust, which is essential to the formation of a strong therapeutic alliance. Furthermore, a worker's critical awareness of the impact of racism and other structural oppression on a client's situation can lead to more comprehensive and empowering interventions, which is more likely to bring better clinical outcomes.

Power

The intensity of the clinical relationship contrasts with the levels of intimacy in most other relationships. Personal disclosure, exploration of socially taboo topics, and even regression are common in clinical work. All relationships involve power, and those who hold greater power have greater control over shaping the nature of the relationship. Power in relationships is manifested by a hierarchy of spoken and unspoken rules (Carter, 1995). These rules are the assumptions about how people are supposed to be in relation to each other.

The rules also dictate patterns of behavior, depending on one's context (e.g., the ways by which one might act at home with friends and family versus the way one acts at work with colleagues and clients). Carter (1995) explored the ways in which power is manifest in the clinical relationship, concluding that therapists who understand their own social identity and are critically aware will be better able to negotiate the therapeutic relationship to help clients effectively.

Racially and ethnically minoritized people often feel pressures to assimilate so they can achieve upward social mobility or even to avoid harassment or overt discrimination. When this pressure to assimilate is combined with respect for authority, group members may seem to be deferential toward people they perceive to be in authority, such as helping professionals. Clinicians, whatever their race, already have a great deal of power in the helping relationship by virtue of their training, status, professional role, authority over eligibility, and appointment schedules, combined with the vulnerabilities implicit in being a client. This power differential can be compounded if the worker is White and has not acknowledged and examined White privilege thoroughly, which can be manifested in an authoritative stance that compels the client to assimilate. If not carefully monitored, the dynamics of internalized racism and internalized White supremacy can come to characterize the therapeutic relationship.

Lee and Bhuyan (2013) illustrate through a discourse analysis of therapy dialogue transcripts how clinicians maintain Whiteness as a cultural norm and produce racialized immigrant clients as subordinate "other" in therapy. The therapists in this study presumably had no conscious intention to enforce Whiteness as a cultural norm; however, the subtle ways in which they encouraged and discouraged different narratives signaled to the clients which ideas and behaviors were approved and which were not, thus shaping their thoughts and actions.

If a clinician continues to fail to be critically reflective of their power and privilege and to act to equalize power, clinical effectiveness diminishes, which results in disservice to clients. Often in these situations, clients ultimately leave therapy prematurely, as they may have difficulty speaking out against or criticizing those whom they perceive to be authority figures. Or, clients might tell the worker that they are finding the work together to be helpful and that they see improvements when there actually is little noticeable change or growth, especially if the worker is perceived to be or is in an evaluative position (e.g., in mandated cases). Clients also may leave therapy because they simply feel unseen in the very relationship where they hoped to be wholly seen, which is disempowering and disappointing. The client in the short vignette in the previous social identity section, for example, decided not to return to therapy because "I can't work with someone if I have to explain racism; I don't need to be teaching my therapist about that when I am there for *her* to help *me*." Therefore, clinicians should be mindful of nuances of power and respect in counseling relationships and actively work to equalize power in the relationship.

LEGACIES OF RACISM SEEN IN CLINICAL WORK

All clinical work engenders a range of complicated emotions for client and worker alike. Cross-racial work, in particular, can elicit powerful affective responses. Particularly in dyads involving a White clinician and a client of color or a multiracial client, racial dynamics of the client's everyday life can be re-enacted in the clinical encounter. When the clinician is a person of color, both White and non-White clients may question, overtly or covertly, the clinician's professional capabilities, which can evoke experiences with racism. Workers, whatever their race, must be mindful of their own feelings, as well as of their own reactions and attitudes toward their client's expression of strong emotions. Otherwise, they might offer unempathic responses to clients, leaving them feeling unheard and misunderstood, or worse, re-experiencing painful racism-based trauma.

Emotional Responses to Racism

Some common emotions and reactions that emerge in clinical relationships are anger, rage, guilt, shame, grief, and mourning. When expressions such as these do emerge, workers must acknowledge, respond to, and be aware of how they can help or hinder therapy. We briefly consider the sources of some common strong emotions, and later in the chapter examine strategies for effective clinical practice in the context of both clinicians and clients working within the context of our society's historical and structural racism.

Anger

We all feel anger, although some do not want to recognize, admit, or respond to this emotion. Here, *anger* is defined as an emotion that arises in the moment and generates an intensity that usually leads to an emotional release of some sort. Anger can be a powerful and productive emotion that propels people to action. For example, activist and author Audrey Lorde (1984) argued that:

Every woman has a well-stocked arsenal of anger potentially useful against those oppressions, personal and institutional, which brought that anger into being. Focused with precision it can become a powerful source of energy serving progress and change. I am speaking of a basic and radical alteration in those assumptions underlying our lives. Anger is loaded with information and energy. (p. 127)

On the other hand, feeling intense anger over a protracted period without an avenue to express and use for productive action can take its toll. Frequent experiences of such anger or holding onto anger can be physically and emotionally taxing and can strain interpersonal and professional relationships.

Rage

Rage is akin to anger but is a more profound and deep-seated emotion than anger (Hardy & Laszloffy, 1995). Rage speaks to incubated, suppressed anger. Rage simmers and lasts over time. It also hides a profound level of despair. It tends to develop gradually and has both functional and dysfunctional dimensions (hooks, 1995). Rage acts as a protective shield in many ways, because people tend to keep a distance from those who are enraged. This can buffer people from the effects of racism, as well as help a person retain a sense of self-respect.

Self-destructive behavior often ensues when rage is internalized and suppressed. By-products of rage can be surges in substance abuse, prolonged sadness or depression, social withdrawal or isolation, and suicidal gestures, ideations, or completions. Fighting can be an external expression of rage, and riots (or rebellions) can be a collective manifestation of rage. Hardy and Laszloffy (1995) described family therapy with an African American family that was punctuated by the family members not talking to one another. For this family, not talking and suppressing anger were protective buffers against the trauma of oppression and the accompanying rage, but it also alienated them from one another and curtailed their capacity to be intimate and supportive.

The expression of rage sometimes releases the pain and humiliation associated with oppression. For people of color, particularly youth of color, these feelings may be attributed to a realization that they indeed are a member of a racial or ethnic group that is not fully valued or appreciated in our society. In discussing the development of the Movement for Black Lives, Copeland (2015) describes it as "the latest stage of a multigenerational marathon for freedom. This marathon has endured since Europeans first started kidnapping Africans for uncompensated labor. This stage emerged among the agony and outrage at the failure to convict George Zimmerman for the killing of Trayvon Martin and accelerated as Ferguson residents faced off against paramilitary police forces after the killing of Mike Brown" (p. 4).

Both anger and rage, when unacknowledged by the larger society, can lead to feelings of isolation and invalidation. Poussaint (2000) described the high numbers of suicides in the Black community as a direct example of rage taken to the extreme, in which people feel that they have no other options. Gripping, "uncontrollable" rage can affect people of color (hooks, 1995, p. 26): "That rage is not pathological. It is an appropriate response to injustice. However, if not processed constructively, it can lead to pathological behavior." She links this to counseling:

Concurrently, without a more sophisticated understanding of those particularly extreme expressions of rage which indicate serious mental disorder, we will not be able to address the complexity and multidimensional nature of Black rage. We will not be able to understand the psychological displacement of grief and pain into rage. And without that understanding the deeper dimensions of Black rage cannot be acknowledged, nor the psychological wounds it masks, attended to. (hooks, 1995, p. 27)

Guilt

Guilt arising from racism is a common emotion that can be manifested in clients, as well as workers, of any race. People of color may feel a sense of guilt over not having done more to challenge racism or to help family members. Guilt also can derive from feelings of doing better than one's family or community, perhaps because of having a lighter skin, or speaking English with an Anglo-American accent, or having achieved a higher level of education. People of color can also experience guilt over their internalized racism or their feelings of prejudice toward other people of color or even those of their own race.

White people may experience guilt about their privilege or because they have internalized racial stereotypes that conflict with their egalitarian values. Dwelling on "White guilt" can lead to denial and rationalization to avoid the uncomfortable feeling. DiAngelo (2018) terms such responses *White fragility* and argues that they come from internalized White supremacy that places primacy on White people's feelings of discomfort over struggles and oppression of people of color. She warns that White guilt often leads to White complicity.

We believe that feelings of guilt, while difficult, can be a helpful signal of internal unrest for both people of color and White people. When we critically reflect upon and understand the source and meaning of the guilt, and take that knowledge and turn it into positive advocacy and action, it can be turned into a productive emotion.

Shame

Shame is to guilt as rage is to anger, with shame being the deeper emotion, the feelings of which often are attached to very early memories. Though guilt can lead to feeling bad about what happened to another person, shame is tied inextricably to feeling bad about oneself (Damasio, 2000). The examples we gave about sources of guilt apply to shame as well, but the impact is more profound, self-negating, and immobilizing. Profound feelings of shame can be overwhelming and make it difficult for people to take the actions necessary to help themselves and others. In clinical situations unexamined shame (and guilt) can lead to clinicians overreacting or underreacting to clients, which we will address in the strategy section.

Grief and Mourning

When an awareness and acknowledgment of racism enters the clinical relationship, it involves getting in touch with something that is profoundly distressing. Such sadness is difficult to tolerate much of the time and thus is often repressed, displaced, or channeled elsewhere. Counseling and therapy create spaces where people can confront, and bring into conscious awareness, that which often has been unexamined. The depth of sadness that can be expressed is akin to the grief and mourning that follow when someone has died. Metaphorically and literally, racism is a process of truncating potential, limiting success, and causing pain, harm, wounds, and suffering which, if left unacknowledged, can take a serious toll on one's physical and emotional well-being.

Unexpressed grief usually finds an outlet, often one that is destabilizing or counterproductive. It can be the source of suppressed anger and rage or lead to chronic anxiety and depression. Thus, it is healthy and helpful to identify, name, and explore grief and to enter a process of mourning. Clients who have experienced racism can mourn the wounds that they and their loved ones have suffered. Those with race privilege can grieve their loss of illusion about the fairness of society or the losses that others have suffered. Processed grief and mourning ultimately can be liberating, freeing people to empower themselves and to work on behalf of others.

Stress and Trauma

Stress is multifaceted, with many causes, types, and levels. Critical incidents (sudden, uncontrollable, overwhelming events) can cause acute stress disorders and even posttraumatic stress disorder (Perrin-Klinger, 2000). Long-term exposure to stressful situations can produce chronic stress disorder. All types of stress disorders have negative consequences—cognitive, emotional, behavioral, physical, interpersonal, and spiritual (Yassen, 1995).

Racism and its consequences should not be reduced to, and labeled as, a medical disorder. Yet, when engaging in clinical work, the psychological and emotional effects of racism on people of color must be recognized (Daniel, 2000). Poussaint (2000) has conceptualized racism as a source of chronic stress and trauma, with severe psychological consequences for African Americans. Carter (2007) argued that "race-based traumatic stress injury" has many of the same symptoms of other forms of trauma (such as intrusion, arousal, and avoidance) but is deeply rooted in repeated exposure to race-based stress. This is compounded by the knowledge that the threats have not ended and are likely to occur again, leading to a loss of a sense of control. The consequences of racism-based stress and trauma on psychological, physical, and social health well-being of people of color are well documented (e.g., Brondolo et al. 2003; Carter, 2007; Carter et al., 2005; Copeland et al., 2011; Gee et al., 2007; Martin et al., 2011; Moradi & Risco, 2006; Nadal et al., 2014; Paradies, 2006; Seaton et al., 2010; Sue et al., 2008; Tucker et al., 2007; Wang et al., 2020).

History of extreme and overwhelming racism, such as genocide, ethnic cleansing, mass incarceration, and slavery, leaves a collective memory of these events that never completely goes away, transmitting intergenerational trauma from one generation to another. The awareness that others could do this to one's ancestors (or you and your children, had you lived in that era) based on who you are (i.e., racial and ethnic identity) can foster a profound sense of dismay, lack of control, and feelings of perpetual vulnerability. And present experiences of racism and ethnic discrimination and microaggression are everyday reminders of historical atrocities. Indeed, scholars such as Brave Heart (2003), Duran and Duran (1995), Evans-Campbell (2008), Hartmann et al. (2019), and Walters et al. (2002) discussed the destructive impact of historical trauma on Indigenous people's emotional, mental, spiritual, and physical health and well-being.

However, clinicians who are trained in a narrower view of posttraumatic stress disorder may focus on childhood abuse, gender-based violence, and war/combat trauma while missing the impact of racism-based trauma (including historical trauma and repeated vicarious racial trauma) in clients' history even though racism-based trauma likely produces the same trauma responses and negative impact on functioning (Kang & Burton, 2014). Therefore, it is essential for clinicians to be aware of and consider racism-based stress and trauma and their consequences on individual's health and wellness.

Historical Mistrust

The history of the helping profession in the United States is complicated by its complicity, overt and covert, in racist policies and practices. For example, the legacy of exploitation of African American people in public health and medical research, such as the Tuskegee experiment, still reverberates, making it difficult for African Americans to trust the medical profession (Royles, 2020). Social workers' compliance with the Indian Adoption Project in the 1950s, which resulted in forced separation of Native American families and cultural displacement of Native American children, still haunts the profession (Hair & Donohue, 2009). Similarly, social workers cooperated with the U.S. government in the incarceration process of Japanese immigrants and Japanese Americans during World War II instead of advocating for their civil rights (Park, 2008). A history of misdiagnosis and mistreatment of African American clients by (predominantly White) mental health clinicians (Suite et al., 2007) presents a significant barrier to trust.

Given this history, it is not difficult to understand why clients of color may have difficulty establishing trust with clinicians, especially those who are White. Clinicians of color must also be aware that they represent the profession with a complicated history. Therefore, clinicians of all races and ethnicities must be cognizant of the historical barriers to trust for clients of color and not take the process of building trust for granted.

THEORETICAL BIASES

In large measure, mental health work in the helping professions reflects dominant, Eurocentric cultural values. The foundation for counseling theory and practice methods developed out of the experience of White clinicians and researchers working almost exclusively with White client systems. The theoretical base for many of the helping professions is predicated on a Eurocentric worldview, a set of assumptions concerning human behavior, and a set of values concerning mental health needs and interventions.

Our ability to be effective clinical workers is severely hampered if we do not recognize and counteract on these limitations. Theoretical biases are manifested in assumptions about human behavior, development, and expression. Even concepts that are basic and taken for granted in most clinical training programs can carry a great deal of cultural bias (Roland, 1996). For example, using psychodynamic theory, the concepts of separation and individuation often are seen as healthy benchmarks of development. Yet these concepts are Westernized and presuppose that differentiating oneself from parents and siblings and attaining an independent sense of self is good and normal. Many cultures, however, emphasize interdependence and do not prioritize an autonomous and freestanding self (Yeh & Hwang, 2000). Another example is a clinical emphasis on disclosure of affect and talking about feelings, which may be a norm in some groups even within Western cultures but are not necessarily in others.

Theoretical biases are buttressed by their fit with assumptions and biases in the dominant culture at large, which makes them appear "normal" while marginalizing other cultures and worldviews. They are replicated and promulgated because most clinicians have been trained in programs where these biases are centralized and privileged. Teachers in clinical programs often have internalized these assumptions from their own training and practice experience. Agencies also reflect theoretical biases through their models of practice and programmatic structure. Thus, interrogating and dislodging Eurocentric clinical assumptions is a difficult thing to do. This relates to our discussion about power, as theory gives clinicians the power to define and diagnose, which is so normalized in our everyday practices that we may scarcely recognize as a function of power.

One way to counter clinical biases is to identify them and offer alternative ways of conceptualizing human development and clinical services that are responsive to cultural diversity. Much has been written about this (Appendix F provides resources). Ultimately, although there are sound practice principles, which this chapter discusses, there are no theoretical recipes to guide us in working with people of all races and cultures. A one-size-fits-all approach to clinical work is not only impossible but also inadvisable. Interventions that are effective with a Vietnamese American immigrant adolescent female who is seeking autonomy from her family of origin in an urban ethnic neighborhood may not be the same as those called for with a European American male in a small rural town struggling with similar issues of autonomy. Clinical case planning relies on an understanding of the client's sociocultural context; their experiences of power, privilege, and social oppression; and a thorough assessment of each person's unique situation (Gaw, 1993).

A final theoretical challenge for clinical work in our society's racial and cultural context, particularly when the client is a person of color or multiracial, is that many theories start with a premise of pathology. The emphasis is on individual problems, unfulfilled wishes and desires, developmental hitches, and interpersonal weaknesses. Certainly, most people do not seek, or are not referred for, therapy because they are feeling good. The impetus for therapy typically comes from dissatisfaction, dysfunction, and disaffection. But when working with anyone who has been subjected to sustained and ongoing pressure from social oppression, which surely stems from racism, we must first try to understand how that person's current problems may relate to structural oppression and learn how they have coped and survived. What sources of strength and resiliency have sustained them? How and when do they thrive? What does healing look like in their tradition and their current community context? A theoretical perspective that recognizes environmental stressors such as racism and identifies and honors strengths instead of pathology is crucial to successful clinical work.

BARRIERS TO EFFECTIVE CLINICAL WORK

This book has already presented many ways by which racism creates barriers between people in communities, schools, workplaces, and society at large, and also has discussed how people internalize racism. This book has already presented many ways by which racism creates barriers between people in communities, schools, workplaces, and society at large, and also has discussed how people internalize racism. In this section, we have identified three major obstacles to successful clinical work: internalized racism, inattention to power and privilege, and defensive racial dynamics. We have identified three major obstacles to successful clinical work: internalized racism, inattention to power and privilege, and defensive racial dynamics.

Internalized Racism

Internalized racism can mean either internalized feelings of superiority and privilege based on one's race or feelings of being less worthy base on one's race or responsible for one's own social oppression (Joseph & Williams, 2008). Multiracial people may experience a mixture of both. As described in Chapter 7, social identity development involves uncovering internalized belief systems and trying to move beyond them. This is particularly important for clinicians as any internalized racism can potentially be enacted with clients and could damage the therapeutic process, or worse, do harm. Unexamined internalized racism also makes the therapist vulnerable to the client's internalized racism (Comas-Diaz & Jacobsen, 2001). Internalized racism can surface and confound transference and counter-transference in a clinical relationship, which we will discuss in depth in the next section.

Inattention to Power and Privilege

Unequal power and privilege are major elements of racism, and they carry over to clinical encounters. One sphere in which the clinician must be attuned to the power dynamic is within the clinical relationship. As discussed in the earlier section, unexamined power and privilege can significantly disrupt the clinical process and undermine the strength of the clinical relationship. Without a conscious critical reflection on power and privilege the therapeutic relationship can mirror the societal power dynamics, and the interactions between the counselor and the client can inadvertently re-enact the racial power dynamics in the larger society. For example, a White female clinician working with a treatment group may let a White male client dominate the conversation and take up more than his share of air time while another client, a woman of color, exasperatedly waits for an opening to get her word in. While this situation may seem as though it is just about the clinician's lack of skill in managing a group, it replicates both the racial and gender dynamics in the larger society.

Another sphere that the worker must be mindful of the power dynamics is the community and the agency where the client and the worker are located. For example, does an intervention intended to help an immigrant South Asian Muslim client adjust to his new environment subtly pressure him to assimilate to the Eurocentric culture and practices of the community? Does an agency, which is located in a predominantly Black neighborhood, have mostly White professional staff and administrators, thus echoing the larger society's racial dynamics?

Not being attentive to these power dynamics can result in losing opportunities for developing a healthy therapeutic relationship and, ultimately, disservice to the client. Thus, clinicians must engage in critical reflection and consciously work to equalize power in the clinical relationship.

Defensive Racial Dynamics

Ridley (1995) has argued that "defensive racial dynamics" pose a big threat to establishing a constructive therapeutic alliance and achieving positive treatment outcomes, particularly with White clinicians and clients of color. In this section, we build on his thesis.

Color-Blindness

Ridley argues that color-blindness is manifested when White clinicians do not recognize or acknowledge a client's race or ethnicity. As stated previously, this can be a consequence of a well-intentioned effort to treat all clients equally. In therapy, however, it can convey a strong lack of empathy about clients' race or ethnicity, cultural heritage, and social experiences that result from their racial or ethnic identity. It also closes off potential discussion of the client's reactions to the therapist's race or ethnicity, which can truncate the relationship and create prohibited zones of discourse.

Although Ridley was addressing White clinicians working with people of color, color-blindness can be problematic for clinicians of color and multiracial clinicians as well. If clinicians of color do not recognize the meaning of a client's race/ethnicity, or the impact that their own race may have on a client's reactions and transference, the same problems identified with White clinicians can emerge.

Essentialism

At the other end of the spectrum from color-blindness is essentialism (which Ridley calls color-consciousness), in which clinicians overly emphasize race and ethnicity. Although race and ethnicity are important, they are not always central to the therapeutic process or the critical area of focus for the client. Race and ethnicity can be overemphasized, or brought up at the wrong time, which changes the agenda and direction to reflect the clinician's ideology or need more than the client's needs. For example, Lydia, a clinician who identifies as an African American woman, is concerned about racism-based stress of Zaid, a 15-year-old African American young man with test anxiety. She raises the "school-to-prison pipeline" phenomenon with Zaid and emphatically educates him about how structural oppression in the school system can affect the mental health of students of color and fail their educational achievement. Zaid, an honor student, listens respectfully to Lydia but is unsure how to address his test anxiety with her.

Similarly, clinicians may narrowly focus on culture, reducing clients' issues to "cultural beliefs and values." While it may stem from a worker's eagerness to practice cultural competence, narrowly focusing on culture poses several problems. First, cultural essentialism truncates a person's complex, intersectional experiences to just one aspect of their social identity (e.g., ethnicity) and interferes with seeing the whole person experience, which is crucial for good clinical practice. Second, it often reduces rich diversity within a culture to a simplistic set of "beliefs and values," (e.g., "ten core values of Asian culture," "five spiritual beliefs of Native Americans"). Again, while it may be from a sincere desire to learn and understand more about the client's culture, doing so results in reducing a complex concept of culture into a one-dimensional caricature. Third, and perhaps most problematic, cultural essentialism results in elevating White, middle-class cultural perspectives and practices as the unspoken norm and rendering other "cultural values, beliefs, and practices" into distinct "others." Nicotera and Kang (2009) argue that this normative view of culture does not acknowledge the power differential between the taken-for-granted norm (the "center") and the "other," thus marginalizing the experiences of those defined as the "other" and upholding the power of the "center" to define what is normal and what is not.

For example, Sue, a second-generation Chinese American woman who is processing trauma issues stemming from witnessing domestic violence perpetuated by her father toward her mother throughout her childhood, is asked by her Latina therapist if "the Chinese culture's Confucian values on patriarchy" perpetuated her family's tolerance of the father's violence and controlling behaviors. Sue says "But I grew up in Boston, and the *American* culture also upholds patriarchy, too." Her therapist then focuses on "the phenomenon of saving face in Asian cultures" and suggests that Sue may have tried to protect her "family's honor" by keeping the domestic violence a secret as a child. Sue feels as though she now has to defend her "culture" to her therapist who is supposed to help her process trauma. In this case, the therapist focused on Chinese "culture" even though the same issues (patriarchy and family secrets) are common in the experiences of family violence, regardless of race and ethnicity.

Rather than seeing patriarchy and family secrets as the problems, the therapist pathologized what she considered *unique* to Chinese culture.

Racial Transference and Countertransference

We use the terms *transference* and *countertransference* broadly here. Transference denotes the client's feelings and reactions toward a clinician, shaped and influenced by earlier experiences and relationships. Thus, the clinician might represent someone else—often a significant person in the client's life—in the client's mind, or the clinician–client relationship unconsciously evokes other relationships. Countertransference refers to the clinician's projections onto the client, as well as the clinician's reactions to client's interactions and transference toward the clinician.

Although Ridley uses the term *cultural transference and countertransference,* transference and countertransference can be attached to race, as well as to ethnicity and culture. Race and culture add to the dimensions of transference and countertransference, potentially heightening and deepening their interaction. This is true particularly if strong feelings or reactions (negative or positive) are attached to the therapist's or client's race, or if either party has had limited exposure to the racial or ethnic group that the other represents. In such situations, stereotypes or symbols gain importance and can become the grist of the mutual process of transference. Here we present a few examples of how racial transference and countertransference may surface in clinical work.

Clients may experience and enact racial transference. An example may be a White client questioning and challenging a clinician's qualifications due to a deeply held yet unconscious bias against people of color coupled with his own fear of being inadequate. One of the authors of this text (Garran, 2013) encountered this dynamic in a family session with a White, Eastern European American, upper-middle-class family. The parents clearly were distressed that their daughter was in psychotherapy, and they were eager for her to be discharged from receiving services. During a particularly volatile family meeting, the father repeatedly maligned the worker, a woman of color, questioning her credentials and her ability to offer help to the family. The worker endured several tacit and overt references to her "lack of adequate preparation" and to the allegation that she held her position only "because of affirmative action." At one point in the session, after the therapist's listening and gentle challenging, the father revealed that he was fearful they had been summoned to participate in their daughter's psychotherapy because the worker was questioning their competence as parents and shaming them for their daughter's difficulties.

Another example may be a client of color who is in an environment where White people predominantly serve as authority figures such as teachers, bosses, and legal authorities, reacting to a White therapist as an authority figure, which leads to not being able assert herself in the clinical interaction even when she feels the therapy is not meeting her needs. In Lee and Bhuyan's (2013) study, an immigrant woman of color tries to discuss her ambivalence about not having followed her parents' wishes for her (to have an arranged marriage), and her White, female, Canadian citizen therapist, re-directs the conversation from exploring the ambivalence to re-enforcing and affirming the client's "personal choice," which is consistent with the mainstream Eurocentric notion of decision-making. Seeing the therapist's response, the client disengages from her exploration and acquiesces to the therapist's re-direction.

Clinicians also may experience and enact racial countertransference. For clinicians of color and multiracial clinicians, the dynamics of internalized racism can play out in racial countertransference. Working with clients of similar racial or ethnic backgrounds can evoke strong responses if a client is exploring an issue of low racial self-esteem. This could strike an empathic chord, resulting in overidentification or, conversely, seem threatening to clinicians, causing them to erect an emotional wall with the client to avoid dealing with their *own* pain, leading to empathic failure. Clients of color from ethnic or racial backgrounds different from the clinician's can also stir up similar reactions or trigger the clinician's internalized biases toward that ethnic or racial group. Racial countertransference may emerge for a clinician of color working with a White client where the differential power and privilege based on race can foster feelings of resentment, as well as less empathy, for the client (Ferguson & King, 1997). It also may surface as a re-enactment of agent-target roles or a power struggle in the clinical relationship.

For White clinicians working with clients of color, racial countertransference may surface as the clinician's enactment of unconscious feelings of privilege and superiority. When working with White clients there is the danger of colluding with racism by virtue of both client and worker carrying internalized racial privilege. Another risk for White clinicians is that of carrying strong feelings of guilt and shame over racism and overreacting to clients of color or acting in ways that assuage the therapist's feelings but are not necessarily responsive to the client's needs.

Racial countertransference may be further complicated by what Ridley calls *cultural ambivalence* where clinicians are conflicted about their reactions toward the client. An example is a White clinician who feels threatened by a client of color and holds tightly to the reins of power but at the same time wants to be seen by the client as empathic and not racially prejudiced. In this case, the client of color represents both a threat to his race-based power and privilege *and* a possible source of absolution and approval of the power and privilege. In all these examples, the clinicians are expressing their own needs and reactions at the expense of clients' progress and well-being.

Transference and countertransference, while potentially perilous to clinical process if unexamined, could be a rich source of information and provide crucial insight to therapy. We will address this point in the next section.

STRATEGIES FOR EFFECTIVE CLINICAL WORK

As illustrated throughout this book, race and racism in the United States are highly complex topics. Because we *all* live in this society with the same complex racial history and dynamics, attending to the impact of race and racism is essential for good clinical practice, no matter the racial identity of the client or the clinician. In this section we present strategies for effective clinical practice that apply a relational, intersubjective, critical, and anti-oppressive approach. Although these approaches are discussed under different subheadings to highlight how they impact specific aspects of clinical practice, they should not be understood in silos. We emphasize that these approaches must be applied concurrently for effective clinical practice.

Critical Approach

As we discussed in the beginning of this chapter, effective clinical practice in our society's racial context requires the clinician's ability and commitment to practice critical reflection to gain more contextual understanding of our own and our clients' intersectional social identities, attend to the power dynamic in the therapeutic relationship, and work toward challenging existing power relations and structures within which both the clinician and the client are located. Thus, critical clinical practice involves: (a) worker's critical awareness of their own intersectional social identities (including relative power and privilege) and how they shape their lived experience and influence their perspectives, including their understanding of the present case; (b) worker's critical consideration of the client's intersectional social identities (including relative power and privilege) that shape their lived experience and influence their perspectives (including their understanding of their own situation); (c) worker's critical examination of the power dynamics in the therapeutic relationship *and* constant effort to equalize power, (d) worker's collaboration with the client to define the clinical issue, identify strengths, imagine what the resolution or healing might look like, determine intervention strategies, and work toward the goal; and (e) advocating for necessary resources and larger systemic changes.

Clearly, critical reflection is an on-going process and must occur throughout the therapeutic process. The authors of this book are often asked by their students what that might look like when they are working on a case. Suarez et al.'s (2008) case study of family work (with the Salam family) provides an excellent illustration of use of critical reflection in every phase of the clinical work, as follows:

Pre-contact reflections (through ongoing engagement)

- Identify own strengths, fears, assumptions in relation to positionalities
- Analyze worker/agency knowledge, values, and assumptions re: Salam family
- Consider power and privilege in the family, agency, and environments
- Assess resources and limitations in agency and larger environments
- Conduct initial self-education re: family, environmental factors

Early contacts and assessments

- Make safety and empowerment of all family members a priority (in all phases)
- Conduct assessments using intersectional criteria (e.g., cultural norms, language, gender alliances)
- Educate self through information from family members *and* research
- Exchange education about environmental factors (e.g., relevant laws, customs, history)
- Identify resources, barriers, potential collaborators
- Question (interrogate/deconstruct) knowledge and theories

Interventions

- Engage with collaborators to implement interventions
- Empower all members through education, reframing histories in larger contexts; articulate choices
- Use supervision and consultation to support critical consciousness development
- Attend to dynamics related to power and privilege in all interactions
- Guard against triggering stereotype threats
- Monitor and reflect at every stage, engaging in praxis

Ongoing reflections about self and social contexts

- Review personal challenges related to own histories and positionalities
- Identify educational gaps and seek relevant knowledge
- Create collaborations with others that support ongoing deconstruction, critical awareness, and struggling with personal resistances. (Suarez et al., 2008, p. 412)

In a critical approach to clinical practice, a constant analysis of the power dynamics between the worker and the client and a conscious effort to equalize and share power is paramount. Thus, the worker–client relationship must be a collaborative partnership where both engage in understanding the issues or uncovering of the story of problems as well as learning about client's individual, familial, and community strengths, resources, and vulnerabilities (i.e., assessment); learning about and imagining what the resolution or healing may look like (i.e., intervention planning); and working to construct a new story of healing and thriving (i.e., intervention).

From a critical perspective, it is important not only to recognize the impact of racism on clients of color (e.g., racism-based stress and trauma) but also to imagine interventions that go beyond addressing and coping with the impact. To paraphrase the famous Maya Angelou quote, while helping people of color cope with the stress and trauma of racism and gain resiliency to cope better and to function at a nonclinical level may be an important first goal of the clinical work but it cannot be the ultimate goal. There must be a higher standard of care. In other words, the clinical work must not only be trauma informed but also be healing promotion oriented. This work includes building or re-building support network to sustain the client's thriving, exploring necessary resources for the client to thrive, and advocacy for those resources at the organizational and systems level.

Relational and Intersubjective Approach

A relational model of clinical practice is grounded in relational theory, which posits that clinical work is rooted in the formation of a working relationship between client and worker. In relational practice, the interpersonal relationship connection between a worker and a client serves as a foundation for change and growth. Clinical relationship serves as the basis for the client to understand and develop a healthy sense of self as well as secure and healthy relationships outside the therapy. In this book, we emphasize an intersubjective approach to relational practice, which acknowledges the intersecting inner worlds (including psychologies, emotions, perspectives, lived experiences, and worldviews) of the clinician and the client in a therapeutic relationship (Fort, 2018). Thus, the therapist and the client affect and are affected by the clinical relationship.

Empathy and Social Identity

All clinical work involves trying to understand another person from that person's perspective. This holds true for psychodynamic and cognitive–behavioral approaches, as well as many other therapeutic orientations that rely on the clinician–client relationship. Therefore, empathy is crucial in the clinical process. Studies on mirror neurons (Jankowiak-Siuda et al., 2011) suggest that the same areas of the brain are activated when we experience our own emotions (e.g., pain) and when we observe the same emotions in others (e.g., others in pain). Studies on social cognition suggest that being able to simulate others' emotions and imagine ourselves in such states allows us to consider others' thoughts or beliefs (Goldman & Sebanz, 2005; Azevedo et al., 2013). Thus, empathy allows us not only to internally simulate ("share") others' emotional experiences but also to take the cognitive perspective of others, thus helping us to understand others' emotions, thoughts, and experiences (Jankowiak-Siuda et al., 2011).

When working with clients, clinicians are asked to take their clients' perspective empathically even though clinician and client have differences in social identity and accompanying power and privilege (Dyche & Zayas, 2001) as well as lived experiences. What clinicians see and hear from clients present access points to the clients' experience, and clinicians may respond to them by empathy, that is, sharing feelings and perspectives of their clients. Clinicians may use their own feelings to try to gauge the clients' feelings and thoughts—wondering if they are experiencing something similar to their own inner maps and libraries of experiences.

However, empathy and altruism may be impacted by whether someone is perceived to be similar to us or not. Mathur et al.'s (2012) found that neural activity differed when ethnic group members observed pain in members of their own ethnic group and when they observed the pain in members of another ethnic group, suggesting that neurocognitive processes associated with self-identity predicted higher empathy and altruism for in-group members. Thus, sharing or not sharing a social identity may influence our empathy toward our clients. We do not know what contributes to the difference in empathy for in-group versus out-group members. It may be that internalized stereotypes and biases that lurk beneath the radar screen of consciousness can cloud our ability to see and hear the client (Perez-Foster, 1998) empathically. This is why we stress critical reflection of our own perceptions and internal processes to recognize our emotional and cognitive responses to what we see and hear from clients. Also, an intersubjective approach to relational practice allows clinicians and clients to develop understanding together. By letting clients know what we see and hear, we convey attentiveness while opening up channels to pursue as the client helps us to understand how they experience their feelings and thoughts, thus co-constructing meaning in the process.

Mirroring

We have described at length the lack of validation and mirroring for many people of color in society. Conversely, White people have internalized a sense of White superiority from the many distorted mirrors that elevate their social status while diminishing or erasing that of people of color. Mirroring is the process whereby a person receives an empathic, nuanced reflection of themselves from others that is positive, affirming, and validating. The concept of mirroring is derived from Heinz Kohut's theory of *self-psychology,* which refers to the reflections that people receive from family members and other significant others (Eagle, 1984). Hertzberg (1990) expanded this theory to include cultural and social markers.

Social mirroring can occur when viewing beauty advertisements, reading greeting cards, or seeing national politicians, celebrated artists, or CEOs, which frequently reflect positive images of White people and either an absence of or negative images of people of color. Hertzberg employs additional concepts from self-psychology, such as "idealizing," which involves internalizing another person as a self-ideal. She argues further that this happens on a public and social level, where fewer affirmative role models are available for people of color.

Therapists can employ mirroring effectively with their clients using a technique similar to Rogers's (1951) client-centered therapy. Here, the clinician makes a sustained effort to maintain an empathic connection with a client, whatever material is being brought up, and to mirror the client's value and worth by communicating empathic understanding. With White clients, attention should be paid to grandiosity or assumptions of supremacy. In this process, if clients do not feel judged or humiliated but rather seen and heard, they are better able to explore feelings or self-concepts that are unpleasant, damaged, or stigmatized. Given the empathy considered in the previous section, mirroring is an effective stance from which to develop a therapeutic alliance and to help repair self-concepts damaged as a consequence of racism.

Mirroring is particularly important for people whose self-concept has been injured or distorted by racism and those who suddenly find themselves in a new situation, where they have difficulty seeing themselves in those around them. Consider a young woman of color from a multiracial city where she was surrounded by people of her ethnic group as she travels to a majority White community to attend college. What are the mirroring needs of this young woman, especially her need for role models that reflect her, and how can they be met? What are her strengths, and how might she draw upon them? What would be the needs for mirroring for an idealistic young White man who grew up in a predominantly White suburb and who is motivated by altruism to work with "inner city kids" as a teacher?

Mirroring also is consistent with an anti-oppressive approach, in which clinicians help clients identify and access their strengths, assets, and coping and healing mechanisms. Clinicians must review with clients how they have survived and endured oppression through their resiliency and how and when they thrived, which can be difficult to retrieve in times of duress. By being reflected on their—and their family's and community's—strengths, a possibility for healing and thriving is also imagined.

Opening Up Space for and Responding to Strong Affect

We have described many of the strong feelings that racism can evoke in clients—anger, rage, guilt, shame, and grief and mourning. When clients express these feelings, counselors may have difficulty tolerating these emotions, and this in turn can elicit strong affective reactions from them. Although therapy is often enhanced by the expression and processing of strong affect, when it comes to racism, the magnitude of the reaction can feel overwhelming, for both people of color and White people.

Many people are uncomfortable with direct and powerful manifestations of feelings such as rage and shame, and others are uneasy with candid confrontations about race and racism. Combining these emotions creates a potent mixture. This is one reason why many people do not have many opportunities to express and process these emotions outside therapy (e.g., many people of color are legitimately concerned that their job or career will be negatively impacted if they discussed racism in a frank manner or express their strong feelings about racial discrimination at work). If experiences of racism and attendant emotions cannot be expressed and supported in counseling and therapy, where can they be processed?

Whatever affect a clinician is unable to handle becomes forbidden territory for clients. This reinforces the social unacceptability of both the feeling and its expression. The wider the range of feelings about racism that a clinician can open up for, accept, and support, the more space is granted for clients to use these feelings as therapeutic levers. So how can clinicians increase their affective capacities? One way is through experience. The more they encounter powerful affect, the better they are able to manage reactions. Another way is to explore one's own experience with these emotions and to use self-reflection and insight to better understand their triggers and their powerful hold. Clinicians can use exercises to explore their reactions to feelings around racism, as well as to develop capacity for themselves to experience being in the presence of strong emotions without feeling overwhelmed.

A final way to work toward increasing affective capacity is through supervision. Supervisors and clinicians should be vigilant about bringing these issues out in the open to further the clinical work. With both cross-racial and racially homogeneous supervisory dyads, supervision can be challenging when it involves processing the powerful affect that tends to arise in cross-racial work. Workers and supervisors must be creative and open to finding ways to negotiate discomfort or powerful affect that might arise from discussing these cases, or that might surface between them as the discussions unfold (Peterson, 1991). Supervisors, too, must demonstrate flexibility and a willingness to examine their own biases and internalized racism, and also to discuss race and racism with supervisees. Goggin et al. (2015) offer a case study of clinical work between a White female worker and an African American adolescent male that was terminated prematurely. In spite of the worker's repeated attempts to discuss the disposition of the case with her supervisor, who also identifies as White and female, the supervisor's unexamined bias and racism-based stereotypes took precedence and her belief that this adolescent posed a threat hastened his transfer to another part of the agency for clients with far more stigmatizing and serious diagnoses. Had the supervisor been more vigilant about critically examining her own biases, and had she been open to discussing the impact of her race and the supervisee's and how this influenced their reactions to this young man, the outcome could have been vastly different.

Once therapists have expanded their affective tolerance, they can use a range of interventions. A helpful one is to connect the emotion with the client's presenting problems (Hardy & Laszloffy, 1995). A discussion of possible transference is another avenue to pursue. Tying emotions with historical and social conditions, such as webs of oppression, helps to externalize the source of unpleasant feelings, and it is a means to validate them as well. Clients can be assisted in sorting out what they are responsible for and what they have no control over. Hardy and Laszloffy (1995) also suggest that seeking underlying feelings, such as the grief and mourning beneath anger, is of value to clients. Clinicians should try to help clients find more constructive expression of feelings (e.g., productive anger) that are less likely to be personally harmful or counterproductive.

Working With Racial Transference and Countertransference

As Ridley (1995) has argued, the cultural dimension of transference and countertransference is always present, and we extrapolate that to racial transference and countertransference. Many therapists, particularly those using psychodynamic methods, discuss transference and countertransference as a means for using the clinical relationship to further client insight, growth, and change. Thus, clinical practice in the context of racism in our society requires making space for consideration of racial transference and countertransference—how it feels and what it means to both client and worker. It should not be treated as the proverbial "elephant in the room." As relational theory emphasizes mutual and interactional processes and posits that our primary goal is to be in relationship with others, it is critical that workers anticipate and pay close attention to potential racialized dynamics inherent in clinical work, and the ways that the transference–countertransference matrix is enacted in these instances (see Altman, 2010; Suchet, 2004, 2007).

Although the clinician does not have to raise the issue immediately, it certainly should be discussed at some point. For the clinician, this means first accessing and tracking one's own transference and countertransference, critically reflecting on them, and developing the capacity to share reflections and explore meanings with clients in a productive way.

In the example of racial transference discussed in the *Barriers to Effective Clinical Work* section of this chapter, Garran (2013) discusses how the therapist recognized the racial transference and countertransference being enacted in the therapy room. The therapist then used empathetic listening to gently challenge the father of the client who had been aggressively challenging the therapist's authority and legitimacy with a coded language of race, ethnicity, gender, and class, and the father revealed that he was fearful he and his wife had been summoned to participate in their daughter's psychotherapy because the worker was questioning their competence as parents and shaming for their daughter's difficulties. The therapist assured the parents that that was not her intent, and they were able to relax and relate to the therapist in a more appropriate and less inflammatory manner. This session was pivotal in the daughter's psychotherapy. Communication within the family improved as each recognized the assumptive styles of interaction that often obstructed truly hearing one another.

Essentially, the therapist in this case used critical reflexivity to observe and understand her own reactions to those aggressive challenges, which enabled her to get to the underlying parental shame and envy that were projected onto her, and how the racial dynamics in the larger society were implicated in the projection. In order to do this, the therapist had to consistently remind herself of the purpose of the session and try to see and hear past the personal attacks in order to more fully understand the clinical reasons for the racist affronts. Only when the therapist was able to do this was she then able to hear the father's quite compromised self-esteem as demonstrated by his virulent projections, and with this information, she moved with the family to a more settled place. Finally, the therapist then sought supervision to more fully process the residue left from such a highly charged session. It is important that the therapist had her own support after the session to process and reflect on such aggressive projection and attack on her social identities that she holds dear.

One possible racial countertransference seen in a cross-racial clinical relationship is when clinicians who identify as White experience impulses to please clients of color or desire to be seen as a "good" White person. This can come from many reasons, including possible reaction formation (for their unconscious or conscious feelings of racism, prejudice, or White superiority), desire to be seen only as an individual, separate from White racism in the society (which paradoxically comes from unexamined White privilege since people of color cannot afford to do so), wish to assuage "White guilt," or any other unconscious reasons. This can produce situations of colluding with clients of color or backing away from situations in which confronting or challenging clients is necessary. Clinicians in this situation may notice that clinical progress is slow or met with impasse. This situation calls for critical self-reflection and seeking supervision or consultation immediately. By processing one's racial countertransference, the clinician can gain rich and productive clinical insight that can be used to improve clinical effectiveness and ultimately help the client to progress toward their goal.

Anti-Oppressive Practice Approach

As discussed at the beginning of this chapter, anti-oppressive practice (AOP) approach involves a critical examination of the various power imbalances that are found in our society, within organizational structures, and between the clinician and their clients (Morgaine & Capous-Desyllas, 2014). In AOP, clinicians consider connections between individual struggles, structural inequalities, and historical oppression. Individual struggles are connected to social identities in terms of how they and their behaviors are perceived and interpreted by others, including clinicians, and types of resources that are available to them. Societal inequities often exacerbate individual's struggles, and experiences of oppression such as racism can lead to trauma reactions and negative health and wellness consequences. Furthermore, policies including social, health, economic, judicial and the like, at all levels (local, state, national, and organizational) constrain or promote individuals' life choices and access to resources. Therefore, AOP compels clinicians to go beyond psychological services to strategize ways to diminish power imbalances through their practice, promoting equity and empowerment for their clients in all contexts.

Situating Clients and Clinicians in Their Historical and Social Context

In the first section of the *Strategies*, we discussed the importance of using critical reflection to understand our own and our clients' intersectional social identities, including attendant issues of power and privilege, and how they impact our perspectives and life experiences. This critical reflection is an essential element of AOP and helps situate both the clinician and the client in their historical and social context. This means that clinicians must consciously consider human development and functioning in the multiple and intersecting contexts of the environment, including community, society, policy, and history. Doing so allows the clinician to see clients' behaviors, choices, and functioning through the lens of interaction between the person and their environment and to understand their vulnerabilities and strengths in a fuller scope, leading to a more contextual assessment. Situating clients in their social and historical contexts also opens up possibilities for clinicians and clients to discover interventions that are more appropriate and empowering.

Consider the vignette that was shared in the earlier section of this chapter about an African American mother who shared her concerns about her pre-teen son riding his bicycle to an unfamiliar, White suburban neighborhood. If the clinician in that case considered the mother's concerns in the historical, social, and political contexts of anti-Black racism and violence, especially against young Black men, how would it have changed her interpretation of the client's concerns? (The consideration of the social and historical context must also be applied to the therapist, and therapist self-reflection would have helped her situate her understanding and perspective in that context.)

Clients may or may not know about the historical and social conditions of racism that have contributed to psychic scars and wounds, and they may or may not be at a place in their clinical process where it would be appropriate to reflect and discuss these issues. However, wherever the client is in their process, it is essential that clinicians have a good understanding of these conditions and of the ways by which webs of racism affect their clients. This helps to avoid missing an important source of trauma and pathologizing and problematizing of what often are normal reactions to exceedingly stressful circumstances. It also helps clinicians to better understand the social conditions to which their clients return upon leaving the consulting room and to enact realistic interventions and follow-up. For example, a client who has relocated to the United States recently from war-torn Syria might not be comfortable speaking of the atrocities witnessed, because of a continuing fear of retribution that the client has internalized. Clinicians should be aware of these nuances so they do not rush clients to tell their stories before they are ready. Instead, clinicians should collaborate with clients to negotiate the pace and scope of the intervention that support client self-determination and empowerment (see Box 12.1).

Bringing Up Issues of Race and Racism

One of the questions that students most commonly ask us is when and how to bring up issues of race and racism. Unfortunately, this question has no simple answer. From experiences of grappling with these issues (Carter, 1995; Ridley, 1995), there is no set rule.

BOX 12.1 Strategies for Effective Clinical Work

▶ Know yourself. Assess your own intersectional social identities and how they influence your perspectives, assumptions, and lived experiences

▶ Know your clients. Assess their intersectional social identities and how they influence their perspectives, assumptions, and lived experiences. Learn from them how they view themselves, the world, and you.

▶ Learn about your clients' social, historical, and cultural contexts to form a nuanced and contextual understanding.

▶ Learn about how webs of racism and oppression or passports of unearned power and privilege have affected both you and your clients and have been internalized.

▶ Practice critical self-reflection to examine and understand the process between yourself and your clients, particularly cultural and racial transference and countertransference.

▶ Enhance your ability to tolerate pain, rage, and client mistrust to develop capacity to open up space for and support clients' expression and processing of difficult emotions about race and racism.

▶ Seek supervision and consultation.

▶ Examine theories for biases and assumptions, and learn about alternative theories and how healing and thriving are conceptualized in the client's traditional perspectives.

▶ Seek organizational support for antiracism and social justice.

▶ Consider interventions that address multilevel (individual, community/organizational, structural/policy) changes.

Clinicians should be willing and able to broach the topic, but they should understand that there is no formula about when and how to do this effectively.

Talk about race and racism should occur within the overall context of counseling and therapy, which includes the client's presenting problems, the organizational context of treatment, treatment goals, the bond between client and worker, and the dynamics of that relationship. We caution against rigid admonitions such as telling clinicians to always bring up race or ethnicity right away, but at the same time are wary that some clinicians seldom or never bring it up.

Certain situations lend themselves to inquiries about this topic, such as when a client of color relates examples of racism or a White client brings up racial stereotypes or expresses negativity or ambivalence about people of color. Both instances present an opening for the clinician to invite reflection and discussion about the salience of these issues in the clinical relationship. At times, indirect yet probing questions can invite clients to talk about race and racism if they choose. Clients must have agency with this process and the clinician should neither close it off nor force it open. This is part of the collaborative process of an intersubjective relational approach of clinical practice.

Clinicians should be self-reflective and mindful of their own inclinations to want to bring up race and racism out of context or avoid talking about race (Cook, 1994). Writing process recordings and reviewing them can allow clinicians to track themes that are either present but unnamed or avoidant maneuvers by the therapist. Supervision, case conferences, and discussions with trusted colleagues are other avenues for exploring and monitoring these themes. Audio and visual recording sessions can assist with tracking the clinical process and highlighting verbal and bodily reactions. This is a useful method of critical reflection.

Ultimately, both client and worker are aware of race and ethnicity on some level (Leary, 1997, 2000). Their relevance and importance vary considerably for each client and therapeutic dyad. As in making most clinical decisions, counselors and therapists should follow the lead of their clients and also use their own judgment, in consultation with others, about the relevance of this topic for treatment, the timing of discussing it, and the best way to frame it.

As with any clinical skills, skills in addressing race and racism in clinical settings takes experience and practice. One of the authors of this text found it helpful to have students role-play, based on a vignette or by imagining themselves having a conversation with a client at their practicum, skills in addressing race and racism in class. First, through a quick writing exercise, students are asked to critically reflect on their own and their client's social identities and their impact and to locate both themselves and their client in social and historical contexts. Students are then paired with another student to role-play addressing race and racism and then share their reflection and feedback with their role-play partner. The exercise can be repeated at different phases of the course so that students can apply what they have learned to the next role-play, gaining more confidence and competence as they practice. Students often find it a bit awkward at first but usually end up feeling relieved that they had a chance to exercise a skill that is new to many of them. This exercise may be helpful for clinicians who are not experienced or would like to strengthen their skills in this area.

Responding to Bias

Racial biases and stereotypes will inevitably surface in clinical work. Workers should not collude with bias and should consider how best to respond in a clinical context. Maintaining the clinical relationship is essential and necessary for helping the client. Rupturing the relationship in response to client bias is not likely to help clients with either their presenting problems or their prejudices. Clients may express bias and prejudice in the consulting room in two ways:

1. By describing their views and feelings toward people outside of the therapeutic dyad.
2. By expressing them directly toward the therapist.

When bias is directed outside of the consulting room, it also may stir up strong reactions in the therapist. A higher risk is that some clinicians may not perceive or acknowledge client bias, which will signal approval either actively or passively through acquiescence.

Clinicians can use several strategies in these situations. One strategy is to continue to work on one's own triggers and to increase the capacity to tolerate feelings of outrage, anger, pain, and disgust engendered by the client's statements. Ideally, clients should not have to consult with clinicians who are so overwhelmed in the moment by such strong emotions. Also fruitful is to question clients' prejudicial attitudes, much as counselors help clients explore other pathogenic or irrational belief systems. This is much more likely to be effective if it can be done in a nonjudgmental and clinically consistent fashion.

Another strategy is to make overt the covert, if the client is raising bias in a coded or indirect manner. Clinicians, too, can make their own values known, as long as they do this in a way that does not attack the client or make them feel less worthy or honorable. If this raises concerns that such a challenge might influence the therapeutic alliance adversely, clinicians can discuss the views and values of others, such as public figures and social scientists, to offer an opposing narrative. Then both client and worker can interrogate the contrast between nonracist viewpoints and the perspective the client expresses.

All of these interventions tend to be more effective if they are linked to the client's presenting problems and the themes and issues of treatment. Also, clinicians must seek supervision and consultation to process their feelings and reactions and to ensure that their responses are crafted to achieve effectiveness for the clinical work.

Responding to bias directed to the clinician is more challenging because of its potential to trigger strong reactions in the clinician. One of the biggest challenges for clinicians of color and multiracial clinicians is being the target of direct racist comments by clients, or hearing clients talk in biased ways against others. Hearing biased comments, including those directed toward one's own race or ethnic group, is particularly common for multiracial clinicians who look White. Clients also may test the clinician's authority and expertise. Clinicians of color often have to work harder than their White counterparts to establish their credentials. This may necessitate confronting clients more frequently, which takes more effort than what their White counterparts have to do. Also, confronting White clients in a social environment that support White superiority and normativity means that clinicians of color experience a higher level of emotional labor, which can be exhausting. In addition, confronting clients has to be balanced with establishing and maintaining therapeutic alliances (Garran, 2013). As we discussed in the *racial transference and countertransference* section, support from supervision or consultation is greatly needed for clinicians of color in such situations.

Situating Clinical Intervention in Sociopolitical Context: Clinical Intervention for Change at Multiple Levels

A vital aspect of AOP is critical analysis of power dynamics. By locating themselves and their clients within the larger social and historical context, clinicians analyze and understand not only the power dynamics between the worker and the client but also the interactions between the worker, the client, and the larger systems (including organizations and social and economic policies). Thus, AOP considers interventions that aim to bring changes at multiple levels (individual, community/organization, and society/policy) as part of clinical work. Traditionally, clinical practice focused on psychological interventions at the individual level, with family therapy and small group treatment methods later developed and added. Many contemporary clinicians recognize the necessity of casework, including resource advocacy, but others do not recognize it as clinical practice. Furthermore, many clinical workers do not consider systems-level change or policy advocacy as part of clinical work. However, people do not live in a psychological vacuum but rather in communities and societies, and their lives and clinical issues are impacted by systemic inequalities and policies. In concert with AOP we argue that interventions that are aimed at multi-level change are often more effective, especially when the client's struggles stem from or are exacerbated by the community or policy level problems.

For example, Kang's (2013) case study of her work with a Korean immigrant elderly client illustrates how multilevel interventions worked together not only to improve the client's functioning but also to help her thrive and find new meaning. In this case, the client developed acute depressive symptoms after learning that she will lose her Medicaid benefits even though she had permanent residency due to the immigrant restrictions in the 1996 Welfare Reform.

Situating the client's story of loss (of identity, security, and belonging) in the sociopolitical context, the worker and the client worked together on a multi-level intervention. On the micro (individual) level, the worker and the client engaged in a narrative psychotherapy; the client was also assisted by medication treatment by a psychiatrist. On the mezzo (community) level, the worker advocated for the client to participate in an English learning class for the elderly who wished to study for the citizenship exam, which was administered only in English at that time. On the macro (policy) level, the worker accompanied and interpreted for the client who participated in the Asian American community Lobby Day at the state legislature, which was organized by the agency. The client and other elderly community members were able to meet with the state legislators to advocate for themselves. In addition, the worker (who is also a Korean immigrant) participated in the Lobby Day to advocate for rights for immigrants. The individual intervention helped the client reduce depressive symptoms and find a new narrative of resiliency, meaning, and identity. The community linkage helped the client gain a community support network and a sense of belonging. Participating in the Lobby Day helped the client situate her story in the larger story of her community's fight for their rights. Also, the Lobby Day advocacy from the community resulted in the state allowing elderly immigrants to take the citizenship exam in their native language, which helped the client eventually gain her citizenship and regain her Medicaid benefits. The multilevel intervention resulted in a significant improvement in the client's mental health as well as in her social and economic well-being; she remained active and thrived in her community after the case was closed due to remission. The case reminds us of the importance of situating the client and the worker in the sociopolitical context, illustrates effectiveness of a multilevel intervention method, and suggests that individual struggles that stem from a structural problem (such as the welfare policy regarding immigrants) may need a macro-level intervention in addition to individual therapies and community resource linkages.

It might seem daunting for clinicians to imagine taking on macro-level advocacy; many workers are already dealing with a high caseload and frustrated by unfair and rigid organizational or governmental policies that limit their clients' access to care or create unnecessary bureaucratic barriers to effective work. The challenge may seem insurmountable. However, as Reynolds (2011) reminds us, it is rarely the client work—even with a high caseload or clients with severe and persistent mental health problems—that leads us to burnout but rather the "the injustices and indignities suffered by clients and [the clinician's] frustrating inability to personally change the unjust structures of society they struggle with and live in" (p. 28) that exhausts us. Reynolds points out that burnout is conceptualized as an individual phenomenon that casts responsibility onto individual workers, and this isolation furthers feelings of exhaustion and despair. Because the exhaustion and frustration are based on facing the structural barriers as an individual worker, Reynolds argues that workers need to reconceptualize self-care to collective care and "justice doing." Working in solidarity with others to resist systemic injustices can help us feel less isolated and individually responsible for what is a community-wide issue. It can also give us a sense of hope and purpose for a long-term change. When working individually in isolation it feels frustrating and sometimes even pointless when changes do not happen, are very slow, or highly incremental. However, working collectively helps us see that we are contributing our share to a long history of activism and larger social change even if we do not see the changes quickly. Also, community care means that we practice care and compassion for one another and to ourselves, which helps sustain us as we engage in anti-oppressive clinical practice.

SUPERVISION AND CONSULTATION

Clearly, anti-oppressive clinical work requires honest self-awareness, the ability to manage strong emotions and reactions, and the capacity to empathize with people who have very different experiences, worldviews, and access to resources. Supervision and consultation are always important and necessary in clinical work. Clinical supervision is a relational and developmental process; thus, many of the issues that have been identified with clients must be negotiated—in a process that often parallels the helping relationship itself. Supervision involves teaching as well as ensuring professional accountability, which includes the capacity to work in a critically reflective and anti-oppressive way.

Supervisors and supervisees alike have to be able to track and analyze the clinical work and to collaboratively explore issues of race and racism. All clinicians should question their theoretical orientations for culturally and racially biased assumptions and principles. White clinicians and supervisors in particular should be cautious about accepting theoretical assumptions because they potentially are consistent with the clinician's own worldview and value system and thus are more difficult to detect.

The supervisory relationship is a space where both worker and supervisor will have to process issues that arise between them, as well as issues between worker and client. To this end, supervisors must be skilled in recognizing the racial power dynamics that emerge in clinical work, and also how they may play out in supervision (Cashwell et al., 1997). Supervisors must also be able to tolerate and reflect on not only the strong affect and reactions originating from clients and supervisees but also their own feelings reactions stirred up in themselves. Thus, supervisors should be able to raise issues of social identities, power, and privilege in the supervisory relationship in a way that does not intimidate or shut down a supervisee. One concern that we have heard from our students with a range of social identities is that their supervisor rarely initiates a consideration of race and ethnicity or even may see this as a diversion from the "real" clinical issues. A supervisor should be able to discuss with workers the implications of race and ethnicity on the clinical material as it unfolds. Supervisors of any racial or ethnic identity have to be able to track the complex levels of transference and countertransference that involve client, worker, supervisor, and other agency personnel.

Supervisors need to demonstrate leadership in broaching the subject of race and ethnicity in clinical work. Workers (both student interns and professional workers) are often uncomfortable doing so or feel unsure about how their comments, observations, or questions might be received by a supervisor. If a supervisor demonstrates their willingness and capacity to discuss the racial dynamics of clinical work, this confidence and willingness will be evident to most supervisees, opening doors for them to explore racial dynamics. Supervisors should be aware, though, that mentioning race and ethnicity just once is never sufficient. These issues and concerns must be addressed consistently so the supervisee will feel permission to discuss them and also to convey a message of acceptance on the part of the supervisor (Black et al., 1997).

At times, supervisors and supervisees will benefit from additional consultation. Consultation can be about the work with the client, the supervisory relationship itself, the clash between agency policies and client well-being, or a combination of these. Consultants may help to clarify roles and expectations, as well as give specific feedback about cultural misunderstandings and unacknowledged racial dynamics. Depending on the racial or cultural mix of client, worker, and supervisor, there are times when more perspectives will be valuable and clinical work will benefit from multiple consultants. White clinicians consulting with colleagues of color should be mindful about not shifting the burden of education to the colleagues of color and should engage in critical reflection and research before asking for consultation with colleagues of color. Adding more people to the clinical process sometimes presents a greater potential for role confusion, conflicting advice, or splitting and triangulation of relationships. This is particularly true with issues of race and culture, which carry strong affect, as well as questions of identity and ideology.

Thus, all professional players must work together to minimize rifts and covert dynamics that undermine colleagues and, ultimately, effective and just services to clients. Direct, open, above-board communication is necessary, along with a willingness to process and negotiate conflicts and differences of opinion.

ENVIRONMENT, ACCESS, AND REPRESENTATION

In Chapter 11, we explored how helping professionals can work to transform their agencies into antiracism organizations. This section briefly considers some issues that particularly apply to those health and human service organizations that offer counseling and therapy.

Environment

The agency environment encompasses the physical building, waiting room, consulting rooms, and accessories such as artwork and magazines. It also includes the climate and culture conveyed to consumers. Is this a place where all people, whatever their social identities, feel welcomed and comfortable? Many agencies take the overall environment for granted, yet it sends distinct messages to clients seeking services. Small details, such as outdated reading materials or magazines and signs only in English in an agency that serves many people who speak Spanish only, influence whether consumers will feel comfortable or legitimate. The condition and appearance of waiting rooms, office spaces, and even restrooms send unspoken yet potent messages to clients about how much they are valued and respected.

Clients also notice if the spaces for workers are in much better condition than those for consumers. The clinical environment should reflect, respect, and respond to various cultures and be one where all consumers feel included and respected.

Access

To take advantage of clinical services, clients must have adequate access to care. As described in previous chapters, people of color are more likely to rely on public transportation and less likely to have sufficient health insurance or the ability to pay for services. Thus, clinical service agencies must be located near adequate public transportation. Extended clinic hours will accommodate consumers who are working early or late shifts and those who have to transfer buses several times to get to work. Safety, too, is important, both in the area surrounding the agency and inside the agency itself. A welcome shift in the delivery of community mental health services in the United States has been that of seeing clients on demand, rather than making them wait for scheduled appointments. However, there are still problems with how such visits are followed up once a crisis has passed.

For financial or cultural reasons, some consumers may not have access to or do not use daycare for their preschool children or after-school care for older children. Providing adequate play spaces for children, or even supervised creches, enables clients to utilize these services and concentrate better while they are attending sessions.

One crucial barrier to accessing clinical services is language differences. While our society has become much more multilingual our clinical and social health care system has not caught up. Often, agencies do not provide services for clients whose language does not match their staff's or provide woefully inadequate services, leading to severe inequity. In some cases, agencies make clients responsible for providing their own interpreters or utilize clients' bilingual children as interpreters, which is problematic in numerous ways. Similarly, clinicians who are bicultural and bilingual often find themselves managing heavy and demanding caseloads and without adequate time for translation, advocacy, and other necessary activities. Agencies must take the responsibility to provide language-appropriate services without unfairly burdening bilingual and bicultural staff. Providing language-appropriate service, especially in an area where there are not many professionals who speak the language, may require building and strengthening relationships with ethnic-linguistic communities and investing in training and developing multilingual staff (such as a para-professional training program where para-professionals with language capabilities are hired to assist in clinical work and receive agency-supported professional education to become professional clinical workers).

Cutbacks in public funding for counseling and mental health programs, as well as tightened eligibility requirements and restrictions by insurance and managed-care companies, have made it more difficult for agencies to serve all of the clients who would benefit from their services, as well as to offer enough sessions. Although this is a difficult issue for financially strapped agencies, it is significant nonetheless. As described many times in this book, as an overall group, people of color have fewer economic and social assets and resources, so they are affected disproportionately by cuts in public services. Even if an agency has done a good job in training the staff to be culturally responsive, it will go for naught if clients cannot access the services. This has to be an ongoing priority for clinical agencies working on their own and in concert with one another to improve access.

Staffing and Board Representation

This topic was addressed in Chapter 11 and is reiterated here only briefly. To effectively serve a multiracial, multicultural population, an organization must have multiracial/multicultural staff represented at all levels. If clients speak languages other than English, the organization should have multilingual staff members as well. Advisory and policy-making boards should reflect the diversity of the clients (including consumer representation on boards) and of the community being served.

CONCLUSION

Clinical practice in our society's racial context can be both complicated and positive and beneficial for clinicians. In this chapter we presented a relational, intersubjective, critical, and anti-oppressive approach to clinical practice. Effective clinical practice requires that workers exercise critical reflection and reflexivity to be aware of their own complex social identities, attendant power and privilege, and their impact on their perspectives and experiences. They must also be mindful of their clients' complex social identities, power and privilege, and their impact on their perspective, functioning, and experiences. Clinicians must attend to power dynamics in the clinical relationship as well as between the client and the larger society. Supervision and consultation, as well as attention to access to services and representation in the agency, are also vital.

Despite the many obstacles to racially just clinical work, staffs of many counseling and mental health services across the country have responded to the challenges and developed the capacity to provide effective clinical services for consumers having a range of ethnic and racial backgrounds. Becoming anti-oppressive practitioners, who confront oppression in themselves as well as others, must be ongoing, but the investments are well worth the gains.

EXERCISE 12.1 Crossed Racial Identity Between Worker and Client

Sofia is a second-generation Chilean American sophomore at a state university who identifies as a cisgender woman and straight. She is seeking counseling about her test anxiety. Upon arriving at the university, she did not view herself as a person of color, but with encouragement from her friends she recently joined the Council for Students of Color. She has been rethinking events and relationships from high school in light of her new awareness of being a Latina in the United States.

The counselor at the college counseling service is a White, gay man who identifies as Irish American and has not thought a lot about his own racial or ethnic identity. When the student tries to talk about her newfound awareness of her racial and ethnic identities, the counselor tries to redirect her to examine her parents' expectations for her when she was younger and whether she has any cognitive or neurological learning disabilities.

The student accuses the counselor of turning her identity into a pathology and says that a number of students in the Council for Students of Color have had this experience at the college counseling service. The therapist feels defensive and believes the student is using her identity as a way to avoid examining important and painful issues.

Questions

1. Using the social identity model presented in Chapter 7, how might you describe both the student's and the counselor's intersectional social identities and their impact on each person's perception of the situation?
2. What kind of work or training might be helpful to the counselor to better prepare him to be more effective with this client?
3. If you are the counselor's supervisor, what would you recommend? And how would you help the counselor to become more effective?

EXERCISE 12.2 Exploring Emotions

The questions following the case vignette will help you explore your reactions to anger and rage. The same questions can be asked about other emotions, such as guilt, shame, and grief.

You are facilitating a socialization group at a university. Several students of color open up during the group to discuss microaggressions and being targeted because of their race and/or ethnicity, both on campus and in the surrounding community. They share multiple stories of the experiences of racism that they have encountered. Several students in the group start to quietly cry. One student in the group, a White Veteran, contributes to the discussion by stating that he knows how the students of color feel because when he was deployed overseas, people threw rocks at him when he walked around in his military uniform because they didn't like Americans. One of the students of color feels immediately triggered and begins to raise her voice in anger, stating that he cannot possibly know what their experiences are like. Several other students of color join her in their dissent. Two White students in the group get up and leave, with one of them saying that he won't be back until "everyone can control themselves." Another White student stays in the room, but remarks that no one had better throw anything and that everyone needed to just relax and calm down and stop shouting.

Questions

1. What are your values about expressing rage and anger?
2. How do you express anger and rage?
3. How do you react when people direct anger and rage at you?
4. What are your thoughts and reactions to rage when a client is expressing rage?
5. How do you validate the client's rage?
6. What are some constructive ways for clients to channel rage and anger?

REFERENCES

Altman, N. (2010). *The analyst in the inner city: Race, class, and culture through a psychoanalytic lens* (2nd ed.). Taylor & Francis.

Azevedo, R. T., Macaluso, E., Avenanti, A., Santangelo, V., Cazzato, V., & Aglioti, S. M. (2013). Their pain is not our pain: Brain and autonomic correlates of empathic resonance with the pain of same and different race individuals. *Human Brain Mapping, 34*, 3168–3181.

Black, J., Maki, M., & Nunn, J. (1997). Does race affect the social work student-field instructor relationship? *Clinical Supervisor, 16*(1), 39–54.

Brave Heart, M. Y H. (2003). The historical trauma response among Natives and its relationship with substance abuse: A Lakota illustration. *Journal of Psychoactive Drugs, 35*, 7–13.

Brondolo, E., Rieppi, R., Kelly, K. P., & Gerin, W. (2003). Perceived racism and blood pressure: A review of the literature and conceptual and methodological critique. *Annals of Behavioral Medicine, 25*, 55–65. https://doi.org/10.1207/S15324796ABM2501_08

Carter, R. T. (1995). Race and psychotherapy: Clinical applications in a sociocultural context. In R. T. Carter (Ed.), *The influence of race and racial identity in psychotherapy: Toward a racially inclusive model* (Chap. 13, pp. 225–241). Wiley.

Carter, R. T., Forsyth, J., Mazzula, S., & Williams, B. (2005). Racial discrimination and race-based traumatic stress. In R. T. Carter (Ed.), *Handbook of racial–cultural psychology and counseling: Training and practice* (Vol. 2, pp. 447–476). Wiley.

Carter, R. T. (2007). Racism and psychological and emotional injury: Recognizing and assessing race-based traumatic stress. *The Counseling Psychologist, 35*, 13–105.

Cashwell, C., Looby, E. J., & Housley, W. (1997). Appreciating cultural diversity through clinical supervision. *Clinical Supervisor, 25*(1), 75–85.

Comas-Diaz, L., & Jacobsen, F. M. (2001). Ethnocultural allodyma. *Journal of Psychotherapy Practice and Research, 10*, 246–252.

Cook, D. A. (1994). Racial identity in supervision. *Counselor Education and Supervision, 34*(2), 132–141.

Copeland, P. (2015). Let's get free: Social work and the movement for Black lives. *Journal of Forensic Social Work, 5*(1–3), 3–19.

Copeland-Linder, N., Lambert, S. F., Chen, Y. F., & Ialongo, N. S. (2011). Contextual stress and health risk behaviors among African American adolescents. *Journal of Youth and Adolescence, 40*, 158–173.

Damasio, A. (2000). *The feeling of what happens: Body, emotions and the making of consciousness.* Vintage.

Daniel, J. H. (2000). The courage to hear: African American women's memories of racial trauma. In L. C. Jackson & B. Greene (Eds.), *Psychotherapy with African American women: Innovations in psychodynamic perspectives and practice.* Guilford Press.

DiAngelo, R. (2018). *White fragility: Why it is so hard for white people to talk about racism.* Beacon Press.

Duran, E, & Duran, B. (1995). *Native American postcolonial psychology.* State University of New York Press.

Dyche, L., & Zayas, L. H. (2001). Cross-cultural empathy and training the contemporary psychotherapist. *Clinical Social Work Journal, 29*(3), 245–258.

Eagle, M. N. (1984). *Recent developments in psychoanalysis: A critical evaluation.* Harvard University Press.

Evans-Campbell, T. (2008). Historical trauma in American Indian/Native Alaska communities: A multilevel framework for exploring impacts on individuals, families, and communities. *Journal of Interpersonal Violence, 23*, 316–338. [PubMed: 18245571]

Ferguson, S. A., & King, T. C. (1997). There but for the grace of God: Two Black women therapists explore privilege. *Women & Therapy, 20*(1), 5–14.

Fook, J. (2002). *Social work: Critical theory and practice.* Sage.

Fook, J. (2016). *Social work: A critical approach to practice.* Sage.

Fort, C. J. (2018). Intersectionality, intersubjectivity and integration: A two person therapy. *Journal of Psychology and Theology, 46*(2), 116–121. https://doi.org/10.1177/0091647118767987

Garran, A. M. (2013). Lessons learned: Racial enactments in the treatment process. *Journal of Social Work Practice, 27*(3), 305–317.

Gaw, A. C. (Ed.). (1993). *Culture, ethnicity, and mental illness.* American Psychiatric Publishing.

Gee, G. C., Spencer, M., Chen, J., Yip, T., & Takeuchi, D. T. (2007). The association between self-reported racial discrimination and 12-month *DSM-IV* mental disorders among Asian Americans nationwide. *Social Science & Medicine, 64*, 1984–1996. https://doi.org/10.1016/j.socscimed.2007.02.013

Goggin, E., Werkmeister Rozas, L., & Garran, A. M. (2015). A case of mistaken identity: What happens when race is a factor. *Journal of Social Work Practice, 30*(4), 349–363. https://doi.org/10.1080/0265053 3.2015.1100596

Goldman, A., & Sebanz, N. (2005). Simulation, mirroring, and a different argument from error. *Trends in Cognitive Sciences, 9*(7), 320.

Goodman, D. (2011). *Promoting diversity and social justice: Educating people from privileged groups* (2nd ed.). Routledge.

Hair, H., & O'Donohue, K. (2009). Culturally relevant, socially just supervision: Becoming visible through a social constructionist lens. *Journal of Ethnicity and Cultural Diversity in Social Work, 18*(1–2), 70–88.

Hardy, K. V., & Laszloffy, T. A. (1995). Therapy with African Americans and the phenomenon of rage. *In Session: Psychotherapy in Practice, 1*(4), 57–70.

Hartmann, W. E., Wendt, D. C., Burrage, R. L., Pomerville, A., & Gone, J. P. (2019). American Indian historical trauma: Anticolonial prescriptions for healing, resilience, and survivance. *American Psychologist, 74*(1), 6–19.

Hertzberg, J. F. (1990). Feminist psychotherapy and diversity: Treatment considerations from a self-psychology perspective. In L. S. Brown & M. P. P. Root (Eds.), *Diversity and complexity in feminist therapy* (pp. 275–297). Haworth.

hooks, B. (1995). *Killing rage: Ending racism.* Henry Holt.

Jankowiak-Siuda, K., Rymarczyk, K., & Grabowska, A. (2011). How we empathize with others: A neurobiological perspective. *Medical Science Monitor: International Medical Journal of Experimental and Clinical Research, 17*(1), RA18–RA24. https://doi.org/10.12659/msm.881324

Joseph, V., & Williams, T. O. (2008). "Good niggers": The struggle to find courage, strength, and confidence to fight internalized racism and internalized dominance. *Democracy and Education, 17*(2), 67–73.

Kang, H. K. & Burton, D. B. (2014). Effects of racial discrimination, childhood trauma, and trauma symptoms on juvenile delinquency in African American incarcerated youth. *Journal of Aggression, Maltreatment and Trauma, 23*(10), 1109–1125.

Kang, H. K. (2013). Claiming immigrant cultural citizenship: Applying postcolonial theories to social work practice with immigrants. *Critical and Radical Social Work, 1*(2), 233–245.

Leary, K. (1997). Race, self-disclosure, and "forbidden talk": Race and ethnicity in contemporary clinical practice. *Psychoanalytic Quarterly, LXVI,* 163–189.

Leary, K. (2000). Racial enactments in dynamic treatment. *Psychoanalytic Dialogues, 20*(4), 639–653.

Lee, E. & Bhuyan, R. (2013). Negotiating within whiteness in cross-cultural clinical encounters. *Social Service Review, 87* (1), 98–130.

Lorde, A. (1984). The uses of anger: Women responding to racism. *Sister Outsider: Essays and speeches.* Crossing Press.

Martin, M. J., McCarthy, B., Conger, R. D., Gibbons, F. X., Simons, R. L., Cutrona, C. E., & Brody, G. H. (2011). The enduring significance of racism: Discrimination and delinquency among Black American youth. *Journal of Research on Adolescence, 21,* 662–676.

Mathur, V. A., Harada, T., & Chiao, J. Y. (2012). Racial identification modulates default network activity for same and other races. *Human Brain Mapping, 33*(8), 1883–1893.

Moffat, K., & Miehls, D. (1999). Development of student identity: Evolution from neutrality to subjectivity. *Journal of Teaching in Social Work, 19*(1/2), 65–76.

Moradi, B., & Risco, C. (2006). Perceived discrimination experiences and mental health of Latina/o American persons. *Journal of Counseling Psychology, 53,* 411–421. https://doi.org/10.1037/0022-0167.53.4.411

Morgaine, K., & Capous-Desyllas, M. (2014). *Anti-Oppressive Social Work Practice.* Sage.

Nadal, K. L., Griffin, K. E., Wong, Y., Hamit, S., & Rasmus, M. (2014). The impact of racial microaggressions on mental health: Counseling implications for clients of color. *Journal of Counseling & Development, 92,* 57–66. https://doi.org/10.1002/j.1556-6676.2014.00130.x

Nicotera, N., & Kang, H.-K. (2009). Beyond diversity courses: Strategies for integrating critical consciousness across social work curriculum. *Journal of Teaching in Social Work, 29*(3), 188–203.

Paradies, Y. (2006). A systematic review of empirical research on self-reported racism and health. *International Journal of Epidemiology, 35,* 888–901. https://doi.org/10.1093/ije/dyl056

Perez-Foster, R. M. (1998). The clinician's cultural countertransference: The psychodynamics of culturally competent practice. *Clinical Social Work Journal, 26*(3), 253–270.

Perrin-Klinger, G. (2000). The integration of traumatic experiences: Culture and resources. In J. M. Violanti, D. Patton, & C. Dunning (Eds.), *Posttraumatic stress intervention* (pp. 43–64). Charles Thomas.

Peterson, F. K. (1991). Issues of race and ethnicity in supervision: Emphasizing who you are, not what you know. *Clinical Supervisor, 9*(1), 15–31.

Park, Y. (2008). Facilitating injustice: Tracing the role of social workers in the World War II internment of Japanese Americans. *Social Service Review, 82*(3), 447–484.

Poussaint, A. (2000). *Lay my burden down: Unraveling suicide and the mental health burden of African Americans.* Beacon Press.

Reynolds, V. (2011). Resisting burn-out with justice doing. *The International Journal of Narrative Therapy and Community Work, 4,* 27–45.

Ridley, C. R. (1995). *Overcoming unintentional racism in counseling and therapy.* Sage.

Rogers, C. (1951). *Client-centered therapy: Its current implications, practice and theory.* Houghton Mifflin.

Roland, A. (1996). *Cultural pluralism and psychoanalysis: The Asian and North American experience.* Routledge.

Royles, D. (2020, December 15). Years of medical abuse make Black Americans less likely to trust the coronavirus vaccine. *The Washington Post.* https://washingtonpost.com/outlook/2020/12/15/years-medical-abuse-make-black-americans-less-likely-trust-covid-vaccine/

Seaton, E. K., Caldwell, C. H., & Sellers, R. M. (2010). An intersectional approach for understanding perceived discrimination and psychological well-being among African American and Caribbean Black youth. *Developmental Psychology, 46,* 1372–1379.

Suarez, Z., Newman, P., & Reed, B. G. (2008). Critical consciousness and cross-cultural/intersectional social work practice: A case analysis. *Families in Society: The Journal of Contemporary Social Services*, *89*(3), 407–417.

Suchet, M. (2004). A relational encounter with race. *Psychoanalytic Dialogues*, *14*, 423–438.

Suchet, M. (2007). Unraveling Whiteness. *Psychoanalytic Dialogues*, *17*(6), 867–886.

Sue, D. W., Nadal, K. L., Capodilupo, C. M., Lin, A. I., Torino, G. C., & Rivera, D. P. (2008). Racial microaggressions against Black Americans: Implications for counseling. *Journal of Counseling & Development*, *86*, 330–338. https://doi.org/10.1002/j.1556-6678.2008.tb00517.x

Suite, D. H., Bril, R. D., Primm, A., & Harrison-Ross, P. (2007). Beyond misdiagnosis, misunderstanding and mistrust: Relevance of the historical perspective in the medical and mental health treatment of people of color. *Journal of the National Medical Association*, *99*(8), 879–885.

Tucker, M. J., Berg, C. J., Callaghan, W. M., & Hsia, J. (2007). The Black-White disparity in pregnancy-related mortality from 5 conditions: Differences in prevalence and case-fatality rates. *American Journal of Public Health*, *97*(2), 247–51. https://doi.org/10.2105/AJPH.2005.072975

Walters, K., Simoni, J., & Evans-Campbell, T. (2002). Substance use among American Indians and Alaska Natives: Incorporating culture in an "Indigenist" stress-coping paradigm. *Public Health Reports*, *117*, S104–S117.

Wang, E, Glazer, K. B., Howell, E. A., & Janevic, T. M. (2020). Social determinants of pregnancy-related mortality and morbidity in the United States: A systematic review. *Obstetric Gynecology*, *135*(4), 896–915. https://doi.org/10.1097/AOG.0000000000003762

Yassen, J. (1995). Preventing secondary traumatic stress disorder. In C. R. Figley (Ed.), *Compassion fatigue: Coping with secondary traumatic stress disorder in those who treat the traumatized* (pp. 178–208). Brunner/Mazel.

Yeh, C. J., & Hwang, M. Y. (2000). Interdependence in ethnic identity and self: Implications for theory and practice. *Journal of Counseling and Development*, *78*, 420–429.

Zúñiga, X., & Nagda, B. A. (2001). Design considerations in intergroup dialogue. In D. Schoem & S. Hurtado (Eds.), *Intergroup dialogue: Deliberative democracy in school, college, community and workplace* (pp. 306–327). University of Michigan Press.

CHAPTER 13

Teaching About Race and Racism

INTRODUCTION

Teaching about race and racism is both complex and rewarding. This chapter is intended for people who may be teaching about racism in a range of settings. There are faculty who teach specific courses on racism or who endeavor to incorporate an antiracism perspective in whatever topic they are teaching. Many professionals offer workshops on racism and antiracism and, within agencies, there are in-service trainings that contribute to an organization's antiracism commitment and activities. Teaching occurs in groups, such as "unlearning racism support groups." We have found that students teach other students about race and racism in both formal and informal, structured and unstructured ways. Teachers often learn from their students. And teaching takes place in relationships and interpersonal interactions. Although this chapter is devoted to teaching in classrooms and workshops, the ideas presented also apply to microinteractions. Teaching and learning about racism and antiracism constitute an ongoing enterprise.

Viewing students as teachers is consistent with the model of relational, interactive learning articulated by educator and philosopher Freire (1970, 1994). Teaching and learning can be similar. For instance, studying about antiracism necessitates self-reflection, listening, understanding and respecting others, and working collaboratively with other people—as does teaching.

Freire made an important distinction between a "banking mode" of education and a dialogic or problem-posing approach (Adams, 2016; Freire, 1970, 1994). The former assumes that teachers are repositories of knowledge that they can transfer or deposit into the vault of a student's mind. A dialogic approach is a collaborative method of posing questions and seeking answers without knowing them in advance. Teaching, then, is not only about obtaining information from an expert. It is also an interactive process in which instructors and students approach education in an open and inquisitive fashion and learn from one another. Social learning does not occur by itself; it requires other people (Wasserman & Doran, 1999). As instructors, we have learned about racism and our own relationship to racism every time we have been in a teaching situation, whether in the classroom or in agencies.

A good place to start is to think about what has helped and hindered your learning about racism.

▶ What have been your most important and significant learning experiences?
▶ What teaching techniques reached you, and which ones did you not respond to?
▶ Have you had experiences with learning about racism in which you shut down or felt overwhelmed by feelings of anger, guilt, hopelessness, or shame?
▶ If you could replay the tape, what would you do differently or hope that others would do differently with you?
▶ Have you been in discussions where you feel like the "group appointed" expert and are weary of people coming to you instead of doing their own work?
▶ Have you been in discussions in which you struggled to say what you believe or lacked the information or confidence to present your case effectively?

As teachers and learners, we all carry reservoirs of experiences upon which we can draw as we pursue antiracism education. Each of us has our own unique mix of learning styles and strengths and weaknesses as communicators. Many, if not most, people learn in multiple ways and integrate knowledge from various sources.

Learning about racism requires not only knowledge about facts and concepts, history, and social patterns, but also introspection, self-awareness, good listening skills, and empathy. Conceptual understanding helps us to discern patterns of communication and intergroup relations. Because of the levels of racism, learning about it requires a combination of cognitive understandings and personal insights. Thus, a variety of teaching strategies, both inside and outside the classroom, leads to a deeper and wider grasp of racism and antiracism.

There are also institutional challenges for those teaching about racism. Institutions of higher learning emphasize the value of objective knowledge, separating rational thought from strong affect and feelings, and balanced neutrality, which ignores the reality of racism and how it is embodied in the construction and maintenance of knowledge, differential power, and privilege, and influences the culture of learning in any classroom (Wagner, 2005). Many White professors and students prefer a classroom climate of comfort and personal comity, but for many students of color, such a consensus is false or a collusion with the inequities wrought by racism (Leonardo & Porter, 2010; Wagner, 2005). Another challenge is that while encouraging students in the helping professions to be self-reflective and committed to social justice, they then encounter the full spectrum of racism in their internships and workplaces (Jeffery, 2005). It is important for antiracism instructors to be mindful of these inconsistencies and contradictions when preparing students for work as antiracism helping professionals. And yet greater awareness of self and other in a racialized society can help students to become antiracism activists, which over time should work in favor of systemic change and social justice.

Teaching about any topic in a group setting necessitates responding to many different learning styles. When teaching about racism, several factors make the enterprise even more complex (Kernahan, 2019). One is the *emotional resonance* of the topic, which invariably activates strong feelings and, at times, defensive maneuvers. Another major dynamic is that students and instructors have all had different experiences of racism and are at different phases of racial and social identity development. Thus, we end up with diverse needs, divergent reactions to material, varying political stances, and different levels of awareness. Powerful crosscurrents, tides, and undertows of interpersonal interactions elevate the importance of good group facilitation and management skills, as people or subgroups can easily become hurt, alienated, angry, and withdrawn—all places from which it is hard to "come back."

Another risk is that instructors will meet the needs of some students at the expense of others. Because Whites and people of color have had dissimilar experiences of racism, their learning goals often are different. For example, a primary learning task for many White students is to learn about White privilege, White supremacy, and internalized stereotypes and racist attitudes and beliefs (DiAngelo, 2012), while for students of color, the task can be to excise internalized racism (David, 2014) and feel validated and empowered (Joseph & Williams, 2008). Responding to all of these needs at once in a racially mixed class is difficult.

This dilemma frequently is resolved by instructors spending a great deal of time helping White students work through resistance or paralyzing emotions such as guilt and shame (Goodman, 2011, 2015). Although this is essential work, it can occur at the expense of the learning needs of students of color in the class. Finding a balance between different students' needs is difficult, but necessary. Not doing so fails to model for students that antiracism work is for all of us and that we all have things to learn from it. It can be inspiring to witness people with privilege working to dismantle it, but also quite painful for people of color to observe White people, perhaps their friends, struggling with their lack of awareness of racism. We must find ways to engage all of our students, regardless of where they are in their journey.

A common classroom dynamic is that White professors and White students carry stereotypes that are expressed through implicit bias (and aversive racism and macroaggressions) which then contribute to racial anxiety and stereotype threat (Godsil, 2015). What Godsil means by racial anxiety is that students of color exposed to implicit and aversive racism become emotionally activated as they seek to protect themselves from racial targeting and micro aggressions. At the same time, White students (and professors) sensing that something is wrong become emotionally activated over the threat of being viewed as "racist." As we described in Chapters 6 to 9, students of color also have to contend with stereotype threat (Steele, 2011), the anxiety over not conforming to stereotypes held by authors, which by this time may have entered the classroom.

While this is going on, White students seek "safety," which often means they hope that they will not be "attacked" for harboring racist stereotypes or lack of awareness of White privilege. Often, students of color respond that they have never had the privilege of being "safe" from the wounds of racism (Garran & Rasmussen, 2014). This highly charged classroom environment often inhibits engagement and learning about racism, particularly when White students conflate *safety* with *consequence-free environment*. Yet White people do need space to explore the complexities of racism and White privilege before "unlearning" it, and students of color need spaces where they can share experiences of racism and support one another in information sharing, healing, and advocacy. These are examples of the complex interactions and group dynamics that have to be considered when teaching about race and racism.

EXAMPLES

Despite the complexities, we do not believe that a person has to wait until they feel "ready" or like a "race expert" to teach about racism—in fact, even after many years of teaching this content, it is important to be wary of overconfidence or hubris. The following are examples of students being teachers.

Regina

A social work student in our experience, whom we will call Regina, grew up White in a predominantly Black community. Initially, she took the stance of knowing a great deal about racism because of her extensive experience with people of color, but she soon opened up to exploring the White privileges that she had, which most of her childhood friends were not accorded.

After taking the antiracism course, Regina entered her field placement, where she, like all students, was expected to conduct a small antiracism project. She decided to offer a miniversion of the antiracism course that she had taken as a brown-bag lunch seminar meeting for the staff in her agency. The group that met was racially and ethnically mixed and numbered about 10 to 15 people.

Regina realized that she did not have extensive teaching skills, nor did she consider herself to be an expert on racism. But she did have a strong commitment to doing meaningful antiracism work and knew that she could draw on her life experiences, knowledge, and self-awareness, having been a student in an antiracism course. She proceeded cautiously and with humility, using articles and handouts from her antiracism course, consulting with her former professors, and working closely with her supervisor, who was a White woman also strongly committed to antiracism work. Regina was open and transparent about her lack of teaching experience and her limited perspective about racism as a White person. And she modeled a willingness to explore her own biases and blind spots.

She first worked with the group to clarify expectations and establish norms—a topic we will consider in greater detail later. Her pedagogical approach was to ask staff members to read one or two articles addressing an important aspect of racism and then to facilitate a discussion. Some difficulties and tensions between staff members surfaced in the seminar, but the overall feedback—formally solicited through anonymous questionnaires—indicated that all staff members had found this to be a productive endeavor. It was a good learning experience about racism in a human service workplace and put antiracism front and center as an organizational undertaking. The seminar opened up a difficult topic of conversation and demonstrated that it could be discussed and considered without huge emotional explosions.

Some staff members became more introspective and began considering issues that often were sidestepped or ignored. The seminar provided a space for people to listen and reflect while forming potential antiracism alliances with one another. It also was a good experience for Regina, who learned more about herself and racism, strengthening her commitment to continue work as an antiracism activist and educator.

The project involved some risks as well: The process could have become ensnared if staff conflicts had erupted. But the staff also had simmering feelings about the failure to explore this issue, and Regina's willingness to pursue it diligently, with caution and the support of allies, led to a meaningful experience and success.

Alicia

Another real-life example of a student teaching others comes from a classroom experience in the graduate social work program where we teach. An advanced institutional racism course was being cotaught by a professor of color and a White professor. On more than one occasion, one White student attempted to find explanations *other* than racism when people of color in the class were describing incidents of racism that they had experienced, including one example given by the professor of color. The White professor confronted the White student strongly, which caused her to shut down and withdraw from class discussion.

A student of color in the classroom, Alicia, was disturbed by this. She emailed the professors, then raised her concerns in a subsequent class. Her major point was that students should be able to make mistakes, and that when the professor confronted a student too strongly, it inhibited learning and personal growth. This prompted class discussion that processed the interactions leading up to the confrontation by the professor, as well as the professor's response, including a fishbowl discussion (see Chapter 8).

Alicia then encouraged the White professor and the student who had been confronted to continue their conversation outside the class, which they did. By the end of the course, many students reported that Alicia's intervention and the subsequent introspection, reflection, dialogue, and reparation of relationships were the most significant "learning moments" of the course. Students also appreciated that the professors were willing to revisit both the content and process of an earlier session (the one in which the professor confronted the student) in the course, and that they opened up the space to have fruitful, albeit challenging, clarifying conversations.

Michael

A final example of a student also being a teacher is Michael. When he was a junior in high school, he was the only teenager participating in a Study Circle group (see Chapter 8) to discuss race and racism. He lived in a town where people of color constituted only 12% of the population but were 25% of the public school population. Michael, who is White, was so affected by his Study Circle dialogue experience that he decided to do an antiracism project as an independent study project while he was a senior. His project was ambitious: to prepare a curriculum to be distributed to all elementary and middle-school teachers, in which teachers would learn how to discuss race and racism in their classes in a developmentally appropriate fashion, including explorations of White privilege.

After research, as well as consulting with antiracism teachers and activists, he produced a 15-page booklet, which he then presented to the town's human rights commission, to an antiracism activist group, to the local school committee, and at a meeting of all of the town's school principals. The *Anti-Racism Handbook* covered many relevant topics: teaching in a diverse classroom, understanding definitions and concepts, breaking down personal prejudices, creating inclusive learning communities, providing examples of antiracism class projects, dealing with resistance, and noting how to frame diversity issues. It also included an extensive bibliography and a survey for teachers to complete about their reactions to the handbook.

In his introduction, Michael used self-disclosure to open up the discussion: When I passed through the public elementary and middle schools in this town, I know that I often picked up on who teachers prioritized and encouraged most in the classroom, and it had an impact on my own personal prejudices that I wish didn't exist. I also internalized a sense that I was more deserving of attention than my classmates of color. It is so necessary for the classroom to create an antiracism culture of resistance, by prioritizing traditionally marginalized groups and challenging racist language, values, assumptions, and behavior.

We do not want to minimize the challenges of teaching about racism or the importance of carefully preparing to engage in this enterprise. These examples illustrate some of the many ways to teach and how people with the status of "student" are able to work effectively as teachers. We now discuss ways to enhance the effectiveness of teaching about race and racism: developing an effective course and class structure, co-creating a positive classroom climate, understanding ourselves as teachers and knowing our students, and employing specific teaching strategies and techniques. We also consider what to do when conflict erupts or teachers feel stuck. The appendices include some exercises that teachers can use in helping students explore racism.

COURSE AND CLASS STRUCTURE

The starting point for teaching about race and racism is to have a framework and format for the course and each class to maximize the chances for success. Like all teaching, this implies thinking carefully about an applicable course description, goals, and objectives, as well as developing a syllabus that clearly outlines and supports attaining these targets. Every course, whether it lasts 14 weeks or is a 1-hour workshop, should have a map that allows students and teachers alike to follow where it is heading.

When creating a structure for a course or class on racism, the sequencing of both content and activities has to be considered. Bell et al. (2016a) recommend moving from lower to higher risk as a course or class progresses. If participants feel too uncomfortable in the early going, they are less likely to invest and take risks as the course progresses. Attendees need a foundation, trust, and a modicum of security to expend the personal energy necessary for deep learning. They look to the instructor for this foundation.

Thus, sequencing has to take into account the importance of establishing confidence and creating a group environment in which norms are established and people are committed to working together. Bell et al. (2016a) also recommend moving from the more concrete to the abstract and from the personal to the institutional. They also have found that beginning with less threatening concepts, such as diversity, is helpful, and then moving on to more challenging and emotionally laden notions, such as power and privilege.

We have found such sequencing to be helpful, with some modifications. Before considering concepts, attendees should be encouraged to first situate themselves, thereby focusing on social identity by exploring the many different identities they carry. Conversations about difference always are easier to initiate than those about privilege, dominance, and exploitation. But examining personal issues of racism, along with social and historical subjects on a parallel track, is also fruitful. For example, a class may look at the history and sociology of the interaction of race and immigration while also leaving space to explore how students have internalized beliefs, narratives, and myths that stem from the immigration and crossing experiences of their ancestors. All areas of content should be linked continually with an ongoing awareness and focus on students' social identities.

Early in the course, it is useful to introduce concepts that act as a lens through which to view material. These concepts provide ways to explain strong reactions and emotions, linking the personal with the social and political. An example is "racial identity," a concept that encapsulates history, sociology, the construction of meaning, relationships, loyalty and affiliation, interpersonal preferences and interactions, self-concept, and one's innermost psychological and emotional life. Encouraging students to dig into this material helps acclimate them to self-reflection and slowly helps them to raise their awareness of the ways that race and identity connect with other concepts that will be discussed.

Another useful concept is to develop a "critical consciousness" (Bell, 2016; Zúñiga & Nagda, 2001). This establishes an expectation that students will interrogate their assumptions, learn about important historical and social contexts, and engage in introspection. It allows for questioning and challenging and asks students to dig deeper without being critical or putting down anyone. As we have said throughout the book, concepts, such as triggers, comfort zone, and learning edge (Adams & Zúñiga, 2016), or the three aspects of a difficult conversation (content, emotions, identity; Stone et al., 1999) help to interpret unsettling or confusing feelings and interactions.

Course structure and meaningful concepts establish a framework for teaching about racism and help to create a holding environment (Winnicott, 1960) for the class. Inevitably, unanticipated issues will come up, such as confrontations between students or between students and teachers, or distracting class undercurrents. At times, it is prudent to let go of a class plan and respond to the circumstance that presents itself in the classroom or workshop. Some of the deepest learning moments can occur at these times.

But we must not let process become an end in itself and lose the thread of the syllabus or agenda. A class is not a dialogue group, and though dialogue should be part of an antiracism curriculum, it is not the entire program. At times a teacher has to acknowledge strong feelings and unresolved conflicts and suggest other places where conversations can be continued, such as after class or through an online chat room, and refocus the class on the course content. The teacher should maintain a balance between adhering to the class structure and taking advantage of learning moments embedded in unforeseen hurdles. It is critical that instructors keep this in mind, as discussion topics can be easily hijacked by those in the group who wish to deflect from talking about racism, particularly as they start to identify themselves or family and friends as people who uphold White supremacy.

Maintaining clear boundaries with time management is essential to any teaching situation, and this is certainly the case when teaching about racism, oppression, and White supremacy. Classes or workshops should begin and end on time. The temptation may be to extend time periods, particularly when misunderstandings, tensions, or conflicts crop up, but this can be counterproductive. Sometimes during an intense discussion, people lock into rigid or redundant patterns of thinking and interacting, so taking a break and providing time for reflection and to regain perspective can be helpful. If racism classes (or classes where racism is being discussed) do not end on time, people may feel emotionally overwhelmed and depleted. Running over time also can take time away from other classes, commitments, and activities, which can fuel pressure or resentment.

At the same time, provisions should be made for the spillover of feelings or leftover dynamics that are not resolved during actual class time. Conversations can (and often will) continue outside the classroom in pairs or small groups. Encouraging students to use journals to write down perplexing questions, confused thoughts, and powerful feelings offers a space for processing, reflection, and capturing important moments or reactions. If participants are able to write about their conflicts or painful emotions, they can let go of them at least temporarily, return to them later, mull them over, and perhaps share them in class later. Establishing websites or learning management systems (e.g., Blackboard, Moodle) as a forum for students to exchange reactions, either with instructors or with the entire class, also can extend learning outside the classroom. Using these platforms also helps students to interact with one another out of class, thus offering the opportunity for a different type of relationship to evolve.

Whenever any of these alternative venues are used, the issues raised should be brought back into the actual classroom eventually. This can be done with a summary at the beginning of the next class or a check-in time during which students share thoughts or feelings that have stayed with them or that they are still working on. Even an acknowledgment that there have been further conversations or unresolved feelings can be a form of validation and allow for the group to tolerate ambiguity and complexity and move forward (Brookfield, 2019).

CLASSROOM CLIMATE

The primary factors affecting classroom climate are student motivation, the ability of teachers to kindle and fan motivation, at whatever level, and the instructor's ability to facilitate. People have various reasons for taking courses or workshops about racism. In some instances, they are required to do so—perhaps to meet a curricular requirement or because a worksite supervisor or boss strongly encourages it. In these situations, motivation may be low and resistance high, with students feeling ambivalent about being in the class. Nevertheless, many students study racism because they are genuinely interested in it. Even those in this group have many different motivations: wanting to explore their own experiences or identity, trying to learn about how institutional racism is manifested, attempting to intellectually grasp the causes and reasons for racism, seeking to develop better intervention skills, or desiring to explore one's internalized biases. In most learning situations, students have mixed motivations for being there.

With student hesitation in mind, it is useful to conduct a survey about why students are attending, what they think about taking the course or workshop, and what they envision getting out of the experience. To enable the discussion, teachers or facilitators must convey and model a nonjudgmental, tolerant stance, creating a space for people to be open and honest. If participants are concerned about politically correct responses, they will self-monitor, hesitate to share, and may withdraw or have their guard up. One way to confront this dynamic is by asking students about their hopes and fears for the course or workshop. This normalizes talking about concerns and reservations while also asking people to identify and articulate goals.

Teachers can gain information about who is in their class and why they are there, allowing instructors to respond empathically and to validate what students are feeling and thinking. Teachers also can clarify what the class is supposed to cover, including what is likely to be addressed and what is not within the purview of the course. Instructors can share their own goals for the course, which also can serve as a bridge to discussing classroom climate, and determine how everyone can work together to create a positive learning environment. Instructors should emphasize that the purpose of the course goes beyond gaining an intellectual and theoretical understanding of racism, to attendees' learning about themselves and gaining the skills and knowledge they need to engage in antiracism activities (Miller et al., 2004b).

Ideally, in any class, a culture is established that is characterized by a community of inquisitive, self-aware, and self-directed learners. For this to happen, students have to feel motivated and inspired to work hard and take risks, moving beyond their "comfort zone." The basis for this is a foundation of trust. How is trust established in the classroom?

Classroom Safety

Perhaps the biggest fear that students express in racism classes, as previously described in the Classroom Climate section, is that they do not trust that they will be "safe." What do they mean by this? Certainly, racism itself creates an unsafe environment for people of color. They may encounter discrimination, prejudice, biases, micro aggressions, or aversive racism; be asked to represent their group; encounter outright hostility; or endure social exclusion (Garran & Rasmussen, 2014). One aspect of safety that students of color seek is that this will not occur in the classroom.

And many students of color wonder if White students will be authentic and honest about their attitudes, beliefs, and experiences. Students of color often are wary of White students who will say what they think instructors and other students want to hear, without sincere self-reflection or disclosure. A related concern is that White students will talk the talk in the classroom but not walk the walk after the class ends. This impinges upon the safety of students of color, who may have taken the risk of sharing their experiences with racism without knowing how White students will use this information. Additionally, White students might quietly bear witness to what students of color are conveying, but they will not respond. This leaves the student(s) of color feeling as those they are supporting a type of "voyeurism" on the part of White participants, who are curious to know the student of color perspective, but are silent when it comes to sharing anything about themselves.

For White students, safety often means that they will not be called a racist or if they accidentally "make a mistake," they will not encounter severe criticism or hostility. They may be concerned about unresolved stereotypes or that if they say the "wrong" thing; they will offend or hurt someone. They also may be concerned that teachers and other students will misunderstand or misjudge them. White students also may be concerned that if they have ideas and values that seem at odds with the instructors or many fellow students, they will suffer academic consequences or group censorship. Again, this fear, and longing for a consequence-free environment is understandable but certainly not helpful if open, honest dialogue and personal introspection are to occur.

All students, regardless of their race, are wary of others labeling or misinterpreting them. Fears for their psychological safety undermine trust. These concerns work against establishing a learning environment that embraces difficult questions, deep listening, complexity, paradox, and subtlety (Goodman, 2011). People who are feeling vulnerable, wary, or unsafe tend to cling to the familiar or they shut down, closing themselves off to new ideas and material. They are less prone to speak honestly and take risks, leading to predictable discourses and "soapbox speeches" with fixed and ritualistic classroom roles.

Classroom Norms

To establish a classroom environment with sufficient trust to enable fruitful discourse and inquiry, the dynamic of safety must be addressed. One way to approach this is to ask students about their concerns and what might help them to feel less fearful or apprehensive. This can lead to a discussion about classroom norms of conduct, which may include, but are not limited to, expecting confidentiality, listening to one another, appreciating differences, speaking for oneself and not having to represent one's group or others, being honest, owning one's feelings, and challenging and criticizing ideas and assumptions while still respecting the person.

Establishing norms often works best when done with the group, as it then can form the basis of a learning contract to which everyone has contributed. Instructors can suggest additional norms that do not emerge in the group discussion (Miller et al., 2004a). Some useful norms that should be included are trying to be fully present, taking responsibility for oneself (including challenging oneself), accepting that another person's frame of reference has meaning for them, and the importance of working through conflict and "leaning into discomfort" (Wasserman & Doran, 1999). It also is helpful to write out the norms, distribute them to all students, and post them on Blackboard or any electronic notice board. The act of generating norms and discussing them in itself begins the conversation about race and racism and explores why talking about this subject is so challenging for so many students. Ultimately, no discussion about race and racism is entirely "safe"—if safety refers to possible misunderstanding, hearing biased and prejudiced comments, or having painful realizations and hurt feelings—but norms can create "safer" learning environments (Garran & Rasmussen, 2014).

When establishing norms, one of the thorniest issues is that, while people are encouraged to take risks, they also will reveal biases. For example, if a White student has stereotypes about African Americans, which were learned from the student's parents, and honestly shares them in a class with African American students, what the student is saying can be painful and offensive to hear. This interaction may be compounded by relationships outside the class.

If the discussion is taking place in an agency, people are expected to continue to work together. At this point, it is helpful to introduce the concept of racial identity formation and to acknowledge how students have had different experiences of racism and are at different phases in their racial identity development. This serves to frame the notion that people taking the course are at different places with their racial identity, with different experiences of racial oppression and privilege, and have a range of ideas, views, feelings, needs, and aspirations (Arao & Clemens, 2013). Facilitators can share examples of when they have made remarks that they later regretted or how they felt hurt by others' statements. This models how instructors as well as students are still engaged in the process of learning and are capable of being wounded or hurting others. It is also important to directly acknowledge when an offensive statement is made, but then to ask for clarification and to also contextualize what has been said. A delicate balance is required between honest sharing and wounding or offending others.

We have managed this balance by reminding people that what they are about to say will have a potential impact on other people. Sometimes it is better to note an idea, thought, or feeling, but to work on it in a different environment. At the same time, students should be gentle with themselves and others when they make missteps and painful revelations, all the while being accountable, as this is all part of the learning process. It can help to look at *intentions*, which often are well meaning, and to acknowledge them. At the same time, it is important that the instructor makes manifest and examines with the class the *impact* of well-meaning but painful interactions, which also is critical to learning about racism. So, students should also be prepared to receive difficult, honest feedback, especially if they have indeed said something offensive, even though their intent was not to do so.

Caucus/Affinity Groups

In our experience, students of any racial/ethnic background can express biased statements and hurt or anger others or be hurt by what others say; however, most students of color contend with racism outside the classroom, which White students do not. As we described in

Chapters 5 to 9, even if White students are targeted by other social oppressions (e.g., homophobia, sexism, anti-Semitism), they do not experience systemic racism. Thus, even though each individual has unique learning needs, generally speaking, there are differences in learning expectations for students of color and White students in a racism class. Any student in the class should be able to explore internalized biases or prejudices as part of unlearning racism, but attempts should be made to protect those who are already exposed to racism from further insults or injuries. This calls for active listening and participation from the instructor.

So how can a class on racism open up space for all students to explore internalized racism, power, and privilege without students of color having to witness or be the target of racist ideas, feelings, or actions? To respond to this dilemma, the facilitator might try to create spaces in classes in which people can explore their prejudices, beliefs, attitudes, and experiences, without placing students of color in unnecessarily vulnerable positions. This can be accomplished in a number of ways. We have already mentioned the value of keeping journals in helping students explore stereotypes and biases without the people who are the targets of such prejudices having to hear them. Another useful strategy is to break up classes into caucus groups in which people who identify as White can examine White privilege, White supremacy, and racism, and where people of color can explore internalized racism and reactions to White racism with less vulnerability and risk of causing harm.

Caucus groups can focus on the varied learning needs of different groups of students. Dividing the group may meet with resistance initially, particularly from White students who want to hear what people of color have to say about racism. This division is a temporary realignment, as it always is important to reconvene as a large group and to share in a larger discussion the themes (although not always the details) that emerged from the caucuses. A great deal of learning can take place in both the small group and in the class as a whole. Caucus groups create a structure that encourages honesty as well as self-awareness about the impact of one's statements on others. Some students might become quite outspoken about not wanting to break up into caucus groups because they want to bear witness to what the other group is saying. Moments like these provide the instructor with the opportunity to reiterate the varied learning needs of different students in the class, and that learning for some should not come at the expense of others. It is also a time to discuss with students if they see differences between caucus groups and wholly White or wholly people of color spaces outside of the classroom. Why are they so perturbed by caucus groups in the classroom, when so many communities are informally running like caucus groups already?

If using caucus groups in a classroom or workshop, we must remain mindful that some students who identify as being multiracial and multiethnic may feel as if dividing into caucus groups pressures them to have to choose one part of their identity over the other. There is no simple way to respond to this tension, but it is helpful to acknowledge it and to encourage people to choose whichever group they wish to participate in or, if there are sufficient numbers, to establish a separate caucus group for those who have a more mixed, complex, or ambivalent racial identity.

When using any of these techniques, instructors should be as transparent as possible about their reasoning. The discussion about *why* and *how* to break up into caucus groups is part of an important conversation about the differential impact of racism on people and their consequent learning needs in a class on racism. If students are merely told to do something without adequate discussion and preparation, an important learning moment may be lost and the community of problem solvers that we seek to create will not evolve. But we as instructors have found that it also is important to confront the inevitable resistance about breaking into caucus groups because students often do not appreciate the potential gains and benefits until they try it.

INSTRUCTOR SELF-AWARENESS

One of the dilemmas for instructors teaching about racism or integrating an antiracism stance into their teaching is not having an adequate awareness of their racial identity, positioning and unresolved stereotypes, and unexamined assumptions. This can be particularly true for White professors. Solomon et al. (2005) found that White teachers in training, when exposed to an article about White privilege, had strategies for denying Whiteness and White privileges. These included minimizing White privilege and retreating to arguments supporting individual achievement without acknowledging social context. They also experienced conflicts between consciously wanting to support equity and fairness but having unexamined negative myths and stereotypes about people of color. In our work teaching and consulting with White professors about incorporating an antiracism stance in their teaching, we have encountered a similar dynamic.

Knowing who we are, our strengths and weaknesses, our vulnerabilities and assets, and our trigger points and hot spots is essential for teaching about racism (Bell et al., 2016b; Miller et al., 2004b). Racism courses certainly are going to challenge students and will test teachers as well. Preparing for this task minimizes the risks and increases effectiveness. Bell et al. (2016a) have identified a number of areas about which all instructors who teach social justice courses should be mindful while preparing for and actually teaching courses. These include:

▶ Making one aware of one's social identity
▶ Confronting one's own biases
▶ Taking an inventory of one's triggers
▶ Preparing for how to respond to biased comments by students
▶ Confronting one's own doubts and anxiety about competency
▶ Being aware of one's need for student approval

They also suggest that teachers prepare for difficult situations in the classroom and fears of losing control of the process, which raises issues about authority and how to exercise it.

Drawing on our own experiences to use as examples can be helpful to students, including sharing times we made mistakes or felt inadequate—as long as we are cautious about not telling too many "war stories," which shifts the spotlight to us and away from our students. Instructors may use their own feelings, reactions, and internal processes effectively as points of discussion and reflection, if this is done selectively and strategically. When teaching by example, instructors should consider what level of self-disclosure is comfortable and use caution. Some personal examples can stir up a lot of feelings within the instructor.

In general, a teacher being able to tolerate strong affect in a group requires practice, whether it is being expressed by someone else or experienced internally. Expanding this capacity and desensitizing trigger points without sacrificing empathy and compassion build confidence in one's capacity to handle most situations.

Resistance

Resistance is common in antiracism courses (Goodman, 2011; Mildred & Zúñiga, 2004). People with race privilege often resist examining racism, and people targeted by racism may hesitate to relive or re-experience painful situations. Students who are ambivalent about their racial identities also may experience resistance. When people feel threatened, they understandably respond with resistance (Goodman, 2011, 2015).

Whatever the sources of resistance, it is often directed at those teaching the course. It can manifest itself as denial, anger, withdrawal, sabotage, or as a direct challenge to the credibility of teachers. When presented with new and disturbing material or insights, participants frequently question the teacher's expertise or the validity of their experience. Thus, antiracism teachers should expect to have their integrity contested. Goodman recommends that educators recall a time when they felt resistant themselves so they can connect empathically with the students' experiences.

People of color and White teachers have reported variations on how this theme affects their teaching experience. Students, particularly White male students, are more likely to challenge the authority and credibility of teachers of color (Goodman, 2011). Whenever professors or facilitators are teaching about a form of oppression they directly experience, students who have unearned and unexamined privileges are likely to be resistant and may try to discredit the teacher's legitimacy and accuse them of being self-serving by advocating for their own cause (Bell et al., 2016). As we considered in Chapters 6 and 7, the interactions of social identity may magnify students' resistance, so women of color face devaluation by White men by virtue of both their race and gender.

White teachers and facilitators also face certain types of resistance when teaching about racism. Miller et al. (2004b) identified three challenges for White educators teaching about racism:

1. Questions about their legitimacy when talking about racism
2. Negotiating their own privileges, including biases
3. Being viewed with hostility as "race traitors" by resistant White students.

A fourth hurdle, which has an impact on all teachers, whatever their race and ethnicity, is the lack of institutional support for teaching such demanding and potentially volatile courses. Racism courses can be marginalized within an undergraduate or graduate program and viewed as an "add-on," rather than being central to the curriculum. When racism courses are required, many students enter them with low motivation and high levels of skepticism. Other professors talk negatively about racism courses, adding to a student's trepidations or low expectations. The volatility of the topic itself presents the possibility of difficult class experiences, potentially resulting in negative course evaluations or even student protests (Miller et al., 2004a). This has happened to the most experienced antiracism teachers. The risks raise concerns about the professional wisdom of taking on this sort of teaching.

Supporting Antiracism Teaching

Fortunately, the teaching risks can be minimalized, both institutionally and within the classroom. Institutions of higher education and human service organizations can make explicit commitments toward antiracism, creating a context in which courses are offered. Part of the commitment should ensure that the courses receive adequate support and resources and that the potential risks and burdens of teaching these courses are recognized and acknowledged administratively.

Multiracial/Co-teaching Teams

One way of providing institutional support to antiracism classes is to offer multiracial teaching teams. This is a pedagogically sound intervention and has many advantages over solo teaching. Co-teaching teams offer a wider range of perspectives, experiences, and models of antiracism professionals (Garran et al., 2015; Miller et al., 2004a, 2004b). These teams allow for greater support and consultation inside and outside the classroom, because co-teachers are able to back up one another and step in if their colleague becomes triggered or the target of strong student resistance. Co-teachers can plan classes together and serve as advisors to each other, providing valuable feedback about the missteps, microaggressions, and prejudices. Co-teaching also allows greater flexibility and creativity about how material is presented and who presents it. If the class breaks up into caucus groups, the teachers are available to split up as well.

We have found that co-teaching offers significant advantages in courses which focus on race and racism. Co-teaching offers students the opportunity to hear multiple points of view and to be exposed to multiple areas of expertise related to one subject area. Additionally, the ability to collaborate with colleagues affords instructors the ability to capitalize on strengths while expanding one's knowledge base in other substantive areas.

One key area where co-teaching has been an effective model is with problem-solving, whether there is a challenge waged by one or more students, or there is a difficult conversation to facilitate. For instance, if a student or group of students angrily challenge one instructor, the other is able to step in and diffuse the tension. Or, if the students are struggling to stay connected to the content and process of a class because of an underlying tension, co-teaching provides important modeling for students about how to dialogue and problem-solve around difficult issues (Garran et al., 2015).

Solomon (2000) conducted a 3-year study of cross-racial teaching dyads. The finding that emerged was that this partnership helped to break down racial barriers between instructors; teachers learned from one another; and when prejudice was directed toward one of the teaching partners, they were able to back each other up and serve as a buffer.

Co-teaching has its own risks and demands. Racial patterns can be re-enacted if White professors take a dominating leadership role. Power must be negotiated (Anti-Defamation League [ADL], 1998). Teachers like to teach and can trip over one another or have difficulty operating within a more circumscribed, shared teaching space. The danger of splitting is always present, with one teacher becoming idealized and the other disparaged. This dynamic also may follow typical patterns of racism. In many situations, White students feel more comfortable sharing things with the White professor, thereby minimizing or marginalizing the role of the professor of color. Co-teachers, too, may have disagreements over topics or teaching strategies, and these can spill over into classes. And they can trigger one another. Finally, co-teaching requires a significant time commitment and use of departmental resources; thus, many institutions may be reticent to support such a model.

If the teaching team becomes stuck and unable to work out tensions between themselves, there should be a fallback mechanism for conflict resolution, involving a third party or a group of peers. This should be set up in advance of any actual tensions or conflict. Again, this is where institutional or departmental support is critical.

Thus, co-teaching should be approached thoughtfully and carefully. Co-teachers need to get to know one another, develop trust, and become familiar with their partner's style. Sufficient time must be allocated for planning classes and debriefing afterward. A game plan should be drawn up for each class, including time frames, roles, and techniques. Co-teachers should plan how they will present themselves to the class: Will they stand up together, or will one sit down while the other is taking the lead role (ADL, 1998)? Both professors should read and comment on all written work. In our experience, co-teaching takes up to twice as much time as teaching solo, but the benefits far outweigh the potential risks, and the time invested in co-teaching is well spent (Garran et al., 2015).

Strong Support Networks

Whether teaching alone or with a partner, all antiracism educators benefit from strong support networks. These might include fellow teachers, supervisors, and other colleagues. Everyone needs space to process difficult emotions and reactions, and teachers should create these places for themselves outside the classroom. Instructor assignments for this type of course need to be made with care; a new hire or a doctoral student with little teaching experience or little exposure to this content would struggle a great deal, especially in the face of no institutional support.

Weekly group meetings of all antiracism teachers are useful, allowing them to share experiences and provide mutual support and consultation. Newer antiracism educators, in particular, benefit from access to support systems, including teaching mentors, who can help with both teaching strategies as well as course content.

UNDERSTANDING STUDENTS

Understanding who our students are and where they are coming from is essential for antiracism educators (Adams et al., 2007). Planning and thinking about this can begin before a course starts.

▶ What do we know about the organizational culture and context for the course?
▶ Is the course required, or have students chosen to take this class?
▶ What classes or experiences in this field have students already had?
▶ Are there any incidents or ongoing dynamics within the organization or within the student cohort that may affect the course?
▶ What are the likely ethnic and racial identities of participants? Is this consistent with the ethnic and racial makeup of the student body?
▶ What other aspects of social identity may be particularly salient for this course?

These are a few examples of questions instructors can ask themselves before classes even start.

Once the course begins, as we mentioned, it is useful to have students situate themselves and to introduce exercises that illuminate the complexities of their social identities and that summarize critical experiences, worldviews, and perspectives relevant to this learning project (see exercises in Chapters 1, 5, 6, and 11; appendix after Chapter 1; as well as Exercise 13.1 at the end of this chapter). Assessing this information and applying concepts such as social identity formation can help instructors anticipate likely learning needs, potential sources of resistance, and interpersonal and group dynamics. We can attempt to match curricular goals with who is actually in the class (Adams et al., 2016). As a caveat, we can only imagine potential scenarios and have to be open to surprises and prepared for the unexpected as the class progresses.

In any class, instructors should track who talks a lot and who is silent. Do any racial or ethnic patterns become apparent in who speaks up and who listens? Some students are quiet because they are sorting through their thoughts and feelings, and as a result they are consciously trying to not take up too much space. But are some students sitting quietly as voyeurs, taking in information but unwilling to take risks and get involved? Are there tacit expectations about who should respond to certain material? Usually, roles emerge after a couple of classes, and it is helpful to map them out along with their impact on group dynamics. Inevitably, when some students talk too much and others too little, what intervention strategy, if any, should the instructor use? Additional questions include:

> What kinds of body language does the teacher notice?
> Which students always arrive quite late or leave quite early from class?
> What kinds of responses do different teaching techniques elicit?
> How does what is happening in the classroom correspond to what a teacher is reading in student journals?
> Who does an instructor feel triggered by or drawn to?

By getting to know the students, instructors are creating pathways for feedback as the course moves along, allowing instructors to adapt and adjust teaching strategies (Adams et al., 2016).

As with all teaching, letting students know that the instructor regards them as individuals is helpful. Simple things, such as learning their names, go a long way. Unfortunately, racism courses sometimes are offered in a large lecture format, which cuts down on the possibilities for experiential learning and makes it more difficult for instructors to develop a textured understanding of who their students are and how to respond to them differentially. However, we believe that any way that an instructor can make an effort to learn who their students are will be noticed and appreciated.

TEACHING STRATEGIES AND TECHNIQUES

In addition to the recommendations presented for structuring antiracism classes, creating a positive learning environment, being aware of ourselves as instructors, and knowing our students, some specific teaching strategies and techniques are more likely to result in positive and meaningful classes for students. Much of what is discussed here pertains to all effective teaching but has been tailored to antiracism courses.

The actual choice and mix of techniques should be influenced by what instructors are trying to convey, their assessment of students' learning needs and styles, and their own skills and strengths as teachers. If the goal is to convey information, such as the history of racism or statistics about the web of institutional racism, a lecture format works well. Slides and handouts can augment learning, as can readings. Materials of this nature, however, are likely to engender student reactions. Small discussion groups and journals can deepen students' personal connection to the content, as can class exercises that highlight patterns of racism or its consequences. Videos, too, can be used to respond to the learning needs of some students and illustrate abstract or dry material with visual images, human faces, and personal narratives. And reading personal accounts humanizes theoretical and historical approaches.

When the learning goals are geared more toward personal exploration and growth, lecture usually is not the pedagogical strategy of choice. Focused small-group discussions, written and in-class exercises, and simulations stimulate reflection and introspection. Journals and web-based discussion groups also further dialogue and self-awareness. Watching a video such as *The Color of Fear, Last Chance for Eden* (Lee & Hunter, 1994; Lee, 2002), *Precious Knowledge* (Palos, 2011), or *Dawnland* (Mazo, 2018) and then breaking into small discussion groups can introduce important themes in a powerful and dramatic way. This allows students to witness intense racial conflict (and reconciliation) without engaging directly in it. Structured racial dialogues or temporarily breaking into racial or ethnic caucus groups can create spaces where students can learn to talk about race and racism while also exploring assumptions and stereotypes and their consequences.

If the topic is White privilege or the types of activities in which antiracism activists can engage, brainstorming and other large-group activities can generate a variety of ideas. Small groups can refine or react to what is generated and deepen understanding. Simulations and exercises can illustrate concepts such as privilege in graphic and visual ways.

Exercises

For example, Adams et al. (2016) describe an activity called "Common Ground" in which students are asked to line up on one side of a room and listen to a series of statements. If a statement applies, such as "I am a woman," the student steps to the other side of the room. This begins to illustrate the different social identities that students bring to the course. If no one crosses the room in response to a statement such as "I am bisexual," it visualizes that the class has no student with that social identity or that students do not feel comfortable disclosing this aspect of their identity publicly. This exercise usually is followed by a class discussion.

A variation on this exercise is to have participants take a step forward in response to questions that ask about privilege, or take a step backward if the question is about lack of privilege and applies to them. This visually illustrates the differential privileges of students in the class, which can prompt illuminating discussions and deep self-realizations. It also can be painful to see these differences, and this exercise can elicit strong emotions that must be acknowledged and processed. But this is an effective way to break through resistance if many students in the class are unaware of their unearned privileges. This type of exercise can be done with any aspect of social identity or a combination of social identity axes.

Interviewing in Pairs

A more gentle and private way to engage in similar explorations is to pair the participants and have them interview each other about aspects of their social identity (see Exercise 1.2 in Chapter 1). This is more intimate and less threatening than some exercises; it also builds relationships between classmates and deepens empathy. When pairs report back themes to the larger class, it can lead to a discussion or lecture about relevant concepts and theories. Exercises should always have a "pass rule," so if students do not feel comfortable saying something or even participating, they can opt out without explanation. Instructors should pay careful attention to students who always "pass," as it may signal distancing from the course and it might become necessary to meet with the student outside class for further discussion.

Maintaining Balance

Most antiracism teachers have found it helpful to mix and vary the types of learning strategies used in any given class. Two hours of lecture by a professor can be counterproductive. Conversely, too many exercises and small-group discussions may represent a lack of focus and clarity, at the expense of the students learning important concepts and ideas. Exploring racism in society and the world, as well as racism that is internalized or expressed interpersonally, requires balance and a variety of teaching approaches.

The use of self as an instructor is another way of achieving balance. As we mentioned, self-disclosure can be valuable as long as it does not unduly trigger a professor or direct too much class attention toward the teacher and away from the students. A teacher's ability to convey passion and optimism without sacrificing realism is a powerful stimulant to learning. Students are seeking role models and looking for ways to be helpful and make a difference, while some are also looking for validation of their lived experiences and empathy. If only the negative consequences of racism are presented, then students can easily feel overwhelmed, hopeless, and despondent.

The other side of the coin is that if the teacher overstates hope and understates the dismal reality of racism, people of color in the class can feel devalued and White students may gloss over the destructiveness of racism and not honestly acknowledge or explore their own White privileges. A balance must be struck. Ultimately, the class has to move and progress toward taking action and feeling empowered. Yet, if the course moves too quickly toward action, students may not adequately grasp the depth of racism or genuinely reflect about how racism has affected them. Without introspection, students may engage in actions that detract from feelings, such as guilt and shame, and in so doing will re-enact prejudices and stereotypes, accompanied by a dismissive attitude that those who wield social power are often unaware of. Additionally, the rush to action impedes with their learning about how to listen without reacting.

Another pedagogical balance is that of validating and supporting while also challenging and confronting. Moving to either end of the spectrum compromises learning. Students have to be confirmed and encouraged, for without these, pessimism or resentment can seep in. Yet all learners can and will get stuck and usually are capable of digging deeper. Effective antiracism teaching inevitably involves some confrontation, but delivering it in a way that will be meaningfully received is an art that takes practice. Institutional and collegial support as well as an ongoing outlet to debrief and develop skills (Garran et al., 2014) are critical here. A direct confrontation that makes a student feel humiliated or put down is not an effective intervention and can compromise a student's learning; the ensuing classroom chaos can interfere with the instructor's pedagogical goals.

However, we do not mean that problematic statements or questions should not be dealt with. Instructors can ask questions about something a student said or invite them to reflect on it. They can solicit reactions from other students in a structured fashion—asking what people agreed with and disagreed with. Another way to confront students is through self-revelation, perhaps by teachers sharing a story about a time when they said or did something they regretted and how they came to understand this. Sometimes, direct confrontation is not ideal but might be needed to de-escalate a situation before it escalates.

Yet another balancing act in antiracism teaching is between process and content. The content about racism is seemingly endless. Most instructors fret over all they think must be covered and the inadequacy of the time to do this. Yet significant learning takes place through the class process, and this will not occur if the process is rushed and does not allow sufficient time for reflection. If teachers do not attend to potholes and grimly drive on, rushing to present content, the class may be in for a rough ride. On the one hand, few antiracism teachers think, in retrospect, that they covered every topic they had hoped to, in as much depth as they wished! On the other hand, too much attention to process can be seductive, and every class has some students who would like to concentrate exclusively on group dynamics, to the detriment of learning important factual and conceptual material.

Another challenge to teaching about race and racism is to set a tone in class that is respectful and dignified while also allowing for participants to relax and even express humor. Because nothing is light or funny about racism, we must be serious and sober about its terrible consequences. Study of this topic often calls for a solemn and somber atmosphere, which is understandable and appropriate. Yet, taken to an extreme, it can feel so heavy and burdensome that students feel deflated by the sheer weight of the subject. In any group situation, humor and self-deprecation can be a helpful lubricant, as long as it is not manifested gratuitously or inappropriately. Again, balance is called for.

Availability of Teachers

Teachers should be available to students outside actual class time, within reasonable limits. Whether this is through office hours, by moderating web-based discussion groups, or by checking informally with students during breaks, teachers must be accessible to their students. Racism courses stir up a great deal of feelings, and at times students need some space outside class to consult with teachers or process their reactions so they can gain sufficient perspective to return to class as fully engaged learners.

We also recommend copious feedback by instructors on student logs and papers. This engages students in a more personal and intimate dialogue with professors, which is validating and spurs motivation. Ample written feedback is one of the most effective ways of encouraging engagement and working through resistance. (Exercise 13.1 and Appendix K offer examples of assignments that can support the course objectives, in addition to those already presented as exercises and appendices in previous chapters.)

FEELING STUCK

Everyone who teaches about race and racism will encounter situations that are unanticipated, challenging, and stump us as educators. Anticipating "stuckness" is important, because it will be less frightening when it occurs if teachers are able to remind themselves that this is normal. The next step is to take a deep breath—maybe a few deep breaths—and let the feeling of panic pass. When we feel stuck, we may not know what to do immediately, but we will think of something eventually, and we and the class will learn from the experience. What are some typical situations that teachers find challenging? These vary but some rise to the top of the list:

- ▶ Intense and unanticipated conflict between students
- ▶ Overt hostility directed toward other students or the instructor
- ▶ Direct challenges to the teacher's authority and credibility
- ▶ Severe emotional reactions, including leaving the room

► Profoundly racist statements and comments
► Behind-the-scenes provocations, including orchestrating group rebellions in class

The power and valence of these scenarios will vary from teacher to teacher and according to the context in which they occur. What makes any of them particularly hard to deal with is the element of surprise, when we fail to see what is coming.

We can prepare in many ways for the unexpected and respond effectively once it happens. As an antiracism educator, a key intervention is to predict teacher's mistakes and invite criticism from the class. This immediately takes away the sting when missteps do occur or if students are challenging or critical. It normalizes and models openness and nondefensiveness. No intervention works in all situations and for all people, and this intervention is not effective if some students are committed to undermining the instructor's credibility, or if their social identity becomes an issue. In these situations, a direct confrontation sometimes is needed, including marshaling administrative resources as backup. But usually it is better to try to avoid unnecessary showdowns with students.

Another way to deal with the unexpected is to call a timeout. This comes in handy if the need arises near the time for a break anyway. Even if it does not, there is nothing wrong with giving the class (and teacher) 5 minutes to reflect on what happened before responding to it. This can break a negative chain of interactions, interrupt ritualized conflict, and give the teacher and everyone else a few moments to become more centered and to think of effective ways to respond in the moment. The timeout option is successful when teaching with others or alone.

A variation is to ask students to write down the answers to some questions before further discussion. Examples of questions are:

► What do you think just happened?
► What did you observe and hear?
► What was your immediate reaction?
► What other reactions do you think people in the class might be having?
► What would be a helpful way to follow-up?
► What did you learn from this incident?

Questions like these offer structure and direction to student reactions. It usually is helpful to pose at least one question in which students are asked to speculate on what other students might be feeling. Although this may seem to be at odds with the classroom norm of speaking for oneself, it can be helpful for students to engage in understanding others' perspectives and explore valid reactions that differ from their own. It is useful to explain to the class the rationale for asking the question.

Breaking up into caucus groups or several small groups is another helpful strategy in a time of stress and uncertainty. The teacher should give small groups specific guidelines about what to cover, and to be clear on time limits, perhaps also reminding students of the norms they constructed at the outset of the course. This allows clusters of people to explore a difficult situation in small groups where they are more likely to take risks while also having their perspectives expanded, modified, and challenged by discussing the situation with others. When the small groups report back to the larger class, students are exposed to an even wider range of narratives generated about the original incident, which adds another layer of reflection about the event and its meaning.

The fishbowl (see Chapter 9) is a variation on breaking up into small groups. Fishbowls allow for smaller, more intimate conversations, but in front of the entire class. The filtering system allows people to enter and leave the fishbowl. Some students find it easier to observe than to participate, and this gives them the opportunity to benefit from a discussion that they think would be threatening if they were mandated to participate.

Still another strategy is to address class issues in a homework assignment, such as having students respond in their journals to questions similar to those we suggested previously for exploring reactions in class. Or students can be asked to link their discussions to some of the concepts and theories that have been presented in the course. This depersonalizes and connects micro-events with macro-processes and helpful concepts. A related strategy is to punt—to acknowledge that a difficult incident arose in class and that at some point it should be revisited, but to acknowledge that the teacher needs some time to think about the best way to do that.

One intervention for instructors that we have found to be effective is a faculty-driven seminar entitled *Pedagogy and Diversity* (P&D; see Garran et al., 2014; Kang & Garran, 2018). The seminar is offered for the entire semester and offers peer consultation and support around teaching social justice and diversity issues. With P&D, which is facilitated by instructors with an expertise in racism, instructors and doctoral students come together to discuss societal events and discourses that present as classroom impasses, challenging dynamics or other issues that have arisen or might be brewing in the classroom, and in turn, they offer collaborative consultation to one another. Those in attendance act as a reflecting team to help the instructor(s) who is bringing a concern(s) forward to examine the underlying dynamics and then offer a range of strategies, insights, and possible solutions. Participants who attend P&D appreciate the institutional commitment, openness of others in the group, and the mutual aid aspects of the seminars. It offers a unique space for teachers to be vulnerable and inquisitive while seeking support from their peers.

When we are stuck, we often feel triggered, stirred up, overwhelmed, numb, at a loss for words, angry, and treated unfairly. Feelings of shame can bring to the surface a narrative of inadequacy, and failure begins to take shape in our mind. These are normal reactions, and the more we are able to be gentle with ourselves and give ourselves time to regain our footing, the more we can turn these situations into learning moments. Deep breathing and meditative techniques can be helpful. Listening to others, rather than talking, can give us space to calm down, but this is not appropriate if an out-of-control, escalating conflict is raging in the class. In these circumstances, a timeout is preferable.

We must remember that we are all learners, teachers, and human beings, with warts, blemishes, and moments of uncertainty. It is not the end of the world if students see that we are upset or flustered. We frequently have received feedback from students that this made us seem more accessible and real, and our willingness to be vulnerable was something that students admired. It does not feel good at the time, and being open and exposed is in conflict with traditional images of teachers and facilitators.

Those teaching about antiracism should expect such moments, and they can lead to unexpected insights. The more we can relax and accept these moments, the better we become at dealing with them. What is important is that we stay in the process when we are feeling beleaguered, and that we encourage our students to do the same. Most antiracism courses and workshops will benefit participants, even when there are painful or disturbing moments, as long as the participants remain authentic and engaged.

CONCLUSION

Students should think of themselves as potential teachers, and teachers always as students. The potential risks and pitfalls of teaching antiracism courses should not be minimized, but a variety of ideas can be applied to designing and facilitating meaningful learning environments.

This work can be immensely rewarding, but both teaching and learning about race and racism require a great deal of commitment and time. Personal experiences and professional experiences alike serve as important learning tools. Ultimately, working together toward a fuller understanding of the history of race and racism in the United States, as well as the implications for helping professionals, can lead to enhanced service delivery for all populations and to greater job satisfaction for all involved. Teaching and learning about race and racism offer important opportunities for helping professionals. They contribute to the larger project of antiracism work, which will be covered in the final chapter.

EXERCISE 13.1 Cultural Audit Field Trip

This assignment can help students identify examples of cultural racism and cultural sensitivity and empowerment that they might usually miss.

Take a field trip and observe the world around you. The trip can be any place where there are cultural markers (public signs and symbols that convey cultural norms, assumptions, values, and expectations)—downtown, around campus, the dorms and dining rooms, the library, the media, and so on.

Do a cultural audit and find *five* examples of cultural, ethnic, or racial bias and *five* examples of racial or ethnic sensitivity or empowerment.

Referring to your audit, what generalizations would you make about how cultural markers can be constructed in an empowering and respectful fashion? Did you notice any stereotypes or hidden assumptions? What was visible and invisible? Did you encounter anything surprising?

Write up your findings in a *two-page* paper.

Source: This exercise was suggested by Andrea Ayvazian and Norma Akamatsu.

REFERENCES

Adams, M. (2016). Pedagogical foundations for social justice education. In M. Adams, L. A. Bell (Eds.), *Teaching for diversity and social justice* (3rd ed., pp. 27–54). Routledge.

Adams, M., Jones, J., & Tatum, B. (2007). Knowing our students. In M. Adams, L. A. Bell, & P. Griffin (Eds.), *Teaching for diversity and social justice* (pp. 395–410). Routledge.

Adams, M., & Zúñiga, X. (2016). Getting started: Core concepts for social justice education. In M. Adams & L. A. Bell (Eds.). *Teaching for diversity and social justice* (3rd ed., pp. 95–130). Routledge.

Anti-Defamation League. (1998). *A classroom of difference trainer's manual.* Author.

Arao, B., & Clemens, K. (2013). From safe spaces to brave spaces: A new way to frame dialogue around diversity and social justice. In L. Landreman (Ed.), *The art of effective facilitation* (pp. 135–150). Stylus.

Bell, L. A. (2016). Theoretical foundations for social justice education. In M. Adams, L. A. Bell, & P. Griffin (Eds.), *Teaching for diversity and social justice* (3rd ed., pp. 3–26). Routledge.

Bell, L. A., Goodman, D. J., & Ouellett, M. L. (2016a). Design and facilitation. In M. Adams & L. A. Bell (Eds.), *Teaching for diversity and social justice* (3rd ed., pp. 55–94). Routledge.

Bell, L. A., Goodman, D. J., & Varghese, R. (2016b). Critical self-knowledge for social justice educators. In M. Adams & L. A. Bell (Eds.), *Teaching for diversity and social justice* (3rd ed., pp. 397–418). Routledge.

Brookfield, S. (2019). The dynamics of teaching race. In S. Brookfield (Ed.). *Teaching race*. John Wiley & Sons.

David, E. J. R. (Ed.). (2014). *Internalized oppression*. Springer.

DiAngelo, R. (2012). *What does it mean to be White? Developing White racial literacy*. Peter Lang Publishers.

Freire, P. (1970). *Pedagogy of the oppressed*. Seabury Press.

Freire, P. (1994). *Pedagogy of hope: Reliving pedagogy of the oppressed*. Continuum.

Garran, A. M., Aymer, S., Gelman, C. R., & Miller, J. L. (2015). Team-teaching anti-oppression with diverse faculty: Challenges and opportunities. *Social Work Education, 34*(7), 799–814.

Garran, A. M., Kang, H. K., & Fraser, E. (2014). Pedagogy and diversity: Enrichment and support for social work instructors engaged in social justice education. *Journal of Teaching in Social Work, 34*(4), 564–574.

Garran, A. M., & Rasmussen, B. (2014). Safety in the classroom: Reconsidered. *Journal of Teaching in Social Work, 34*(4), 401–412.

Godsil, R. D. (2015, January/February). Breaking the cycle: Implicit bias, racial anxiety and stereotype threat. *Poverty & Race, 24*(1), 1–2, 8–10.

Goodman, D. (2011). *Promoting diversity and social justice: Educating people from privileged groups* (2nd ed.). Routledge.

Goodman, D. (2015). Can you love them enough to help them learn? Reflections of a social justice educator on addressing resistance from White students to anti-racism education. *Understanding and Dismantling Privilege, 5*(1), 62–73.

Jeffery, D. (2005). "What good is anti-racist social work if you can't master it?" Exploring a paradox in anti-racist social work education. *Race, Ethnicity and Education, 8*(4), 409–425.

Joseph, V., & Williams, T. O. (2008). "Good niggers": The struggle to find courage, strength, and confidence to fight internalized racism and internalized dominance. *Democracy and Education, 17*(2), 67–73.

Kang, H. K., & Garran, A. M. (2018). Microaggressions in social work classrooms: Strategies for pedagogical intervention. *Journal of Ethnic and Cultural Diversity in Social Work, 27*(1), 1–13. https://doi.org/10.1080/15313204.2017.1413608

Kernahan, C. (2019). *Teaching about race and racism in the college classroom*. West Virginia University Press.

Lee, M. W. (Director & Producer). (2002). *Last chance for Eden [DVD]*. StirFry Productions.

Lee, M. W. (Director & Co-Producer), & Hunter, M. (Co-Producer). (1994). *The color of fear [VHS]*. StirFry Productions.

Leonardo, Z., & Porter, R. K. (2010). Pedagogy of fear: Toward a Fanonian theory of "safety" in race dialogue. *Race, Ethnicity and Education, 13*(2), 139–157.

Mazo, A. (2018). *Dawnland [Documentary]*. United States: Upstander Project.

Mildred, J., & Zúñiga, X. (2004). Working with resistance to diversity issues in the classroom: Lessons from teacher training and multicultural education. *Smith College Studies in Social Work, 74*(2), 359–375.

Miller, J., Donner, S., & Fraser, E. (2004a). Talking when talking is tough: Taking on conversations about race, sexual orientation, gender, class, and other aspects of social identity. *Smith College Studies in Social Work, 74*(2), 377–392.

Miller, J., Hyde, C., & Ruth, B. J. (2004b). Teaching about race and racism in social work: Challenges for White educators. *Smith College Studies in Social Work, 74*(2), 409–426.

Palos, A. (2011). *Precious knowledge [Documentary]. United States: A Dos Vatos Film.*

Solomon, R. P. (2000). Exploring cross-race dyad partnerships in learning to teach. *Teachers College Record, 102*(6), 953–979.

Solomon, R. P., Portelli, J. P., Daniel, B., & Campbell, A. (2005). The discourse of denial: How White teacher candidates construct race, racism and "White privilege." *Race, Ethnicity and Education, 8*(2), 147–169.

Steele, C. (2011). *Whistling Vivaldi: How stereotypes affect us and what we can do*. W. W. Norton.

Stone, D., Patton, B., & Heen, S. (1999). *Difficult conversations: How to discuss what matters most*. Viking.

Wagner, A. E. (2005). Unsettling the academy: Working through the challenges of anti-racist pedagogy. *Race, Ethnicity and Education, 8*(3), 261–275.

Wasserman, I. C., & Doran, R. F. (1999). Creating inclusive learning communities. In A. L. Cooke, M. Brazzel, A. S. Craig, & B. Greig (Eds.), *Reading book for human relations training* (8th ed., pp. 307–310). NTL Institute for Applied Behavioral Science.

Winnicott, D. W. (1960). The theory of the parent-infant relationship. In D. W. Winnicott (Ed.), *The maturational processes and the facilitating environment: Studies in the theory of emotional development* (pp. 37–55). International Universities Press.

Zúñiga, X., & Nagda, B. A. (2001). Design considerations in intergroup dialogue. In D. Schoem & S. Hurtado (Eds.), *Intergroup dialogue: Deliberative democracy in school, college, community and workplace* (pp. 306–327). University of Michigan Press.

CHAPTER 14

Dismantling Racism: Creating the Web of Resistance

The persistence of racism relies on the collusion of the majority of White people in the United States, a form of by-standing that allows existing racial privileges for Whites and the web of racism for people of color to remain unchallenged. Although this inactivity may stem in part from an unwillingness to give up group advantages based on race, it also may be a result of White people either being unaware of race privilege or not knowing what to do about it. Racism is complex and intractable. It is not easily remedied by a few reforms, and it migrates, shifts, and reconfigures when confronted (Massey, 2005), much like a virus or bacteria that has altered in response to antibiotics.

Despite the persistence of racism, progress has been forthcoming, although it may be more difficult to recognize given President Trump's divisiveness and unwillingness to condemn acts and rhetoric of White supremacy. More and more people in the United States consider the most egregious forms of racism to be wrong and abhorrent. The mass protests demanding the murders of Black and Brown men and women by police be investigated and the perpetrators brought to justice, which blossomed during the summer of 2020, are evidence of the growing solidarity. The values of racial equity, nondiscrimination, and integration now are part of a national consensus, a marked shift in the past half-century (Bobo, 2001).

In the wake of the Great Society, affirmative action led to breaking down long-standing racial barriers and dislodged the embedded "affirmative action" of White privilege in many sectors of the economy. The African American middle class has grown markedly. Although much of this book has described the persistence of racism and what remains to be achieved, we must acknowledge what has been accomplished.

Before moving to create a web of resistance to racism, however, we must acknowledge some of the biggest challenges. A major one is the feeling of inevitability and hopelessness instilled by such a profound, multifaceted, adaptable, and durable form of oppression and social inequality. Racism is pervasive and suffuses all of American society, to the extent that it seems to be a normal state of affairs. By bestowing privileges and granting social and economic passports for White people while creating webs of oppression for people of color, racism has divided us. The greatest risks are that people targeted by racism will despair or be so consumed with survival that they have little energy left to confront the sources of their oppression, while people with privilege have an impaired capacity to see racism or become apathetic and indifferent to its injustices. We must not underestimate the enormity of the antiracism project.

Perhaps the biggest challenge to dismantling racism is that it is inside of us as well as outside of us. The social structure of racism is predicated on generalizations and stereotypes based on the appearance of our bodies, but its poisonous fumes actually *invade* our bodies. The vapors of racism sap our spirit, damage the psyche, and cloud the mind. It distorts how we see ourselves and others, particularly our ability to promote change. So we must repair the damage to our thoughts, feelings, and self-concepts and reconnect with our belief in our capacity for compassion, empathy, and our desire to manifest racial justice.

Apathy leads to acquiescence with racism and hopelessness begets apathy. By contrast, resisting racism is an act of liberation and engenders hope. Every steel thread in the web of racism can be dissolved in nonviolent ways, replacing the web with a tapestry of resistance. Racism relies on isolation, division, dehumanization—turning sisters and brothers into "others." A web of resistance to racism starts with humanizing everyone, including humanizing ourselves.

Humanizing ourselves implies being compassionate and gentle toward our flaws while also having the courage to move beyond our comfort zones, extending that compassion to others through our actions. Racism alienates us from ourselves, divides us, and isolates us from others. By contrast, forming groups of allies unites us so we can provide support, encouragement, and assistance to one another. The dams of racism block opportunity while ripples of actions create waves of liberation.

Helping professionals work to engender hope in their clients. Social and psychological challenges and problems deflate individuals' belief in themselves and in the beneficence of others. Every human service worker has encountered situations in which their clients' inability to feel optimistic and to envision a better future hinders their progress as much as the presenting problems that led to their demoralization. Empowerment comes from acknowledging real barriers and limitations and recognizing our inability to control everything, while also believing in our capacity to have some influence over the course of our lives.

Helping professionals must abide by mandates in codes of ethics about social justice, respect for diverse cultures, and the worth and dignity of all people. Spurred by professional mandates and buoyed by a belief in our ability to make a difference, helping professionals are positioned to take a leadership role in the move to dismantle racism, empowering ourselves and seeking to inspire our clients.

CREATING THE WEB OF RESISTANCE

If there's a web of racism, there also must be a web of resistance (Werkmeister Rozas & Miller, 2009). We have developed this idea further and presented it in a diagram Figure 14.1 a web of resistance to racism. Within this web we list the ABCDs of core values and skills that exist in both the internal and external realm; when employed these core values and skills can assist in combating the web of institutional racism. We will examine the ABCD of core values and skills and what takes place in each realm.

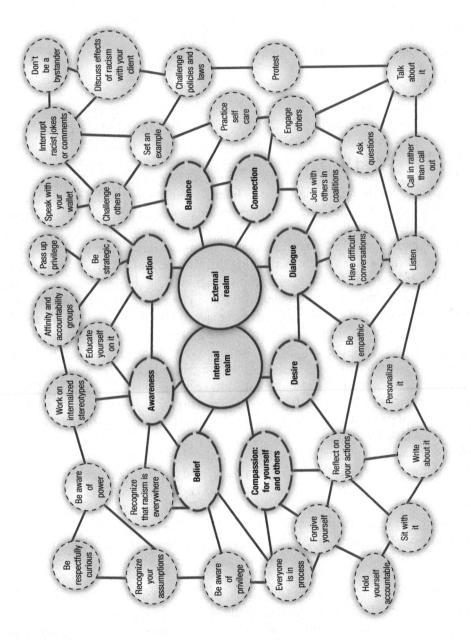

FIGURE 14.1 The web of resistance.

INTERNAL REALM

ABCDs of core values:

1. Awareness of the existence of racism
2. Belief in the deleterious effects of racism
3. Compassion for ourselves and others
4. Desire to advocate for change through activism

Awareness

Antiracism work requires an awareness of racism and all of its forms. If we do not see or hear racism, it is difficult to confront. Harro (2013) calls this "waking up." Although most people of color are acutely aware of racism, most White people are not attuned to its vicissitudes. One way of thinking about this is that many White people have severe vision problems when it comes to seeing racism. Therefore, a precise lens can bring into view things previously undetected. The brain then has to develop new frames to make sense of the new information being observed. And if the lens is removed too quickly, we will revert to visual impairment.

We also urge readers to listen for the more subtle manifestations of racism in the main-stream media, particularly the "liberal" media. Racism is clear and overt when listening to AM talk radio when hosts are White men railing against people of color. But when a liberal media outlet does a story and a White perspective is assumed, or the announcers and guests for a program consistently are predominantly White, or people of color only are called upon when there is an "ethnic story," or there is a determination to be "color blind" when consider-ing the impact of programs or policies—it is important to ask questions, to invite reflection and inquiry, to point out patterns or hidden assumptions, to hold producers accountable, and to confront the unexamined White privilege which saturates all mainstream media.

Those who do not encounter racism have difficulty seeing it and understanding what they are viewing. Antiracism work is ongoing, as the obfuscating fog of racism is always in the air. What can be instrumental in developing a person's awareness around racism and anti-racism is the practice of introspection and self-reflection.

Much can be said about how racism is internalized and can distort our view of ourselves and others. Introspection can take many forms. Keeping a journal allows us to express our-selves and explore what we are thinking and feeling. The act of writing is illuminating in itself. When we share our narratives with trusted others, we receive feedback and learn from what others see and hear; others learn from us in this process as well. Structured exercises, such as those described in the appendices to previous chapters, are useful ways to explore what is inside of us. These can be done alone or in the presence of others, such as discussion groups or pairs.

Other acts of introspection include participating in support groups that focus on unlearn-ing racism or on how to be a better ally, reading and reflecting about others' experiences, and mapping out goals for ourselves that move us out of our comfort zone and engage us in action. Talking with partners, children, friends, and colleagues is another vehicle for learning about ourselves and others.

Introspection will take different forms for different people. One influential factor is our experience with racism. For those who have encountered racism and have developed strengths, resiliency, and effective coping strategies, a task of introspection can be to build on these capacities and become even stronger. Or perhaps a coping strategy has mixed results, such as dealing with racism in the moment but leaving a lingering sense of pain or self-doubt. Exposing our vulnerabilities and recognizing our assumptions can be difficult, even to ourselves, yet by doing so, we heighten our awareness and become even more adaptive and effective in advocating for ourselves and the rights and needs of others.

For people who have experienced race privilege, or have not had experiences of racism, introspection can help to uncover hidden biases or stereotypes. Introspection also involves taking risks and exploring painful and unpleasant internalizations. Yet, without insight and awareness, we are vulnerable to the power of unexamined prejudice. People with race privilege also should have an education plan, to learn about the history, manifestations, and consequences of racism.

Although we have described different tasks for people with different racial identities, we are not suggesting that some tasks are exclusively for either people of color or White people. For example, people of color also internalize prejudices or stereotypes and can learn more about the history of racism and how to conceptualize it, while Whites benefit from reflecting on how best to respond to racism in the moment. We recommend a personal plan of education and reflection for all antiracism activists and offer an antiracism activist audit in Exercise 14.1.

Believing

It is not enough to be aware of racism. Just as important is believing in its pervasive and insidious existence on multiple levels. Racism lurks in the unconscious, affecting individual behaviors without intention or cognitive awareness. This is often difficult for well-intentioned people to admit. The systemic and cultural aspects of racism, often imperceptible to those who are not directly affected by racist policies and practices, are real and do irreparable damage. Just as it is vital to validate and believe people of color who have experienced microaggressions, it is crucial to acknowledge the racism that occurs on a systemic and cultural level. When people fail to believe that racism exists on levels that are not evidenced by individual behaviors, they perpetuate racist socialization processes and continue to support racist ideas and policies.

We not only have to believe in the existence of racism, we have to believe that things can change in the direction of racial justice. Part of the challenge to the persistence of racism is to articulate a vision of a society without racism. In such a world, people would live wherever they want and there would be much greater racial integration. The homes owned by people of color and the neighborhoods where they reside would be as valuable as those of White people. These neighborhoods would be served by banks rather than by predatory lenders. Educational achievement at all levels would not reflect racial gaps. All occupations and professions would have a range of racial representation consistent with the demographics of the country. Health, infant mortality, access to healthcare, and life expectancy would not reflect racial patterns. Fewer people would be in jail, and jails would not be grossly over-populated by African Americans and other people of color. Broken treaties with Indigenous tribes would be revisited and repaired. Salaries and wealth would not reflect racial inequities. Policing would be a community-based enterprise, working with community leaders and being accountable to the community, and police officers would reflect the ethnic-racial demographics of those being policed. There would be cultural pluralism. Everyone would have a right to vote, and their votes would be counted. And politicians, particularly at state and national levels, would not be overwhelmingly White. Every office of government, including the presidency, would be truly open and accessible to anyone, regardless of race. Social opportunity and access would be available to people of all races, and everyone could make choices about their occupations, neighborhoods, and lifestyles as individuals, not as representatives of their race.

Lastly, we need to believe in ourselves; our ability to survive and thrive, have compassion for ourselves and others, and that in concert with allies we can be part of the centuries-old movement to achieve racial justice.

Compassion

Compassion for Others

Antiracism calls for having compassion for everyone and dissolving artificial boundaries that cause us to extend compassion to some but not others. This means having compassion for ourselves as well as for people who are similar to and different from us. In our view, it also extends to people who are perpetuating racism consciously or unconsciously. We condemn racism while trying to maintain compassion for those it damages, including those with race privilege.

One way of demonstrating compassion for others is recognizing that we are all a work in progress. All people are potential antiracism allies and, like ourselves, have flaws. We can commit to holding others and ourselves accountable without participating in the call out or cancel culture that has infiltrated our media saturated society. To be clear, no act of racism should be ignored or go unchallenged. What is important is to consider what type of response would bring forth the most profit in the fight against racism. Once a person is tasked with facing up to their racist actions the way they respond should be considered in what steps come next. A person who negates their action or contends that they are now the victim requires a different response than one who acknowledges their wrong-doing and commits to personal change. Sometimes, past racist statements or actions performed by individuals when they were young come to light later in life. The "guilty" are publicly condemned by contemporary media and people are propelled to denounce not only the action or statement, but the person themselves. This dynamic creates a situation where the person can do nothing to redeem themselves, even if their current work and behavior does not support racism. Not only does calling people out dismiss the potential for a person to change, it prohibits others from discussing race and racism for fear that they may say something wrong and be cancelled, slowing the anti-racist movement.

We also are tempted to dismiss someone if we think they are just "not getting it" and never will "get it." This response is typical and understandable. Sometimes we do need to disengage from a person because we are so frustrated or estranged from them. This distancing should be a temporary response, and hopefully we will be able to re-establish our compassion for that person and engage in authentic and productive dialogue at some point. The scenarios in Exercise 14.2, taken from conversations with students, illustrate the tension between confronting racism and not humiliating others.

Compassion for Self

Antiracism helping professionals know how racism damages people and are aware of its capacity to distort perceptions of self and others. So it can be particularly frustrating and discouraging to be reminded of one's own unfinished personal business when an ethnic or racial stereotype bubbles up or a wound of racism is reopened. Helping professionals who are people of color know how painful and dispiriting it can be to continually engage in talking about racism and trying to "educate" White people, even if the cause is just. Helping professionals who are White at times feel appalled at their unresolved biases or a sense of shame when they inadvertently engage in microaggressions with colleagues of color. To retreat from activism when criticized by others can be tempting.

We encourage antiracism activists to be compassionate and gentle with themselves. Although we are working for a fair and just society, we are all "works in progress" and imperfect people. Of course, our own personal work is an important part of the struggle against racism, but mistakes and unresolved issues are inevitable, and becoming overly self-critical can diminish our energy and motivation. If we are feeling tired or burdened by antiracism work, or upset with our own internalized stereotypes and racism, we may take out these feelings on other people, criticizing or even verbally attacking them, which alienates potential allies. Sometimes antiracism activists should take a deep breath or even take a break from the intensity of the work. Self-compassion is an important stance to develop.

Desire

The positive changes in the struggle against racism to date have resulted from the sustained engagement of dedicated people. In short, people had a desire to bring about change through advocacy and activism. Monumental transformations take place at seams in history, but even these moments of profound change depend on concerted efforts leading up to them and collective vigilance afterward. The dissolution of racism requires a society-wide effort, desire and commitment from a multitude of individuals, groups, and organizations who are willing to remain engaged for the long haul.

EXTERNAL REALM

The ABCDs of Core Skills

1. Action
2. Balance
3. Connection
4. Dialogue

Action

As a former colleague of ours Jerry Sachs used to say, the most important thing we can do as helping professionals is "show up." Making ourselves available to do what needs to be done is the first step in engaging in any type of resistance. Anytime you work with individuals, groups, or communities there are a variety of tasks that need to be done in order to accomplish a specific task, goal, or initiative. Wanting or having the desire to accomplish something is not enough; we have to learn new skills, enhance those we already possess, and put them into active practice. There are myriad roles to be filled when confronting racist acts or policies. What is needed may not always be what someone envisioned themselves doing. The most important task for White allies is showing up and asking what it is they can do. Such action ought not be initiated with an expectation of a reward. When individuals telegraph their virtue, but participate in ally behaviors that either do not help or actively harm people of color, they are participating in what is called *performance allyship*. Activities such as public declarations of support for antiracism efforts on social media using hashtags or Facebook filters/ frames may feel virtuous in the short run but in the long run can feed the beast of complicity. It allows people with White privilege to believe that they have done their part in the fight against racism, without making the sustained commitment necessary to do the real work that has to be done, which involves time and tolerance of discomfort, or experiencing the consequences of going against White dominance, which people of color continually encounter.

Balance

Engaging in antiracism activism can be enlivening and liberating, but it also involves commitment and dedication. Taking a stand against injustice and working for racial equality imparts a sense of empowerment. As a person becomes more actively engaged in this work, the investment in dismantling racism deepens. High motivation and passion fuel the level of energy that this work takes. As with any strong commitments, frustration can set in when progress is slow or there are setbacks.

Tensions between fellow activists can arise over differences in opinion about priorities and tactics. Misunderstandings crop up because of cultural differences and unexamined stereotypes, as well as reflexive patterns of assuming roles or patterns of group conflict. Struggles over power and leadership increase the frustration and pressure. The antiracism movement needs all of the help it can muster and, thus, we must consider strategies that can encourage activists to stay involved and be effective in their work. One key strategy is to find a balance in your life while pursuing this work. If you burn yourself out, who will be there to continue the work?

Helping professionals can become engaged in a number of antiracism strategies that will erode the web of institutional racism. These involve making legal challenges to racism, supporting laws that foster equality, and backing affirmative action and some form of reparations. The recent protests against the murders of George Floyd, Breonna Taylor, and others under the banner of Black Lives Matter have the potential to ignite a social movement in the 21st century, belying the belief that the power of the Civil Rights Movement of the past can never be restored. Helping professionals must be aware of such coalescing factors and recognize the various options available to them by joining the web of resistance: This is what ethical practice looks like!

All activism requires taking care of oneself. Many helping professionals are already struggling with self-care, as they are endowed with deep reservoirs of compassion and are working with clients, agencies, and organizations who have pressing needs. Engaging in antiracism work usually increases concern for the well-being of consumers and fires up fervor for fairness and social justice. Under these circumstances, self-care may be viewed as a luxury or as a failure of will. But without self-care, burnout becomes a distinct risk.

Self-care may take many different forms, ranging from vigorous physical exercise to reading, meditating, or socializing with friends (see Box 14.1). Although individuals must identify what works best for them, helping professionals should build in activities and time that allow for a break from the intensity of antiracism work. We all function with greater strength and acuity if we can nurture ourselves periodically *before* becoming fried and frazzled.

> ## BOX 14.1 Self-Care When Doing Antiracism Work
>
> 1. Do regular self-audits about stress and burnout. Monitor for preoccupation, difficulty sleeping, and not eating properly.
> 2. Set realistic goals. You can't do everything all of the time.
> 3. Seek regular supervision, consultation, peer consultation, support, and ally groups. Accountability matters.
> 4. Seek balance between professional and personal lives. Set limits.
> 5. Pay attention to your physical health, and exercise.
> 6. Use meditation, mindfulness, and other techniques for self-awareness, self-relaxation, and self-healing.
> 7. Attend to your spiritual needs.
> 8. Don't lose contact with joy, beauty, humor, pleasure, and sources of enjoyment.
> 9. Stay connected with others.
> 10. Keep a journal about how your antiracism work is going.

Self-care can involve an extraordinary range of activities, of which we highlight three here.

1. Nurture your spiritual life if that is a meaningful part of your being. Participate in public organized religious activities or in personal, regular meditation. Having a larger philosophical and spiritual worldview can provide motivation for antiracism activities, as well as to offer hope and help to deal with setbacks.
2. Engage in physical activity. Any kind of work or activism that involves strong commitments and deep passions can deplete the body or foster a build up of unhealthy toxins. Some form of physical activity, however vigorous or gentle, can be restorative and offer balance and ballast to the life of an antiracism activist.
3. Connect with others and join in collective action. The power of social networks and social advocacy are both forms of self-care and effective means of achieving social change. At the same time, it is important to also connect with other people socially and recreationally and to have times when one is not on-duty as an activist.

Part of the motivation for antiracism work is to improve the health and opportunities for people targeted by racism. How ironic it would be if activists were to physically compromise their own health in the process.

Connection

We are not alone in this fight, and yet racism can cause us to feel isolated, divided, and deflated. Antiracism work is more effective when we do it with others. All of us, people of color and White people both, need other people to form coalitions, transform organizations, change communities, and have a political impact. Being connected with others who are confronting racism enhances our power and increases our effectiveness, and the actual process of resisting with others is empowering as well. Connections to organizations and communities are also a vital piece in resisting racism.

Helping professionals who have connections to organizations can challenge institutional racism within programs and agencies, as well as within funding entities and professional associations. We also can challenge racist practices that are embedded in systems that serve clients and lobby for changes and reforms. Most of us work for agencies, and all of us are members, or potential members, of professional associations. As we work with others to dismantle racism, we must ensure that our own houses are in order.

Helping professionals can work to foster connections within communities that are inclusive and in which people of all races and ethnicities are treated fairly and equitably and have equal access to resources. All human service professionals live and work in communities and through their connections can engage in this work as residents as well as professionals. Connection within communities and across communities can create some of the most powerful and active forms of resistance to racism.

Interracial coalitions are effective mechanisms in confronting racism. Coalitions offer more resources, generate a wider range of ideas, have greater access to a variety of people and systems, and can establish more credibility than disparate clusters of individuals. Coalitions have clout! Antiracism coalitions that bring in a wide range of people and organizations increase the number of stakeholders actively committed and working together toward common goals.

There are a range of coalitions that antiracism activists can join. Some are long-standing national organizations, such as the National Association for the Advancement of Colored People (NAACP) and the Urban League, which have local chapters in many communities. A more recent nationwide coalition has been the Black Lives Matter movement.

Black Lives Matter is a response to the wave of killing of unarmed Black people, mostly by law enforcement officials but not limited to them. Some of the recent murders that have contributed to the momentum of this movement are the killing of Trayvon Martin by George Zimmerman in Sanford, Florida, in 2012; the murder of Michael Brown by police in Ferguson, Missouri, in 2014; and the murder of Eric Garner by police in Staten Island, New York, in 2014 (McLaughlin, 2016). In all three instances, the perpetrators were acquitted by mostly White juries. The movement was further fueled by the murder of Freddie Gray while in the custody of the Baltimore police, the mysterious death of Sandra Bland while in police custody in Waller County, Texas, in 2015; the shooting death of Rekia Boyd by an off-duty officer as she walked with friends from a party in 2012; the 2015 massacre of nine African American worshippers during Bible study in their church in Charleston, South Carolina, by White supremacist Dylan Roof (Cobb, 2016); Philando Castile, shot by Minnesota police, reaching for his drivers license after being pulled over during a routine check; in March 2020, 26-year-old Breonna Taylor was shot eight times in Louisville when police raided her apartment without announcing themselves; and in Minneapolis, in May 2020 George Floyd was held down by three police officers, one of whom had his knee on Mr. Floyd's neck for almost 10 minutes resulting in his death. George Floyd's death sparked protests worldwide with people demanding the officers be indicted for murder. Of these deaths only the police officer who held his knee on Mr. Floyd's neck was actually charged with second-degree murder and manslaughter. The Black Lives Matter website specifies that their mission is to eliminate White supremacy and to bolster community power that can intercede on behalf of Black communities where violence has been exacted by individual actors and hegemonic structures (Black Lives Matter, 2020).

Black Lives Matter espouses a commitment to being a global and national movement with local chapters and is wary of organizational hierarchies (Cobb, 2016). It also has a commitment to intersectionality when addressing social oppression. It is too early yet to assess the ongoing impact of this movement but already it has galvanized thousands, if not millions, of followers through the use of social media and has made racism against Black people a central social concern through publicizing murders, highlighting the extent and many forms of racism, and contributing to campus and community protests focusing on a mixture of local and national issues (Copeland, 2015). It has spread from the United States around the world and there are chapters in many countries. The movement is committed to documenting police brutality, demilitarizing police forces, and lowering the arrest and incarceration rates for people of color accused of minor crimes (Cobb, 2016). Some activists are also running for local political offices, although within the movement there is skepticism about the legitimacy and effectiveness of the political process (Cobb, 2016).

Other groups are local and address specific community issues. Some examples are working to support documented and undocumented immigrants living in the community or creating groups that examine White privilege, police brutality, reparations or how to challenge all forms of local institutional racism. When no local coalition is addressing pressing issues pertaining to racism, human service professionals can link with other concerned groups and individuals to form one. Communities usually have a critical mass of helping professionals, clergy, activists, local political leaders, educators, and students, progressive business leaders, and residents who are concerned about racism and are willing to work on it. To draw attention to critical issues, coalitions can arrange press conferences, teach-ins, and demonstrations.

Any work with groups and coalitions takes patience and willingness to share and compromise. Coalitions working against racism must be particularly cognizant of who is and is not represented in their ranks and who ends up in positions of leadership. White members must not dominate the coalition, set the agenda, or assume power.

Dialogue

Being aware of social identities and social group memberships, and the differential power surrounding such identities and memberships is important in order for any real dialogue about race and racism to occur. It is human nature to identify with groups and for identity to be influenced by our group affiliations. This can be a positive source of norms, values, mutual support, and validation. Groups can buffer people from social assaults and violations. Feeling positive about one's group need not lead to fearing, disliking, exploiting, or oppressing members of another group (Brewer, 2001). An example of how group identity can have deleterious effects on intergroup cooperation and racial justice is the emboldened public acts of White supremacist/nationalist groups, such as the Proud Boys founded in 2016. Such groups spout indefensible racist, sexist, xenophobic, homo/transphobic, Islamophobic rhetoric while disavowing their bigotry and hate toward historically underrepresented and marginazied groups. A recent example is how respectfully the White insurrectionists who stormed the U.S. capitol were treated by law enforcement in contrast to how peaceful Black Lives Matter demonstrators were tear gassed and beaten a few months earlier when President Trump wanted to walk across the street for a photo-op.

Racism is an extreme example of in-group validation and social privileges for White people, at the expense of people of color. Thus, a major task for antiracism work is to repair and reconstruct intergroup relationships. One way to facilitate intergroup connections is through providing opportunities for individuals from different racial groups to participate in structured dialogues. One of the main barriers to dismantling racism is the inability many have to dialogue about the subject due to a lack of training and experience.

This concept is important because less intergroup hostility, particularly from Whites toward people of color, diminishes collusion with racist practices. Greater intergroup cooperation fosters mutual respect and compassion extending beyond one's own ethnic or racial group.

Dialogues can occur within educational settings, community settings, and organizational settings.

Successful coalitions usually have democratic mechanisms to resolve disputes and foster dialogue and understanding among members. And, as discussed in Chapter 8, structured conversations about race and racism increase the ability of people to work together, as well as respect and understand one another.

BEING HEARD: THE REALM OF DIALOGUE, DISCOURSE, AND CULTURE

The webs of racism and coloniality of power explain how U.S. culture privileges Western, Eurocentric worldviews and values and how other cultures are marginalized or subjected to negative stereotypes. It also considers how public discourses reinforce dominant cultural patterns and serve to normalize White race privilege while also denigrating and blaming people of color for their social exclusion. Therefore, antiracism work by human professionals should seek to address public discourses, dialogues, and narratives about racism and to expand and diversify the vision of what constitutes USAmerican culture to value and include non-White, non-Western groups. Although this task initially may appear abstract and daunting, helping professionals can participate in antiracism discourses in many ways. This book already has mentioned how coalitions can do this through demonstrations, teach-ins, press releases, and many other activities for individuals and groups. As Martin Luther King, Jr. stated, [violence] leads to monologue rather than dialogue.

Helping professionals have access to clients' stories. We can encourage them to tell their stories by publishing letters, blogs and submitting journal articles, as well as arranging events to give them access to the media. We can write our own stories, too, along with letters to the editor and op-ed pieces. We can call radio comment lines to highlight issues of race and racism. We can conduct research about the impact of racism on the lives of clients and publish the results in journals, magazines, and newspapers. Human service professionals can prepare leaflets and brochures that inform the public about racism and ways to confront it both interpersonally and institutionally. We can discuss racism online in chat rooms. Social media platforms offer a means for conveying one's commitment to antiracism while engaging others in self-reflection and collective action. These are examples of ways that helping professionals can contribute to public discourses about race and racism utilizing our unique position of working directly with clients, as well as with the social service systems that affect them.

Further, we can make noise through our conversations with colleagues, friends, and family. We can show videos and sponsor discussion groups. We can start antiracism discussion threads on social media and other web-based discussion forums. We can challenge racist assumptions that come up in staff meetings. Just as microaggressions of racism take their cumulative toll, we can offer micro-acts of antiracism that contribute to a discourse of liberation.

To be active in resisting racism through dialogue it is important to be aware of which topics may inspire more division and then acquire the needed training or expertise to offer such dialogue. For example, although a policy like affirmative action or a concept such as reparations may, for many, be perceived as mechanisms that allow for the opportunity for equality and access to resources that have historically been denied to people of color, many Whites may describe it as "reverse racism." How can this be deconstructed so that the historic and ongoing affirmative action for White people is surfaced and there are mechanisms for discussing and reflecting on this inversion.

AFFIRMATIVE ACTION

Affirmative action has been grossly distorted in public discourses and by conservative politicians appealing to economic and social insecurities of White voters. Affirmative action does not take away college seats and jobs from Whites. It opens up semi-closed systems to people of all races.

We will use the integration of baseball as an example. A cartel of owners of major league teams fielded all White rosters until Jackie Robinson joined the Brooklyn Dodgers in 1947. It was not that up until then there were no talented and qualified Black and Latino players. There were no laws forbidding integration. There was a "gentleman's agreement" to keep baseball segregated. If Branch Rickey, the Dodgers' general manager, had not affirmatively sought to end this practice, segregation would have remained.

And although baseball teams are integrated, inequality in baseball continues 70 years later. April 15 has been designated "Jackie Robinson Day" and all major league players wear his number, 42, a celebration of his historic role in integrating the major leagues. It is a day that helps the Major League Baseball organization to feel good about itself. However, only in late 2020 did Major League Baseball decide to include Negro League Baseball statistics in the game's official historical records. The number of African American players in the game has dropped precipitously over the past few decades and is currently at 7.7% (infogram, 2020), and there are scarcely any managers, general managers, or executives of color (Rhoden, 2016). There are even fewer people of color who own major league teams. In baseball in 2014, 98% of majority owners were White as were 87% of managers (Chalabi, 2014). The same pattern holds true in other major league sports with the exception of basketball, where 43% of head coaches were African American (Chalabi, 2014). For there to be qualified leaders in any industry, including baseball, there needs to be an intentional program that extends throughout the system, training and preparing people for leadership jobs while ensuring that an old boy's network does not continue to replicate itself.

The real affirmative action in the United States has been the knapsack of privileges carried by all White citizens. What has been called "affirmative action" since the Great Society in the 1960s has over time penetrated virtually all-White niches and enclaves. Without it, college campuses doubtless would not be as integrated as they are and police and fire departments would not have more than a token representation of people of color. If affirmative action continues to come under attack and be diluted, we likely will regress to pre-affirmative action racial patterns. Affirmative action is needed to ensure that all of the forms of racism discussed in this book do not block and impede the opportunities for people of color to succeed in this country. This is a nation committed to equal rights and opportunity; affirmative action is one way of ensuring that endemic and persistent racism, which is counter to those values, is offset.

REPARATIONS

The notion of reparations is exceedingly complex and controversial. We support a national dialogue about reparations because, as we have tried to illustrate, the historical legacies of racism have created profound structural imbalances that disadvantage many people of color. The U.S. government is highly unlikely to return in full the land appropriated from Native Americans or Mexican Americans. There is no way to restore the many resources lost by African Americans (Coates, 2014). But, as a nation, we can examine the economic and social consequences of these and other historical heritages and consider policies that will acknowledge their impact, seek to repair the social and psychological damage, and work to reverse current economic inequalities that can be linked to slavery, Jim Crow, gerrymandering, redlining, and other manifestations of racism. Much of the wealth of this nation comes from stealing land from Indigenous people and giving it to White people and generating wealth based on enslaved African American labor: This enriched White capitalists, raised the living standards of White workers, and helped to fund and build government offices and colleges and universities. How can such thefts and unpaid labor be paid back? A small example of the attempt to do this were the reparations finally granted to Japanese Americans who were incarcerated during World War II.

Some readers will support all of these priorities, while others may support only some or envision other initiatives crucial to dismantling institutional racism. We have shared our views. What is most important is that helping professionals work to intervene with laws, policies, and institutions and not resort to being bystanders to racial injustice. Policy formation involves setting agendas and lobbying by various interest groups. If human service professionals are hesitant or opt out of full participation, the vacuum created by inaction will be filled by other interest groups, including those committed to maintaining White privilege and dominance.

USING THE WEB OF RESISTANCE IN THE POLITICAL AND SOCIAL REALM: LAWS, INSTITUTIONS, AND PRACTICES

The web of institutional racism described in Chapter 5 is the level of pervasive, societal racism that eventually must be transformed to ensure that the United States lives up to its ideals of equality, justice, and freedom.

When we consider the Spectrum of Racism in Chapter 2 (Figure 2.1) and look at the left-hand side of the diagram, we can see the most egregious, extreme forms of state-supported racism: genocide, apartheid, slavery, and ethnic cleansing. All of these have occurred in the past in this country, and we still witness with horror their presence in other parts of the world today.

State-supported racism includes racist codes and laws, legal segregation and exclusion, and Jim Crow laws. These were part of our nation's more recent history, extending well into the 1960s in some parts of the country. Although there are remnants of state-supported racism— such as the disenfranchisement of significant numbers of African American men by virtue of voter suppression laws and criminal convictions in certain states—the national consensus for many years was that these practices were wrong, unlawful, and un-American (Anderson, 2018; Bobo, 2001). Sadly, with the Supreme Court decision known as Holder in 2013 gutted the Voting Rights Act and voter suppression against Black, Indigenous, and people of color has risen ever since. In the 2020 Presidential election, the sitting president openly tried to "find" votes while throwing out votes from predominantly African American precincts.

Today, institutional racism, also called structural racism, is the most entrenched, destructive, and enduring form of racism on the spectrum of racism in the United States. Because it is so omnipresent and complex, confronting it feels daunting. Yet, just as with the extreme forms of racism that no longer are acceptable in this nation, institutional racism can be dismantled.

What sustains this web? Many things, including ignorance and lack of awareness by White people, cultural discourses legitimizing it, economic inequalities and advantages that accrue for Whites, intergroup competition, political manipulation, and the persistence of both intentional and unintentional segregation. Many of the strategies already mentioned work to undermine some of these forces. But more is needed.

When we consider the web of institutional racism, the default setting for all institutions and organizations is to reflect the structure and practices of racism in society. Active and dynamic efforts are required to negate and transform this. One of the most insidious facets of the web of racism is how the steel threads connect: For example, residential racism leads to educational and transportation racism, which contribute to a lack of employment opportunities as well as the capacity to accumulate wealth.

The web is so huge and linked that working to dismantle all of it at once would be a Herculean task. Still, because it is so connected, if progress can be made in one part of the web, it starts to pull on the other strands, starting a process of unraveling that eventually can lead to the web's collapse. For example, if political racism is confronted successfully, more lawmakers are likely to understand the importance of equal access to healthcare, and of protecting poor people of color from environmental hazards, which will give rise to challenges to healthcare and environmental racism. But in order to succeed, there need to be lawmakers, presidents, and supreme court justices who realize that the United States has never been a color-blind society. White supremacists like Donald Trump have to be prevented from assuming office and seizing power, while voter registration drives can help elect people such as Raphael Warnock, Georgia's first African American Senator. This takes dedication, commitment and action. If communities become truly racially integrated, a foundation will be laid from which to confront educational and occupational racism. The successes of the Gautreaux program, mentioned in Chapter 10, is encouraging in this regard.

Granted, this is only a partial vision, but it illustrates the types of activities in which helping professionals can engage. Wherever we work (and live), we can challenge practices by real estate firms, banks, and local municipalities that continue segregation. For those of us who work in or with public schools, ending the racial achievement gap can be our highest priority. We can join coalitions, parent–teacher organizations, and police review boards; run for school committee positions; and exert our influence as professionals and parents. We can ensure that our own professions do not have racial patterns of staffing, promotion, and leadership. We all have interactions with the health system, and we can work with healthcare providers and systems to serve all people equally, regardless of race. We can help to form task forces and coalitions to lower infant mortality rates, reduce pollution and increase access to healthy food in all communities. After the election of Donald Trump in 2016, small neighborhood grassroots groups called Rapid Organized Active Response (ROAR) sprang up across the country. One such group was organized in the Northeast, is still in existence today, and has a membership of 54 people. This group was responsible for writing a total of 1,500 postcards to constituents across the country who did not vote in 2016 mobilizing them to vote and wrote to registered independent constituents in Georgia, urging them to vote Democratic.

All of these local actions are significant. Also, we can advocate for state and national priorities—universal healthcare coverage, adequate minimum wages, an end to racial profiling, and policies geared to ensure that people of color attend college and have access to jobs in industries that still are predominantly White. Everyone in the United States has the right to vote, and we can advocate for that right and ensure that it is respected and validated. These are huge national issues in the struggle for racial justice.

An inescapable conclusion is that helping professionals must be politically active. The conservative trend in this country has been a regression in the struggle for civil rights. Without leadership from presidents, senators, members of Congress, governors, and state lawmakers, the agenda we are calling for will be blocked, stalled, and derailed. Helping professionals are a large group, a growing sector of the U.S. economy. We need to exercise our political muscle through our own efforts and those of our professional organizations. Helping professionals can join national organizations, form local chapters, and work with politicians to advocate for these issues. National organizations such as the National Association of Social Workers (NASW) and the American Psychological Association (APA) are already lobbying for these and similar policies and should be encouraged to do even more. Professional associations need to band with other professional associations; this requires professional intersectionality and unity in the fight against racism rather than professional competition. All helping professionals can contribute to helping clients and consumers to register to vote, open up organizations and institutions through affirmative action, and join with meaningful efforts toward reparations.

WORKING TOGETHER

Helping professionals who choose to become antiracism activists are not alone, as many people are engaged in this work in a variety of ways. Antiracism work requires a great deal of energy, a willingness to confront racism consistently, and a commitment to stay active for the long haul. At times, this can feel isolating and lonely.

This chapter already has described the many advantages of working in coalitions. Also helpful is to develop personal support systems and antiracism allies—people to whom we can turn when things become complicated or overwhelming and who can also turn to us. Groups that help people of color feel buffered from the effects of racism and groups that support White people committed to unlearning racism offer validation and support.

Taking the Long View

Kivel (1996) has urged antiracism activists not to confuse the battle with the war. Antiracism work involves many losses and setbacks, as well as achievements. Progress toward social justice has not moved forward rapidly or consistently. Therefore, we must see antiracism work as part of a chain of resistance and liberation that has taken place over hundreds of years. We have witnessed in our own nation how the most extreme manifestations of racism that were morally, socially, and politically unacceptable have rapidly seeped back into the politics and public discourses.

Taking the long view involves a Janus-like perspective, looking both backward and ahead, noting progress and at the same time identifying what work remains to be done. Remembering that this kind of work is most likely to have an effect when it is sustained over time, as the late congressman John Lewis believed, it is better to be a pilot light than a firecracker. Our progress must be steady and deliberate and, like a pilot light, keep burning. We should celebrate successes and not become overly discouraged when encountering roadblocks. Dismantling racism is a massive historical project, and many acts of activism are necessary for it to happen. Placing our work within the larger historical context can connect us with our predecessors while illuminating the path for our successors.

Valuing the Process as Well as the Product

We value working together to confront racism to change racist policies and practices. We also seek to overcome the group divisions and conflict that racism fosters, as well as the schisms that develop between individuals. Working together to overcome racism, particularly in multiracial teams, illustrates how the process becomes part of the product. However, as DeMott (1995) has argued, focusing on just becoming "friends" can obscure the social and economic consequences of racism by making it seem as if the problem is solely one of our "just getting along." When we say that the process is the product, we mean that through the act of authentic engagement, through multiracial coalitions, we can embody and live our vision of racial justice.

Breaking down the interpersonal barriers of racism is vital to creating a racially just society. To take just one example: Interpersonal connections have a great deal to do with who does and does not get certain jobs or other opportunities (Steinberg, 2001). When interpersonal preferences are based on the construction of race, structural racism is buttressed and reified. Working together against racism has the potential to dissolve the divisive and negative intergroup comparisons that are central to maintaining racism, and leads to greater equity of opportunity.

Growing as Activists

All of us can continue to develop and hone our skills as antiracism activists. What are our strengths, and what challenges us? What more can we learn about racism or antiracism? How can people of color remain engaged with antiracism work without getting hurt or becoming drained? For White people in particular, what will help to sharpen and deepen the critical consciousness needed to observe and apprehend racism? Exercise 14.1 presents a self-audit for antiracism activists to use. Working with others and seeking and soliciting feedback offers opportunities for growth. Keeping a journal is another useful tool for self-reflection and processing complex and difficult reactions.

ETERNAL VIGILANCE

The sociologist Lieberson (1985) warned that when a group is used to having power and is pressured or required to cede some of its advantages, it will seek to regain its favored position either by changing the rules or by moving the playing field. Ever since the high-water mark of the Great Society in the mid-1960s, we have witnessed the veracity of Lieberson's analysis, through consistent attempts to dismantle affirmative action by reframing diversity on campus to increase the numbers of conservative White male professors, eviscerating voting rights, and defunding and privatizing public services that offered a safety net to people of color. Since the passage of the Affordable Care Act ("Obamacare"), 20 million more people became insured, many of them people of color, and yet the Republican party has consistently committed itself to repealing this act and even greater progress to cover poor people, many of them of color, has been stymied in states controlled by Republicans who have refused Medicaid expansion (Tavernise & Gebeloff, 2016). Of note, we have repeatedly criticized the contemporary Republican party in this book, not because we are Democrats or believe that Democrats always do the right thing on behalf of people of color. The Republican party made a strategic decision beginning with Richard Nixon to court White voters by appealing to their racism and have since then supported the suppression of voters of color, dismantled affirmative action, and tried to block legislation, such as the Affordable Care Act and relief funds to compensate for the significant financial losses during the 2020 pandemic that significantly benefits people of color. Similarly during the tenure of the Trump administration, White supremacist ideology was fueled by the president's rhetoric and refusal to quell racist attacks on people of color, culminating in his supporters storming the U.S. Capitol, carrying Confederate flags and hangman's nooses!

Enforcement of discrimination laws and policies has become more lax, voter suppression laws have metastasized, and many school districts have abandoned attempts at desegregation, supported by an extremely conservative judiciary. And while there is a public discourse accompanying this backlash that heralds the achievement of racial equality in the nation, civil rights struggles are relegated as historical artifacts.

Massey (2005) concluded that Lieberson's prediction is at work with housing discrimination as well. Now people of color have an easier time getting housing loans than they did in the past (which is progress), but they disproportionately receive their loans from predatory lenders rather than banks, the former of which charge exorbitant interest rates and carry severe default penalties. Further, the loans are for properties that are less valuable than those in predominantly White neighborhoods. So even when one hurdle is cleared, other obstacles appear.

All of us engaged in antiracism work must forge ahead, breaking new ground while securing what has been achieved and guarding against an inevitable backlash. We do this not only for ourselves but for our neighbors and for those who have the right to be our neighbors; not only for *our* children but for *all* children; not only for the present generation but for generations to come. We are not alone. We are all connected and part of a chain that predates us and will continue with our nieces and nephews, children and grandchildren, long after we no longer can walk or raise our voices. They, in particular, need to see us lighting the torch so they know how to do it, as the flame of hope is passed on, match by match, person by person.

As Massey (2005) said:

Whenever one social group derives systematic benefits from an institutionalized system of subordination, its members can be expected to resist efforts to dismantle the system despite its injustice. Instead, as old forms of discrimination are curtailed, new mechanisms will be invented. The struggle to achieve civil rights may thus be expected to be a long, drawn-out affair. As with liberty, the price of racial justice is eternal vigilance.

CONCLUSION

The work of dismantling racism requires constant vigilance and self-reflection. There are elements that exist in our internal as well as external realms of reality that must be developed and enhanced. The web of resistance illustrates the various elements that can help individuals participating in authentic activism, allyship, and advocacy. Working with others in sustained coalitions provides much needed strength and support to attain racial justice and equity.

EXERCISE 14.1 Antiracism Activist Self-Audit

This audit can be responded to alone, in pairs, or in small groups.

1. Strengths as an antiracism activist
2. Resources that I bring to this work
3. Support systems that I can draw upon
4. Triggers I need to be mindful of
5. Areas I need to learn more about
6. Concerns I have about my role as an antiracism ally (After listing concerns, develop a strategy to respond to each one.)
7. Goals for myself

EXERCISE 14.2 Confronting Racism Without Humiliating Others

The following situations raise questions about how to confront racism without humiliating others. Responses to the questions can be done alone, in pairs, or in small groups.

Situation One

A professor of color is teaching a human behavior class. After presenting a lecture about race and identity development, three or four White students ask challenging questions that seem to you to be a cross-examination of the professor. One student suggests that the professor may not adequately understand identity theory. You notice that the professor is becoming tense. What are some ways in which you can intervene? What might you be concerned about saying? What would be your goal in this situation, and what would be a productive outcome? If you decide to do or say nothing, what goes into that decision?

Situation Two

After hearing a lecture about microaggressions, students were invited to give an example they had witnessed or had been a victim or perpetrator. A Black student described a situation where they were told that they were not offered a job because they did not present in a professional manner. Since the student had worn a suit, they were surprised by the comment. Another student offered that perhaps it was the way she walked or wore her hair (which were in cornrows). The Black student responded, stating that she didn't feel there was anything wrong with her hair or the way she walked. The professor chimes in, signaling to move on by asking if anyone else had another example adding that hair can be a tricky situation since some organizations have policies on tidiness. How might you respond to the professor's call to "move on" to another example? What do you think the Black student might be feeling? What messages do you think the students in the class received? How could you intervene as an ally to the Black student?

Situation Three

A White professor makes a remark in the classroom about how racism is not central to a consideration of housing segregation, which makes you feel that he is insensitive to people of color and the profound influence of racism in this country. After his statement, the room becomes noticeably silent, and some students fidget and look uncomfortable. How might you bring up the content of what the professor said? Would you address the group dynamic you perceive? If yes, how would you do this? If you decide to do or say nothing, what goes into that decision? How would your response differ if the remark was made by a fellow classmate?

Situation Four

After you return home for a holiday, a close relative (or friend) with whom you have a good relationship starts making jokes that disparage a racial or ethnic group. You used to listen to these jokes, but now, after studying about racism, you have a strong negative reaction. You care about the person but think you must speak up. How might you raise this issue? What would be your fears or concerns? What positive outcome might come from your confrontation? If you decide to do or say nothing, what goes into that decision?

Situation Five

You overhear a conversation in the dining room between three people, two of whom you know and one of whom you do not. The person you do not know is making stereotypical and offensive remarks about a colleague, generalizing about that colleague's racial or ethnic group. What might you be feeling at this time? Would it be appropriate to say something in the moment? If so, what might you say? If you did not intervene, can you envision any kind of follow-up that would be helpful? If you decide to do or say nothing, what goes into that decision?

REFERENCES

Anderson, C. (2018). *One person, no vote: How voter suppression is destroying our democracy.* Bloomsbury Publishing USA.

Black Lives Matter (2020). http://blacklivesmatter.com/about/

Bobo, L. D. (2001). Racial attitudes and relations at the close of the twentieth century. In N. J. Smelser, W. J. Wilson, & F. Mitchell (Eds.), *America becoming: Racial trends and their consequences* (Vol. 1, pp. 265–301). Washington, DC: National Academies Press.

Brewer, M. B. (2001). Ingroup identification and intergroup conflict: When does in group love become out-group hate? In R. D. Ashmore, L. Jussim, & D. Wilder (Eds.), *Social identity, intergroup conflict, and conflict resolution* (pp. 17–41). Oxford University Press.

Chalabi, M. (2014, April 28). *Three leagues, 92 teams and one Black principle owner.* Five Thirty Eight. http://fivethirtyeight.com/datalab/diversity-in-the-nba-the-nfl-and-mlb

Coates, T. (2014, June). *The case for reparations.* The Atlantic.

Cobb, J. (2016, March 14). *The matter of Black lives.* The New Yorker. www.newyorker.com/magazine/2016/03/14/where-is-black-lives-matter-headed

Copeland, P. (2015). Let's get free: Social work and the movement for Black lives. *Journal of Forensic Social Work, 5*(1–3), 3–19.

DeMott, B. (1995). *The trouble with friendship: Why Americans can't think straight about race.* Atlantic Monthly Press.

Harro, B. (2013). The cycle of liberation. In M. Adams, W. J. Blumenfeld, R. Casteñeda, H. W. Hackman, M. L. Peters, & X. Zúñiga (Eds.), *Readings for diversity and social justice* (pp. 618–624). Routledge.

Kivel, P. (1996). *Uprooting racism: How White people can work for racial justice.* New Society Publishers.

Lieberson, S. (1985). *Making it count: The improvement of social research and theory.* University of California Press.

Massey, D. S. (2005). Racial discrimination and housing: A moving target. *Social Problems, 52*(2), 149–151.

McLaughlin, M. (2016, February 29). *The dynamic history of #BlackLivesMatter explained.* The Huffington Post. www.huffingtonpost.com/entry/history-black-lives-matter_us_56d0a3b0e4b0871f60eb4af5

Rhoden, W. C. (2016, April 14). Baseball has yet to deliver its biggest tribute to Jackie Robinson. *The New York Times.* www.nytimes.com/2016/04/17/sports/baseball/baseball-has-yet-to-deliver-greatest-tribute-to-jackie-robinson.html

Steinberg, S. (2001). *The ethnic myth: Race, ethnicity and class in America* (3rd ed.). Beacon Press.

Tavernise, S., & Gebeloff, R. (2016, April 17). Immigrants, the poor and minorities gain sharply under the Affordable Care Act. *The New York Times.* www.nytimes.com/2016/04/18/health/immigrants-the-poor-and-minorities-gain-sharply-under-health-act.html?hpw&rref=health&action=click&pgtype=Homepage&module=well-region&region=bottom-well&WT.nav=bottom-well

Werkmeister Rozas, L. M., & Miller, J. L. (2009). Discourses for social justice education: The web of racism and the web of resistance. *Journal of Ethnic and Cultural Diversity in Social Work, 18*(1–2), 24–39.

Appendices

Everyday Democracy

Everyday Democracy is a nonprofit organization, a project of the Paul J. Aicher Foundation, that trains people to facilitate racial dialogues in communities, schools, and workplaces, using a racial equity lens. They help groups to focus in particular on how structural racism and other oppressive structural forces affect issues in communities across the country. They seek to create positive community change that is inclusive. They achieve this by giving people tools, skills, and resources that target problematic, divisive community issues and help to give everyone a voice.

Everyday Democracy believes that equitable change occurs when diverse groups of people join together and have the opportunity to share ideas, shape policy, and give voice to those who are usually marginalized, dismissed, and devalued. People come together to share their access to resources, networks, and even power—and in so doing, they work to foster an understanding of the ways that structural racism gives way to social, cultural, and economic inequities. With this shared knowledge, these individuals work to advocate for a stronger democracy to eradicate all inequity.

Summary from: (https://everyday-democracy.org/about/vision-reach).

APPENDIX B

Steps to Successful Intergroup Conversation: A Critical-Dialogic Model

This model is used for small groups of 12 to 16 students who meet for 7 to 12 weeks in 2-hour sessions. They are coded by facilitators who represent target and agent identities in the area being considered.

Step One: Group beginnings: Forming and building relationships

- ▶ Establishment of an environment conducive to honest and meaningful dialogue
- ▶ Identity work (Who am I? Who are you? How will we talk as a group?)

Step Two: Exploring differences and commonalities of experience

▶ Builds on the identity work of the first step
▶ Challenges individuals to examine the advantages and disadvantages of social group membership and status as members of privileged and targeted social groups
▶ Allows group building activities with increased opportunities for talking and listening to each other's experiences and perspectives

Step Three: Exploring and dialoguing about *Hot Topics*

▶ Encourages individuals to explore questions or issues from various perspectives
▶ Examination of personal, interpersonal, cultural, institutional, and historical factors that cause tensions or estrangement between social identity groups

Step Four: Action planning and alliance building

▶ Shifts the focus from dialogue and conflict exploration to action planning and alliance building
▶ Individuals identify necessary steps to address injustices and to bridge differences

Based on a model developed by Zúñiga et al. (2002). Intergroup dialogues: An educational model for cultivating engagement across difference. *Equity and Excellence in Education, 35*(1), 7–17.

APPENDIX C

Activities Toward Becoming a Racially Just Organization

Following each statement, indicate the level of activity for your organization as: (A) Accomplished, (IP) In Process, (U) Unaddressed.

	Kinds of activities	
	Writing a mission statement that articulates racial justice goals	
	Hiring more faculty and/or staff of color	
	Providing opportunities for mentoring, support and advancement for Black, Indigenous and people of color staff	
	Establishing racial identity based affinity groups for buffering, support, and feedback	
	Analyze how Black, Indigenous and people of color workers pay an "identity tax"—expend greater effort and emotional energy and have a plan to mitigate or offset this.	
	Analyze power distribution and racial patterns and develop a plan to address inequities	
	Making a commitment to become a racially just organization in almost all organizational literature	

	Reviewing curricula and policies for colonial legacies and White supremacist biases. Having a plan to decolonize the organization	
	Increasing financial resources allocated toward antiracism initiatives	
	Holding ongoing discussions about White supremacy, racism, and race for staff, including having caucus groups reporting back to the full staff	
	Increasing training for all staff about White supremacy and racism and how this impacts the work of the organization	
	Establishing mechanisms to hear the voices of consumers of color and Black, Indigenous and people of color community residents	
	Engaging in public dialogues on race and racism that include all organizational constituencies, including volunteers, consumers, community members, boards, and trustees	
	Creating and facilitating alliances between individuals, groups, and organizations within and outside of the organization to challenge policies and practices that perpetuate systemic discrimination, prejudice, and targeting or marginalization of people of color	
	Supporting practices, policies, and mechanisms needed to create an inclusive environment and culture	
	Having a mechanism to address racialized ruptures and impasses among employees	
	Creating opportunities and structures for addressing and resolving inequitable or discriminatory behavior, policies, or practices related to race that have the trust and support of all staff	
	Review models of practice or service delivery for Eurocentric, White biases and ensure that they address the needs of diverse clients, students, staff and consumers	
	Having an ongoing review of the racial justice commitment that is made public to all constituents	
	Creating space to explore worldviews, biases, and assumptions of staff	

Source: Adapted from Donner and Miller (2005). The road to becoming an anti-racism organization. In A. Lightburn & P. Sessions (Eds.), *Community based clinical practice*. Oxford University Press.

APPENDIX D

Issues to Consider When Confronting Institutional Racism

► Have a vision with both a long-term and short-term plan.
► Map out steps toward achieving the long-term goal.
► Determine what level of institutions, organizations, laws, or policies you will concentrate on influencing and changing.
► Assess your relationship with those who hold formal power and decide on the most productive strategy.

- ▶ Decide who will constitute the group working on this strategy. (For example, do you work with a few people who think like you [allies] or a larger, more diverse group?)
- ▶ Assess what is feasible within the current historical/social/economic/political context.
- ▶ Develop strategies for resolving conflict.
- ▶ Review previous efforts for their strengths and areas for improvement.
- ▶ Define what role clients and consumers will play.
- ▶ Analyze formal and informal power.
- ▶ Anticipate unintended consequences.
- ▶ Determine ways to sustain momentum, monitor progress, and have an idea of what constitutes success.
- ▶ If collaboration is ineffective, explore other available options.
- ▶ Consider the risks to you and others and understand your limitations.

APPENDIX E

Cultural Values and Worldviews

VALUES

Some areas where cultures have different values:

- ▶ Privacy versus being part of a group
- ▶ Well-being of the individual versus the well-being of the group
- ▶ Independence versus interdependence
- ▶ Seeking help versus managing your own problems
- ▶ Where help is sought and what are the expectations
- ▶ Children should be encouraged to express themselves versus children should be seen but not heard
- ▶ What to do when a child is sick
- ▶ The roles of men and women in the family
- ▶ How to express respect
- ▶ Whether authority is to be trusted and respected or challenged
- ▶ The meaning of time and punctuality

Questions

1. What are your values in these areas?
2. Where have you noticed differences between your values and those of your clients?
3. How have these differences in values caused misunderstandings or conflict between you and your clients?
4. How have you tried to bridge these differences? What has worked and what has not worked?

SAYINGS

In most of our families, we grew up hearing sayings or expressions that reflected the family's values. Here are some common North American sayings:

- ► Pull yourself up by your own bootstraps.
- ► Don't beat around the bush.
- ► Time is money.
- ► A man's home is his castle.
- ► He's all talk and no action.
- ► A stitch in time saves nine.
- ► Stand on your own two feet.
- ► God helps those who help themselves.
- ► Loosen up.
- ► The ball is in your court.
- ► Don't put all of your eggs in one basket.
- ► Don't burn your bridges.
- ► What is the bottom line?
- ► He will have to face the music.
- ► Let's bury the hatchet.
- ► You've made your bed, now lie in it.

Questions

1. Did you ever hear these expressions while you were growing up?
2. If yes, what did they mean and what did you think of them now?
3. What values and worldviews are implicit in these sayings?
4. Did you grow up with other expressions? If so, what were they and what values did they reflect?

APPENDIX F

For Further Reading About Racism and Clinical Practice

Abrams, L. S., & Moio, J. A. (2009). Critical race theory and the cultural competence dilemma in social work education. *Journal of Social Work Education, 45*(2), 245–261.

Carter, R. T. (2007). Racism and psychological and emotional injury: Recognizing and assessing race-based traumatic stress. *The Counseling Psychologist, 35,* 13–105.

Coates, T. (2015). *Between the world and me.* Spiegel & Grau.

Comas-Diaz, L., & Greene, B. (Eds.). (1994). *Women of color: Integrating ethnic and gender identities in psycho-therapy.* Guilford Press.

Comas-Diaz, L. & Hall, G. (2019). Racial trauma: Theory, research and healing: Introduction to the special issue. *American Psychologist, 74*(1), 1–5.

Comas-Diaz, L., & Jacobsen, F. M. (1995). The therapist of color and the White patient dyad: Contradictions and recognitions. *Cultural Diversity and Mental Health, 1*(2), 93–106.

DiAngelo, R. (2017). *White fragility.* Beacon Press.

Dyson, M. (2017). *Tears we cannot stop: A sermon to White America.* St. Martin's Press.

Franklin, A. J., Boyd-Franklin, N., & Kelly, S. (2006). Racism and invisibility: Race-related stress, emotional abuse and psychological trauma for people of color. *Journal of Emotional Abuse, 6*(2–3), 9–30.

Fuertes, J. N. (1999). Asian Americans' and African Americans' initial perceptions of Hispanic counselors. *Journal of Multicultural Counseling and Development, 27,* 122–135.

Garran, A. M. (2013). Lessons learned: Racial enactments in the treatment process. *Journal of Social Work Practice: Psychotherapeutic Approaches in Health, Welfare and the Community, 27*(3), 305–317.

Garran, A.M. & Rasmussen, B.M. (2016). In the line of duty: Racism in health care. *Social Work, 61*(2), 175–177.

Garran, A. M. (2013). Lessons learned: Racial enactments in the treatment process. *Journal of Social Work Practice, 27*(3), 305–317.

Garran, A. M., & Werkmeister Rozas, L. (2013). Cultural competence revisited. *Journal of Ethnic and Cultural Diversity in Social Work, 22*(2), 97–111.

Goggin, E., Werkmeister Rozas, L. & Garran, A. M. (2015). A case of mistaken identity: What happens when race is a factor. *Journal of Social Work Practice. Psychotherapeutic Approaches in Health, Welfare and the Community.* https://doi.org/10.1080/02650533.2015.1100596

Goodman, D. (2011). *Promoting diversity and social justice: Educating People From Privileged Groups* (2nd ed., pp. 157–177). Routledge.

Hall, C. (2018). Black women talk about stereotypical transference enactments in cross-cultural supervision. *Journal of Human Behavior in the Social Environment, 28*(8), 1019–1032.

Hosken, N. (2013). Social work supervision and discrimination. *Advances in Social Work & Welfare Education, 15*(1), 91–103.

Kendi, I. X. (2019). *How to be an antiracist.* One World.

King, T. (2012). *The inconvenient Indian: A curious account of Native people in North America.* Doubleday.

Kirschner, S. R., & Martin, J. (Eds.). (2010). *The sociocultural turn in psychology: The contextual emergence of self and mind.* Columbia University Press.

Leary, K. (1997). Race, self-disclosure, and "forbidden talk": Race and ethnicity in contemporary clinical practice. *Psychoanalytic Quarterly, 66*(2), 163–189.

Leary, K. (2000). Racial enactments in dynamic treatment. *Psychoanalytic Dialogues, 10*(4), 639–653.

Leary, K. (2007). Racial insult and repair. *Psychoanalytic Dialogues, 17*(4), 539–549.

Lijtmaer, R. M. (2001). Countertransference and ethnicity: The analyst's psychic changes. *Journal of the American Academy of Psychoanalysis, 29*(1), 73–83.

Loya, M. (2012). Racial attitudes in White social workers: Implications for culturally sensitive practice. *PB&J: Politics, Bureaucracy, and Justice, 3*(1), 23–31.

Manning, M., Cornelius, L., & Okundaye, J. (2004). Empowering African Americans through social work practice: Integrating an Afrocentric perspective, ego psychology, and spirituality. *Families in Society, 85*(2), 229–235.

Menakem, R. (2017). *My grandmother's hands.* Central Recovery Press.

Oluo, I. (2018). *So you want to talk about race.* Basic Books.

Perez-Foster, R. M. (1998). The clinician's cultural countertransference: The psychodynamics of culturally competent practice. *Clinical Social Work Journal, 26*(3), 253–270.

Perez-Foster, R. M., Moskowitz, M., & Javier, R. A. (Eds.). (1996). *Reaching across boundaries of culture and class: Widening the scope of psychotherapy.* Jason Aronson.

Rasmussen, B. (2013). Making sense of Walt: A psychoanalytic understanding of racism. *Psychoanalytic Social Work, 20*(1), 50–61.

Rasmussen, B., & Garran, A.M. (2019) Psychodynamic analysis of racialized interactions: The *Get Out* case study, *Smith College Studies in Social Work, 89,* 2, 179–196.

Rasmussen, B., & Salhani, D. (2010). A contemporary Kleinian contribution to understanding racism. *Social Service Review, 84*(3), 491–513.

Ridley, C. R. (1995). *Overcoming unintentional racism in counseling and therapy.* Sage.

Saad, L. (2020). *Me and white supremacy: Combat racism, change the world, and become a good ancestor.* Sourcebooks.

Sakamoto, I., & Pitner, R. O. (2005). Use of critical consciousness in anti-oppressive social work practice: Disentangling power dynamics at personal and structural levels. *British Journal of Social Work, 35*(4), 435–452.

Schroeder, M., Andrews, J. J., & Hindes, Y. L. (2009). Cross-racial supervision: Critical issues in the supervisory relationship. *Canadian Journal of Counselling, 43*(4), 295.

Spencer, M. S. (2008). A social worker's reflections on power, privilege, and oppression. *Social Work, 53*(2), 99–101.

Suchet, M. (2007). Uncovering Whiteness. *Psychoanalytic Dialogues, 17*(6), 887–894.

Tang, N., & Gardner, J. (1999). Race, culture, and psychotherapy: Transference to minority therapists. *The Psychoanalytic Quarterly, 68*(1), 1–20 [especially relevant for clinicians of color].

Vontress, C. E., & Epp, L. R. (1997). Historical hostility in the African American client: Implications for counseling. *Journal of Multicultural Counseling and Development, 25*(3), 170–184.

Wachtel, P. L. (2011). *Therapeutic communication: Knowing what to say, when* (2nd ed.). Guilford Press.

Winters, M-F. (2020) *Black fatigue: How racism erodes the mind, body, and spirit.* Berrett-Koehler Publ.

Yuval-Davis, N. (2006). Intersectionality and feminist politics. *European Journal of Women's Studies, 13*(3), 193–209.

APPENDIX G

Culturally Influenced Behaviors

Examine your own values and the origin of these values in the following sections. Discuss with colleagues and compare similarities and differences.

Help seeking behavior
Medical care and illness
Gender roles
Role of family
Behavior toward authority
Time and punctuality

Source: Based on the work of Lynch and Hanson (1992). *Developing cross-cultural competence.* Paul H. Brookes Publishing.

APPENDIX H

Questions About Cross-Cultural Contacts

1. Describe your first contacts with members of other racial and ethnic groups.
2. What was your most positive encounter with a person from another ethnic or racial group?
3. What is your most negative encounter with a person from another ethnic or racial group? If you could replay the tape of what happened, what do you wish that you could do differently?

4. Which clients have you found to be most challenging and why?
5. Which ethnic, religious, or cultural groups would you like to learn more about?
6. What is the best way for you to learn about other cultures (e.g., discussion groups, dialogue groups, classes, reading, visiting different neighborhoods, attending films, listening to music)?

APPENDIX I

Imaginary Letter

This assignment can help students to empathize with a person who may be racially or ethnically different from them. It involves perspective taking and searching for strengths as well as struggles.

Read one of the assigned narratives or stories. Write a *two-page* imaginary letter reacting to the narrative to either a character in the narrative or the narrator, with particular attention to the importance or unimportance of race and ethnicity. How is the character's or narrator's culture and worldview similar or different from your own? Are there any concerns about your subject's well-being or encouragement about your subject's strengths that you care to share with them? Please ask any questions about your subject and share what you learned about them and yourself.

Examples of Narratives

Adichie, C. N. (2013). *Americanah* (Chapter 4). Knopf.

Beatty, P. (2001). *The White boy shuffle*. Picador.

Brown, A. C. (2020). I'm Still Here: Black dignity in a world made for Whiteness: "A leading new voice on racial justice" LAYLA SAAD, author of ME AND WHITE SUPREMACY. Hachette UK.

Coates, T. N. (2015). Letter to my son. *The Atlantic, 316*(2), 82–91.

Cose, E. (2012). *The end of anger: A new generation's take on race and rage*. Ecco Press.

Easton, S. (2012). On being special. In G. Gutiérrez y Muhs, Y. F. Niemann, C. G. González, & A. P. Harris (Eds.), *Presumed incompetent: The intersections of race and class for women in academia* (pp. 152–163). University Press of Colorado.

Ignatiev, N., & Pendragon, A. (1996). Exchange with a national socialist. *Race Traitor, 5*, 17–48.

Fair, R. (1972). *We can't breathe*. Harper Collins.

Garciá, M. (2016). *The Latino generation: Voices of the New America*. University of North Carolina Press (Story of Alma Cortez-Lara).

Goffman, A. (2014). *On the run: Fugitive life in an American city*. Picador.

Hale, J. C. (1993). *Bloodlines: Odyssey of a native daughter* ("Daughter of winter," pp. 25–87). Random House.

Harris-Perry, M. V. (2011). Shame. In M. V. Harris-Perry (Ed.), *Sister citizen: Shame, stereotypes and Black women in America* (Chap. 3, pp. 101–133). Yale University Press.

Hassenback, I. (1996, January 8). How Nazis are made. *The New Yorker*, 36–56.

Hobbs, J. (2015). *The short and tragic life of Robert Pease: A brilliant young man who left Newark for the Ivy League*. Scribner.

Kendall, M. (2020). *Hood feminism: Notes from the women that a movement forgot*. Random House.

Kingston, M. H. (1991). No name woman. In Minnesota Humanities Commission. (Eds.), *Braided lives*. Humanities Commission.

McMillan, T. (1990). Ma' Dear. In T. McMillan (Ed.), *Breaking ice: An anthology of contemporary African–American fiction* (pp. 457–465). Penguin.

Nathan, D. (2016). What happened to Sandra Bland? *The Nation, 302*(19/20), 12–18.

Piper, A. (1993). Passing for White, passing for Black. *Transition, 58,* 4–33.

Rankin, C. (2014). *Citizen: An American lyric* (pp. 23–36, 131–156). Graywolf Press.

Silko, L. M. (2006). *Ceremony.* Penguin Classics.

Skloot, R. (2010). *The immortal life of Henrietta Lacks* (Chap. 5). Crown (Random House).

Index